THE DARK KNIGHT RETURNS

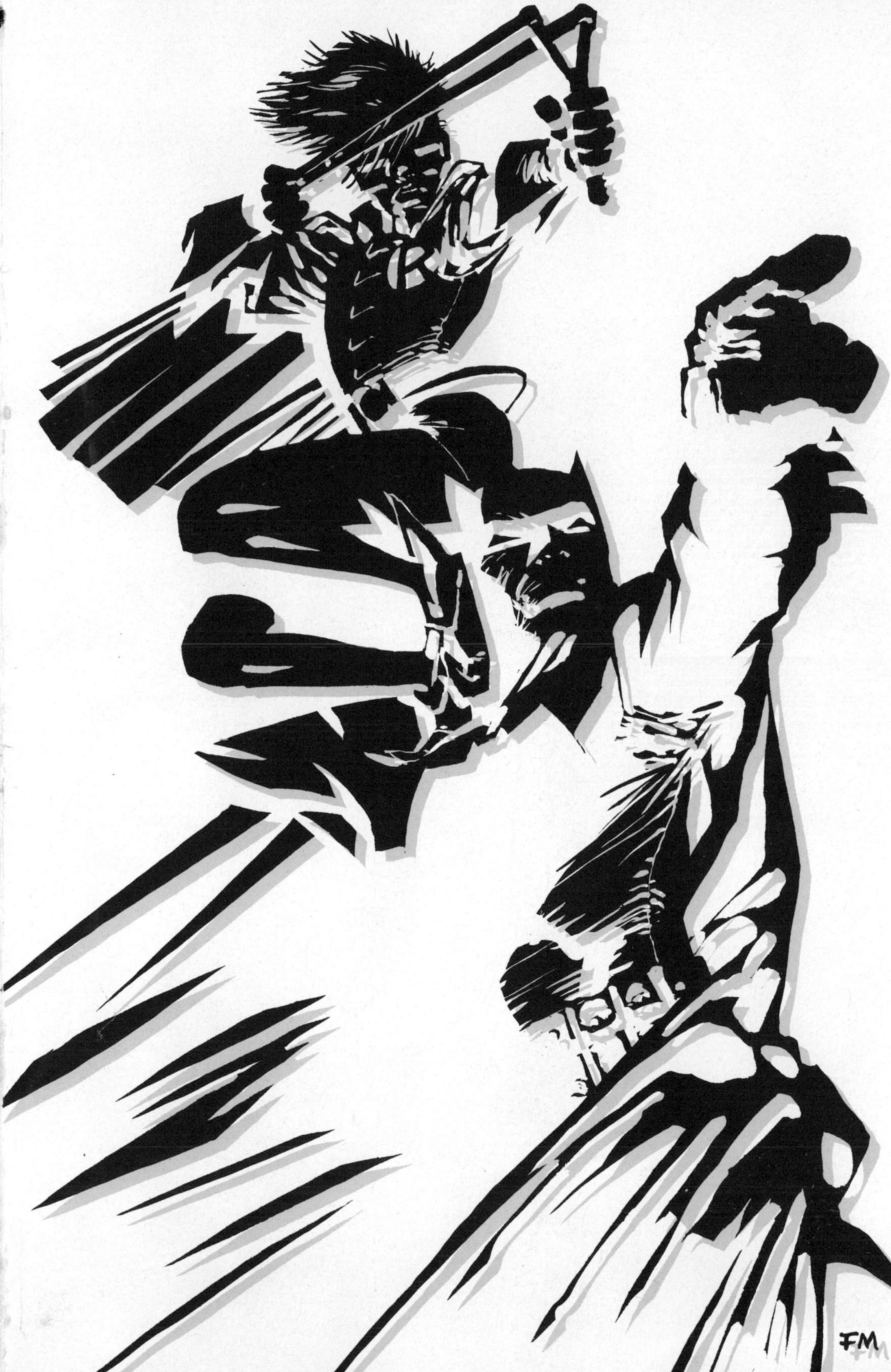
FM

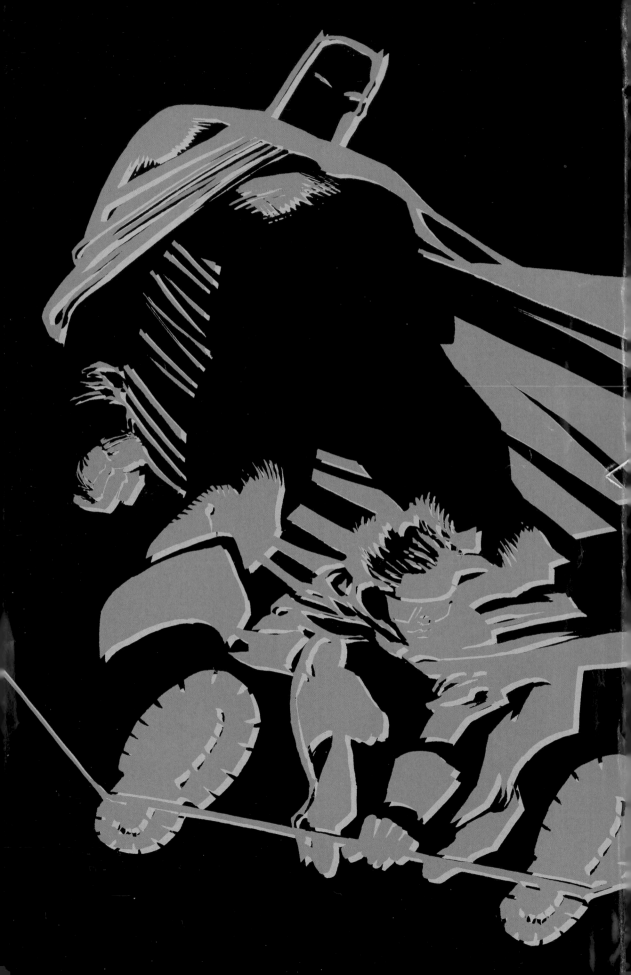

BATMAN

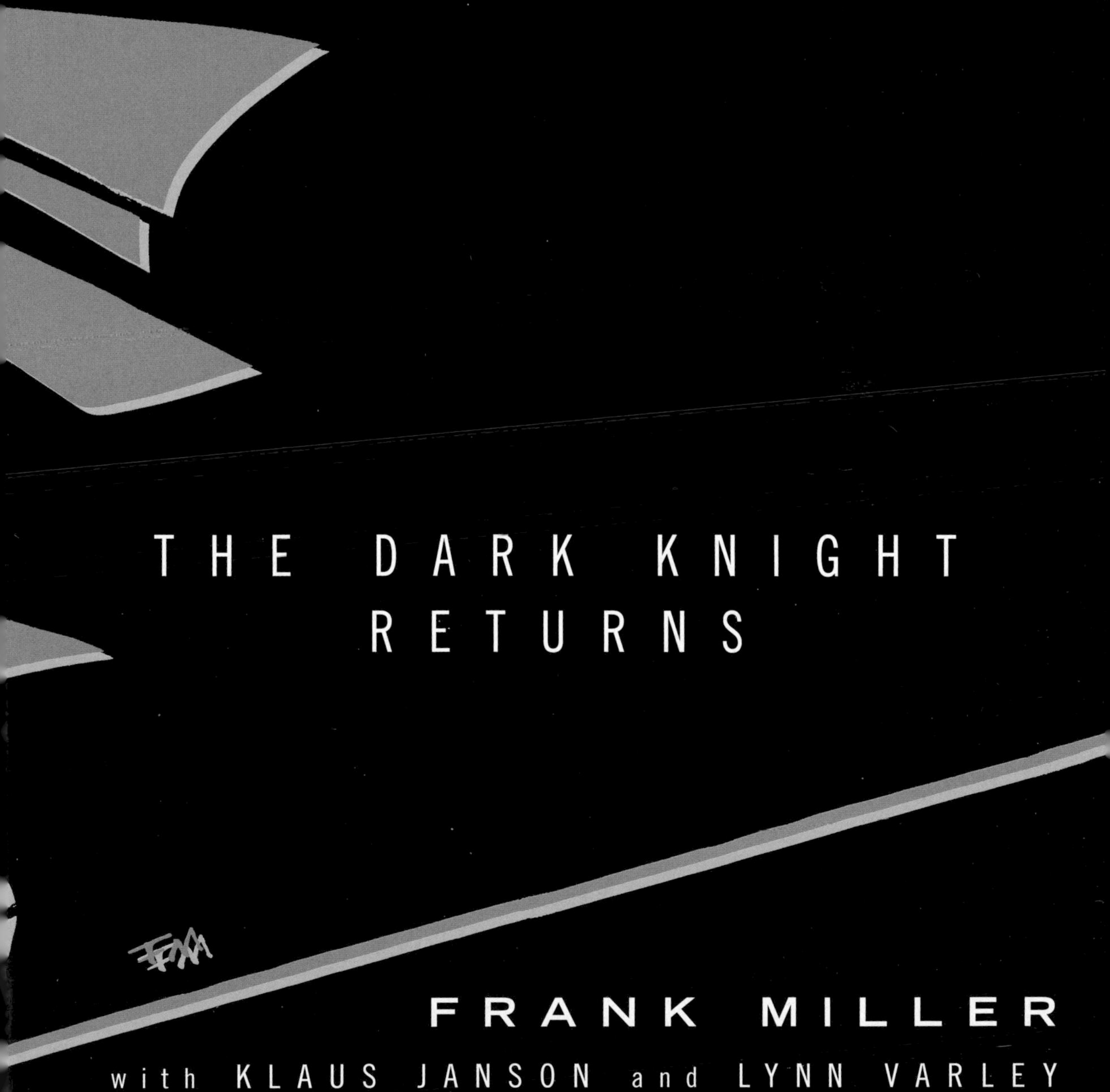

THE DARK KNIGHT RETURNS

FRANK MILLER

with KLAUS JANSON and LYNN VARLEY

Lettered by JOHN COSTANZA

Batman created by BOB KANE

Dick Giordano and **Dennis O'Neil**
Editors – Original Series

Dale Crain
Senior Editor

Scott Nybakken
Associate Editor

Robbin Brosterman
Design Director – Books

Bob Harras
VP – Editor-in-Chief

Diane Nelson
President

Dan DiDio and **Jim Lee**
Co-Publishers

Geoff Johns
Chief Creative Officer

John Rood
Executive VP – Sales, Marketing and Business Development

Amy Genkins
Senior VP – Business and Legal Affairs

Nairi Gardiner
Senior VP – Finance

Jeff Boison
VP – Publishing Operations

Mark Chiarello
VP – Art Direction and Design

John Cunningham
VP – Marketing

Terri Cunningham
VP – Talent Relations and Services

Alison Gill
Senior VP – Manufacturing and Operations

Hank Kanalz
Senior VP – Digital

Jay Kogan
VP – Business and Legal Affairs, Publishing

Jack Mahan
VP – Business Affairs, Talent

Nick Napolitano
VP – Manufacturing Administration

Sue Pohja
VP – Book Sales

Courtney Simmons
Senior VP – Publicity

Bob Wayne
Senior VP – Sales

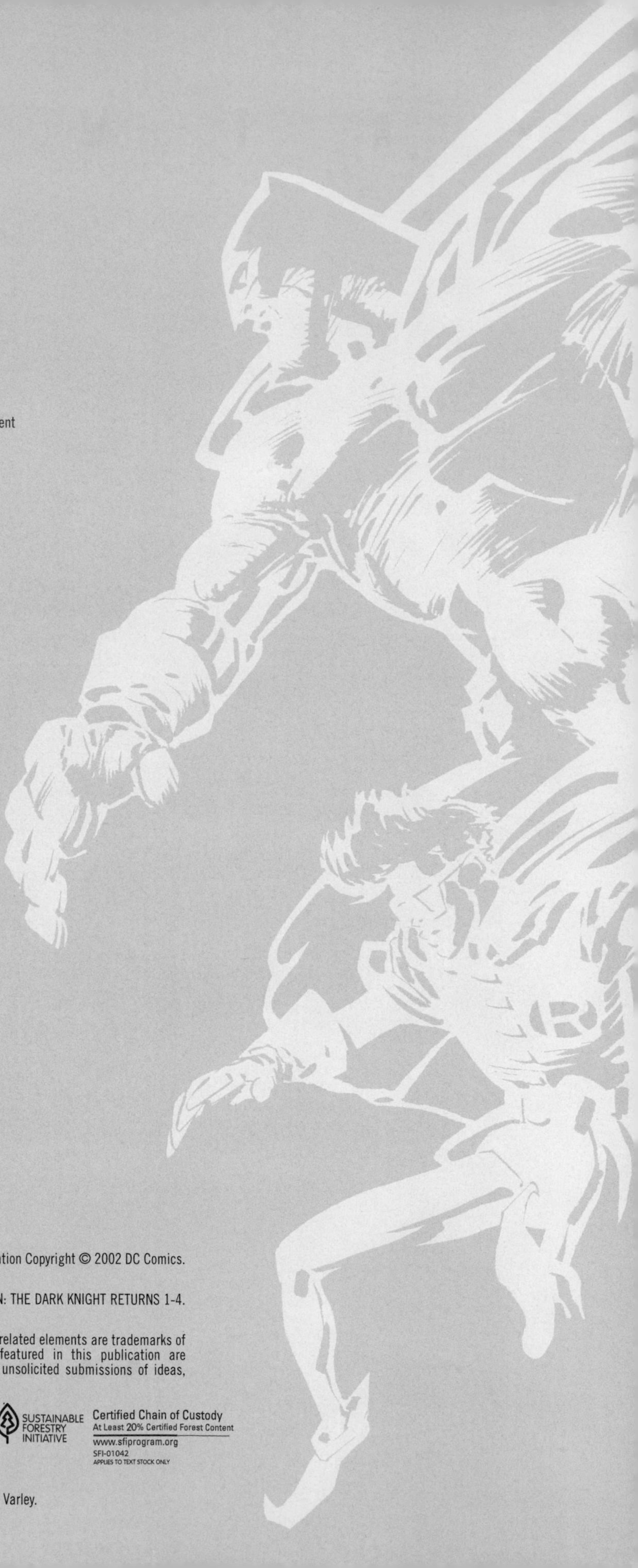

BATMAN: THE DARK KNIGHT RETURNS

DC Comics, 1700 Broadway, New York, NY 10019
A Warner Bros. Entertainment Company
Printed by RR Donnelley, Salem, VA, USA. 2/22/13.
Fifteenth Printing.
ISBN: 978-1-56389-342-1

SUSTAINABLE FORESTRY INITIATIVE
Certified Chain of Custody
At Least 20% Certified Forest Content
www.sfiprogram.org
SFI-01042
APPLIES TO TEXT STOCK ONLY

Cover Illustration by Frank Miller, Klaus Janson and Lynn Varley.

Table of Contents

There's this little saloon you'll find up and running and packed with patrons before most of us are ready for our morning coffee.

The joint's two subway levels beneath the streets of downtown Metropolis.

Step out at the Schuster stop on the south-bound side, take two lefts, walk maybe fifteen feet and you're right on top of it.

But you could just as easily walk right past it and never know it was there.

There's no sign up. Not even a door. Just a dark hallway that looks like a good place for a murder.

Take a breath. Follow the cigarette stink and the bluesy jukebox sounds inside.

It's a tolerable little gin mill. Get there before the morning rush, and you're likely to find a stool.

TRUTH TO POWER

JAMES OLSEN

Your first clue that there's some-thing wrong about the place is the bartender. You'll never forget his face. He's a hulk of a guy who's seen way too much. A broken man with laser-red eyes. His forehead's a fractured cantilever, an avalanche waiting to happen. His skin's gone a little gray from its natural chartreuse.

He's got a voice like Coke bottles getting ground up under a door.

His name is Jones.

He says he's from Mars.

And nobody tells him he's nuts, not one of these sad old barflies. It's not that they're scared of him, either.

They've seen and done things that are supposed to be impossible.

They're not the kind to out-and-out brag about being able to bench-press cars or run faster than a speeding bullet or jump up into the air and stay there. Nah. Not these guys.

These guys, they've got nothing to prove. Been there. Done that.

Except for old "Snapper" always at the same stool at the end, living up to his nickname, snap-ping his fingers in time to the music and rattling on and on and on about mighty powers, globe-spanning

continued

continued from page 21

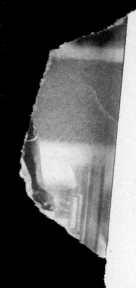

adventures, nefarious world conquerors, you name it.

He never stops snapping his damn fingers. And he never stops sucking back the sauce and jabbering about the old days. The glory days.

The "Golden Age" he calls it.

The age of heroes.

And all the other old farts, they grunt and nod and grumble at each other, swapping old jokes they've swapped a thousand times. Even fat, beet-red old "Penguin" chirps out a curse or two before bursting into tears.

Then they get talking. And if you've got half a brain, you listen.

They talk about amazing adventures, sounding like a bunch of retired car mechanics the whole time.

They talk about a Man of Steel. An Amazon Princess.

But they never talk about the mean one. The cruel one. The one who couldn't fly or bend steel in his bare hands. The one who scared the crap out of everybody and laughed at all of the rest of us for being the envious cowards we were.

No, they never talk about him. Say his name and watch Dibny's face sag so bad his jaw hits the bar.

Not a man among them wants to hear about Batman.

Was he quietly assassinated? Or did he just decide we weren't worth the grief?

The question hangs in the air for a moment or two, then Jones springs for a round for everybody and himself.

They get talking again. About the old days. The glory days.

They remember.

They were right there. In the thick of it.

Back then.

It wasn't so long ago.

We had heroes.

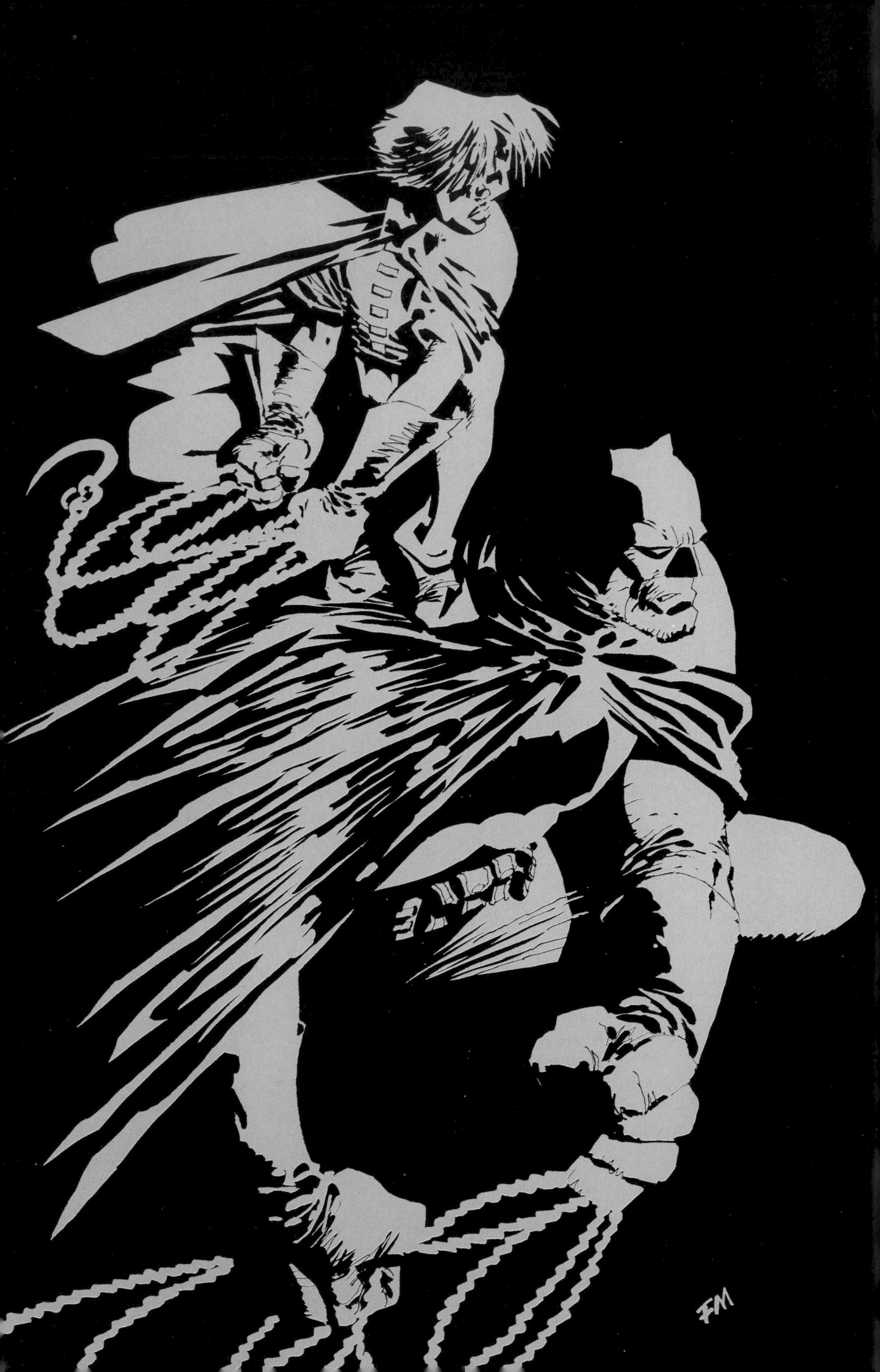
FM

BOOK ONE

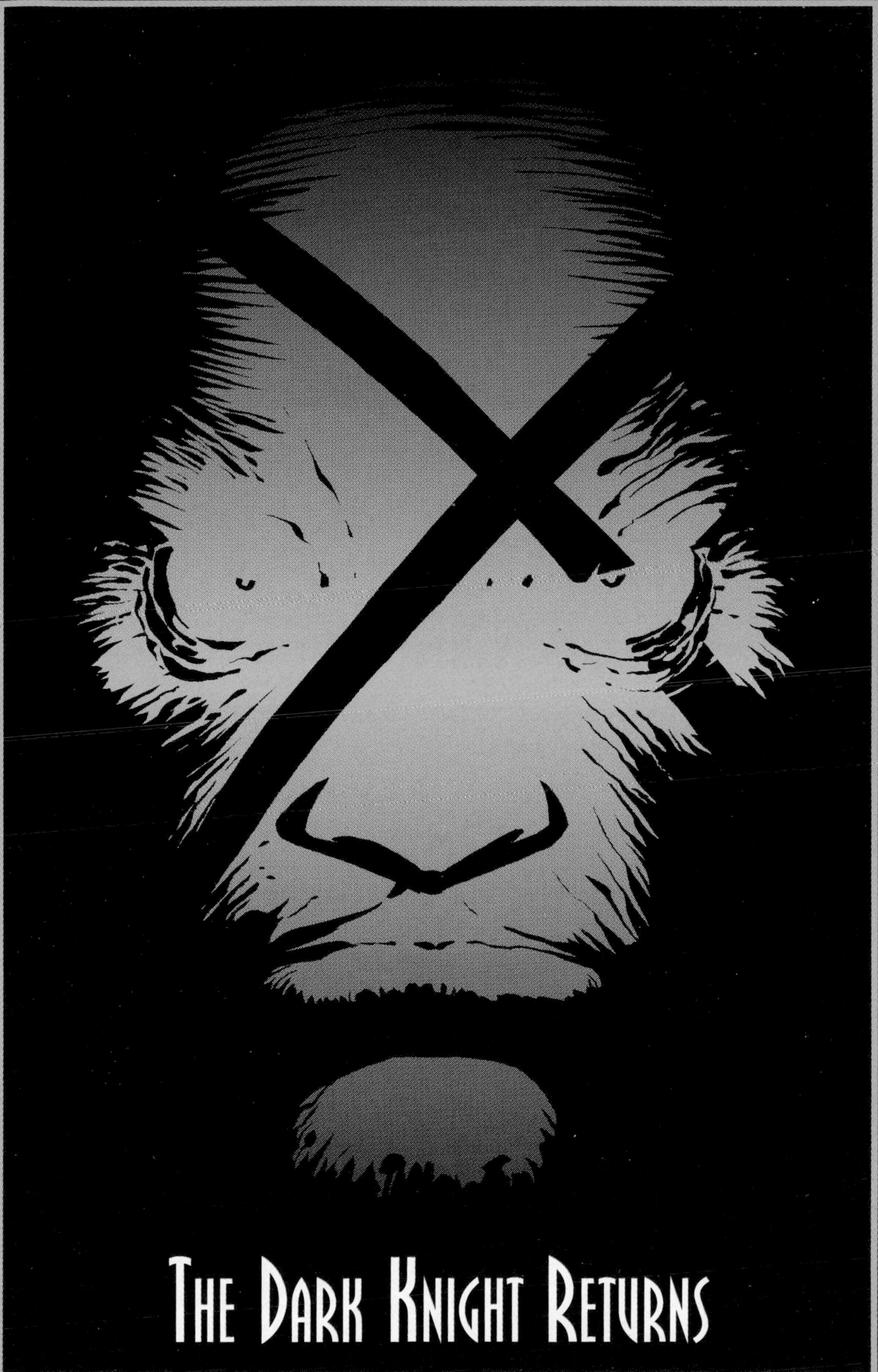

THE DARK KNIGHT RETURNS

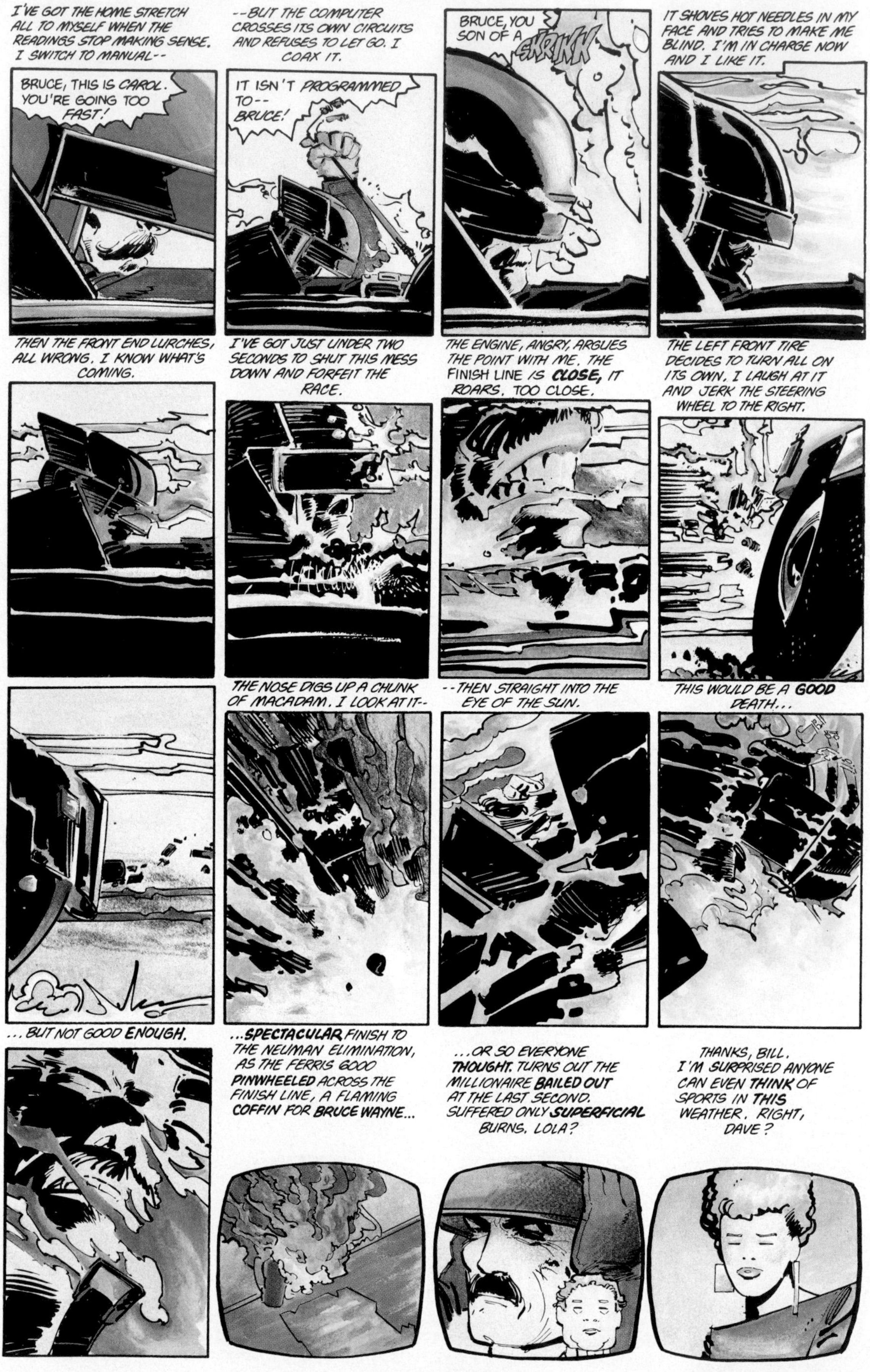

I'VE GOT THE HOME STRETCH ALL TO MYSELF WHEN THE READINGS STOP MAKING SENSE. I SWITCH TO MANUAL--
BRUCE, THIS IS CAROL. YOU'RE GOING TOO FAST!
--BUT THE COMPUTER CROSSES ITS OWN CIRCUITS AND REFUSES TO LET GO. I COAX IT.
IT ISN'T PROGRAMMED TO-- BRUCE!
BRUCE, YOU SON OF A
SKRIKK
IT SHOVES HOT NEEDLES IN MY FACE AND TRIES TO MAKE ME BLIND. I'M IN CHARGE NOW AND I LIKE IT.
THEN THE FRONT END LURCHES, ALL WRONG. I KNOW WHAT'S COMING.
I'VE GOT JUST UNDER TWO SECONDS TO SHUT THIS MESS DOWN AND FORFEIT THE RACE.
THE ENGINE, ANGRY, ARGUES THE POINT WITH ME. THE FINISH LINE IS CLOSE, IT ROARS. TOO CLOSE.
THE LEFT FRONT TIRE DECIDES TO TURN ALL ON ITS OWN. I LAUGH AT IT AND JERK THE STEERING WHEEL TO THE RIGHT.
THE NOSE DIGS UP A CHUNK OF MACADAM. I LOOK AT IT--
--THEN STRAIGHT INTO THE EYE OF THE SUN.
THIS WOULD BE A GOOD DEATH...
...BUT NOT GOOD ENOUGH.
...SPECTACULAR FINISH TO THE NEUMAN ELIMINATION, AS THE FERRIS 6000 PINWHEELED ACROSS THE FINISH LINE, A FLAMING COFFIN FOR BRUCE WAYNE...
...OR SO EVERYONE THOUGHT. TURNS OUT THE MILLIONAIRE BAILED OUT AT THE LAST SECOND. SUFFERED ONLY SUPERFICIAL BURNS. LOLA?
THANKS, BILL. I'M SURPRISED ANYONE CAN EVEN THINK OF SPORTS IN THIS WEATHER. RIGHT, DAVE?

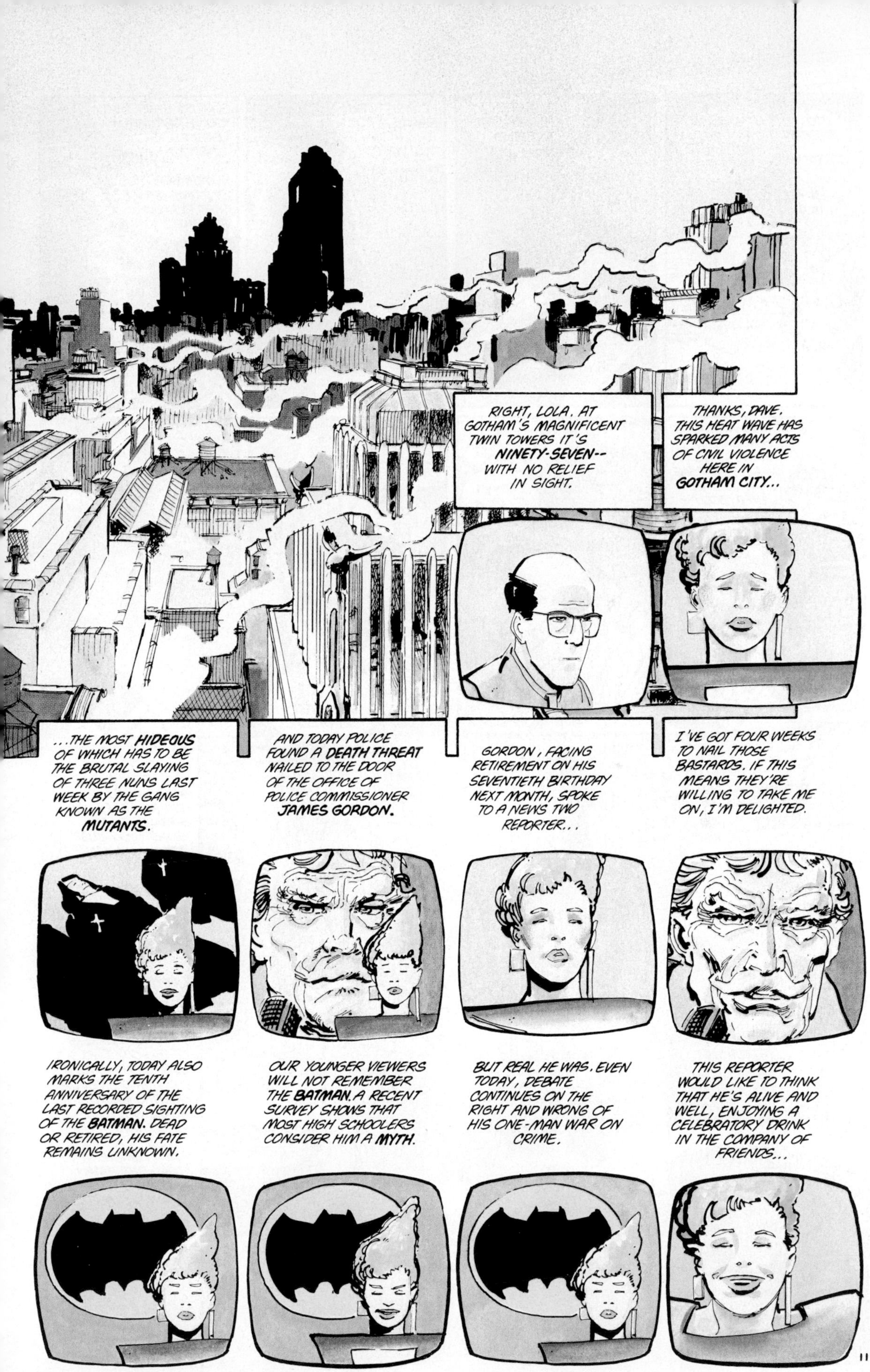
RIGHT, LOLA. AT GOTHAM'S MAGNIFICENT TWIN TOWERS IT'S NINETY-SEVEN-- WITH NO RELIEF IN SIGHT.
THANKS, DAVE. THIS HEAT WAVE HAS SPARKED MANY ACTS OF CIVIL VIOLENCE HERE IN GOTHAM CITY...
...THE MOST HIDEOUS OF WHICH HAS TO BE THE BRUTAL SLAYING OF THREE NUNS LAST WEEK BY THE GANG KNOWN AS THE MUTANTS.
AND TODAY POLICE FOUND A DEATH THREAT NAILED TO THE DOOR OF THE OFFICE OF POLICE COMMISSIONER JAMES GORDON.
GORDON, FACING RETIREMENT ON HIS SEVENTIETH BIRTHDAY NEXT MONTH, SPOKE TO A NEWS TWO REPORTER...
I'VE GOT FOUR WEEKS TO NAIL THOSE BASTARDS. IF THIS MEANS THEY'RE WILLING TO TAKE ME ON, I'M DELIGHTED.
IRONICALLY, TODAY ALSO MARKS THE TENTH ANNIVERSARY OF THE LAST RECORDED SIGHTING OF THE BATMAN. DEAD OR RETIRED, HIS FATE REMAINS UNKNOWN.
OUR YOUNGER VIEWERS WILL NOT REMEMBER THE BATMAN. A RECENT SURVEY SHOWS THAT MOST HIGH SCHOOLERS CONSIDER HIM A MYTH.
BUT REAL HE WAS. EVEN TODAY, DEBATE CONTINUES ON THE RIGHT AND WRONG OF HIS ONE-MAN WAR ON CRIME.
THIS REPORTER WOULD LIKE TO THINK THAT HE'S ALIVE AND WELL, ENJOYING A CELEBRATORY DRINK IN THE COMPANY OF FRIENDS...

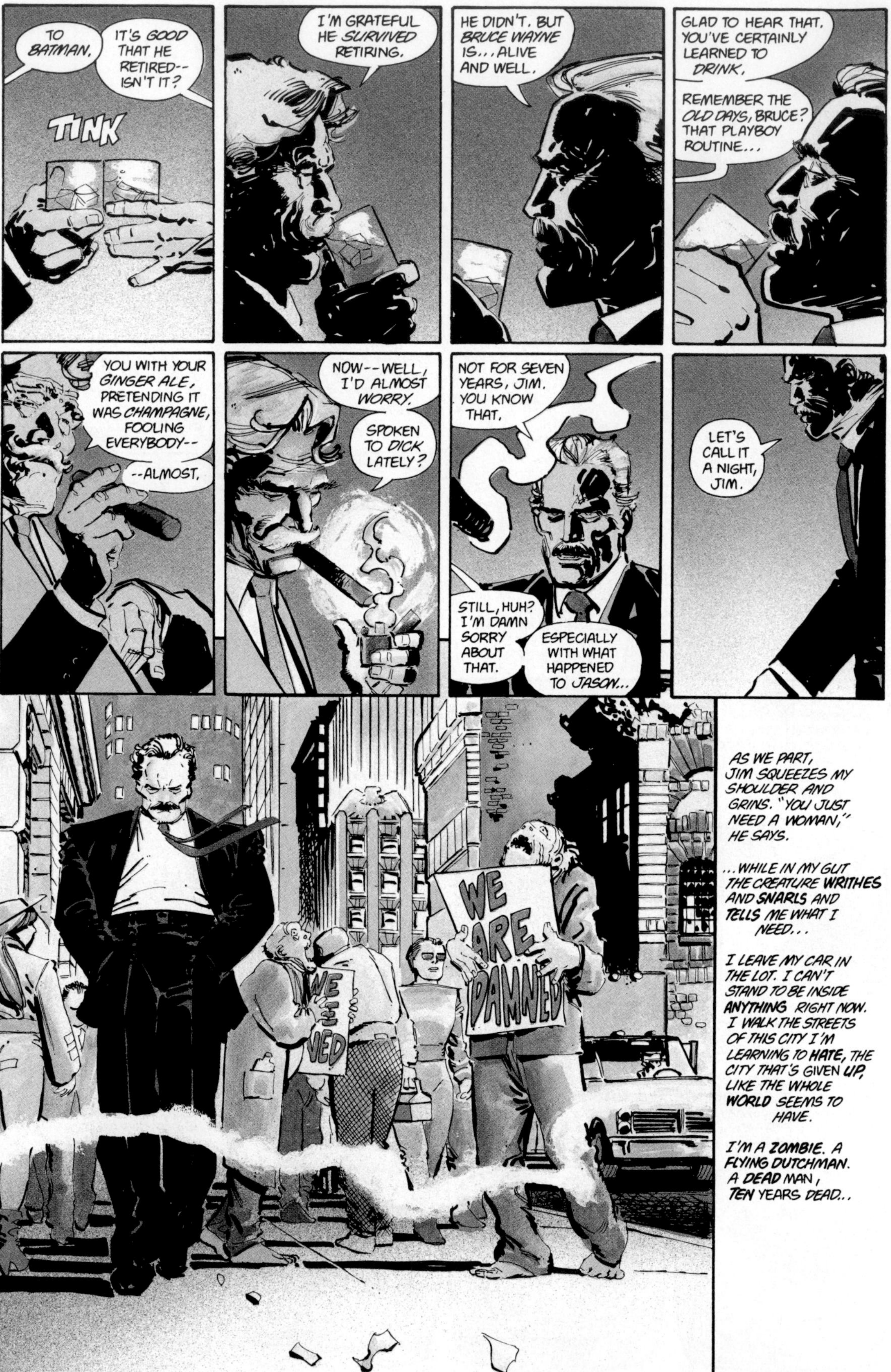
TO BATMAN.
IT'S GOOD THAT HE RETIRED-- ISN'T IT?
TINK
I'M GRATEFUL HE SURVIVED RETIRING.
HE DIDN'T. BUT BRUCE WAYNE IS... ALIVE AND WELL.
GLAD TO HEAR THAT. YOU'VE CERTAINLY LEARNED TO DRINK.
REMEMBER THE OLD DAYS, BRUCE? THAT PLAYBOY ROUTINE...
YOU WITH YOUR GINGER ALE, PRETENDING IT WAS CHAMPAGNE, FOOLING EVERYBODY--
--ALMOST.
NOW--WELL, I'D ALMOST WORRY.
SPOKEN TO DICK LATELY?
NOT FOR SEVEN YEARS, JIM. YOU KNOW THAT.
STILL, HUH? I'M DAMN SORRY ABOUT THAT.
ESPECIALLY WITH WHAT HAPPENED TO JASON...
LET'S CALL IT A NIGHT, JIM.
WE ARE DAMNED
AS WE PART, JIM SQUEEZES MY SHOULDER AND GRINS. "YOU JUST NEED A WOMAN," HE SAYS.
...WHILE IN MY GUT THE CREATURE WRITHES AND SNARLS AND TELLS ME WHAT I NEED...
I LEAVE MY CAR IN THE LOT. I CAN'T STAND TO BE INSIDE ANYTHING RIGHT NOW. I WALK THE STREETS OF THIS CITY I'M LEARNING TO HATE, THE CITY THAT'S GIVEN UP, LIKE THE WHOLE WORLD SEEMS TO HAVE.
I'M A ZOMBIE. A FLYING DUTCHMAN. A DEAD MAN, TEN YEARS DEAD...

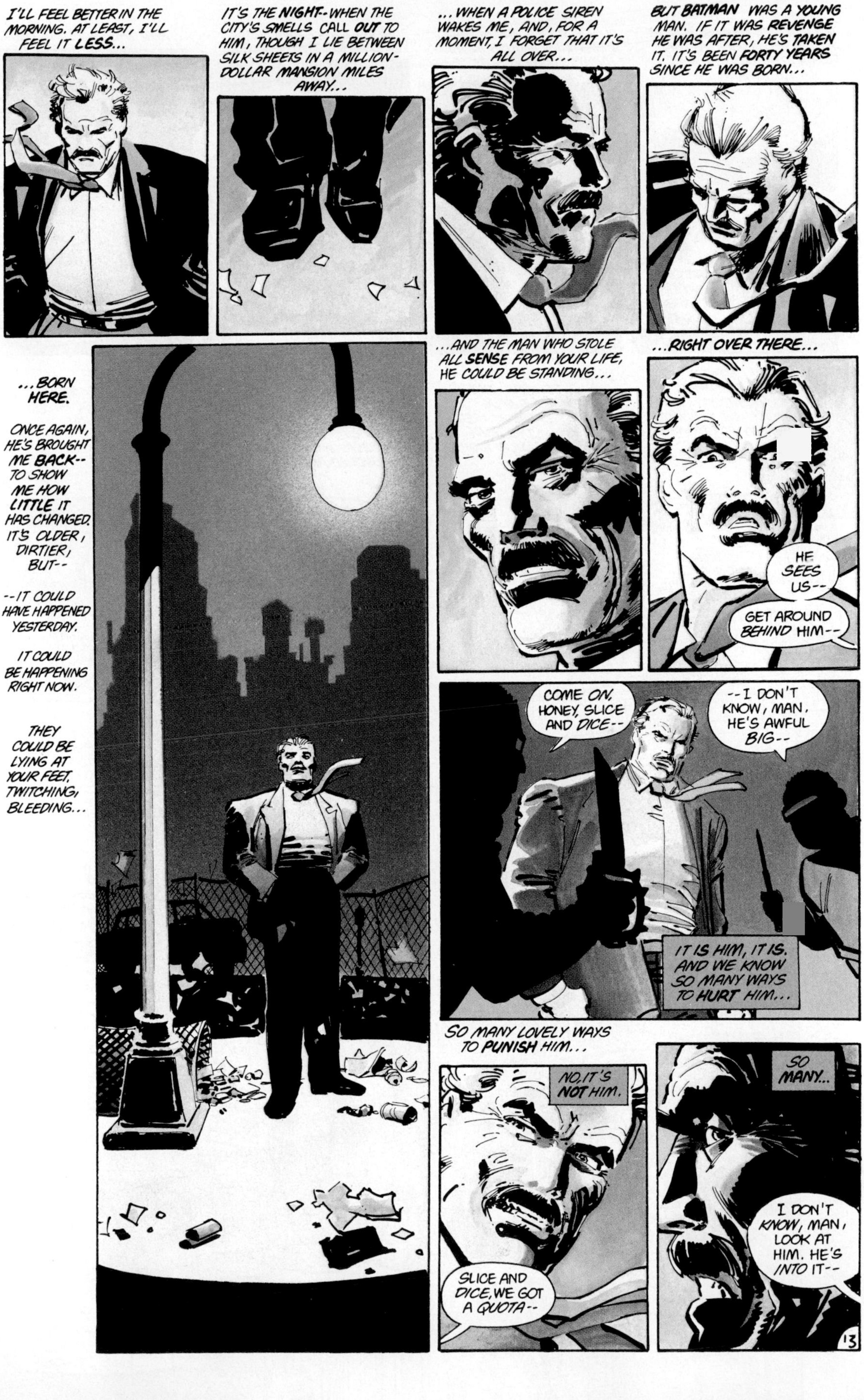
I'LL FEEL BETTER IN THE MORNING. AT LEAST, I'LL FEEL IT LESS...
IT'S THE NIGHT-- WHEN THE CITY'S SMELLS CALL OUT TO HIM, THOUGH I LIE BETWEEN SILK SHEETS IN A MILLION-DOLLAR MANSION MILES AWAY...
...WHEN A POLICE SIREN WAKES ME, AND, FOR A MOMENT, I FORGET THAT IT'S ALL OVER...
BUT BATMAN WAS A YOUNG MAN. IF IT WAS REVENGE HE WAS AFTER, HE'S TAKEN IT. IT'S BEEN FORTY YEARS SINCE HE WAS BORN...
...BORN HERE.
ONCE AGAIN, HE'S BROUGHT ME BACK-- TO SHOW ME HOW LITTLE IT HAS CHANGED. IT'S OLDER, DIRTIER, BUT--
--IT COULD HAVE HAPPENED YESTERDAY.
IT COULD BE HAPPENING RIGHT NOW.
THEY COULD BE LYING AT YOUR FEET, TWITCHING, BLEEDING...
...AND THE MAN WHO STOLE ALL SENSE FROM YOUR LIFE, HE COULD BE STANDING...
...RIGHT OVER THERE...
HE SEES US--
GET AROUND BEHIND HIM--
COME ON, HONEY, SLICE AND DICE--
--I DON'T KNOW, MAN. HE'S AWFUL BIG--
IT IS HIM, IT IS. AND WE KNOW SO MANY WAYS TO HURT HIM...
SO MANY LOVELY WAYS TO PUNISH HIM...
NO, IT'S NOT HIM.
SLICE AND DICE, WE GOT A QUOTA--
SO MANY...
I DON'T KNOW, MAN, LOOK AT HIM. HE'S INTO IT--
13

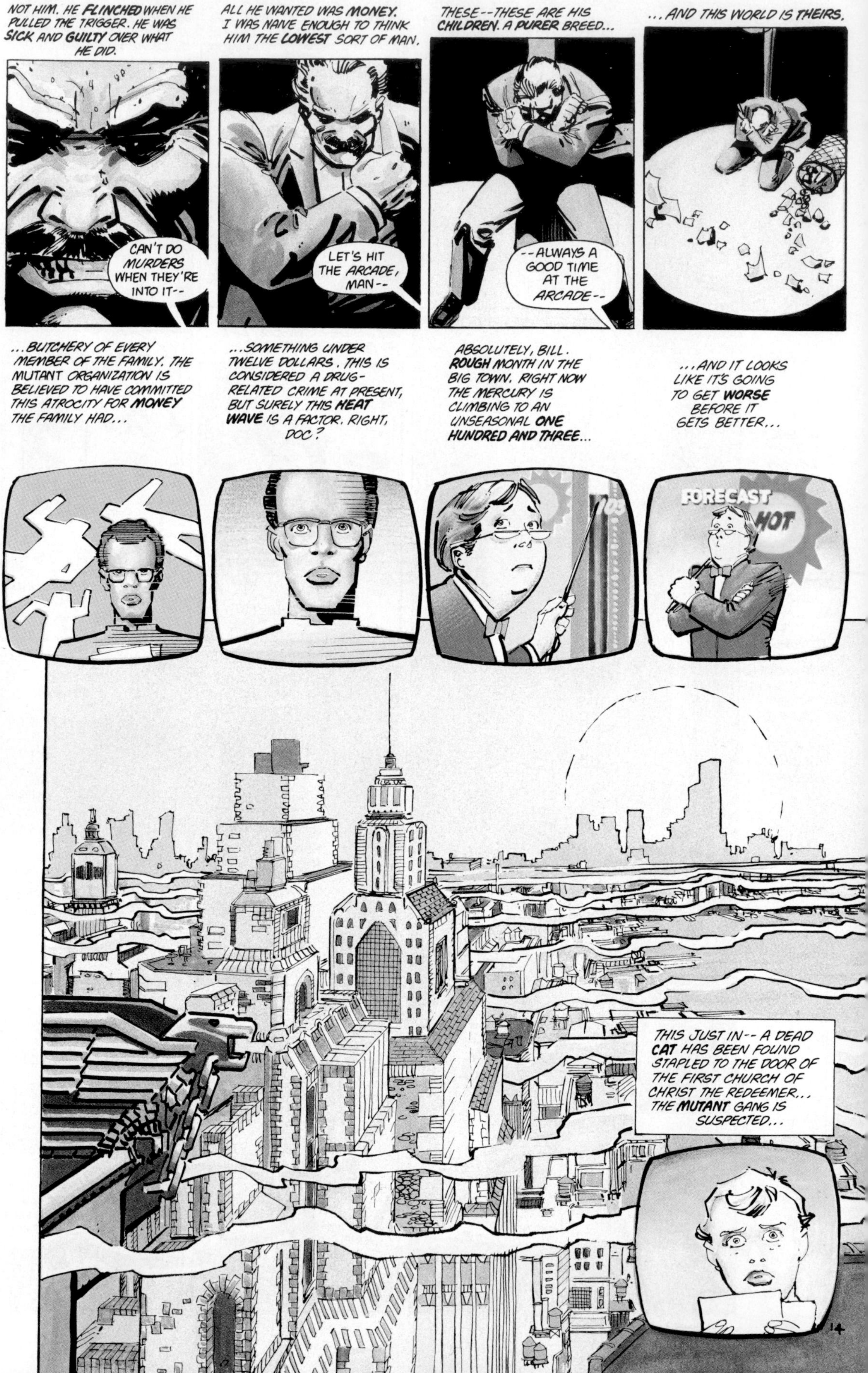

NOT HIM. HE FLINCHED WHEN HE PULLED THE TRIGGER. HE WAS SICK AND GUILTY OVER WHAT HE DID.
CAN'T DO MURDERS WHEN THEY'RE INTO IT--
ALL HE WANTED WAS MONEY. I WAS NAIVE ENOUGH TO THINK HIM THE LOWEST SORT OF MAN.
LET'S HIT THE ARCADE, MAN--
THESE--THESE ARE HIS CHILDREN. A PURER BREED...
--ALWAYS A GOOD TIME AT THE ARCADE--
...AND THIS WORLD IS THEIRS.
...BUTCHERY OF EVERY MEMBER OF THE FAMILY. THE MUTANT ORGANIZATION IS BELIEVED TO HAVE COMMITTED THIS ATROCITY FOR MONEY THE FAMILY HAD...
...SOMETHING UNDER TWELVE DOLLARS. THIS IS CONSIDERED A DRUG-RELATED CRIME AT PRESENT, BUT SURELY THIS HEAT WAVE IS A FACTOR. RIGHT, DOC?
ABSOLUTELY, BILL. ROUGH MONTH IN THE BIG TOWN. RIGHT NOW THE MERCURY IS CLIMBING TO AN UNSEASONAL ONE HUNDRED AND THREE...
...AND IT LOOKS LIKE IT'S GOING TO GET WORSE BEFORE IT GETS BETTER...
FORECAST
HOT
THIS JUST IN-- A DEAD CAT HAS BEEN FOUND STAPLED TO THE DOOR OF THE FIRST CHURCH OF CHRIST THE REDEEMER... THE MUTANT GANG IS SUSPECTED...

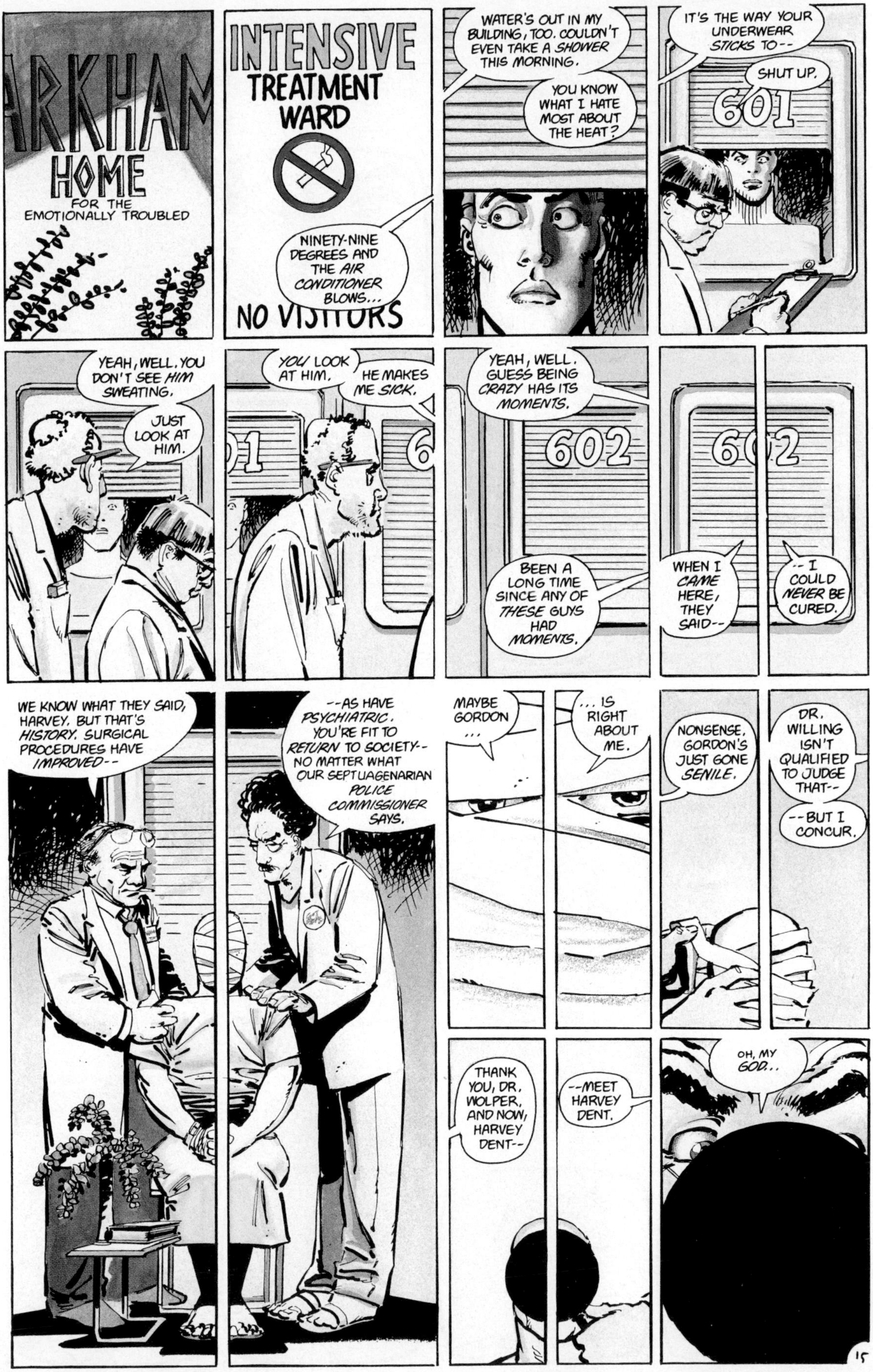
ARKHAM HOME FOR THE EMOTIONALLY TROUBLED
INTENSIVE TREATMENT WARD
NO VISITORS
NINETY-NINE DEGREES AND THE AIR CONDITIONER BLOWS...
WATER'S OUT IN MY BUILDING, TOO. COULDN'T EVEN TAKE A SHOWER THIS MORNING.
YOU KNOW WHAT I HATE MOST ABOUT THE HEAT?
IT'S THE WAY YOUR UNDERWEAR STICKS TO--
SHUT UP.
601
YEAH, WELL, YOU DON'T SEE HIM SWEATING.
JUST LOOK AT HIM.
YOU LOOK AT HIM.
HE MAKES ME SICK.
YEAH, WELL. GUESS BEING CRAZY HAS ITS MOMENTS.
602
BEEN A LONG TIME SINCE ANY OF THESE GUYS HAD MOMENTS.
WHEN I CAME HERE, THEY SAID--
--I COULD NEVER BE CURED.
WE KNOW WHAT THEY SAID, HARVEY. BUT THAT'S HISTORY. SURGICAL PROCEDURES HAVE IMPROVED--
--AS HAVE PSYCHIATRIC. YOU'RE FIT TO RETURN TO SOCIETY--NO MATTER WHAT OUR SEPTUAGENARIAN POLICE COMMISSIONER SAYS.
MAYBE GORDON ...
...IS RIGHT ABOUT ME.
NONSENSE. GORDON'S JUST GONE SENILE.
DR. WILLING ISN'T QUALIFIED TO JUDGE THAT--
--BUT I CONCUR.
THANK YOU, DR. WOLPER. AND NOW, HARVEY DENT--
--MEET HARVEY DENT.
OH, MY GOD...

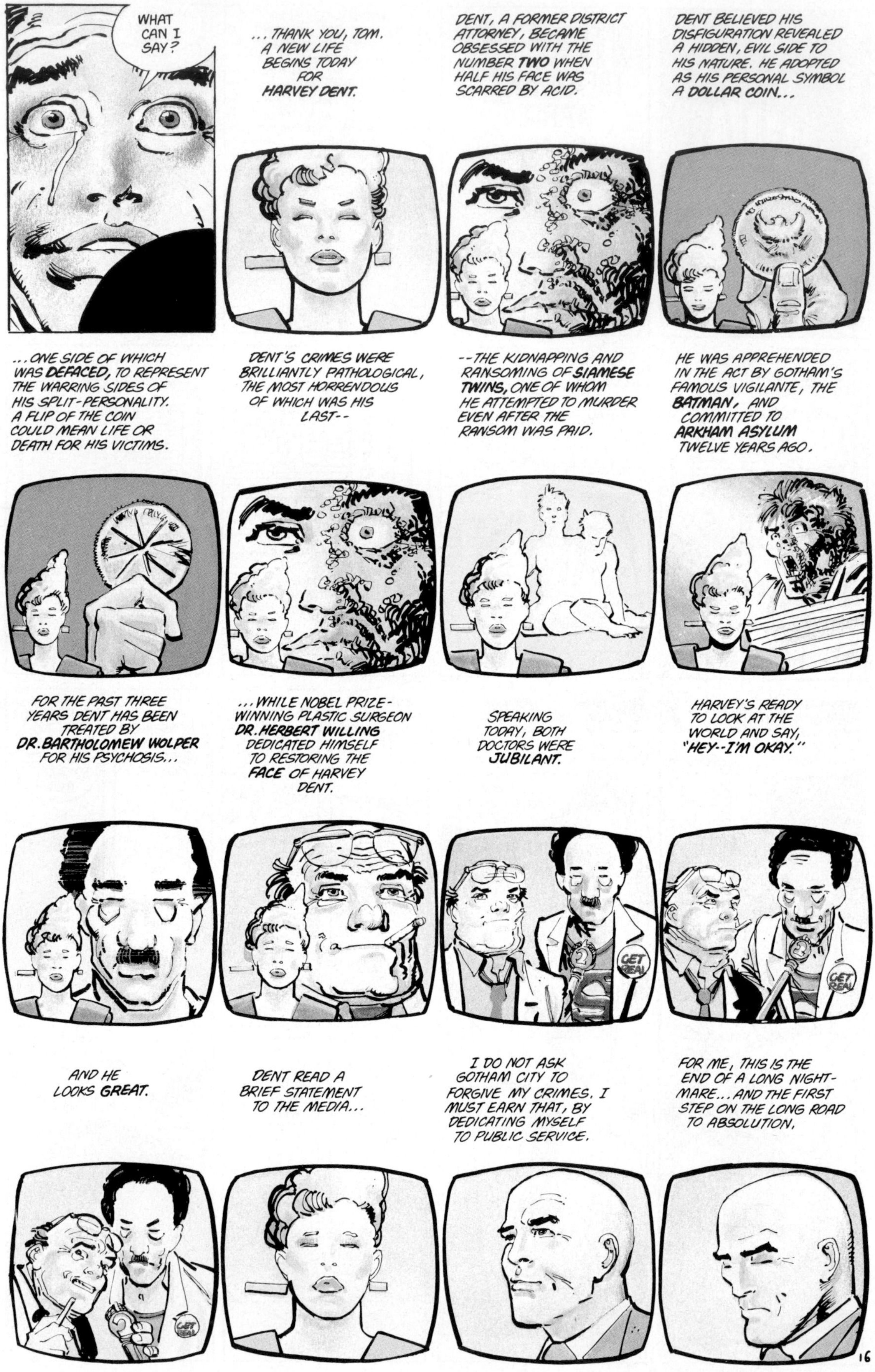

WHAT CAN I SAY?
...THANK YOU, TOM. A NEW LIFE BEGINS TODAY FOR HARVEY DENT.
DENT, A FORMER DISTRICT ATTORNEY, BECAME OBSESSED WITH THE NUMBER TWO WHEN HALF HIS FACE WAS SCARRED BY ACID.
DENT BELIEVED HIS DISFIGURATION REVEALED A HIDDEN, EVIL SIDE TO HIS NATURE. HE ADOPTED AS HIS PERSONAL SYMBOL A DOLLAR COIN...
...ONE SIDE OF WHICH WAS DEFACED, TO REPRESENT THE WARRING SIDES OF HIS SPLIT-PERSONALITY. A FLIP OF THE COIN COULD MEAN LIFE OR DEATH FOR HIS VICTIMS.
DENT'S CRIMES WERE BRILLIANTLY PATHOLOGICAL, THE MOST HORRENDOUS OF WHICH WAS HIS LAST--
--THE KIDNAPPING AND RANSOMING OF SIAMESE TWINS, ONE OF WHOM HE ATTEMPTED TO MURDER EVEN AFTER THE RANSOM WAS PAID.
HE WAS APPREHENDED IN THE ACT BY GOTHAM'S FAMOUS VIGILANTE, THE BATMAN, AND COMMITTED TO ARKHAM ASYLUM TWELVE YEARS AGO.
FOR THE PAST THREE YEARS DENT HAS BEEN TREATED BY DR. BARTHOLOMEW WOLPER FOR HIS PSYCHOSIS...
...WHILE NOBEL PRIZE-WINNING PLASTIC SURGEON DR. HERBERT WILLING DEDICATED HIMSELF TO RESTORING THE FACE OF HARVEY DENT.
SPEAKING TODAY, BOTH DOCTORS WERE JUBILANT.
HARVEY'S READY TO LOOK AT THE WORLD AND SAY, "HEY--I'M OKAY."
GET REAL
GET REAL
AND HE LOOKS GREAT.
DENT READ A BRIEF STATEMENT TO THE MEDIA...
I DO NOT ASK GOTHAM CITY TO FORGIVE MY CRIMES. I MUST EARN THAT, BY DEDICATING MYSELF TO PUBLIC SERVICE.
FOR ME, THIS IS THE END OF A LONG NIGHT-MARE... AND THE FIRST STEP ON THE LONG ROAD TO ABSOLUTION.
GET REAL

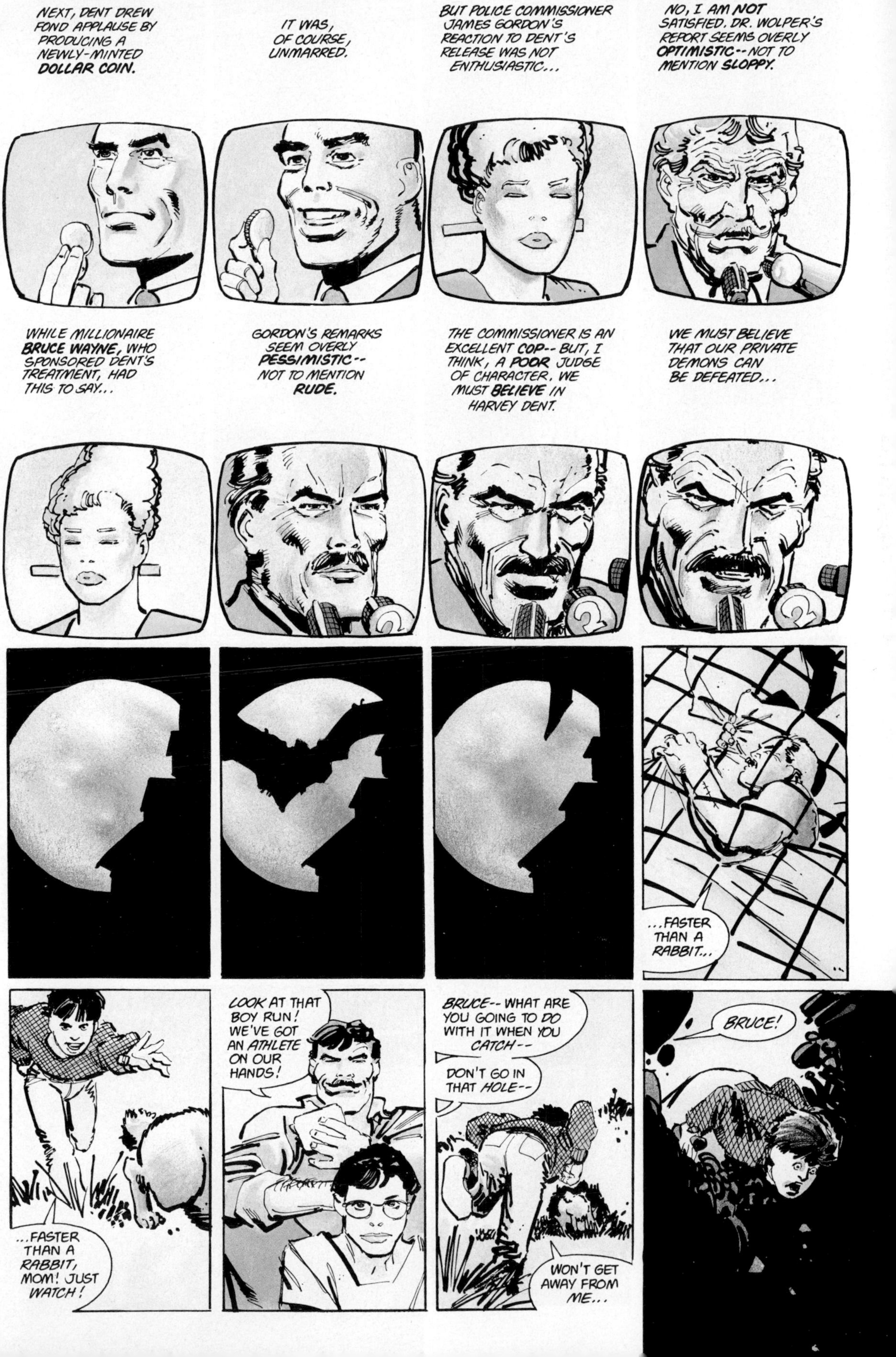

NEXT, DENT DREW FOND APPLAUSE BY PRODUCING A NEWLY-MINTED **DOLLAR COIN.**
IT WAS, OF COURSE, UNMARRED.
BUT POLICE COMMISSIONER JAMES GORDON'S REACTION TO DENT'S RELEASE WAS NOT ENTHUSIASTIC...
NO, I AM **NOT** SATISFIED. DR. WOLPER'S REPORT SEEMS OVERLY **OPTIMISTIC**-- NOT TO MENTION **SLOPPY.**
WHILE MILLIONAIRE **BRUCE WAYNE,** WHO SPONSORED DENT'S TREATMENT, HAD THIS TO SAY...
GORDON'S REMARKS SEEM OVERLY **PESSIMISTIC**-- NOT TO MENTION **RUDE.**
THE COMMISSIONER IS AN EXCELLENT **COP**-- BUT, I THINK, A **POOR** JUDGE OF CHARACTER. WE MUST **BELIEVE** IN HARVEY DENT.
WE MUST **BELIEVE** THAT OUR PRIVATE DEMONS CAN BE DEFEATED...
...FASTER THAN A RABBIT...
...FASTER THAN A RABBIT, MOM! JUST WATCH!
LOOK AT THAT BOY RUN! WE'VE GOT AN *ATHLETE* ON OUR HANDS!
BRUCE-- WHAT ARE YOU GOING TO *DO* WITH IT WHEN YOU *CATCH*--
DON'T GO IN THAT *HOLE*--
WON'T GET AWAY FROM ME...
BRUCE!

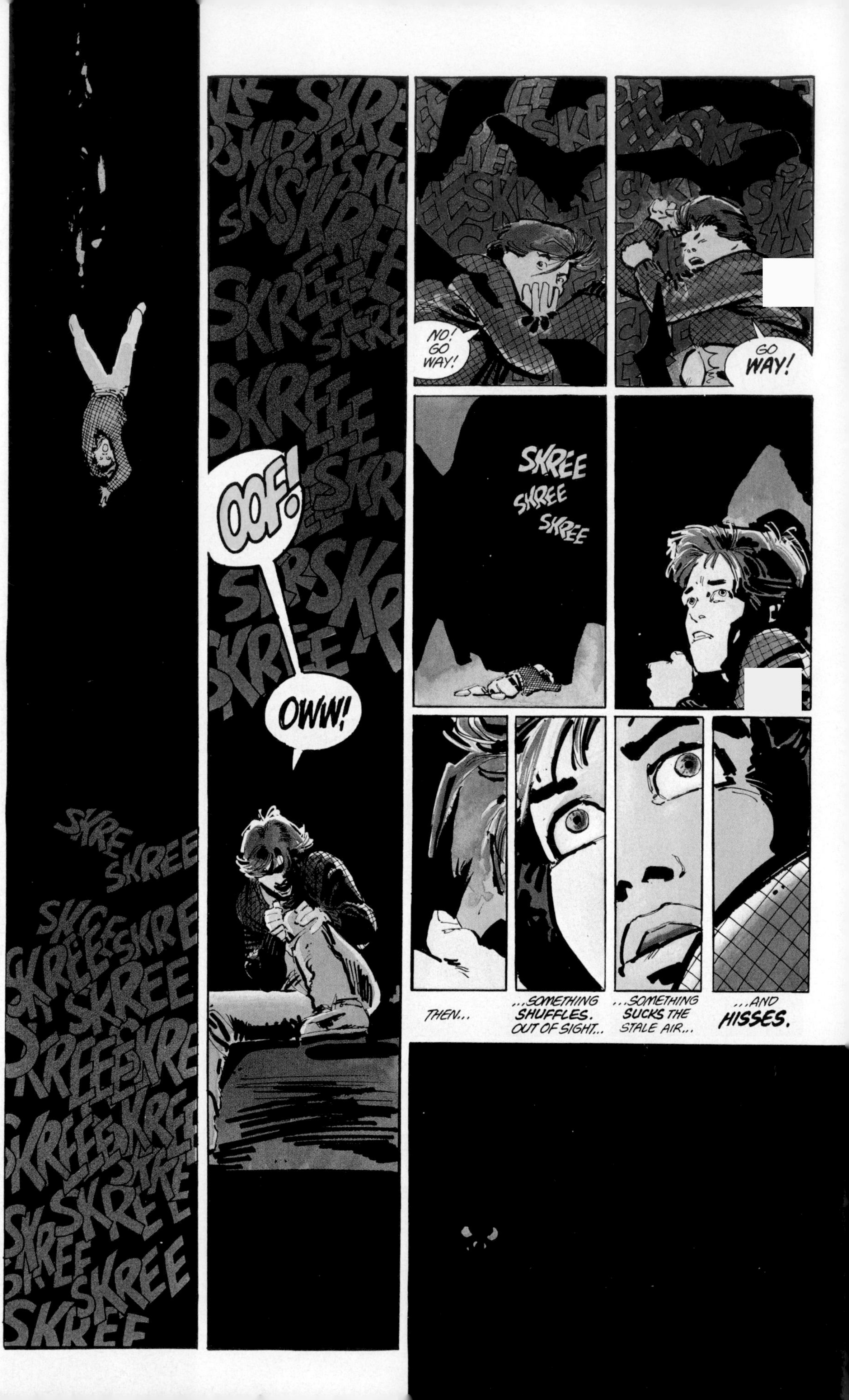
OOF!
OWW!
NO! GO WAY!
GO WAY!
SKREE
SKREE
SKREE
THEN...
...SOMETHING SHUFFLES. OUT OF SIGHT...
...SOMETHING SUCKS THE STALE AIR...
...AND HISSES.

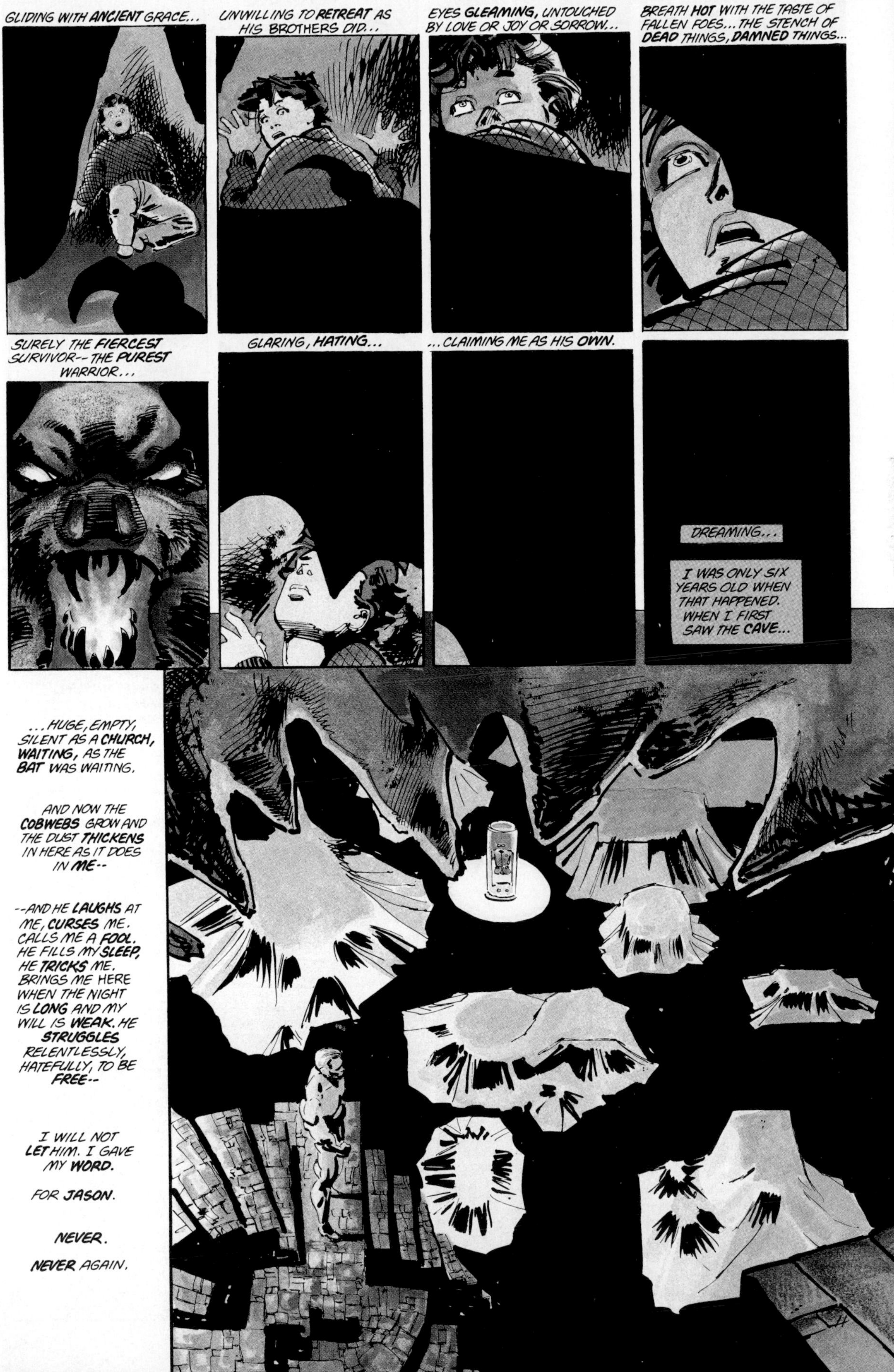
GLIDING WITH ANCIENT GRACE...
UNWILLING TO RETREAT AS HIS BROTHERS DID...
EYES GLEAMING, UNTOUCHED BY LOVE OR JOY OR SORROW...
BREATH HOT WITH THE TASTE OF FALLEN FOES...THE STENCH OF DEAD THINGS, DAMNED THINGS...
SURELY THE FIERCEST SURVIVOR--THE PUREST WARRIOR...
GLARING, HATING...
...CLAIMING ME AS HIS OWN.
DREAMING...
I WAS ONLY SIX YEARS OLD WHEN THAT HAPPENED. WHEN I FIRST SAW THE CAVE...
...HUGE, EMPTY, SILENT AS A CHURCH, WAITING, AS THE BAT WAS WAITING.
AND NOW THE COBWEBS GROW AND THE DUST THICKENS IN HERE AS IT DOES IN ME--
--AND HE LAUGHS AT ME, CURSES ME. CALLS ME A FOOL. HE FILLS MY SLEEP, HE TRICKS ME. BRINGS ME HERE WHEN THE NIGHT IS LONG AND MY WILL IS WEAK. HE STRUGGLES RELENTLESSLY, HATEFULLY, TO BE FREE--
I WILL NOT LET HIM. I GAVE MY WORD.
FOR JASON.
NEVER.
NEVER AGAIN.

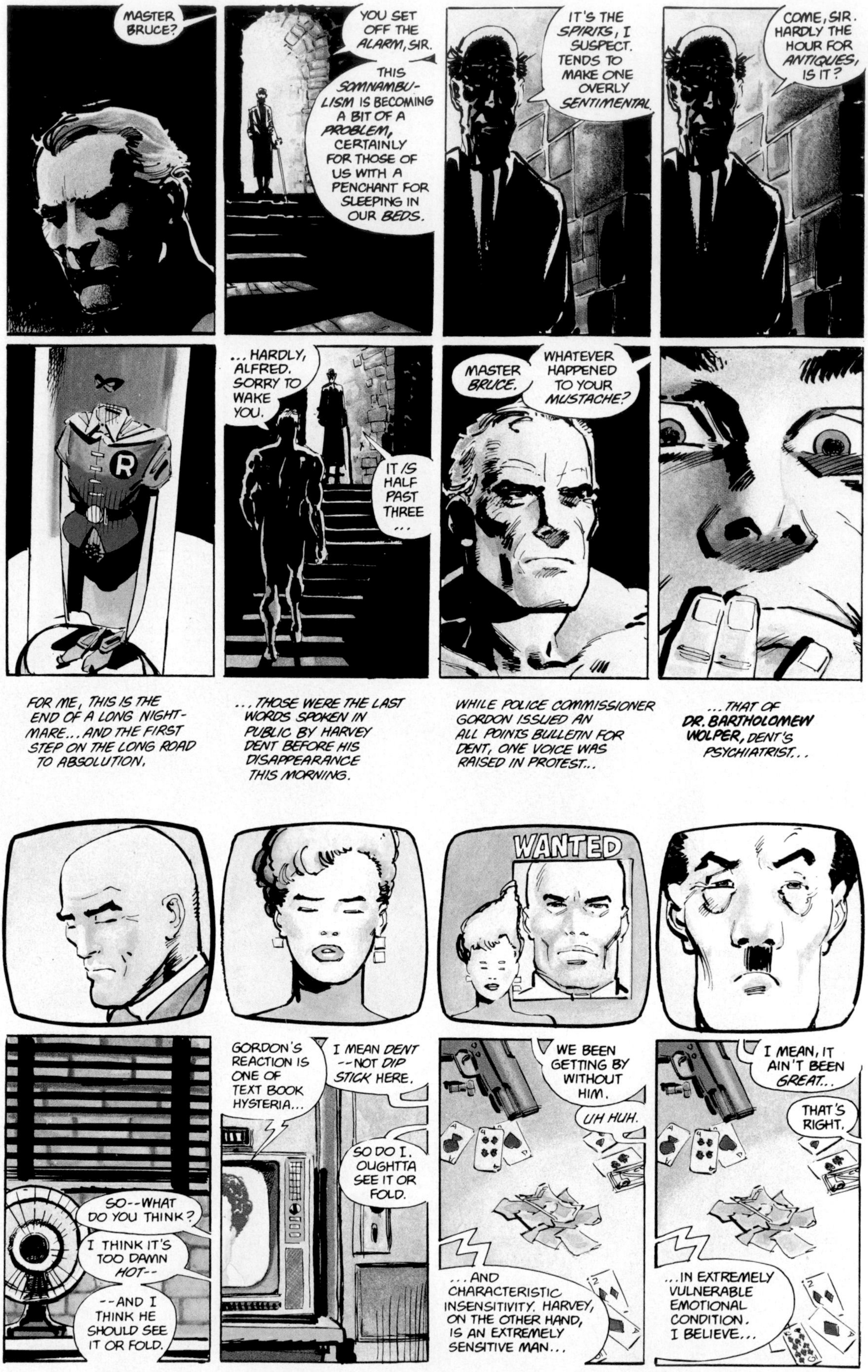
MASTER BRUCE?
YOU SET OFF THE ALARM, SIR.
THIS SOMNAMBULISM IS BECOMING A BIT OF A PROBLEM, CERTAINLY FOR THOSE OF US WITH A PENCHANT FOR SLEEPING IN OUR BEDS.
IT'S THE SPIRITS, I SUSPECT. TENDS TO MAKE ONE OVERLY SENTIMENTAL.
COME, SIR. HARDLY THE HOUR FOR ANTIQUES, IS IT?
...HARDLY, ALFRED. SORRY TO WAKE YOU.
IT IS HALF PAST THREE ...
MASTER BRUCE.
WHATEVER HAPPENED TO YOUR MUSTACHE?
FOR ME, THIS IS THE END OF A LONG NIGHTMARE... AND THE FIRST STEP ON THE LONG ROAD TO ABSOLUTION.
...THOSE WERE THE LAST WORDS SPOKEN IN PUBLIC BY HARVEY DENT BEFORE HIS DISAPPEARANCE THIS MORNING.
WHILE POLICE COMMISSIONER GORDON ISSUED AN ALL POINTS BULLETIN FOR DENT, ONE VOICE WAS RAISED IN PROTEST...
...THAT OF DR. BARTHOLOMEW WOLPER, DENT'S PSYCHIATRIST...
WANTED
SO--WHAT DO YOU THINK?
I THINK IT'S TOO DAMN HOT--
--AND I THINK HE SHOULD SEE IT OR FOLD.
GORDON'S REACTION IS ONE OF TEXT BOOK HYSTERIA...
I MEAN DENT --NOT DIP STICK HERE.
SO DO I. OUGHTTA SEE IT OR FOLD.
WE BEEN GETTING BY WITHOUT HIM.
UH HUH.
...AND CHARACTERISTIC INSENSITIVITY. HARVEY, ON THE OTHER HAND, IS AN EXTREMELY SENSITIVE MAN...
I MEAN, IT AIN'T BEEN GREAT...
THAT'S RIGHT.
...IN EXTREMELY VULNERABLE EMOTIONAL CONDITION. I BELIEVE...

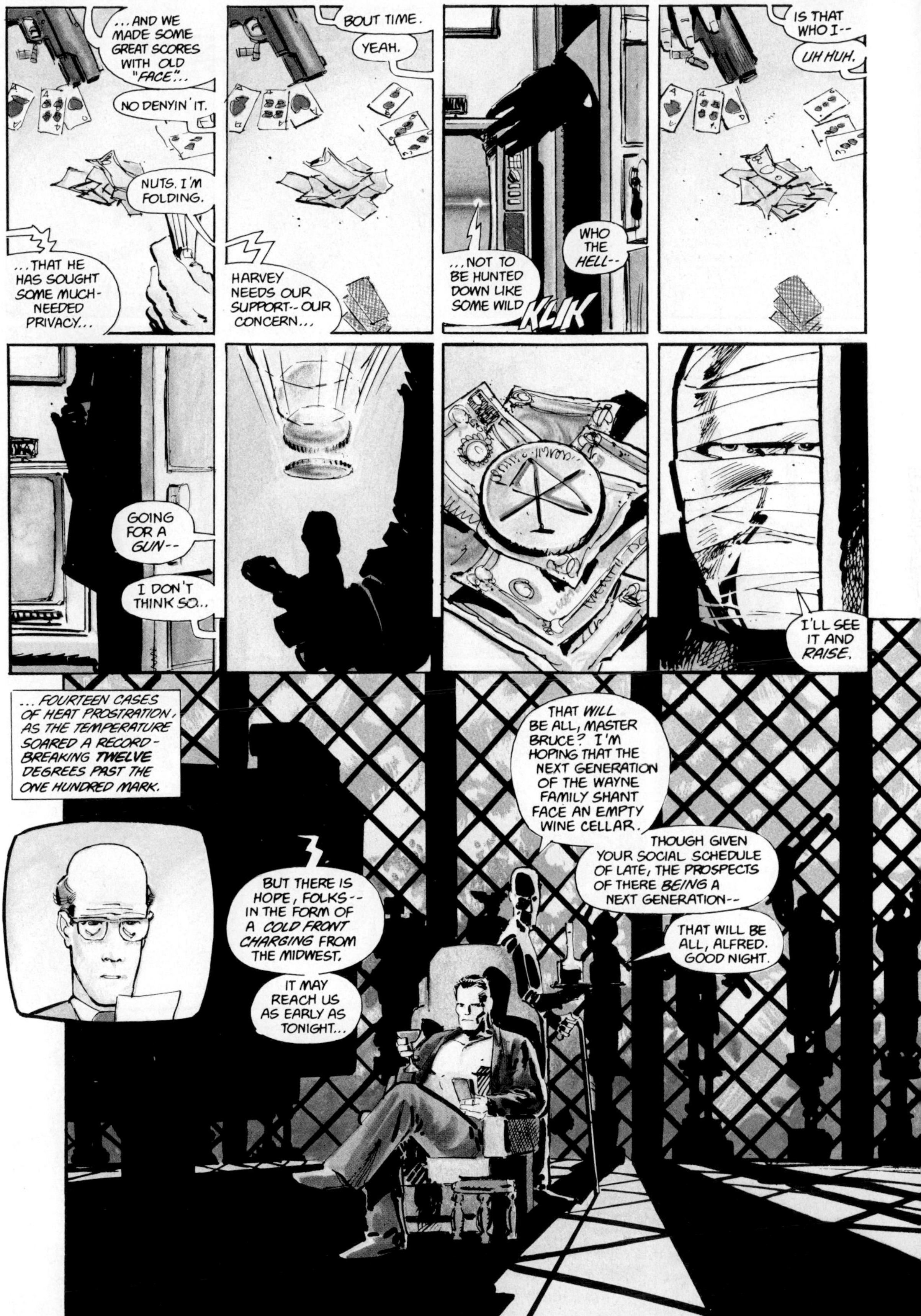
...AND WE MADE SOME GREAT SCORES WITH OLD "FACE"...
NO DENYIN' IT.
NUTS. I'M FOLDING.
...THAT HE HAS SOUGHT SOME MUCH-NEEDED PRIVACY...
BOUT TIME.
YEAH.
HARVEY NEEDS OUR SUPPORT--OUR CONCERN...
...NOT TO BE HUNTED DOWN LIKE SOME WILD
WHO THE HELL--
KLIK
IS THAT WHO I--
UH HUH.
GOING FOR A GUN--
I DON'T THINK SO...
I'LL SEE IT AND RAISE.
...FOURTEEN CASES OF HEAT PROSTRATION, AS THE TEMPERATURE SOARED A RECORD-BREAKING TWELVE DEGREES PAST THE ONE HUNDRED MARK.
BUT THERE IS HOPE, FOLKS--IN THE FORM OF A COLD FRONT CHARGING FROM THE MIDWEST.
IT MAY REACH US AS EARLY AS TONIGHT...
THAT WILL BE ALL, MASTER BRUCE? I'M HOPING THAT THE NEXT GENERATION OF THE WAYNE FAMILY SHANT FACE AN EMPTY WINE CELLAR.
THOUGH GIVEN YOUR SOCIAL SCHEDULE OF LATE, THE PROSPECTS OF THERE BEING A NEXT GENERATION--
THAT WILL BE ALL, ALFRED. GOOD NIGHT.

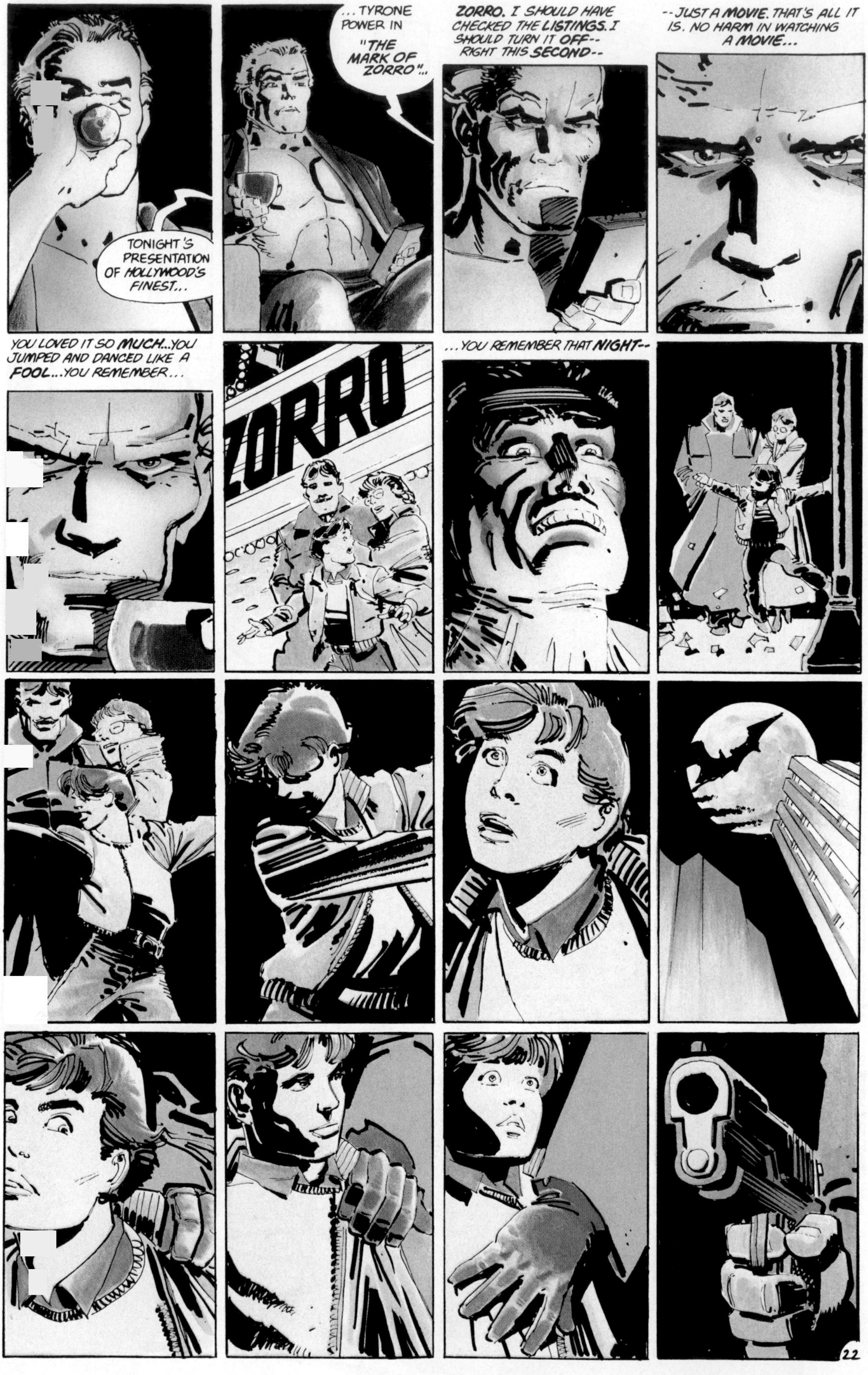

TONIGHT'S PRESENTATION OF HOLLYWOOD'S FINEST...
...TYRONE POWER IN "THE MARK OF ZORRO"...
ZORRO. I SHOULD HAVE CHECKED THE LISTINGS. I SHOULD TURN IT OFF-- RIGHT THIS SECOND--
--JUST A MOVIE. THAT'S ALL IT IS. NO HARM IN WATCHING A MOVIE...
YOU LOVED IT SO MUCH...YOU JUMPED AND DANCED LIKE A FOOL...YOU REMEMBER...
ZORRO
...YOU REMEMBER THAT NIGHT--

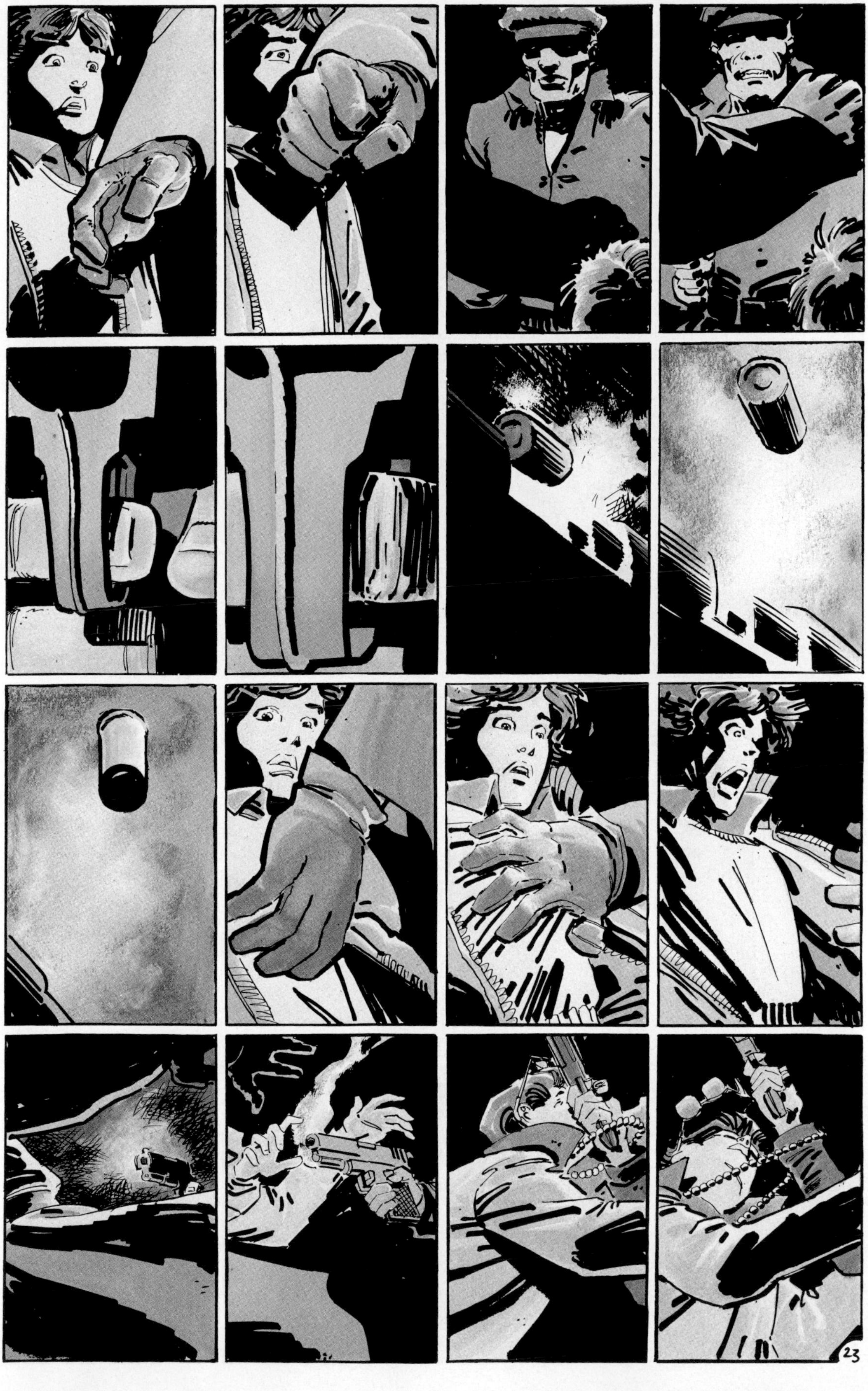

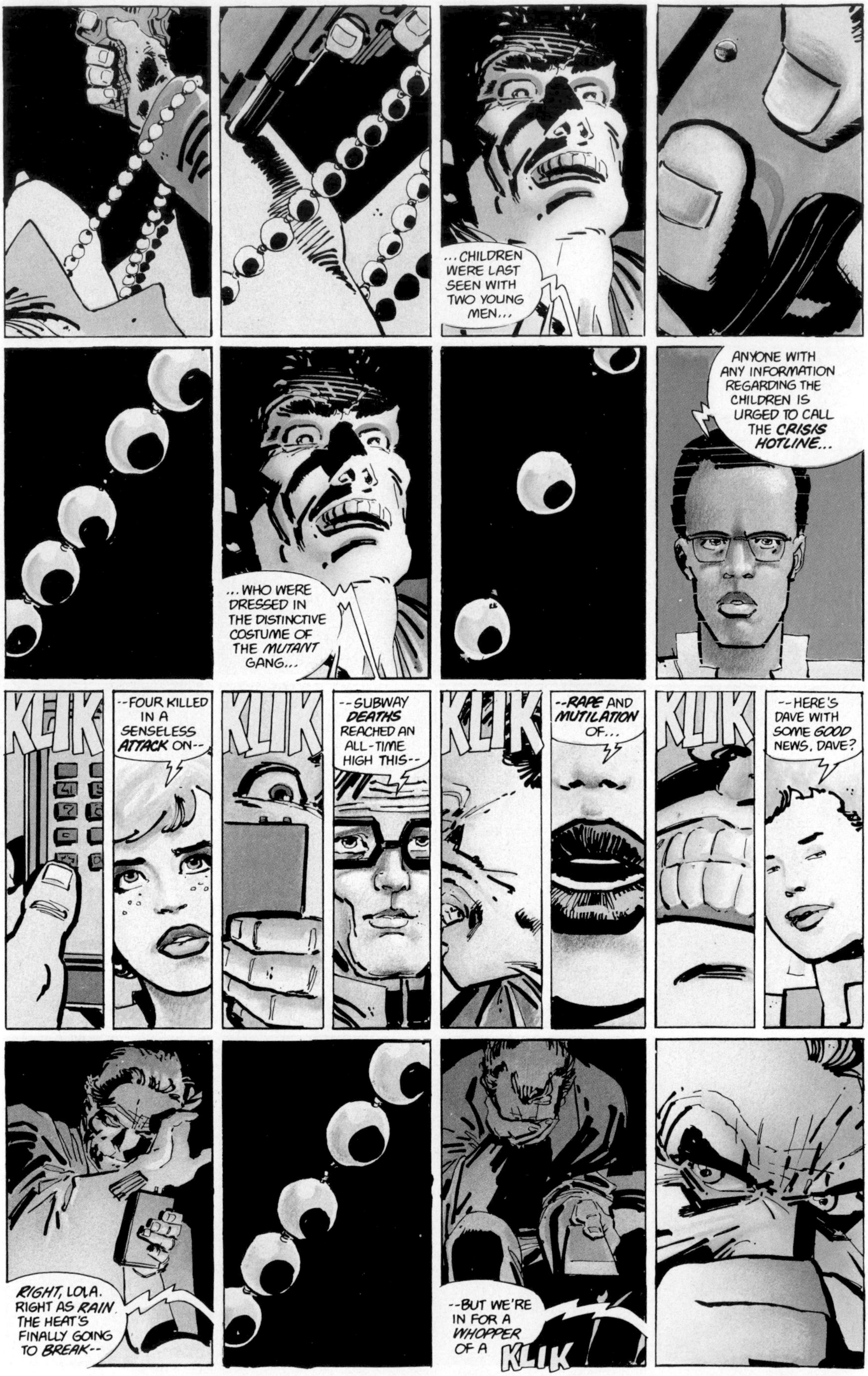
...CHILDREN WERE LAST SEEN WITH TWO YOUNG MEN...
...WHO WERE DRESSED IN THE DISTINCTIVE COSTUME OF THE MUTANT GANG...
ANYONE WITH ANY INFORMATION REGARDING THE CHILDREN IS URGED TO CALL THE CRISIS HOTLINE...
KLIK
--FOUR KILLED IN A SENSELESS ATTACK ON--
KLIK
--SUBWAY DEATHS REACHED AN ALL-TIME HIGH THIS--
KLIK
--RAPE AND MUTILATION OF...
KLIK
--HERE'S DAVE WITH SOME GOOD NEWS, DAVE?
RIGHT, LOLA. RIGHT AS RAIN. THE HEAT'S FINALLY GOING TO BREAK--
--BUT WE'RE IN FOR A WHOPPER OF A
KLIK

THE TIME HAS COME.

YOU KNOW IT IN YOUR SOUL.

FOR I AM YOUR SOUL...

YOU CANNOT ESCAPE ME...

YOU ARE PUNY, YOU ARE SMALL--

YOU ARE NOTHING--A HOLLOW SHELL, A RUSTY TRAP THAT CANNOT HOLD ME--

SMOLDERING, I BURN YOU-- BURNING YOU, I FLARE, HOT AND BRIGHT AND FIERCE AND BEAUTIFUL--

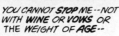
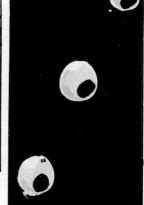

YOU CANNOT STOP ME--NOT WITH WINE OR VOWS OR THE WEIGHT OF AGE--

YOU CANNOT STOP ME BUT STILL YOU TRY-- STILL YOU RUN--

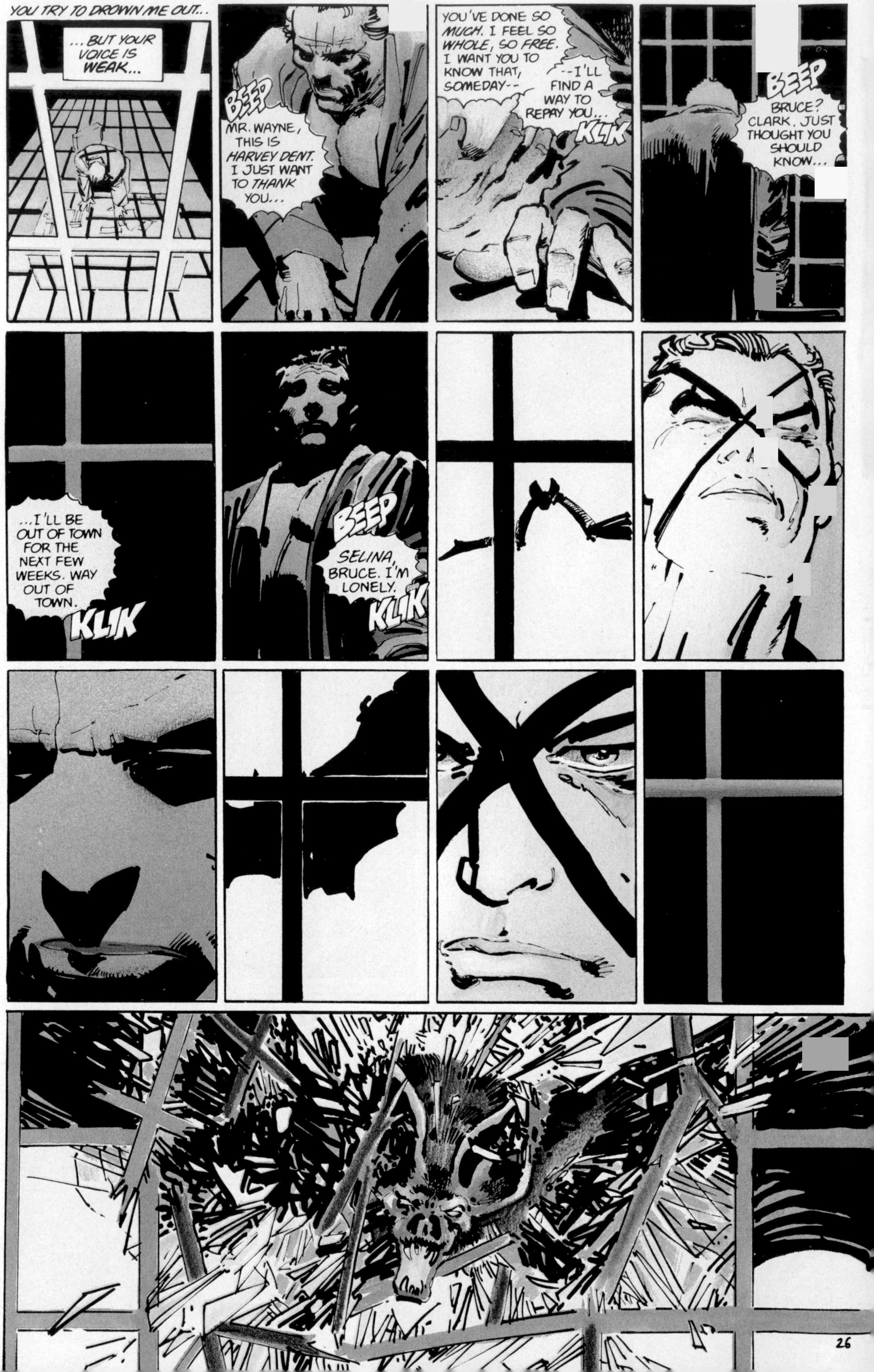
YOU TRY TO DROWN ME OUT...
...BUT YOUR VOICE IS WEAK...
BEEP
MR. WAYNE, THIS IS HARVEY DENT. I JUST WANT TO THANK YOU...
YOU'VE DONE SO MUCH. I FEEL SO WHOLE, SO FREE. I WANT YOU TO KNOW THAT, SOMEDAY--
--I'LL FIND A WAY TO REPAY YOU...
KLIK
BEEP
BRUCE? CLARK. JUST THOUGHT YOU SHOULD KNOW...
...I'LL BE OUT OF TOWN FOR THE NEXT FEW WEEKS. WAY OUT OF TOWN.
KLIK
BEEP
SELINA. BRUCE. I'M LONELY.
KLIK

RRRRMMMMBBBLLLLLL

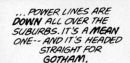

... POWER LINES ARE **DOWN** ALL OVER THE SUBURBS. IT'S A **MEAN** ONE-- AND IT'S HEADED STRAIGHT FOR GOTHAM.

LIKE THE WRATH OF GOD IT'S HEADED FOR GOTHAM...

... STRAIGHT OUT OF **NOWHERE** THIS COMES. AND HAVE I MY UMBRELLA?

SURELY **NOT**, AND HAD I MY UMBRELLA WOULD IT NOW BE RAINING?

SURELY NOT--

HEY, MOMMIE...

... COME IN HERE WHERE IT'S WARM.

I NEED YOU, MOMMIE.

MAKE ME FEEL SAFE.

OH NO PLEASE...

PLEASE GOD NO--

TALK SOFT...

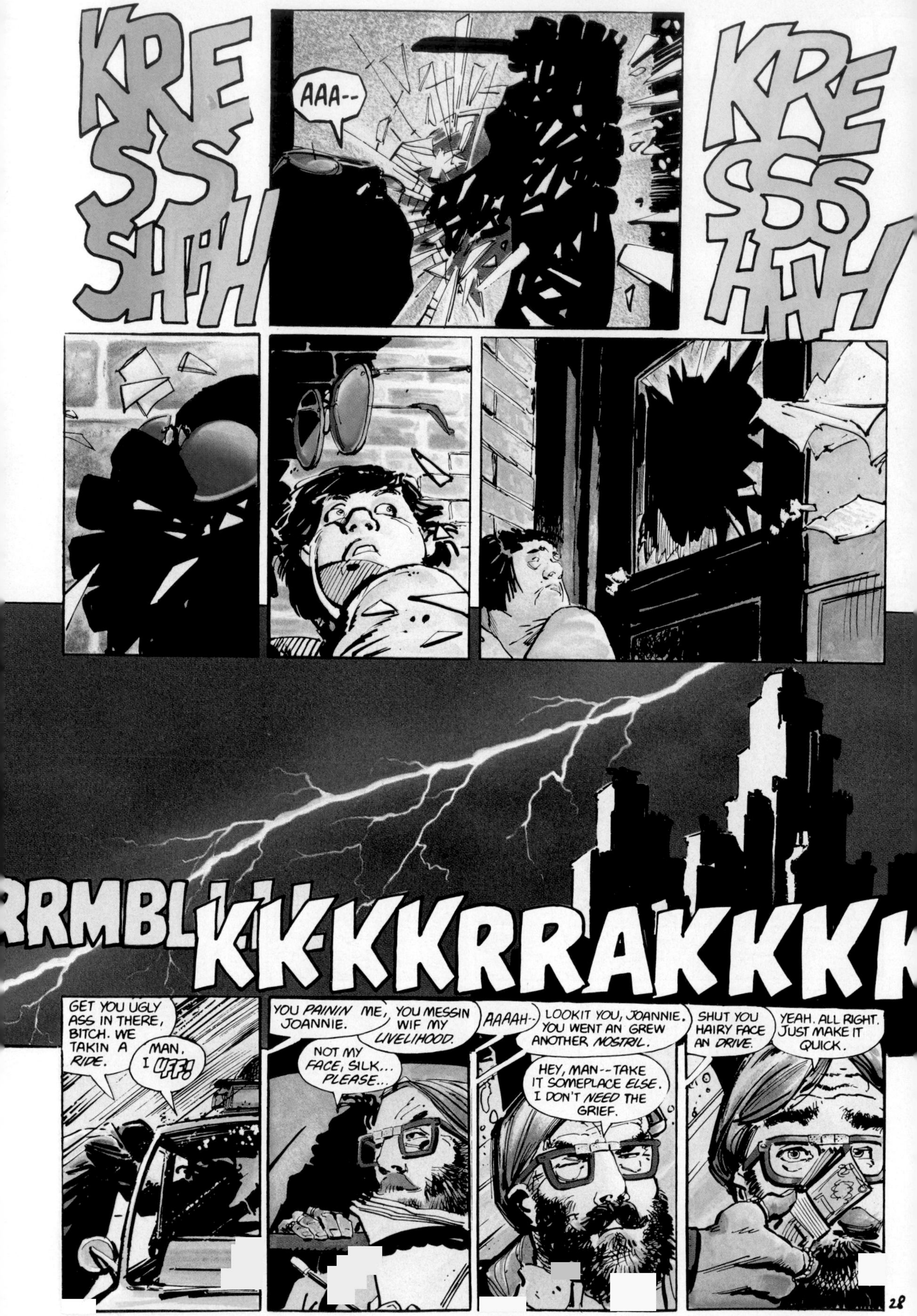

KRESSSHHH
AAA--
KRESSSSHHH
RRMBL
KKKKRRAKKKK
GET YOU UGLY ASS IN THERE, BITCH. WE TAKIN A RIDE.
MAN. I UFF!
YOU PAININ ME, JOANNIE.
YOU MESSIN WIF MY LIVELIHOOD.
NOT MY FACE, SILK... PLEASE...
AAAAH--
LOOKIT YOU, JOANNIE. YOU WENT AN GREW ANOTHER NOSTRIL.
HEY, MAN--TAKE IT SOMEPLACE ELSE. I DON'T NEED THE GRIEF.
SHUT YOU HAIRY FACE AN DRIVE.
YEAH. ALL RIGHT. JUST MAKE IT QUICK.

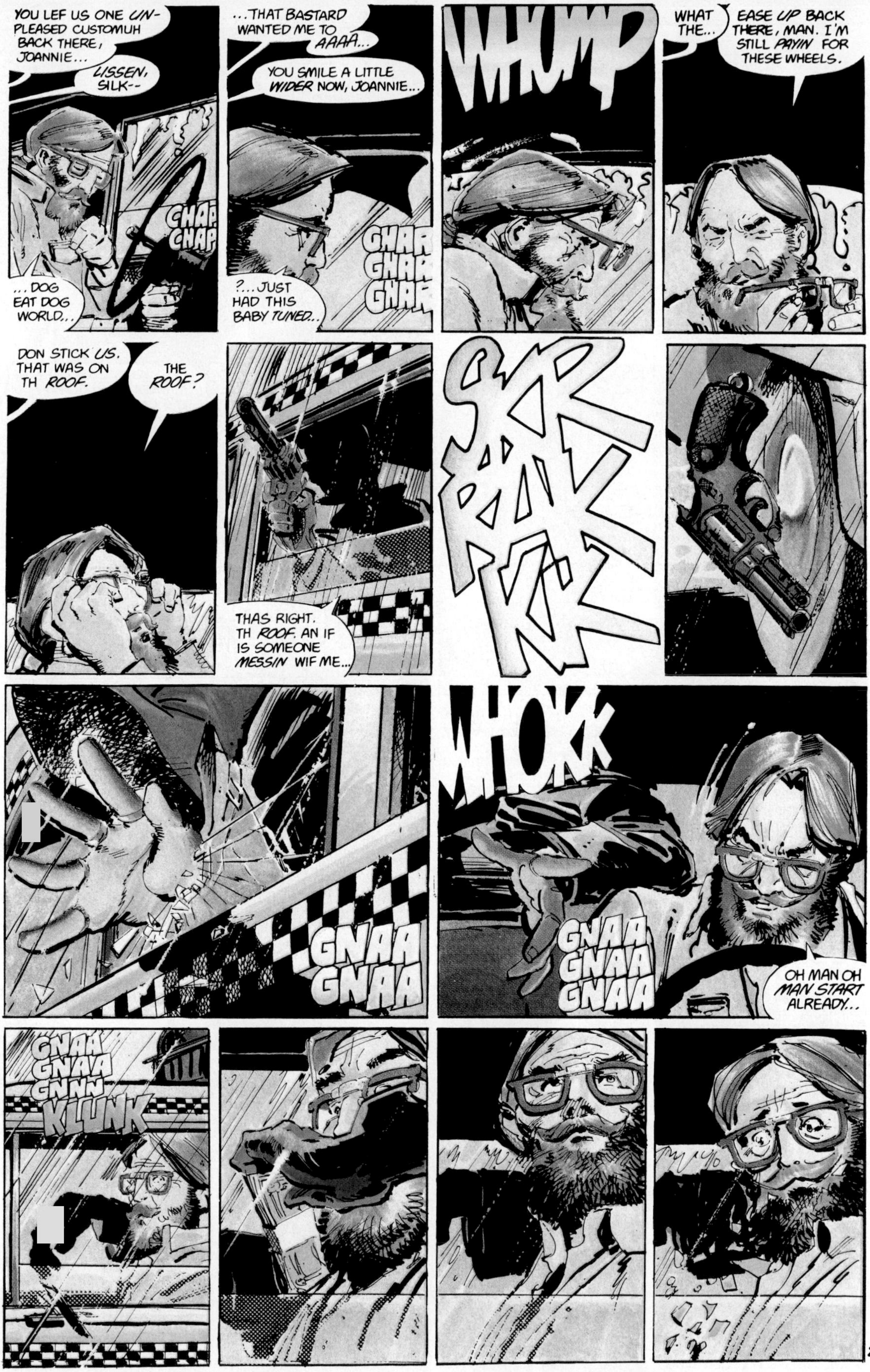

YOU LEF US ONE UN-PLEASED CUSTOMUH BACK THERE, JOANNIE...
LISSEN, SILK--
CHAP CHAP
...DOG EAT DOG WORLD...
...THAT BASTARD WANTED ME TO AAAA...
YOU SMILE A LITTLE WIDER NOW, JOANNIE...
GNAR GNAR GNAR
?...JUST HAD THIS BABY TUNED...
WHUMP
WHAT THE...
EASE UP BACK THERE, MAN. I'M STILL PAYIN FOR THESE WHEELS.
DON STICK US. THAT WAS ON TH ROOF.
THE ROOF?
THAS RIGHT. TH ROOF. AN IF IS SOMEONE MESSIN WIF ME...
SKR RAK KK
GNAA GNAA
WHOKK
GNAA GNAA GNAA
OH MAN OH MAN START ALREADY...
GNAA GNAA GNNN
KLUNK

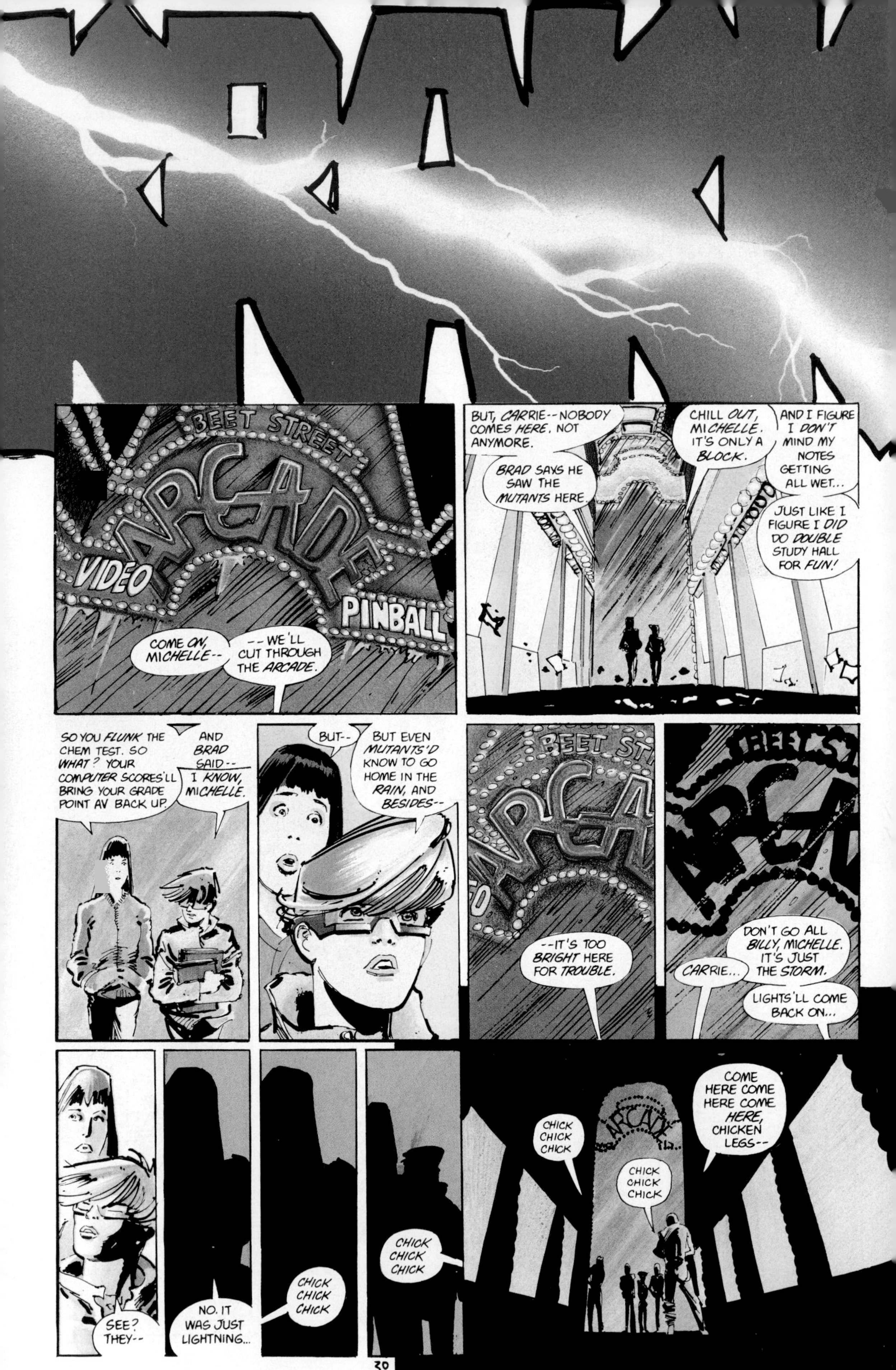
BEET STREET
ARCADE
VIDEO
PINBALL
COME ON, MICHELLE--
--WE'LL CUT THROUGH THE ARCADE.
BUT, CARRIE--NOBODY COMES HERE. NOT ANYMORE.
BRAD SAYS HE SAW THE MUTANTS HERE.
CHILL OUT, MICHELLE. IT'S ONLY A BLOCK.
AND I FIGURE I DON'T MIND MY NOTES GETTING ALL WET...
JUST LIKE I FIGURE I DID DO DOUBLE STUDY HALL FOR FUN!
SO YOU FLUNK THE CHEM TEST. SO WHAT? YOUR COMPUTER SCORES'LL BRING YOUR GRADE POINT AV BACK UP.
AND BRAD SAID--
I KNOW, MICHELLE.
BUT--
BUT EVEN MUTANTS'D KNOW TO GO HOME IN THE RAIN, AND BESIDES--
--IT'S TOO BRIGHT HERE FOR TROUBLE.
CARRIE...
DON'T GO ALL BILLY, MICHELLE. IT'S JUST THE STORM.
LIGHTS'LL COME BACK ON...
SEE? THEY--
NO. IT WAS JUST LIGHTNING...
CHICK CHICK CHICK
CHICK CHICK CHICK
CHICK CHICK CHICK
COME HERE COME HERE COME HERE, CHICKEN LEGS--
CHICK CHICK CHICK
ARCADE

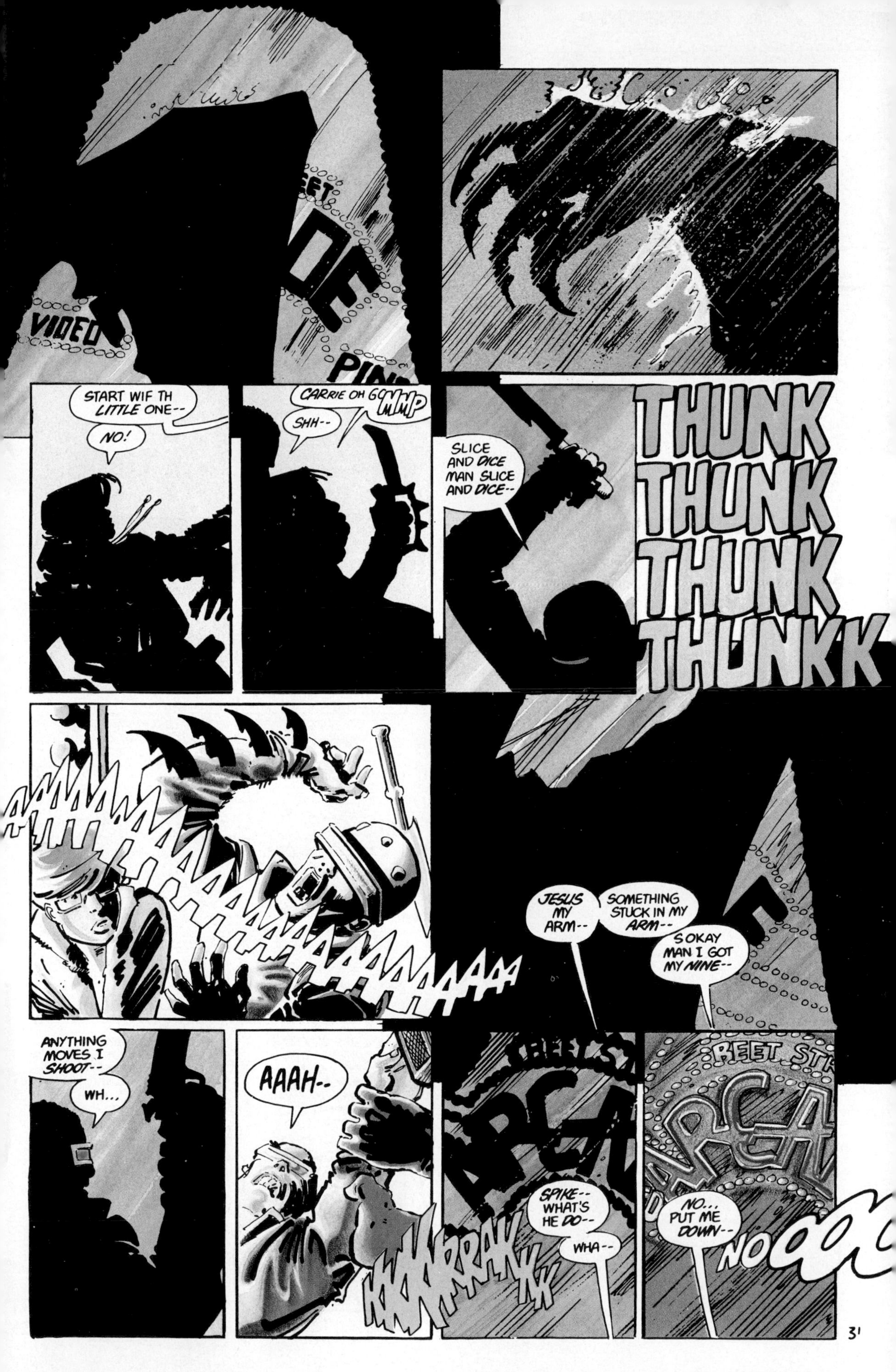
VIDEO
START WIF TH LITTLE ONE--
NO!
CARRIE OH GMMMP
SHH--
SLICE AND DICE MAN SLICE AND DICE--
THUNK
THUNK
THUNK
THUNKK
JESUS MY ARM--
SOMETHING STUCK IN MY ARM--
S OKAY MAN I GOT MY NINE--
ANYTHING MOVES I SHOOT--
WH...
AAAH--
SPIKE-- WHAT'S HE DO--
WHA--
NO... PUT ME DOWN--
NOOOO

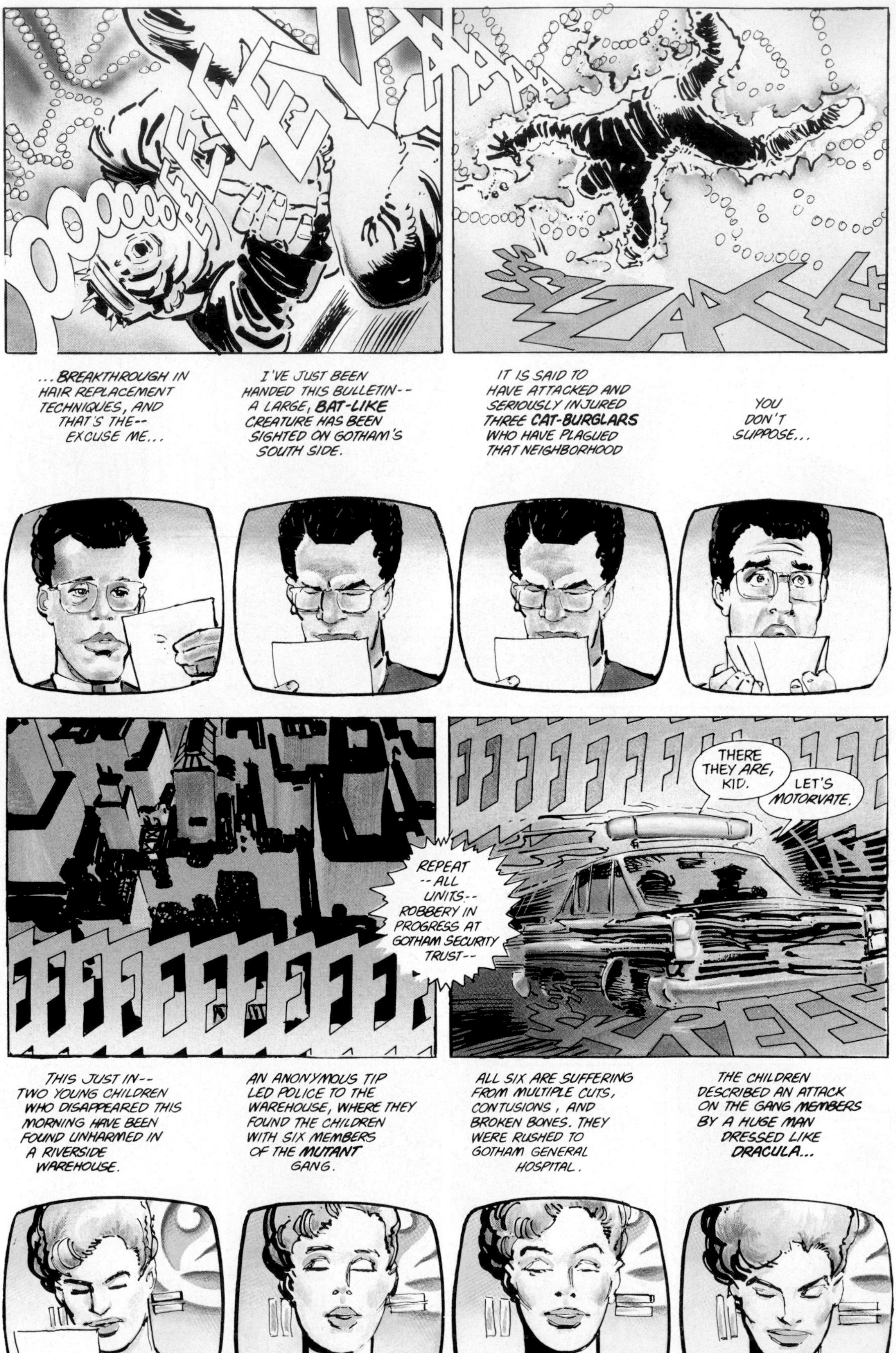
...BREAKTHROUGH IN HAIR REPLACEMENT TECHNIQUES, AND THAT'S THE-- EXCUSE ME...
I'VE JUST BEEN HANDED THIS BULLETIN-- A LARGE, BAT-LIKE CREATURE HAS BEEN SIGHTED ON GOTHAM'S SOUTH SIDE.
IT IS SAID TO HAVE ATTACKED AND SERIOUSLY INJURED THREE CAT-BURGLARS WHO HAVE PLAGUED THAT NEIGHBORHOOD
YOU DON'T SUPPOSE...
REPEAT --ALL UNITS-- ROBBERY IN PROGRESS AT GOTHAM SECURITY TRUST--
THERE THEY ARE, KID.
LET'S MOTORVATE.
THIS JUST IN-- TWO YOUNG CHILDREN WHO DISAPPEARED THIS MORNING HAVE BEEN FOUND UNHARMED IN A RIVERSIDE WAREHOUSE.
AN ANONYMOUS TIP LED POLICE TO THE WAREHOUSE, WHERE THEY FOUND THE CHILDREN WITH SIX MEMBERS OF THE MUTANT GANG.
ALL SIX ARE SUFFERING FROM MULTIPLE CUTS, CONTUSIONS, AND BROKEN BONES. THEY WERE RUSHED TO GOTHAM GENERAL HOSPITAL.
THE CHILDREN DESCRIBED AN ATTACK ON THE GANG MEMBERS BY A HUGE MAN DRESSED LIKE DRACULA...

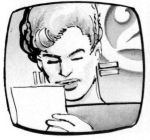

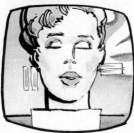

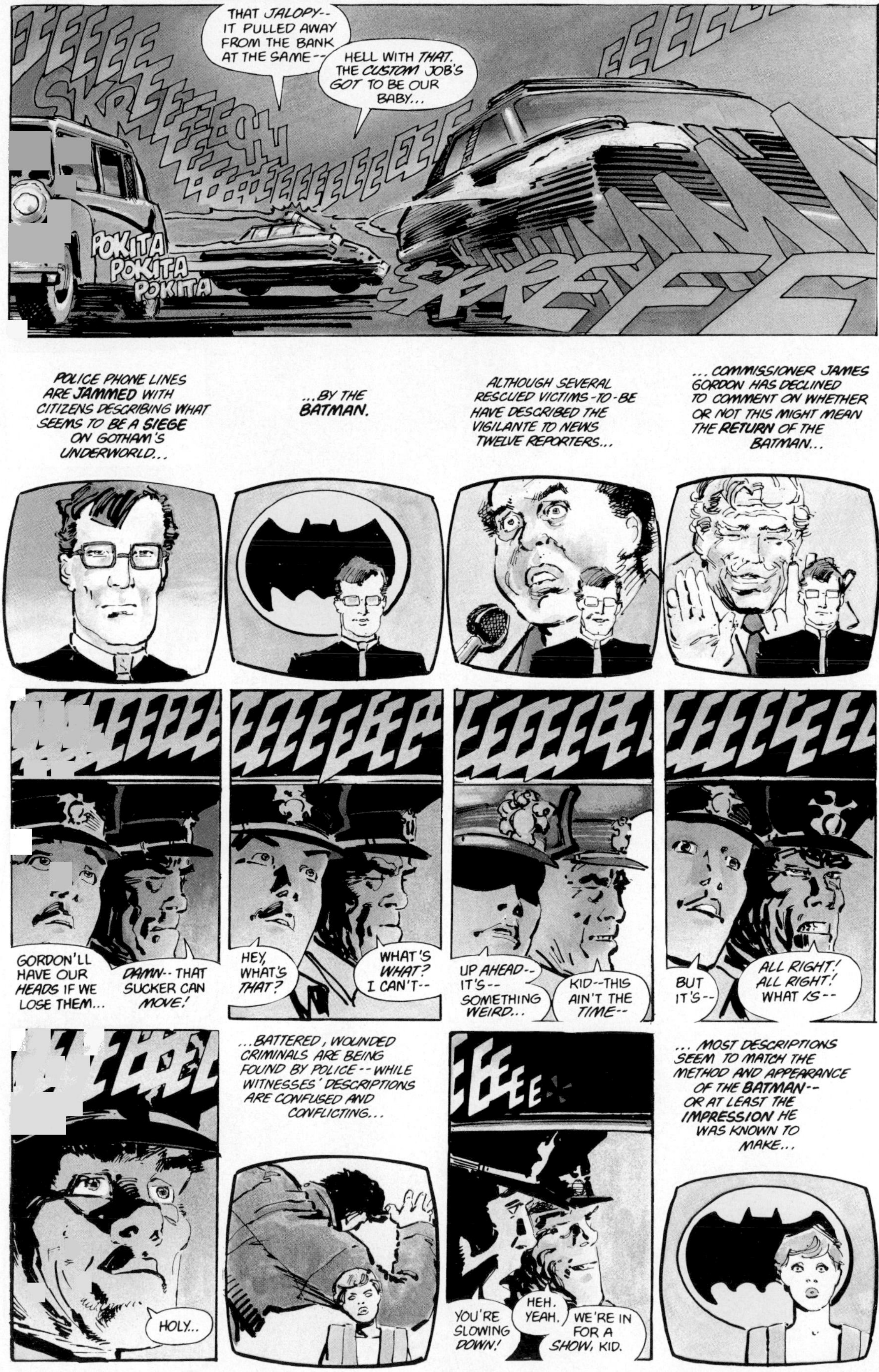
THAT JALOPY-- IT PULLED AWAY FROM THE BANK AT THE SAME--
HELL WITH THAT. THE CUSTOM JOB'S GOT TO BE OUR BABY...
POKITA POKITA POKITA
POLICE PHONE LINES ARE JAMMED WITH CITIZENS DESCRIBING WHAT SEEMS TO BE A SIEGE ON GOTHAM'S UNDERWORLD...
...BY THE BATMAN.
ALTHOUGH SEVERAL RESCUED VICTIMS-TO-BE HAVE DESCRIBED THE VIGILANTE TO NEWS TWELVE REPORTERS...
...COMMISSIONER JAMES GORDON HAS DECLINED TO COMMENT ON WHETHER OR NOT THIS MIGHT MEAN THE RETURN OF THE BATMAN...
GORDON'LL HAVE OUR HEADS IF WE LOSE THEM...
DAMN-- THAT SUCKER CAN MOVE!
HEY, WHAT'S THAT?
WHAT'S WHAT? I CAN'T--
UP AHEAD-- IT'S-- SOMETHING WEIRD...
KID--THIS AIN'T THE TIME--
BUT IT'S--
ALL RIGHT! ALL RIGHT! WHAT IS--
HOLY...
...BATTERED, WOUNDED CRIMINALS ARE BEING FOUND BY POLICE--WHILE WITNESSES' DESCRIPTIONS ARE CONFUSED AND CONFLICTING...
YOU'RE SLOWING DOWN!
HEH. YEAH.
WE'RE IN FOR A SHOW, KID.
...MOST DESCRIPTIONS SEEM TO MATCH THE METHOD AND APPEARANCE OF THE BATMAN-- OR AT LEAST THE IMPRESSION HE WAS KNOWN TO MAKE...

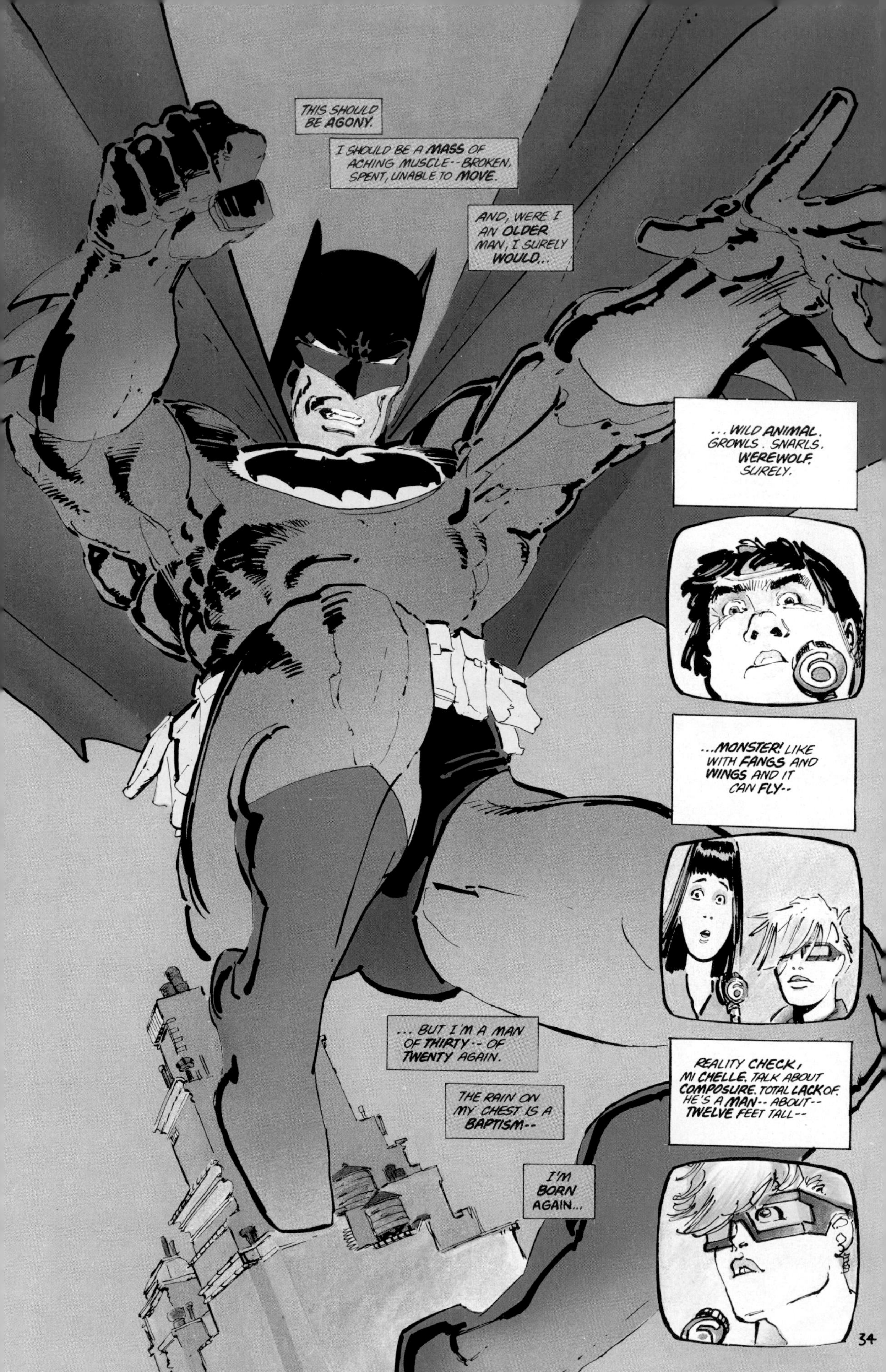

THIS SHOULD BE AGONY.
I SHOULD BE A MASS OF ACHING MUSCLE--BROKEN, SPENT, UNABLE TO MOVE.
AND, WERE I AN OLDER MAN, I SURELY WOULD...
...WILD ANIMAL. GROWLS. SNARLS. WEREWOLF. SURELY.
...MONSTER! LIKE WITH FANGS AND WINGS AND IT CAN FLY--
...BUT I'M A MAN OF THIRTY--OF TWENTY AGAIN.
THE RAIN ON MY CHEST IS A BAPTISM--
REALITY CHECK, MI CHELLE. TALK ABOUT COMPOSURE. TOTAL LACK OF. HE'S A MAN--ABOUT--TWELVE FEET TALL--
I'M BORN AGAIN...

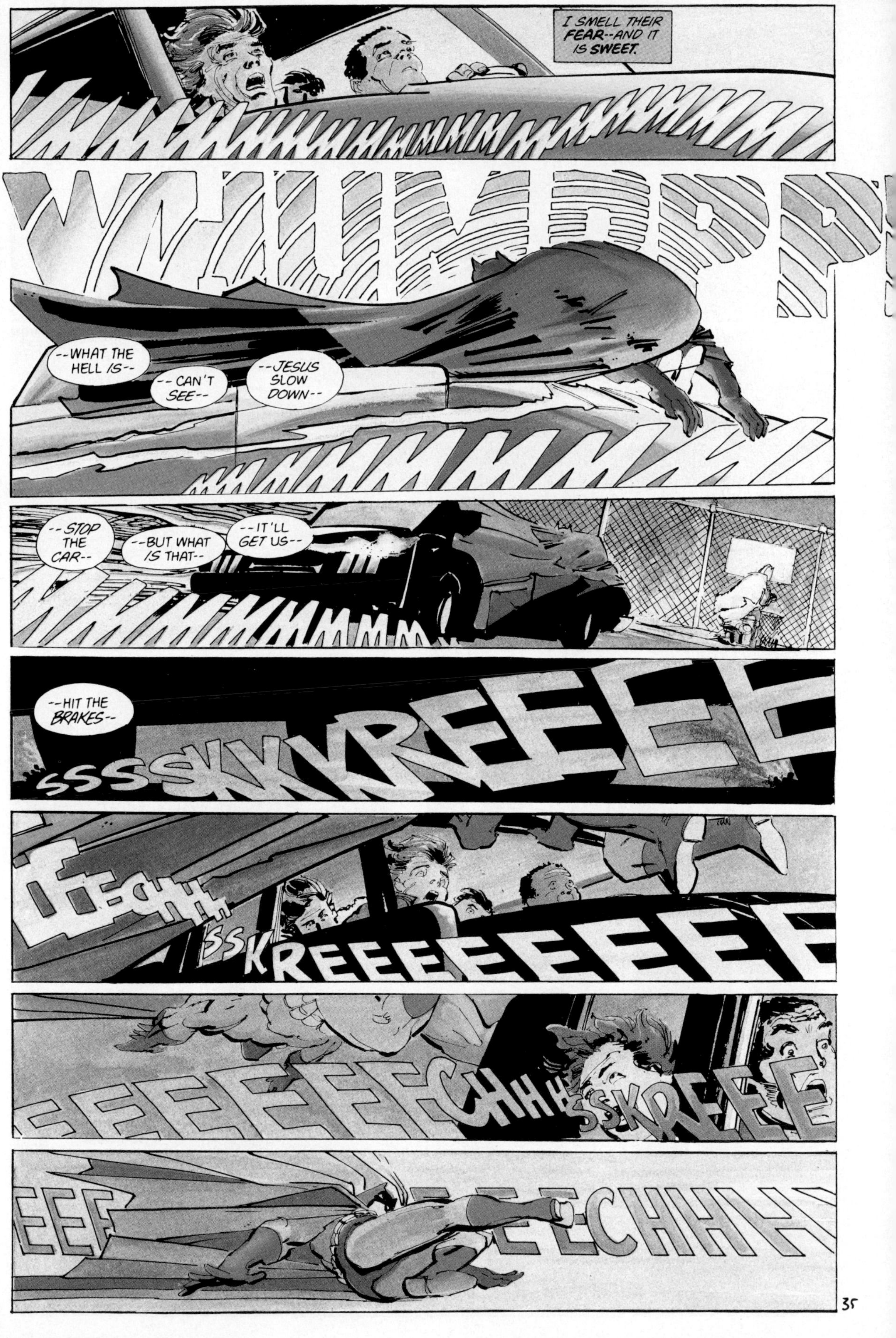
I SMELL THEIR FEAR--AND IT IS SWEET.
--WHAT THE HELL IS--
--CAN'T SEE--
--JESUS SLOW DOWN--
--STOP THE CAR--
--BUT WHAT IS THAT--
--IT'LL GET US--
--HIT THE BRAKES--

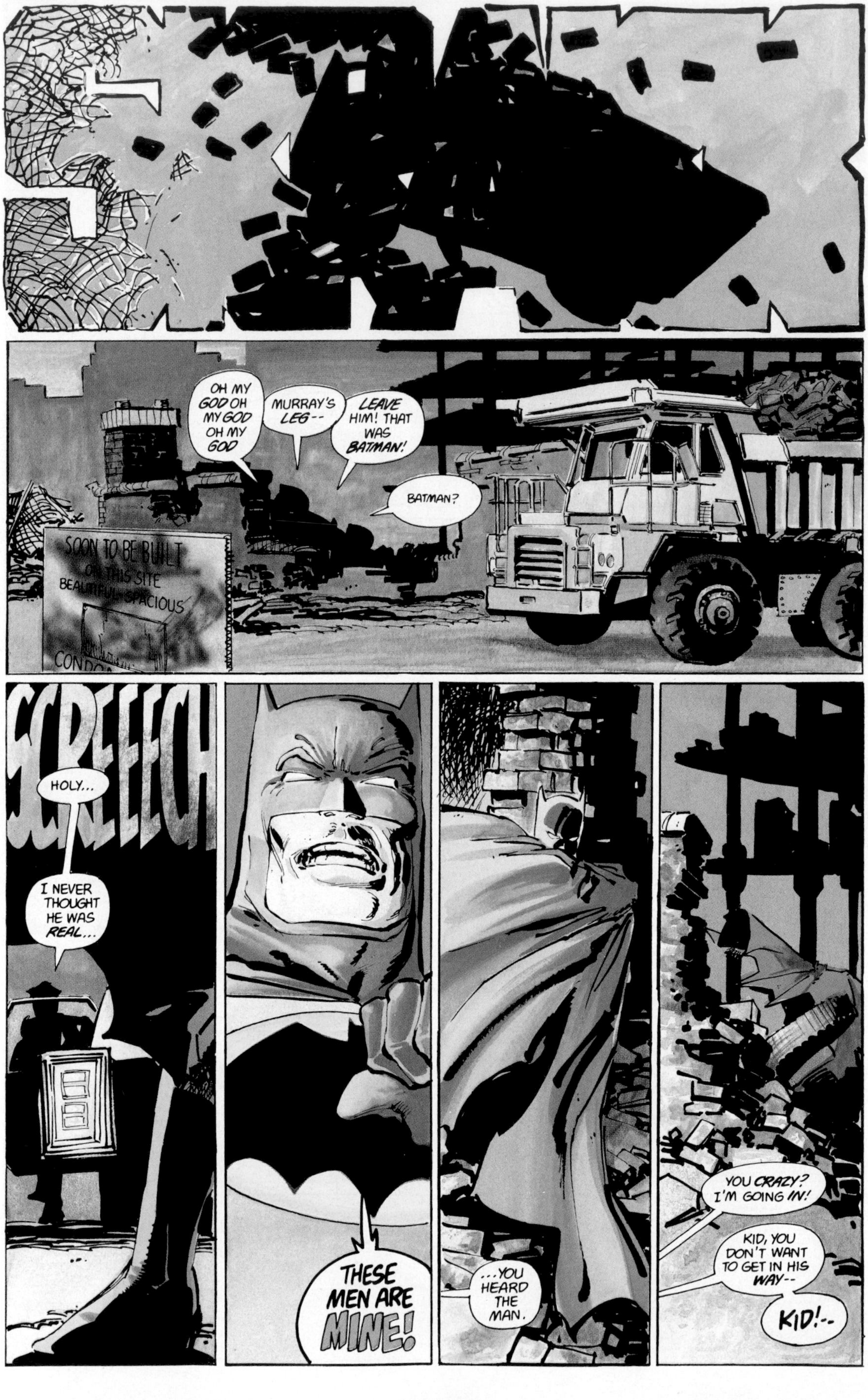
OH MY GOD OH MY GOD OH MY GOD
MURRAY'S LEG--
LEAVE HIM! THAT WAS BATMAN!
BATMAN?
SOON TO BE BUILT
ON THIS SITE
BEAUTIFUL SPACIOUS
SCREECH
HOLY...
I NEVER THOUGHT HE WAS REAL...
THESE MEN ARE MINE!
...YOU HEARD THE MAN.
YOU CRAZY? I'M GOING IN!
KID, YOU DON'T WANT TO GET IN HIS WAY--
KID!--

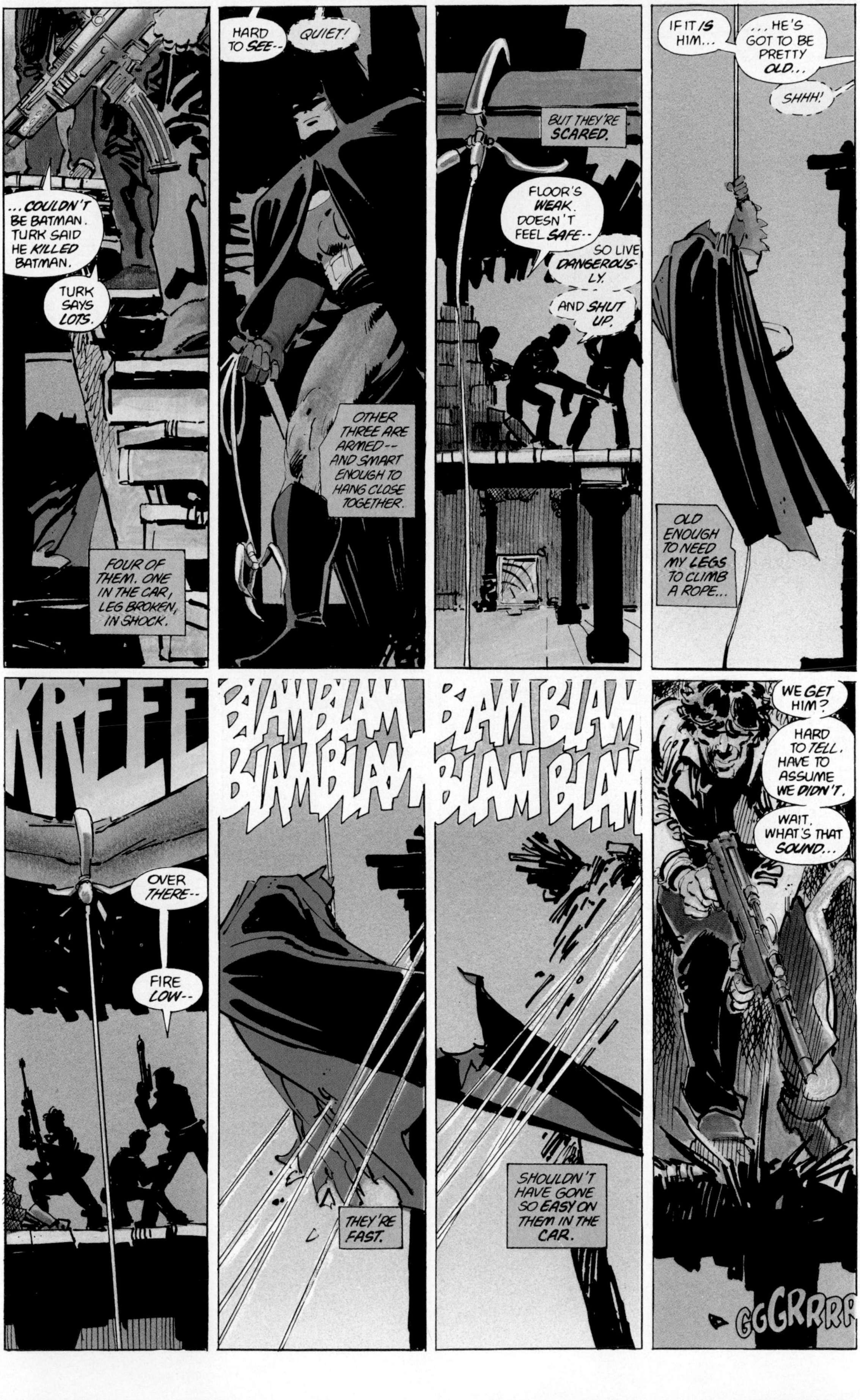
...COULDN'T BE BATMAN. TURK SAID HE KILLED BATMAN.
TURK SAYS LOTS.
FOUR OF THEM. ONE IN THE CAR, LEG BROKEN, IN SHOCK.
HARD TO SEE--
QUIET!
OTHER THREE ARE ARMED-- AND SMART ENOUGH TO HANG CLOSE TOGETHER.
BUT THEY'RE SCARED.
FLOOR'S WEAK. DOESN'T FEEL SAFE--
SO LIVE DANGEROUSLY.
AND SHUT UP.
IF IT IS HIM...
...HE'S GOT TO BE PRETTY OLD...
SHHH!
OLD ENOUGH TO NEED MY LEGS TO CLIMB A ROPE...
KREEE
OVER THERE--
FIRE LOW--
BLAMBLAM BLAMBLAM
THEY'RE FAST.
BLAM BLAM BLAM BLAM
SHOULDN'T HAVE GONE SO EASY ON THEM IN THE CAR.
WE GET HIM?
HARD TO TELL. HAVE TO ASSUME WE DIDN'T.
WAIT. WHAT'S THAT SOUND...
GGGRRRR

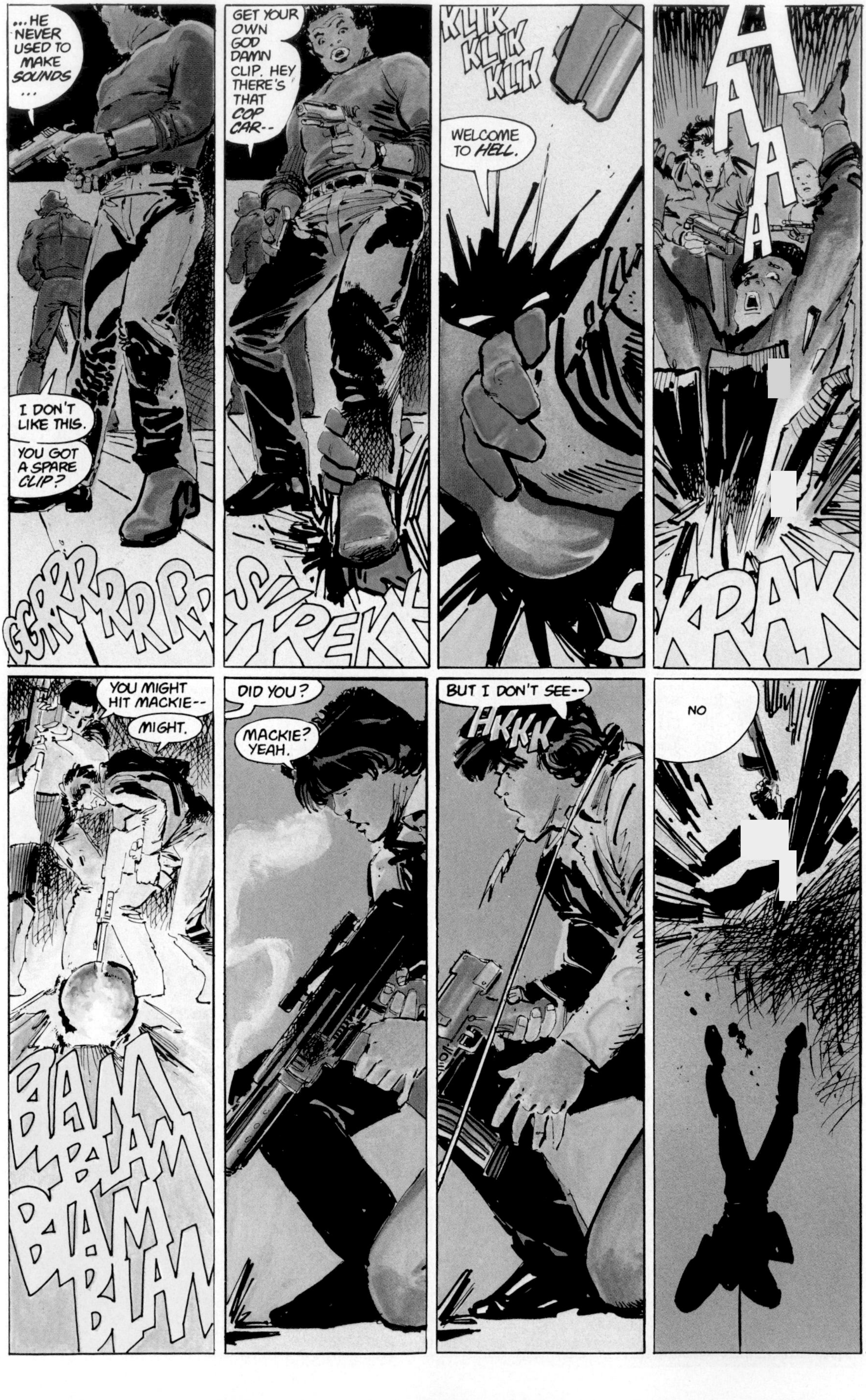
...HE NEVER USED TO MAKE SOUNDS ...
I DON'T LIKE THIS.
YOU GOT A SPARE CLIP?
GGRRRRRRRR
GET YOUR OWN GOD DAMN CLIP. HEY THERE'S THAT COP CAR--
SKREK
KLIK KLIK KLIK
WELCOME TO HELL.
SKRAK
AAAAA
YOU MIGHT HIT MACKIE--
MIGHT.
BLAM BLAM BLAM BLAM BLAM
DID YOU?
MACKIE? YEAH.
BUT I DON'T SEE--
HKKK
NO

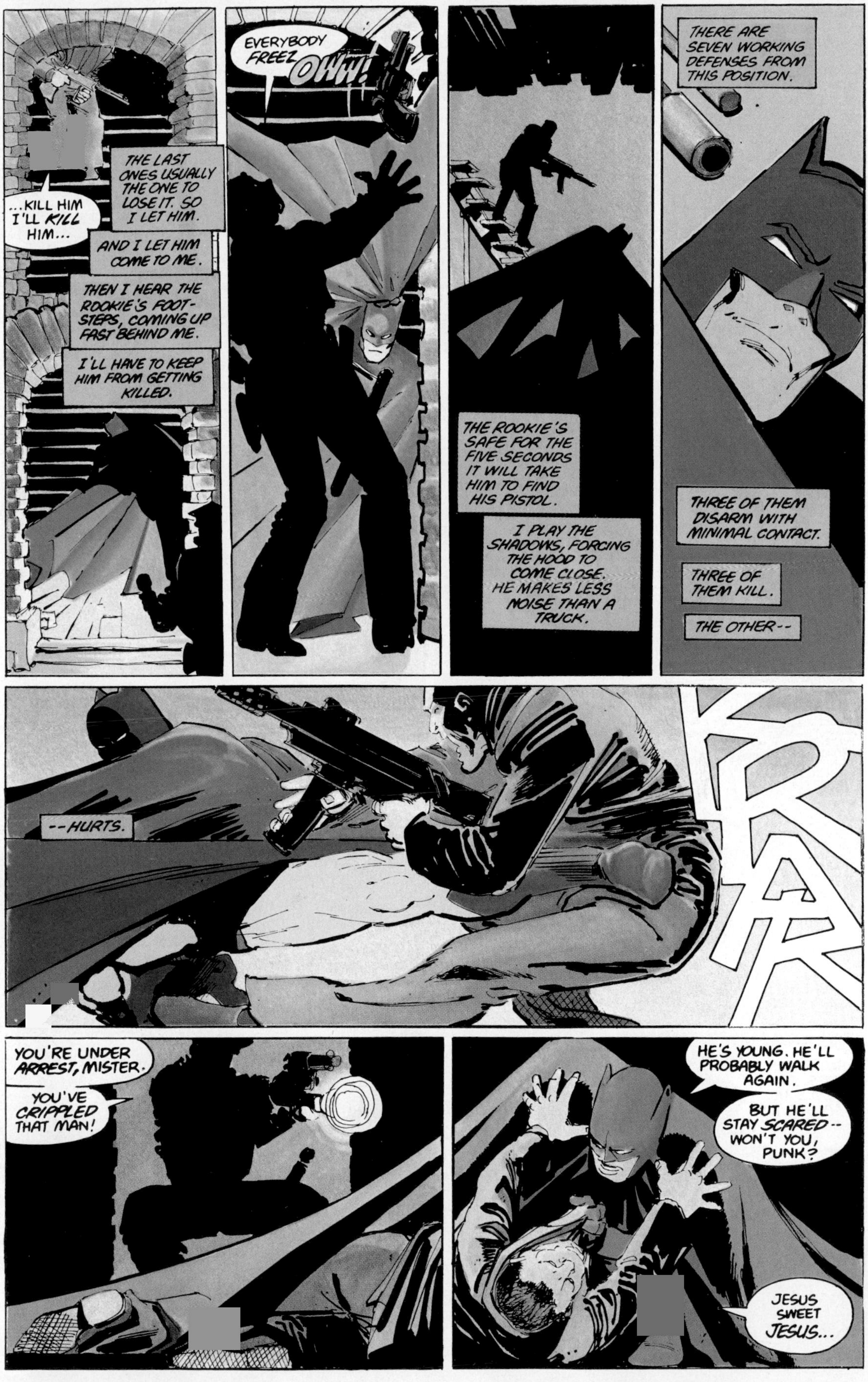
...KILL HIM I'LL KILL HIM...
THE LAST ONES USUALLY THE ONE TO LOSE IT. SO I LET HIM.
AND I LET HIM COME TO ME.
THEN I HEAR THE ROOKIE'S FOOT-STEPS, COMING UP FAST BEHIND ME.
I'LL HAVE TO KEEP HIM FROM GETTING KILLED.
EVERYBODY FREEZ
OWW!
THE ROOKIE'S SAFE FOR THE FIVE SECONDS IT WILL TAKE HIM TO FIND HIS PISTOL.
I PLAY THE SHADOWS, FORCING THE HOOD TO COME CLOSE. HE MAKES LESS NOISE THAN A TRUCK.
THERE ARE SEVEN WORKING DEFENSES FROM THIS POSITION.
THREE OF THEM DISARM WITH MINIMAL CONTACT.
THREE OF THEM KILL.
THE OTHER--
--HURTS.
KRAK
YOU'RE UNDER ARREST, MISTER.
YOU'VE CRIPPLED THAT MAN!
HE'S YOUNG. HE'LL PROBABLY WALK AGAIN.
BUT HE'LL STAY SCARED-- WON'T YOU, PUNK?
JESUS SWEET JESUS...

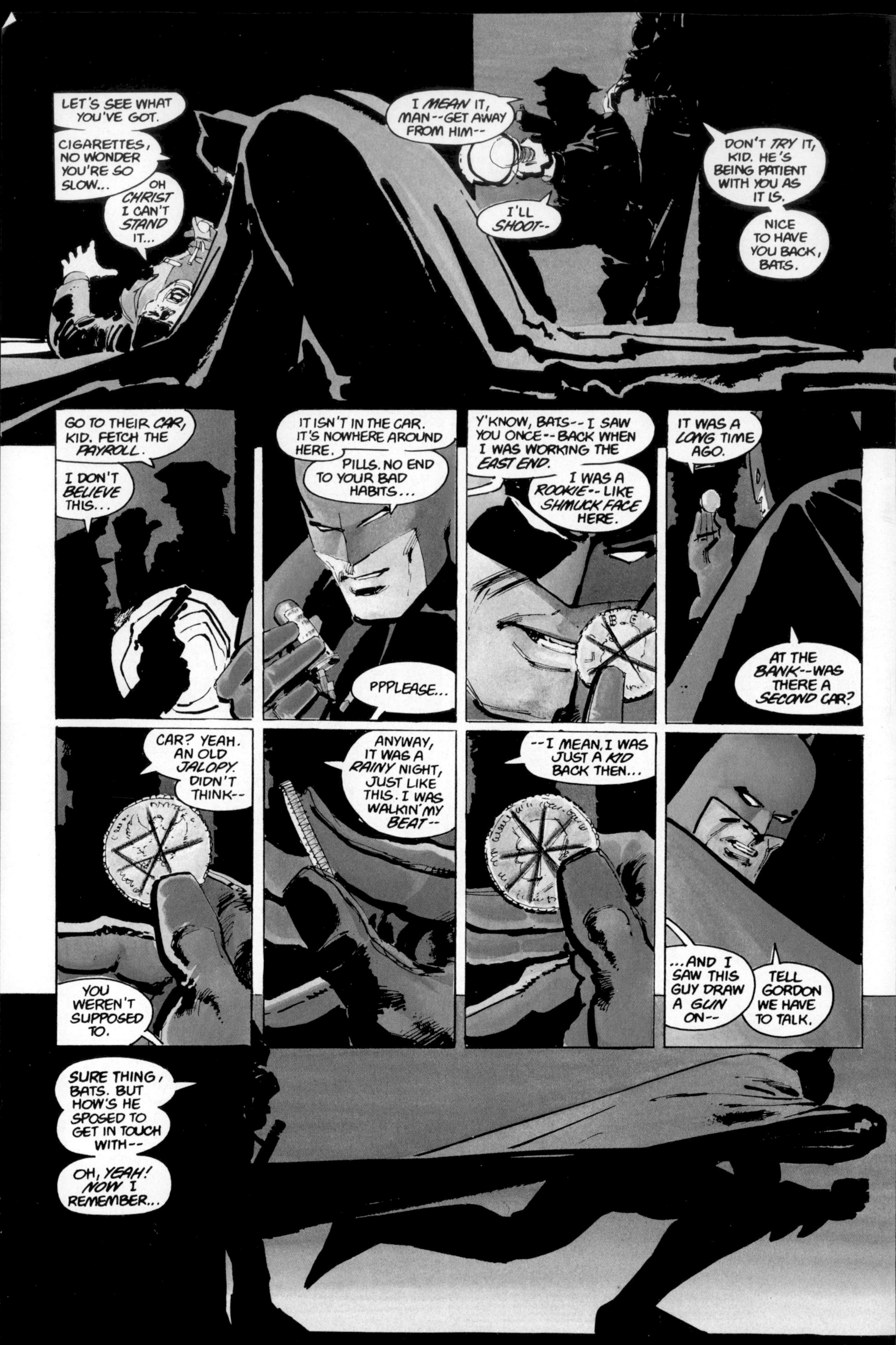

LET'S SEE WHAT YOU'VE GOT.
CIGARETTES, NO WONDER YOU'RE SO SLOW...
OH CHRIST I CAN'T STAND IT...
I MEAN IT, MAN--GET AWAY FROM HIM--
I'LL SHOOT--
DON'T TRY IT, KID. HE'S BEING PATIENT WITH YOU AS IT IS.
NICE TO HAVE YOU BACK, BATS.
GO TO THEIR CAR, KID. FETCH THE PAYROLL.
I DON'T BELIEVE THIS...
IT ISN'T IN THE CAR. IT'S NOWHERE AROUND HERE.
PILLS. NO END TO YOUR BAD HABITS...
PPPLEASE...
Y'KNOW, BATS--I SAW YOU ONCE--BACK WHEN I WAS WORKING THE EAST END.
I WAS A ROOKIE--LIKE SHMUCK FACE HERE.
IT WAS A LONG TIME AGO.
AT THE BANK--WAS THERE A SECOND CAR?
CAR? YEAH. AN OLD JALOPY. DIDN'T THINK--
YOU WEREN'T SUPPOSED TO.
ANYWAY, IT WAS A RAINY NIGHT, JUST LIKE THIS. I WAS WALKIN' MY BEAT--
--I MEAN, I WAS JUST A KID BACK THEN...
...AND I SAW THIS GUY DRAW A GUN ON--
TELL GORDON WE HAVE TO TALK.
SURE THING, BATS. BUT HOW'S HE SPOSED TO GET IN TOUCH WITH--
OH, YEAH! NOW I REMEMBER...

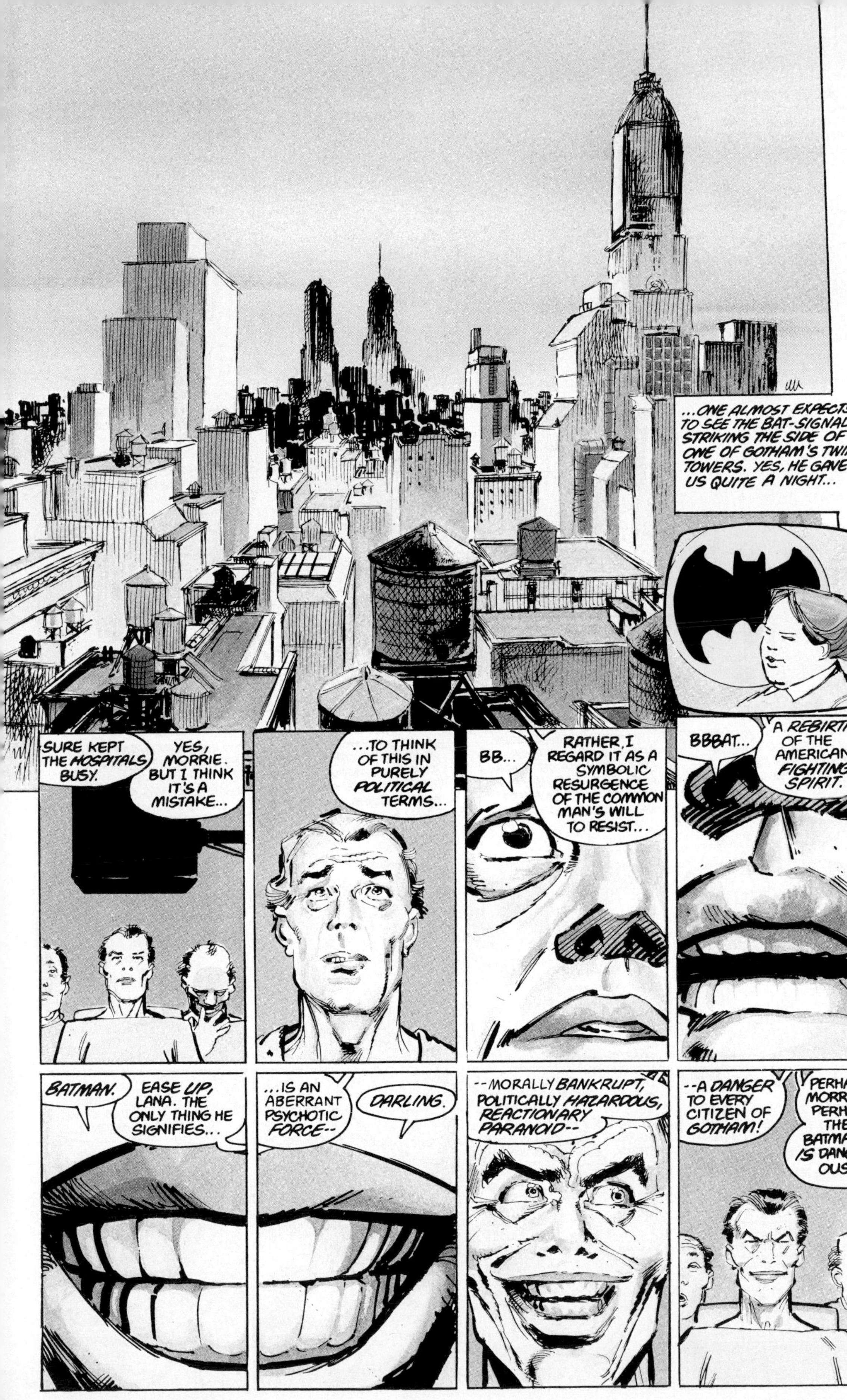
...ONE ALMOST EXPECTS TO SEE THE BAT-SIGNAL STRIKING THE SIDE OF ONE OF GOTHAM'S TWIN TOWERS. YES, HE GAVE US QUITE A NIGHT...
SURE KEPT THE HOSPITALS BUSY.
YES, MORRIE. BUT I THINK IT'S A MISTAKE...
...TO THINK OF THIS IN PURELY POLITICAL TERMS...
BB...
RATHER, I REGARD IT AS A SYMBOLIC RESURGENCE OF THE COMMON MAN'S WILL TO RESIST...
BBBAT...
A REBIRTH OF THE AMERICAN FIGHTING SPIRIT.
BATMAN.
EASE UP, LANA. THE ONLY THING HE SIGNIFIES...
...IS AN ABERRANT PSYCHOTIC FORCE--
DARLING.
--MORALLY BANKRUPT, POLITICALLY HAZARDOUS, REACTIONARY PARANOID--
--A DANGER TO EVERY CITIZEN OF GOTHAM!
PERHAPS, MORRIE. PERHAPS THE BATMAN IS DANGEROUS...

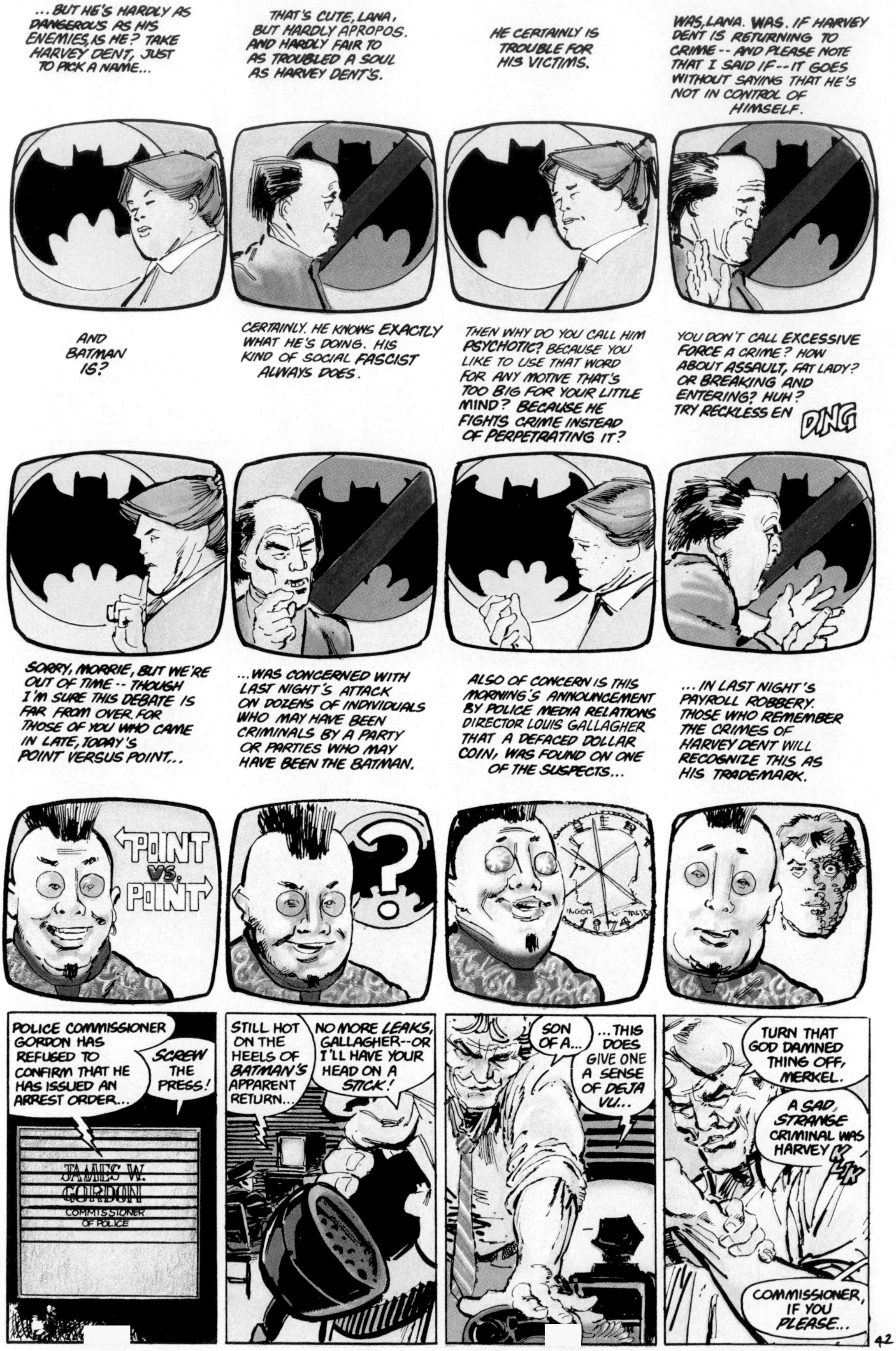
...BUT HE'S HARDLY AS DANGEROUS AS HIS ENEMIES, IS HE? TAKE HARVEY DENT, JUST TO PICK A NAME...
THAT'S CUTE, LANA, BUT HARDLY APROPOS. AND HARDLY FAIR TO AS TROUBLED A SOUL AS HARVEY DENT'S.
HE CERTAINLY IS TROUBLE FOR HIS VICTIMS.
WAS, LANA. WAS. IF HARVEY DENT IS RETURNING TO CRIME -- AND PLEASE NOTE THAT I SAID IF -- IT GOES WITHOUT SAYING THAT HE'S NOT IN CONTROL OF HIMSELF.
AND BATMAN IS?
CERTAINLY. HE KNOWS EXACTLY WHAT HE'S DOING. HIS KIND OF SOCIAL FASCIST ALWAYS DOES.
THEN WHY DO YOU CALL HIM PSYCHOTIC? BECAUSE YOU LIKE TO USE THAT WORD FOR ANY MOTIVE THAT'S TOO BIG FOR YOUR LITTLE MIND? BECAUSE HE FIGHTS CRIME INSTEAD OF PERPETRATING IT?
YOU DON'T CALL EXCESSIVE FORCE A CRIME? HOW ABOUT ASSAULT, FAT LADY? OR BREAKING AND ENTERING? HUH? TRY RECKLESS EN
DNG
SORRY, MORRIE, BUT WE'RE OUT OF TIME -- THOUGH I'M SURE THIS DEBATE IS FAR FROM OVER. FOR THOSE OF YOU WHO CAME IN LATE, TODAY'S POINT VERSUS POINT...
...WAS CONCERNED WITH LAST NIGHT'S ATTACK ON DOZENS OF INDIVIDUALS WHO MAY HAVE BEEN CRIMINALS BY A PARTY OR PARTIES WHO MAY HAVE BEEN THE BATMAN.
ALSO OF CONCERN IS THIS MORNING'S ANNOUNCEMENT BY POLICE MEDIA RELATIONS DIRECTOR LOUIS GALLAGHER THAT A DEFACED DOLLAR COIN, WAS FOUND ON ONE OF THE SUSPECTS...
...IN LAST NIGHT'S PAYROLL ROBBERY. THOSE WHO REMEMBER THE CRIMES OF HARVEY DENT WILL RECOGNIZE THIS AS HIS TRADEMARK.
POINT VS. POINT
POLICE COMMISSIONER GORDON HAS REFUSED TO CONFIRM THAT HE HAS ISSUED AN ARREST ORDER...
SCREW THE PRESS!
JAMES W. GORDON
COMMISSIONER OF POLICE
STILL HOT ON THE HEELS OF BATMAN'S APPARENT RETURN...
NO MORE LEAKS, GALLAGHER--OR I'LL HAVE YOUR HEAD ON A STICK!
SON OF A...
...THIS DOES GIVE ONE A SENSE OF DEJA VU...
TURN THAT GOD DAMNED THING OFF, MERKEL.
A SAD, STRANGE CRIMINAL WAS HARVEY
COMMISSIONER, IF YOU PLEASE...

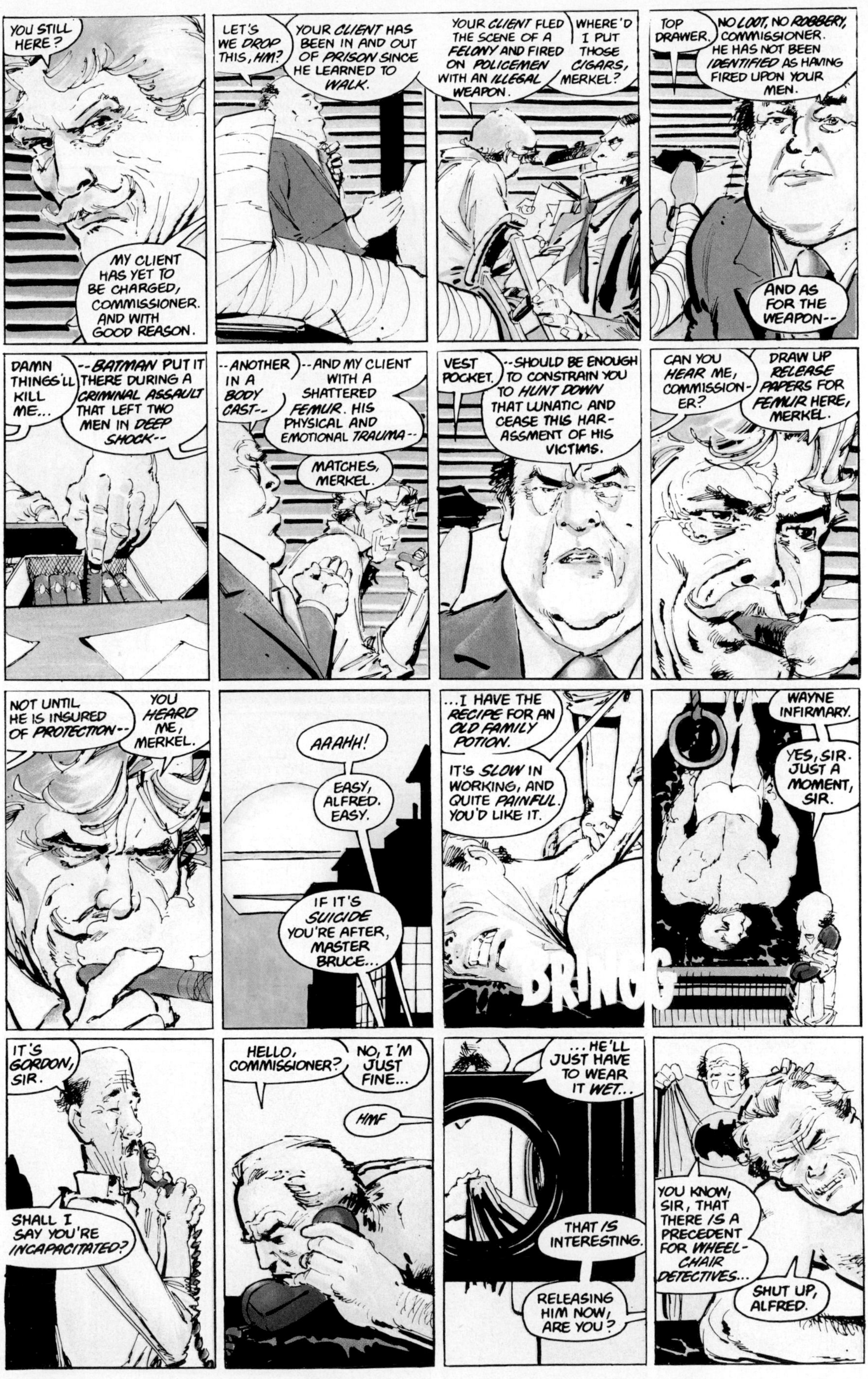

YOU STILL HERE?
MY CLIENT HAS YET TO BE CHARGED, COMMISSIONER. AND WITH GOOD REASON.
LET'S WE DROP THIS, HM?
YOUR CLIENT HAS BEEN IN AND OUT OF PRISON SINCE HE LEARNED TO WALK.
YOUR CLIENT FLED THE SCENE OF A FELONY AND FIRED ON POLICEMEN WITH AN ILLEGAL WEAPON.
WHERE'D I PUT THOSE CIGARS, MERKEL?
TOP DRAWER.
NO LOOT, NO ROBBERY, COMMISSIONER. HE HAS NOT BEEN IDENTIFIED AS HAVING FIRED UPON YOUR MEN.
AND AS FOR THE WEAPON--
DAMN THINGS'LL KILL ME...
--BATMAN PUT IT THERE DURING A CRIMINAL ASSAULT THAT LEFT TWO MEN IN DEEP SHOCK--
--ANOTHER IN A BODY CAST--
--AND MY CLIENT WITH A SHATTERED FEMUR. HIS PHYSICAL AND EMOTIONAL TRAUMA--
MATCHES, MERKEL.
VEST POCKET.
--SHOULD BE ENOUGH TO CONSTRAIN YOU TO HUNT DOWN THAT LUNATIC AND CEASE THIS HAR-ASSMENT OF HIS VICTIMS.
CAN YOU HEAR ME, COMMISSION-ER?
DRAW UP RELEASE PAPERS FOR FEMUR HERE, MERKEL.
NOT UNTIL HE IS INSURED OF PROTECTION--
YOU HEARD ME, MERKEL.
AAAHH!
EASY, ALFRED. EASY.
IF IT'S SUICIDE YOU'RE AFTER, MASTER BRUCE...
...I HAVE THE RECIPE FOR AN OLD FAMILY POTION.
IT'S SLOW IN WORKING, AND QUITE PAINFUL. YOU'D LIKE IT.
BRINGG
WAYNE INFIRMARY.
YES, SIR. JUST A MOMENT, SIR.
IT'S GORDON, SIR.
SHALL I SAY YOU'RE INCAPACITATED?
HELLO, COMMISSIONER?
NO, I'M JUST FINE...
HMF
...HE'LL JUST HAVE TO WEAR IT WET...
THAT IS INTERESTING.
RELEASING HIM NOW, ARE YOU?
YOU KNOW, SIR, THAT THERE IS A PRECEDENT FOR WHEEL-CHAIR DETECTIVES...
SHUT UP, ALFRED.

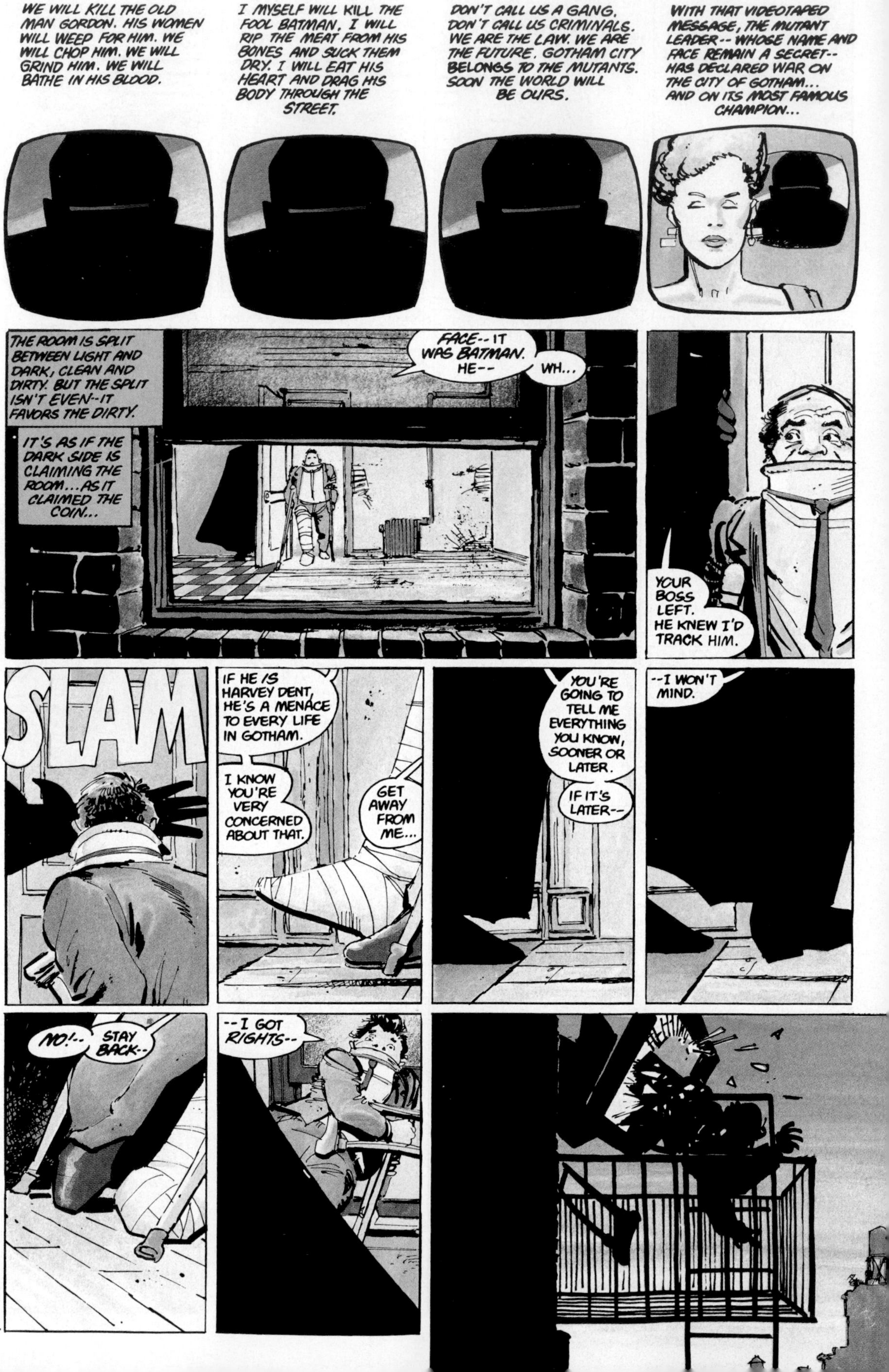
WE WILL KILL THE OLD MAN GORDON. HIS WOMEN WILL WEEP FOR HIM. WE WILL CHOP HIM. WE WILL GRIND HIM. WE WILL BATHE IN HIS BLOOD.
I MYSELF WILL KILL THE FOOL BATMAN. I WILL RIP THE MEAT FROM HIS BONES AND SUCK THEM DRY. I WILL EAT HIS HEART AND DRAG HIS BODY THROUGH THE STREET.
DON'T CALL US A GANG. DON'T CALL US CRIMINALS. WE ARE THE LAW. WE ARE THE FUTURE. GOTHAM CITY BELONGS TO THE MUTANTS. SOON THE WORLD WILL BE OURS.
WITH THAT VIDEOTAPED MESSAGE, THE MUTANT LEADER-- WHOSE NAME AND FACE REMAIN A SECRET-- HAS DECLARED WAR ON THE CITY OF GOTHAM... AND ON ITS MOST FAMOUS CHAMPION...
THE ROOM IS SPLIT BETWEEN LIGHT AND DARK, CLEAN AND DIRTY. BUT THE SPLIT ISN'T EVEN--IT FAVORS THE DIRTY.
IT'S AS IF THE DARK SIDE IS CLAIMING THE ROOM... AS IT CLAIMED THE COIN...
FACE-- IT WAS BATMAN. HE--
WH...
YOUR BOSS LEFT. HE KNEW I'D TRACK HIM.
SLAM
IF HE IS HARVEY DENT, HE'S A MENACE TO EVERY LIFE IN GOTHAM.
I KNOW YOU'RE VERY CONCERNED ABOUT THAT.
GET AWAY FROM ME...
YOU'RE GOING TO TELL ME EVERYTHING YOU KNOW, SOONER OR LATER.
IF IT'S LATER--
--I WON'T MIND.
NO!-- STAY BACK--
--I GOT RIGHTS--

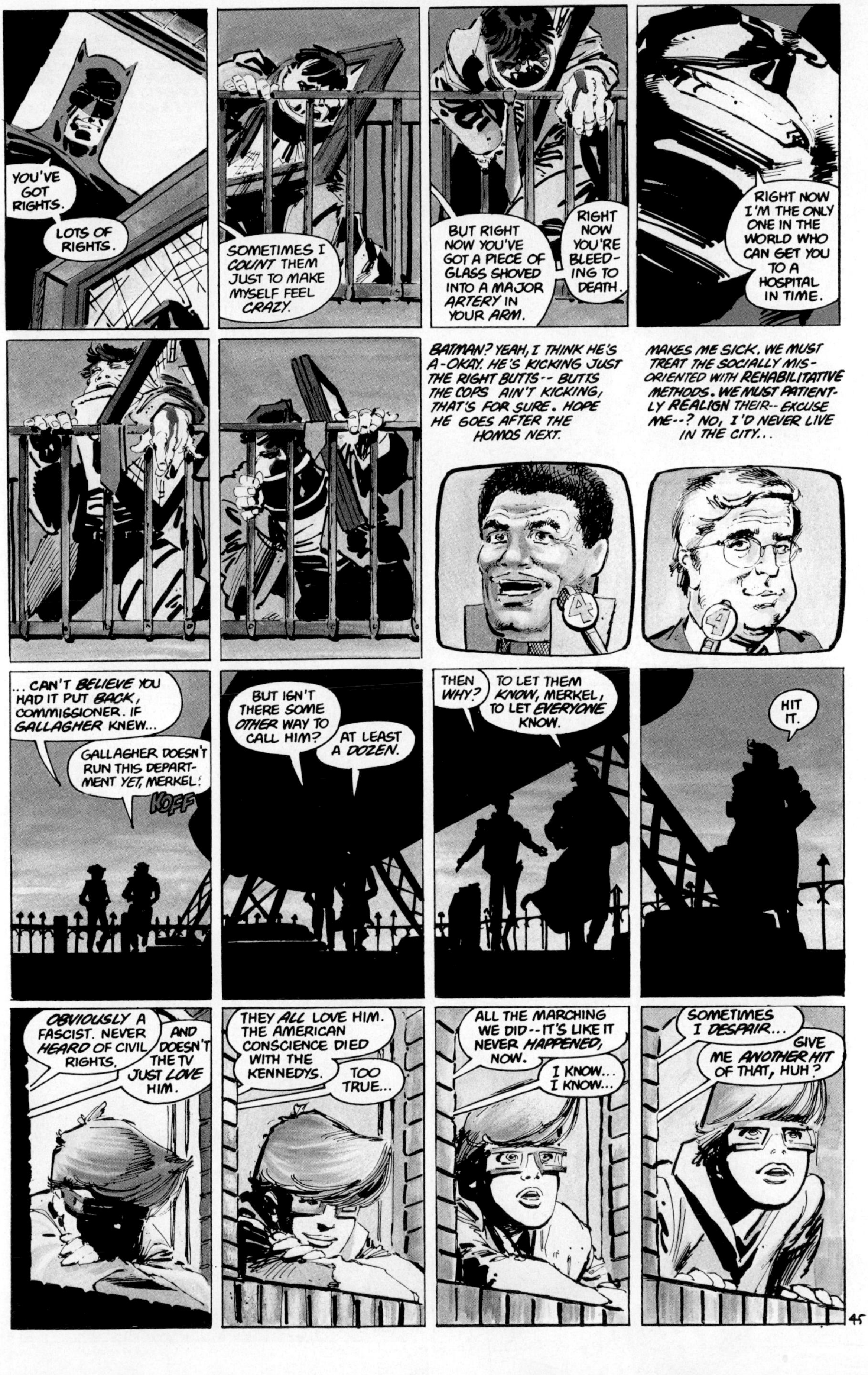
YOU'VE GOT RIGHTS.
LOTS OF RIGHTS.
SOMETIMES I COUNT THEM JUST TO MAKE MYSELF FEEL CRAZY.
BUT RIGHT NOW YOU'VE GOT A PIECE OF GLASS SHOVED INTO A MAJOR ARTERY IN YOUR ARM.
RIGHT NOW YOU'RE BLEED-ING TO DEATH.
RIGHT NOW I'M THE ONLY ONE IN THE WORLD WHO CAN GET YOU TO A HOSPITAL IN TIME.
BATMAN? YEAH, I THINK HE'S A-OKAY. HE'S KICKING JUST THE RIGHT BUTTS-- BUTTS THE COPS AIN'T KICKING, THAT'S FOR SURE. HOPE HE GOES AFTER THE HOMOS NEXT.
4
MAKES ME SICK. WE MUST TREAT THE SOCIALLY MIS-ORIENTED WITH REHABILITATIVE METHODS. WE MUST PATIENT-LY REALIGN THEIR-- EXCUSE ME--? NO, I'D NEVER LIVE IN THE CITY...
4
... CAN'T BELIEVE YOU HAD IT PUT BACK, COMMISSIONER. IF GALLAGHER KNEW...
GALLAGHER DOESN'T RUN THIS DEPART-MENT YET, MERKEL!
KOFF
BUT ISN'T THERE SOME OTHER WAY TO CALL HIM?
AT LEAST A DOZEN.
THEN WHY?
TO LET THEM KNOW, MERKEL, TO LET EVERYONE KNOW.
HIT IT.
OBVIOUSLY A FASCIST. NEVER HEARD OF CIVIL RIGHTS.
AND DOESN'T THE TV JUST LOVE HIM.
THEY ALL LOVE HIM. THE AMERICAN CONSCIENCE DIED WITH THE KENNEDYS.
TOO TRUE...
ALL THE MARCHING WE DID--IT'S LIKE IT NEVER HAPPENED, NOW.
I KNOW... I KNOW...
SOMETIMES I DESPAIR...
GIVE ME ANOTHER HIT OF THAT, HUH?

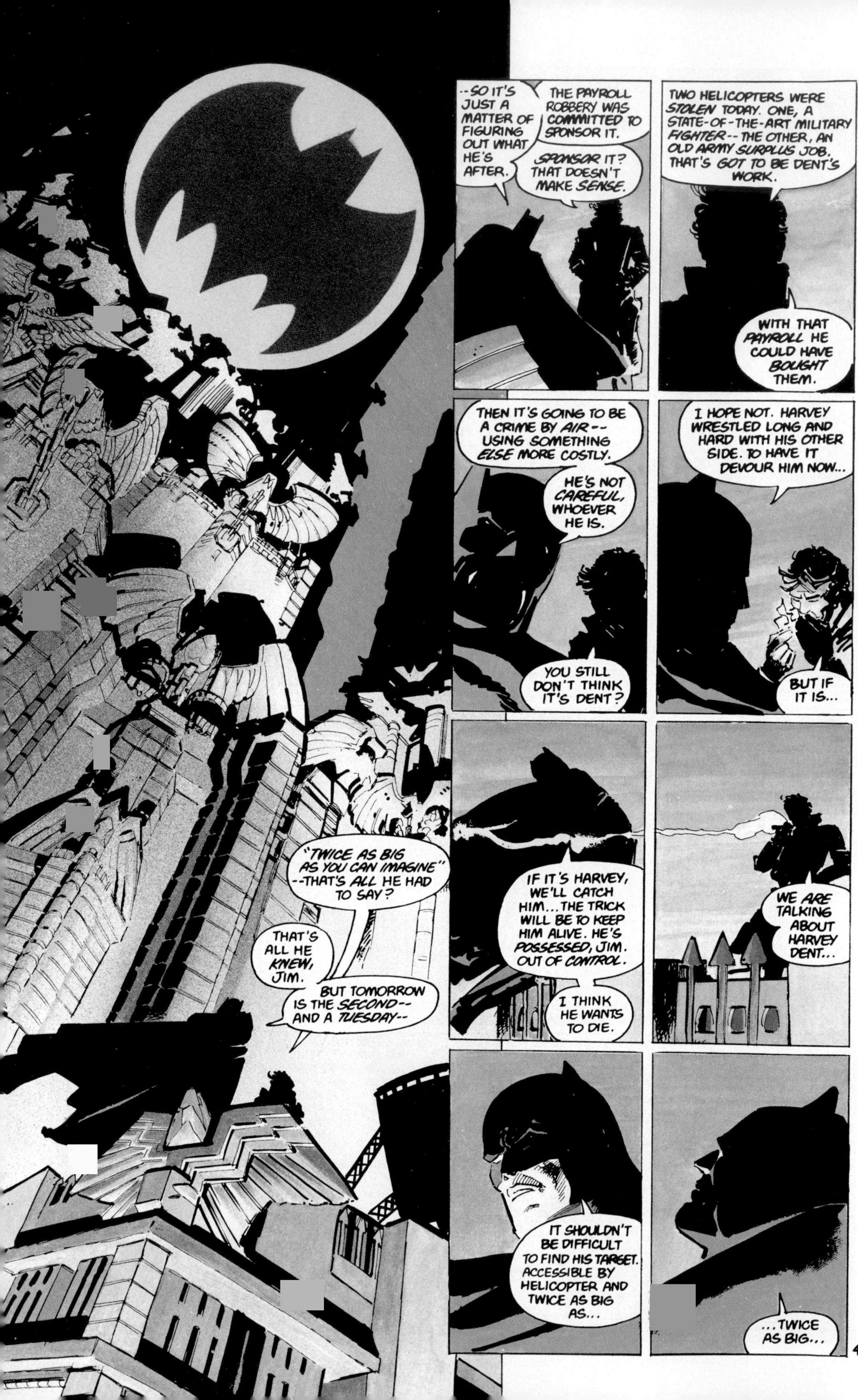

--SO IT'S JUST A MATTER OF FIGURING OUT WHAT HE'S AFTER.
THE PAYROLL ROBBERY WAS COMMITTED TO SPONSOR IT.
SPONSOR IT? THAT DOESN'T MAKE SENSE.
TWO HELICOPTERS WERE STOLEN TODAY. ONE, A STATE-OF-THE-ART MILITARY FIGHTER--THE OTHER, AN OLD ARMY SURPLUS JOB. THAT'S GOT TO BE DENT'S WORK.
WITH THAT PAYROLL HE COULD HAVE BOUGHT THEM.
THEN IT'S GOING TO BE A CRIME BY AIR--USING SOMETHING ELSE MORE COSTLY.
HE'S NOT CAREFUL, WHOEVER HE IS.
YOU STILL DON'T THINK IT'S DENT?
I HOPE NOT. HARVEY WRESTLED LONG AND HARD WITH HIS OTHER SIDE. TO HAVE IT DEVOUR HIM NOW...
BUT IF IT IS...
IF IT'S HARVEY, WE'LL CATCH HIM... THE TRICK WILL BE TO KEEP HIM ALIVE. HE'S POSSESSED, JIM. OUT OF CONTROL.
I THINK HE WANTS TO DIE.
WE ARE TALKING ABOUT HARVEY DENT...
IT SHOULDN'T BE DIFFICULT TO FIND HIS TARGET. ACCESSIBLE BY HELICOPTER AND TWICE AS BIG AS...
...TWICE AS BIG...
"TWICE AS BIG AS YOU CAN IMAGINE" --THAT'S ALL HE HAD TO SAY?
THAT'S ALL HE KNEW, JIM.
BUT TOMORROW IS THE SECOND--AND A TUESDAY--

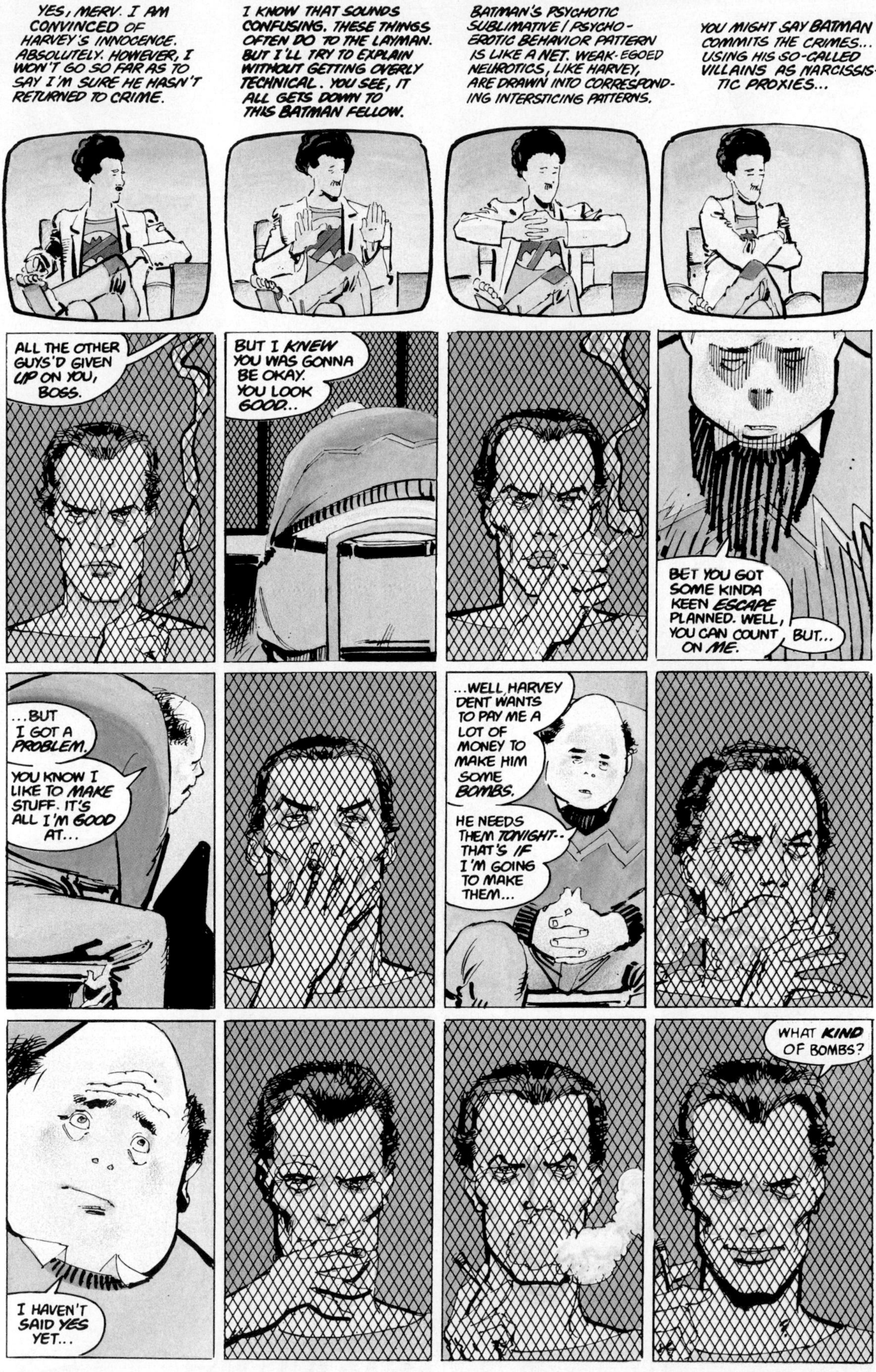
YES, MERV. I AM CONVINCED OF HARVEY'S INNOCENCE. ABSOLUTELY. HOWEVER, I WON'T GO SO FAR AS TO SAY I'M SURE HE HASN'T RETURNED TO CRIME.
I KNOW THAT SOUNDS CONFUSING. THESE THINGS OFTEN DO TO THE LAYMAN. BUT I'LL TRY TO EXPLAIN WITHOUT GETTING OVERLY TECHNICAL. YOU SEE, IT ALL GETS DOWN TO THIS BATMAN FELLOW.
BATMAN'S PSYCHOTIC SUBLIMATIVE/PSYCHO-EROTIC BEHAVIOR PATTERN IS LIKE A NET. WEAK-EGOED NEUROTICS, LIKE HARVEY, ARE DRAWN INTO CORRESPONDING INTERSTICING PATTERNS.
YOU MIGHT SAY BATMAN COMMITS THE CRIMES... USING HIS SO-CALLED VILLAINS AS NARCISSISTIC PROXIES...
ALL THE OTHER GUYS'D GIVEN UP ON YOU, BOSS.
BUT I KNEW YOU WAS GONNA BE OKAY. YOU LOOK GOOD...
BET YOU GOT SOME KINDA KEEN ESCAPE PLANNED. WELL, YOU CAN COUNT ON ME.
BUT...
...BUT I GOT A PROBLEM.
YOU KNOW I LIKE TO MAKE STUFF. IT'S ALL I'M GOOD AT...
...WELL HARVEY DENT WANTS TO PAY ME A LOT OF MONEY TO MAKE HIM SOME BOMBS.
HE NEEDS THEM TONIGHT-- THAT'S IF I'M GOING TO MAKE THEM...
I HAVEN'T SAID YES YET...
WHAT KIND OF BOMBS?

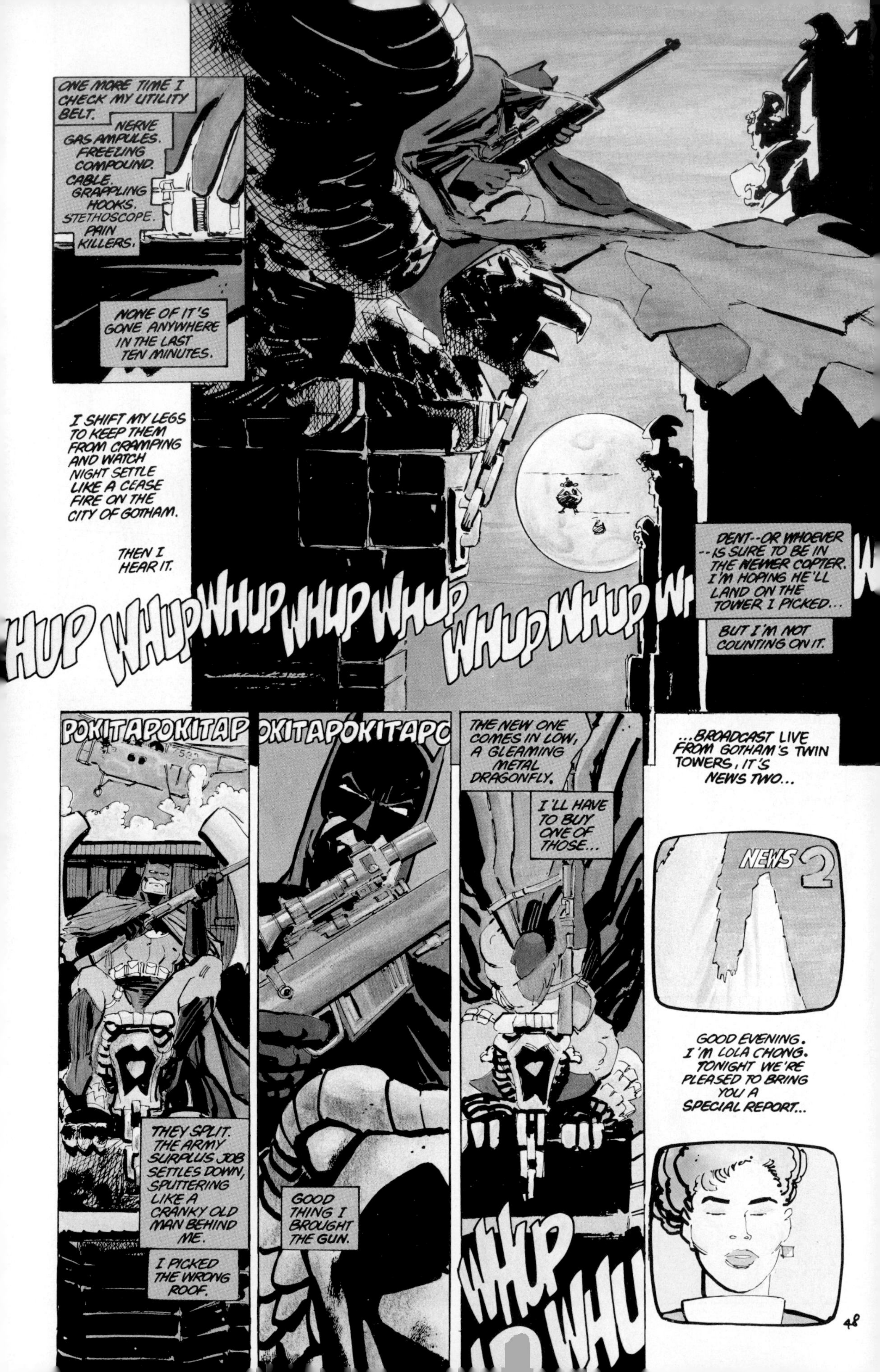

ONE MORE TIME I CHECK MY UTILITY BELT.
NERVE GAS AMPULES. FREEZING COMPOUND. CABLE. GRAPPLING HOOKS. STETHOSCOPE. PAIN KILLERS.
NONE OF IT'S GONE ANYWHERE IN THE LAST TEN MINUTES.
I SHIFT MY LEGS TO KEEP THEM FROM CRAMPING AND WATCH NIGHT SETTLE LIKE A CEASE FIRE ON THE CITY OF GOTHAM.
THEN I HEAR IT.
HUP WHUP WHUP WHUP WHUP WHUP WHUP
DENT--OR WHOEVER--IS SURE TO BE IN THE NEWER COPTER. I'M HOPING HE'LL LAND ON THE TOWER I PICKED...
BUT I'M NOT COUNTING ON IT.
POKITAPOKITAP
THEY SPLIT. THE ARMY SURPLUS JOB SETTLES DOWN, SPUTTERING LIKE A CRANKY OLD MAN BEHIND ME.
I PICKED THE WRONG ROOF.
OKITAPOKITAPO
GOOD THING I BROUGHT THE GUN.
THE NEW ONE COMES IN LOW, A GLEAMING METAL DRAGONFLY.
I'LL HAVE TO BUY ONE OF THOSE...
WHUP WHU
...BROADCAST LIVE FROM GOTHAM'S TWIN TOWERS, IT'S NEWS TWO...
NEWS 2
GOOD EVENING. I'M LOLA CHONG. TONIGHT WE'RE PLEASED TO BRING YOU A SPECIAL REPORT...

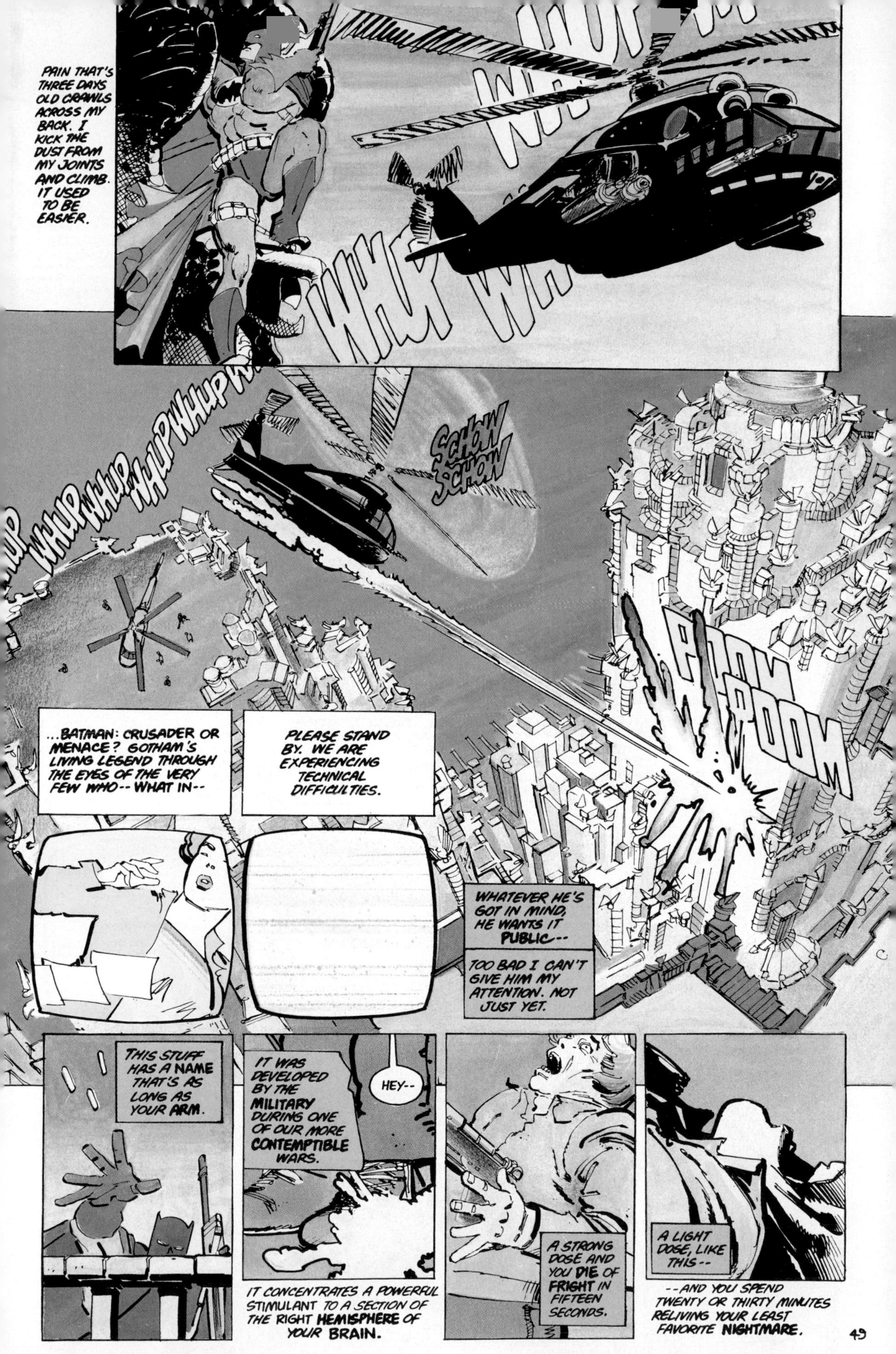

PAIN THAT'S THREE DAYS OLD CRAWLS ACROSS MY BACK. I KICK THE DUST FROM MY JOINTS AND CLIMB. IT USED TO BE EASIER.
WHUP WHUP
WHUPWHUPWHUPWHUPWH
SCHOW SCHOW
...BATMAN: CRUSADER OR MENACE? GOTHAM'S LIVING LEGEND THROUGH THE EYES OF THE VERY FEW WHO-- WHAT IN--
PLEASE STAND BY. WE ARE EXPERIENCING TECHNICAL DIFFICULTIES.
BOOM BOOM
WHATEVER HE'S GOT IN MIND, HE WANTS IT PUBLIC--
TOO BAD I CAN'T GIVE HIM MY ATTENTION. NOT JUST YET.
THIS STUFF HAS A NAME THAT'S AS LONG AS YOUR ARM.
IT WAS DEVELOPED BY THE MILITARY DURING ONE OF OUR MORE CONTEMPTIBLE WARS.
HEY--
IT CONCENTRATES A POWERFUL STIMULANT TO A SECTION OF THE RIGHT HEMISPHERE OF YOUR BRAIN.
A STRONG DOSE AND YOU DIE OF FRIGHT IN FIFTEEN SECONDS.
A LIGHT DOSE, LIKE THIS--
--AND YOU SPEND TWENTY OR THIRTY MINUTES RELIVING YOUR LEAST FAVORITE NIGHTMARE.

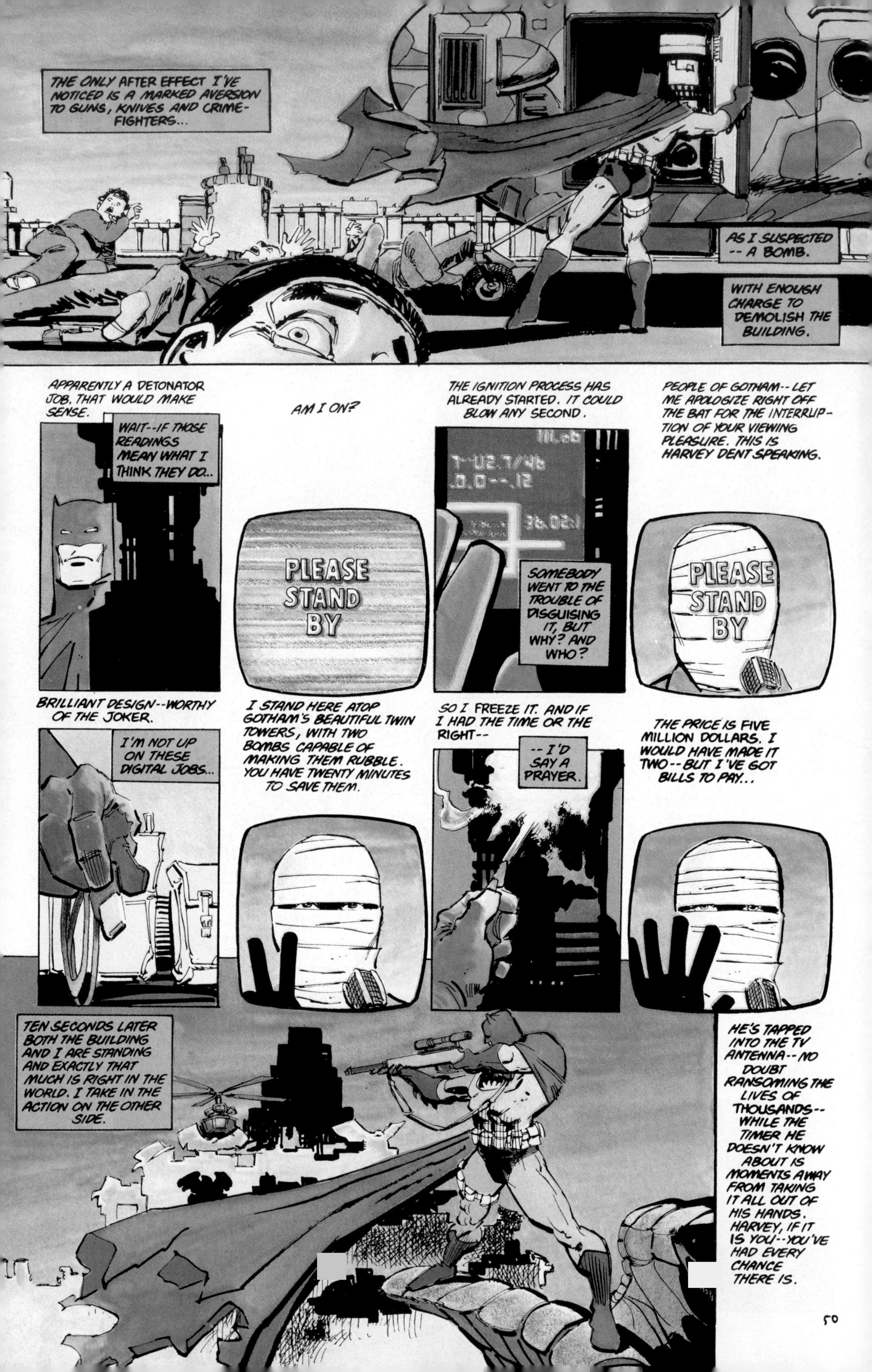
THE ONLY AFTER EFFECT I'VE NOTICED IS A MARKED AVERSION TO GUNS, KNIVES AND CRIME-FIGHTERS...
AS I SUSPECTED -- A BOMB.
WITH ENOUGH CHARGE TO DEMOLISH THE BUILDING.
APPARENTLY A DETONATOR JOB. THAT WOULD MAKE SENSE.
WAIT--IF THOSE READINGS MEAN WHAT I THINK THEY DO...
AM I ON?
PLEASE STAND BY
THE IGNITION PROCESS HAS ALREADY STARTED. IT COULD BLOW ANY SECOND.
SOMEBODY WENT TO THE TROUBLE OF DISGUISING IT, BUT WHY? AND WHO?
PEOPLE OF GOTHAM--LET ME APOLOGIZE RIGHT OFF THE BAT FOR THE INTERRUPTION OF YOUR VIEWING PLEASURE. THIS IS HARVEY DENT SPEAKING.
PLEASE STAND BY
BRILLIANT DESIGN--WORTHY OF THE JOKER.
I'M NOT UP ON THESE DIGITAL JOBS...
I STAND HERE ATOP GOTHAM'S BEAUTIFUL TWIN TOWERS, WITH TWO BOMBS CAPABLE OF MAKING THEM RUBBLE. YOU HAVE TWENTY MINUTES TO SAVE THEM.
SO I FREEZE IT. AND IF I HAD THE TIME OR THE RIGHT--
--I'D SAY A PRAYER.
THE PRICE IS FIVE MILLION DOLLARS. I WOULD HAVE MADE IT TWO--BUT I'VE GOT BILLS TO PAY...
TEN SECONDS LATER BOTH THE BUILDING AND I ARE STANDING AND EXACTLY THAT MUCH IS RIGHT IN THE WORLD. I TAKE IN THE ACTION ON THE OTHER SIDE.
HE'S TAPPED INTO THE TV ANTENNA--NO DOUBT RANSOMING THE LIVES OF THOUSANDS--WHILE THE TIMER HE DOESN'T KNOW ABOUT IS MOMENTS AWAY FROM TAKING IT ALL OUT OF HIS HANDS. HARVEY, IF IT IS YOU--YOU'VE HAD EVERY CHANCE THERE IS.

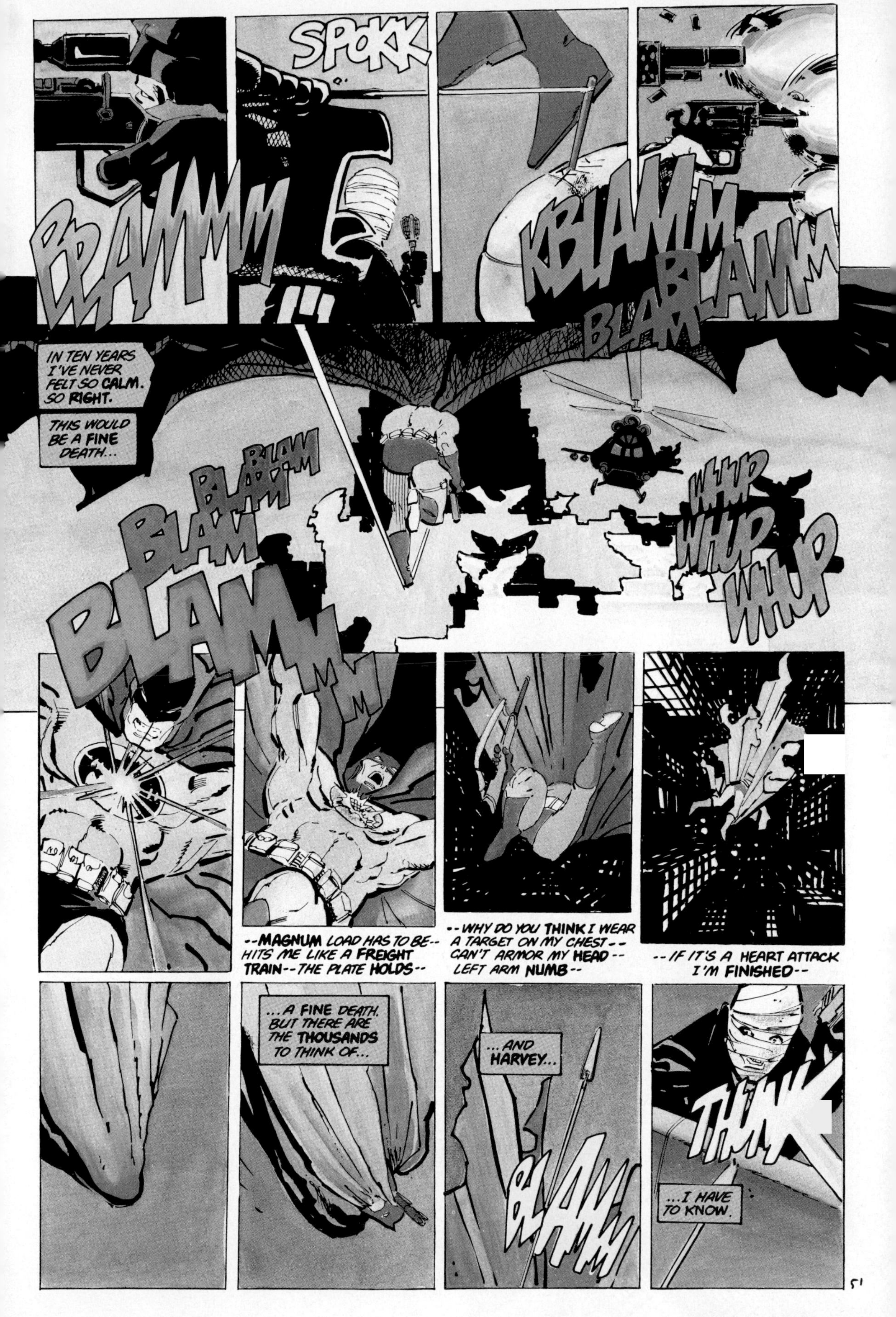

BRAMMM
SPOKK
KBLAMM
BLAMBLAMM
IN TEN YEARS I'VE NEVER FELT SO CALM. SO RIGHT.
THIS WOULD BE A FINE DEATH...
BLAM
BLAM
BLAM
BLAMMM
WHUP
WHUP
WHUP
--MAGNUM LOAD HAS TO BE-- HITS ME LIKE A FREIGHT TRAIN--THE PLATE HOLDS--
--WHY DO YOU THINK I WEAR A TARGET ON MY CHEST-- CAN'T ARMOR MY HEAD-- LEFT ARM NUMB--
--IF IT'S A HEART ATTACK I'M FINISHED--
...A FINE DEATH. BUT THERE ARE THE THOUSANDS TO THINK OF...
...AND HARVEY...
BLAMM
THUNK
...I HAVE TO KNOW.

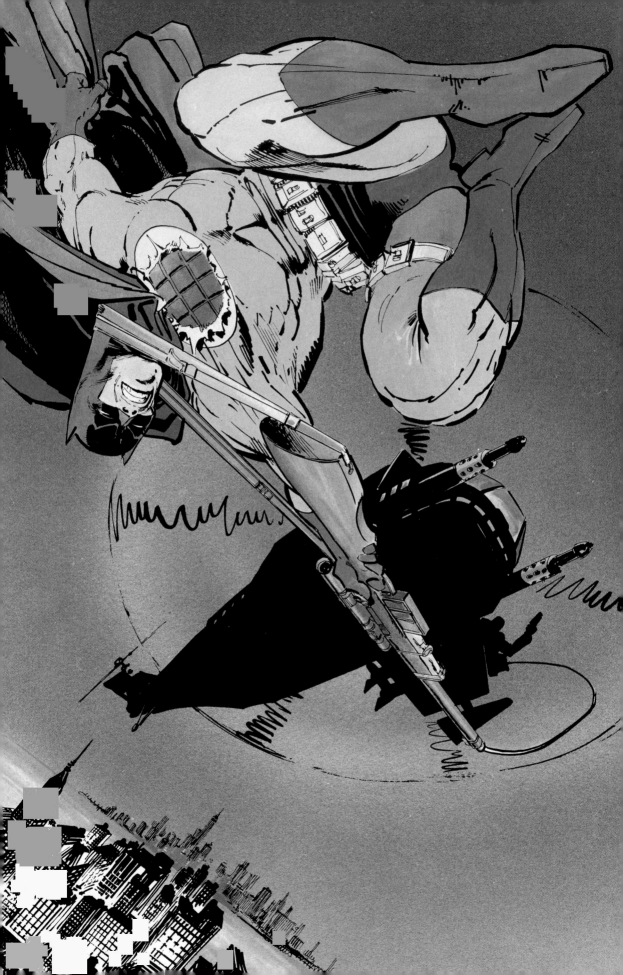

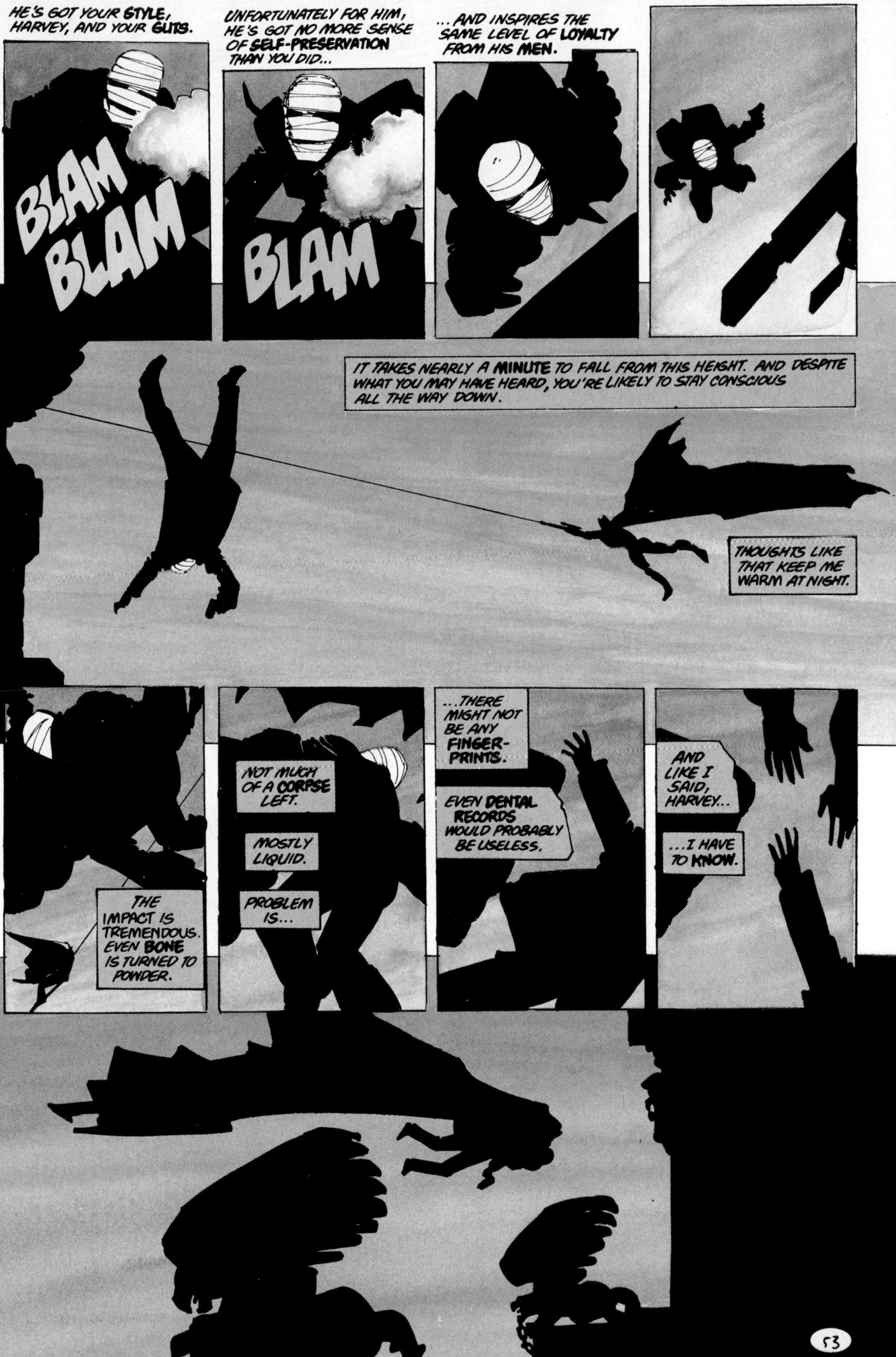
HE'S GOT YOUR STYLE, HARVEY, AND YOUR GUTS.
BLAM BLAM
UNFORTUNATELY FOR HIM, HE'S GOT NO MORE SENSE OF SELF-PRESERVATION THAN YOU DID...
BLAM
...AND INSPIRES THE SAME LEVEL OF LOYALTY FROM HIS MEN.
IT TAKES NEARLY A MINUTE TO FALL FROM THIS HEIGHT. AND DESPITE WHAT YOU MAY HAVE HEARD, YOU'RE LIKELY TO STAY CONSCIOUS ALL THE WAY DOWN.
THOUGHTS LIKE THAT KEEP ME WARM AT NIGHT.
THE IMPACT IS TREMENDOUS. EVEN BONE IS TURNED TO POWDER.
NOT MUCH OF A CORPSE LEFT.
MOSTLY LIQUID.
PROBLEM IS...
...THERE MIGHT NOT BE ANY FINGER-PRINTS.
EVEN DENTAL RECORDS WOULD PROBABLY BE USELESS.
AND LIKE I SAID, HARVEY...
...I HAVE TO KNOW.

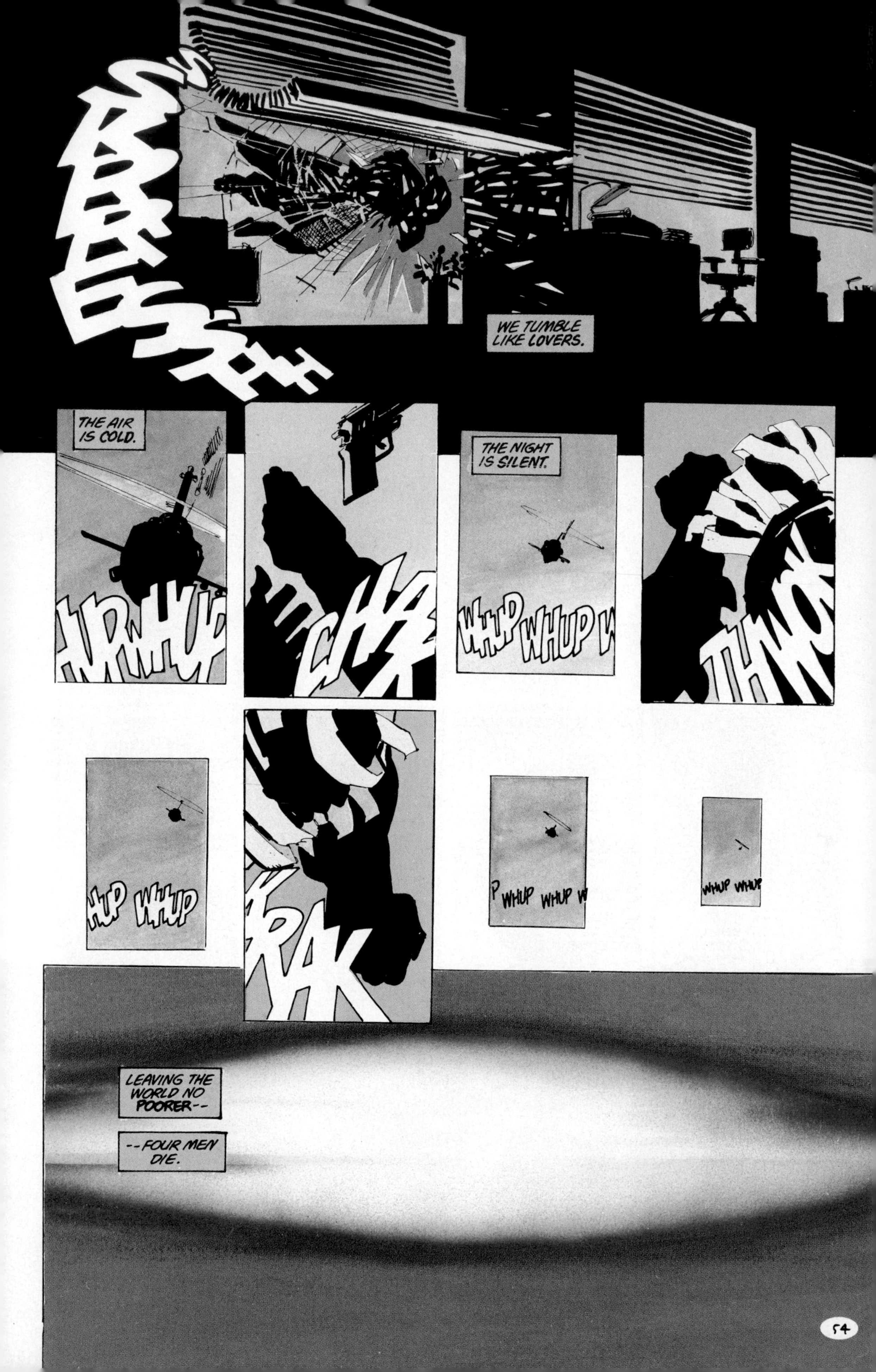
WE TUMBLE LIKE LOVERS.
THE AIR IS COLD.
THE NIGHT IS SILENT.
WHUP WHUP
WHUP WHUP
WHUP WHUP
WHUP WHUP
LEAVING THE WORLD NO POORER--
--FOUR MEN DIE.

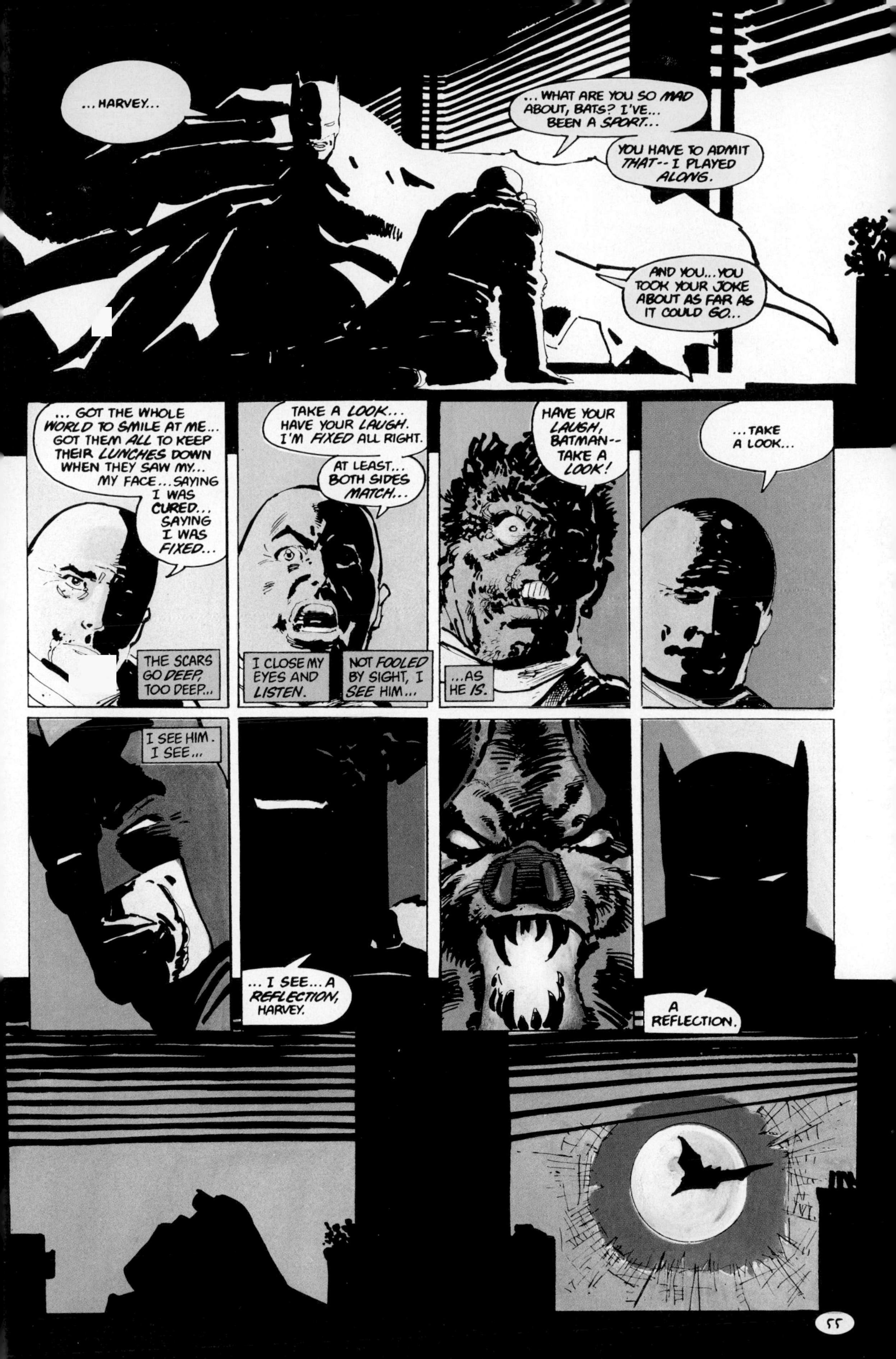

...HARVEY...
...WHAT ARE YOU SO MAD ABOUT, BATS? I'VE... BEEN A SPORT...
YOU HAVE TO ADMIT THAT-- I PLAYED ALONG.
AND YOU...YOU TOOK YOUR JOKE ABOUT AS FAR AS IT COULD GO...
...GOT THE WHOLE WORLD TO SMILE AT ME... GOT THEM ALL TO KEEP THEIR LUNCHES DOWN WHEN THEY SAW MY... MY FACE...SAYING I WAS CURED... SAYING I WAS FIXED...
THE SCARS GO DEEP, TOO DEEP...
TAKE A LOOK... HAVE YOUR LAUGH. I'M FIXED ALL RIGHT.
AT LEAST... BOTH SIDES MATCH...
I CLOSE MY EYES AND LISTEN.
NOT FOOLED BY SIGHT, I SEE HIM...
HAVE YOUR LAUGH, BATMAN-- TAKE A LOOK!
...AS HE IS.
...TAKE A LOOK...
I SEE HIM. I SEE...
...I SEE...A REFLECTION, HARVEY.
A REFLECTION.

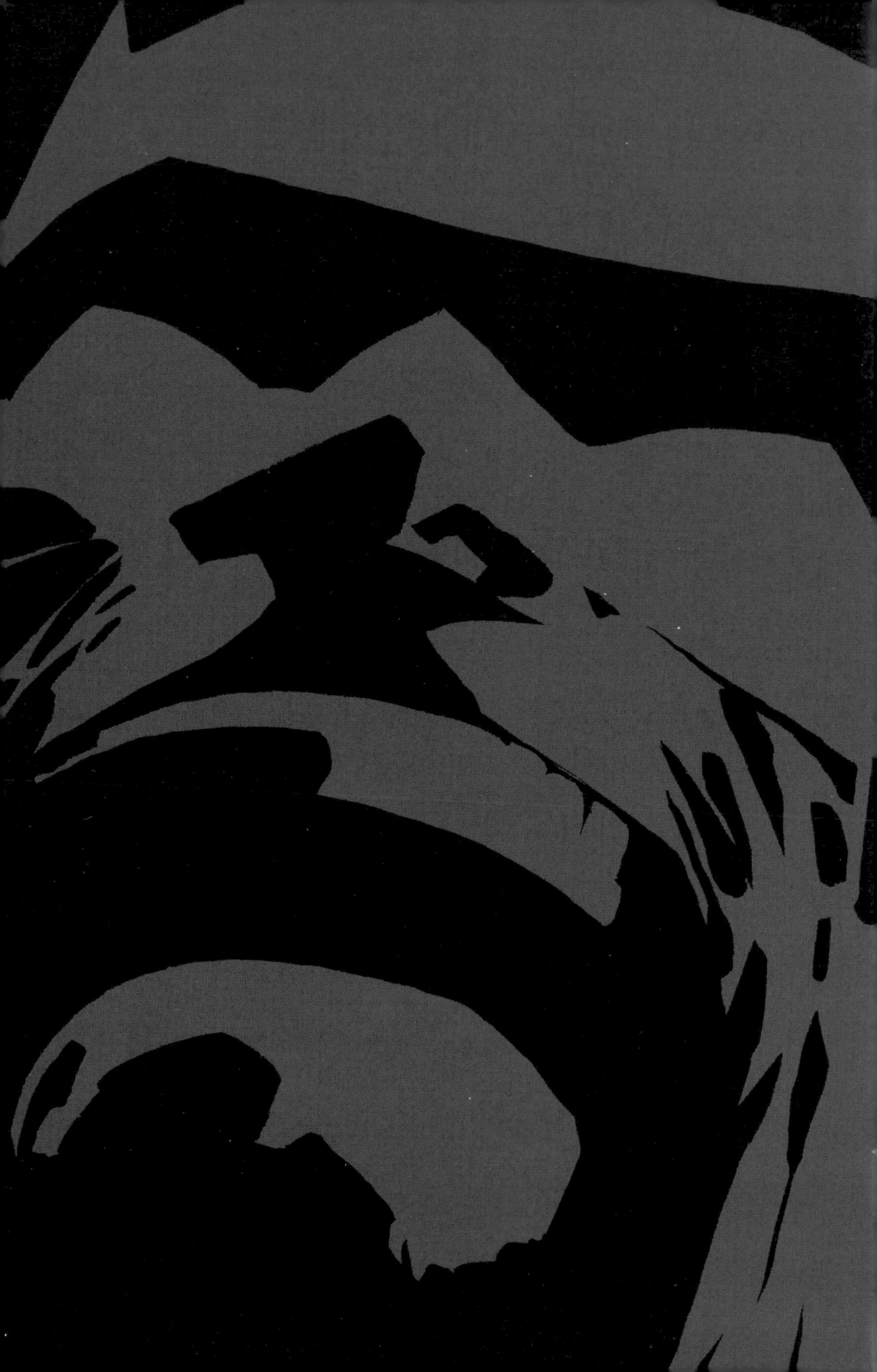

BOOK TWO

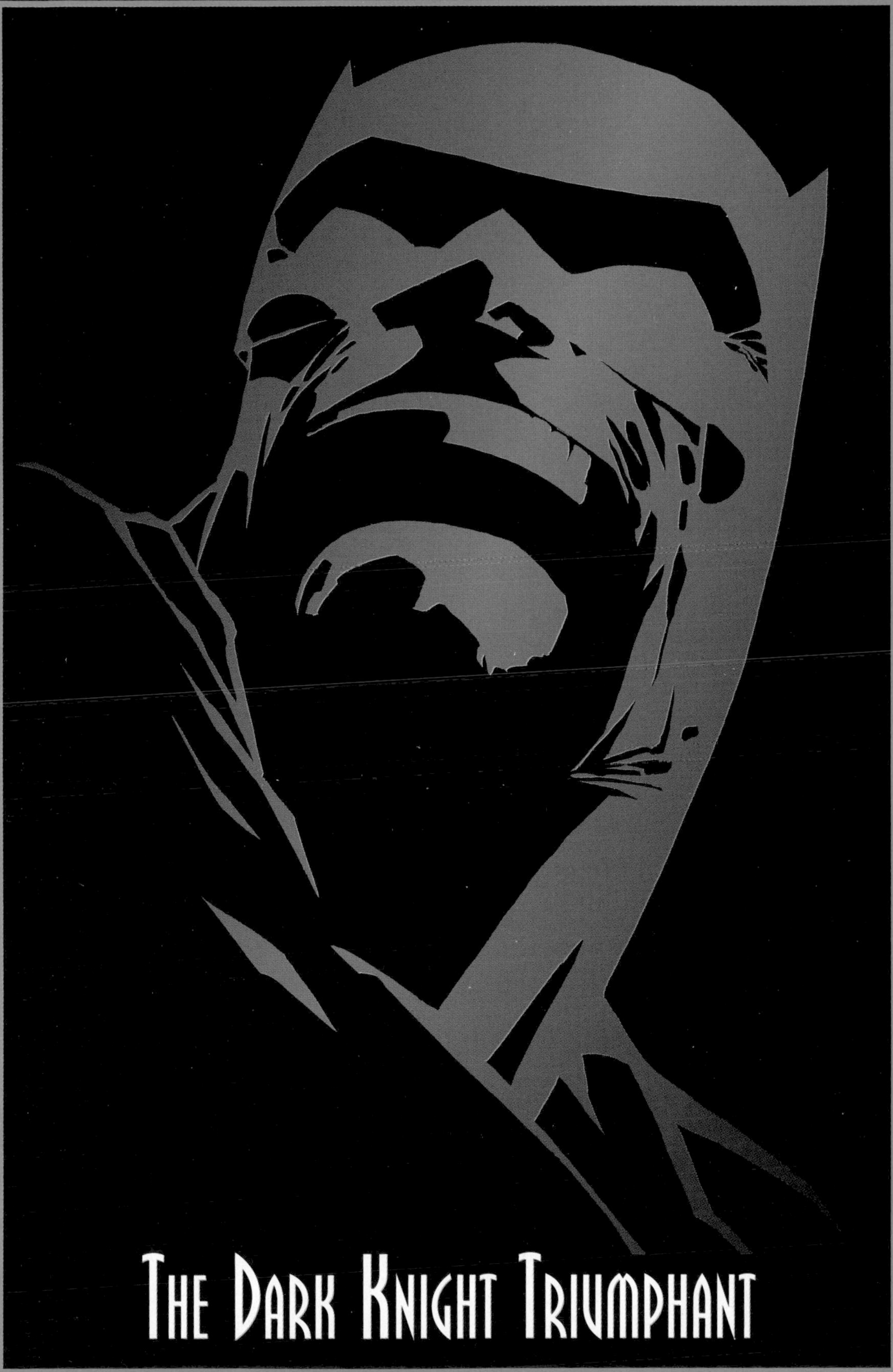

THE DARK KNIGHT TRIUMPHANT

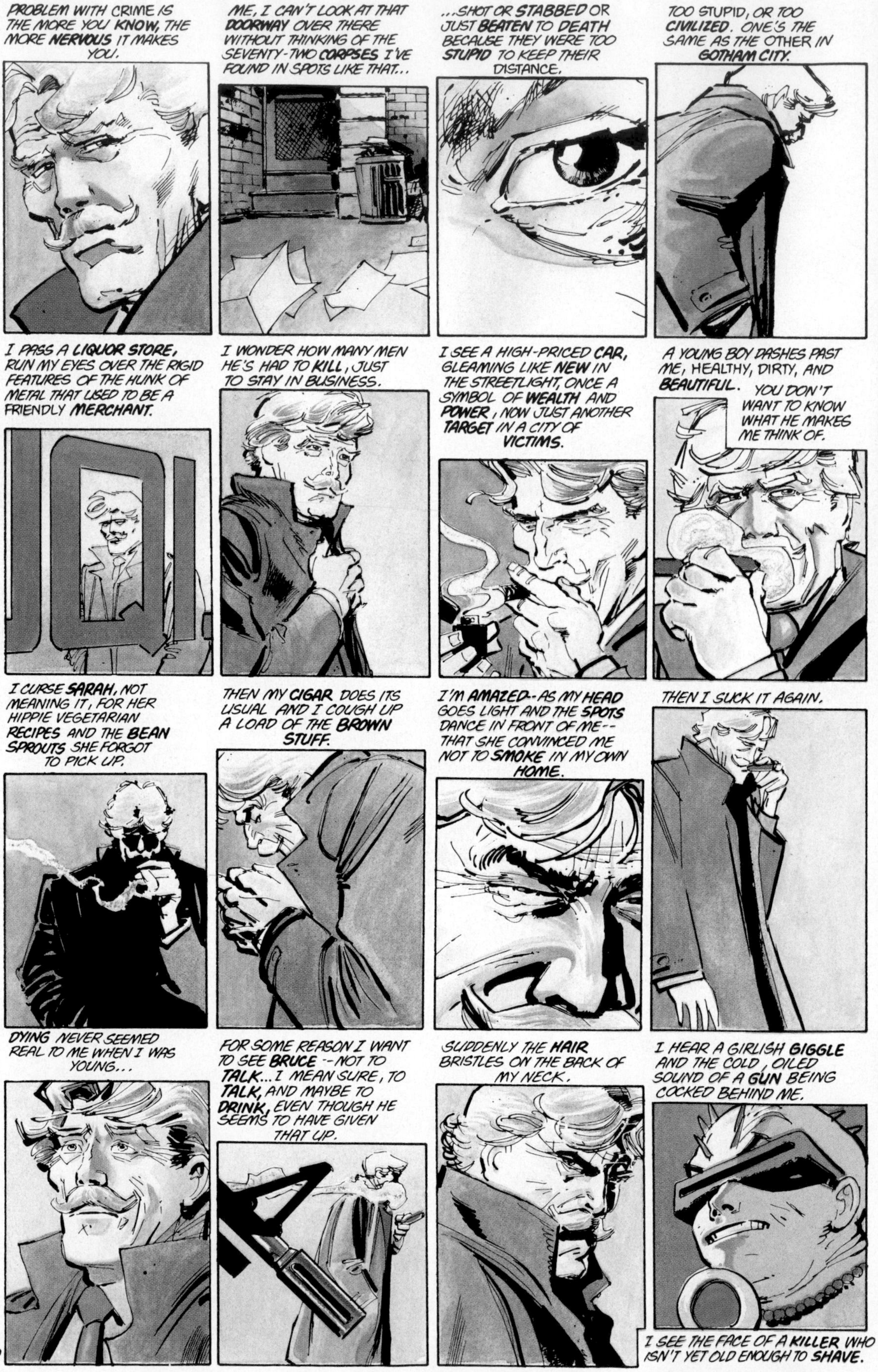
PROBLEM WITH CRIME IS THE MORE YOU KNOW, THE MORE NERVOUS IT MAKES YOU.
ME, I CAN'T LOOK AT THAT DOORWAY OVER THERE WITHOUT THINKING OF THE SEVENTY-TWO CORPSES I'VE FOUND IN SPOTS LIKE THAT...
...SHOT OR STABBED OR JUST BEATEN TO DEATH BECAUSE THEY WERE TOO STUPID TO KEEP THEIR DISTANCE.
TOO STUPID, OR TOO CIVILIZED. ONE'S THE SAME AS THE OTHER IN GOTHAM CITY.
I PASS A LIQUOR STORE, RUN MY EYES OVER THE RIGID FEATURES OF THE HUNK OF METAL THAT USED TO BE A FRIENDLY MERCHANT.
I WONDER HOW MANY MEN HE'S HAD TO KILL, JUST TO STAY IN BUSINESS.
I SEE A HIGH-PRICED CAR, GLEAMING LIKE NEW IN THE STREETLIGHT, ONCE A SYMBOL OF WEALTH AND POWER, NOW JUST ANOTHER TARGET IN A CITY OF VICTIMS.
A YOUNG BOY DASHES PAST ME, HEALTHY, DIRTY, AND BEAUTIFUL.
YOU DON'T WANT TO KNOW WHAT HE MAKES ME THINK OF.
I CURSE SARAH, NOT MEANING IT, FOR HER HIPPIE VEGETARIAN RECIPES AND THE BEAN SPROUTS SHE FORGOT TO PICK UP.
THEN MY CIGAR DOES ITS USUAL AND I COUGH UP A LOAD OF THE BROWN STUFF.
I'M AMAZED--AS MY HEAD GOES LIGHT AND THE SPOTS DANCE IN FRONT OF ME--THAT SHE CONVINCED ME NOT TO SMOKE IN MY OWN HOME.
THEN I SUCK IT AGAIN.
DYING NEVER SEEMED REAL TO ME WHEN I WAS YOUNG...
FOR SOME REASON I WANT TO SEE BRUCE--NOT TO TALK...I MEAN SURE, TO TALK, AND MAYBE TO DRINK, EVEN THOUGH HE SEEMS TO HAVE GIVEN THAT UP.
SUDDENLY THE HAIR BRISTLES ON THE BACK OF MY NECK.
I HEAR A GIRLISH GIGGLE AND THE COLD, OILED SOUND OF A GUN BEING COCKED BEHIND ME.
I SEE THE FACE OF A KILLER WHO ISN'T YET OLD ENOUGH TO SHAVE.

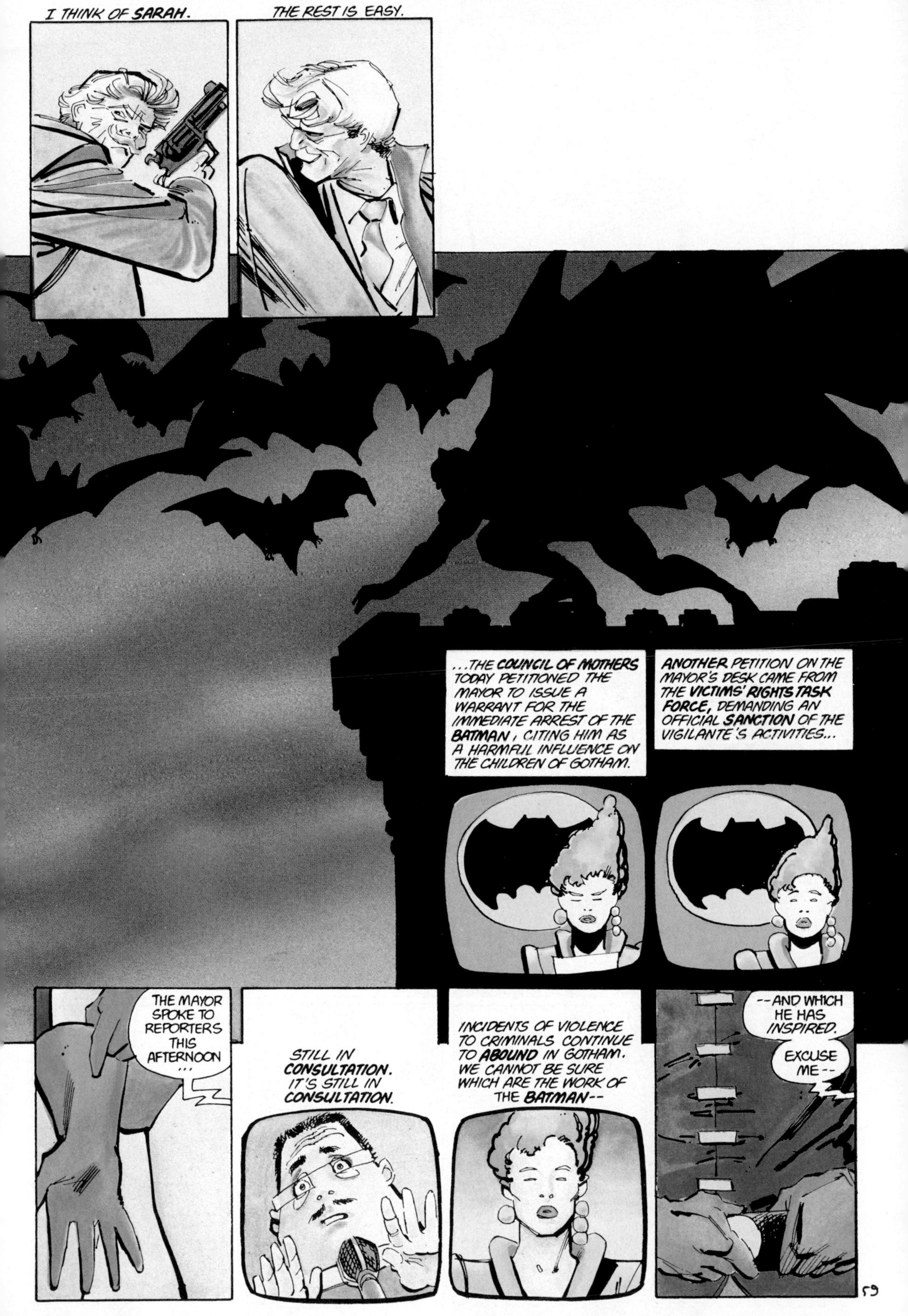
I THINK OF SARAH.
THE REST IS EASY.
...THE COUNCIL OF MOTHERS TODAY PETITIONED THE MAYOR TO ISSUE A WARRANT FOR THE IMMEDIATE ARREST OF THE BATMAN, CITING HIM AS A HARMFUL INFLUENCE ON THE CHILDREN OF GOTHAM.
ANOTHER PETITION ON THE MAYOR'S DESK CAME FROM THE VICTIMS' RIGHTS TASK FORCE, DEMANDING AN OFFICIAL SANCTION OF THE VIGILANTE'S ACTIVITIES...
THE MAYOR SPOKE TO REPORTERS THIS AFTERNOON ...
STILL IN CONSULTATION. IT'S STILL IN CONSULTATION.
INCIDENTS OF VIOLENCE TO CRIMINALS CONTINUE TO ABOUND IN GOTHAM. WE CANNOT BE SURE WHICH ARE THE WORK OF THE BATMAN--
--AND WHICH HE HAS INSPIRED.
EXCUSE ME--

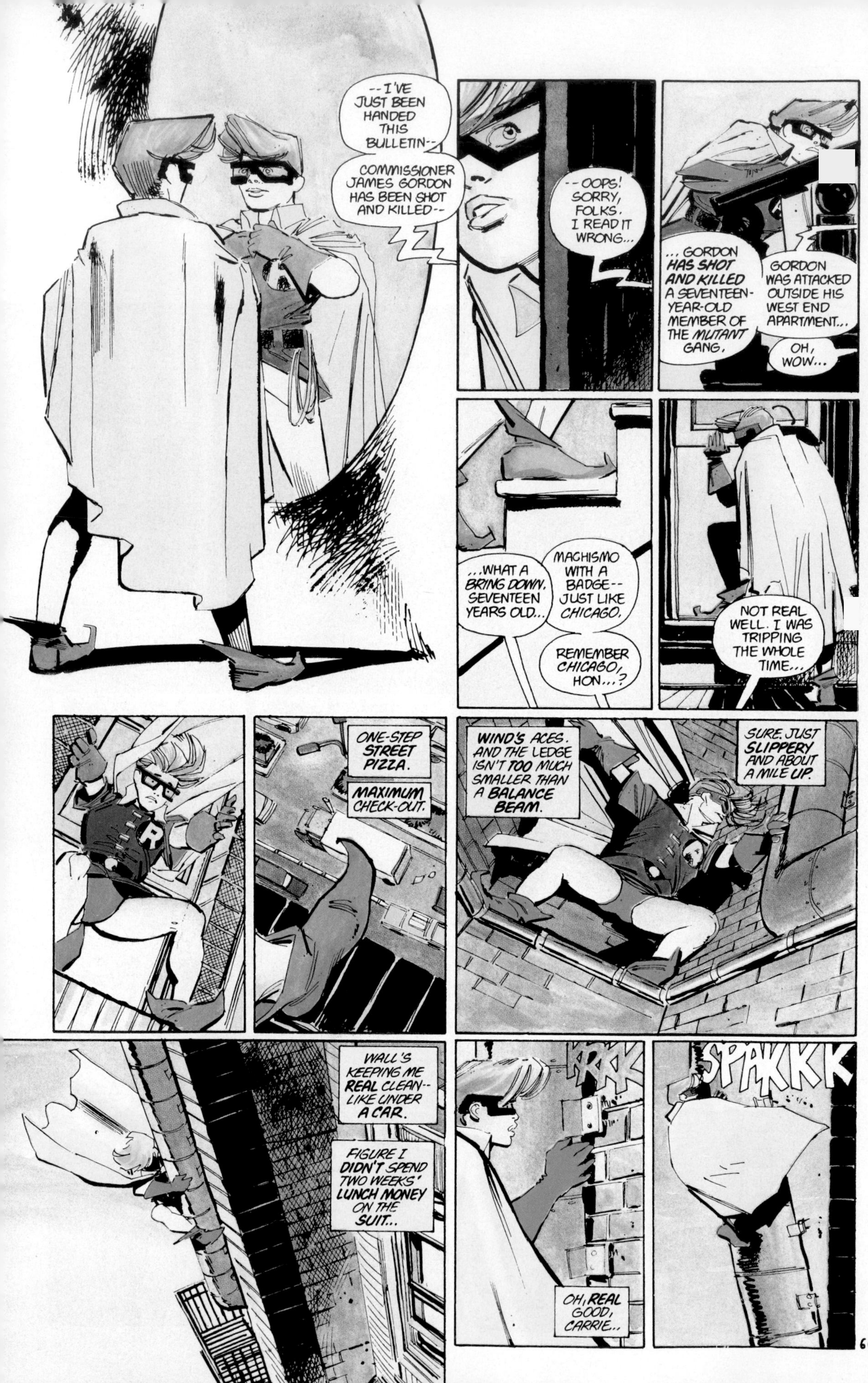
--I'VE JUST BEEN HANDED THIS BULLETIN--
COMMISSIONER JAMES GORDON HAS BEEN SHOT AND KILLED--
--OOPS! SORRY, FOLKS. I READ IT WRONG...
...GORDON **HAS SHOT AND KILLED** A SEVENTEEN-YEAR-OLD MEMBER OF THE *MUTANT* GANG.
GORDON WAS ATTACKED OUTSIDE HIS WEST END APARTMENT...
OH, WOW...
...WHAT A *BRING DOWN*. SEVENTEEN YEARS OLD...
MACHISMO WITH A BADGE--JUST LIKE *CHICAGO*.
REMEMBER *CHICAGO*, HON...?
NOT REAL WELL. I WAS TRIPPING THE WHOLE TIME...
ONE-STEP **STREET PIZZA**.
MAXIMUM CHECK-OUT.
WIND'S ACES. AND THE LEDGE ISN'T **TOO MUCH** SMALLER THAN A **BALANCE BEAM**.
SURE. JUST **SLIPPERY** AND ABOUT A MILE **UP**.
WALL'S KEEPING ME **REAL** CLEAN--LIKE UNDER **A CAR**.
FIGURE I **DIDN'T** SPEND TWO WEEKS' **LUNCH MONEY** ON THE **SUIT**...
SPAKKK
OH, **REAL** GOOD, CARRIE...

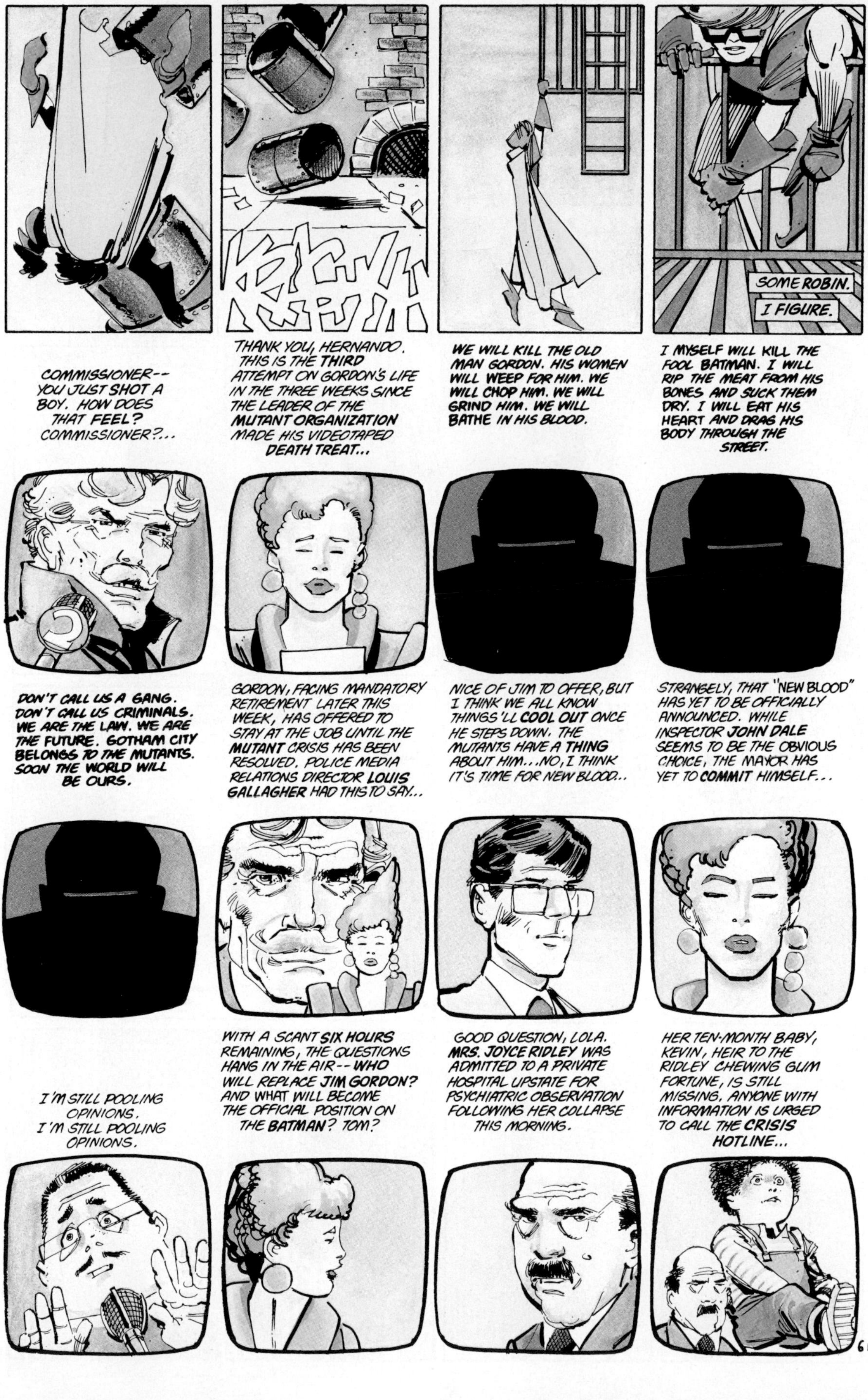

KRRAKK
SOME ROBIN.
I FIGURE.
COMMISSIONER-- YOU JUST SHOT A BOY. HOW DOES THAT FEEL? COMMISSIONER?...
THANK YOU, HERNANDO. THIS IS THE THIRD ATTEMPT ON GORDON'S LIFE IN THE THREE WEEKS SINCE THE LEADER OF THE MUTANT ORGANIZATION MADE HIS VIDEOTAPED DEATH TREAT...
WE WILL KILL THE OLD MAN GORDON. HIS WOMEN WILL WEEP FOR HIM. WE WILL CHOP HIM. WE WILL GRIND HIM. WE WILL BATHE IN HIS BLOOD.
I MYSELF WILL KILL THE FOOL BATMAN. I WILL RIP THE MEAT FROM HIS BONES AND SUCK THEM DRY. I WILL EAT HIS HEART AND DRAG HIS BODY THROUGH THE STREET.
DON'T CALL US A GANG. DON'T CALL US CRIMINALS. WE ARE THE LAW. WE ARE THE FUTURE. GOTHAM CITY BELONGS TO THE MUTANTS. SOON THE WORLD WILL BE OURS.
GORDON, FACING MANDATORY RETIREMENT LATER THIS WEEK, HAS OFFERED TO STAY AT THE JOB UNTIL THE MUTANT CRISIS HAS BEEN RESOLVED. POLICE MEDIA RELATIONS DIRECTOR LOUIS GALLAGHER HAD THIS TO SAY...
NICE OF JIM TO OFFER, BUT I THINK WE ALL KNOW THINGS'LL COOL OUT ONCE HE STEPS DOWN. THE MUTANTS HAVE A THING ABOUT HIM...NO, I THINK IT'S TIME FOR NEW BLOOD...
STRANGELY, THAT "NEW BLOOD" HAS YET TO BE OFFICIALLY ANNOUNCED. WHILE INSPECTOR JOHN DALE SEEMS TO BE THE OBVIOUS CHOICE, THE MAYOR HAS YET TO COMMIT HIMSELF...
I'M STILL POOLING OPINIONS. I'M STILL POOLING OPINIONS.
WITH A SCANT SIX HOURS REMAINING, THE QUESTIONS HANG IN THE AIR-- WHO WILL REPLACE JIM GORDON? AND WHAT WILL BECOME THE OFFICIAL POSITION ON THE BATMAN? TOM?
GOOD QUESTION, LOLA. MRS. JOYCE RIDLEY WAS ADMITTED TO A PRIVATE HOSPITAL UPSTATE FOR PSYCHIATRIC OBSERVATION FOLLOWING HER COLLAPSE THIS MORNING.
HER TEN-MONTH BABY, KEVIN, HEIR TO THE RIDLEY CHEWING GUM FORTUNE, IS STILL MISSING. ANYONE WITH INFORMATION IS URGED TO CALL THE CRISIS HOTLINE...

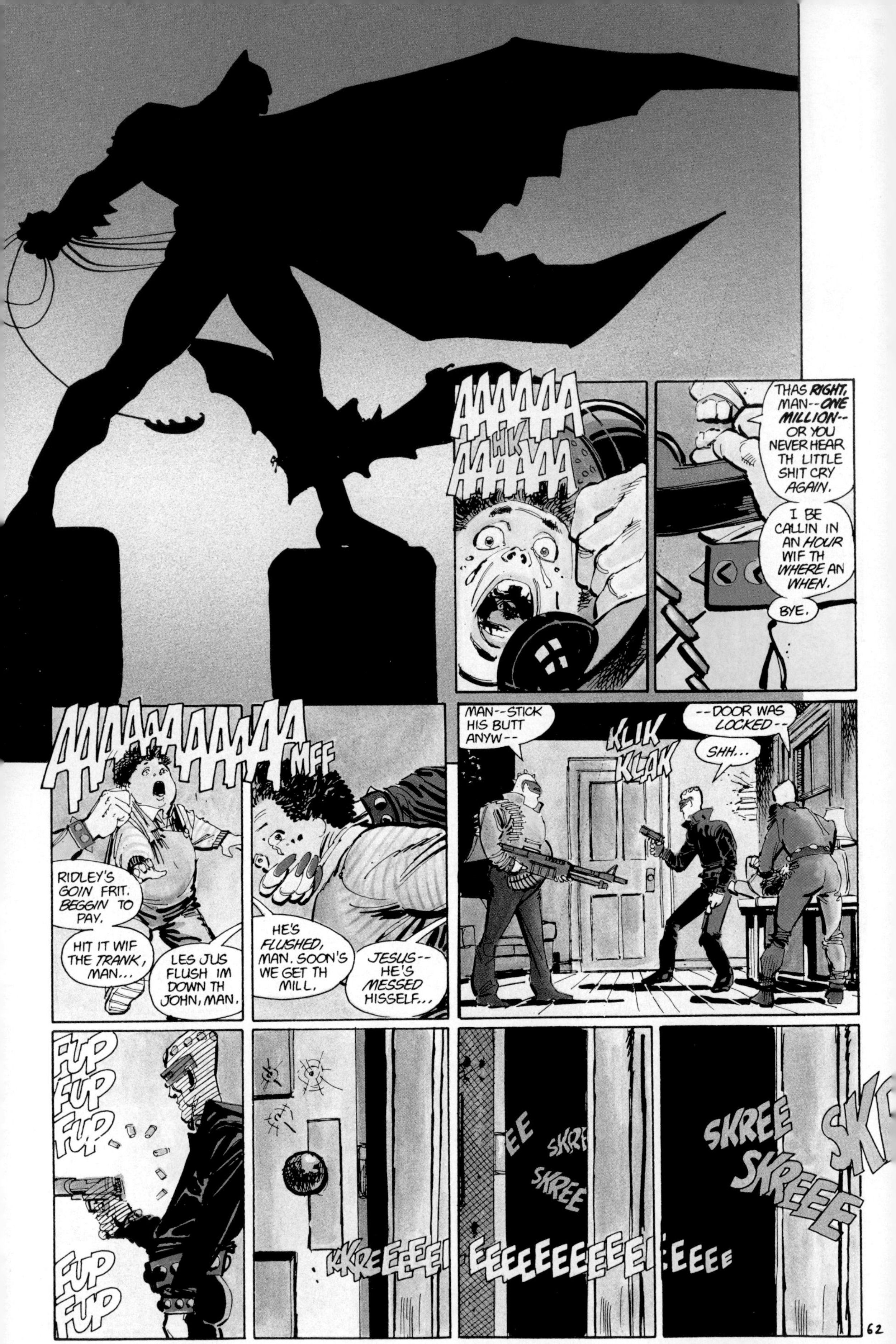

AAAAAA HK AAAAAA
THAS RIGHT, MAN--ONE MILLION-- OR YOU NEVER HEAR TH LITTLE SHIT CRY AGAIN.
I BE CALLIN IN AN HOUR WIF TH WHERE AN WHEN.
BYE.
AAAAAAAAAA
RIDLEY'S GOIN FRIT. BEGGIN TO PAY.
HIT IT WIF THE TRANK, MAN...
LES JUS FLUSH IM DOWN TH JOHN, MAN.
MFF
HE'S FLUSHED, MAN. SOON'S WE GET TH MILL.
JESUS-- HE'S MESSED HISSELF...
MAN--STICK HIS BUTT ANYW--
KLIK KLAK
--DOOR WAS LOCKED--
SHH...
FUP FUP FUP
FUP FUP
KKREEEEEI
EEEEEEEEEEI
EEEEE
EE
SKRE
SKREE
SKREE
SKREE
SKREEEE

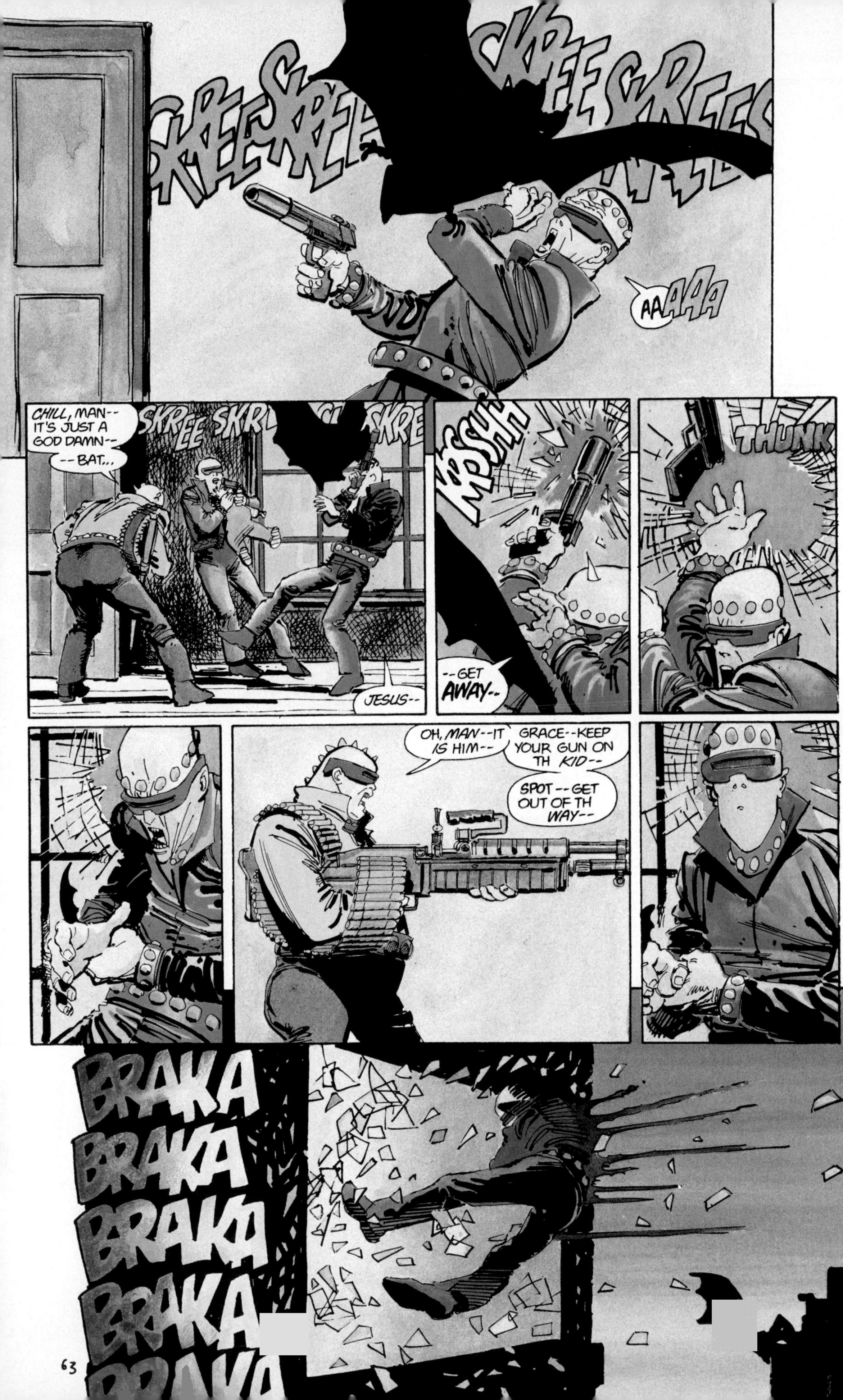
AAAAA
CHILL, MAN-- IT'S JUST A GOD DAMN--
--BAT...
JESUS--
--GET AWAY--
THUNK
OH, MAN--IT IS HIM--
GRACE--KEEP YOUR GUN ON TH KID--
SPOT--GET OUT OF TH WAY--
BRAKA
BRAKA
BRAKA
BRAKA

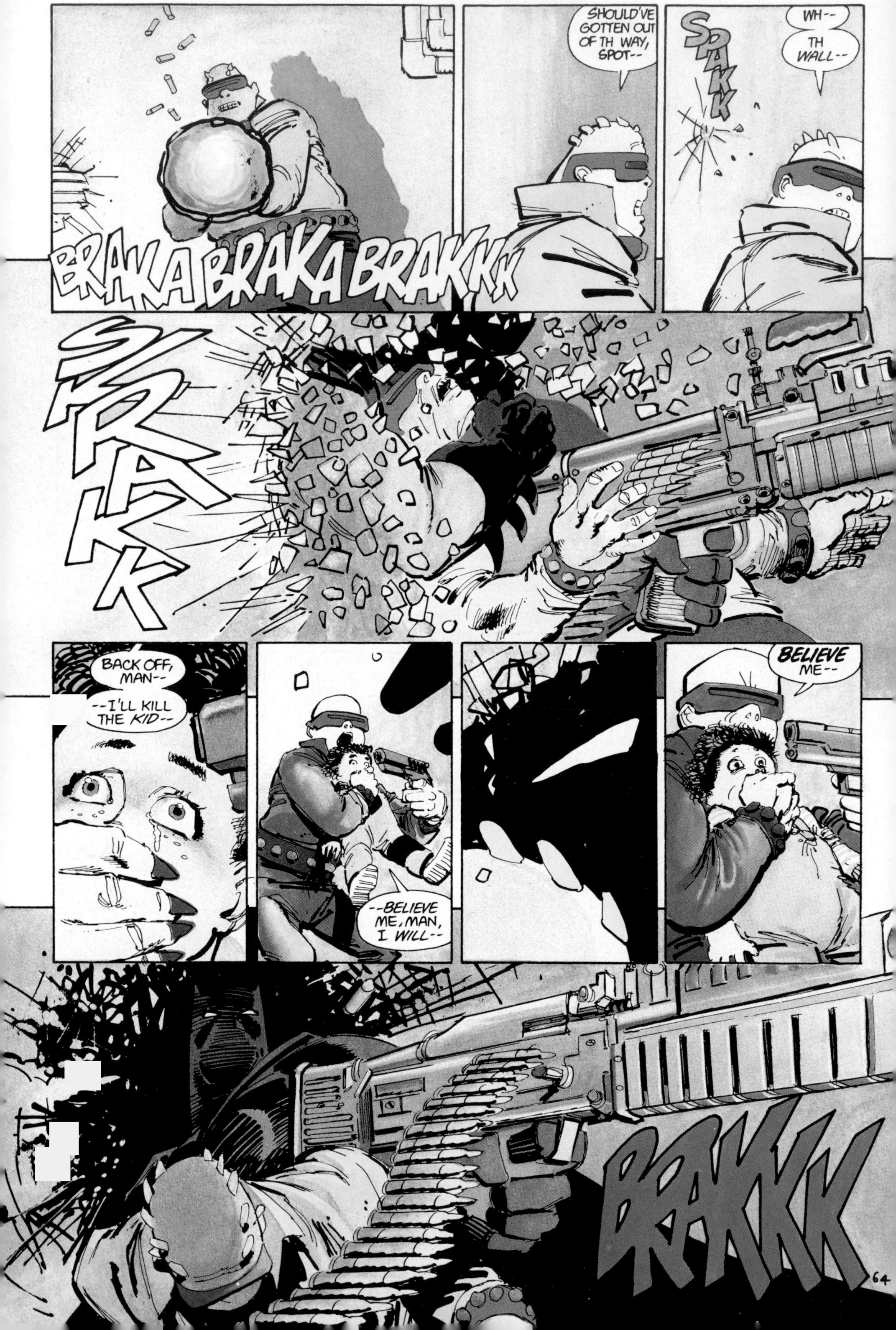
BRAKA BRAKA BRAKKKK
SHOULD'VE GOTTEN OUT OF TH WAY, SPOT--
SPAKK
WH--
TH WALL--
SPRAKK
BACK OFF, MAN--
--I'LL KILL THE KID--
--BELIEVE ME, MAN, I WILL--
BELIEVE ME--
BRAKKK

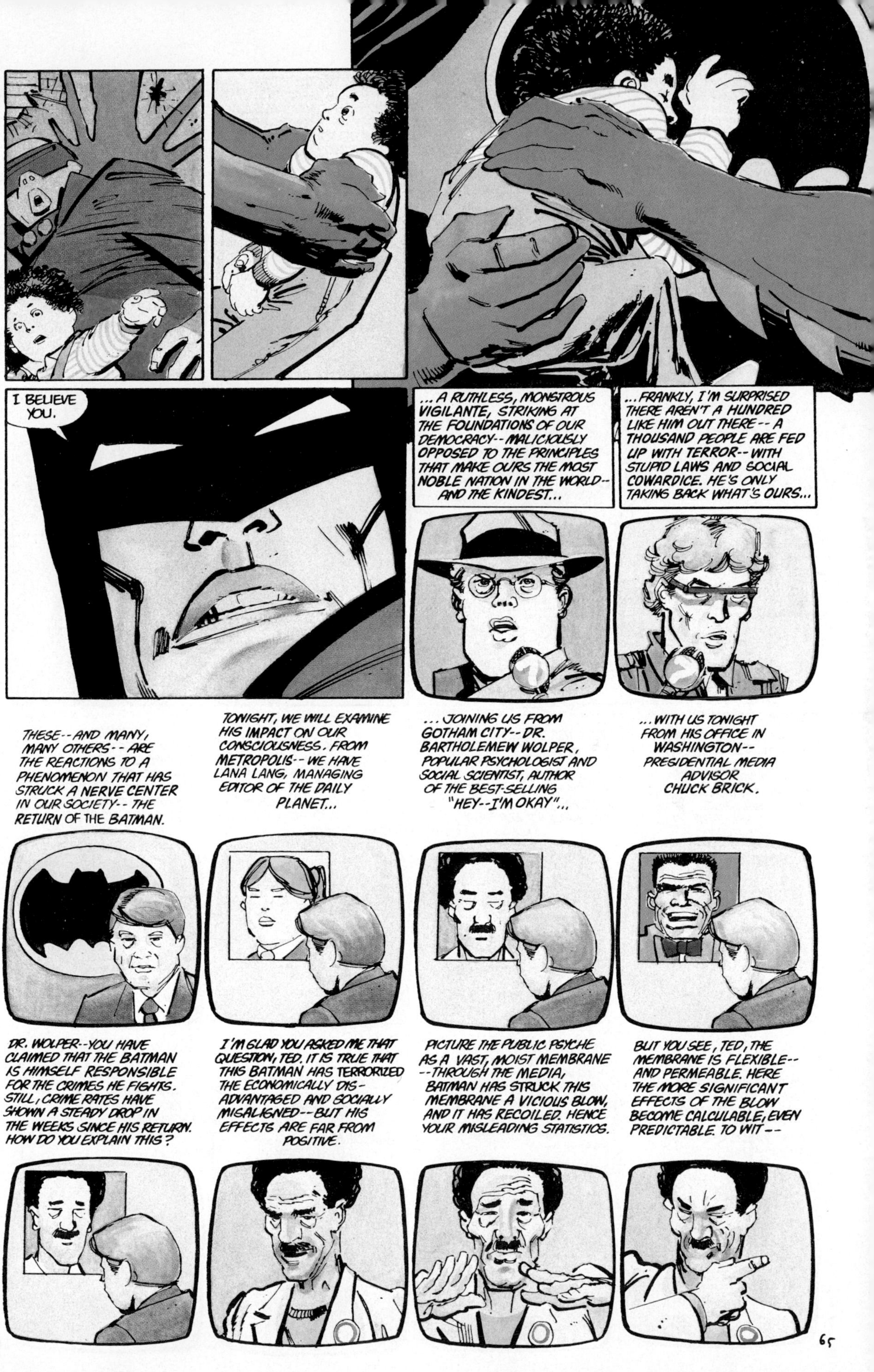
I BELIEVE YOU.
... A RUTHLESS, MONSTROUS VIGILANTE, STRIKING AT THE FOUNDATIONS OF OUR DEMOCRACY-- MALICIOUSLY OPPOSED TO THE PRINCIPLES THAT MAKE OURS THE MOST NOBLE NATION IN THE WORLD-- AND THE KINDEST...
...FRANKLY, I'M SURPRISED THERE AREN'T A HUNDRED LIKE HIM OUT THERE-- A THOUSAND PEOPLE ARE FED UP WITH TERROR-- WITH STUPID LAWS AND SOCIAL COWARDICE. HE'S ONLY TAKING BACK WHAT'S OURS...
THESE--AND MANY, MANY OTHERS--ARE THE REACTIONS TO A PHENOMENON THAT HAS STRUCK A NERVE CENTER IN OUR SOCIETY-- THE RETURN OF THE BATMAN.
TONIGHT, WE WILL EXAMINE HIS IMPACT ON OUR CONSCIOUSNESS. FROM METROPOLIS-- WE HAVE LANA LANG, MANAGING EDITOR OF THE DAILY PLANET...
... JOINING US FROM GOTHAM CITY-- DR. BARTHOLEMEW WOLPER, POPULAR PSYCHOLOGIST AND SOCIAL SCIENTIST, AUTHOR OF THE BEST-SELLING "HEY--I'M OKAY"...
...WITH US TONIGHT FROM HIS OFFICE IN WASHINGTON-- PRESIDENTIAL MEDIA ADVISOR CHUCK BRICK.
DR. WOLPER--YOU HAVE CLAIMED THAT THE BATMAN IS HIMSELF RESPONSIBLE FOR THE CRIMES HE FIGHTS. STILL, CRIME RATES HAVE SHOWN A STEADY DROP IN THE WEEKS SINCE HIS RETURN. HOW DO YOU EXPLAIN THIS?
I'M GLAD YOU ASKED ME THAT QUESTION, TED. IT IS TRUE THAT THIS BATMAN HAS TERRORIZED THE ECONOMICALLY DIS-ADVANTAGED AND SOCIALLY MISALIGNED-- BUT HIS EFFECTS ARE FAR FROM POSITIVE.
PICTURE THE PUBLIC PSYCHE AS A VAST, MOIST MEMBRANE --THROUGH THE MEDIA, BATMAN HAS STRUCK THIS MEMBRANE A VICIOUS BLOW, AND IT HAS RECOILED. HENCE YOUR MISLEADING STATISTICS.
BUT YOU SEE, TED, THE MEMBRANE IS FLEXIBLE-- AND PERMEABLE. HERE THE MORE SIGNIFICANT EFFECTS OF THE BLOW BECOME CALCULABLE, EVEN PREDICTABLE. TO WIT--

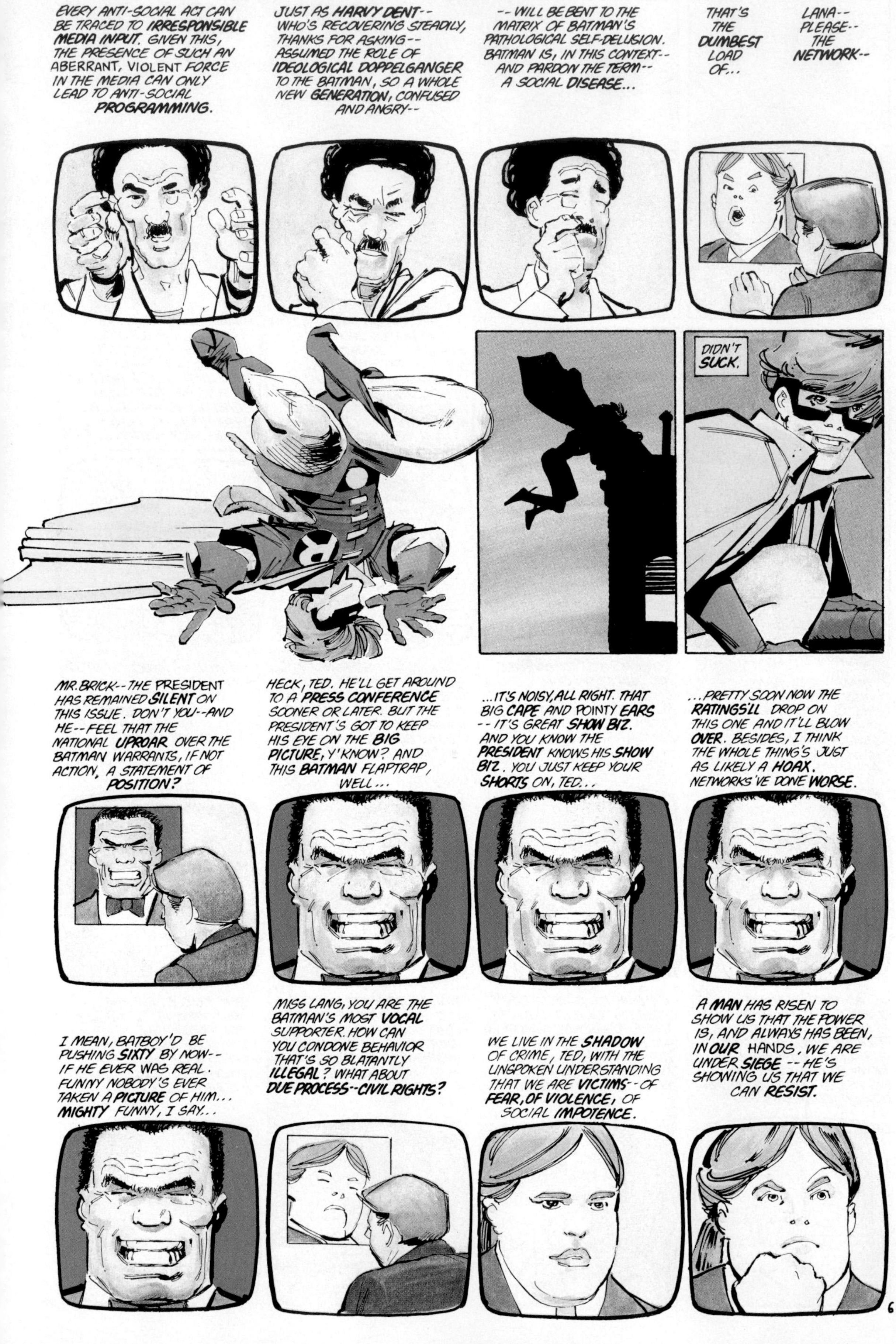
EVERY ANTI-SOCIAL ACT CAN BE TRACED TO IRRESPONSIBLE MEDIA INPUT. GIVEN THIS, THE PRESENCE OF SUCH AN ABERRANT, VIOLENT FORCE IN THE MEDIA CAN ONLY LEAD TO ANTI-SOCIAL PROGRAMMING.
JUST AS HARVY DENT-- WHO'S RECOVERING STEADILY, THANKS FOR ASKING-- ASSUMED THE ROLE OF IDEOLOGICAL DOPPELGANGER TO THE BATMAN, SO A WHOLE NEW GENERATION, CONFUSED AND ANGRY--
--WILL BE BENT TO THE MATRIX OF BATMAN'S PATHOLOGICAL SELF-DELUSION. BATMAN IS, IN THIS CONTEXT-- AND PARDON THE TERM-- A SOCIAL DISEASE...
THAT'S THE DUMBEST LOAD OF...
LANA-- PLEASE-- THE NETWORK--
DIDN'T SUCK.
MR. BRICK--THE PRESIDENT HAS REMAINED SILENT ON THIS ISSUE. DON'T YOU--AND HE--FEEL THAT THE NATIONAL UPROAR OVER THE BATMAN WARRANTS, IF NOT ACTION, A STATEMENT OF POSITION?
HECK, TED. HE'LL GET AROUND TO A PRESS CONFERENCE SOONER OR LATER. BUT THE PRESIDENT'S GOT TO KEEP HIS EYE ON THE BIG PICTURE, Y'KNOW? AND THIS BATMAN FLAPTRAP, WELL...
...IT'S NOISY, ALL RIGHT. THAT BIG CAPE AND POINTY EARS --IT'S GREAT SHOW BIZ. AND YOU KNOW THE PRESIDENT KNOWS HIS SHOW BIZ. YOU JUST KEEP YOUR SHORTS ON, TED...
...PRETTY SOON NOW THE RATINGS'LL DROP ON THIS ONE AND IT'LL BLOW OVER. BESIDES, I THINK THE WHOLE THING'S JUST AS LIKELY A HOAX. NETWORKS'VE DONE WORSE.
I MEAN, BATBOY'D BE PUSHING SIXTY BY NOW-- IF HE EVER WAS REAL. FUNNY NOBODY'S EVER TAKEN A PICTURE OF HIM... MIGHTY FUNNY, I SAY...
MISS LANG, YOU ARE THE BATMAN'S MOST VOCAL SUPPORTER. HOW CAN YOU CONDONE BEHAVIOR THAT'S SO BLATANTLY ILLEGAL? WHAT ABOUT DUE PROCESS--CIVIL RIGHTS?
WE LIVE IN THE SHADOW OF CRIME, TED, WITH THE UNSPOKEN UNDERSTANDING THAT WE ARE VICTIMS--OF FEAR, OF VIOLENCE, OF SOCIAL IMPOTENCE.
A MAN HAS RISEN TO SHOW US THAT THE POWER IS, AND ALWAYS HAS BEEN, IN OUR HANDS. WE ARE UNDER SIEGE --HE'S SHOWING US THAT WE CAN RESIST.

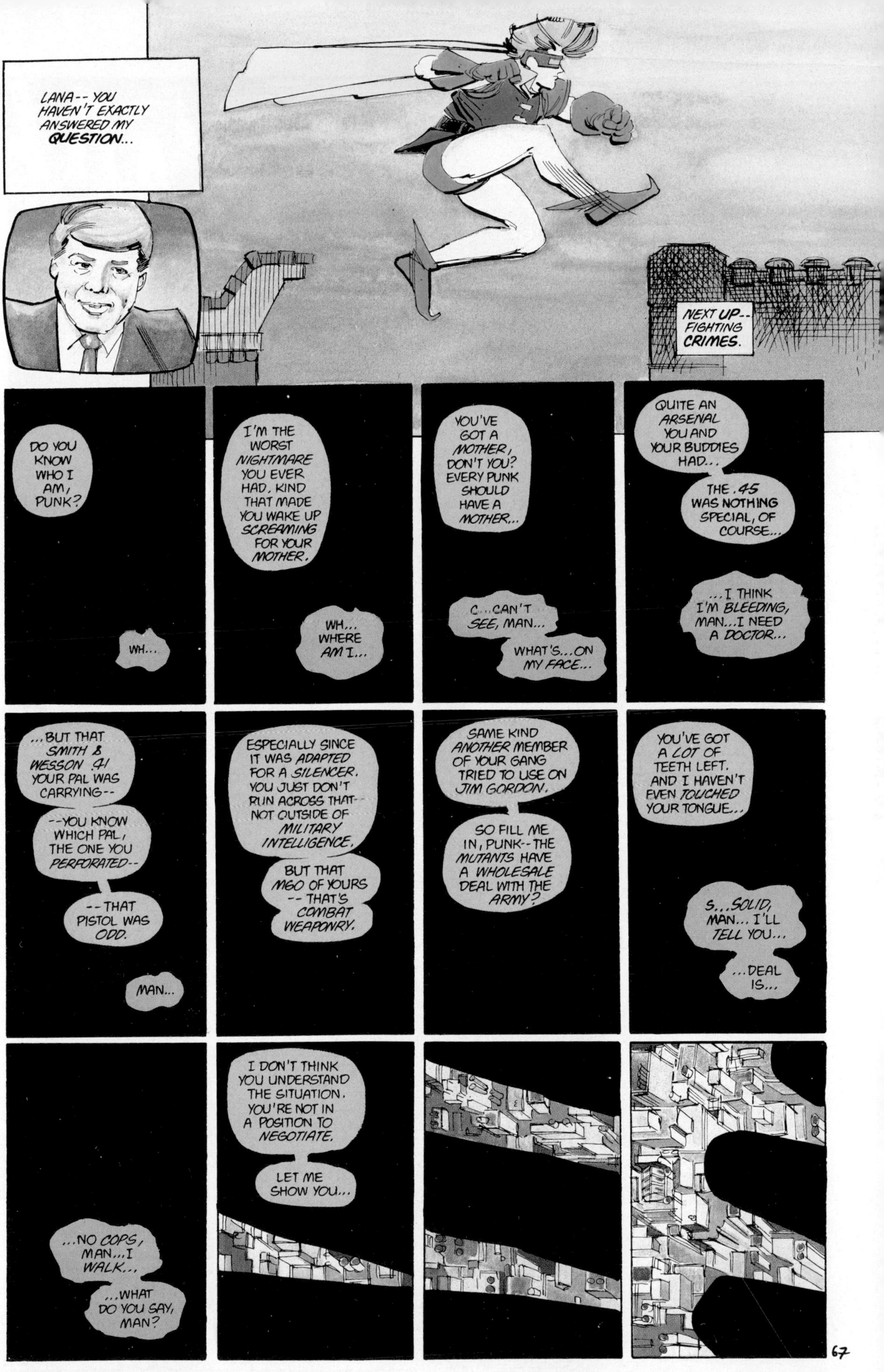

LANA-- YOU HAVEN'T EXACTLY ANSWERED MY QUESTION...
NEXT UP-- FIGHTING CRIMES.
DO YOU KNOW WHO I AM, PUNK?
WH...
I'M THE WORST NIGHTMARE YOU EVER HAD. KIND THAT MADE YOU WAKE UP SCREAMING FOR YOUR MOTHER.
WH... WHERE AM I...
YOU'VE GOT A MOTHER, DON'T YOU? EVERY PUNK SHOULD HAVE A MOTHER...
C...CAN'T SEE, MAN...
WHAT'S...ON MY FACE...
QUITE AN ARSENAL YOU AND YOUR BUDDIES HAD...
THE .45 WAS NOTHING SPECIAL, OF COURSE...
...I THINK I'M BLEEDING, MAN...I NEED A DOCTOR...
...BUT THAT SMITH & WESSON .41 YOUR PAL WAS CARRYING--
--YOU KNOW WHICH PAL, THE ONE YOU PERFORATED--
--THAT PISTOL WAS ODD.
MAN...
ESPECIALLY SINCE IT WAS ADAPTED FOR A SILENCER. YOU JUST DON'T RUN ACROSS THAT-- NOT OUTSIDE OF MILITARY INTELLIGENCE.
BUT THAT M60 OF YOURS -- THAT'S COMBAT WEAPONRY.
SAME KIND ANOTHER MEMBER OF YOUR GANG TRIED TO USE ON JIM GORDON.
SO FILL ME IN, PUNK--THE MUTANTS HAVE A WHOLESALE DEAL WITH THE ARMY?
YOU'VE GOT A LOT OF TEETH LEFT. AND I HAVEN'T EVEN TOUCHED YOUR TONGUE...
S...SOLID, MAN... I'LL TELL YOU...
...DEAL IS...
...NO COPS, MAN...I WALK...
...WHAT DO YOU SAY, MAN?
I DON'T THINK YOU UNDERSTAND THE SITUATION. YOU'RE NOT IN A POSITION TO NEGOTIATE.
LET ME SHOW YOU...

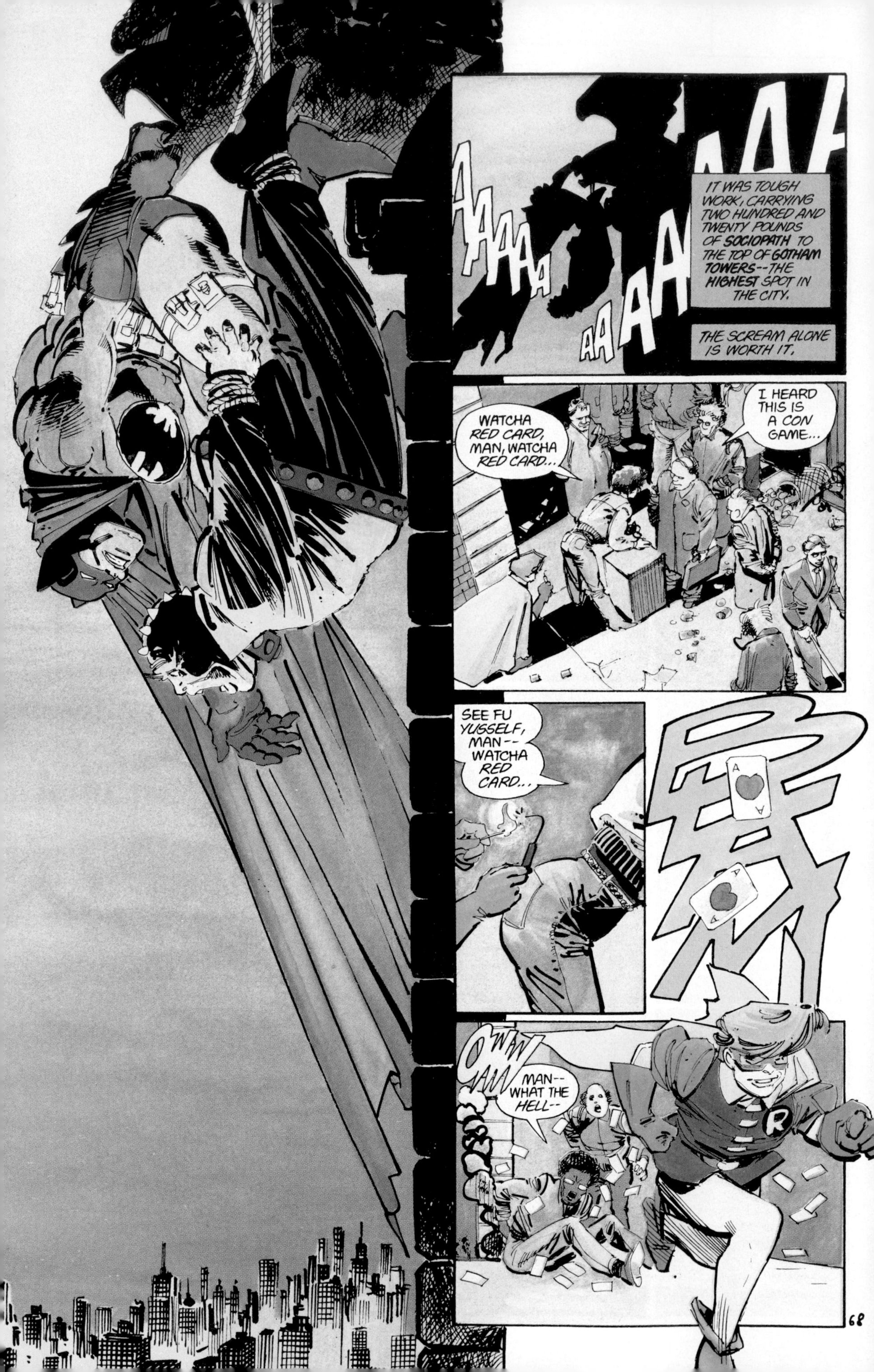
AAAAAAAAAAAAA
IT WAS TOUGH WORK, CARRYING TWO HUNDRED AND TWENTY POUNDS OF SOCIOPATH TO THE TOP OF GOTHAM TOWERS--THE HIGHEST SPOT IN THE CITY.
THE SCREAM ALONE IS WORTH IT.
WATCHA RED CARD, MAN, WATCHA RED CARD...
I HEARD THIS IS A CON GAME...
SEE FU YUSSELF, MAN-- WATCHA RED CARD...
OWW
MAN-- WHAT THE HELL--

IT'S THE **TRAIN**, THINKS MARGARET CORCORAN. MY LEGS NEVER HURT LIKE THIS WHEN I WAIT THE TABLES.

THE **TRAIN**-- IT WON'T LET THE PAIN LIE IN MY **CALVES** WHERE I'M **USED** TO IT.

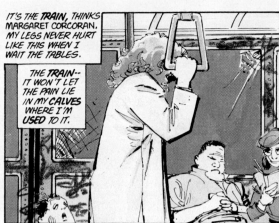

VARICOSE VEINS, THE DOCTOR SAID. EASY FOR HIM TO TELL HER TO QUIT HER JOB. EASY FOR **HIM** TO TALK ABOUT **SURGERY**.

SURGERY. WITH NO INSURANCE AND TWO PAYMENTS LEFT ON JAMIE'S BRACES AND THE TURN-OFF NOTICE FROM THE ELECTRIC COMPANY WITH WINTER ON ITS WAY.

SHE FEELS THE METAL SQUARE INSIDE HER PURSE AND SMILES.

ALMOST NOBODY TIPS ANYMORE. BUT AN UPTOWN DRUNK LEFT TEN DOLLARS ON THE TABLE TONIGHT. WHAT WITH THE TURN-OFF NOTICE IT WAS WRONG TO SPEND THE TIP ON THE PAIN.

BUT YOUNG ROBERT'S **ART TEACHER** SAYS HE HAS **TALENT**...

SHE PICTURES ROBERT'S ABLE LITTLE HANDS, HIS EAGER SMILE...

HER **PURSE STRAP** BITES INTO HER SHOULDER...

...AND MARGARET CORCORAN, WHO HAD NOT PLEADED WITH BLUE CROSS WHEN THEY CANCELLED HER INSURANCE OR WITH **CITICORP** WHEN THEY REPOSSESSED HER CAR...

...BEGS LIKE A WINO FOR A TEN-DOLLAR PAINT SET.

SHE FEELS HER PURSE HIT HER STOMACH AS THE TRAIN RUMBLES TO A STOP. SHE HEARS THEM LAUGH.

SHE LANDS HARD ON THE CEMENT, BUT IT ONLY HURTS.

SHE FEELS THE SQUARE OF METAL AND THANKS GOD AND CAN'T HELP BUT CRY.

THEN SHE FEELS SOMETHING HEAVY AND ROUND LIKE AN APPLE IN HER PURSE...

WOMAN EXPLODES IN SUBWAY STATION-- FILM AT ELEVEN.

69

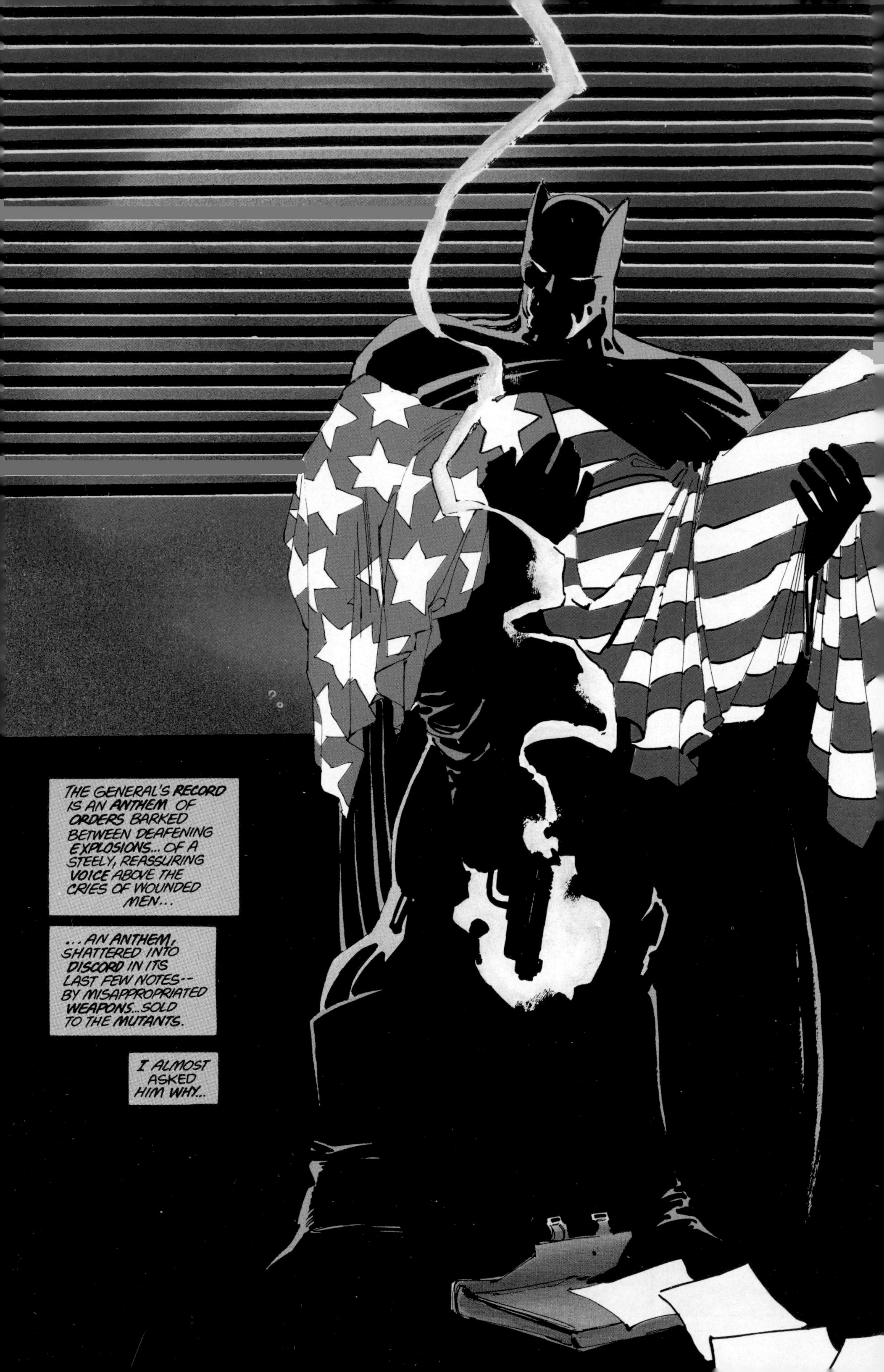
THE GENERAL'S RECORD IS AN ANTHEM OF ORDERS BARKED BETWEEN DEAFENING EXPLOSIONS... OF A STEELY, REASSURING VOICE ABOVE THE CRIES OF WOUNDED MEN...
...AN ANTHEM, SHATTERED INTO DISCORD IN ITS LAST FEW NOTES-- BY MISAPPROPRIATED WEAPONS...SOLD TO THE MUTANTS.
I ALMOST ASKED HIM WHY...

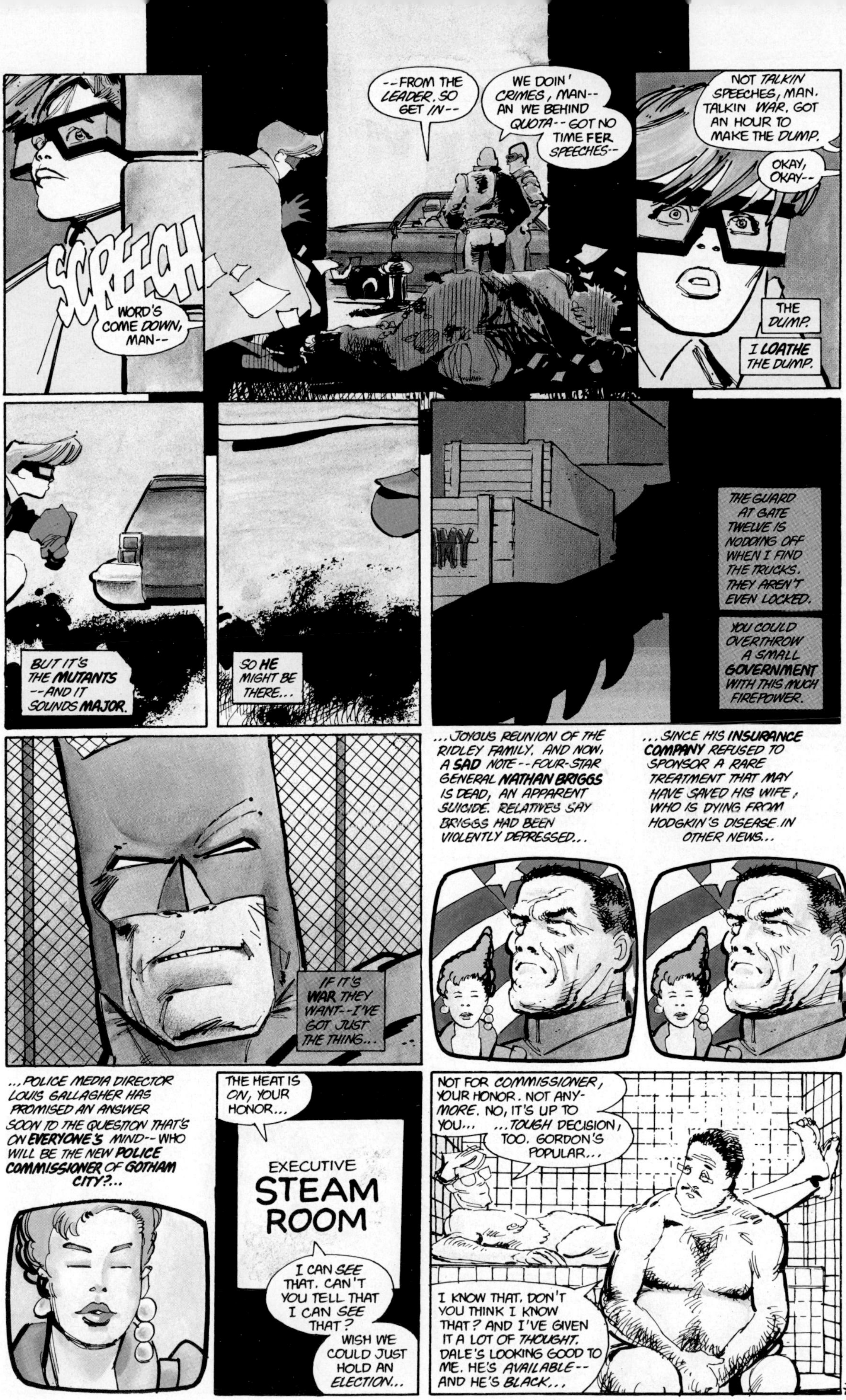
SCREECH
WORD'S COME DOWN, MAN--
--FROM THE LEADER. SO GET IN--
WE DOIN' CRIMES, MAN-- AN WE BEHIND QUOTA-- GOT NO TIME FER SPEECHES--
NOT TALKIN SPEECHES, MAN. TALKIN WAR. GOT AN HOUR TO MAKE THE DUMP.
OKAY, OKAY--
THE DUMP.
I LOATHE THE DUMP.
BUT IT'S THE MUTANTS --AND IT SOUNDS MAJOR.
SO HE MIGHT BE THERE...
THE GUARD AT GATE TWELVE IS NODDING OFF WHEN I FIND THE TRUCKS. THEY AREN'T EVEN LOCKED.
YOU COULD OVERTHROW A SMALL GOVERNMENT WITH THIS MUCH FIREPOWER.
IF IT'S WAR THEY WANT--I'VE GOT JUST THE THING...
...JOYOUS REUNION OF THE RIDLEY FAMILY. AND NOW, A SAD NOTE--FOUR-STAR GENERAL NATHAN BRIGGS IS DEAD, AN APPARENT SUICIDE. RELATIVES SAY BRIGGS HAD BEEN VIOLENTLY DEPRESSED...
...SINCE HIS INSURANCE COMPANY REFUSED TO SPONSOR A RARE TREATMENT THAT MAY HAVE SAVED HIS WIFE, WHO IS DYING FROM HODGKIN'S DISEASE. IN OTHER NEWS...
...POLICE MEDIA DIRECTOR LOUIS GALLAGHER HAS PROMISED AN ANSWER SOON TO THE QUESTION THAT'S ON EVERYONE'S MIND-- WHO WILL BE THE NEW POLICE COMMISSIONER OF GOTHAM CITY?...
THE HEAT IS ON, YOUR HONOR...
EXECUTIVE STEAM ROOM
I CAN SEE THAT. CAN'T YOU TELL THAT I CAN SEE THAT?
WISH WE COULD JUST HOLD AN ELECTION...
NOT FOR COMMISSIONER, YOUR HONOR. NOT ANY-MORE. NO, IT'S UP TO YOU... ...TOUGH DECISION, TOO. GORDON'S POPULAR...
I KNOW THAT. DON'T YOU THINK I KNOW THAT? AND I'VE GIVEN IT A LOT OF THOUGHT. DALE'S LOOKING GOOD TO ME. HE'S AVAILABLE-- AND HE'S BLACK...

BLACK'S PASSÉ, YOUR HONOR. BESIDES, DALE'S *NEUTRAL* ON THE *BATMAN* THING. AND YOU KNOW WHAT YOUR OWN NEUTRALITY IS COSTING YOU...

I'M NOT *NEUTRAL*. WHO SAYS I'M *NEUTRAL*? I'M *CONFLICTED*.

SEEMS TO ME THAT THIS IS YOUR BIG *CHANCE*, YOUR HONOR--TO SHOW WHAT A *LEADER* YOU ARE--TO MAKE A *BOLD DECISION* ABOUT BATMAN...

DECISIONS--YOU'D THINK ALL THERE IS TO RUNNING A CITY IS MAKING *DECISIONS*...

WELL, ALL *RIGHT*, GALLAGHER--I'LL MAKE A *DECISION*. I'LL SHOW THEM WHO'S BOSS, ON MY OWN PRIVATE *AUTHORITY*---- I ASSIGN YOU THE TASK OF FINDING ME A *POLICE COMMISSIONER*.

I ALREADY *HAVE*, SIR.

MASTER BRUCE?

WHO *ELSE*, ALFRED?

OF COURSE, SIR. IT'S JUST THAT THE SIGNAL IS COMING FROM INSIDE THE--

THAT'S *RIGHT*, ALFRED. I'M TAKING HER *OUT*.

I HIT THE *ENGINE*. SHE RESPONDS LIKE IT WAS *YESTERDAY*.

IT *IS* YESTERDAY...

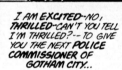

I AM *EXCITED*--NO, *THRILLED*--CAN'T YOU TELL I'M THRILLED?--TO GIVE YOU THE NEXT *POLICE COMMISSIONER* OF GOTHAM CITY...

...CAPTAIN *ELLEN YINDEL*.

THE *YOUNGEST* EVER TO HOLD THE OFFICE--AND, OF COURSE, THE FIRST *WOMAN*--*ELLEN YINDEL* BRINGS WITH HER AN *ASTONISHING ARREST RECORD* FROM CHICAGO. SHE WAS QUICK TO ANSWER ON THE SUBJECT OF *BATMAN*...

I'M SURPRISED THERE *IS* A CONTROVERSY. HIS ACTIONS ARE CATEGORICALLY *CRIMINAL*. I WILL HAVE HIM BROUGHT TO TRIAL. EXCUSE ME?...

...YES. I'LL BE SPECIFIC. MY FIRST ACT AS *POLICE COMMISSIONER* WILL BE TO ISSUE AN *ARREST WARRANT* FOR THE BATMAN ON CHARGES OF *ASSAULT, BREAKING AND ENTERING, CREATING A PUBLIC HAZARD*...

LITTLE MORE THAN *HALF* THE AGE OF THE MAN SHE'S *REPLACING*, ELLEN YINDEL IS--

KLIK

A WOMAN. CHRIST ALMIGHTY...

DID YOU SAY SOMETHING, JIM?

...NOTHING, SWEETHEART...

72

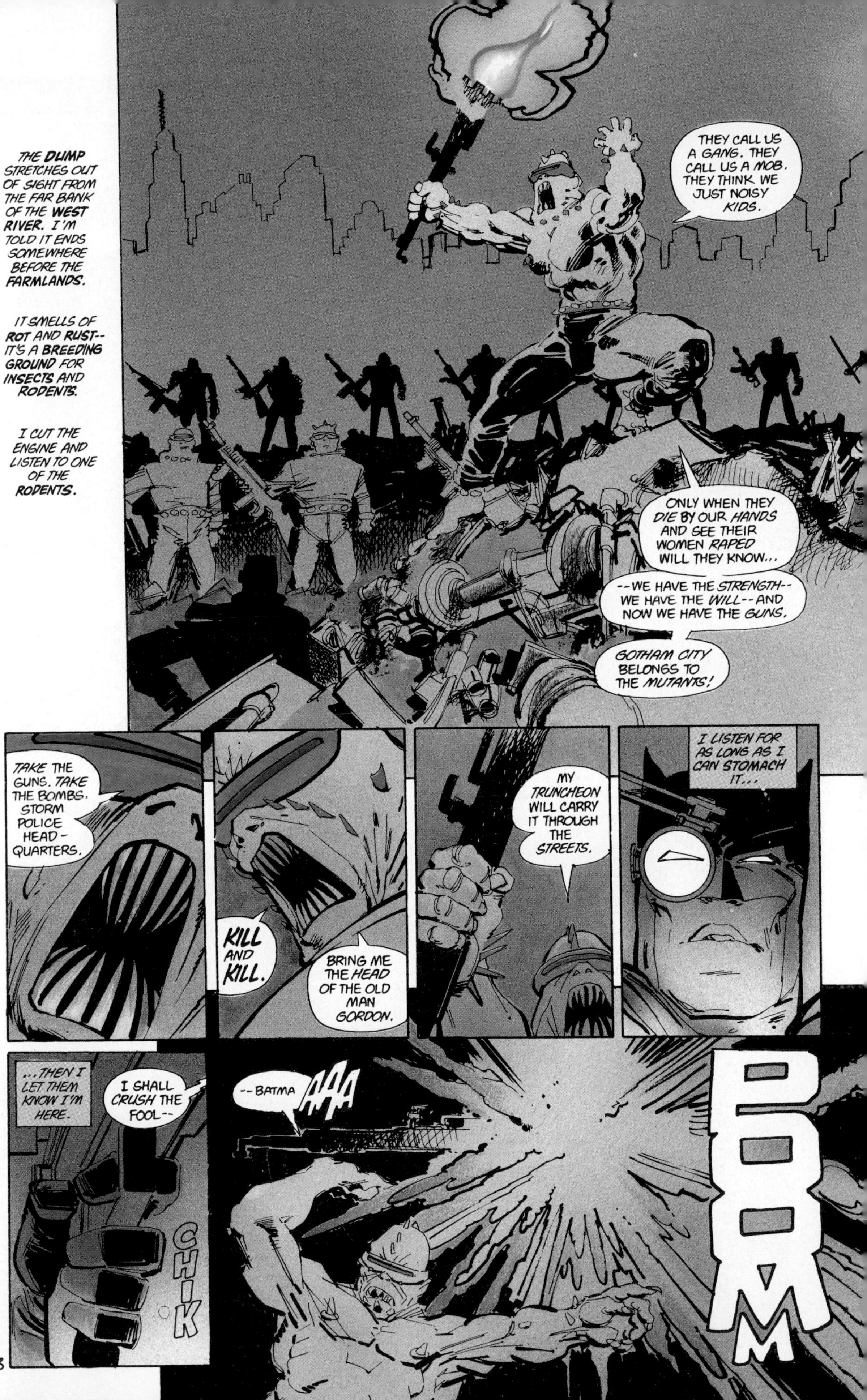
THE DUMP STRETCHES OUT OF SIGHT FROM THE FAR BANK OF THE WEST RIVER. I'M TOLD IT ENDS SOMEWHERE BEFORE THE FARMLANDS.
IT SMELLS OF ROT AND RUST-- IT'S A BREEDING GROUND FOR INSECTS AND RODENTS.
I CUT THE ENGINE AND LISTEN TO ONE OF THE RODENTS.
THEY CALL US A GANG. THEY CALL US A MOB. THEY THINK WE JUST NOISY KIDS.
ONLY WHEN THEY DIE BY OUR HANDS AND SEE THEIR WOMEN RAPED WILL THEY KNOW...
--WE HAVE THE STRENGTH-- WE HAVE THE WILL--AND NOW WE HAVE THE GUNS.
GOTHAM CITY BELONGS TO THE MUTANTS!
TAKE THE GUNS. TAKE THE BOMBS. STORM POLICE HEAD-QUARTERS.
KILL AND KILL.
BRING ME THE HEAD OF THE OLD MAN GORDON.
MY TRUNCHEON WILL CARRY IT THROUGH THE STREETS.
I LISTEN FOR AS LONG AS I CAN STOMACH IT...
...THEN I LET THEM KNOW I'M HERE.
I SHALL CRUSH THE FOOL--
CHIK
--BATMA AAAA
BOOM

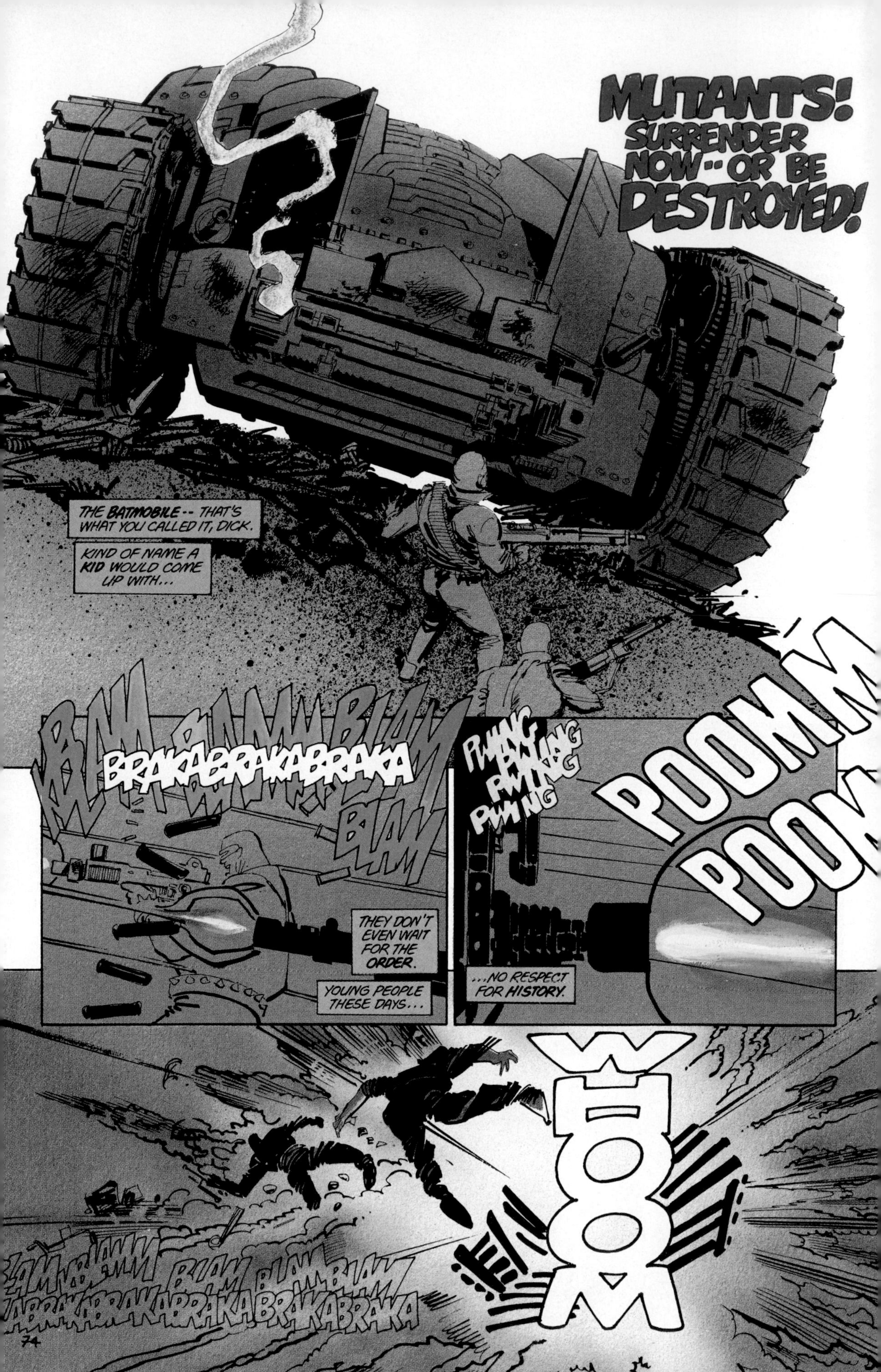

MUTANTS! SURRENDER NOW-- OR BE DESTROYED!
THE BATMOBILE -- THAT'S WHAT YOU CALLED IT, DICK.
KIND OF NAME A KID WOULD COME UP WITH...
BLAM BLAM BLAM
BRAKABRAKABRAKA
BLAM
THEY DON'T EVEN WAIT FOR THE ORDER.
YOUNG PEOPLE THESE DAYS...
PWING PWING PWING PWING
POOMM POOM
...NO RESPECT FOR HISTORY.
WHOOM
BLAM BLAM BLAM BLAM
BRAKABRAKA BRAKABRAKA

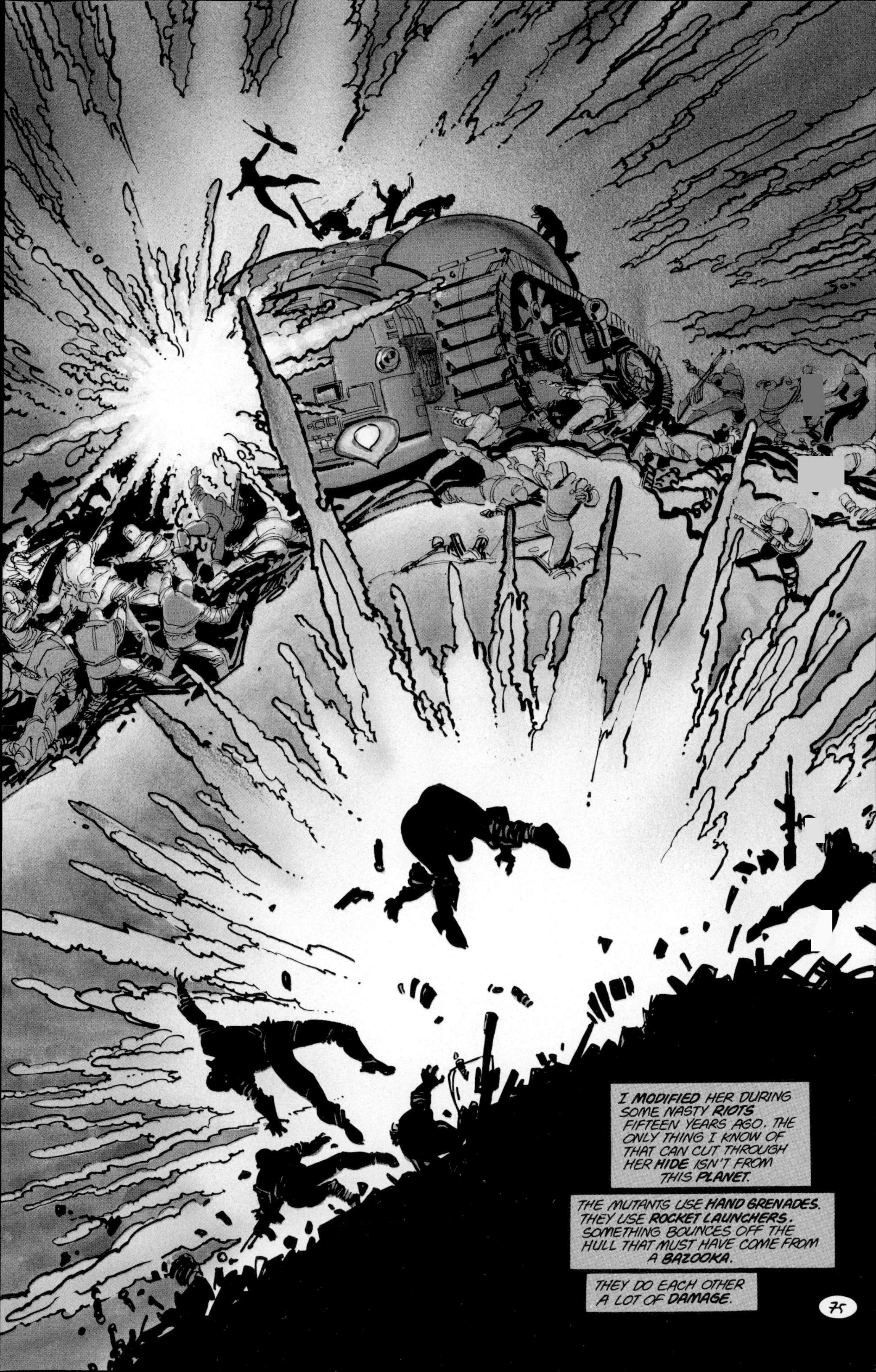
I MODIFIED HER DURING SOME NASTY RIOTS FIFTEEN YEARS AGO. THE ONLY THING I KNOW OF THAT CAN CUT THROUGH HER HIDE ISN'T FROM THIS PLANET.
THE MUTANTS USE HAND GRENADES. THEY USE ROCKET LAUNCHERS. SOMETHING BOUNCES OFF THE HULL THAT MUST HAVE COME FROM A BAZOOKA.
THEY DO EACH OTHER A LOT OF DAMAGE.

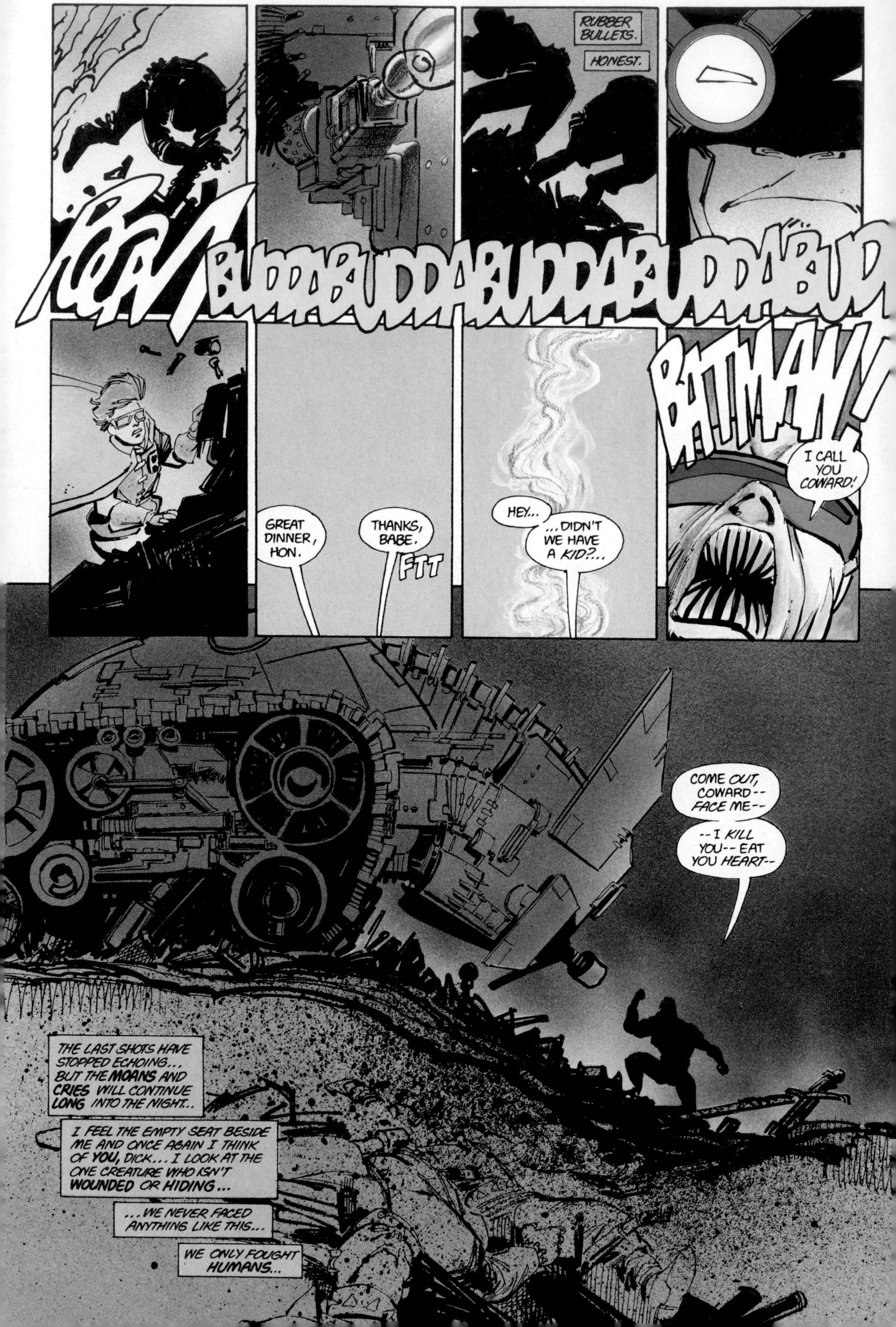
RUBBER BULLETS.
HONEST.
POOM
BUDDABUDDABUDDABUDDABUD
BATMAN!
I CALL YOU COWARD!
GREAT DINNER, HON.
THANKS, BABE.
FTT
HEY...
...DIDN'T WE HAVE A KID?...
COME OUT, COWARD-- FACE ME--
--I KILL YOU-- EAT YOU HEART--
THE LAST SHOTS HAVE STOPPED ECHOING... BUT THE MOANS AND CRIES WILL CONTINUE LONG INTO THE NIGHT...
I FEEL THE EMPTY SEAT BESIDE ME AND ONCE AGAIN I THINK OF YOU, DICK... I LOOK AT THE ONE CREATURE WHO ISN'T WOUNDED OR HIDING...
...WE NEVER FACED ANYTHING LIKE THIS...
WE ONLY FOUGHT HUMANS...

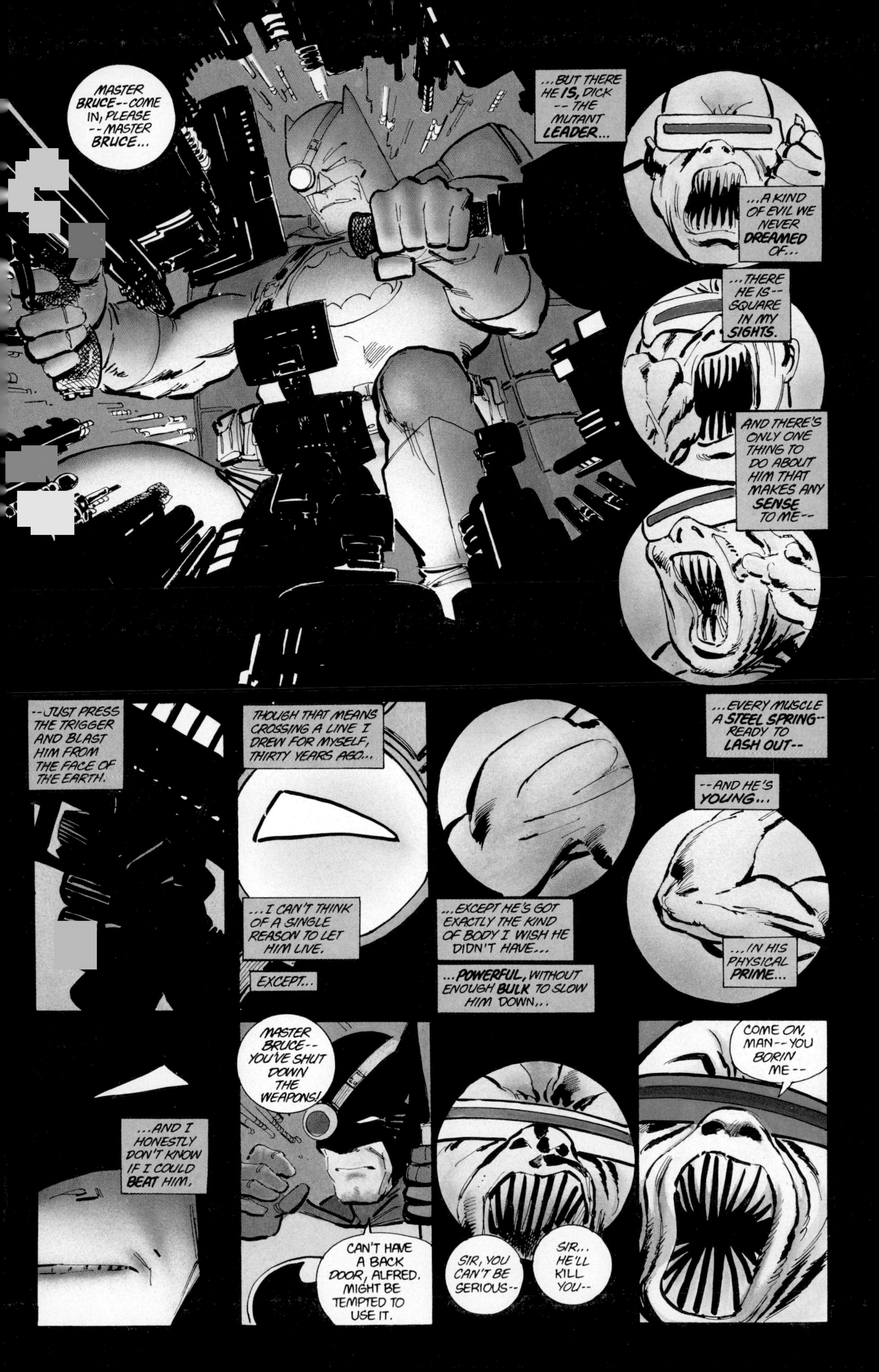

MASTER BRUCE--COME IN, PLEASE --MASTER BRUCE...
...BUT THERE HE IS, DICK --THE MUTANT LEADER...
...A KIND OF EVIL WE NEVER DREAMED OF...
...THERE HE IS SQUARE IN MY SIGHTS.
AND THERE'S ONLY ONE THING TO DO ABOUT HIM THAT MAKES ANY SENSE TO ME--
--JUST PRESS THE TRIGGER AND BLAST HIM FROM THE FACE OF THE EARTH.
THOUGH THAT MEANS CROSSING A LINE I DREW FOR MYSELF, THIRTY YEARS AGO...
...I CAN'T THINK OF A SINGLE REASON TO LET HIM LIVE.
EXCEPT...
...EXCEPT HE'S GOT EXACTLY THE KIND OF BODY I WISH HE DIDN'T HAVE...
...POWERFUL, WITHOUT ENOUGH BULK TO SLOW HIM DOWN...
...EVERY MUSCLE A STEEL SPRING-- READY TO LASH OUT--
--AND HE'S YOUNG...
...IN HIS PHYSICAL PRIME...
...AND I HONESTLY DON'T KNOW IF I COULD BEAT HIM.
MASTER BRUCE-- YOU'VE SHUT DOWN THE WEAPONS!
CAN'T HAVE A BACK DOOR, ALFRED. MIGHT BE TEMPTED TO USE IT.
SIR, YOU CAN'T BE SERIOUS--
SIR... HE'LL KILL YOU--
COME ON, MAN--YOU BORIN ME--

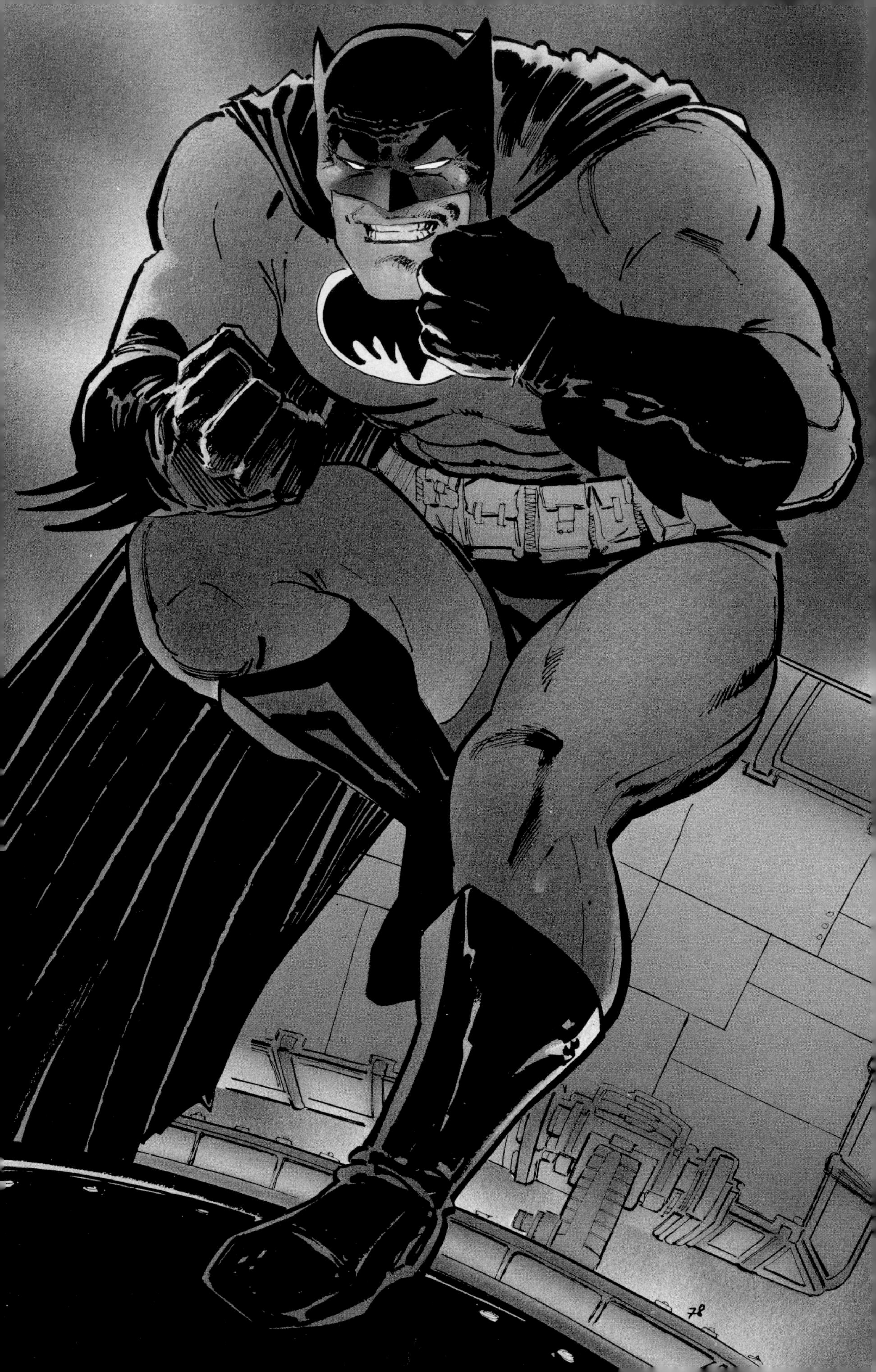

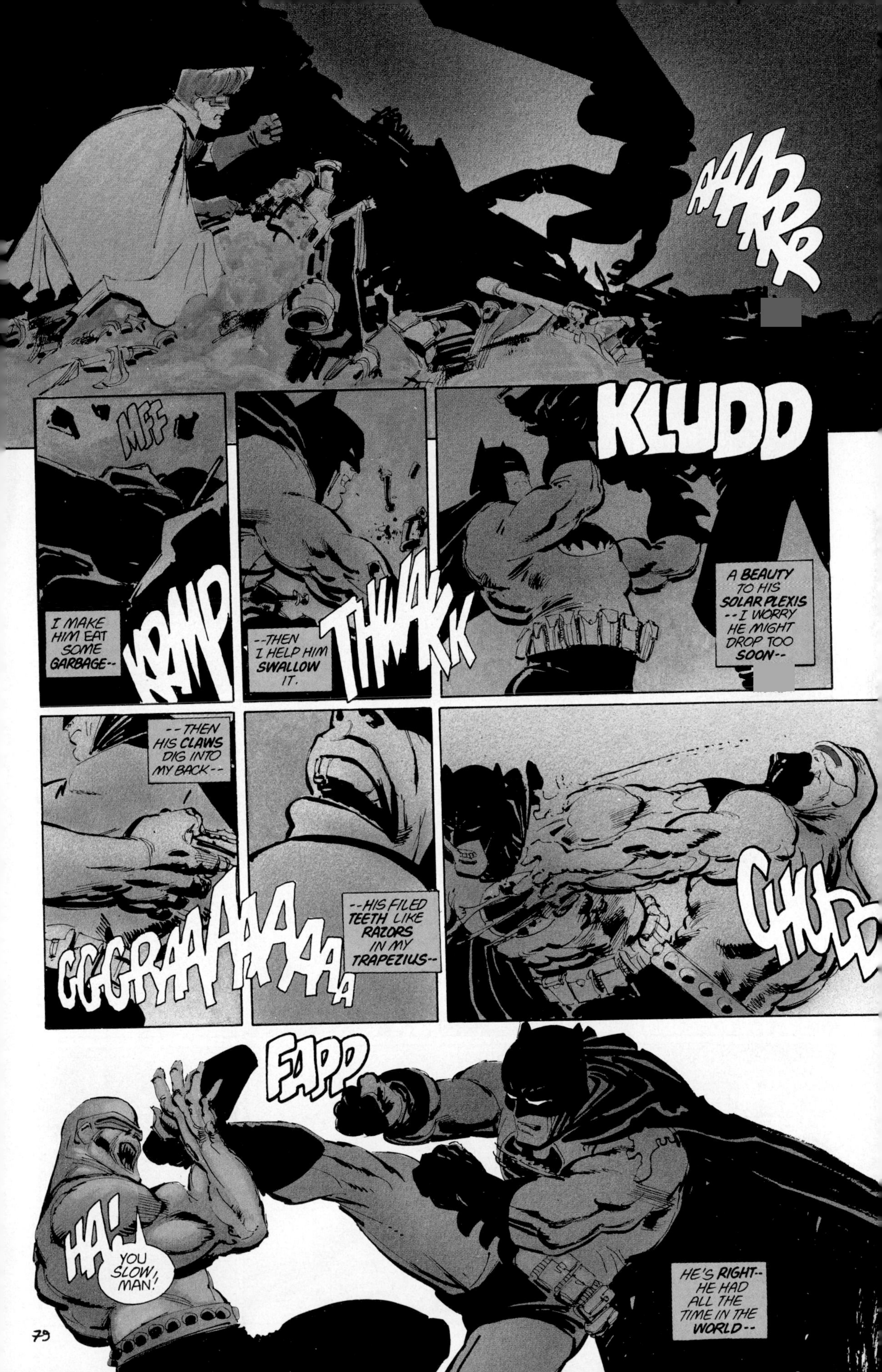
MFF
I MAKE HIM EAT SOME GARBAGE--
KRMP
--THEN I HELP HIM SWALLOW IT.
THWAKK
KLUDD
A BEAUTY TO HIS SOLAR PLEXIS --I WORRY HE MIGHT DROP TOO SOON--
--THEN HIS CLAWS DIG INTO MY BACK--
GGGRAAAAAAAAAA
--HIS FILED TEETH LIKE RAZORS IN MY TRAPEZIUS--
CHUDD
FAPP
HA!
YOU SLOW, MAN!
HE'S RIGHT-- HE HAD ALL THE TIME IN THE WORLD--

--HE SHOWS ME WHAT A FAST KICK IS--

WHUKK

--SOMETHING EXPLODES IN MY MIDSECTION--

--SUNLIGHT BEHIND MY EYES AS THE PAIN RISES--

--A MOMENT OF BLACKNESS-- TOO SOON FOR THAT--

--TOO SOON-- WHAT'S WRONG WITH ME--

NO--

--RIBS INTACT--

--NO INTERNAL BLEEDING--

--LET IT LOOK WORSE THAN IT IS--

--LET HIM-- GET CLOSE--

--NOT YET--

--NOT YET--

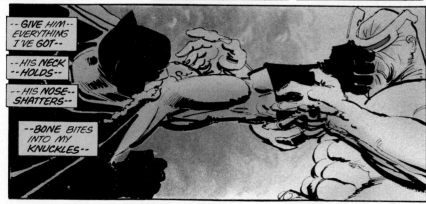

--GIVE HIM-- EVERYTHING I'VE GOT--

--HIS NECK --HOLDS--

--HIS NOSE-- SHATTERS--

--BONE BITES INTO MY KNUCKLES--

--THE IDIOT--

--STARTS LAUGHING--

80

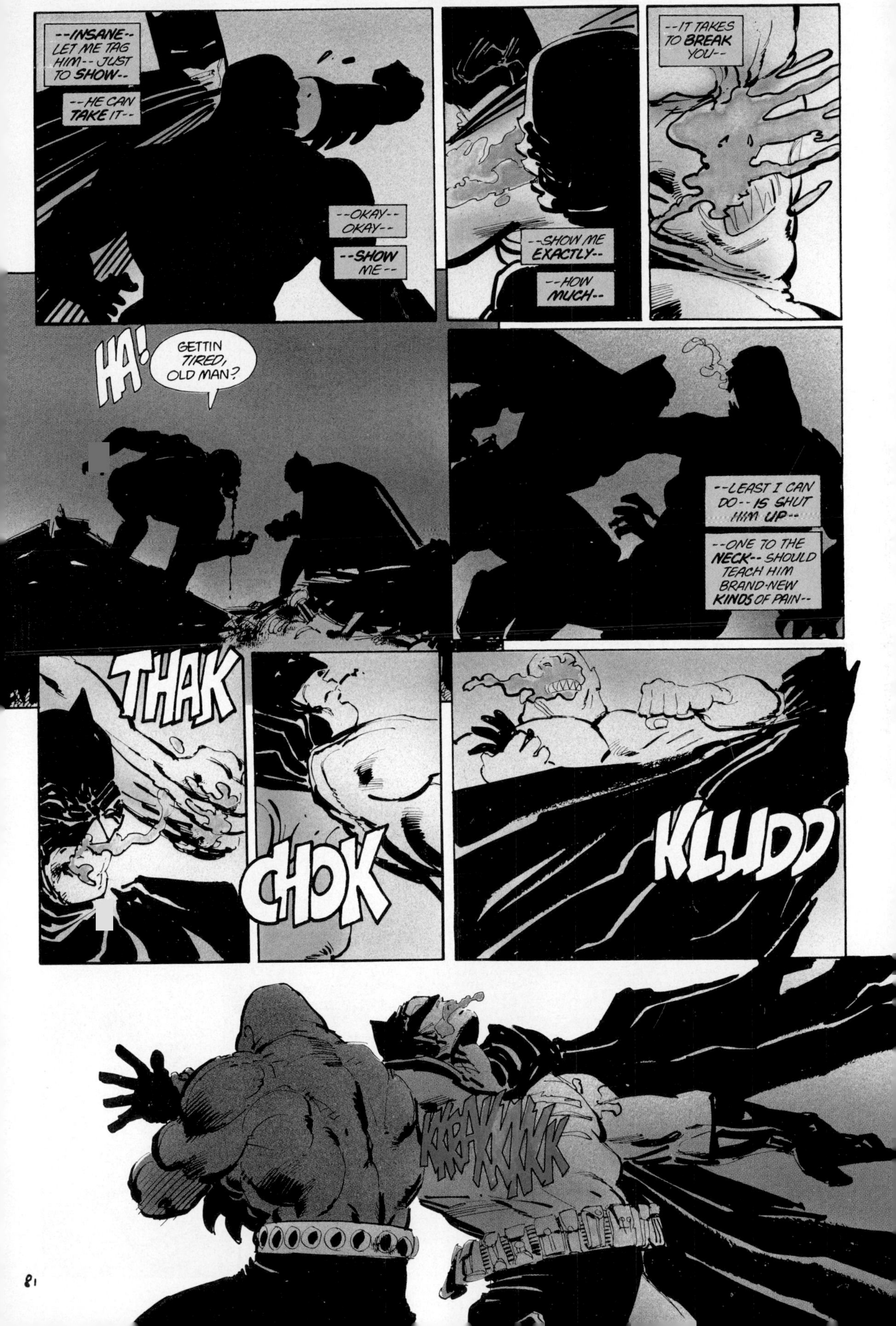
--INSANE-- LET ME TAG HIM-- JUST TO SHOW--
--HE CAN TAKE IT--
--OKAY-- OKAY--
--SHOW ME--
--SHOW ME EXACTLY--
--HOW MUCH--
--IT TAKES TO BREAK YOU--
HA!
GETTIN TIRED, OLD MAN?
--LEAST I CAN DO-- IS SHUT HIM UP--
--ONE TO THE NECK-- SHOULD TEACH HIM BRAND-NEW KINDS OF PAIN--
THAK
CHOK
KLUDD
KRAKKKKKK

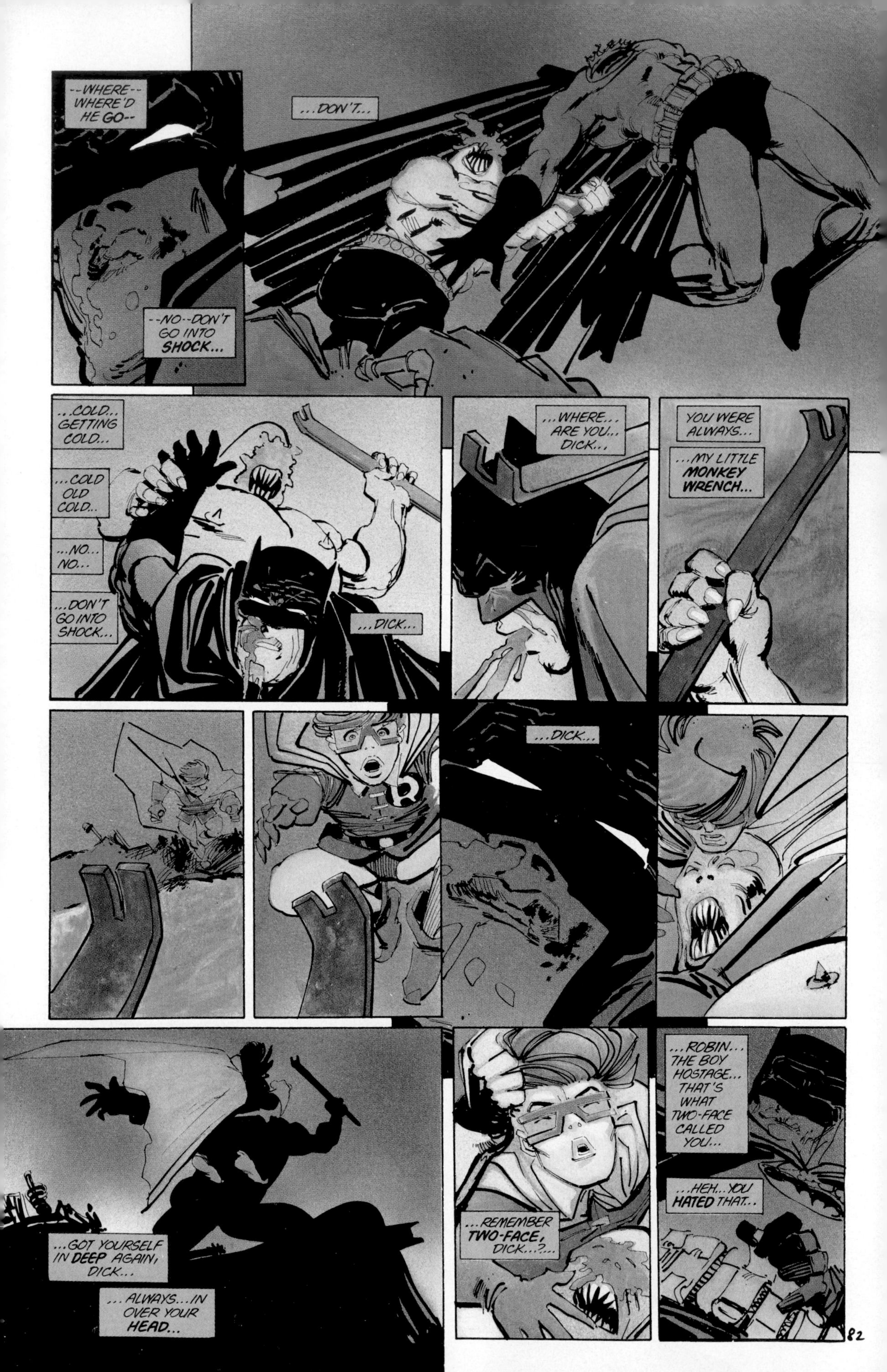
--WHERE--
WHERE'D
HE GO--
...DON'T...
--NO--DON'T
GO INTO
SHOCK...
...COLD...
GETTING
COLD...
...COLD
OLD
COLD...
...NO...
NO...
...DON'T
GO INTO
SHOCK...
...DICK...
...WHERE...
ARE YOU...
DICK...
YOU WERE
ALWAYS...
...MY LITTLE
MONKEY
WRENCH...
...DICK...
...GOT YOURSELF
IN DEEP AGAIN,
DICK...
...ALWAYS...IN
OVER YOUR
HEAD...
...REMEMBER
TWO-FACE,
DICK...?...
...ROBIN...
THE BOY
HOSTAGE...
THAT'S
WHAT
TWO-FACE
CALLED
YOU...
...HEH...YOU
HATED THAT...

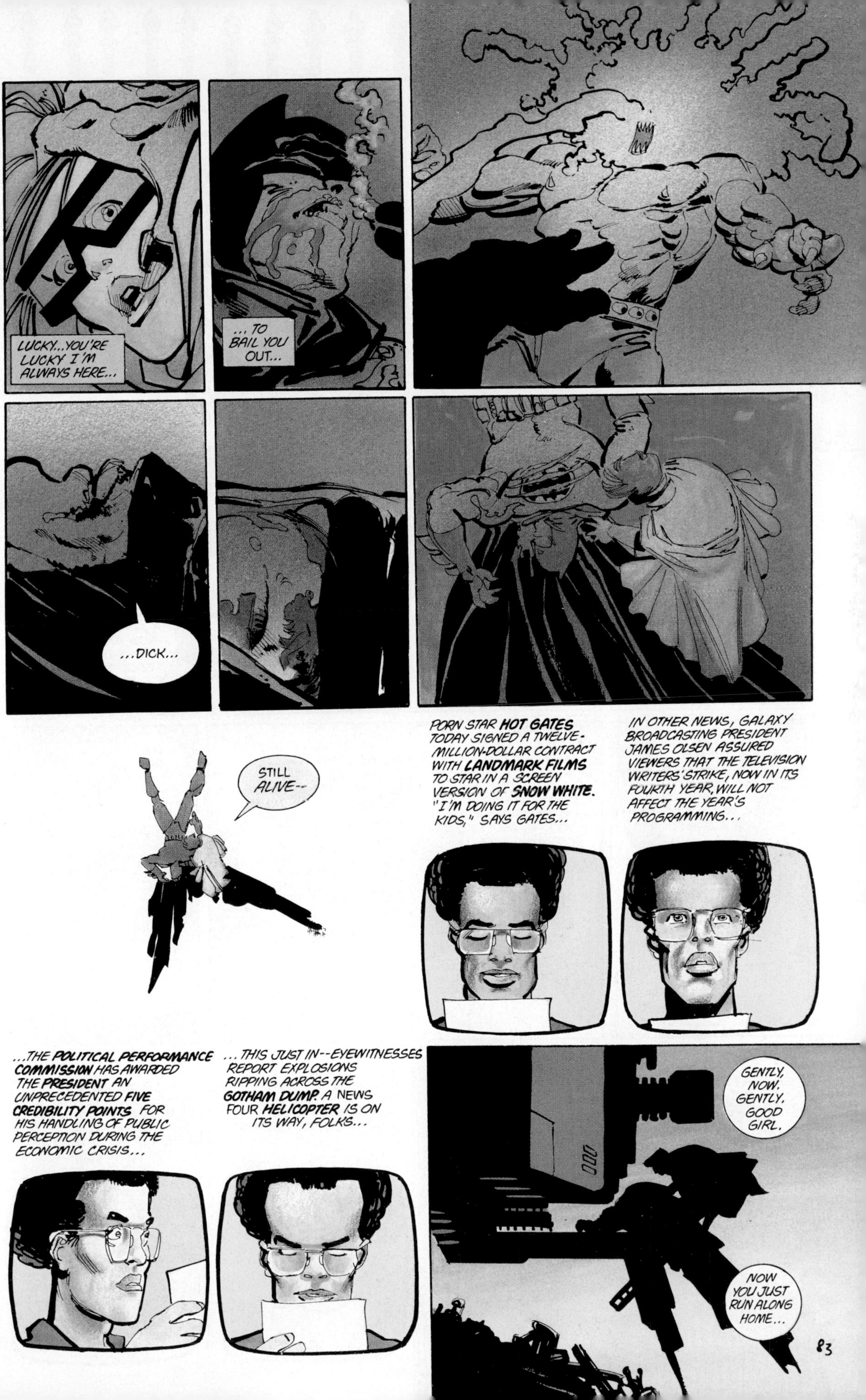

LUCKY...YOU'RE LUCKY I'M ALWAYS HERE...
...TO BAIL YOU OUT...
...DICK...
STILL ALIVE--
PORN STAR HOT GATES TODAY SIGNED A TWELVE-MILLION-DOLLAR CONTRACT WITH LANDMARK FILMS TO STAR IN A SCREEN VERSION OF SNOW WHITE. "I'M DOING IT FOR THE KIDS," SAYS GATES...
IN OTHER NEWS, GALAXY BROADCASTING PRESIDENT JAMES OLSEN ASSURED VIEWERS THAT THE TELEVISION WRITERS' STRIKE, NOW IN ITS FOURTH YEAR, WILL NOT AFFECT THE YEAR'S PROGRAMMING...
...THE POLITICAL PERFORMANCE COMMISSION HAS AWARDED THE PRESIDENT AN UNPRECEDENTED FIVE CREDIBILITY POINTS FOR HIS HANDLING OF PUBLIC PERCEPTION DURING THE ECONOMIC CRISIS...
...THIS JUST IN--EYEWITNESSES REPORT EXPLOSIONS RIPPING ACROSS THE GOTHAM DUMP. A NEWS FOUR HELICOPTER IS ON ITS WAY, FOLKS...
GENTLY, NOW. GENTLY. GOOD GIRL.
NOW YOU JUST RUN ALONG HOME...

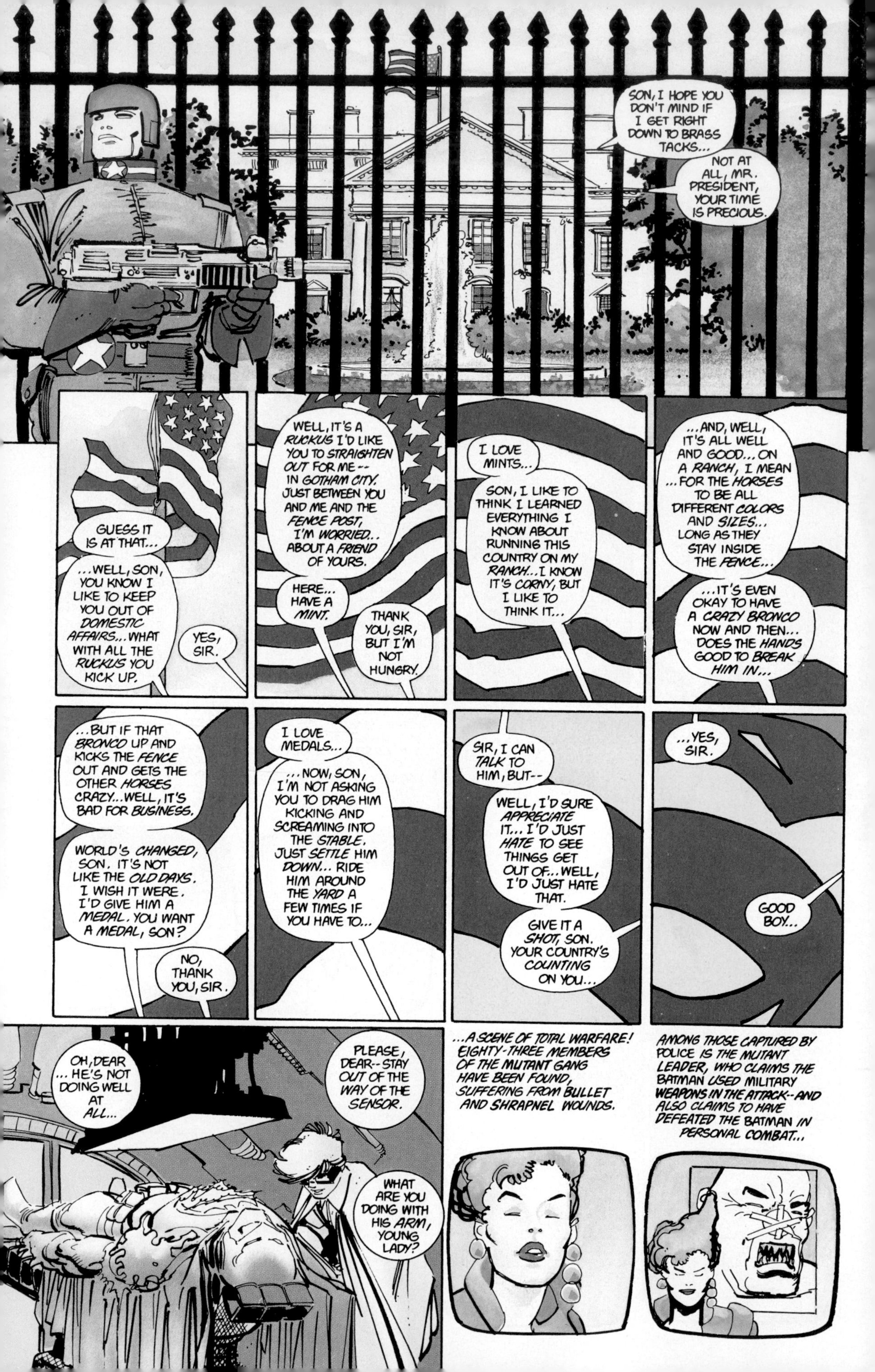

SON, I HOPE YOU DON'T MIND IF I GET RIGHT DOWN TO BRASS TACKS...
NOT AT ALL, MR. PRESIDENT, YOUR TIME IS PRECIOUS.
GUESS IT IS AT THAT...
...WELL, SON, YOU KNOW I LIKE TO KEEP YOU OUT OF DOMESTIC AFFAIRS... WHAT WITH ALL THE RUCKUS YOU KICK UP.
YES, SIR.
WELL, IT'S A RUCKUS I'D LIKE YOU TO STRAIGHTEN OUT FOR ME -- IN GOTHAM CITY. JUST BETWEEN YOU AND ME AND THE FENCE POST, I'M WORRIED... ABOUT A FRIEND OF YOURS.
HERE... HAVE A MINT.
THANK YOU, SIR, BUT I'M NOT HUNGRY.
I LOVE MINTS...
SON, I LIKE TO THINK I LEARNED EVERYTHING I KNOW ABOUT RUNNING THIS COUNTRY ON MY RANCH... I KNOW IT'S CORNY, BUT I LIKE TO THINK IT...
...AND, WELL, IT'S ALL WELL AND GOOD... ON A RANCH, I MEAN ...FOR THE HORSES TO BE ALL DIFFERENT COLORS AND SIZES... LONG AS THEY STAY INSIDE THE FENCE...
...IT'S EVEN OKAY TO HAVE A CRAZY BRONCO NOW AND THEN... DOES THE HANDS GOOD TO BREAK HIM IN...
...BUT IF THAT BRONCO UP AND KICKS THE FENCE OUT AND GETS THE OTHER HORSES CRAZY... WELL, IT'S BAD FOR BUSINESS.
WORLD'S CHANGED, SON. IT'S NOT LIKE THE OLD DAYS. I WISH IT WERE. I'D GIVE HIM A MEDAL. YOU WANT A MEDAL, SON?
NO, THANK YOU, SIR.
I LOVE MEDALS...
...NOW, SON, I'M NOT ASKING YOU TO DRAG HIM KICKING AND SCREAMING INTO THE STABLE. JUST SETTLE HIM DOWN... RIDE HIM AROUND THE YARD A FEW TIMES IF YOU HAVE TO...
SIR, I CAN TALK TO HIM, BUT--
WELL, I'D SURE APPRECIATE IT... I'D JUST HATE TO SEE THINGS GET OUT OF... WELL, I'D JUST HATE THAT.
GIVE IT A SHOT, SON. YOUR COUNTRY'S COUNTING ON YOU...
...YES, SIR.
GOOD BOY...
OH, DEAR ... HE'S NOT DOING WELL AT ALL...
PLEASE, DEAR-- STAY OUT OF THE WAY OF THE SENSOR.
WHAT ARE YOU DOING WITH HIS ARM, YOUNG LADY?
...A SCENE OF TOTAL WARFARE! EIGHTY-THREE MEMBERS OF THE MUTANT GANG HAVE BEEN FOUND, SUFFERING FROM BULLET AND SHRAPNEL WOUNDS.
AMONG THOSE CAPTURED BY POLICE IS THE MUTANT LEADER, WHO CLAIMS THE BATMAN USED MILITARY WEAPONS IN THE ATTACK--AND ALSO CLAIMS TO HAVE DEFEATED THE BATMAN IN PERSONAL COMBAT...

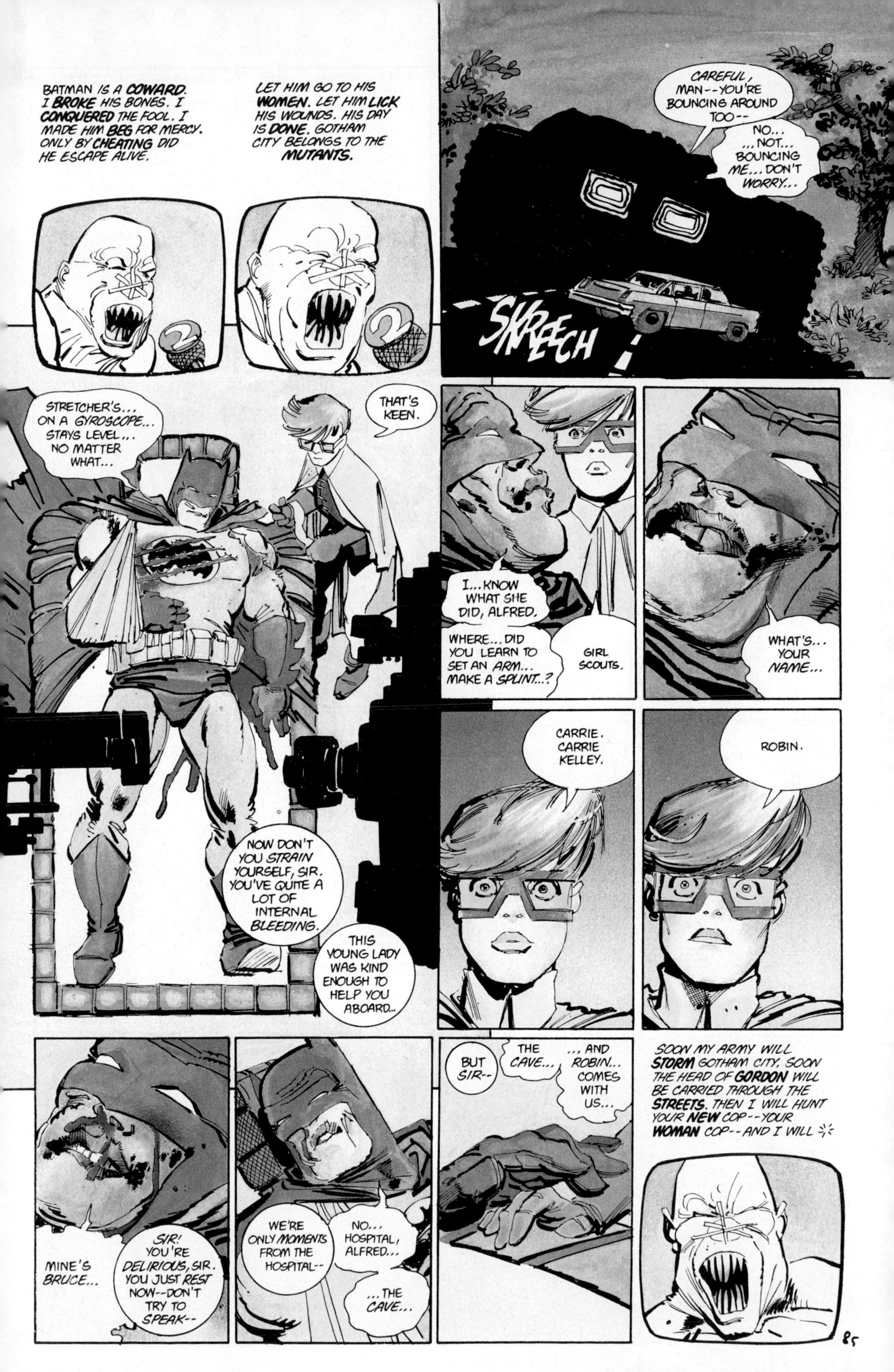

BATMAN IS A COWARD. I BROKE HIS BONES. I CONQUERED THE FOOL. I MADE HIM BEG FOR MERCY. ONLY BY CHEATING DID HE ESCAPE ALIVE.
LET HIM GO TO HIS WOMEN. LET HIM LICK HIS WOUNDS. HIS DAY IS DONE. GOTHAM CITY BELONGS TO THE MUTANTS.
CAREFUL, MAN--YOU'RE BOUNCING AROUND TOO--
NO... ...NOT... BOUNCING ME... DON'T WORRY...
SKREECH
STRETCHER'S... ON A GYROSCOPE... STAYS LEVEL... NO MATTER WHAT...
THAT'S KEEN.
NOW DON'T YOU STRAIN YOURSELF, SIR. YOU'VE QUITE A LOT OF INTERNAL BLEEDING.
THIS YOUNG LADY WAS KIND ENOUGH TO HELP YOU ABOARD...
I...KNOW WHAT SHE DID, ALFRED.
WHERE...DID YOU LEARN TO SET AN ARM... MAKE A SPLINT...?
GIRL SCOUTS.
WHAT'S... YOUR NAME...
CARRIE. CARRIE KELLEY.
ROBIN.
MINE'S BRUCE...
SIR! YOU'RE DELIRIOUS, SIR. YOU JUST REST NOW--DON'T TRY TO SPEAK--
WE'RE ONLY MOMENTS FROM THE HOSPITAL--
NO... HOSPITAL, ALFRED...
...THE CAVE...
BUT SIR--
THE CAVE...
..., AND ROBIN... COMES WITH US...
SOON MY ARMY WILL STORM GOTHAM CITY. SOON THE HEAD OF GORDON WILL BE CARRIED THROUGH THE STREETS. THEN I WILL HUNT YOUR NEW COP--YOUR WOMAN COP--AND I WILL

THE REST OF THE MUTANT LEADER'S STATEMENT IS UNFIT FOR BROADCAST.

I DON'T THINK YOU REALIZE WHAT YOU'RE *SUGGESTING,* DR. WOLPER.

HARVEY DENT DIDN'T EXACTLY BRING US *POSITIVE* PUBLICITY. AND *THIS* ONE...

I *KNOW,* GLEN. I *KNOW*--

--BUT I'M NOT TALKING ABOUT A *RELEASE.* THIS WILL BE A *CONTROLLED ENVIRONMENT*--AND IT WOULD BE SO GOOD FOR HIM.

HIM I'M NOT WORRIED ABOUT.

COME *NOW,* GLEN! HE'S BEEN NEARLY *COMATOSE* FOR MORE THAN A *DECADE.* IF YOU'D JUST *TALK* WITH HIM... FOR *FIVE MINUTES,* GLEN...

I DON'T *KNOW,* THERE'S SOMETHING ...WELL... SOMETHING *SUPERNATURAL* ABOUT THAT ONE.

·ARKHAM·
·HOME·
FOR THE EMOTIONALLY TROUBLED

DR.GLEN
CHIEF ADMI

CHIEF ADMINIS

NOW THAT'S A *FINE* WAY TO SPEAK IN A HOUSE OF *MEDICINE,* ISN'T IT? LISTEN-- PUT ALL THE GUARDS YOU *WANT* IN THE STUDIO, IF IT WILL MAKE YOU FEEL BETTER.

FIVE MINUTES, GLEN. HE *IS* A PATIENT.

LEN FORB
ADMINISTRATOR

OKAY, ALL RIGHT. *FIVE MINUTES.*

'SCUSE ME, WE'RE HEADING STRAIGHT FOR A BRICK WALL.

DON'T... WORRY, ROBIN...

...IT'S JUST ...A HOLOGRAM...

SIR--I URGE YOU TO *REJECT* DR. WOLPER'S SUGGESTION. I DON'T *DESERVE* THIS CHARITY... MY CRIMES...WERE *HORRIBLE* BEYOND ALL WORDS... I AM *BEYOND REDEMPTION.*

PLEASE-- JUST LOCK ME *AWAY*-- FROM HUMAN MEMORY...

SOB

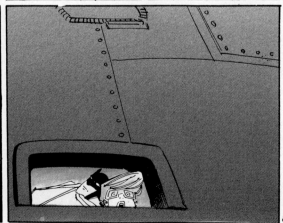

86

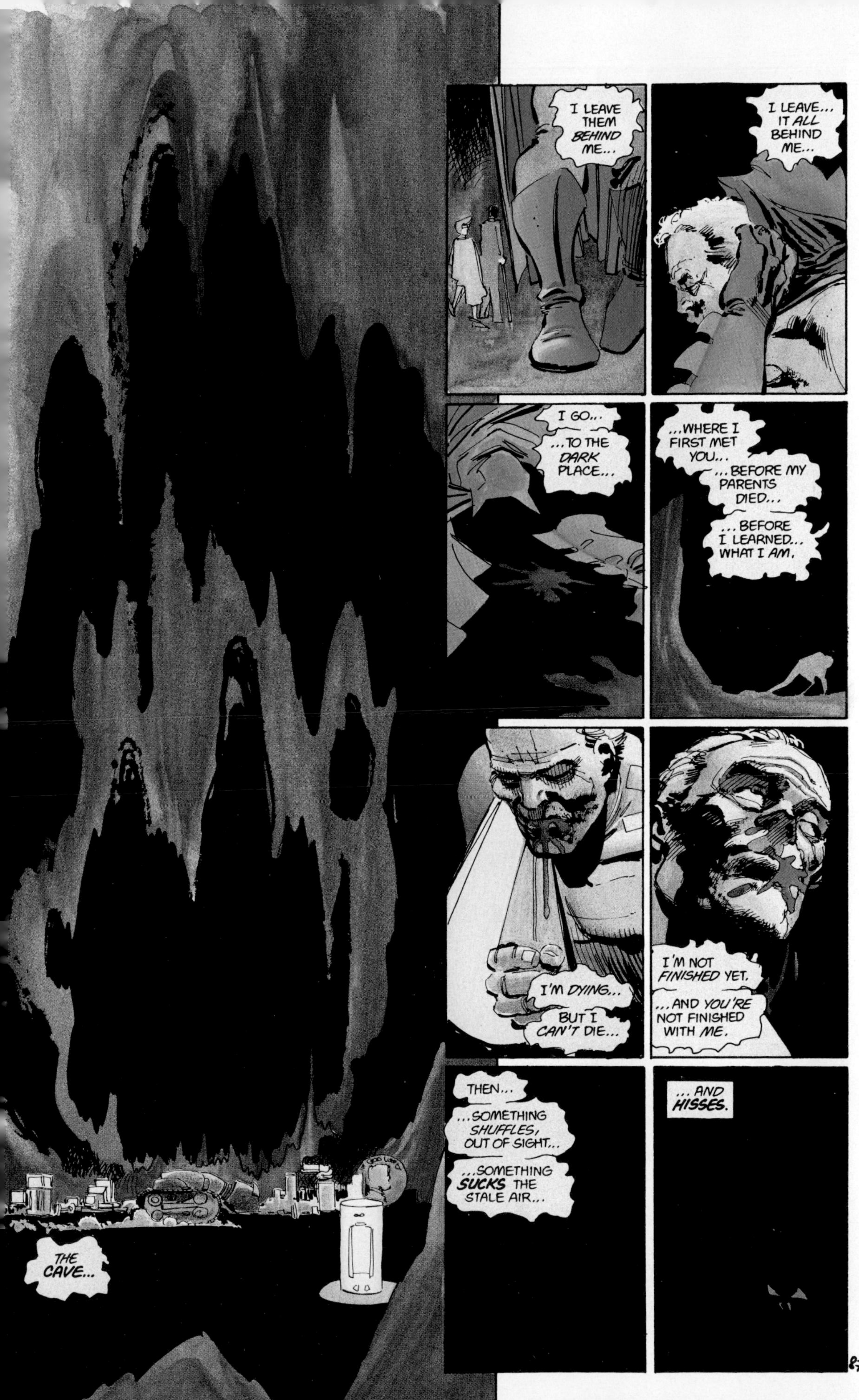

I LEAVE THEM BEHIND ME...
I LEAVE... IT ALL BEHIND ME...
I GO...
...TO THE DARK PLACE...
...WHERE I FIRST MET YOU...
...BEFORE MY PARENTS DIED...
...BEFORE I LEARNED... WHAT I AM.
I'M DYING...
BUT I CAN'T DIE...
I'M NOT FINISHED YET.
...AND YOU'RE NOT FINISHED WITH ME.
THE CAVE...
THEN...
...SOMETHING SHUFFLES, OUT OF SIGHT...
...SOMETHING SUCKS THE STALE AIR...
...AND HISSES.

GLIDING WITH **ANCIENT** GRACE...

EYES **GLEAMING**, UNTOUCHED BY LOVE OR JOY OR SORROW...

BREATH HOT WITH THE TASTE OF FALLEN FOES... THE STENCH OF DEAD THINGS, **DAMNED** THINGS...

SURELY THE FIERCEST SURVIVOR ...THE **PUREST**...

GLARING, **HATING**...

...CLAIMING ME AS YOUR **OWN**.

WE WILL COME FOR OUR LEADER. WE WILL **RAZE** GOTHAM. WE WILL **RAPE** GOTHAM. WE WILL TASTE GOTHAM'S **BLOOD**.

ON HEARING THIS MESSAGE FROM THE MUTANTS, COMMISSIONER GORDON PUT HIMSELF AND HIS MEN ON TWENTY-FOUR HOUR ALERT-- WHILE THE MAYOR WAS QUICK TO SPEAK OUT...

THIS WHOLE SITUATION IS THE RESULT OF GORDON'S **INCOMPETENCE**-- AND OF THE TERRORIST ACTIONS OF THE **BATMAN**. I WISH TO SIT DOWN WITH THE MUTANT LEADER... TO NEGOTIATE A **SETTLEMENT**...

WHAT DO YOU THINK, TRISH? HIS HONOR GONE **NUTS?**

NOT AT ALL, BILL. FRANKLY I EXPECT THE MAYOR'S CREDIBILITY RATING TO GO THROUGH THE **ROOF**, **ESPECIALLY** IF HE'S **SUCCESSFUL** IN THE NEGOTIATIONS.

THIS, COMBINED WITH HIS STRONG STAND ON **BATMAN**-- AND MAKING A WOMAN THE NEXT POLICE COMMISSIONER-- WELL, I THINK WE'VE GOT A WHOLE NEW **MAYOR** ON OUR HANDS--

--PUBLIC PERCEPTION- WISE, THAT IS.

ALL THIS AND BRAINS TOO!

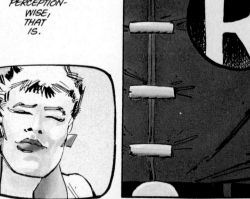

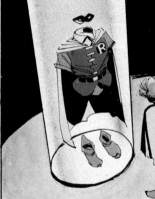

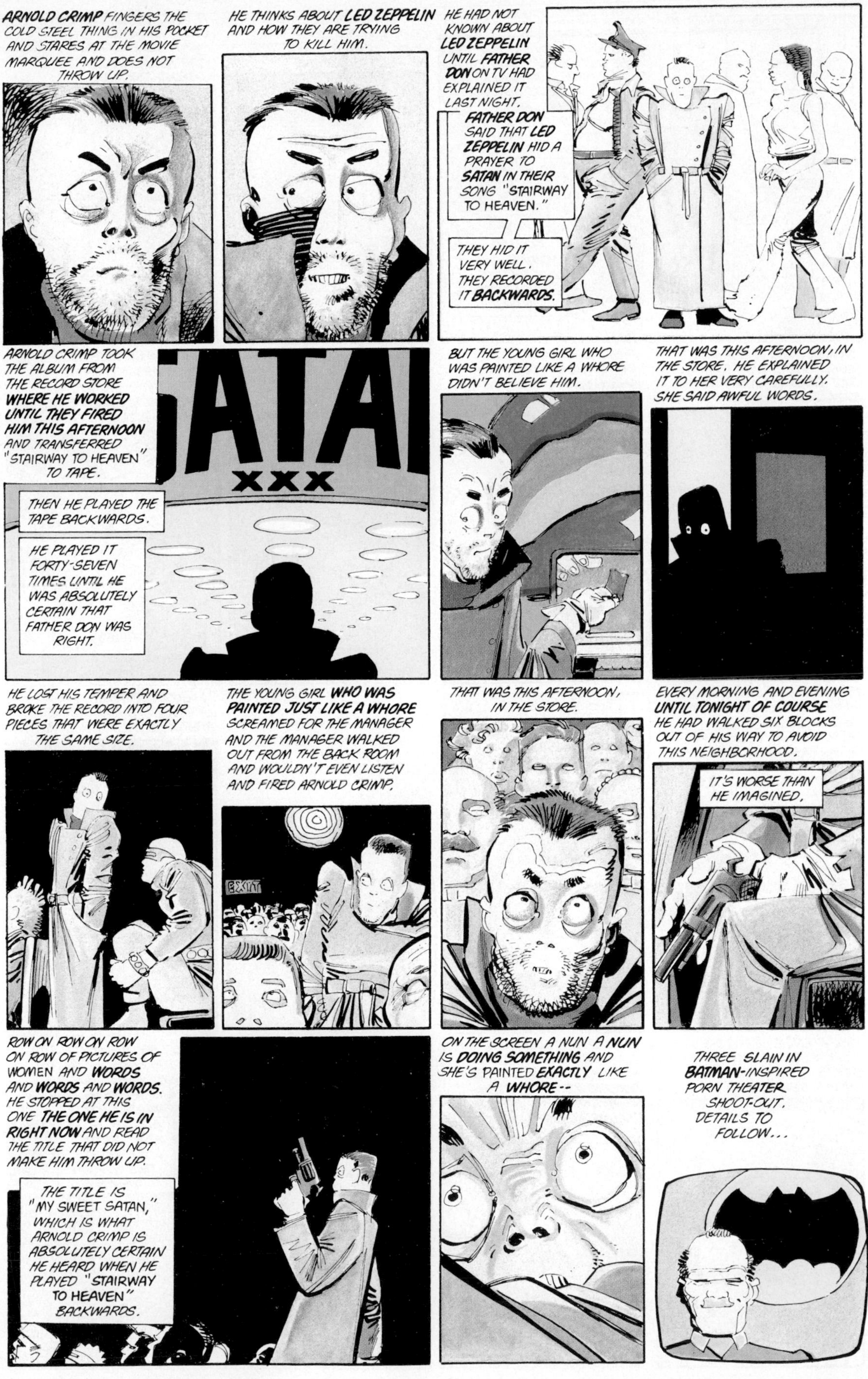
ARNOLD CRIMP FINGERS THE COLD STEEL THING IN HIS POCKET AND STARES AT THE MOVIE MARQUEE AND DOES NOT THROW UP.
HE THINKS ABOUT LED ZEPPELIN AND HOW THEY ARE TRYING TO KILL HIM.
HE HAD NOT KNOWN ABOUT LED ZEPPELIN UNTIL FATHER DON ON TV HAD EXPLAINED IT LAST NIGHT.
FATHER DON SAID THAT LED ZEPPELIN HID A PRAYER TO SATAN IN THEIR SONG "STAIRWAY TO HEAVEN."
THEY HID IT VERY WELL. THEY RECORDED IT BACKWARDS.
ARNOLD CRIMP TOOK THE ALBUM FROM THE RECORD STORE WHERE HE WORKED UNTIL THEY FIRED HIM THIS AFTERNOON AND TRANSFERRED "STAIRWAY TO HEAVEN" TO TAPE.
SATA
XXX
THEN HE PLAYED THE TAPE BACKWARDS.
HE PLAYED IT FORTY-SEVEN TIMES UNTIL HE WAS ABSOLUTELY CERTAIN THAT FATHER DON WAS RIGHT.
BUT THE YOUNG GIRL WHO WAS PAINTED LIKE A WHORE DIDN'T BELIEVE HIM.
THAT WAS THIS AFTERNOON, IN THE STORE. HE EXPLAINED IT TO HER VERY CAREFULLY. SHE SAID AWFUL WORDS.
HE LOST HIS TEMPER AND BROKE THE RECORD INTO FOUR PIECES THAT WERE EXACTLY THE SAME SIZE.
THE YOUNG GIRL WHO WAS PAINTED JUST LIKE A WHORE SCREAMED FOR THE MANAGER AND THE MANAGER WALKED OUT FROM THE BACK ROOM AND WOULDN'T EVEN LISTEN AND FIRED ARNOLD CRIMP.
EXIT
THAT WAS THIS AFTERNOON, IN THE STORE.
EVERY MORNING AND EVENING UNTIL TONIGHT OF COURSE HE HAD WALKED SIX BLOCKS OUT OF HIS WAY TO AVOID THIS NEIGHBORHOOD.
IT'S WORSE THAN HE IMAGINED.
ROW ON ROW ON ROW ON ROW OF PICTURES OF WOMEN AND WORDS AND WORDS AND WORDS. HE STOPPED AT THIS ONE THE ONE HE IS IN RIGHT NOW AND READ THE TITLE THAT DID NOT MAKE HIM THROW UP.
THE TITLE IS "MY SWEET SATAN," WHICH IS WHAT ARNOLD CRIMP IS ABSOLUTELY CERTAIN HE HEARD WHEN HE PLAYED "STAIRWAY TO HEAVEN" BACKWARDS.
ON THE SCREEN A NUN A NUN IS DOING SOMETHING AND SHE'S PAINTED EXACTLY LIKE A WHORE--
THREE SLAIN IN BATMAN-INSPIRED PORN THEATER SHOOT-OUT. DETAILS TO FOLLOW...

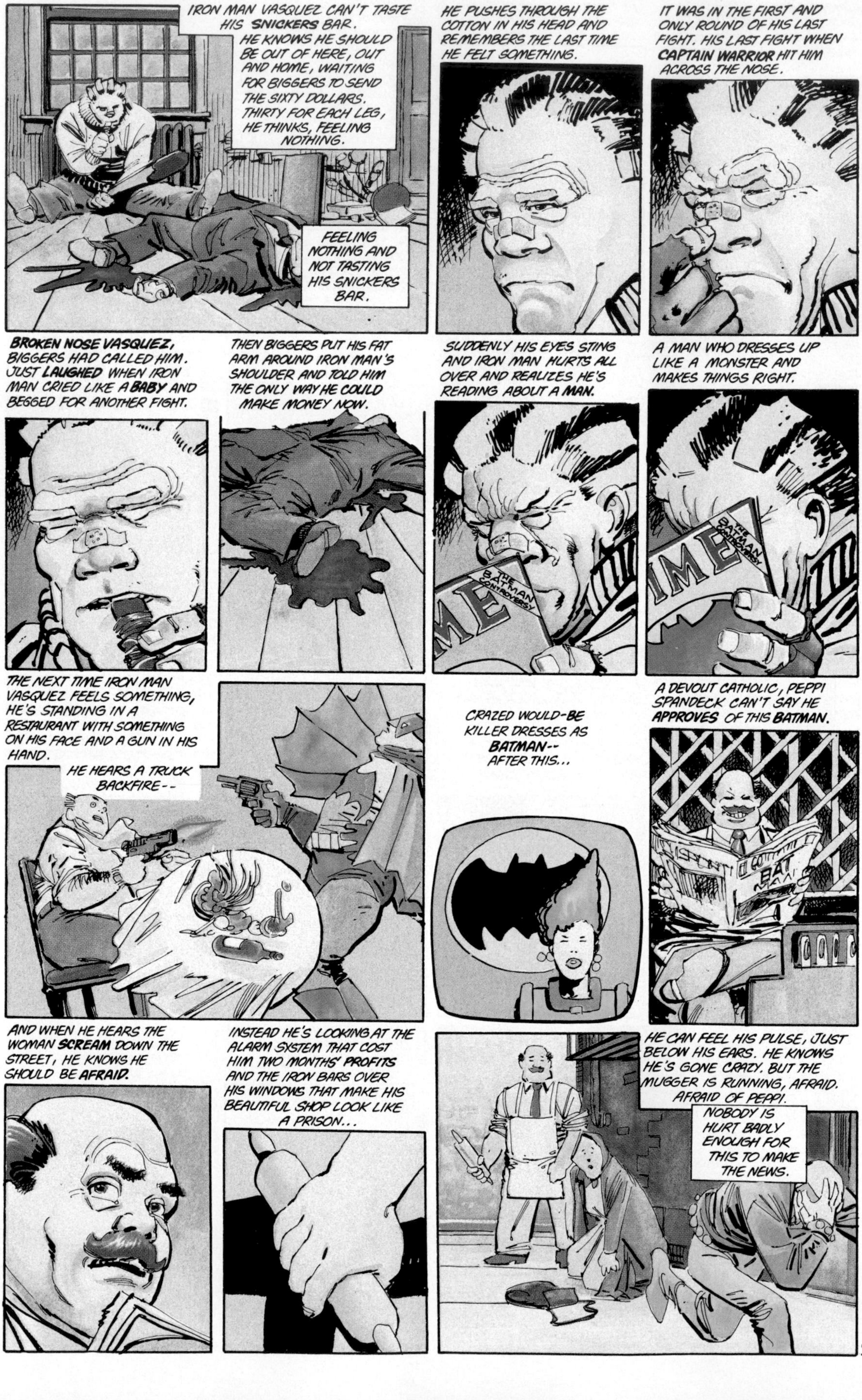
IRON MAN VASQUEZ CAN'T TASTE HIS SNICKERS BAR.
HE KNOWS HE SHOULD BE OUT OF HERE, OUT AND HOME, WAITING FOR BIGGERS TO SEND THE SIXTY DOLLARS. THIRTY FOR EACH LEG, HE THINKS, FEELING NOTHING.
FEELING NOTHING AND NOT TASTING HIS SNICKERS BAR.
HE PUSHES THROUGH THE COTTON IN HIS HEAD AND REMEMBERS THE LAST TIME HE FELT SOMETHING.
IT WAS IN THE FIRST AND ONLY ROUND OF HIS LAST FIGHT. HIS LAST FIGHT WHEN CAPTAIN WARRIOR HIT HIM ACROSS THE NOSE.
BROKEN NOSE VASQUEZ, BIGGERS HAD CALLED HIM. JUST LAUGHED WHEN IRON MAN CRIED LIKE A BABY AND BEGGED FOR ANOTHER FIGHT.
THEN BIGGERS PUT HIS FAT ARM AROUND IRON MAN'S SHOULDER AND TOLD HIM THE ONLY WAY HE COULD MAKE MONEY NOW.
SUDDENLY HIS EYES STING AND IRON MAN HURTS ALL OVER AND REALIZES HE'S READING ABOUT A MAN.
THE BATMAN CONTROVERSY
A MAN WHO DRESSES UP LIKE A MONSTER AND MAKES THINGS RIGHT.
THE BATMAN CONTROVERSY
THE NEXT TIME IRON MAN VASQUEZ FEELS SOMETHING, HE'S STANDING IN A RESTAURANT WITH SOMETHING ON HIS FACE AND A GUN IN HIS HAND.
HE HEARS A TRUCK BACKFIRE--
CRAZED WOULD-BE KILLER DRESSES AS BATMAN-- AFTER THIS...
A DEVOUT CATHOLIC, PEPPI SPANDECK CAN'T SAY HE APPROVES OF THIS BATMAN.
AND WHEN HE HEARS THE WOMAN SCREAM DOWN THE STREET, HE KNOWS HE SHOULD BE AFRAID.
INSTEAD HE'S LOOKING AT THE ALARM SYSTEM THAT COST HIM TWO MONTHS' PROFITS AND THE IRON BARS OVER HIS WINDOWS THAT MAKE HIS BEAUTIFUL SHOP LOOK LIKE A PRISON...
HE CAN FEEL HIS PULSE, JUST BELOW HIS EARS. HE KNOWS HE'S GONE CRAZY. BUT THE MUGGER IS RUNNING, AFRAID. AFRAID OF PEPPI.
NOBODY IS HURT BADLY ENOUGH FOR THIS TO MAKE THE NEWS.

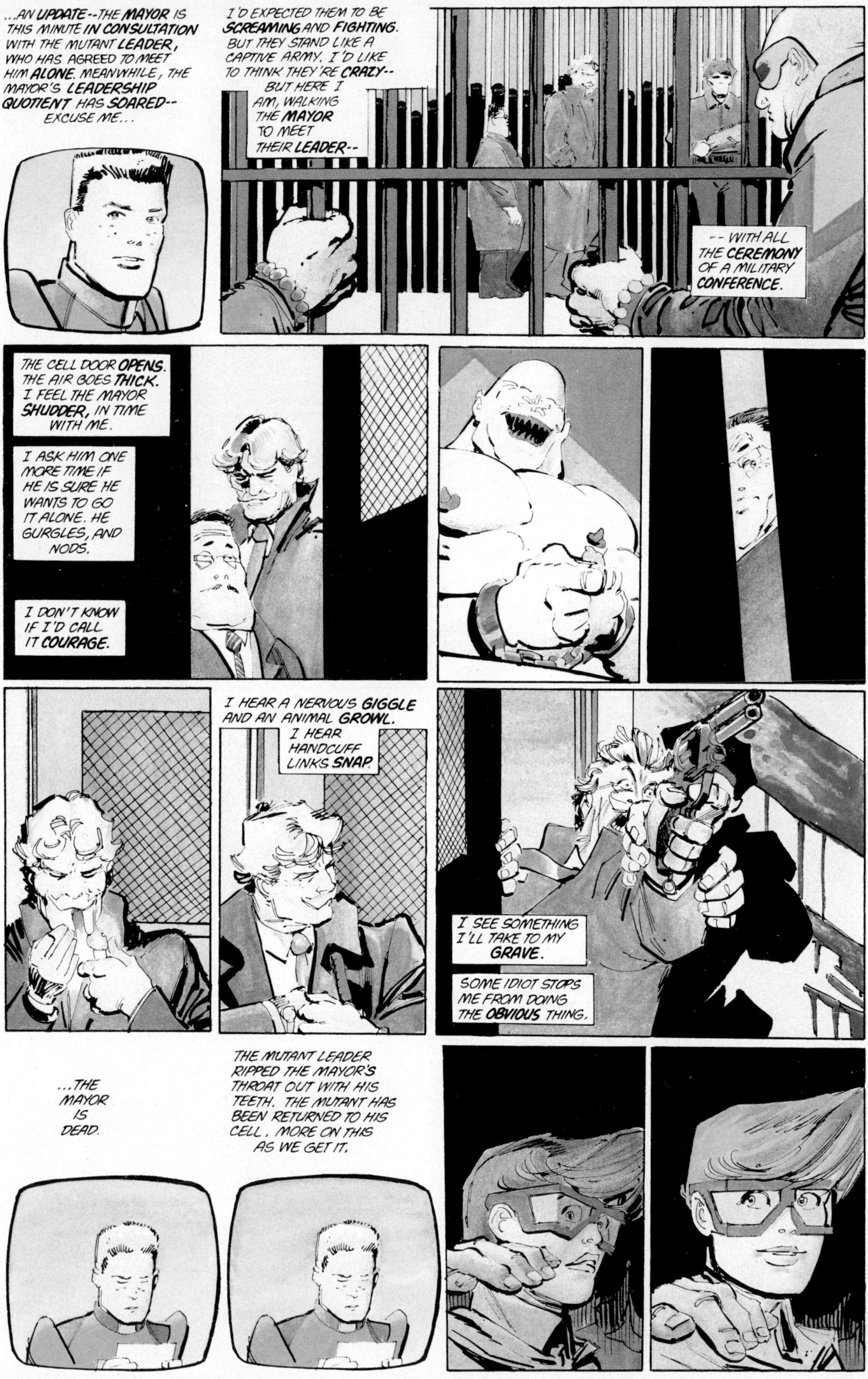
...AN UPDATE--THE MAYOR IS THIS MINUTE IN CONSULTATION WITH THE MUTANT LEADER, WHO HAS AGREED TO MEET HIM ALONE. MEANWHILE, THE MAYOR'S LEADERSHIP QUOTIENT HAS SOARED-- EXCUSE ME...
I'D EXPECTED THEM TO BE SCREAMING AND FIGHTING. BUT THEY STAND LIKE A CAPTIVE ARMY. I'D LIKE TO THINK THEY'RE CRAZY--
BUT HERE I AM, WALKING THE MAYOR TO MEET THEIR LEADER--
--WITH ALL THE CEREMONY OF A MILITARY CONFERENCE.
THE CELL DOOR OPENS. THE AIR GOES THICK. I FEEL THE MAYOR SHUDDER, IN TIME WITH ME.
I ASK HIM ONE MORE TIME IF HE IS SURE HE WANTS TO GO IT ALONE. HE GURGLES, AND NODS.
I DON'T KNOW IF I'D CALL IT COURAGE.
I HEAR A NERVOUS GIGGLE AND AN ANIMAL GROWL.
I HEAR HANDCUFF LINKS SNAP.
I SEE SOMETHING I'LL TAKE TO MY GRAVE.
SOME IDIOT STOPS ME FROM DOING THE OBVIOUS THING.
...THE MAYOR IS DEAD.
THE MUTANT LEADER RIPPED THE MAYOR'S THROAT OUT WITH HIS TEETH. THE MUTANT HAS BEEN RETURNED TO HIS CELL. MORE ON THIS AS WE GET IT.

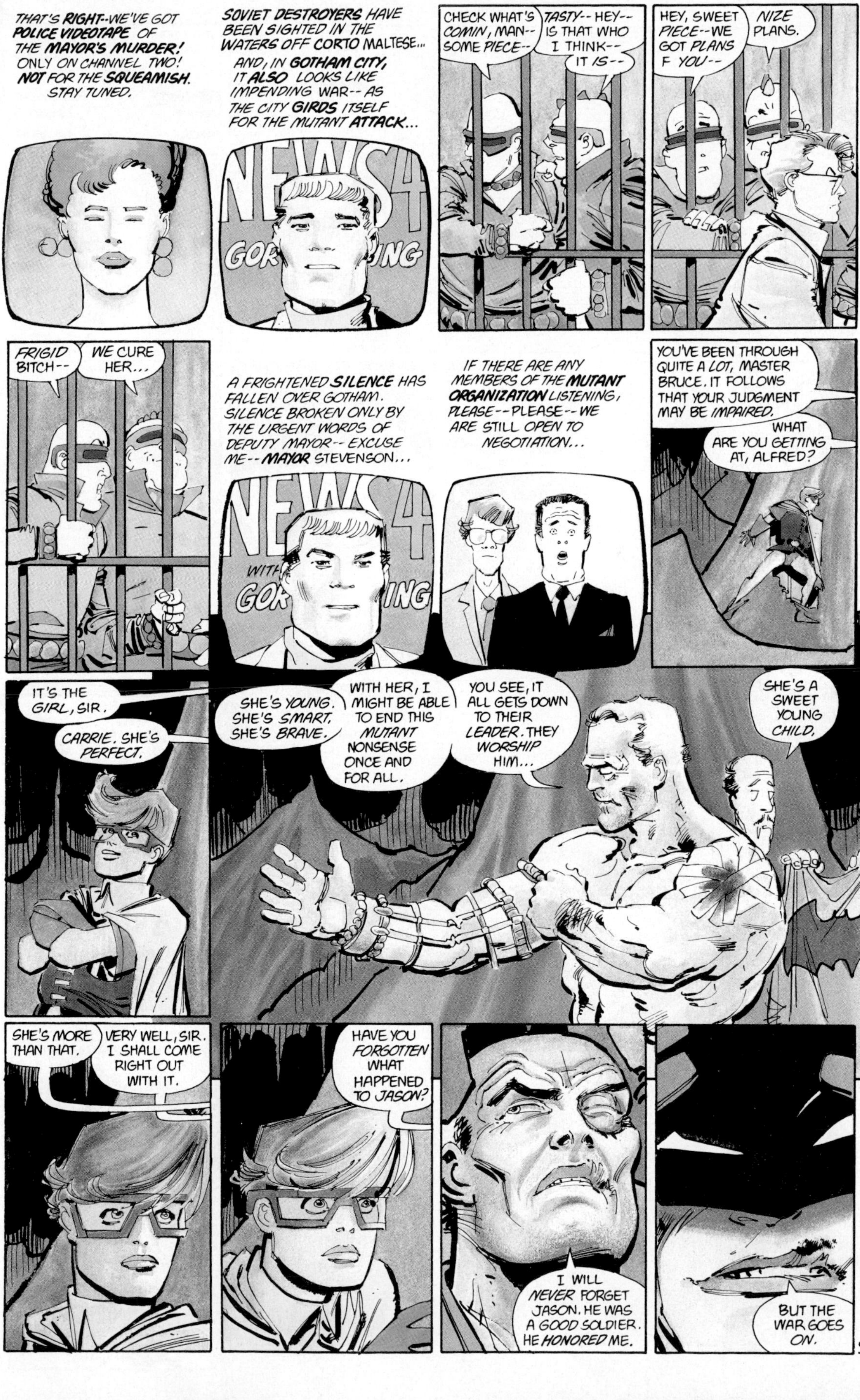
THAT'S RIGHT--WE'VE GOT POLICE VIDEOTAPE OF THE MAYOR'S MURDER! ONLY ON CHANNEL TWO! NOT FOR THE SQUEAMISH. STAY TUNED.
SOVIET DESTROYERS HAVE BEEN SIGHTED IN THE WATERS OFF CORTO MALTESE...
AND, IN GOTHAM CITY, IT ALSO LOOKS LIKE IMPENDING WAR-- AS THE CITY GIRDS ITSELF FOR THE MUTANT ATTACK...
NEWS 4
GOR ING
CHECK WHAT'S COMIN, MAN-- SOME PIECE--
TASTY-- HEY-- IS THAT WHO I THINK-- IT IS--
HEY, SWEET PIECE--WE GOT PLANS F YOU--
NIZE PLANS.
FRIGID BITCH--
WE CURE HER...
A FRIGHTENED SILENCE HAS FALLEN OVER GOTHAM. SILENCE BROKEN ONLY BY THE URGENT WORDS OF DEPUTY MAYOR-- EXCUSE ME-- MAYOR STEVENSON...
NEWS 4
WITH GOR ING
IF THERE ARE ANY MEMBERS OF THE MUTANT ORGANIZATION LISTENING, PLEASE--PLEASE--WE ARE STILL OPEN TO NEGOTIATION...
YOU'VE BEEN THROUGH QUITE A LOT, MASTER BRUCE. IT FOLLOWS THAT YOUR JUDGMENT MAY BE IMPAIRED.
WHAT ARE YOU GETTING AT, ALFRED?
IT'S THE GIRL, SIR.
CARRIE. SHE'S PERFECT.
SHE'S YOUNG. SHE'S SMART, SHE'S BRAVE.
WITH HER, I MIGHT BE ABLE TO END THIS MUTANT NONSENSE ONCE AND FOR ALL.
YOU SEE, IT ALL GETS DOWN TO THEIR LEADER. THEY WORSHIP HIM...
SHE'S A SWEET YOUNG CHILD.
SHE'S MORE THAN THAT.
VERY WELL, SIR. I SHALL COME RIGHT OUT WITH IT.
HAVE YOU FORGOTTEN WHAT HAPPENED TO JASON?
I WILL NEVER FORGET JASON. HE WAS A GOOD SOLDIER. HE HONORED ME.
BUT THE WAR GOES ON.

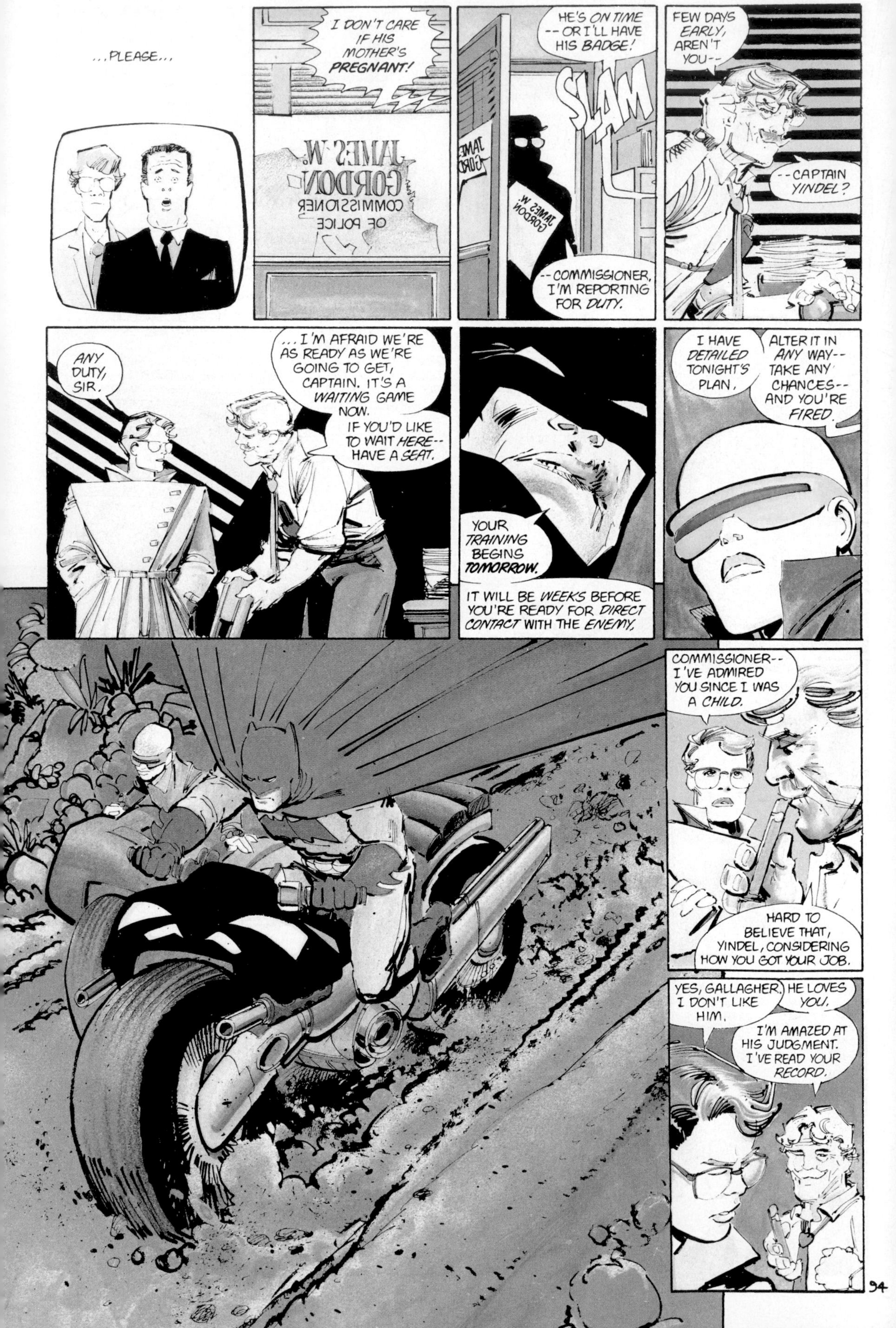
...PLEASE...
I DON'T CARE IF HIS MOTHER'S PREGNANT!
JAMES W. GORDON COMMISSIONER OF POLICE
HE'S ON TIME -- OR I'LL HAVE HIS BADGE!
SLAM
JAMES W. GORDON
--COMMISSIONER, I'M REPORTING FOR DUTY.
FEW DAYS EARLY, AREN'T YOU--
--CAPTAIN YINDEL?
ANY DUTY, SIR.
...I'M AFRAID WE'RE AS READY AS WE'RE GOING TO GET, CAPTAIN. IT'S A WAITING GAME NOW.
IF YOU'D LIKE TO WAIT HERE-- HAVE A SEAT.
YOUR TRAINING BEGINS TOMORROW.
IT WILL BE WEEKS BEFORE YOU'RE READY FOR DIRECT CONTACT WITH THE ENEMY.
I HAVE DETAILED TONIGHT'S PLAN.
ALTER IT IN ANY WAY-- TAKE ANY CHANCES-- AND YOU'RE FIRED.
COMMISSIONER-- I'VE ADMIRED YOU SINCE I WAS A CHILD.
HARD TO BELIEVE THAT, YINDEL, CONSIDERING HOW YOU GOT YOUR JOB.
YES, GALLAGHER. I DON'T LIKE HIM.
HE LOVES YOU.
I'M AMAZED AT HIS JUDGMENT. I'VE READ YOUR RECORD.

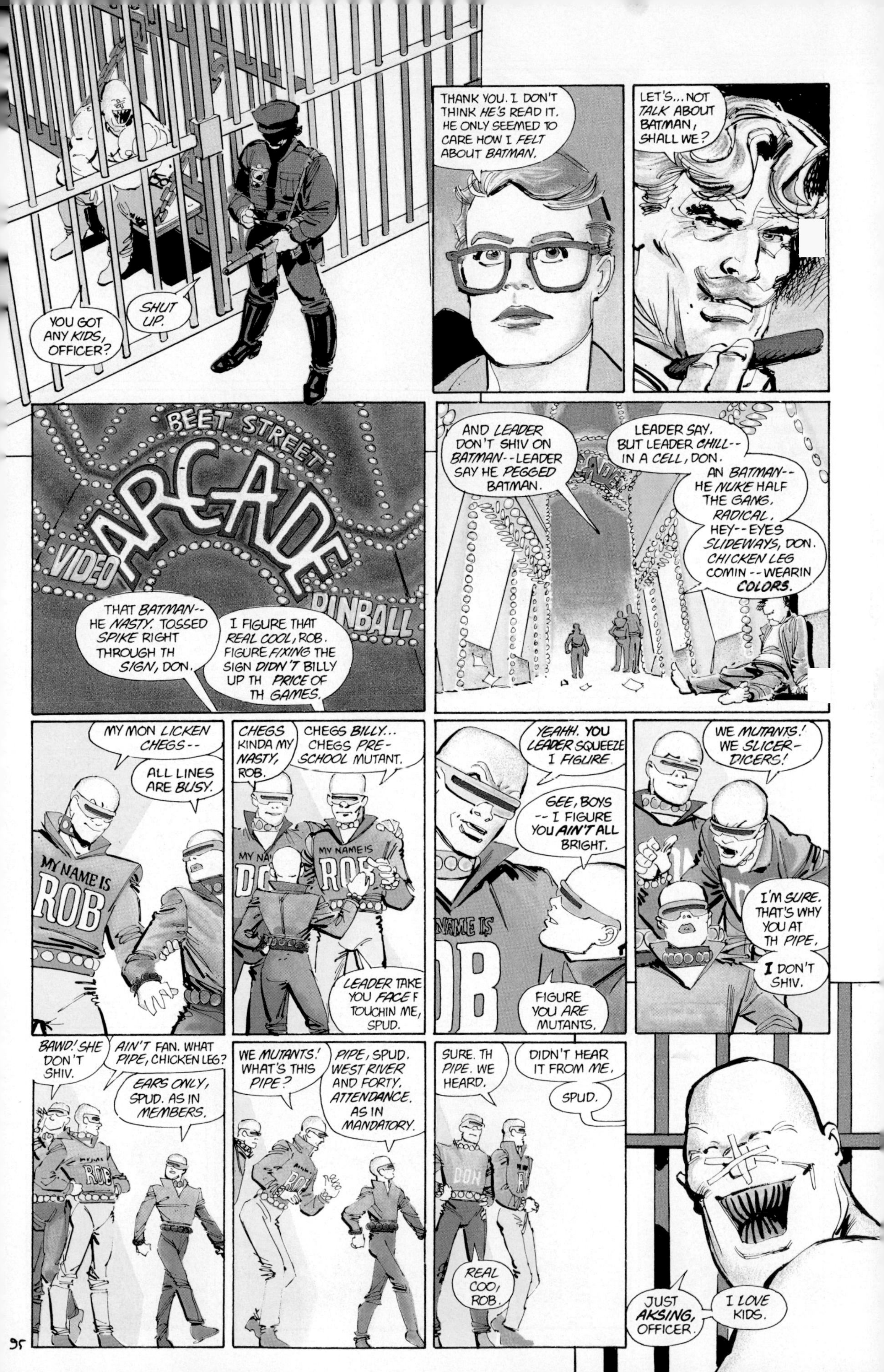
YOU GOT ANY KIDS, OFFICER?
SHUT UP.
THANK YOU. I DON'T THINK HE'S READ IT. HE ONLY SEEMED TO CARE HOW I FELT ABOUT BATMAN.
LET'S... NOT TALK ABOUT BATMAN, SHALL WE?
BEET STREET
ARCADE
VIDEO
PINBALL
THAT BATMAN-- HE NASTY. TOSSED SPIKE RIGHT THROUGH TH SIGN, DON.
I FIGURE THAT REAL COOL, ROB. FIGURE FIXING THE SIGN DIDN'T BILLY UP TH PRICE OF TH GAMES.
AND LEADER DON'T SHIV ON BATMAN--LEADER SAY HE PEGGED BATMAN.
LEADER SAY. BUT LEADER CHILL-- IN A CELL, DON.
AN BATMAN-- HE NUKE HALF THE GANG. RADICAL. HEY--EYES SLIDEWAYS, DON. CHICKEN LEG COMIN--WEARIN COLORS.
MY MON LICKEN CHEGS--
ALL LINES ARE BUSY.
MY NAME IS ROB
CHEGS KINDA MY NASTY, ROB.
CHEGS BILLY... CHEGS PRE-SCHOOL MUTANT.
LEADER TAKE YOU FACE F TOUCHIN ME, SPUD.
YEAHH. YOU LEADER SQUEEZE I FIGURE.
GEE, BOYS --I FIGURE YOU AIN'T ALL BRIGHT.
FIGURE YOU ARE MUTANTS.
WE MUTANTS! WE SLICER-DICERS!
I'M SURE. THAT'S WHY YOU AT TH PIPE.
I DON'T SHIV.
BAWD! SHE DON'T SHIV.
AIN'T FAN. WHAT PIPE, CHICKEN LEG?
EARS ONLY, SPUD. AS IN MEMBERS.
WE MUTANTS! WHAT'S THIS PIPE?
PIPE, SPUD. WEST RIVER AND FORTY. ATTENDANCE. AS IN MANDATORY.
SURE. TH PIPE. WE HEARD.
DIDN'T HEAR IT FROM ME,
SPUD.
REAL COO, ROB.
JUST AKSING, OFFICER.
I LOVE KIDS.

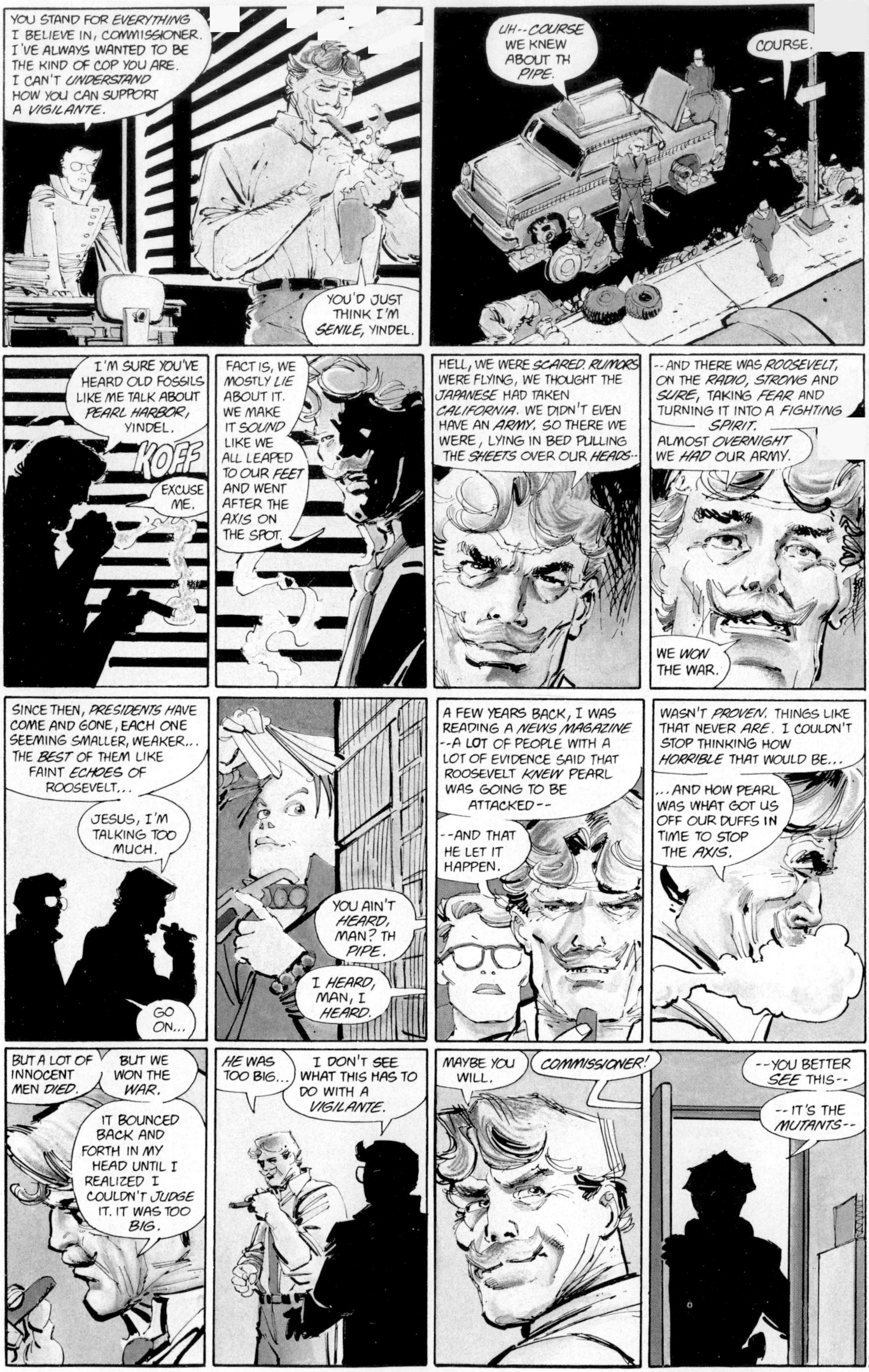
YOU STAND FOR EVERYTHING I BELIEVE IN, COMMISSIONER. I'VE ALWAYS WANTED TO BE THE KIND OF COP YOU ARE. I CAN'T UNDERSTAND HOW YOU CAN SUPPORT A VIGILANTE.
YOU'D JUST THINK I'M SENILE, YINDEL.
UH--COURSE WE KNEW ABOUT TH PIPE.
COURSE.
I'M SURE YOU'VE HEARD OLD FOSSILS LIKE ME TALK ABOUT PEARL HARBOR, YINDEL.
KOFF
EXCUSE ME.
FACT IS, WE MOSTLY LIE ABOUT IT. WE MAKE IT SOUND LIKE WE ALL LEAPED TO OUR FEET AND WENT AFTER THE AXIS ON THE SPOT.
HELL, WE WERE SCARED. RUMORS WERE FLYING, WE THOUGHT THE JAPANESE HAD TAKEN CALIFORNIA. WE DIDN'T EVEN HAVE AN ARMY. SO THERE WE WERE, LYING IN BED PULLING THE SHEETS OVER OUR HEADS--
--AND THERE WAS ROOSEVELT, ON THE RADIO, STRONG AND SURE, TAKING FEAR AND TURNING IT INTO A FIGHTING SPIRIT. ALMOST OVERNIGHT WE HAD OUR ARMY.
WE WON THE WAR.
SINCE THEN, PRESIDENTS HAVE COME AND GONE, EACH ONE SEEMING SMALLER, WEAKER... THE BEST OF THEM LIKE FAINT ECHOES OF ROOSEVELT...
JESUS, I'M TALKING TOO MUCH.
GO ON...
YOU AIN'T HEARD, MAN? TH PIPE.
I HEARD, MAN, I HEARD.
A FEW YEARS BACK, I WAS READING A NEWS MAGAZINE --A LOT OF PEOPLE WITH A LOT OF EVIDENCE SAID THAT ROOSEVELT KNEW PEARL WAS GOING TO BE ATTACKED--
--AND THAT HE LET IT HAPPEN.
WASN'T PROVEN. THINGS LIKE THAT NEVER ARE. I COULDN'T STOP THINKING HOW HORRIBLE THAT WOULD BE...
...AND HOW PEARL WAS WHAT GOT US OFF OUR DUFFS IN TIME TO STOP THE AXIS.
BUT A LOT OF INNOCENT MEN DIED.
BUT WE WON THE WAR.
IT BOUNCED BACK AND FORTH IN MY HEAD UNTIL I REALIZED I COULDN'T JUDGE IT. IT WAS TOO BIG.
HE WAS TOO BIG...
I DON'T SEE WHAT THIS HAS TO DO WITH A VIGILANTE.
MAYBE YOU WILL.
COMMISSIONER!
--YOU BETTER SEE THIS--
--IT'S THE MUTANTS--

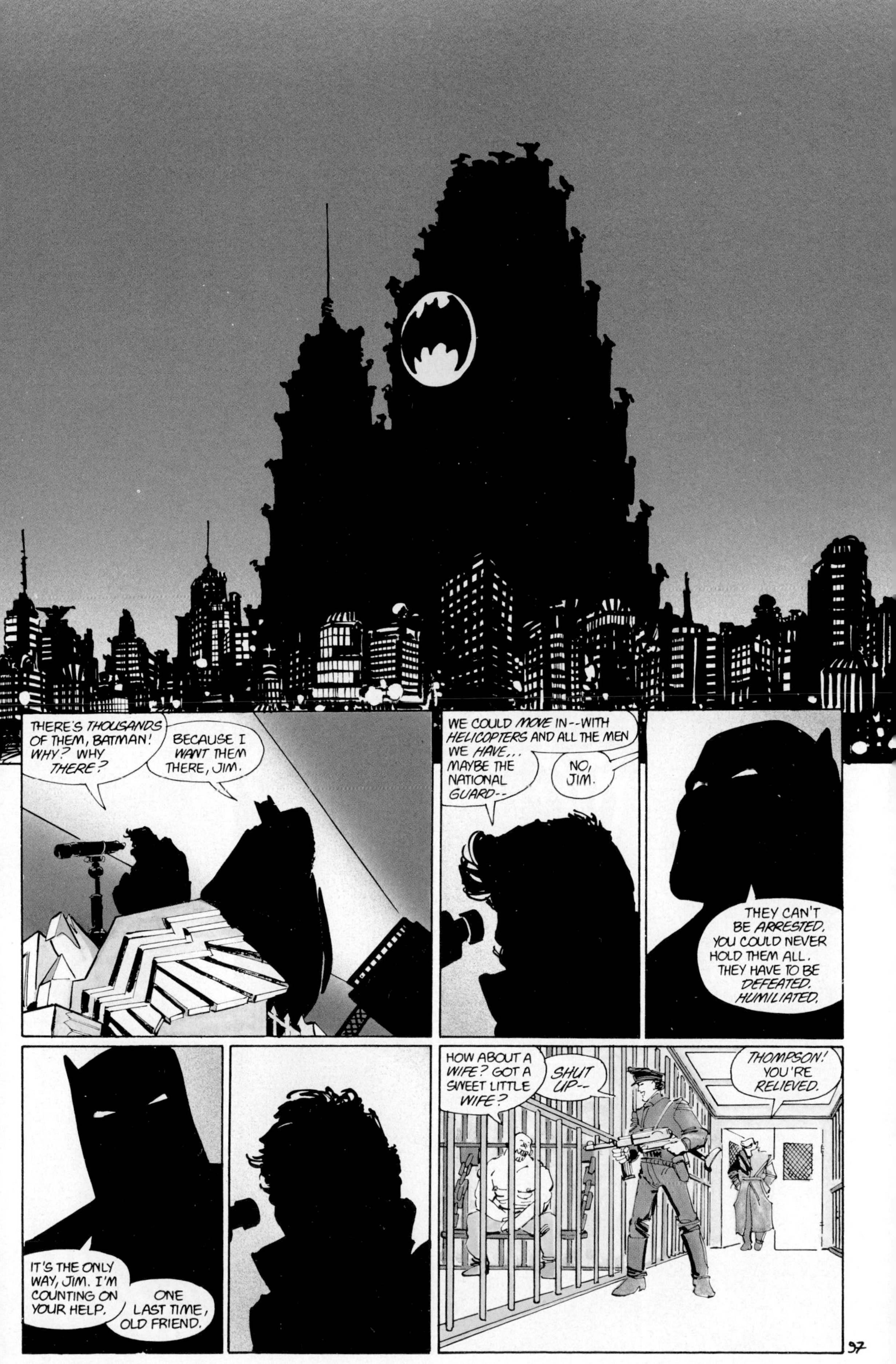
THERE'S THOUSANDS OF THEM, BATMAN! WHY? WHY THERE?
BECAUSE I WANT THEM THERE, JIM.
WE COULD MOVE IN--WITH HELICOPTERS AND ALL THE MEN WE HAVE... MAYBE THE NATIONAL GUARD--
NO, JIM.
THEY CAN'T BE ARRESTED. YOU COULD NEVER HOLD THEM ALL. THEY HAVE TO BE DEFEATED. HUMILIATED.
IT'S THE ONLY WAY, JIM. I'M COUNTING ON YOUR HELP.
ONE LAST TIME, OLD FRIEND.
HOW ABOUT A WIFE? GOT A SWEET LITTLE WIFE?
SHUT UP--
THOMPSON! YOU'RE RELIEVED.

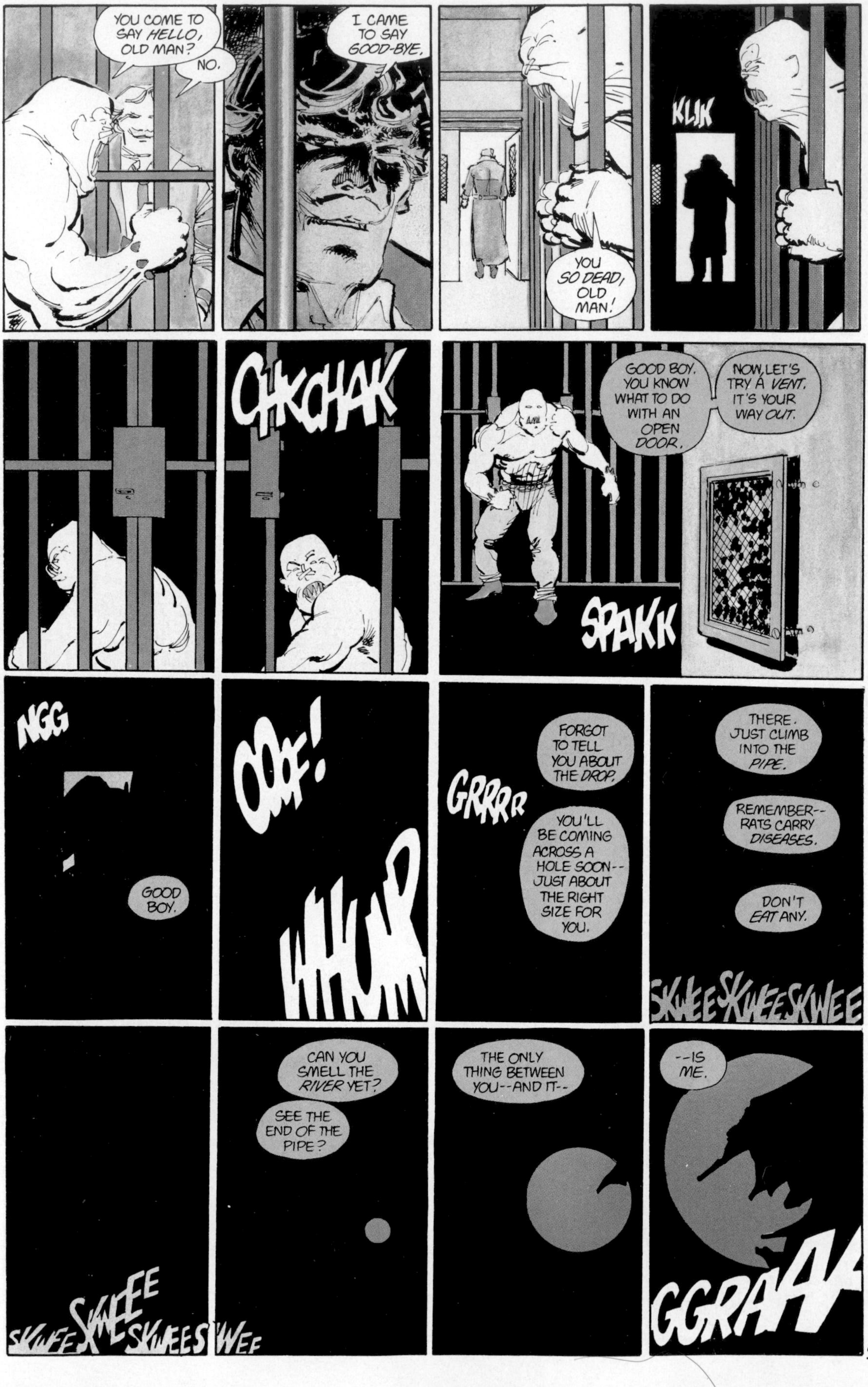

YOU COME TO SAY HELLO, OLD MAN?
NO.
I CAME TO SAY GOOD-BYE.
YOU SO DEAD, OLD MAN!
KLIK
CHKCHAK
GOOD BOY. YOU KNOW WHAT TO DO WITH AN OPEN DOOR.
NOW, LET'S TRY A VENT. IT'S YOUR WAY OUT.
SPAKK
NGG
GOOD BOY.
OOOF!
WHUMP
GRRRR
FORGOT TO TELL YOU ABOUT THE DROP.
YOU'LL BE COMING ACROSS A HOLE SOON-- JUST ABOUT THE RIGHT SIZE FOR YOU.
THERE. JUST CLIMB INTO THE PIPE.
REMEMBER-- RATS CARRY DISEASES.
DON'T EAT ANY.
SKWEE SKWEE SKWEE
SKWEE SKWEE SKWEE SKWEE SKWEE
CAN YOU SMELL THE RIVER YET?
SEE THE END OF THE PIPE?
THE ONLY THING BETWEEN YOU--AND IT--
--IS ME.
GGRAAK

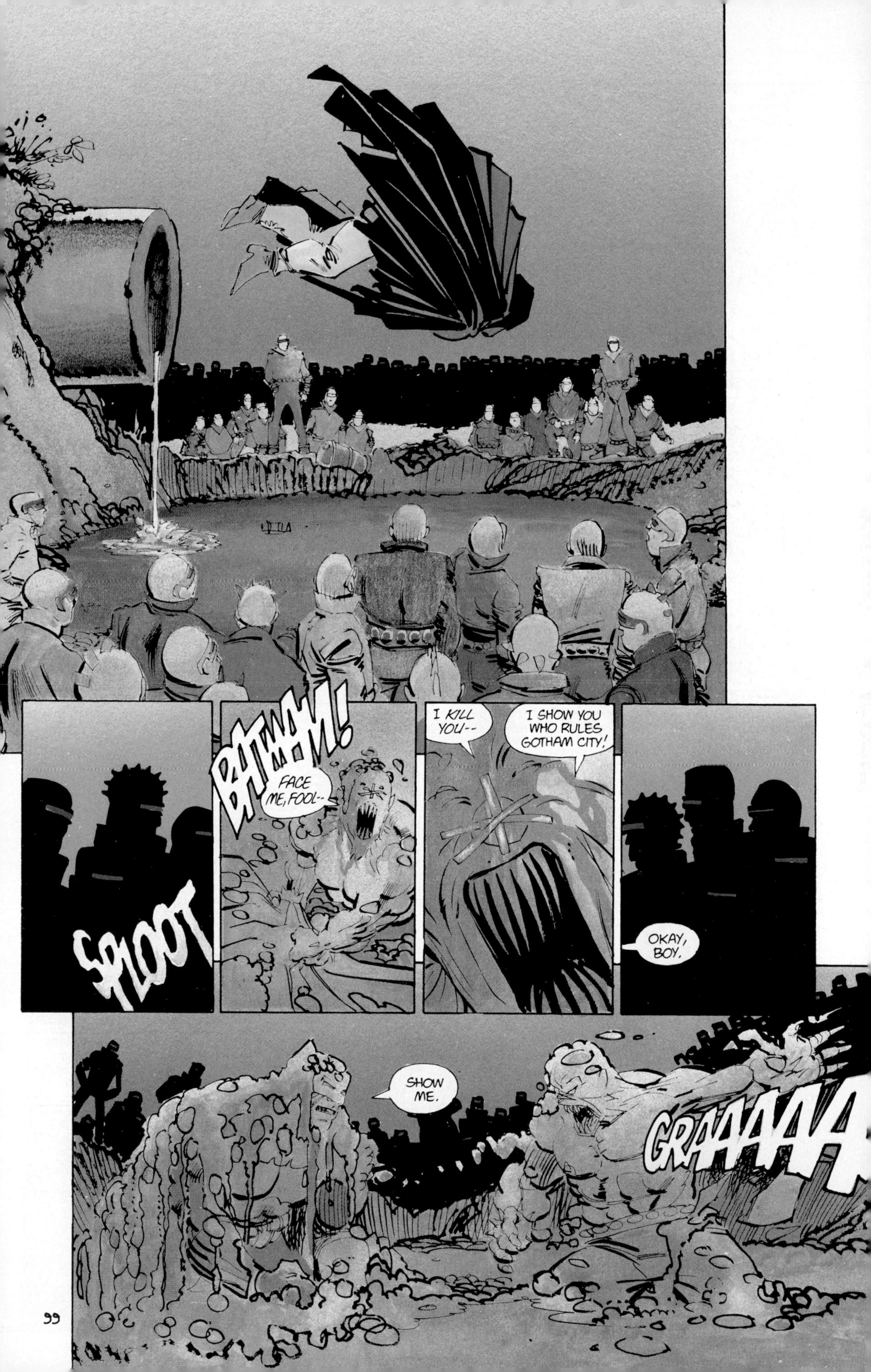
SPLOOT
BATMAN!
FACE ME, FOOL--
I KILL YOU--
I SHOW YOU WHO RULES GOTHAM CITY!
OKAY, BOY.
SHOW ME.
GRAAAAA

YOU SEE, DON. BATMAN --HE *NASTY*.

HOPE ROB DON'T SAY *BALLS NASTY*.

BALLS NASTY.

SHH!

MY NAME AME
ROBI

MY NAME ME
ROBI

HE'S FAST -- FASTER THAN I AM. AND STRONGER--

--AND SEEMINGLY IMPERVIOUS TO PAIN.

BUT THEY DO COME SMARTER.

--AND NOBODY'S VERY FAST WHEN HE'S THIGH-DEEP IN MUD.

I WAIT FOR HIM TO TRY A KICK--

-- GIVE HIM JUST THE *RIGHT* KIND OF CUT ABOVE THE EYES.

THE KIND THAT BLEEDS.

MY MISTAKE WAS TO TRY TO MATCH HIS SAVAGERY.

TO FIGHT LIKE A YOUNG MAN.

RIGHT ON SCHEDULE THE BLOOD HITS HIS EYES.

I GRAB A CLUMP OF MUD.

SPLOOT

LEADER'S BOGGIN'!

LEADER BILLY BERSERK, SPUD. LEADER PEG BATMAN. YOU SEE.

SHH!

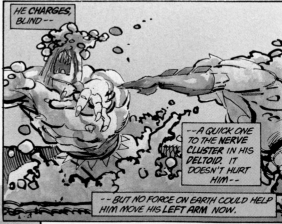

HE CHARGES, BLIND --

--A QUICK ONE TO THE NERVE CLUSTER IN HIS DELTOID. IT DOESN'T HURT HIM --

-- BUT NO FORCE ON EARTH COULD HELP HIM MOVE HIS LEFT ARM NOW.

HIS RIGHT--
--IT'S FAST--
--TOO FAST--

HE DUSTED! HE DUSTED!

MY MON *BATS* DON'T SHIV.

YOU SEE.

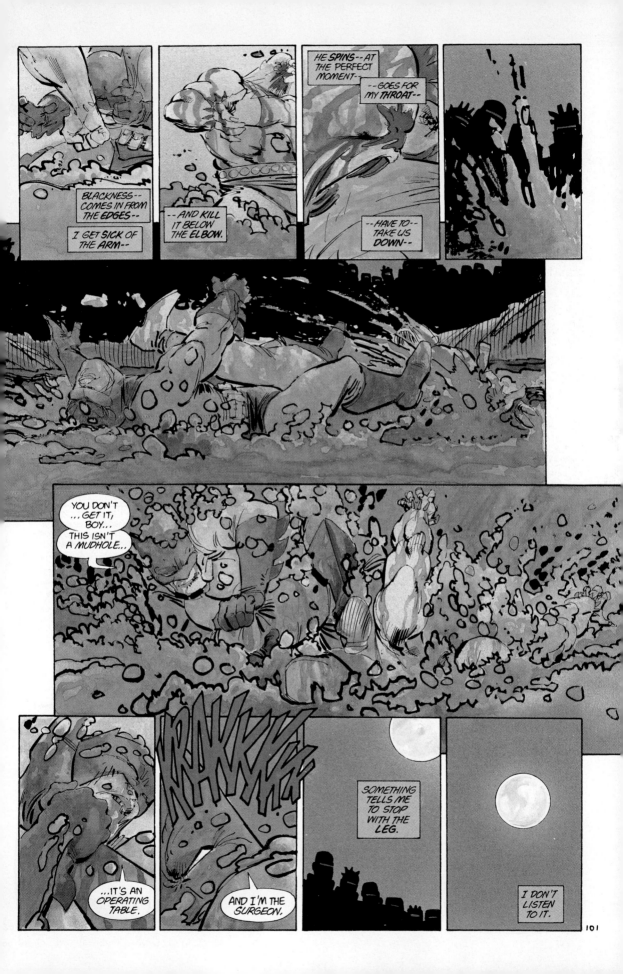

BLACKNESS-- COMES IN FROM THE EDGES--

I GET SICK OF THE ARM--

--AND KILL IT BELOW THE ELBOW.

HE SPINS-- AT THE PERFECT MOMENT--

--GOES FOR MY *THROAT*--

--HAVE TO-- TAKE US *DOWN*--

YOU DON'T ...GET IT, BOY... THIS ISN'T A MUDHOLE...

...IT'S AN OPERATING TABLE.

AND I'M THE SURGEON.

SOMETHING TELLS ME TO STOP WITH THE LEG.

I DON'T LISTEN TO IT.

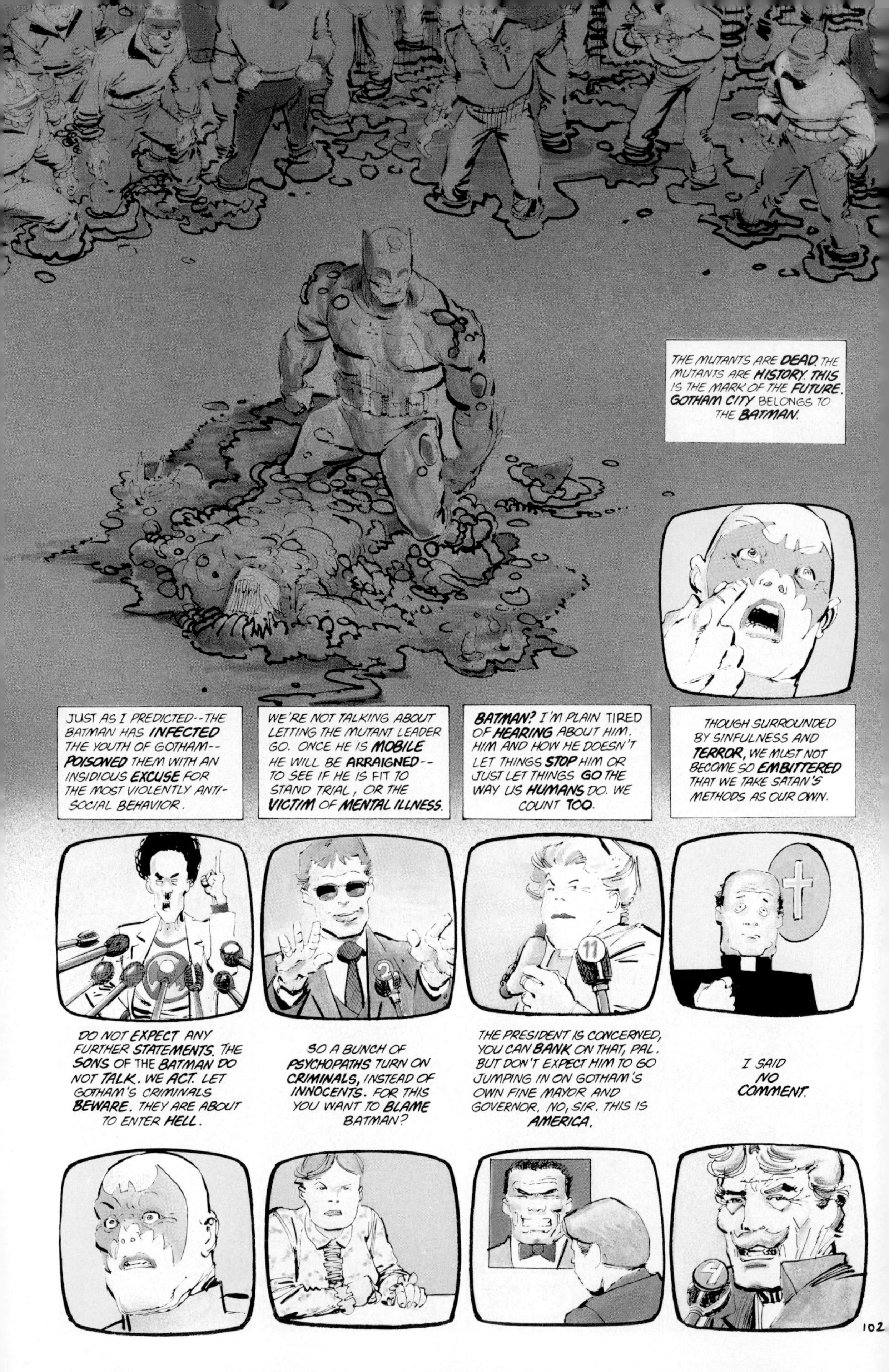
THE MUTANTS ARE DEAD. THE MUTANTS ARE HISTORY. THIS IS THE MARK OF THE FUTURE. GOTHAM CITY BELONGS TO THE BATMAN.
JUST AS I PREDICTED--THE BATMAN HAS INFECTED THE YOUTH OF GOTHAM--POISONED THEM WITH AN INSIDIOUS EXCUSE FOR THE MOST VIOLENTLY ANTI-SOCIAL BEHAVIOR.
WE'RE NOT TALKING ABOUT LETTING THE MUTANT LEADER GO. ONCE HE IS MOBILE HE WILL BE ARRAIGNED--TO SEE IF HE IS FIT TO STAND TRIAL, OR THE VICTIM OF MENTAL ILLNESS.
BATMAN? I'M PLAIN TIRED OF HEARING ABOUT HIM. HIM AND HOW HE DOESN'T LET THINGS STOP HIM OR JUST LET THINGS GO THE WAY US HUMANS DO. WE COUNT TOO.
THOUGH SURROUNDED BY SINFULNESS AND TERROR, WE MUST NOT BECOME SO EMBITTERED THAT WE TAKE SATAN'S METHODS AS OUR OWN.
11
2
DO NOT EXPECT ANY FURTHER STATEMENTS. THE SONS OF THE BATMAN DO NOT TALK. WE ACT. LET GOTHAM'S CRIMINALS BEWARE. THEY ARE ABOUT TO ENTER HELL.
SO A BUNCH OF PSYCHOPATHS TURN ON CRIMINALS, INSTEAD OF INNOCENTS. FOR THIS YOU WANT TO BLAME BATMAN?
THE PRESIDENT IS CONCERNED, YOU CAN BANK ON THAT, PAL. BUT DON'T EXPECT HIM TO GO JUMPING IN ON GOTHAM'S OWN FINE MAYOR AND GOVERNOR. NO, SIR. THIS IS AMERICA.
I SAID NO COMMENT.
4

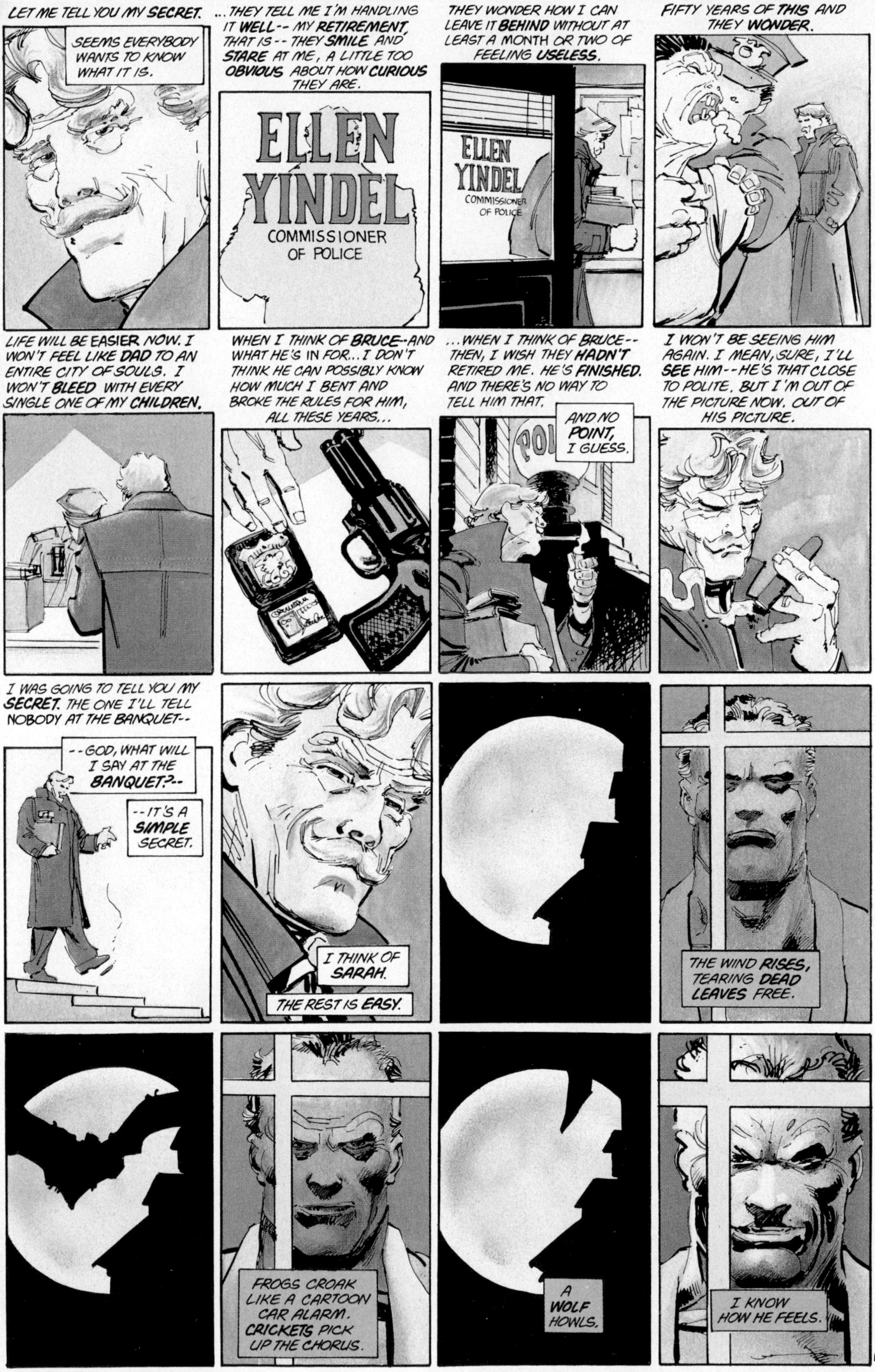
LET ME TELL YOU MY SECRET.
SEEMS EVERYBODY WANTS TO KNOW WHAT IT IS.
...THEY TELL ME I'M HANDLING IT WELL-- MY RETIREMENT, THAT IS-- THEY SMILE AND STARE AT ME, A LITTLE TOO OBVIOUS ABOUT HOW CURIOUS THEY ARE.
ELLEN YINDEL
COMMISSIONER OF POLICE
THEY WONDER HOW I CAN LEAVE IT BEHIND WITHOUT AT LEAST A MONTH OR TWO OF FEELING USELESS.
ELLEN YINDEL
COMMISSIONER OF POLICE
FIFTY YEARS OF THIS AND THEY WONDER.
LIFE WILL BE EASIER NOW. I WON'T FEEL LIKE DAD TO AN ENTIRE CITY OF SOULS. I WON'T BLEED WITH EVERY SINGLE ONE OF MY CHILDREN.
WHEN I THINK OF BRUCE--AND WHAT HE'S IN FOR... I DON'T THINK HE CAN POSSIBLY KNOW HOW MUCH I BENT AND BROKE THE RULES FOR HIM, ALL THESE YEARS...
...WHEN I THINK OF BRUCE-- THEN, I WISH THEY HADN'T RETIRED ME. HE'S FINISHED. AND THERE'S NO WAY TO TELL HIM THAT.
AND NO POINT, I GUESS.
I WON'T BE SEEING HIM AGAIN. I MEAN, SURE, I'LL SEE HIM--HE'S THAT CLOSE TO POLITE. BUT I'M OUT OF THE PICTURE NOW. OUT OF HIS PICTURE.
I WAS GOING TO TELL YOU MY SECRET. THE ONE I'LL TELL NOBODY AT THE BANQUET--
--GOD, WHAT WILL I SAY AT THE BANQUET?--
--IT'S A SIMPLE SECRET.
I THINK OF SARAH.
THE REST IS EASY.
THE WIND RISES, TEARING DEAD LEAVES FREE.
FROGS CROAK LIKE A CARTOON CAR ALARM. CRICKETS PICK UP THE CHORUS.
A WOLF HOWLS.
I KNOW HOW HE FEELS.

BOOK THREE

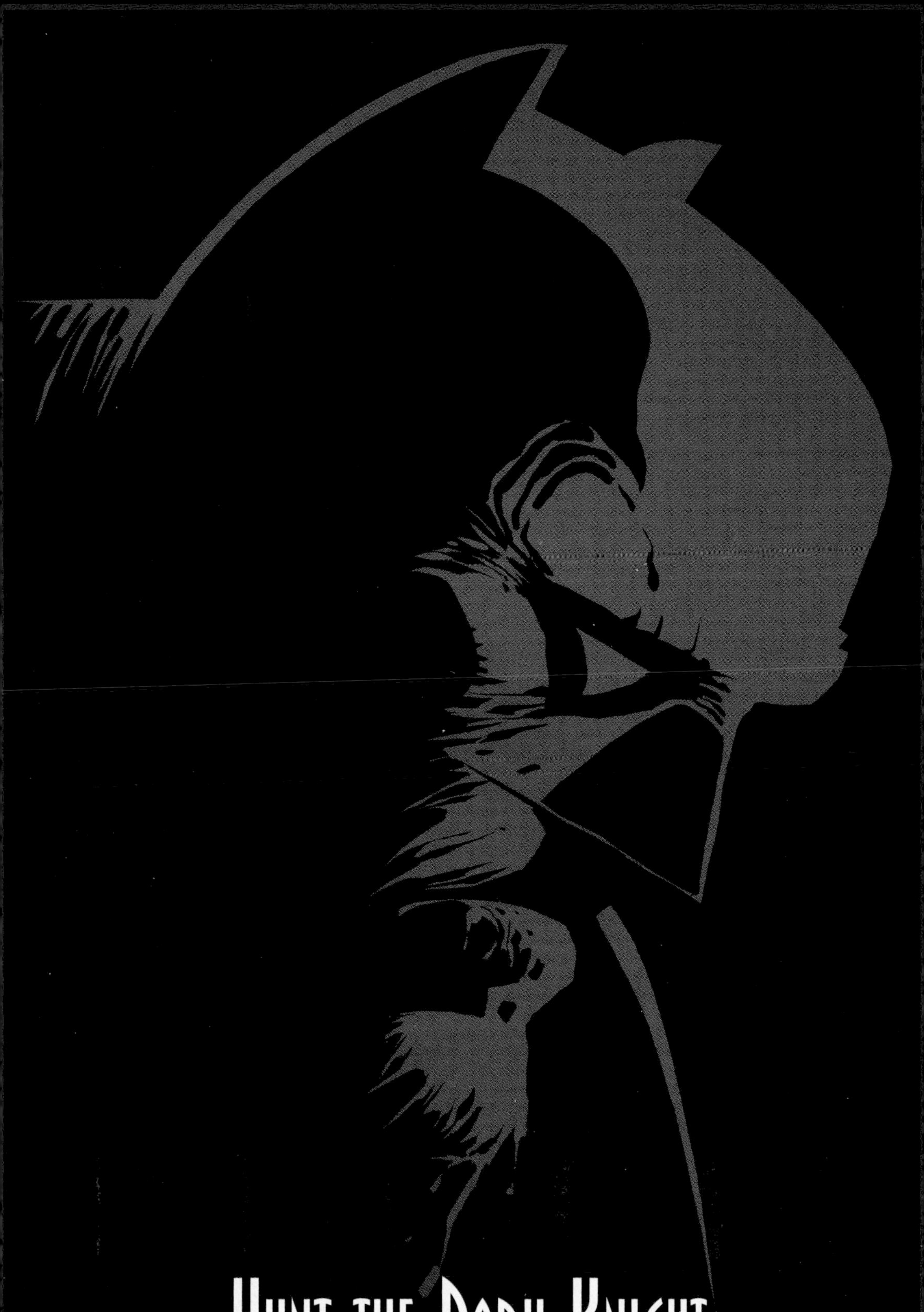

Hunt the Dark Knight

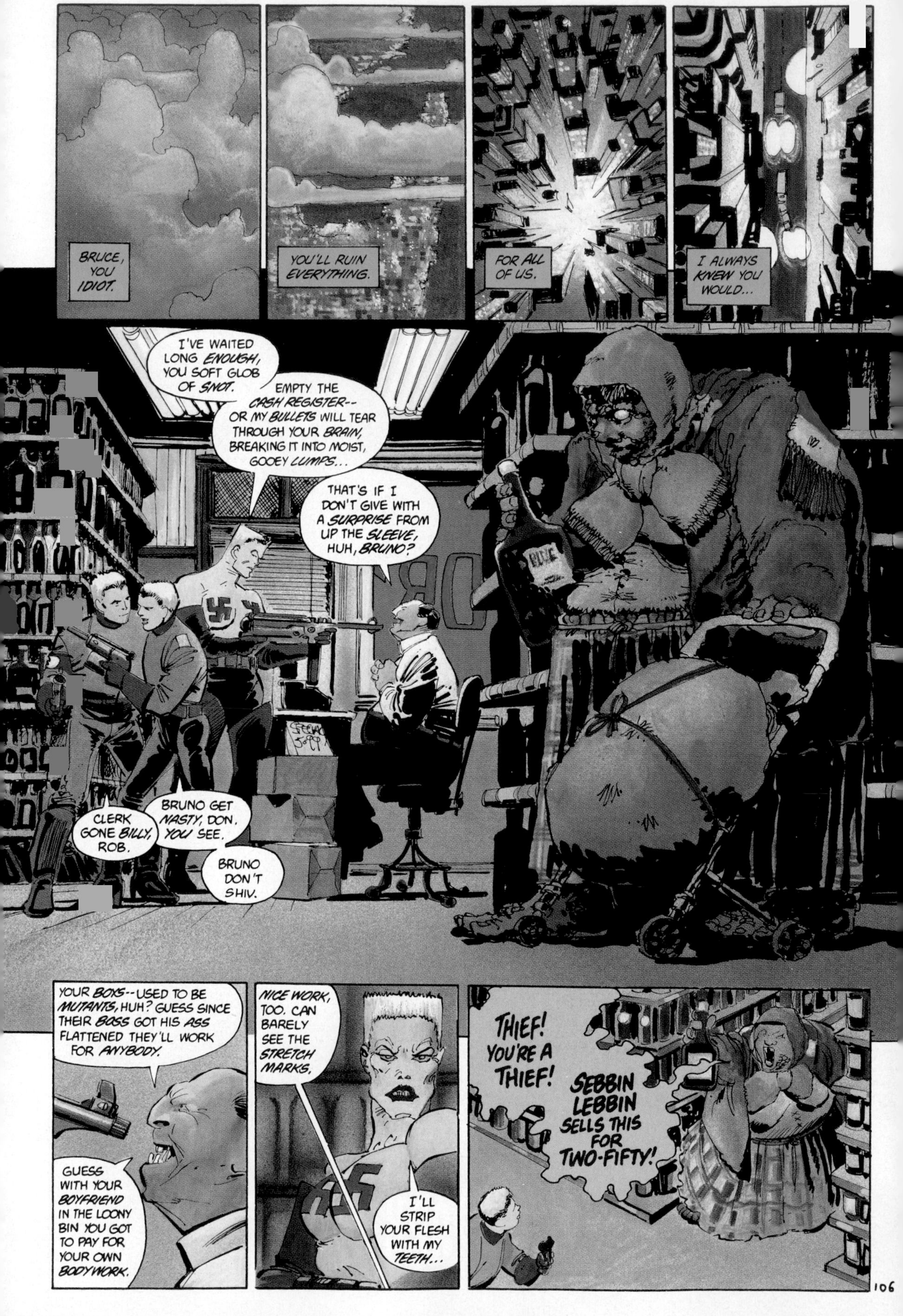

BRUCE, YOU IDIOT.
YOU'LL RUIN EVERYTHING.
FOR ALL OF US.
I ALWAYS KNEW YOU WOULD...
I'VE WAITED LONG ENOUGH, YOU SOFT GLOB OF SNOT.
EMPTY THE CASH REGISTER-- OR MY BULLETS WILL TEAR THROUGH YOUR BRAIN, BREAKING IT INTO MOIST, GOOEY LUMPS...
THAT'S IF I DON'T GIVE WITH A SURPRISE FROM UP THE SLEEVE, HUH, BRUNO?
CLERK GONE BILLY, ROB.
BRUNO GET NASTY, DON. YOU SEE.
BRUNO DON'T SHIV.
YOUR BOYS--USED TO BE MUTANTS, HUH? GUESS SINCE THEIR BOSS GOT HIS ASS FLATTENED THEY'LL WORK FOR ANYBODY.
GUESS WITH YOUR BOYFRIEND IN THE LOONY BIN YOU GOT TO PAY FOR YOUR OWN BODYWORK.
NICE WORK, TOO. CAN BARELY SEE THE STRETCH MARKS.
I'LL STRIP YOUR FLESH WITH MY TEETH...
THIEF! YOU'RE A THIEF!
SEBBIN LEBBIN SELLS THIS FOR TWO-FIFTY!

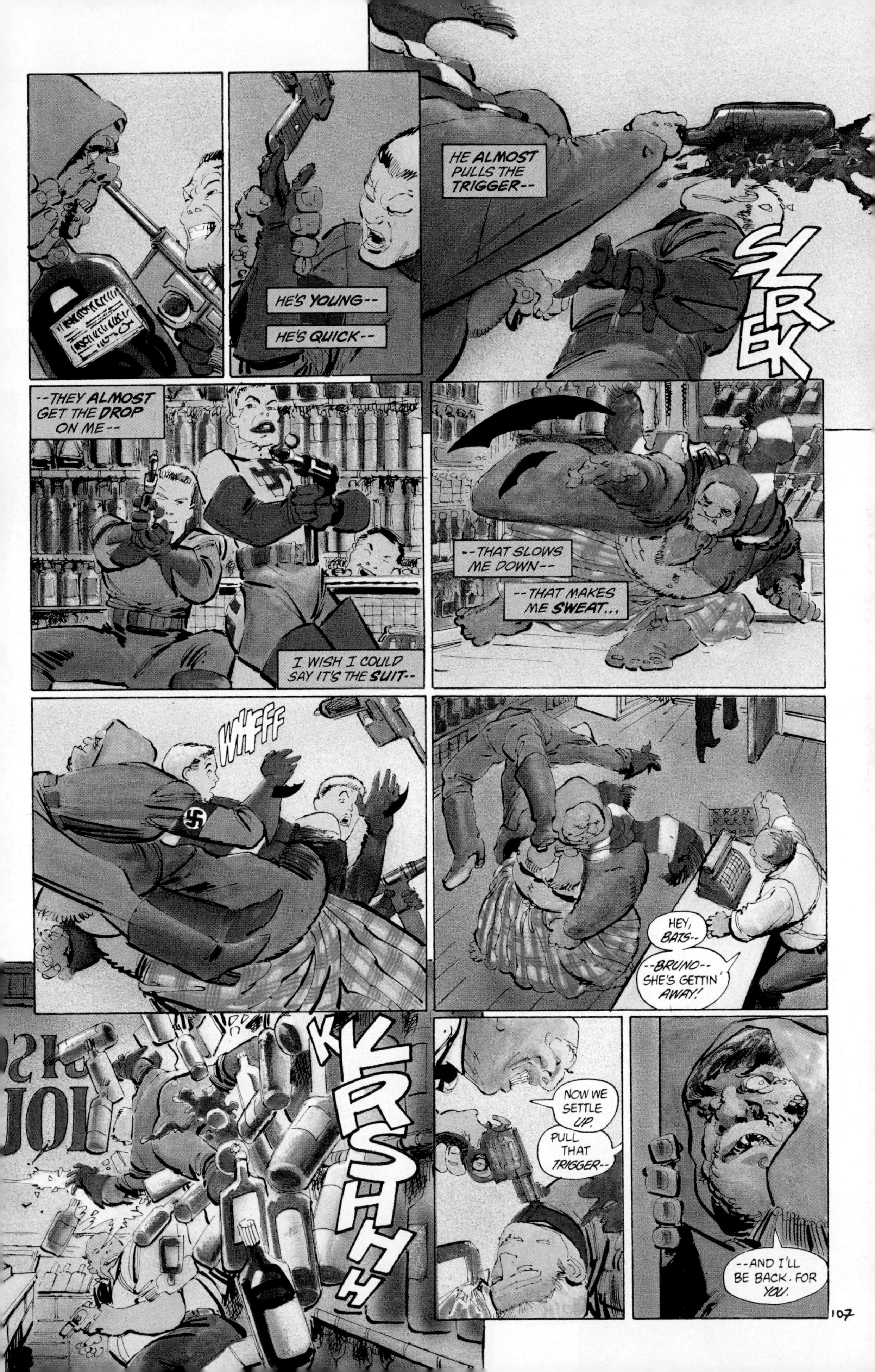
HE'S YOUNG--
HE'S QUICK--
HE ALMOST PULLS THE TRIGGER--
SLREK
--THEY ALMOST GET THE DROP ON ME--
I WISH I COULD SAY IT'S THE SUIT--
--THAT SLOWS ME DOWN--
--THAT MAKES ME SWEAT...
WHFFF
HEY, BATS--
--BRUNO-- SHE'S GETTIN' AWAY!
KKRSHHH
NOW WE SETTLE UP.
PULL THAT TRIGGER--
--AND I'LL BE BACK. FOR YOU.

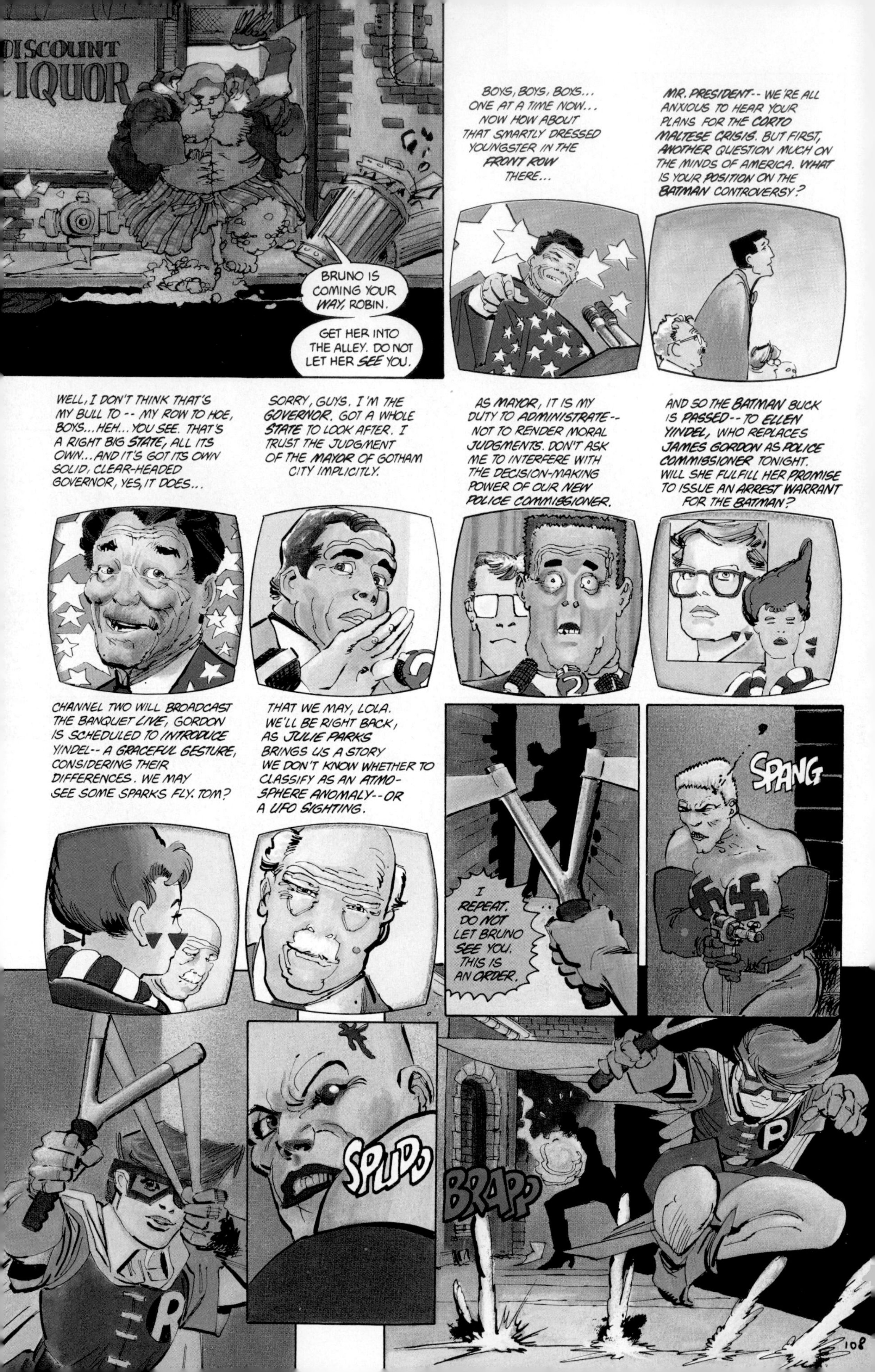
DISCOUNT
LIQUOR
BRUNO IS COMING YOUR WAY, ROBIN.
GET HER INTO THE ALLEY. DO NOT LET HER SEE YOU.
BOYS, BOYS, BOYS... ONE AT A TIME NOW... NOW HOW ABOUT THAT SMARTLY DRESSED YOUNGSTER IN THE FRONT ROW THERE...
MR. PRESIDENT-- WE'RE ALL ANXIOUS TO HEAR YOUR PLANS FOR THE CORTO MALTESE CRISIS. BUT FIRST, ANOTHER QUESTION MUCH ON THE MINDS OF AMERICA. WHAT IS YOUR POSITION ON THE BATMAN CONTROVERSY?
WELL, I DON'T THINK THAT'S MY BULL TO -- MY ROW TO HOE, BOYS... HEH... YOU SEE. THAT'S A RIGHT BIG STATE, ALL ITS OWN... AND IT'S GOT ITS OWN SOLID, CLEAR-HEADED GOVERNOR, YES, IT DOES...
SORRY, GUYS. I'M THE GOVERNOR. GOT A WHOLE STATE TO LOOK AFTER. I TRUST THE JUDGMENT OF THE MAYOR OF GOTHAM CITY IMPLICITLY.
AS MAYOR, IT IS MY DUTY TO ADMINISTRATE-- NOT TO RENDER MORAL JUDGMENTS. DON'T ASK ME TO INTERFERE WITH THE DECISION-MAKING POWER OF OUR NEW POLICE COMMISSIONER.
AND SO THE BATMAN BUCK IS PASSED-- TO ELLEN YINDEL, WHO REPLACES JAMES GORDON AS POLICE COMMISSIONER TONIGHT. WILL SHE FULFILL HER PROMISE TO ISSUE AN ARREST WARRANT FOR THE BATMAN?
CHANNEL TWO WILL BROADCAST THE BANQUET LIVE, GORDON IS SCHEDULED TO INTRODUCE YINDEL-- A GRACEFUL GESTURE, CONSIDERING THEIR DIFFERENCES. WE MAY SEE SOME SPARKS FLY. TOM?
THAT WE MAY, LOLA. WE'LL BE RIGHT BACK, AS JULIE PARKS BRINGS US A STORY WE DON'T KNOW WHETHER TO CLASSIFY AS AN ATMO-SPHERE ANOMALY-- OR A UFO SIGHTING.
I REPEAT. DO NOT LET BRUNO SEE YOU. THIS IS AN ORDER.
SPANG
SPUDD
BRAPP

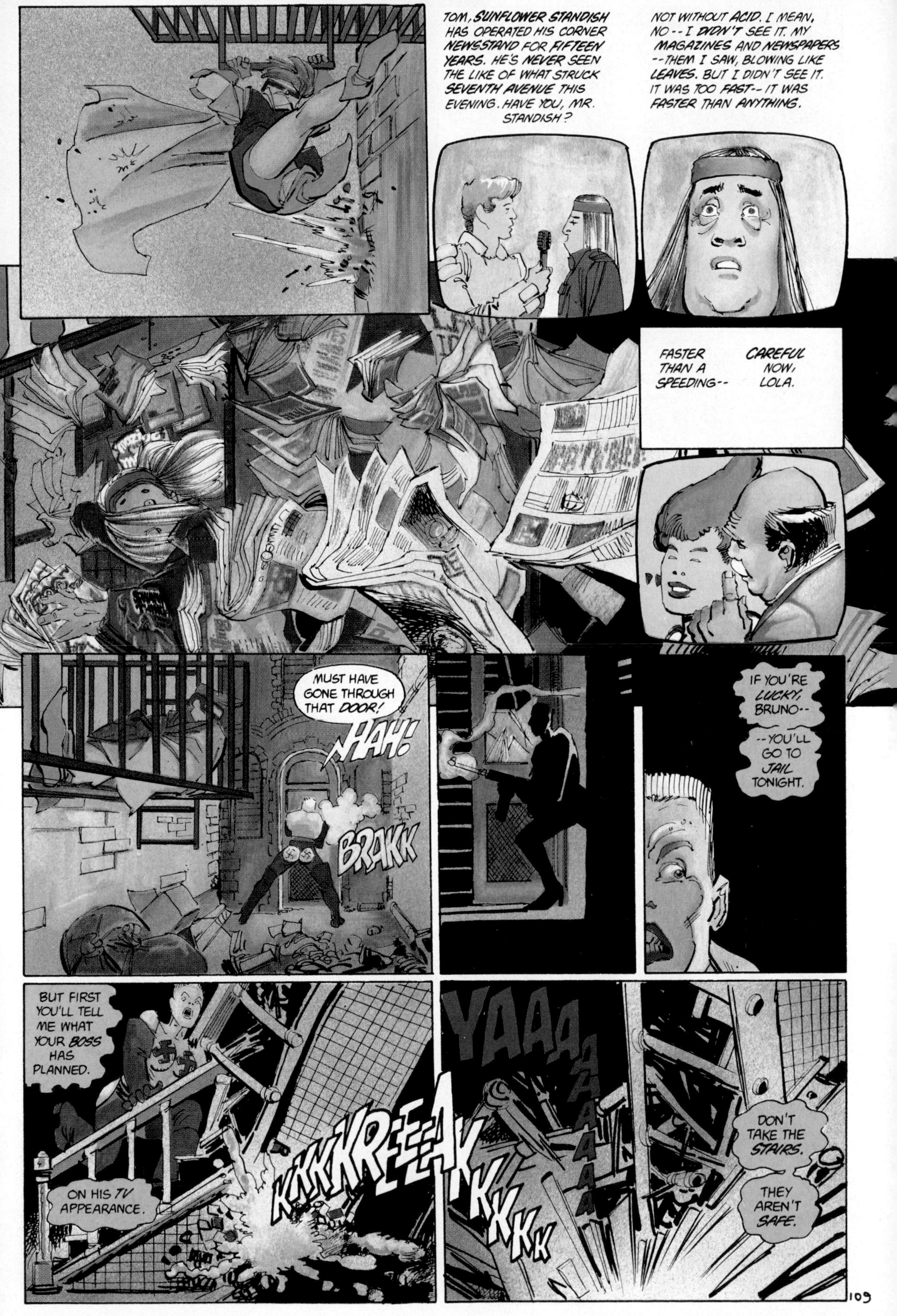
TOM, SUNFLOWER STANDISH HAS OPERATED HIS CORNER NEWSSTAND FOR FIFTEEN YEARS. HE'S NEVER SEEN THE LIKE OF WHAT STRUCK SEVENTH AVENUE THIS EVENING. HAVE YOU, MR. STANDISH?
NOT WITHOUT ACID. I MEAN, NO -- I DIDN'T SEE IT. MY MAGAZINES AND NEWSPAPERS -- THEM I SAW, BLOWING LIKE LEAVES. BUT I DIDN'T SEE IT. IT WAS TOO FAST -- IT WAS FASTER THAN ANYTHING.
FASTER THAN A SPEEDING--
CAREFUL NOW, LOLA.
MUST HAVE GONE THROUGH THAT DOOR!
HAH!
BRAKK
IF YOU'RE LUCKY, BRUNO--
--YOU'LL GO TO JAIL TONIGHT.
BUT FIRST YOU'LL TELL ME WHAT YOUR BOSS HAS PLANNED.
ON HIS TV APPEARANCE.
KKKKREEEAKKKKK
YAAAAAAAAAA
DON'T TAKE THE STAIRS.
THEY AREN'T SAFE.

NEVER MEANT-- TO GIVE HER TIME--

CHKCHAKK

-- TO COCK THAT THING--

BRAPP

THIS-- WOULD BE A STUPID DEATH...

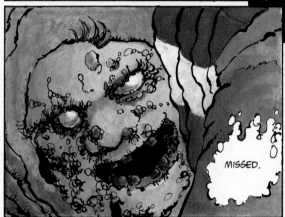

MISSED.

LUCKY--

--LUCKY OLD MAN...

ANOTHER BIZARRE INCIDENT--THIS ONE IN THE SOUTH STREET SUBWAY STATION. ADVERTISING AGENT BYRON BRASSBALLS TOLD REPORTERS...

I DIDN'T DO ANYTHING WRONG. I WAS JUST TRYING TO PROTECT MYSELF. THE SUBWAYS ARE DANGEROUS. YOU DON'T NEED ME TO TELL YOU THAT. SO THERE I WAS, ALONE IN THE STATION EXCEPT FOR THIS "BEGGAR"--I WANT THAT IN QUOTES--

--WHAT?...HOW WAS I TO KNOW HE DIDN'T HAVE A GUN? THEY NEVER SHOW YOU THAT UNTIL THEY'RE READY TO KILL YOU-- WHAT?...OH, SURE. THE CRUTCHES. A LOT OF THEM USE CRUTCHES. YOU KNOW WHAT I MEAN.

HEY--HE STARTED IT. AND IT WAS HIS CRUTCHES THAT TRIPPED HIM UP, BABE-- WHAT?...YOU BET HE YELLED. WANTED ME TO JUMP DOWN AND DIE WITH HIM. OF COURSE I RAN. WHO WOULDN'T? THEN SOMETHING HIT ME HARD--IN THE CHEST--

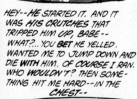

--HAVEN'T SEEN A **DOCTOR** YET, BUT I'M **SURE** I SLIPPED A **DISC** LANDING ON THE **TRACKS**... NO, I COULDN'T SEE. NOT A FRIGGING THING. THAT **WIND** KICKED UP TOO MUCH SOOT. SPENT A SECOND LISTENING TO THAT **BEGGAR** PRAY LIKE AN IDIOT...

...YES, I **AM** RELIGIOUS. BUT I'VE GOT THE **DECENCY** TO KEEP IT IN **CHURCH**. THEN I HEARD THE **SCREAM** OF TWISTING **METAL**-- **SHOUTS** FROM INSIDE THE TRAIN, PEOPLE **BITCHING**. FINALLY THE **SOOT** SETTLED...

...AND THERE IT **WAS**-- THE **TRAIN**, I MEAN--ITS FRONT END CRUSHED **INWARD**, LIKE IT RAN INTO SOMETHING... WELL, SOMETHING...

SOMETHING MORE POWERFUL THAN A LOCOMOTIVE, RIGHT, TOM?

LOLA--THE **LAST** THING WE NEED IS **TROUBLE** WITH THE **F.C.C.** ...

SOFTENING **UP**-- SHE'LL START **TALKING** SOON--

--WHAT'S THAT **SOUND**--

--THE **FLOOR**--

--IT'S **SHAKING**--

--NOT AN EARTHQUAKE. DO **NOT** PANIC. WHATEVER IT IS, IT'S **LOCALIZED**-- AND MOVING ACROSS GOTHAM'S **SOUTH** SIDE...

ONE WAY

NEWS4
WITH GORD... ...ING

RRRRRRRRAAMMMMBBBBB...

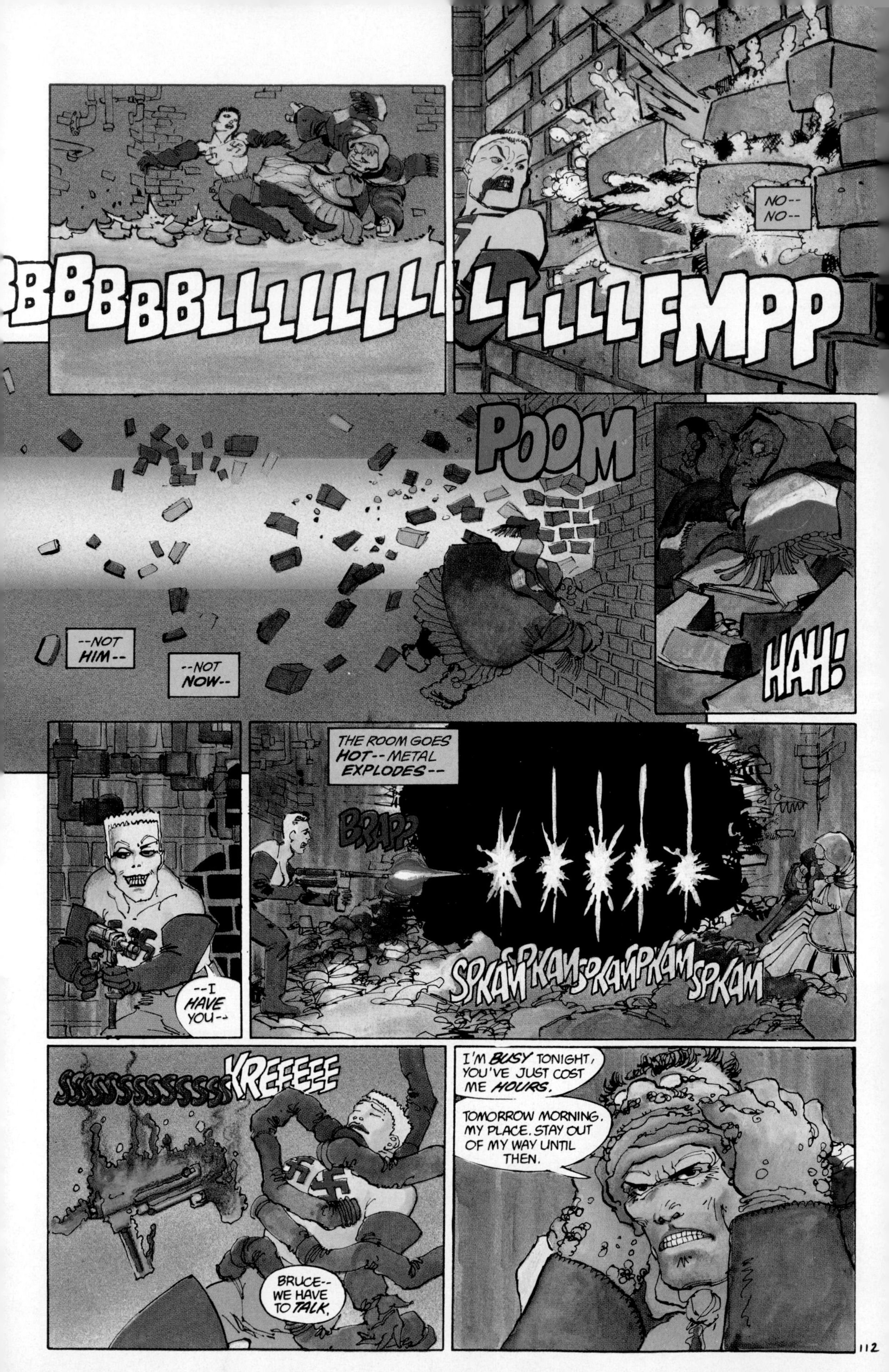
NO--
NO--
BBBBBLLLLLLLLLLLLLLFMPP
POOM
--NOT HIM--
--NOT NOW--
HAH!
THE ROOM GOES HOT-- METAL EXPLODES--
BRAPP
--I HAVE YOU--
SPKAM SPKAM SPKAM SPKAM SPKAM
SSSSSSSSSSSSKREEEEE
BRUCE-- WE HAVE TO TALK.
I'M BUSY TONIGHT, YOU'VE JUST COST ME HOURS.
TOMORROW MORNING. MY PLACE. STAY OUT OF MY WAY UNTIL THEN.

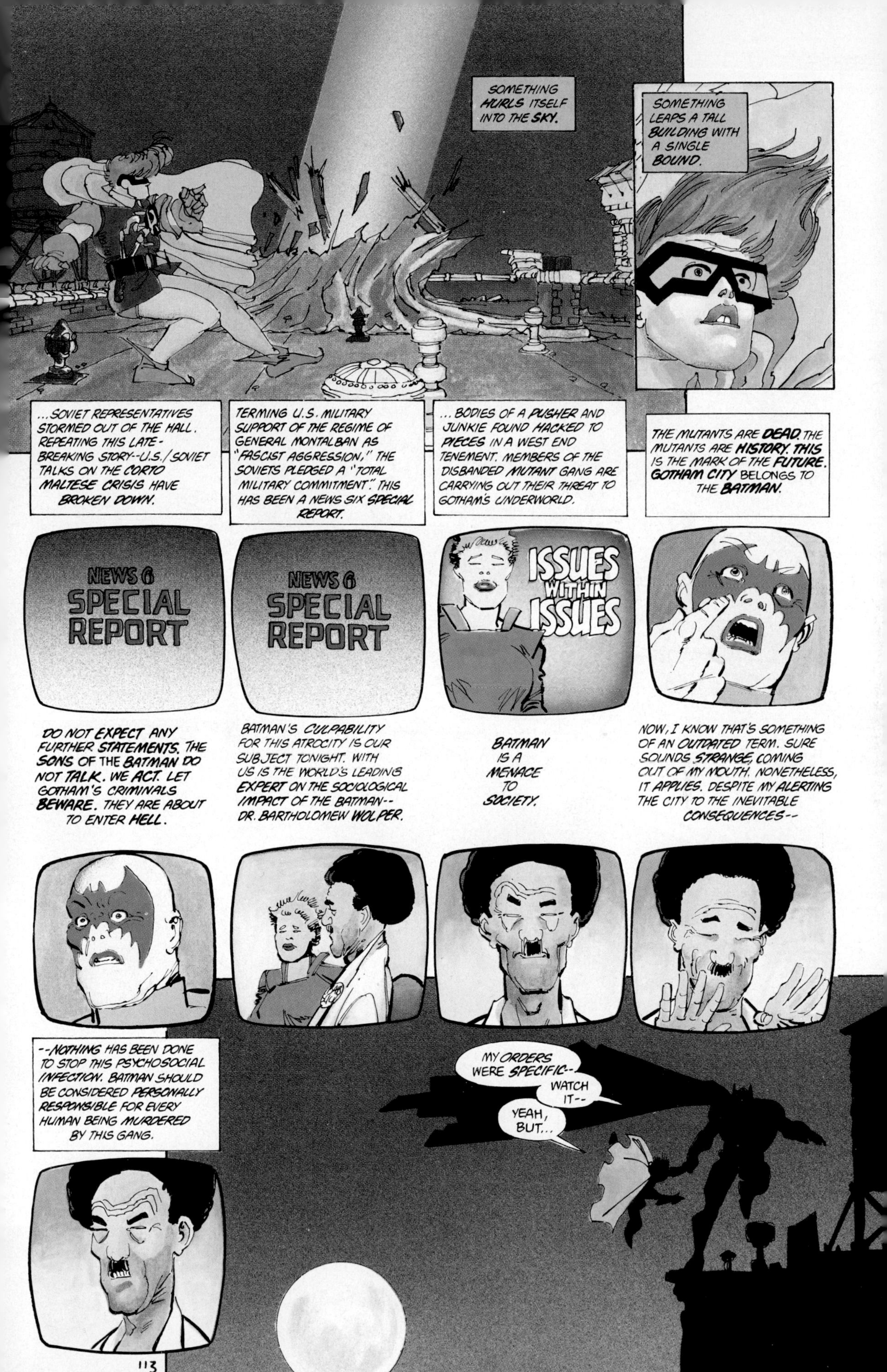

SOMETHING HURLS ITSELF INTO THE SKY.
SOMETHING LEAPS A TALL BUILDING WITH A SINGLE BOUND.
...SOVIET REPRESENTATIVES STORMED OUT OF THE HALL. REPEATING THIS LATE-BREAKING STORY--U.S./SOVIET TALKS ON THE CORTO MALTESE CRISIS HAVE BROKEN DOWN.
TERMING U.S. MILITARY SUPPORT OF THE REGIME OF GENERAL MONTALBAN AS "FASCIST AGGRESSION," THE SOVIETS PLEDGED A "TOTAL MILITARY COMMITMENT." THIS HAS BEEN A NEWS SIX SPECIAL REPORT.
...BODIES OF A PUSHER AND JUNKIE FOUND HACKED TO PIECES IN A WEST END TENEMENT. MEMBERS OF THE DISBANDED MUTANT GANG ARE CARRYING OUT THEIR THREAT TO GOTHAM'S UNDERWORLD.
THE MUTANTS ARE DEAD. THE MUTANTS ARE HISTORY. THIS IS THE MARK OF THE FUTURE. GOTHAM CITY BELONGS TO THE BATMAN.
NEWS 6 SPECIAL REPORT
NEWS 6 SPECIAL REPORT
ISSUES WITHIN ISSUES
DO NOT EXPECT ANY FURTHER STATEMENTS. THE SONS OF THE BATMAN DO NOT TALK. WE ACT. LET GOTHAM'S CRIMINALS BEWARE. THEY ARE ABOUT TO ENTER HELL.
BATMAN'S CULPABILITY FOR THIS ATROCITY IS OUR SUBJECT TONIGHT. WITH US IS THE WORLD'S LEADING EXPERT ON THE SOCIOLOGICAL IMPACT OF THE BATMAN-- DR. BARTHOLOMEW WOLPER.
BATMAN IS A MENACE TO SOCIETY.
NOW, I KNOW THAT'S SOMETHING OF AN OUTDATED TERM. SURE SOUNDS STRANGE, COMING OUT OF MY MOUTH. NONETHELESS, IT APPLIES. DESPITE MY ALERTING THE CITY TO THE INEVITABLE CONSEQUENCES--
--NOTHING HAS BEEN DONE TO STOP THIS PSYCHOSOCIAL INFECTION. BATMAN SHOULD BE CONSIDERED PERSONALLY RESPONSIBLE FOR EVERY HUMAN BEING MURDERED BY THIS GANG.
MY ORDERS WERE SPECIFIC--
WATCH IT--
YEAH, BUT...

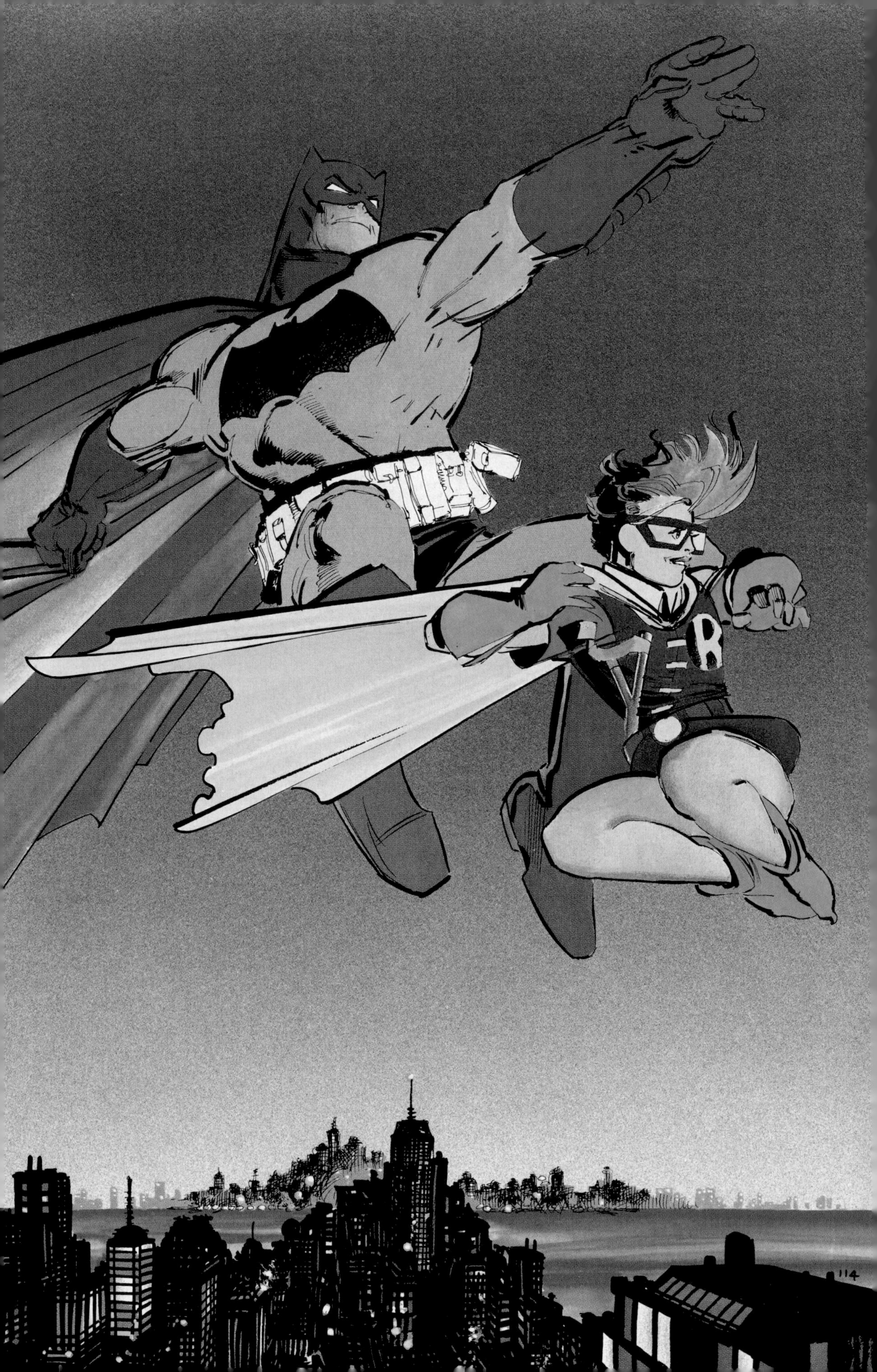
114

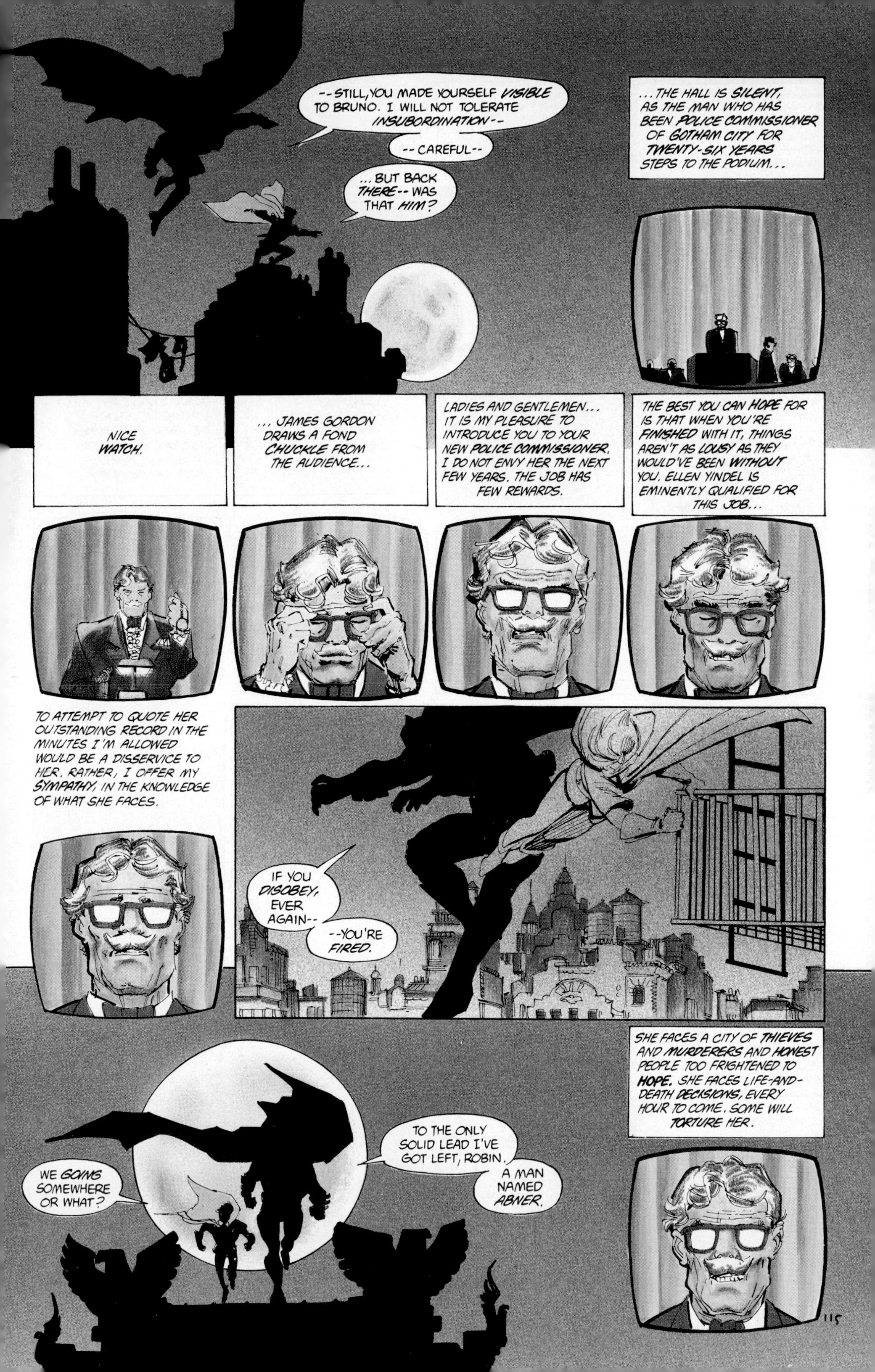
--STILL, YOU MADE YOURSELF VISIBLE TO BRUNO. I WILL NOT TOLERATE INSUBORDINATION--
--CAREFUL--
...BUT BACK THERE-- WAS THAT HIM?
...THE HALL IS SILENT, AS THE MAN WHO HAS BEEN POLICE COMMISSIONER OF GOTHAM CITY FOR TWENTY-SIX YEARS STEPS TO THE PODIUM...
NICE WATCH.
...JAMES GORDON DRAWS A FOND CHUCKLE FROM THE AUDIENCE...
LADIES AND GENTLEMEN... IT IS MY PLEASURE TO INTRODUCE YOU TO YOUR NEW POLICE COMMISSIONER. I DO NOT ENVY HER THE NEXT FEW YEARS. THE JOB HAS FEW REWARDS.
THE BEST YOU CAN HOPE FOR IS THAT WHEN YOU'RE FINISHED WITH IT, THINGS AREN'T AS LOUSY AS THEY WOULD'VE BEEN WITHOUT YOU. ELLEN YINDEL IS EMINENTLY QUALIFIED FOR THIS JOB...
TO ATTEMPT TO QUOTE HER OUTSTANDING RECORD IN THE MINUTES I'M ALLOWED WOULD BE A DISSERVICE TO HER. RATHER, I OFFER MY SYMPATHY, IN THE KNOWLEDGE OF WHAT SHE FACES.
IF YOU DISOBEY, EVER AGAIN--
--YOU'RE FIRED.
SHE FACES A CITY OF THIEVES AND MURDERERS AND HONEST PEOPLE TOO FRIGHTENED TO HOPE. SHE FACES LIFE-AND-DEATH DECISIONS, EVERY HOUR TO COME. SOME WILL TORTURE HER.
WE GOING SOMEWHERE OR WHAT?
TO THE ONLY SOLID LEAD I'VE GOT LEFT, ROBIN.
A MAN NAMED ABNER.

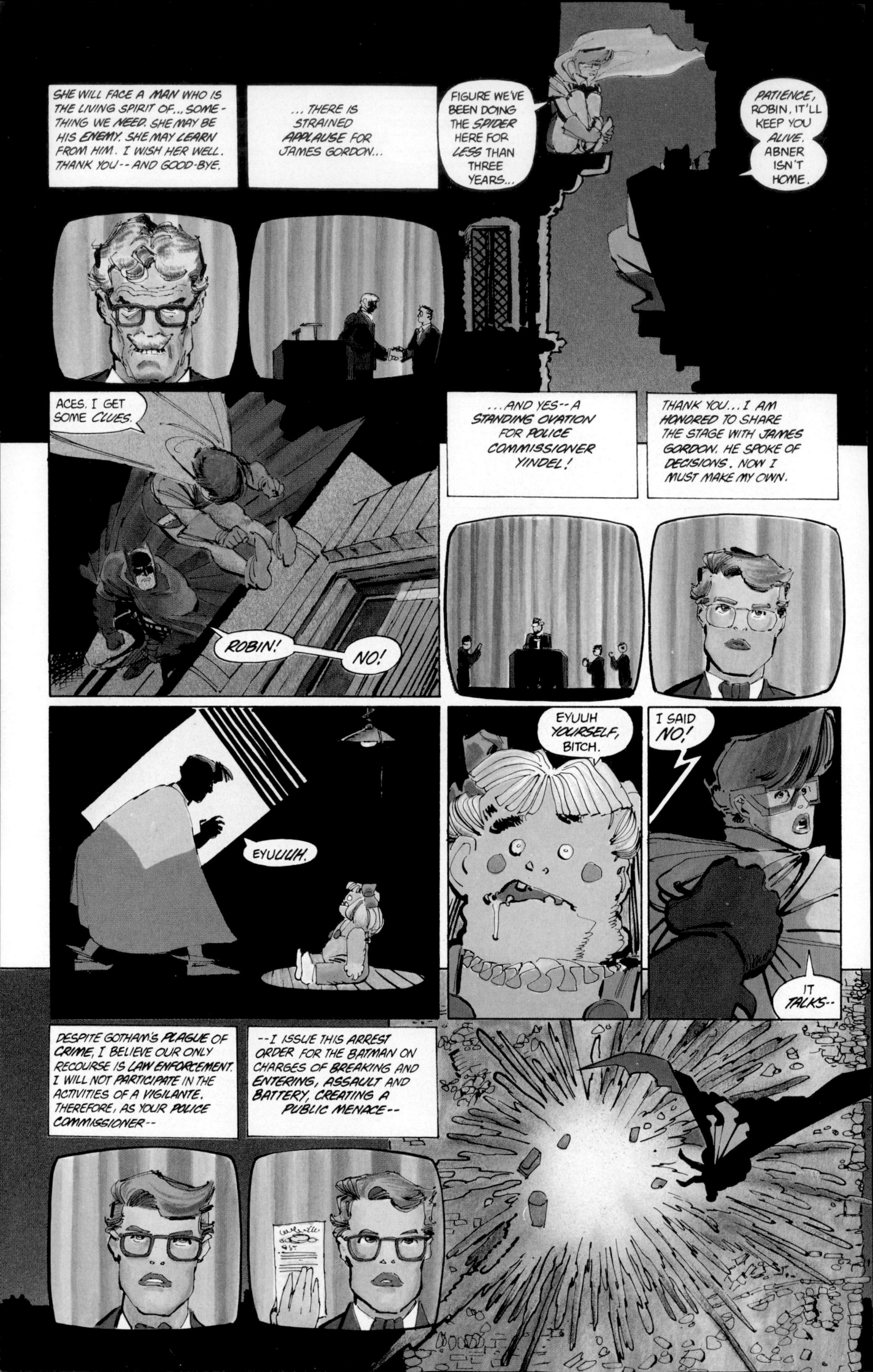

SHE WILL FACE A MAN WHO IS THE LIVING SPIRIT OF... SOME-THING WE NEED. SHE MAY BE HIS ENEMY. SHE MAY LEARN FROM HIM. I WISH HER WELL. THANK YOU-- AND GOOD-BYE.
... THERE IS STRAINED APPLAUSE FOR JAMES GORDON...
FIGURE WE'VE BEEN DOING THE SPIDER HERE FOR LESS THAN THREE YEARS...
PATIENCE, ROBIN, IT'LL KEEP YOU ALIVE. ABNER ISN'T HOME.
ACES. I GET SOME CLUES.
ROBIN!
NO!
...AND YES-- A STANDING OVATION FOR POLICE COMMISSIONER YINDEL!
THANK YOU... I AM HONORED TO SHARE THE STAGE WITH JAMES GORDON. HE SPOKE OF DECISIONS. NOW I MUST MAKE MY OWN.
EYUUUH.
EYUUH YOURSELF, BITCH.
I SAID NO!
IT TALKS--
DESPITE GOTHAM'S PLAGUE OF CRIME, I BELIEVE OUR ONLY RECOURSE IS LAW ENFORCEMENT. I WILL NOT PARTICIPATE IN THE ACTIVITIES OF A VIGILANTE. THEREFORE, AS YOUR POLICE COMMISSIONER--
--I ISSUE THIS ARREST ORDER FOR THE BATMAN ON CHARGES OF BREAKING AND ENTERING, ASSAULT AND BATTERY, CREATING A PUBLIC MENACE--

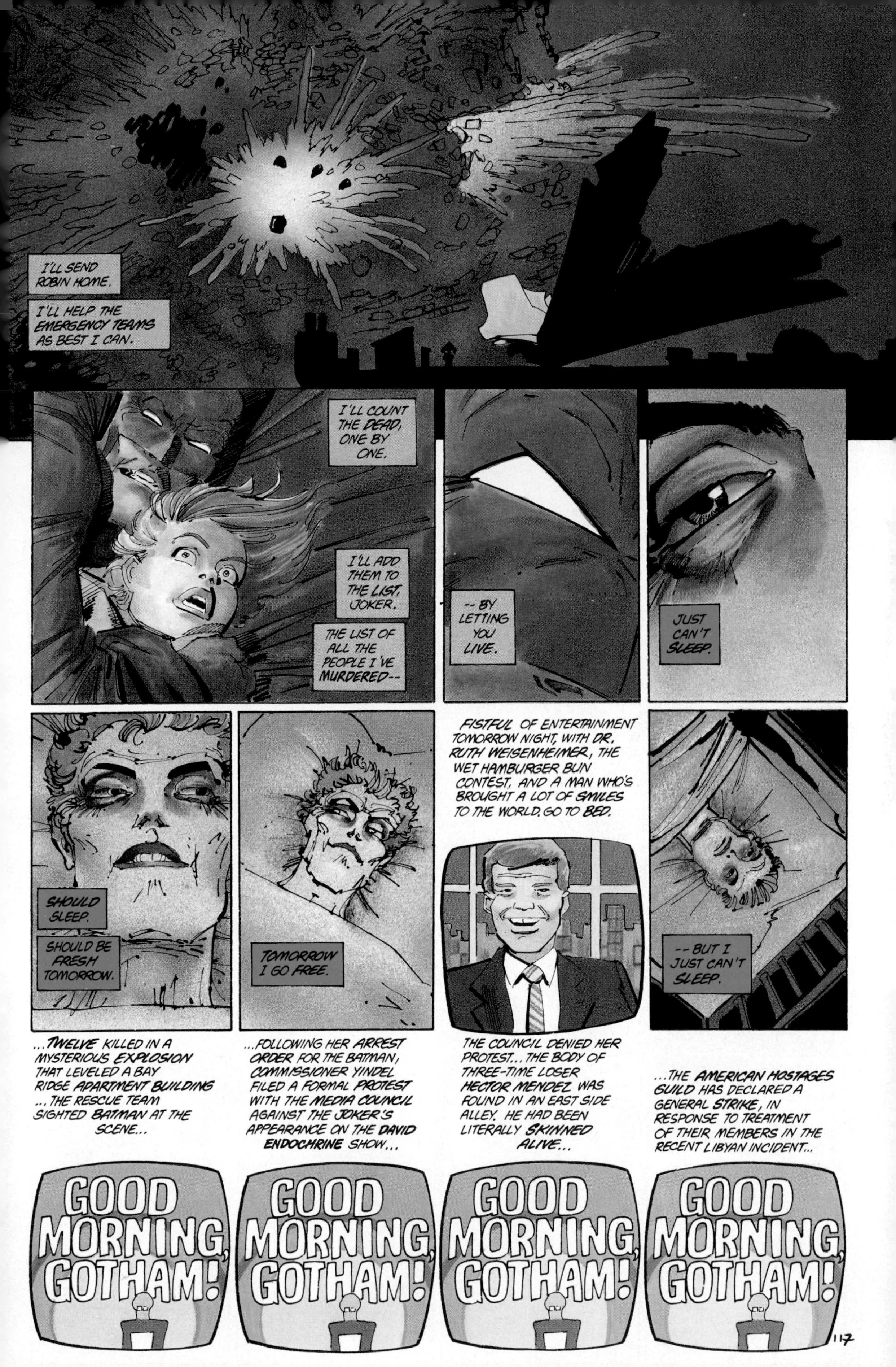

I'LL SEND ROBIN HOME.
I'LL HELP THE EMERGENCY TEAMS AS BEST I CAN.
I'LL COUNT THE DEAD, ONE BY ONE.
I'LL ADD THEM TO THE LIST, JOKER.
THE LIST OF ALL THE PEOPLE I'VE MURDERED--
--BY LETTING YOU LIVE.
JUST CAN'T SLEEP.
SHOULD SLEEP.
SHOULD BE FRESH TOMORROW.
TOMORROW I GO FREE.
FISTFUL OF ENTERTAINMENT TOMORROW NIGHT, WITH DR. RUTH WEISENHEIMER, THE WET HAMBURGER BUN CONTEST, AND A MAN WHO'S BROUGHT A LOT OF SMILES TO THE WORLD. GO TO BED.
--BUT I JUST CAN'T SLEEP.
...TWELVE KILLED IN A MYSTERIOUS EXPLOSION THAT LEVELED A BAY RIDGE APARTMENT BUILDING ...THE RESCUE TEAM SIGHTED BATMAN AT THE SCENE...
...FOLLOWING HER ARREST ORDER FOR THE BATMAN, COMMISSIONER YINDEL FILED A FORMAL PROTEST WITH THE MEDIA COUNCIL AGAINST THE JOKER'S APPEARANCE ON THE DAVID ENDOCHRINE SHOW...
THE COUNCIL DENIED HER PROTEST... THE BODY OF THREE-TIME LOSER HECTOR MENDEZ WAS FOUND IN AN EAST SIDE ALLEY. HE HAD BEEN LITERALLY SKINNED ALIVE...
...THE AMERICAN HOSTAGES GUILD HAS DECLARED A GENERAL STRIKE, IN RESPONSE TO TREATMENT OF THEIR MEMBERS IN THE RECENT LIBYAN INCIDENT...
GOOD MORNING, GOTHAM!
GOOD MORNING, GOTHAM!
GOOD MORNING, GOTHAM!
GOOD MORNING, GOTHAM!

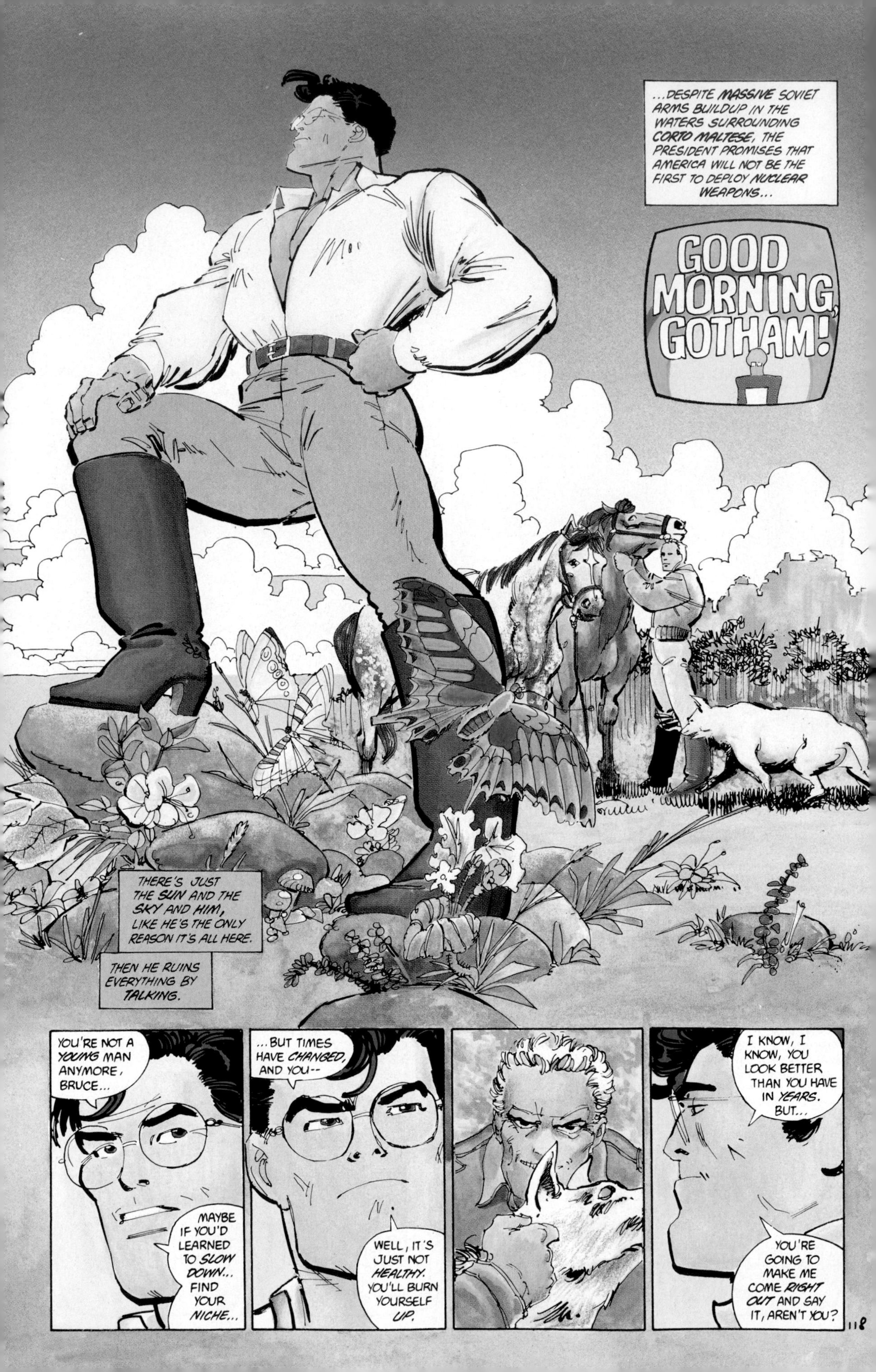

...DESPITE MASSIVE SOVIET ARMS BUILDUP IN THE WATERS SURROUNDING CORTO MALTESE, THE PRESIDENT PROMISES THAT AMERICA WILL NOT BE THE FIRST TO DEPLOY NUCLEAR WEAPONS...
GOOD MORNING, GOTHAM!
THERE'S JUST THE SUN AND THE SKY AND HIM, LIKE HE'S THE ONLY REASON IT'S ALL HERE.
THEN HE RUINS EVERYTHING BY TALKING.
YOU'RE NOT A YOUNG MAN ANYMORE, BRUCE...
MAYBE IF YOU'D LEARNED TO SLOW DOWN... FIND YOUR NICHE...
...BUT TIMES HAVE CHANGED, AND YOU--
WELL, IT'S JUST NOT HEALTHY. YOU'LL BURN YOURSELF UP.
I KNOW, I KNOW, YOU LOOK BETTER THAN YOU HAVE IN YEARS. BUT...
YOU'RE GOING TO MAKE ME COME RIGHT OUT AND SAY IT, AREN'T YOU?

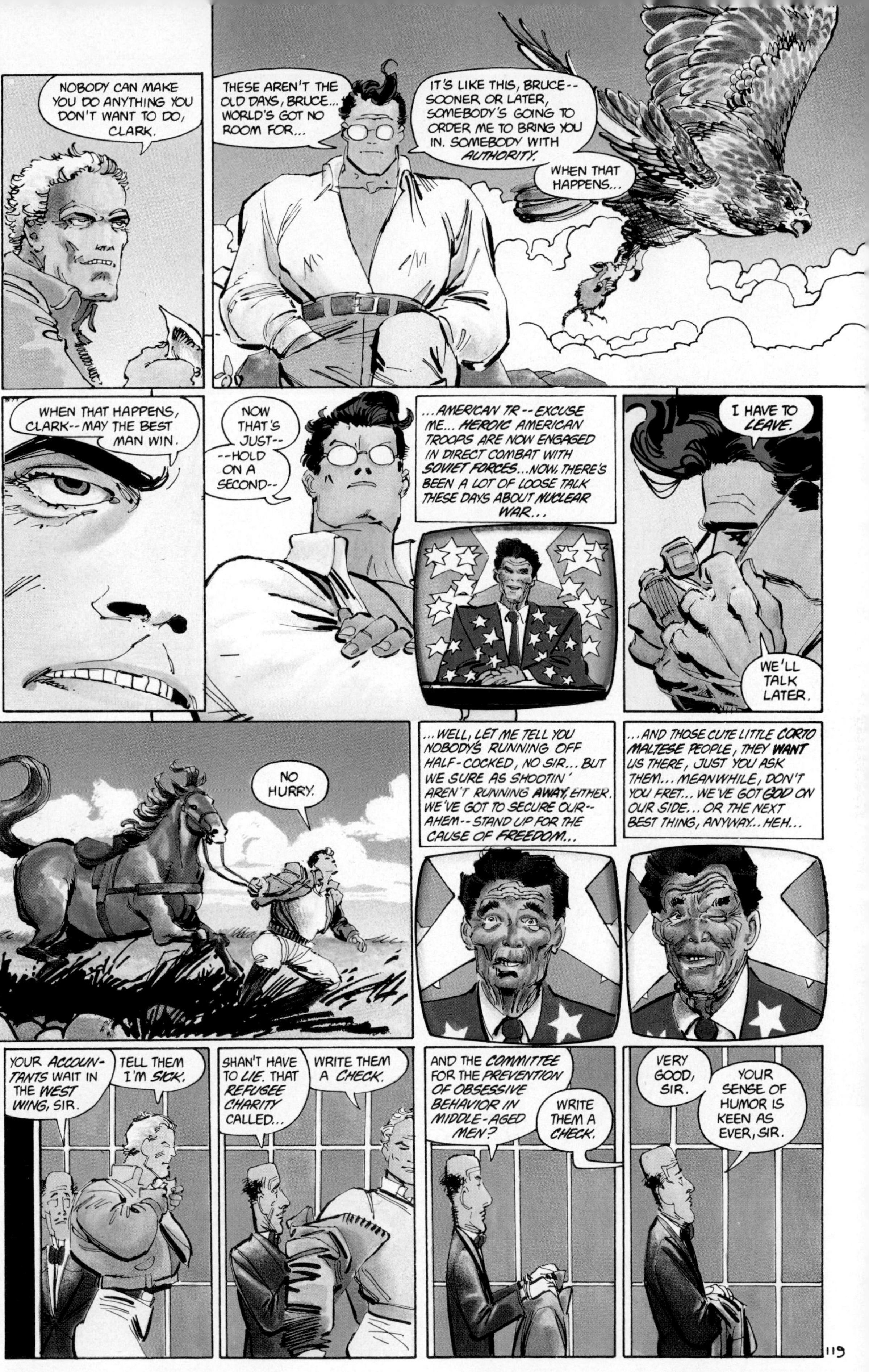
NOBODY CAN MAKE YOU DO ANYTHING YOU DON'T WANT TO DO, CLARK.
THESE AREN'T THE OLD DAYS, BRUCE... WORLD'S GOT NO ROOM FOR...
IT'S LIKE THIS, BRUCE-- SOONER OR LATER, SOMEBODY'S GOING TO ORDER ME TO BRING YOU IN. SOMEBODY WITH AUTHORITY.
WHEN THAT HAPPENS...
WHEN THAT HAPPENS, CLARK-- MAY THE BEST MAN WIN.
NOW THAT'S JUST--
--HOLD ON A SECOND--
...AMERICAN TR--EXCUSE ME... HEROIC AMERICAN TROOPS ARE NOW ENGAGED IN DIRECT COMBAT WITH SOVIET FORCES...NOW, THERE'S BEEN A LOT OF LOOSE TALK THESE DAYS ABOUT NUCLEAR WAR...
I HAVE TO LEAVE.
WE'LL TALK LATER.
NO HURRY.
...WELL, LET ME TELL YOU NOBODY'S RUNNING OFF HALF-COCKED, NO SIR... BUT WE SURE AS SHOOTIN' AREN'T RUNNING AWAY, EITHER. WE'VE GOT TO SECURE OUR-- AHEM-- STAND UP FOR THE CAUSE OF FREEDOM...
...AND THOSE CUTE LITTLE CORTO MALTESE PEOPLE, THEY WANT US THERE, JUST YOU ASK THEM... MEANWHILE, DON'T YOU FRET... WE'VE GOT GOD ON OUR SIDE... OR THE NEXT BEST THING, ANYWAY... HEH...
YOUR ACCOUNTANTS WAIT IN THE WEST WING, SIR.
TELL THEM I'M SICK.
SHAN'T HAVE TO LIE. THAT REFUGEE CHARITY CALLED...
WRITE THEM A CHECK.
AND THE COMMITTEE FOR THE PREVENTION OF OBSESSIVE BEHAVIOR IN MIDDLE-AGED MEN?
WRITE THEM A CHECK.
VERY GOOD, SIR.
YOUR SENSE OF HUMOR IS KEEN AS EVER, SIR.

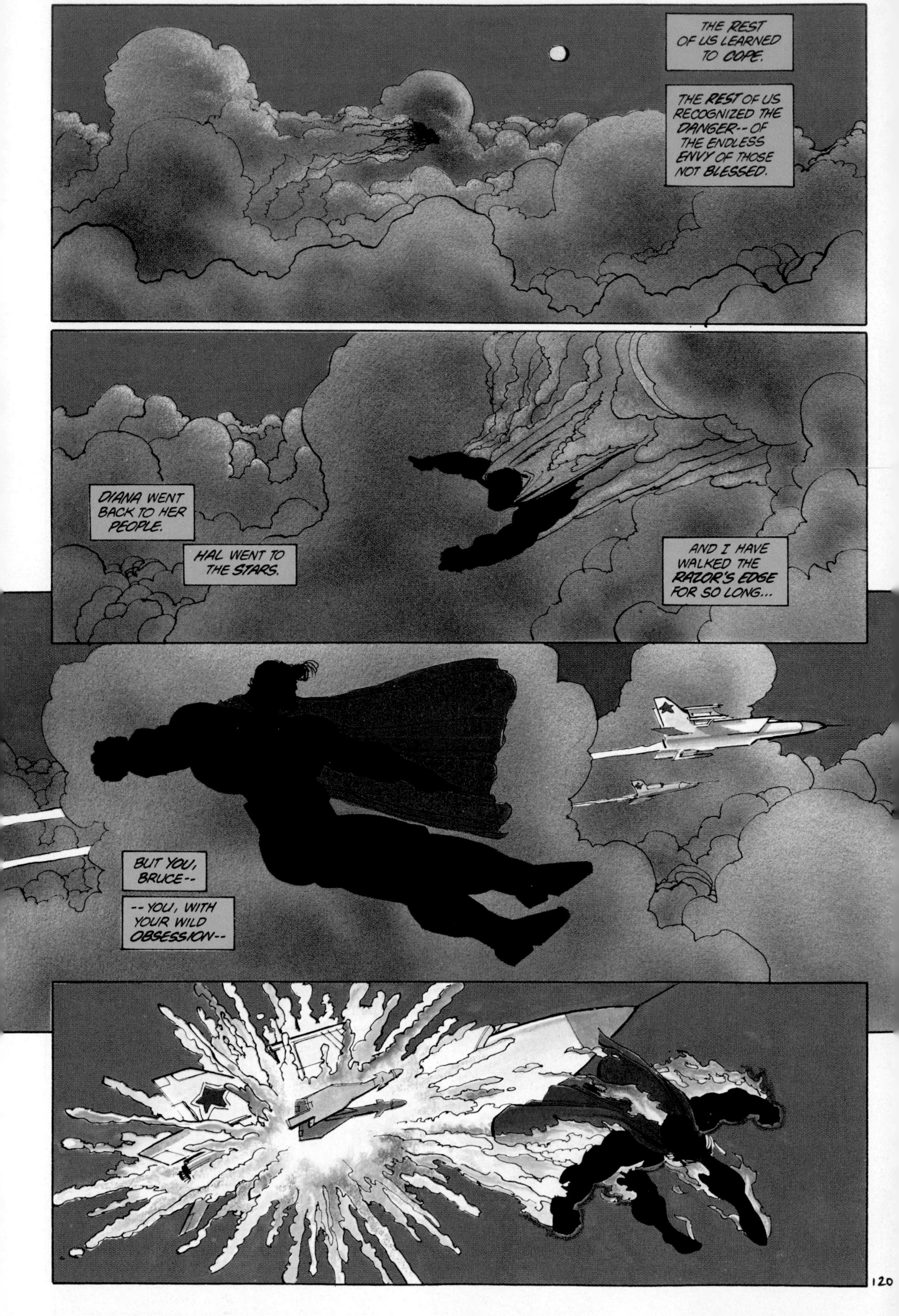
THE REST OF US LEARNED TO COPE.
THE REST OF US RECOGNIZED THE DANGER-- OF THE ENDLESS ENVY OF THOSE NOT BLESSED.
DIANA WENT BACK TO HER PEOPLE.
HAL WENT TO THE STARS.
AND I HAVE WALKED THE RAZOR'S EDGE FOR SO LONG...
BUT YOU, BRUCE--
--YOU, WITH YOUR WILD OBSESSION--

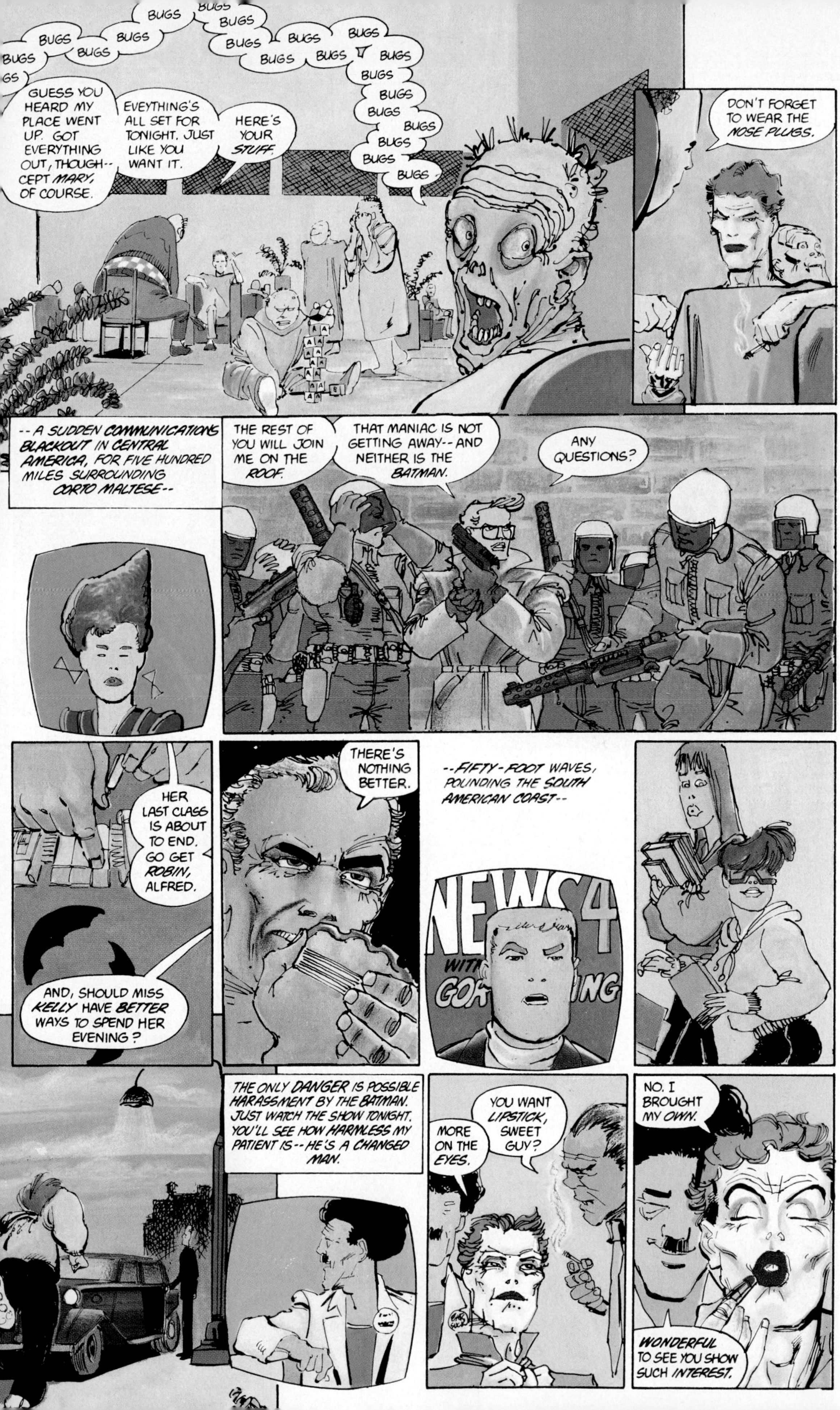
BUGS BUGS BUGS BUGS BUGS BUGS BUGS BUGS BUGS BUGS BUGS BUGS BUGS BUGS BUGS BUGS BUGS BUGS
GUESS YOU HEARD MY PLACE WENT UP. GOT EVERYTHING OUT, THOUGH-- CEPT MARY, OF COURSE.
EVEYTHING'S ALL SET FOR TONIGHT. JUST LIKE YOU WANT IT.
HERE'S YOUR STUFF.
DON'T FORGET TO WEAR THE NOSE PLUGS.
--A SUDDEN COMMUNICATIONS BLACKOUT IN CENTRAL AMERICA, FOR FIVE HUNDRED MILES SURROUNDING CORTO MALTESE--
THE REST OF YOU WILL JOIN ME ON THE ROOF.
THAT MANIAC IS NOT GETTING AWAY-- AND NEITHER IS THE BATMAN.
ANY QUESTIONS?
HER LAST CLASS IS ABOUT TO END. GO GET ROBIN, ALFRED.
AND, SHOULD MISS KELLY HAVE BETTER WAYS TO SPEND HER EVENING?
THERE'S NOTHING BETTER.
--FIFTY-FOOT WAVES, POUNDING THE SOUTH AMERICAN COAST--
NEWS 4
THE ONLY DANGER IS POSSIBLE HARASSMENT BY THE BATMAN. JUST WATCH THE SHOW TONIGHT. YOU'LL SEE HOW HARMLESS MY PATIENT IS-- HE'S A CHANGED MAN.
MORE ON THE EYES.
YOU WANT LIPSTICK, SWEET GUY?
NO. I BROUGHT MY OWN.
WONDERFUL TO SEE YOU SHOW SUCH INTEREST.

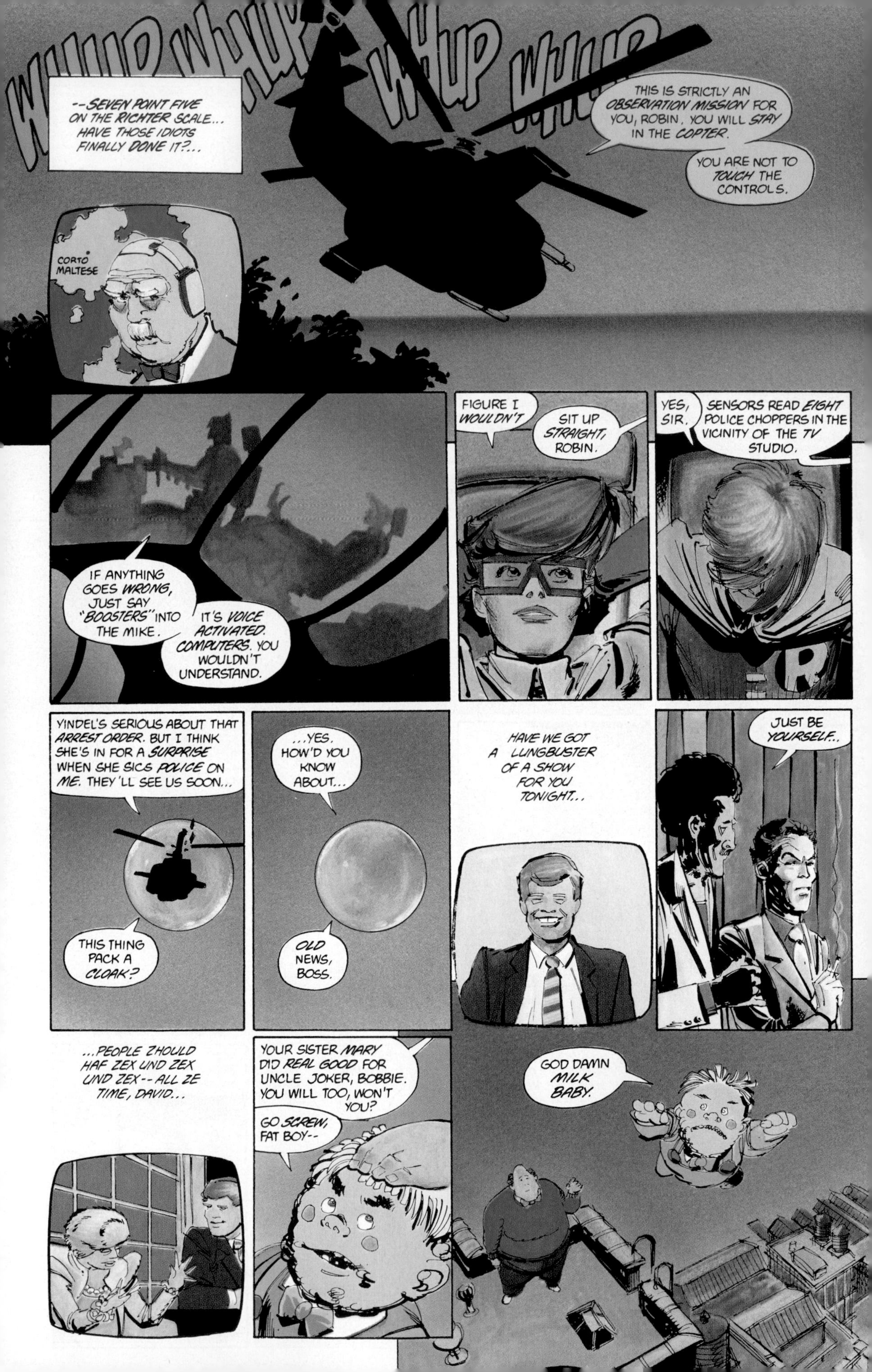
WHUP WHUP WHUP WHUP
--SEVEN POINT FIVE ON THE RICHTER SCALE... HAVE THOSE IDIOTS FINALLY DONE IT?...
THIS IS STRICTLY AN OBSERVATION MISSION FOR YOU, ROBIN. YOU WILL STAY IN THE COPTER.
YOU ARE NOT TO TOUCH THE CONTROLS.
CORTO MALTESE
IF ANYTHING GOES WRONG, JUST SAY "BOOSTERS" INTO THE MIKE.
IT'S VOICE ACTIVATED. COMPUTERS. YOU WOULDN'T UNDERSTAND.
FIGURE I WOULDN'T
SIT UP STRAIGHT, ROBIN.
YES, SIR.
SENSORS READ EIGHT POLICE CHOPPERS IN THE VICINITY OF THE TV STUDIO.
YINDEL'S SERIOUS ABOUT THAT ARREST ORDER. BUT I THINK SHE'S IN FOR A SURPRISE WHEN SHE SICS POLICE ON ME. THEY'LL SEE US SOON...
THIS THING PACK A CLOAK?
...YES. HOW'D YOU KNOW ABOUT...
OLD NEWS, BOSS.
HAVE WE GOT A LUNGBUSTER OF A SHOW FOR YOU TONIGHT...
JUST BE YOURSELF...
...PEOPLE ZHOULD HAF ZEX UND ZEX UND ZEX--ALL ZE TIME, DAVID...
YOUR SISTER MARY DID REAL GOOD FOR UNCLE JOKER, BOBBIE. YOU WILL TOO, WON'T YOU?
GO SCREW, FAT BOY--
GOD DAMN MILK BABY.

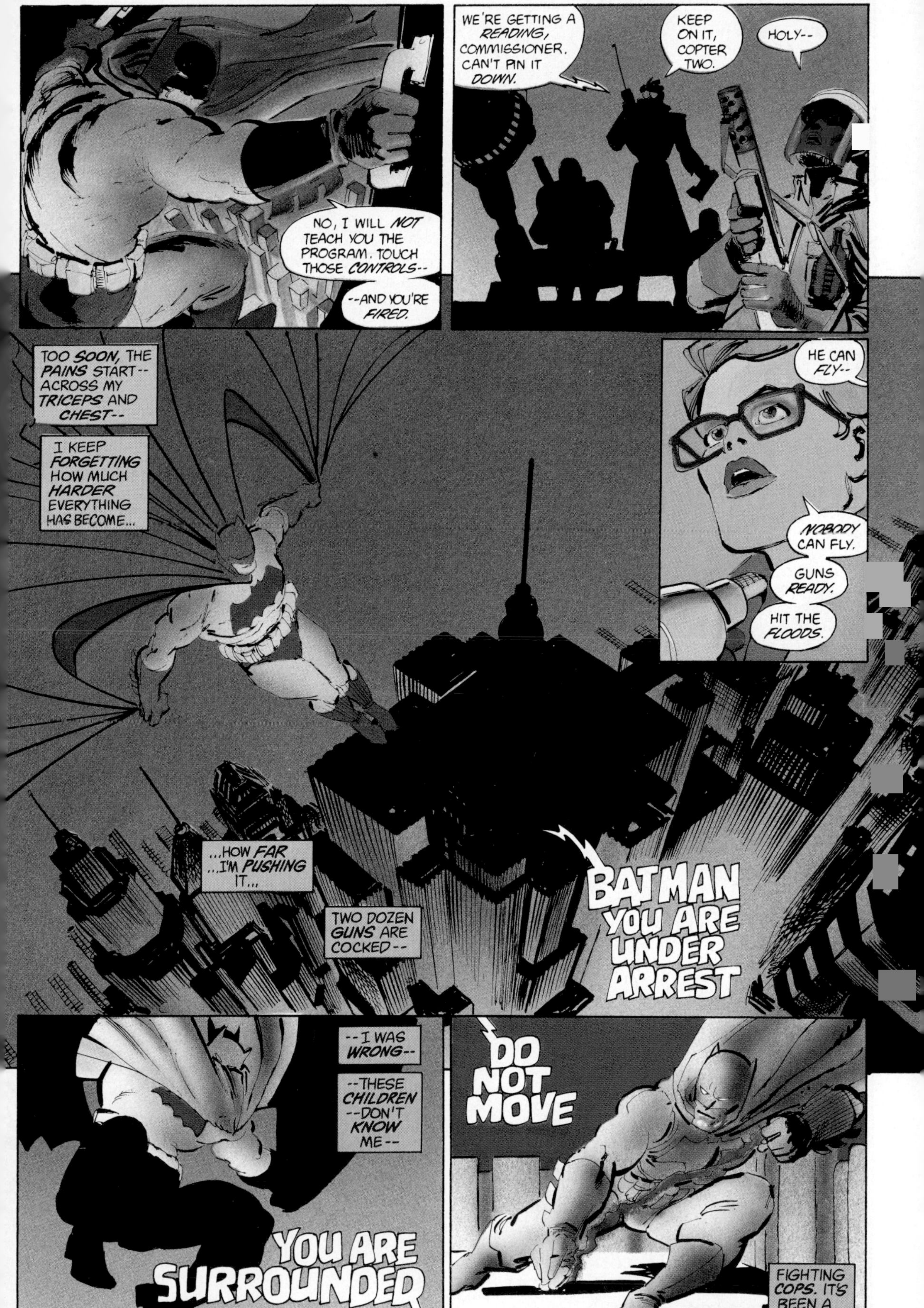
NO, I WILL NOT TEACH YOU THE PROGRAM. TOUCH THOSE CONTROLS--
--AND YOU'RE FIRED.
WE'RE GETTING A READING, COMMISSIONER. CAN'T PIN IT DOWN.
KEEP ON IT, COPTER TWO.
HOLY--
TOO SOON, THE PAINS START-- ACROSS MY TRICEPS AND CHEST--
I KEEP FORGETTING HOW MUCH HARDER EVERYTHING HAS BECOME...
HE CAN FLY--
NOBODY CAN FLY.
GUNS READY.
HIT THE FLOODS.
...HOW FAR ...I'M PUSHING IT...
TWO DOZEN GUNS ARE COCKED--
BATMAN YOU ARE UNDER ARREST
--I WAS WRONG--
--THESE CHILDREN --DON'T KNOW ME--
YOU ARE SURROUNDED
DO NOT MOVE
FIGHTING COPS. IT'S BEEN A WHILE...

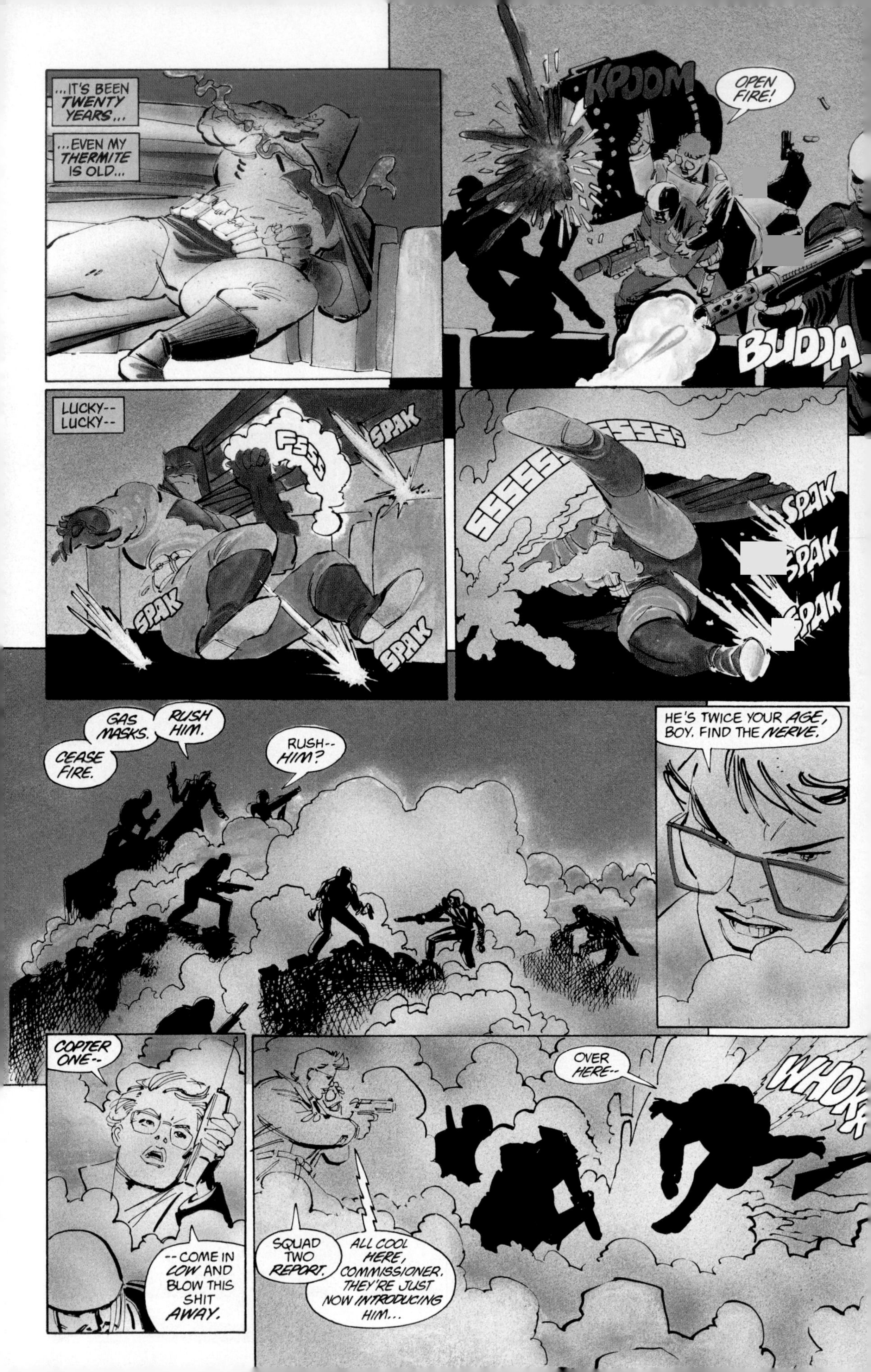

...IT'S BEEN TWENTY YEARS...
...EVEN MY THERMITE IS OLD...
KPJOOM
OPEN FIRE!
BUDDA
LUCKY-- LUCKY--
FSSS
SPAK
SPAK
SPAK
SSSSSSSSSSS
SPAK
SPAK
SPAK
GAS MASKS.
RUSH HIM.
CEASE FIRE.
RUSH-- HIM?
HE'S TWICE YOUR AGE, BOY. FIND THE NERVE.
COPTER ONE--
--COME IN LOW AND BLOW THIS SHIT AWAY.
OVER HERE--
WHOK
SQUAD TWO REPORT.
ALL COOL HERE, COMMISSIONER. THEY'RE JUST NOW INTRODUCING HIM...

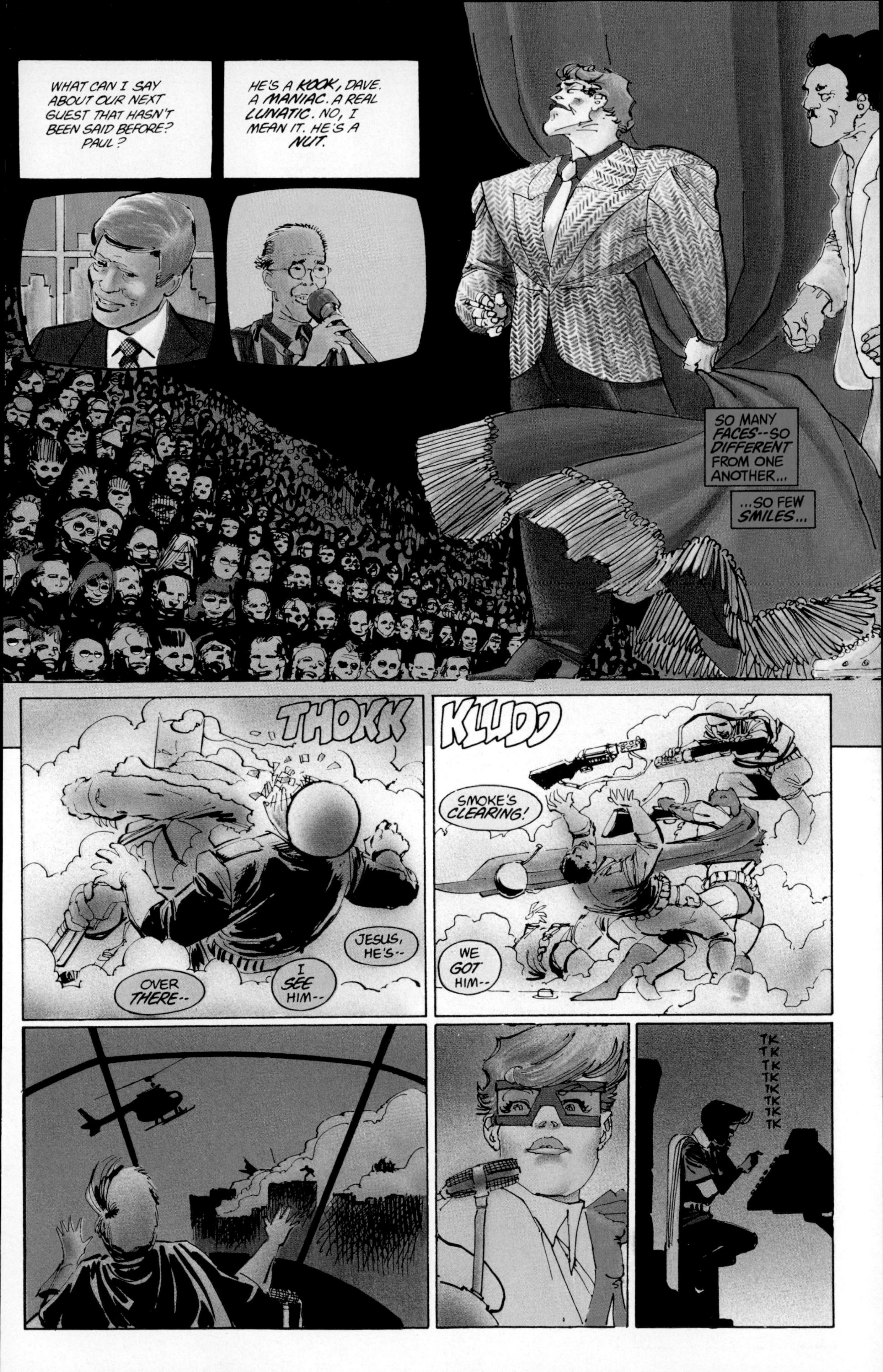
WHAT CAN I SAY ABOUT OUR NEXT GUEST THAT HASN'T BEEN SAID BEFORE? PAUL?
HE'S A KOOK, DAVE. A MANIAC. A REAL LUNATIC. NO, I MEAN IT. HE'S A NUT.
SO MANY FACES--SO DIFFERENT FROM ONE ANOTHER...
...SO FEW SMILES...
THOKK
OVER THERE--
I SEE HIM--
JESUS, HE'S--
KLUDD
SMOKE'S CLEARING!
WE GOT HIM--
TK TK TK TK TK TK TK TK TK TK TK TK TK TK

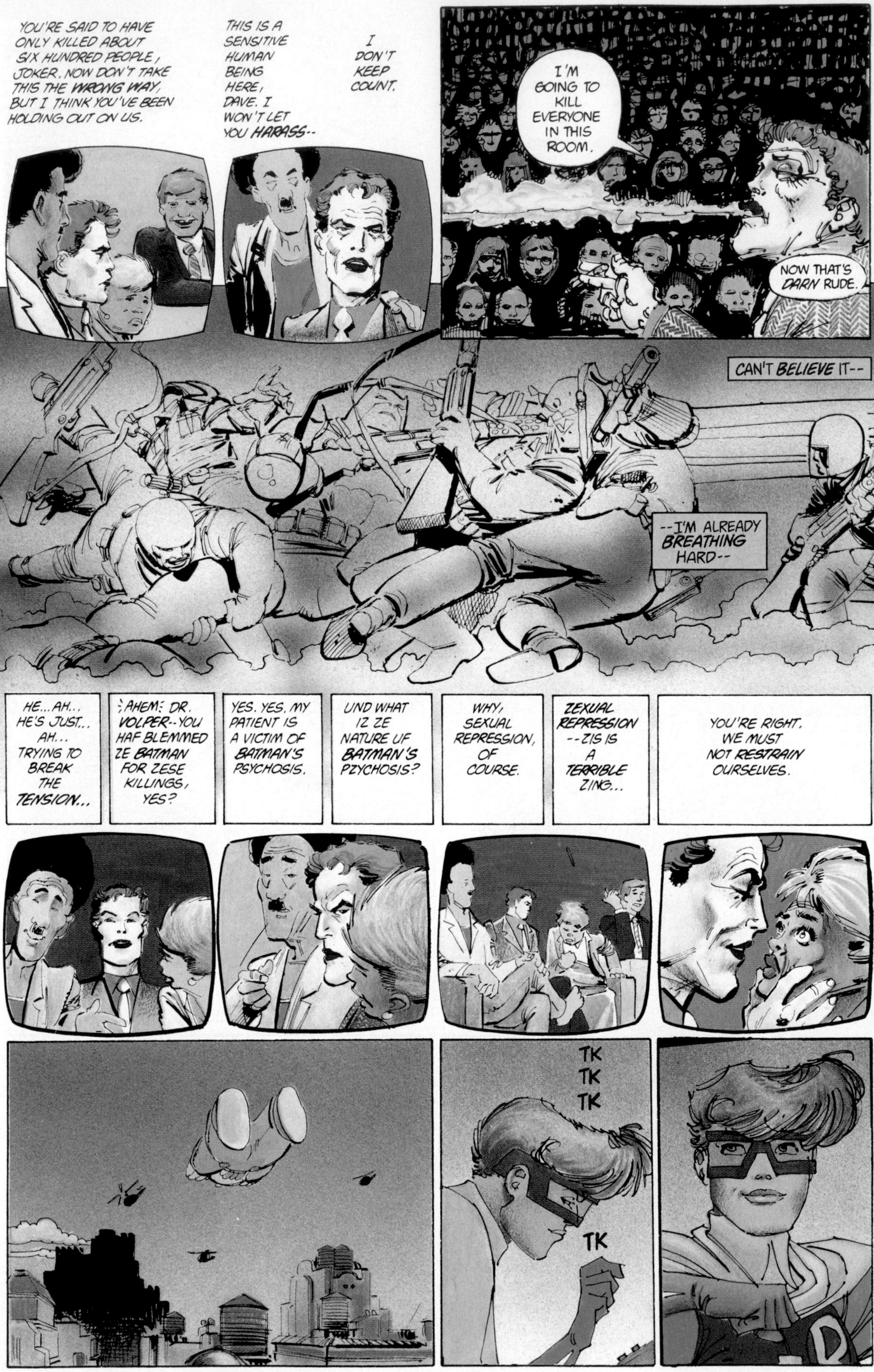
YOU'RE SAID TO HAVE ONLY KILLED ABOUT SIX HUNDRED PEOPLE, JOKER. NOW DON'T TAKE THIS THE WRONG WAY, BUT I THINK YOU'VE BEEN HOLDING OUT ON US.
THIS IS A SENSITIVE HUMAN BEING HERE, DAVE. I WON'T LET YOU HARASS--
I DON'T KEEP COUNT.
I'M GOING TO KILL EVERYONE IN THIS ROOM.
NOW THAT'S DARN RUDE.
CAN'T BELIEVE IT--
--I'M ALREADY BREATHING HARD--
HE...AH... HE'S JUST... AH... TRYING TO BREAK THE TENSION...
:AHEM: DR. VOLPER--YOU HAF BLEMMED ZE BATMAN FOR ZESE KILLINGS, YES?
YES. YES. MY PATIENT IS A VICTIM OF BATMAN'S PSYCHOSIS.
UND WHAT IZ ZE NATURE UF BATMAN'S PZYCHOSIS?
WHY, SEXUAL REPRESSION, OF COURSE.
ZEXUAL REPRESSION --ZIS IS A TERRIBLE ZING...
YOU'RE RIGHT. WE MUST NOT RESTRAIN OURSELVES.
TK
TK
TK
TK

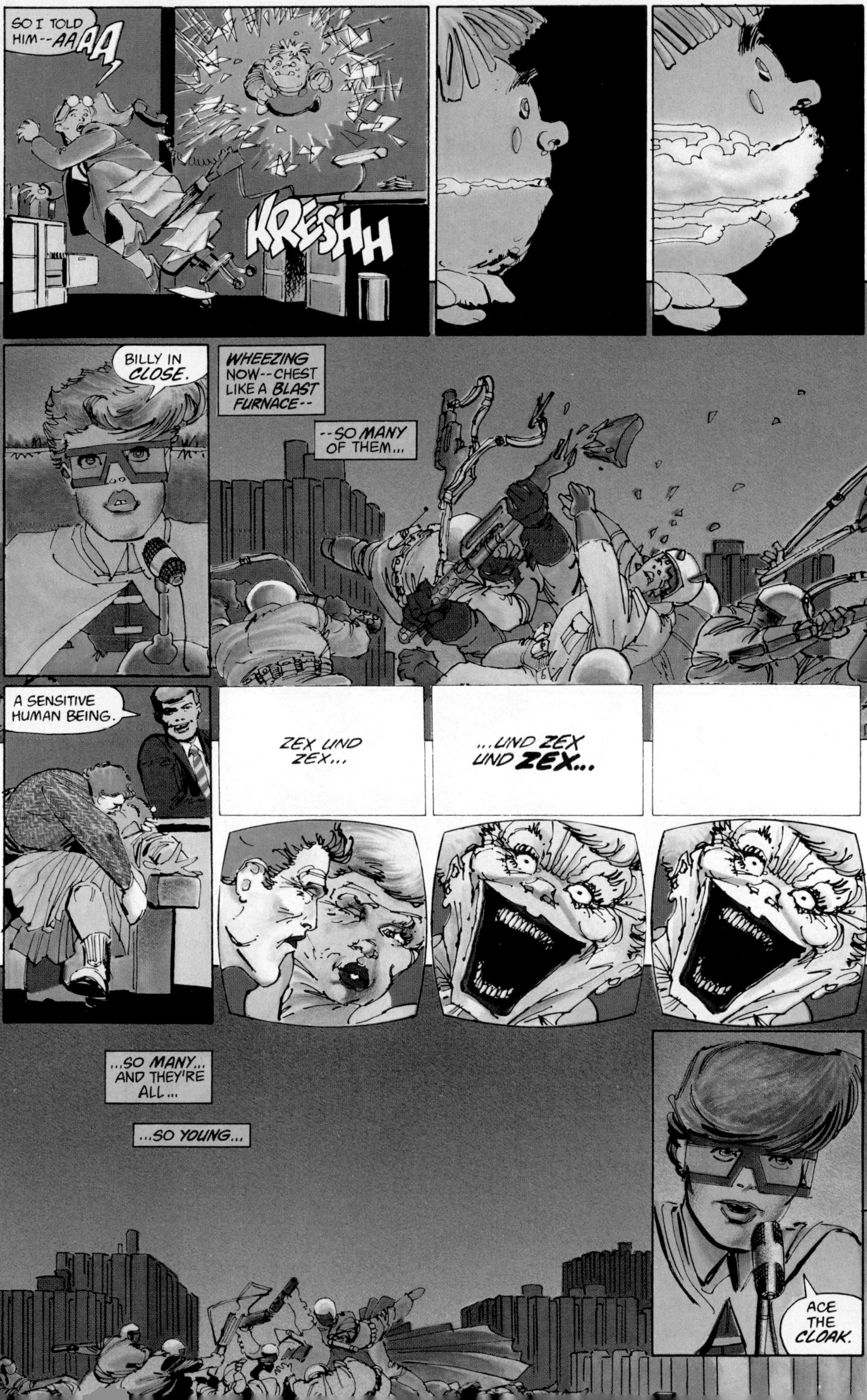
SO I TOLD HIM--AAAA
KRESHH
BILLY IN CLOSE.
WHEEZING NOW--CHEST LIKE A BLAST FURNACE--
--SO MANY OF THEM...
A SENSITIVE HUMAN BEING.
ZEX UND ZEX...
...UND ZEX UND ZEX...
...SO MANY... AND THEY'RE ALL...
...SO YOUNG...
ACE THE CLOAK.

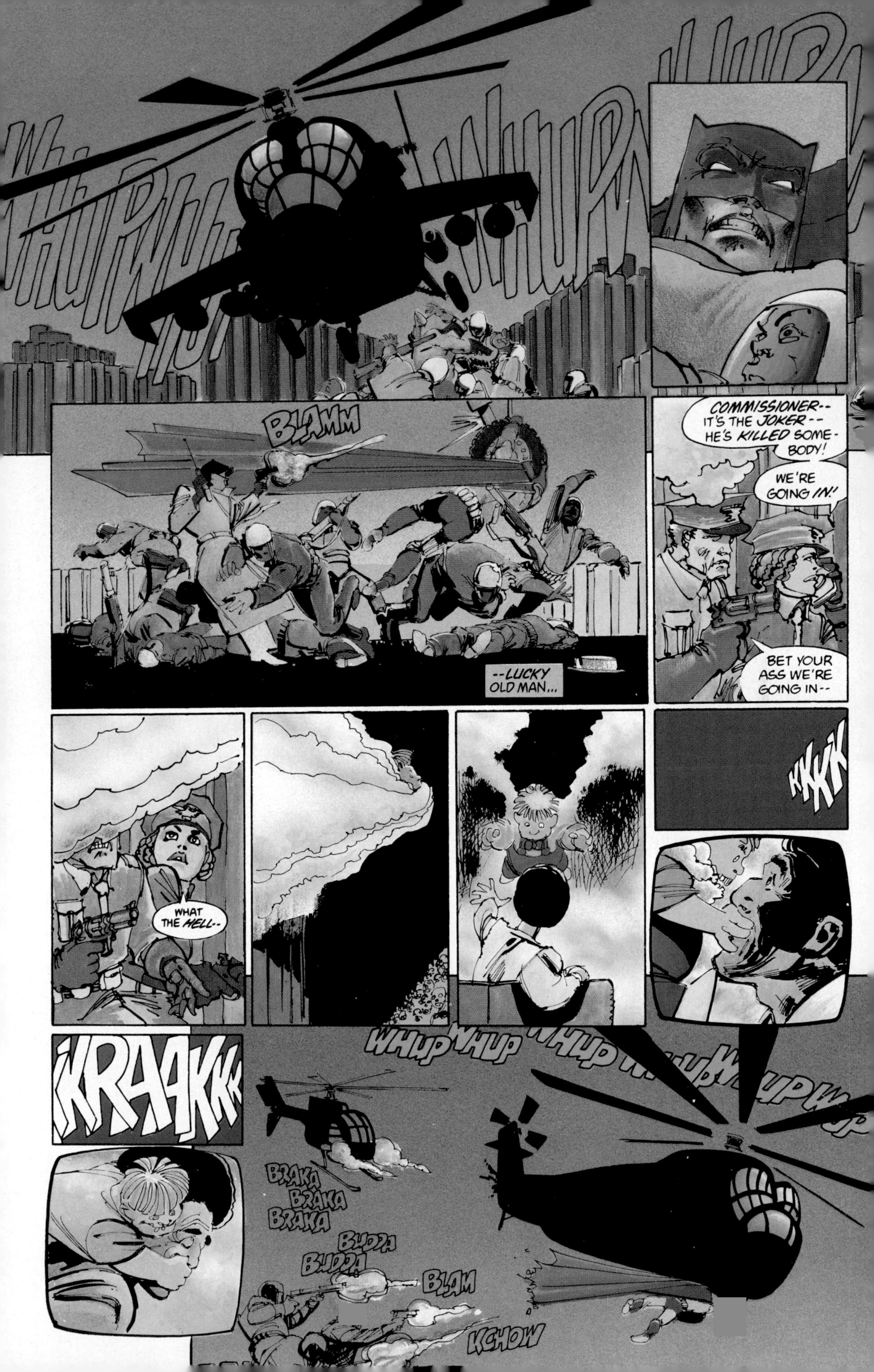

WHUPWHUPWHUP
BLAMM
--LUCKY OLD MAN...
COMMISSIONER-- IT'S THE JOKER-- HE'S KILLED SOMEBODY!
WE'RE GOING IN!
BET YOUR ASS WE'RE GOING IN--
WHAT THE HELL--
KKKK
KRAAKKK
WHUP WHUP WHUP
BRAKA BRAKA BRAKA
BUDDA BUDDA
BLAM
KCHOW

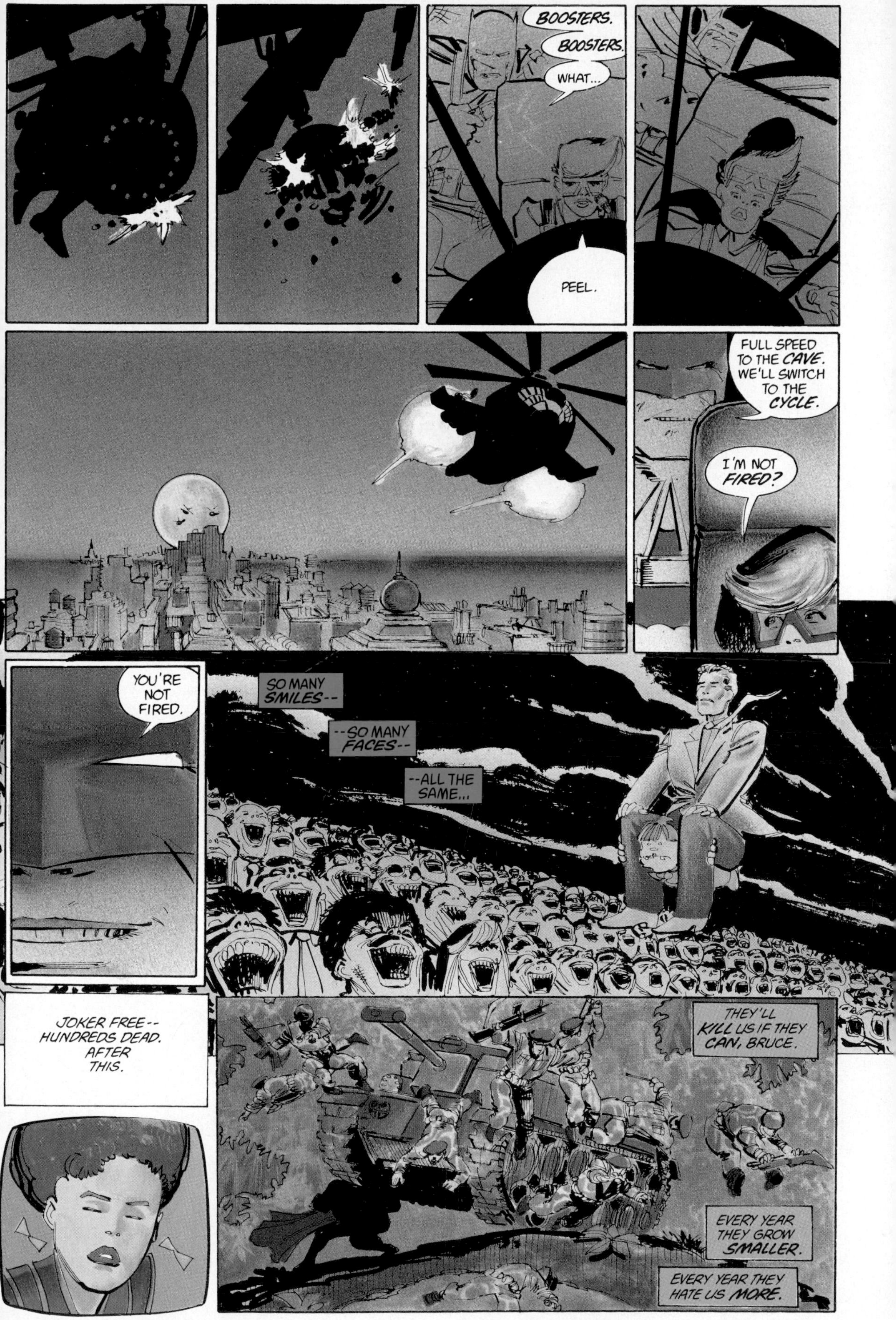
BOOSTERS.
BOOSTERS.
WHAT...
PEEL.
FULL SPEED TO THE CAVE. WE'LL SWITCH TO THE CYCLE.
I'M NOT FIRED?
YOU'RE NOT FIRED.
SO MANY SMILES--
--SO MANY FACES--
--ALL THE SAME...
JOKER FREE-- HUNDREDS DEAD. AFTER THIS.
THEY'LL KILL US IF THEY CAN, BRUCE.
EVERY YEAR THEY GROW SMALLER.
EVERY YEAR THEY HATE US MORE.

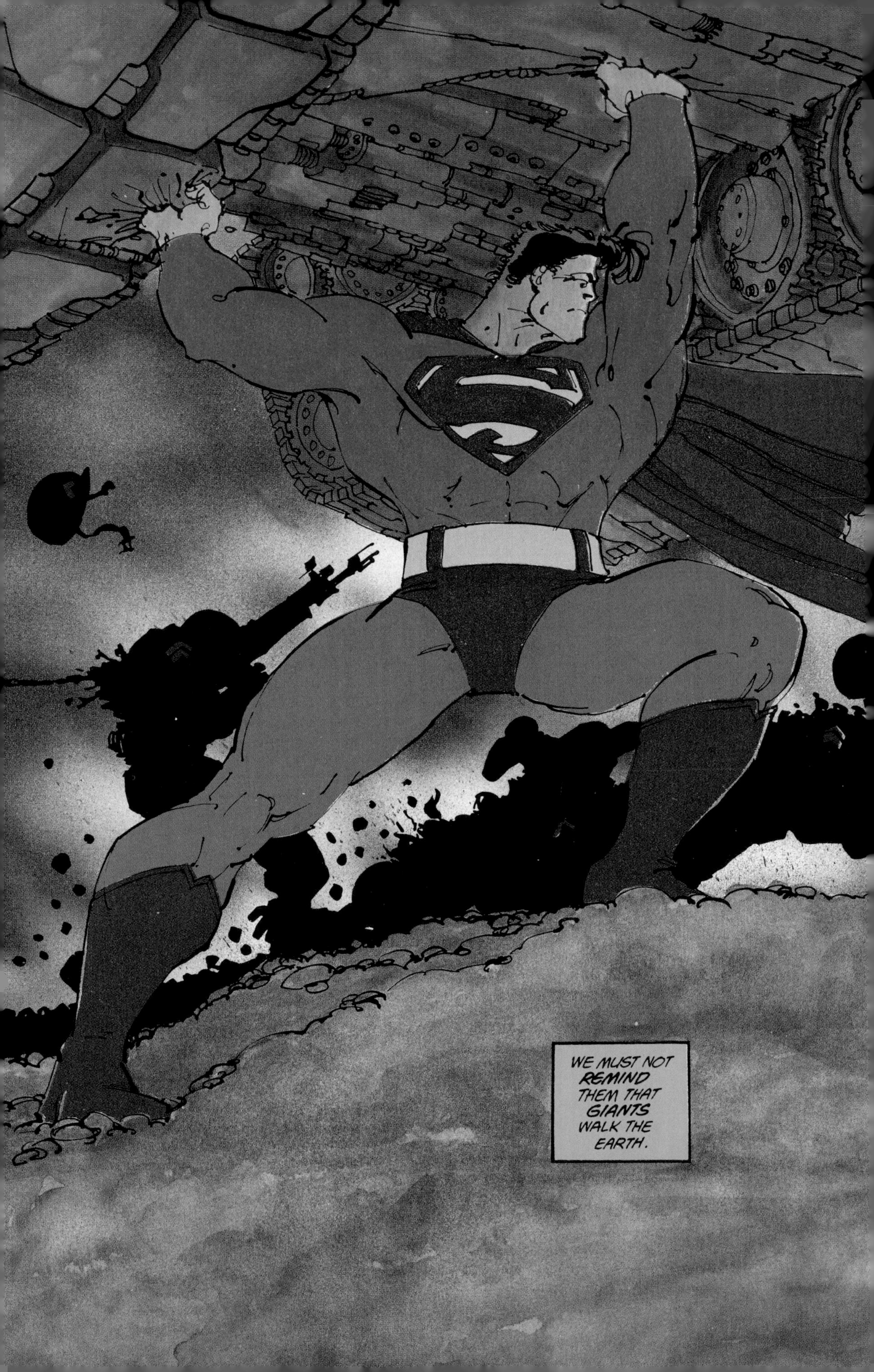
WE MUST NOT REMIND THEM THAT GIANTS WALK THE EARTH.

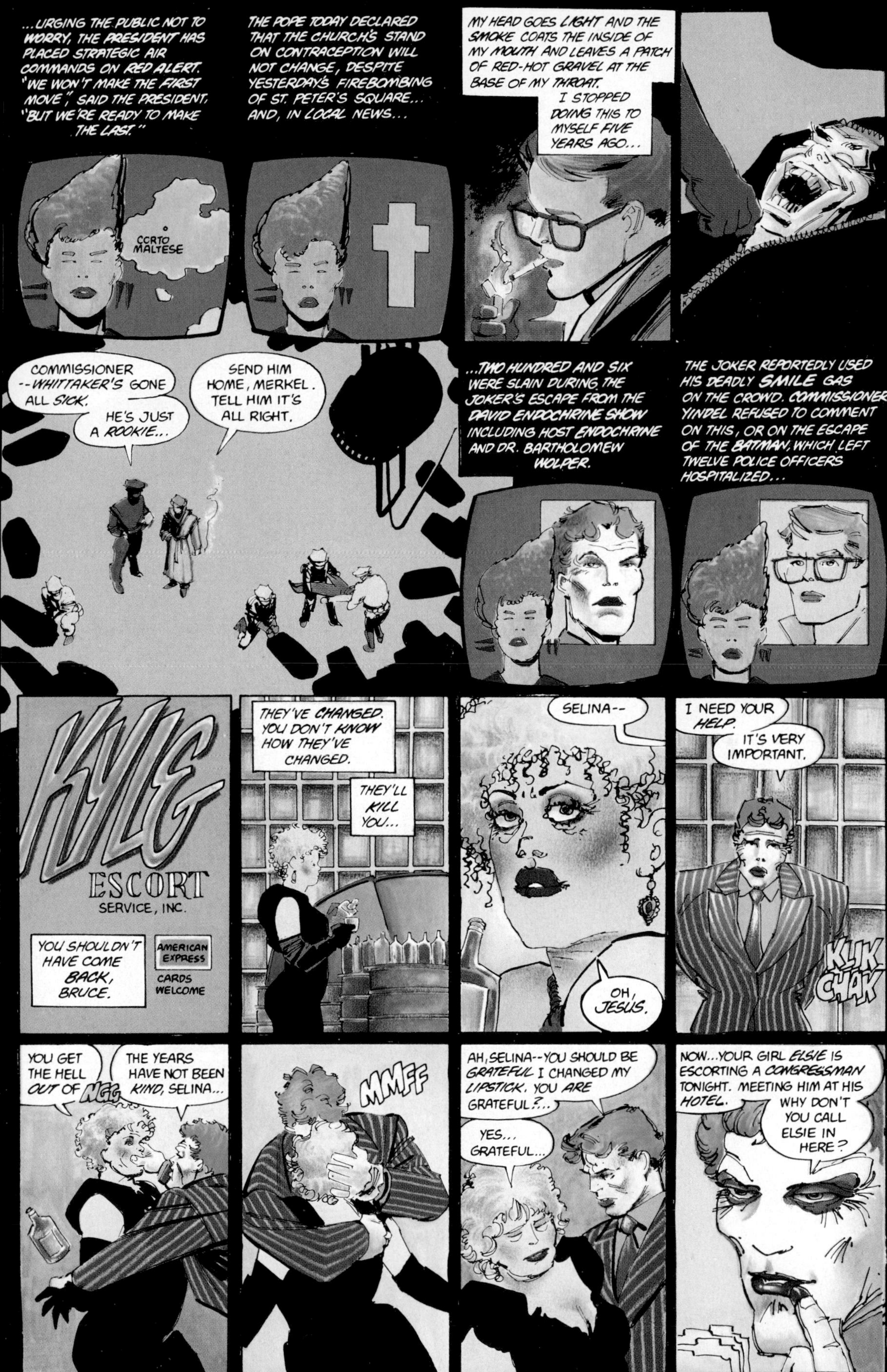
...URGING THE PUBLIC NOT TO WORRY, THE PRESIDENT HAS PLACED STRATEGIC AIR COMMANDS ON RED ALERT. "WE WON'T MAKE THE FIRST MOVE", SAID THE PRESIDENT, "BUT WE'RE READY TO MAKE THE LAST."
CORTO MALTESE
THE POPE TODAY DECLARED THAT THE CHURCH'S STAND ON CONTRACEPTION WILL NOT CHANGE, DESPITE YESTERDAY'S FIREBOMBING OF ST. PETER'S SQUARE... AND, IN LOCAL NEWS...
MY HEAD GOES LIGHT AND THE SMOKE COATS THE INSIDE OF MY MOUTH AND LEAVES A PATCH OF RED-HOT GRAVEL AT THE BASE OF MY THROAT.
I STOPPED DOING THIS TO MYSELF FIVE YEARS AGO...
COMMISSIONER --WHITTAKER'S GONE ALL SICK.
HE'S JUST A ROOKIE...
SEND HIM HOME, MERKEL. TELL HIM IT'S ALL RIGHT.
...TWO HUNDRED AND SIX WERE SLAIN DURING THE JOKER'S ESCAPE FROM THE DAVID ENDOCHRINE SHOW INCLUDING HOST ENDOCHRINE AND DR. BARTHOLOMEW WOLPER.
THE JOKER REPORTEDLY USED HIS DEADLY SMILE GAS ON THE CROWD. COMMISSIONER YINDEL REFUSED TO COMMENT ON THIS, OR ON THE ESCAPE OF THE BATMAN, WHICH LEFT TWELVE POLICE OFFICERS HOSPITALIZED...
KYLE
ESCORT
SERVICE, INC.
YOU SHOULDN'T HAVE COME BACK, BRUCE.
AMERICAN EXPRESS
CARDS WELCOME
THEY'VE CHANGED. YOU DON'T KNOW HOW THEY'VE CHANGED.
THEY'LL KILL YOU...
SELINA--
OH, JESUS.
I NEED YOUR HELP.
IT'S VERY IMPORTANT.
KLIK
CHAK
YOU GET THE HELL OUT OF NGG
THE YEARS HAVE NOT BEEN KIND, SELINA...
MMFF
AH, SELINA--YOU SHOULD BE GRATEFUL I CHANGED MY LIPSTICK. YOU ARE GRATEFUL?...
YES... GRATEFUL...
NOW...YOUR GIRL ELSIE IS ESCORTING A CONGRESSMAN TONIGHT. MEETING HIM AT HIS HOTEL.
WHY DON'T YOU CALL ELSIE IN HERE?

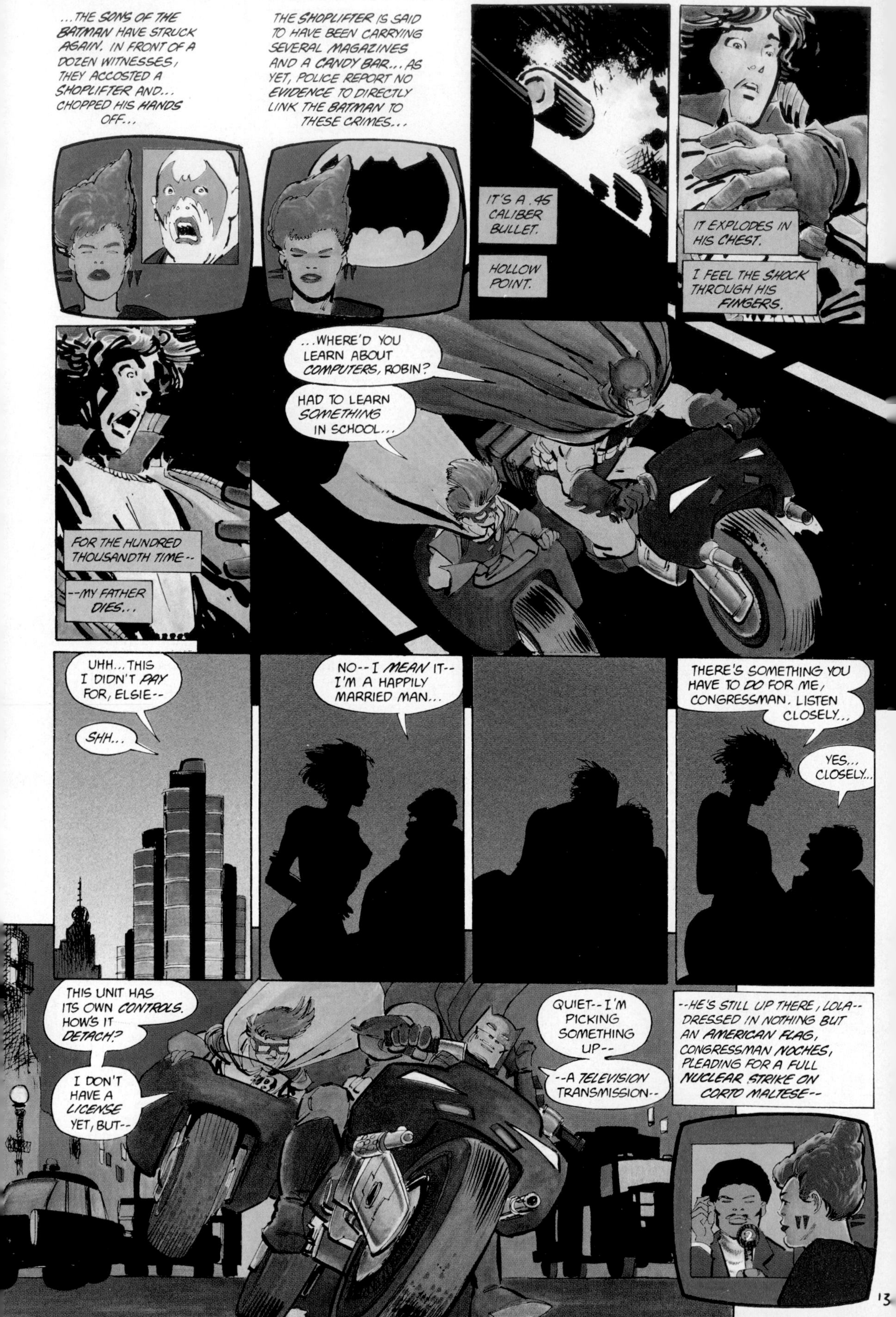
...THE SONS OF THE BATMAN HAVE STRUCK AGAIN. IN FRONT OF A DOZEN WITNESSES, THEY ACCOSTED A SHOPLIFTER AND... CHOPPED HIS HANDS OFF...
THE SHOPLIFTER IS SAID TO HAVE BEEN CARRYING SEVERAL MAGAZINES AND A CANDY BAR... AS YET, POLICE REPORT NO EVIDENCE TO DIRECTLY LINK THE BATMAN TO THESE CRIMES...
IT'S A .45 CALIBER BULLET.
HOLLOW POINT.
IT EXPLODES IN HIS CHEST.
I FEEL THE SHOCK THROUGH HIS FINGERS.
FOR THE HUNDRED THOUSANDTH TIME--
--MY FATHER DIES...
...WHERE'D YOU LEARN ABOUT COMPUTERS, ROBIN?
HAD TO LEARN SOMETHING IN SCHOOL...
UHH... THIS I DIDN'T PAY FOR, ELSIE--
SHH...
NO--I MEAN IT--I'M A HAPPILY MARRIED MAN...
THERE'S SOMETHING YOU HAVE TO DO FOR ME, CONGRESSMAN. LISTEN CLOSELY...
YES... CLOSELY...
THIS UNIT HAS ITS OWN CONTROLS. HOW'S IT DETACH?
I DON'T HAVE A LICENSE YET, BUT--
QUIET--I'M PICKING SOMETHING UP--
--A TELEVISION TRANSMISSION--
--HE'S STILL UP THERE, LOLA--DRESSED IN NOTHING BUT AN AMERICAN FLAG, CONGRESSMAN NOCHES, PLEADING FOR A FULL NUCLEAR STRIKE ON CORTO MALTESE--

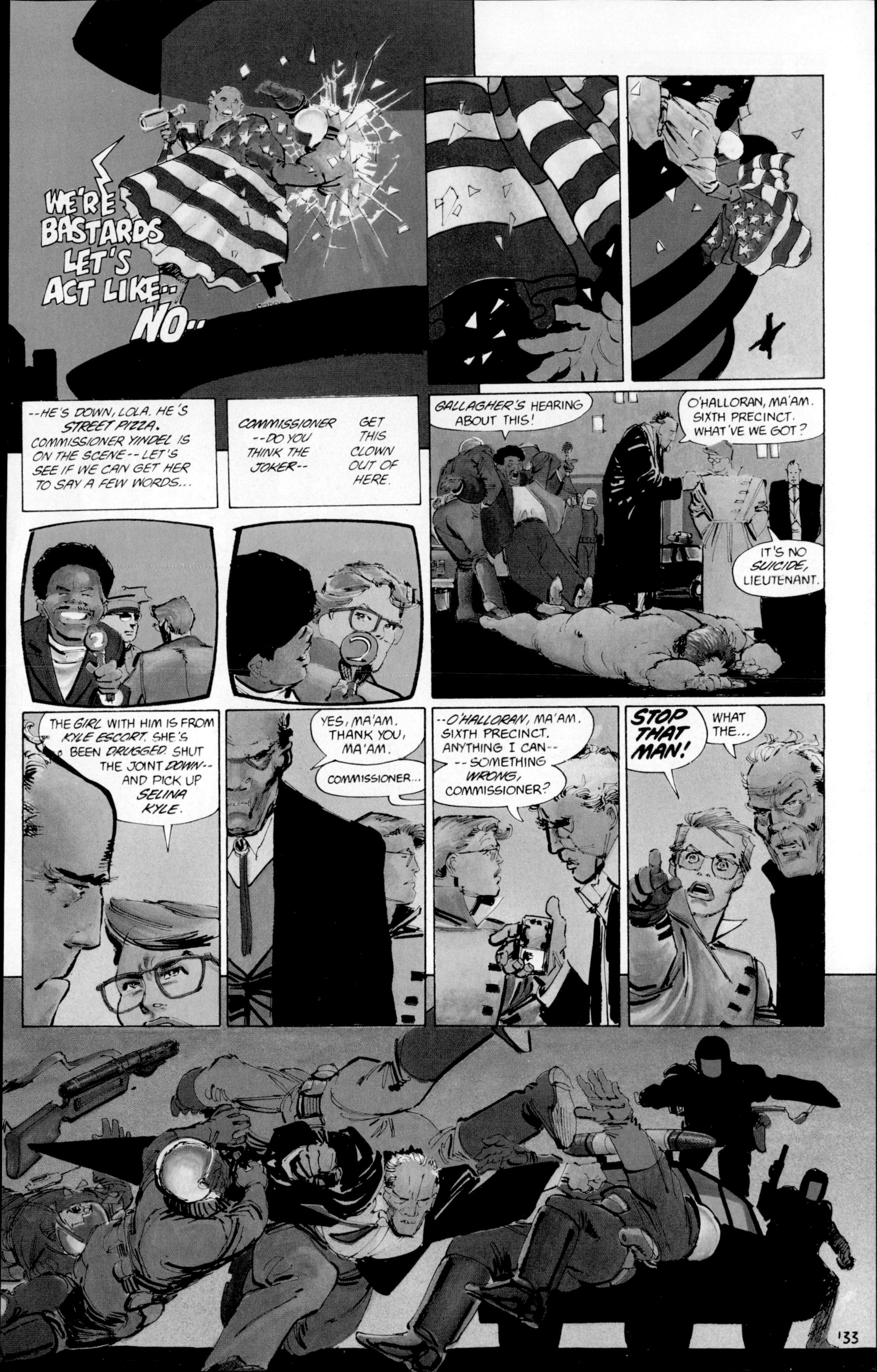
WE'RE BASTARDS LET'S ACT LIKE.. NO..
--HE'S DOWN, LOLA. HE'S STREET PIZZA. COMMISSIONER YINDEL IS ON THE SCENE--LET'S SEE IF WE CAN GET HER TO SAY A FEW WORDS...
COMMISSIONER --DO YOU THINK THE JOKER--
GET THIS CLOWN OUT OF HERE.
GALLAGHER'S HEARING ABOUT THIS!
O'HALLORAN, MA'AM. SIXTH PRECINCT. WHAT'VE WE GOT?
IT'S NO SUICIDE, LIEUTENANT.
THE GIRL WITH HIM IS FROM KYLE ESCORT. SHE'S BEEN DRUGGED. SHUT THE JOINT DOWN-- AND PICK UP SELINA KYLE.
YES, MA'AM. THANK YOU, MA'AM.
COMMISSIONER...
--O'HALLORAN, MA'AM. SIXTH PRECINCT. ANYTHING I CAN-- --SOMETHING WRONG, COMMISSIONER?
STOP THAT MAN!
WHAT THE...

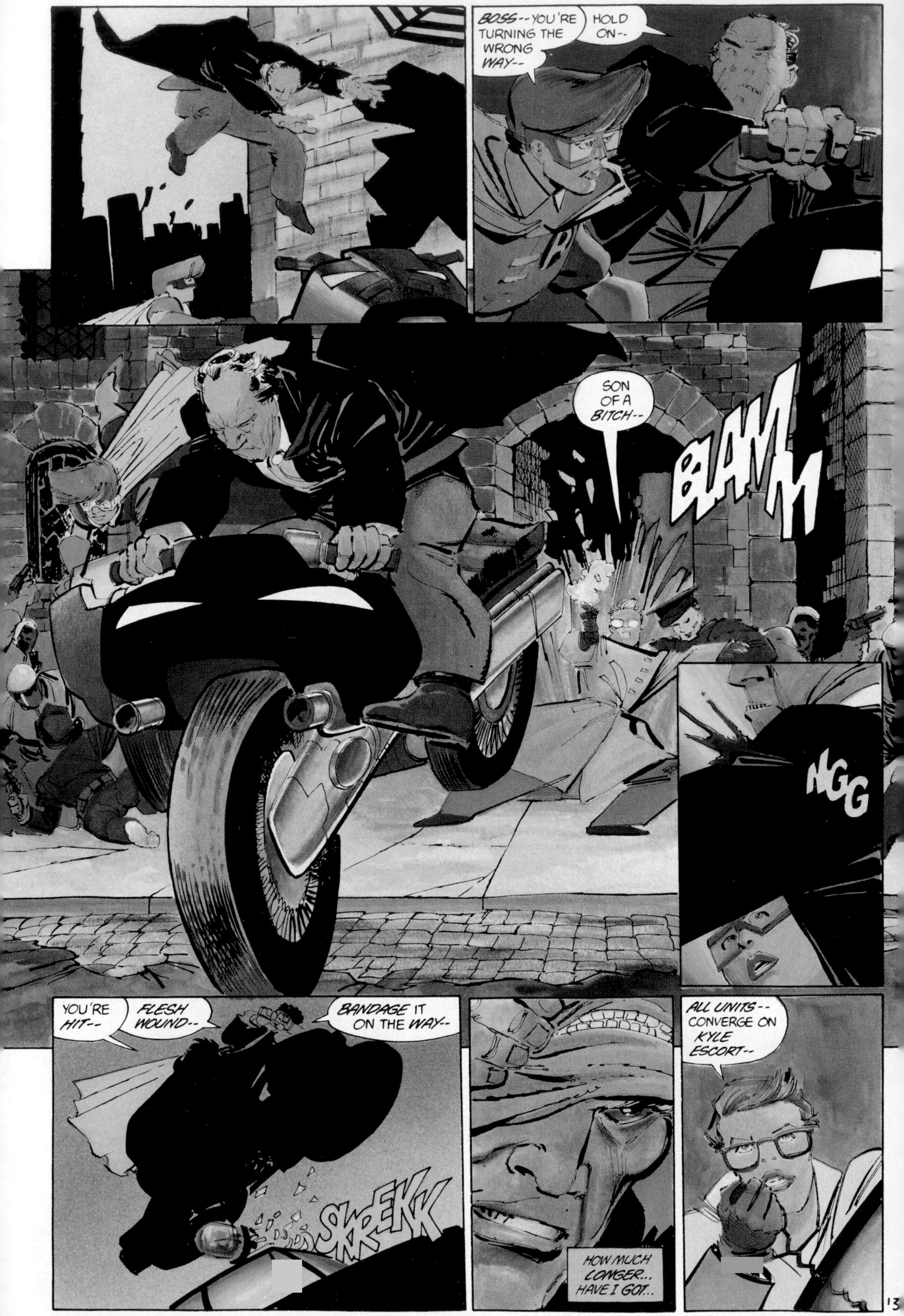
BOSS--YOU'RE TURNING THE WRONG WAY--
HOLD ON--
SON OF A BITCH--
BLAMM
NGG
YOU'RE HIT--
FLESH WOUND--
BANDAGE IT ON THE WAY--
SKREEKK
HOW MUCH LONGER... HAVE I GOT...
ALL UNITS--CONVERGE ON KYLE ESCORT--

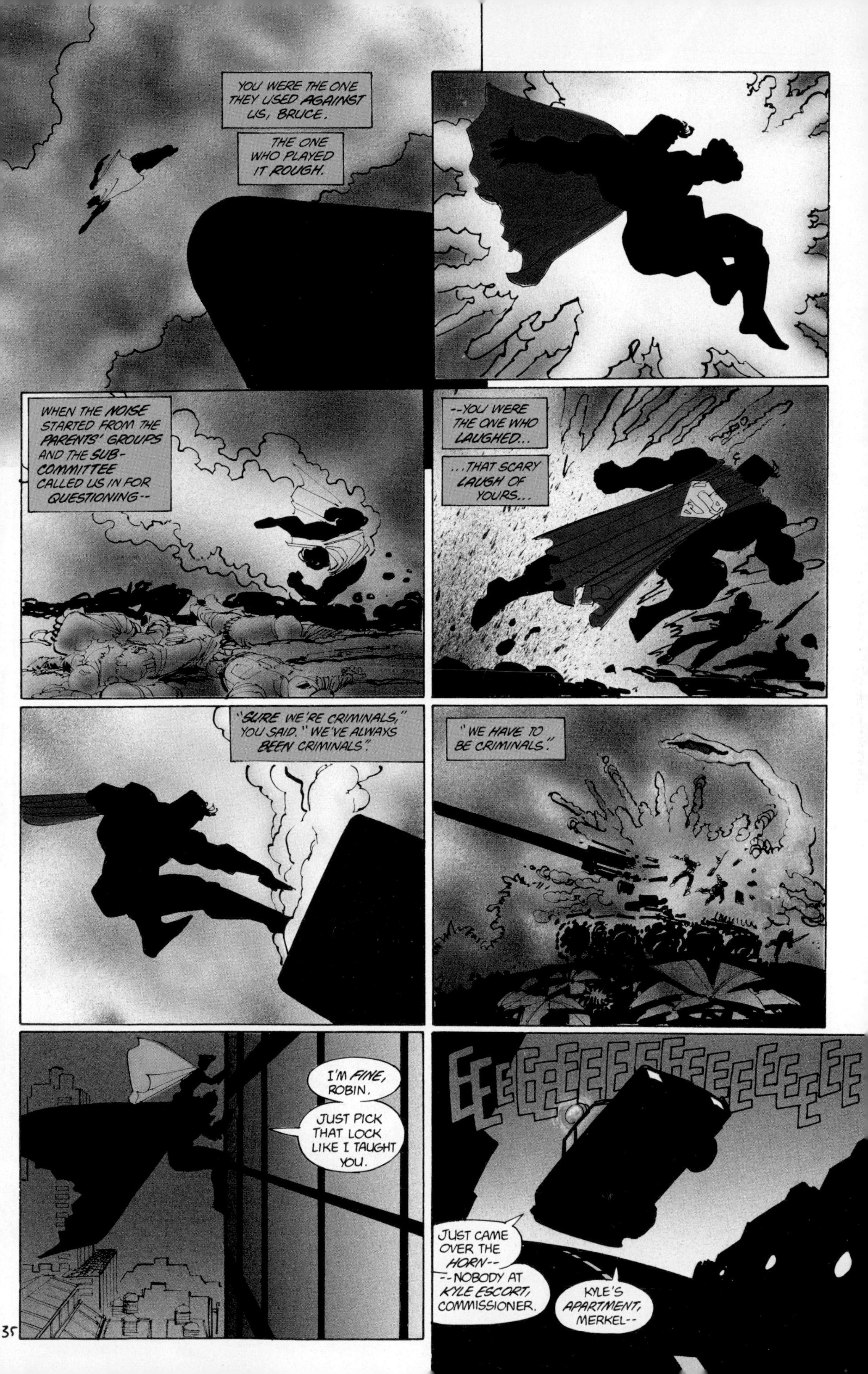

YOU WERE THE ONE THEY USED AGAINST US, BRUCE.
THE ONE WHO PLAYED IT ROUGH.
WHEN THE NOISE STARTED FROM THE PARENTS' GROUPS AND THE SUB-COMMITTEE CALLED US IN FOR QUESTIONING--
--YOU WERE THE ONE WHO LAUGHED...
...THAT SCARY LAUGH OF YOURS...
"SURE WE'RE CRIMINALS," YOU SAID. "WE'VE ALWAYS BEEN CRIMINALS".
"WE HAVE TO BE CRIMINALS."
I'M FINE, ROBIN.
JUST PICK THAT LOCK LIKE I TAUGHT YOU.
EEEEEEEEEEEEEEEEEEEE
JUST CAME OVER THE HORN--
--NOBODY AT KYLE ESCORT, COMMISSIONER.
KYLE'S APARTMENT, MERKEL--

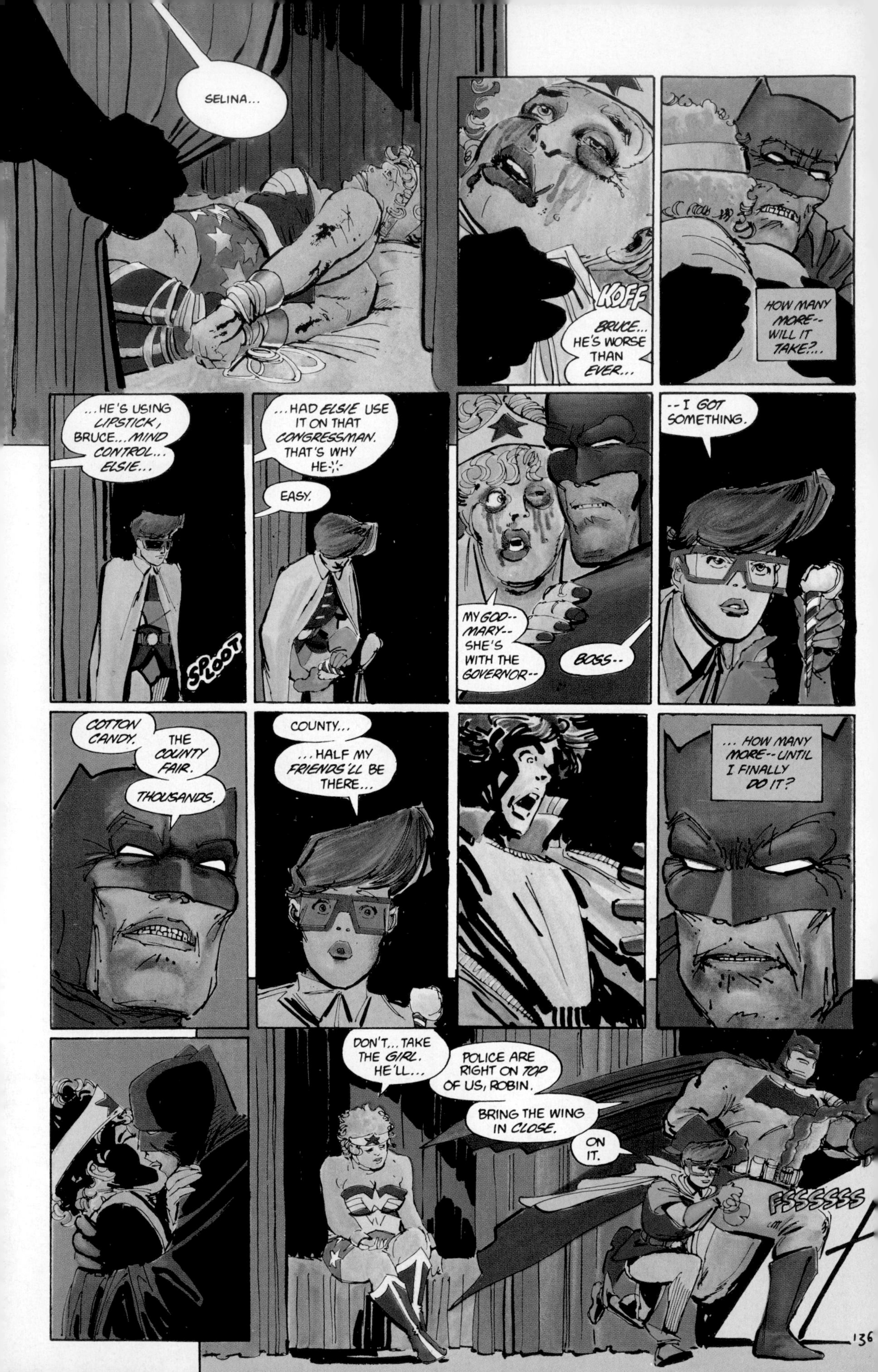
SELINA...
KOFF
BRUCE... HE'S WORSE THAN EVER...
HOW MANY MORE-- WILL IT TAKE?...
...HE'S USING LIPSTICK, BRUCE... MIND CONTROL... ELSIE...
SPLOOT
...HAD ELSIE USE IT ON THAT CONGRESSMAN. THAT'S WHY HE-
EASY.
MY GOD-- MARY-- SHE'S WITH THE GOVERNOR--
BOSS--
--I GOT SOMETHING.
COTTON CANDY.
THE COUNTY FAIR.
THOUSANDS.
COUNTY...
...HALF MY FRIENDS'LL BE THERE...
... HOW MANY MORE-- UNTIL I FINALLY DO IT?
DON'T... TAKE THE GIRL. HE'LL...
POLICE ARE RIGHT ON TOP OF US, ROBIN.
BRING THE WING IN CLOSE.
ON IT.
FSSSSSS

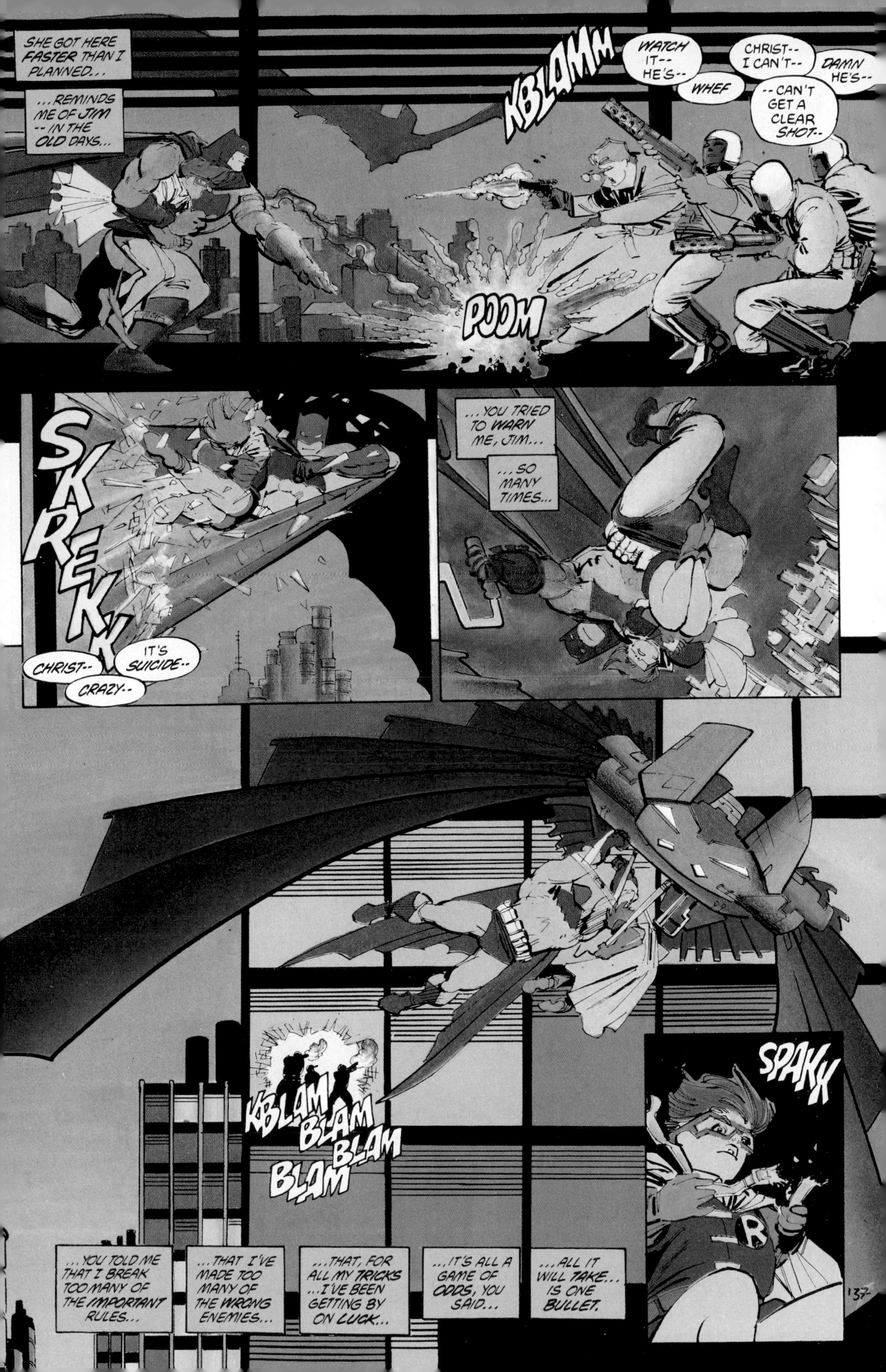

SHE GOT HERE FASTER THAN I PLANNED...
...REMINDS ME OF JIM -- IN THE OLD DAYS...
KBLAMM
WATCH IT-- HE'S--
WHEF
CHRIST-- I CAN'T--
DAMN HE'S--
--CAN'T GET A CLEAR SHOT--
POOM
SKREKK
CHRIST--
IT'S SUICIDE--
CRAZY--
...YOU TRIED TO WARN ME, JIM...
...SO MANY TIMES...
KBLAM
BLAM
BLAM
BLAM
SPAKK
...YOU TOLD ME THAT I BREAK TOO MANY OF THE IMPORTANT RULES...
...THAT I'VE MADE TOO MANY OF THE WRONG ENEMIES...
...THAT, FOR ALL MY TRICKS ...I'VE BEEN GETTING BY ON LUCK...
...IT'S ALL A GAME OF ODDS, YOU SAID...
...ALL IT WILL TAKE... IS ONE BULLET.

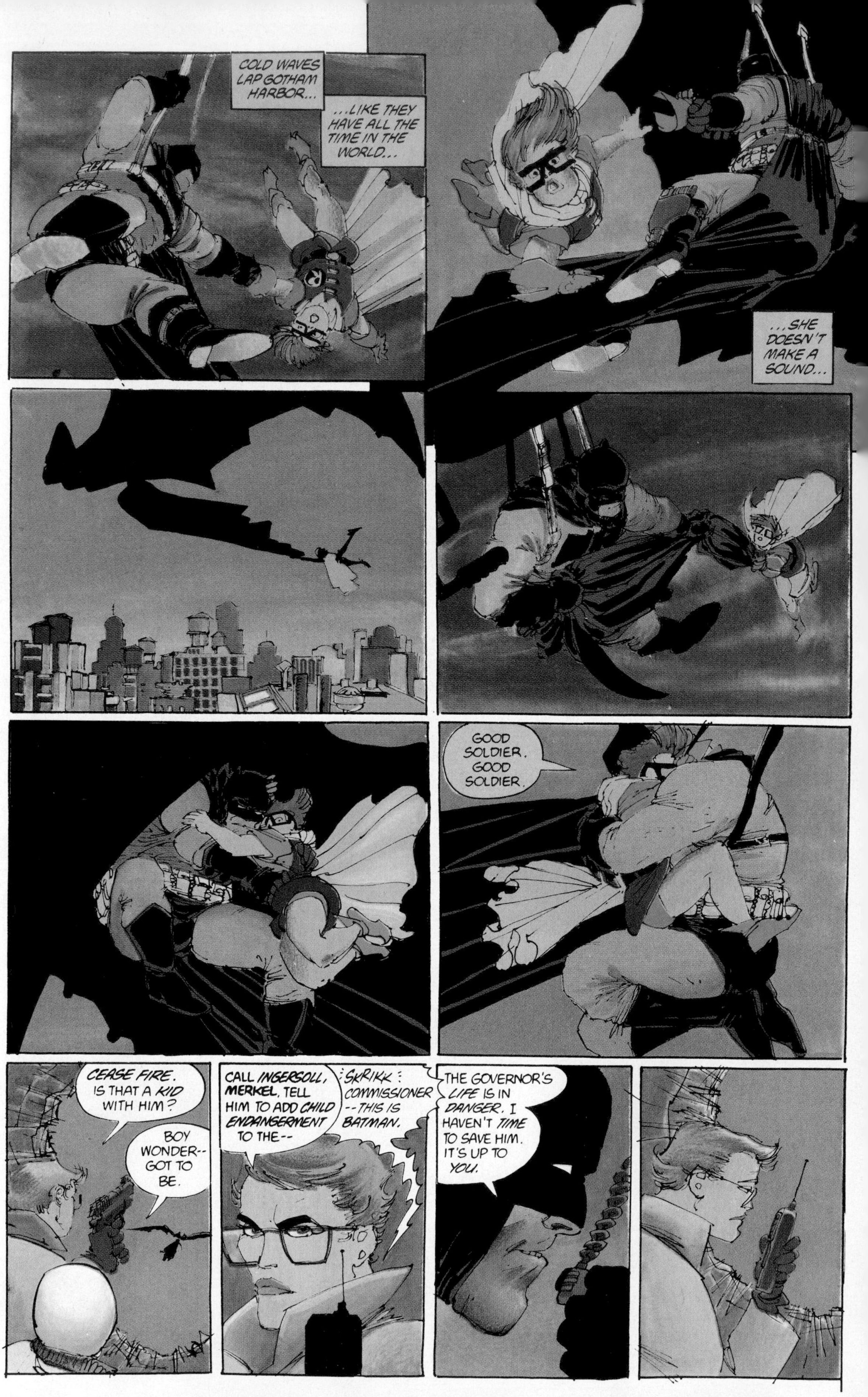

COLD WAVES LAP GOTHAM HARBOR...
...LIKE THEY HAVE ALL THE TIME IN THE WORLD...
...SHE DOESN'T MAKE A SOUND...
GOOD SOLDIER. GOOD SOLDIER.
CEASE FIRE. IS THAT A KID WITH HIM?
BOY WONDER-- GOT TO BE.
CALL INGERSOLL, MERKEL. TELL HIM TO ADD CHILD ENDANGERMENT TO THE--
SKRIKK: COMMISSIONER --THIS IS BATMAN.
THE GOVERNOR'S LIFE IS IN DANGER. I HAVEN'T TIME TO SAVE HIM. IT'S UP TO YOU.

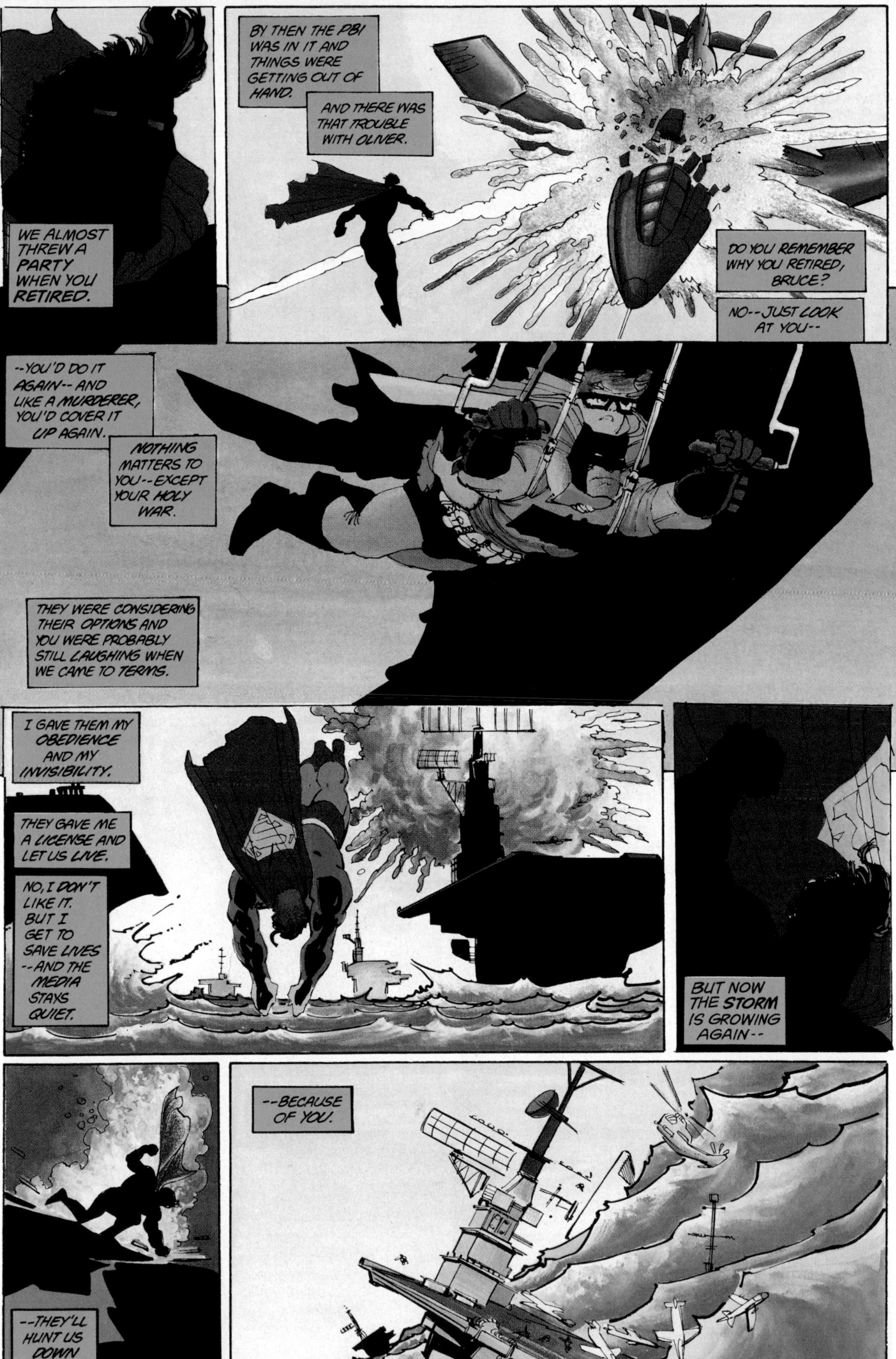
WE ALMOST THREW A PARTY WHEN YOU RETIRED.
BY THEN THE FBI WAS IN IT AND THINGS WERE GETTING OUT OF HAND.
AND THERE WAS THAT TROUBLE WITH OLIVER.
DO YOU REMEMBER WHY YOU RETIRED, BRUCE?
NO--JUST LOOK AT YOU--
--YOU'D DO IT AGAIN--AND LIKE A MURDERER, YOU'D COVER IT UP AGAIN.
NOTHING MATTERS TO YOU--EXCEPT YOUR HOLY WAR.
THEY WERE CONSIDERING THEIR OPTIONS AND YOU WERE PROBABLY STILL LAUGHING WHEN WE CAME TO TERMS.
I GAVE THEM MY OBEDIENCE AND MY INVISIBILITY.
THEY GAVE ME A LICENSE AND LET US LIVE.
NO, I DON'T LIKE IT. BUT I GET TO SAVE LIVES --AND THE MEDIA STAYS QUIET.
BUT NOW THE STORM IS GROWING AGAIN--
--BECAUSE OF YOU.
--THEY'LL HUNT US DOWN AGAIN--

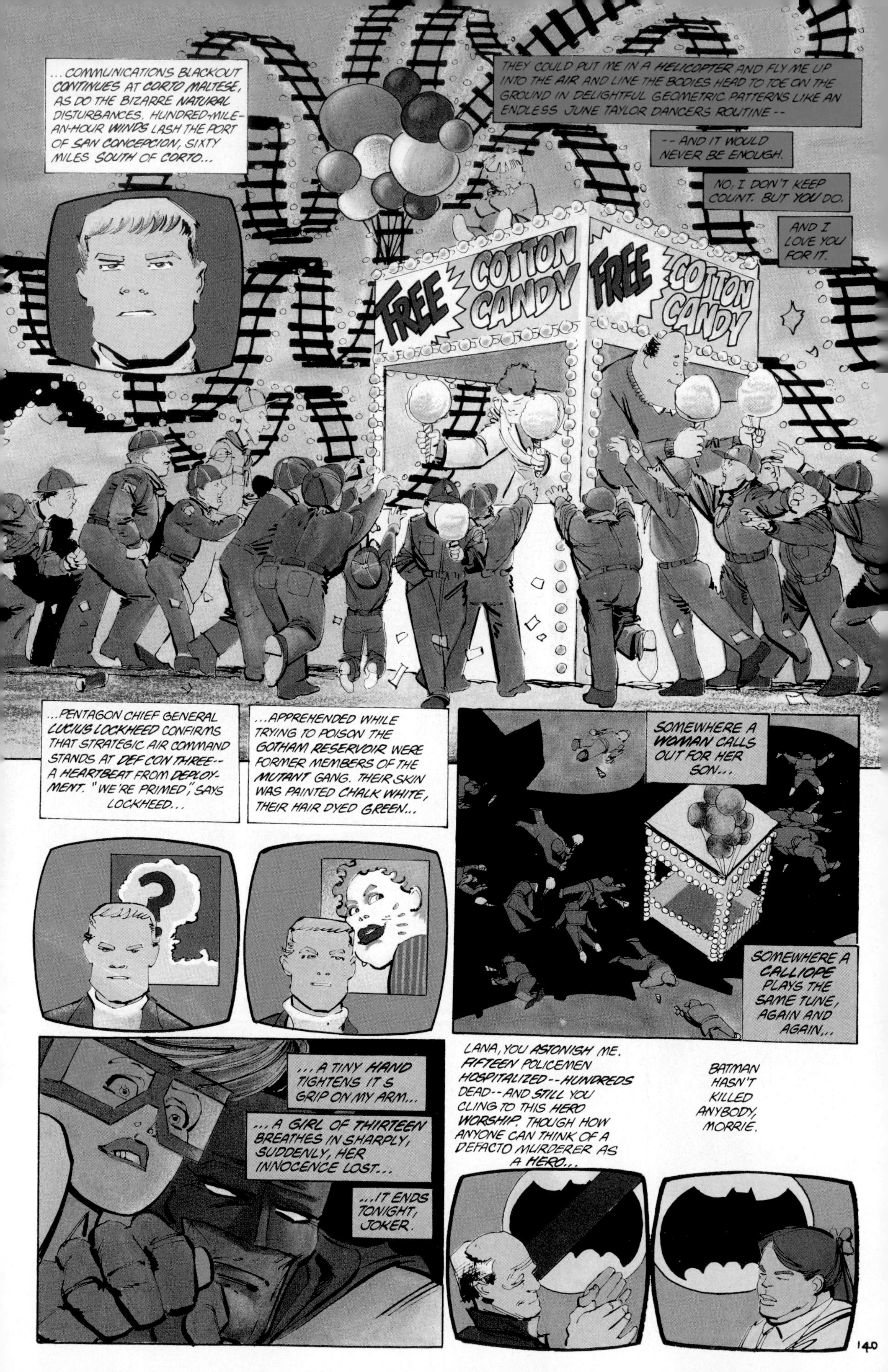
...COMMUNICATIONS BLACKOUT CONTINUES AT CORTO MALTESE, AS DO THE BIZARRE NATURAL DISTURBANCES. HUNDRED-MILE-AN-HOUR WINDS LASH THE PORT OF SAN CONCEPCION, SIXTY MILES SOUTH OF CORTO...
THEY COULD PUT ME IN A HELICOPTER AND FLY ME UP INTO THE AIR AND LINE THE BODIES HEAD TO TOE ON THE GROUND IN DELIGHTFUL GEOMETRIC PATTERNS LIKE AN ENDLESS JUNE TAYLOR DANCERS ROUTINE --
-- AND IT WOULD NEVER BE ENOUGH.
NO, I DON'T KEEP COUNT. BUT YOU DO.
AND I LOVE YOU FOR IT.
FREE COTTON CANDY
FREE COTTON CANDY
...PENTAGON CHIEF GENERAL LUCIUS LOCKHEED CONFIRMS THAT STRATEGIC AIR COMMAND STANDS AT DEF CON THREE-- A HEARTBEAT FROM DEPLOYMENT. "WE'RE PRIMED," SAYS LOCKHEED...
...APPREHENDED WHILE TRYING TO POISON THE GOTHAM RESERVOIR WERE FORMER MEMBERS OF THE MUTANT GANG. THEIR SKIN WAS PAINTED CHALK WHITE, THEIR HAIR DYED GREEN...
SOMEWHERE A WOMAN CALLS OUT FOR HER SON...
SOMEWHERE A CALLIOPE PLAYS THE SAME TUNE, AGAIN AND AGAIN...
...A TINY HAND TIGHTENS IT'S GRIP ON MY ARM...
...A GIRL OF THIRTEEN BREATHES IN SHARPLY, SUDDENLY, HER INNOCENCE LOST...
...IT ENDS TONIGHT, JOKER.
LANA, YOU ASTONISH ME. FIFTEEN POLICEMEN HOSPITALIZED--HUNDREDS DEAD--AND STILL YOU CLING TO THIS HERO WORSHIP. THOUGH HOW ANYONE CAN THINK OF A DEFACTO MURDERER AS A HERO...
BATMAN HASN'T KILLED ANYBODY, MORRIE.

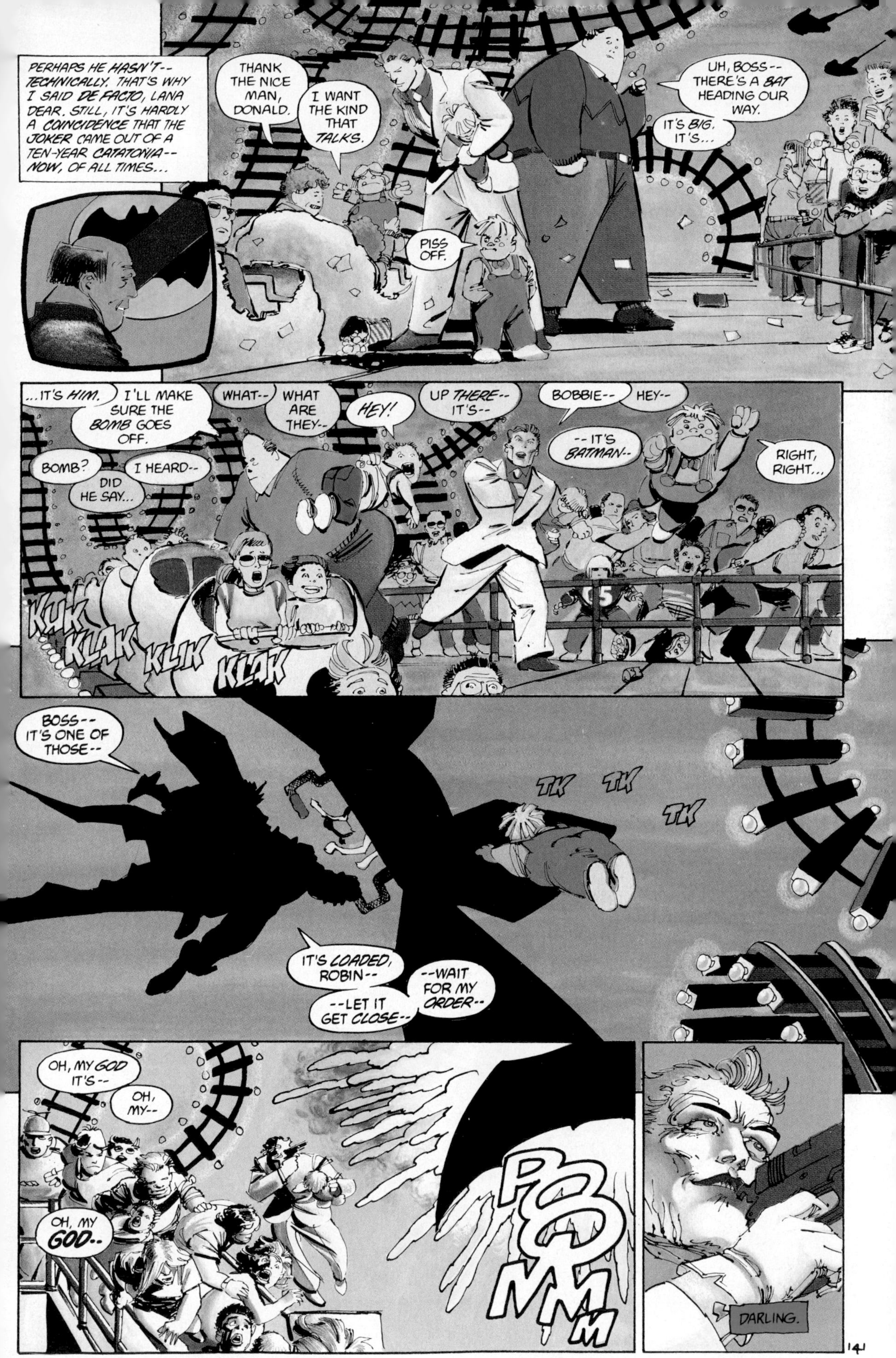

PERHAPS HE HASN'T-- TECHNICALLY. THAT'S WHY I SAID DE FACTO, LANA DEAR. STILL, IT'S HARDLY A COINCIDENCE THAT THE JOKER CAME OUT OF A TEN-YEAR CATATONIA-- NOW, OF ALL TIMES...
THANK THE NICE MAN, DONALD.
I WANT THE KIND THAT TALKS.
PISS OFF.
UH, BOSS-- THERE'S A BAT HEADING OUR WAY.
IT'S BIG. IT'S...
...IT'S HIM.
I'LL MAKE SURE THE BOMB GOES OFF.
WHAT--
WHAT ARE THEY--
HEY!
UP THERE-- IT'S--
BOBBIE--
HEY--
--IT'S BATMAN--
RIGHT, RIGHT...
BOMB?
DID HE SAY...
I HEARD--
KUK
KLAK
KLIK
KLAK
BOSS-- IT'S ONE OF THOSE--
TK
TK
TK
IT'S LOADED, ROBIN--
--LET IT GET CLOSE--
--WAIT FOR MY ORDER--
OH, MY GOD IT'S--
OH, MY--
OH, MY GOD..
POOMMM
DARLING.

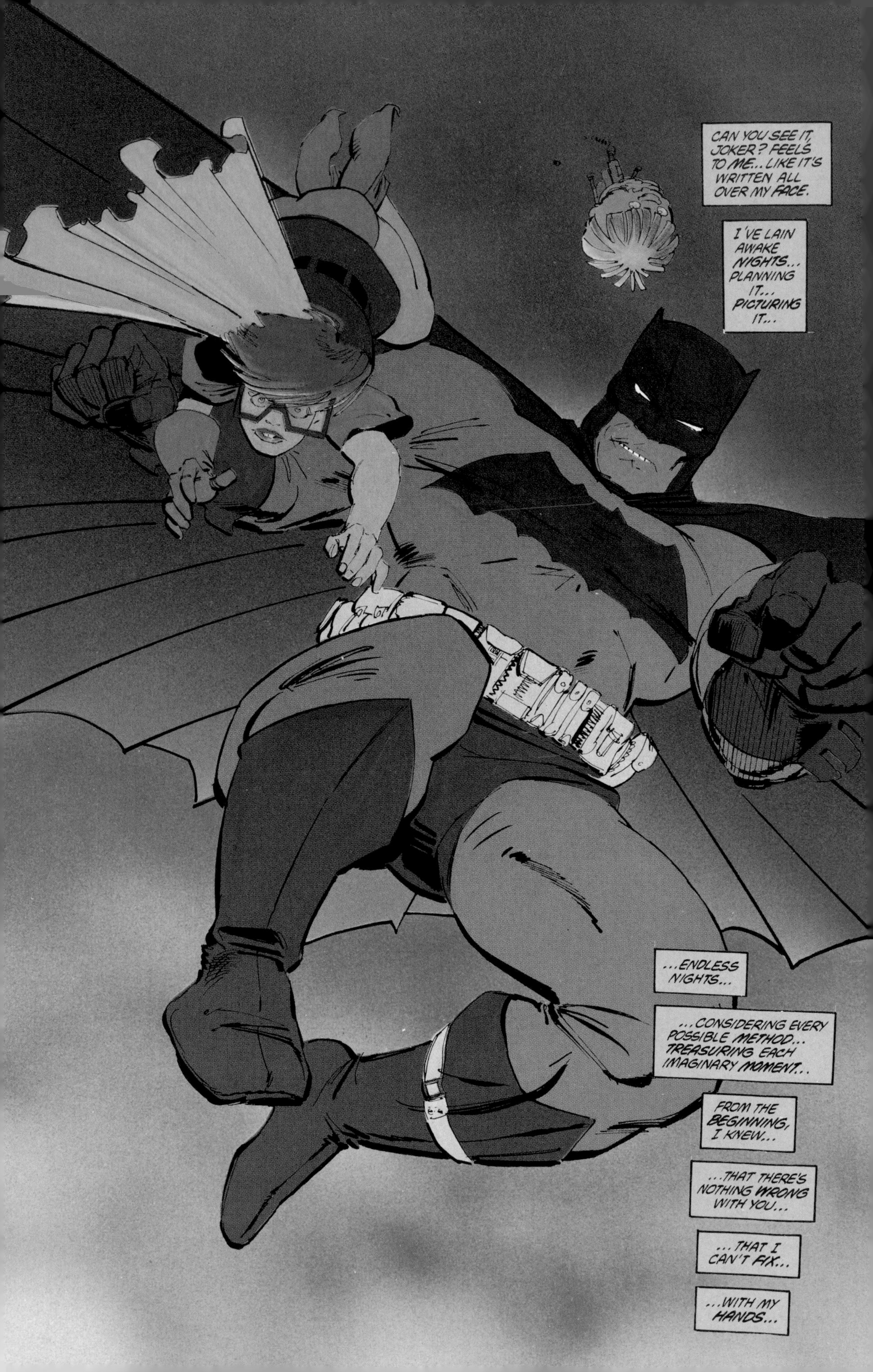
CAN YOU SEE IT, JOKER? FEELS TO ME... LIKE IT'S WRITTEN ALL OVER MY FACE.
I'VE LAIN AWAKE NIGHTS... PLANNING IT... PICTURING IT...
...ENDLESS NIGHTS...
...CONSIDERING EVERY POSSIBLE METHOD... TREASURING EACH IMAGINARY MOMENT...
FROM THE BEGINNING, I KNEW...
...THAT THERE'S NOTHING WRONG WITH YOU...
...THAT I CAN'T FIX...
...WITH MY HANDS...

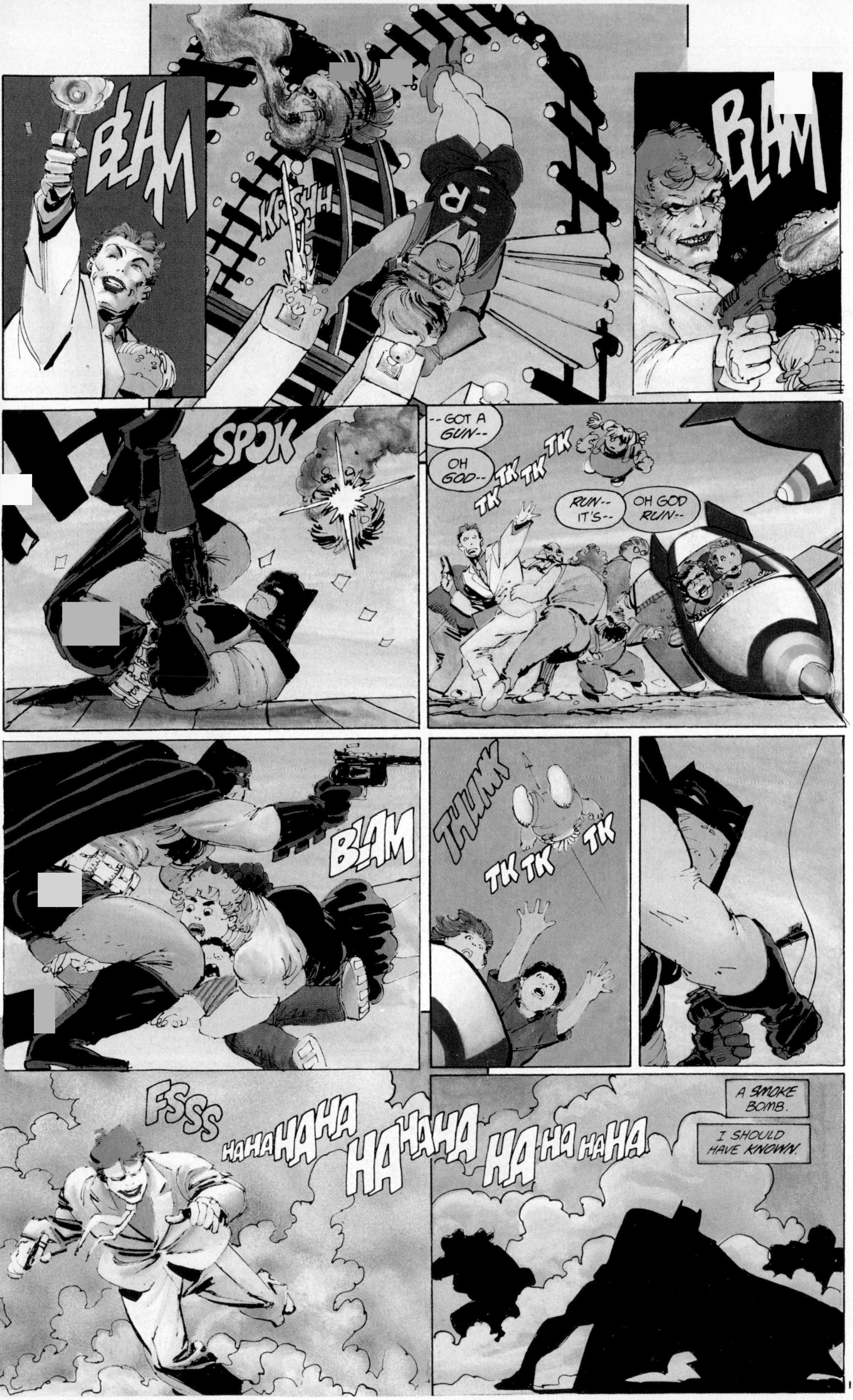
BLAM
KRSHH
BLAM
SPOK
--GOT A GUN--
OH GOD--
TK TK TK TK
RUN-- IT'S--
OH GOD RUN--
BLAM
THUNK
TK TK TK
FSSS
HAHAHAHAHA HAHAHAHA HAHAHAHAHA
A SMOKE BOMB.
I SHOULD HAVE KNOWN.

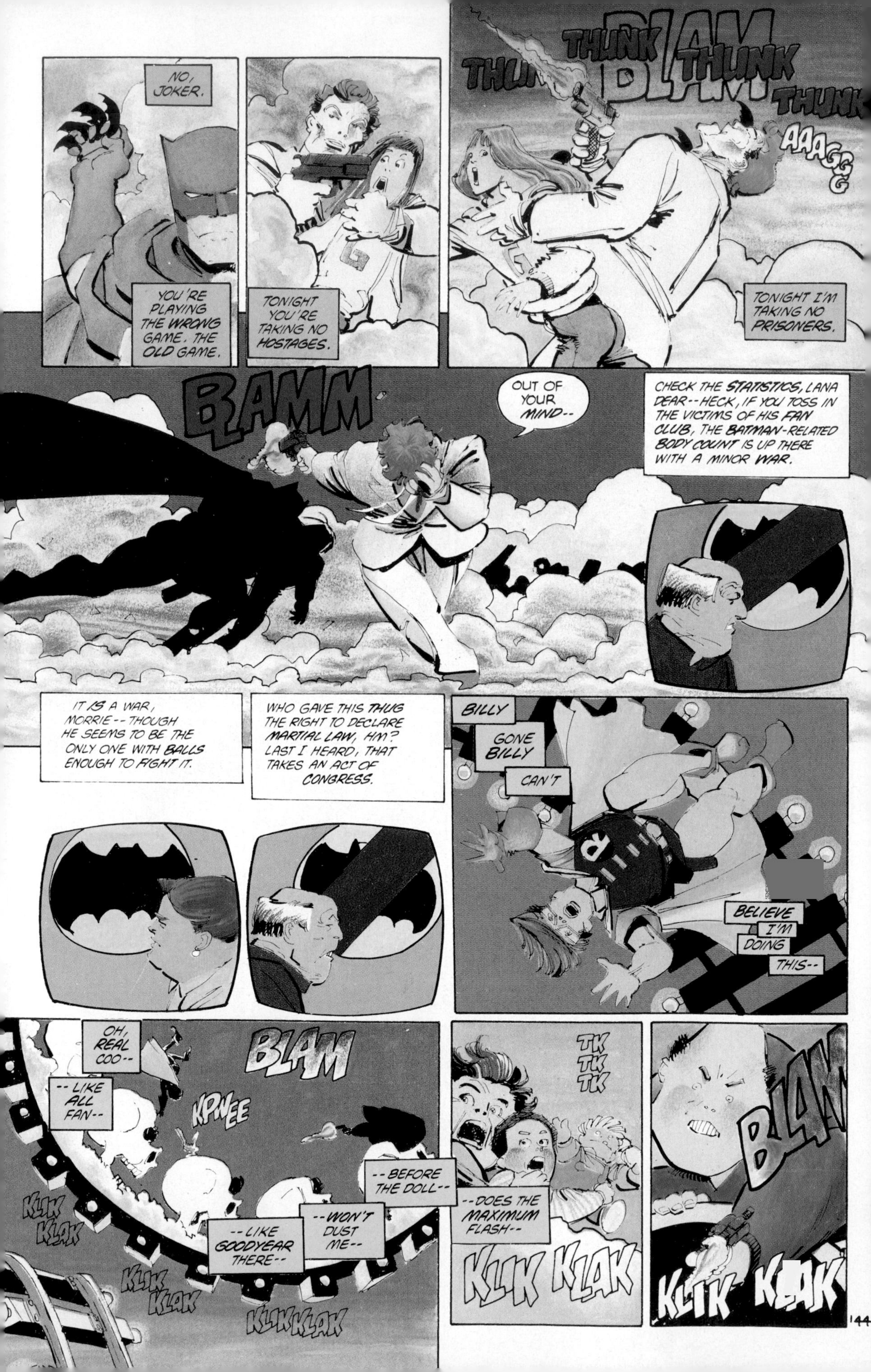
NO, JOKER.
YOU'RE PLAYING THE WRONG GAME, THE OLD GAME.
TONIGHT YOU'RE TAKING NO HOSTAGES.
THUNK
BLAM
THUNK
BLAM
THUNK
THUNK
AAAGGG
TONIGHT I'M TAKING NO PRISONERS.
BLAMM
OUT OF YOUR MIND--
CHECK THE STATISTICS, LANA DEAR--HECK, IF YOU TOSS IN THE VICTIMS OF HIS FAN CLUB, THE BATMAN-RELATED BODY COUNT IS UP THERE WITH A MINOR WAR.
IT IS A WAR, MORRIE--THOUGH HE SEEMS TO BE THE ONLY ONE WITH BALLS ENOUGH TO FIGHT IT.
WHO GAVE THIS THUG THE RIGHT TO DECLARE MARTIAL LAW, HM? LAST I HEARD, THAT TAKES AN ACT OF CONGRESS.
BILLY
GONE BILLY
CAN'T
BELIEVE
I'M
DOING
THIS--
OH, REAL COO--
--LIKE ALL FAN--
BLAM
KPWEE
--BEFORE THE DOLL--
--WON'T DUST ME--
--LIKE GOODYEAR THERE--
KLIK KLAK
KLIK KLAK
KLIK KLAK
TK TK TK
--DOES THE MAXIMUM FLASH--
KLIK KLAK
BLAM
KLIK KLAK

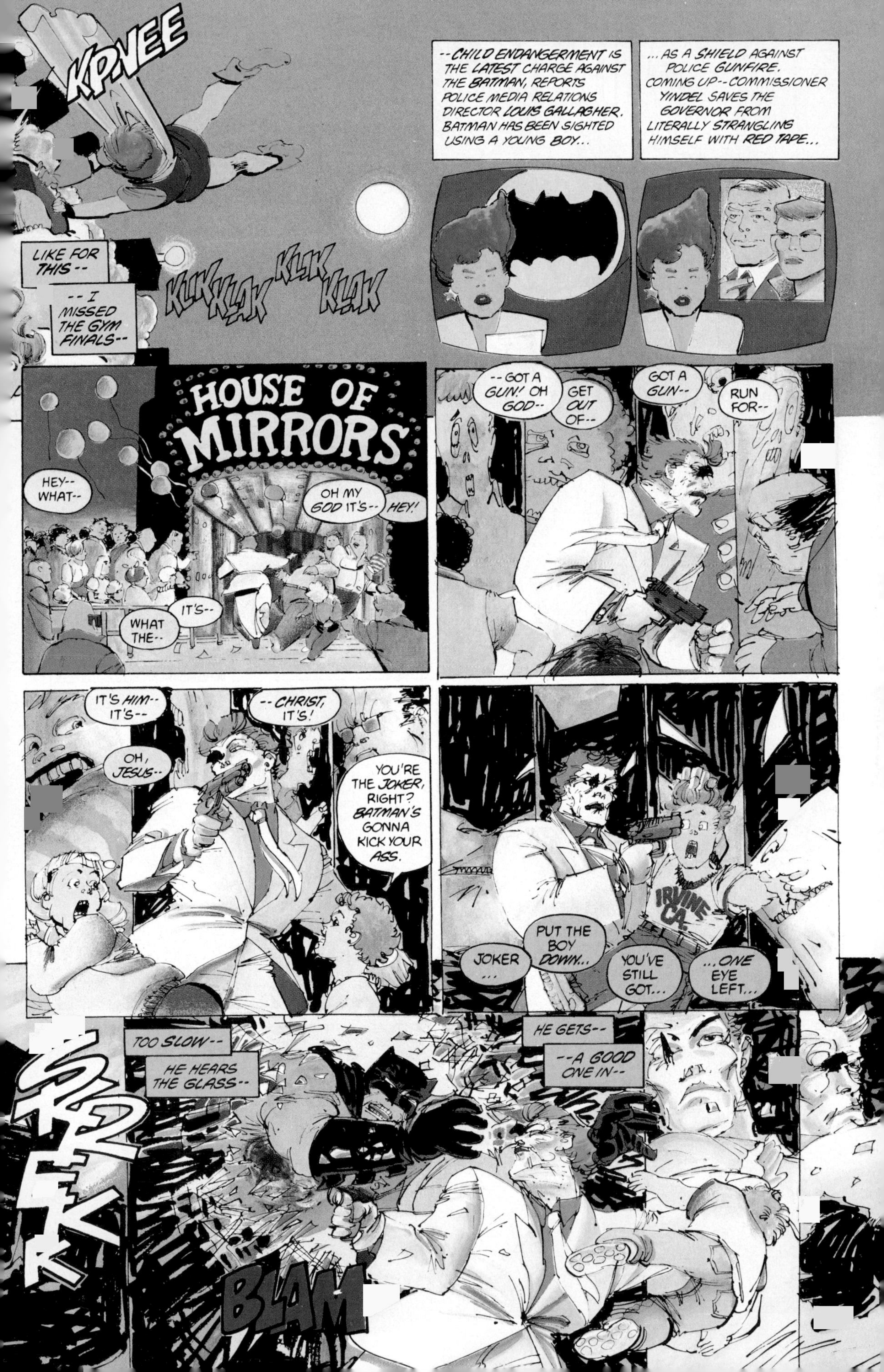
KPWEE
LIKE FOR THIS--
--I MISSED THE GYM FINALS--
KLIK KLAK KLIK KLAK
--CHILD ENDANGERMENT IS THE LATEST CHARGE AGAINST THE BATMAN, REPORTS POLICE MEDIA RELATIONS DIRECTOR LOUIS GALLAGHER. BATMAN HAS BEEN SIGHTED USING A YOUNG BOY...
...AS A SHIELD AGAINST POLICE GUNFIRE. COMING UP--COMMISSIONER YINDEL SAVES THE GOVERNOR FROM LITERALLY STRANGLING HIMSELF WITH RED TAPE...
HOUSE OF MIRRORS
HEY-- WHAT--
OH MY GOD IT'S--
HEY!
WHAT THE--
IT'S--
--GOT A GUN! OH GOD--
GET OUT OF--
GOT A GUN--
RUN FOR--
IT'S HIM-- IT'S--
--CHRIST, IT'S!
OH, JESUS--
YOU'RE THE JOKER, RIGHT? BATMAN'S GONNA KICK YOUR ASS.
IRVINE CA.
JOKER ...
PUT THE BOY DOWN...
YOU'VE STILL GOT...
...ONE EYE LEFT...
TOO SLOW--
HE HEARS THE GLASS--
HE GETS--
--A GOOD ONE IN--
SKRZEEK
BLAM

WHOKK

BLAM

--GLANCED OFF A RIB--

--TOOK SOME MEAT WITH IT--

KLIK KLIK

HE'S FAST-- AS EVER--

--WOULD HAVE GOTTEN ME--

--DIZZY--

--NOT DIZZY --NOT ALREADY--

KSHH

--I'M TAKING TOO LONG--

GIVING HIM--

--TOO MANY CHANCES--

CHK CHAK

BAM

SPAKK

--THAT COULD HAVE BEEN ME--

--INSTEAD OF A MIRROR--

--THAT'S RIGHT, JOKER--

SPAK

BLAM SPAKK BLAM

--WASTE THOSE BULLETS--

BATMAN-- HE'S GETTING AWAY-- GET UP.

YOU GOT TO KICK HIS--

WATCH...

THIS IS TOO WEIRD...

...WATCH YOUR LANGUAGE, SON...

YES, SIR.

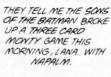

THEY TELL ME THE SONS OF THE BATMAN BROKE UP A THREE CARD MONTY GAME THIS MORNING, LANA. WITH NAPALM.

WHY HASN'T BATMAN DONE SOMETHING ABOUT THOSE LUNATICS? UNLESS, OF COURSE, HE APPROVES...

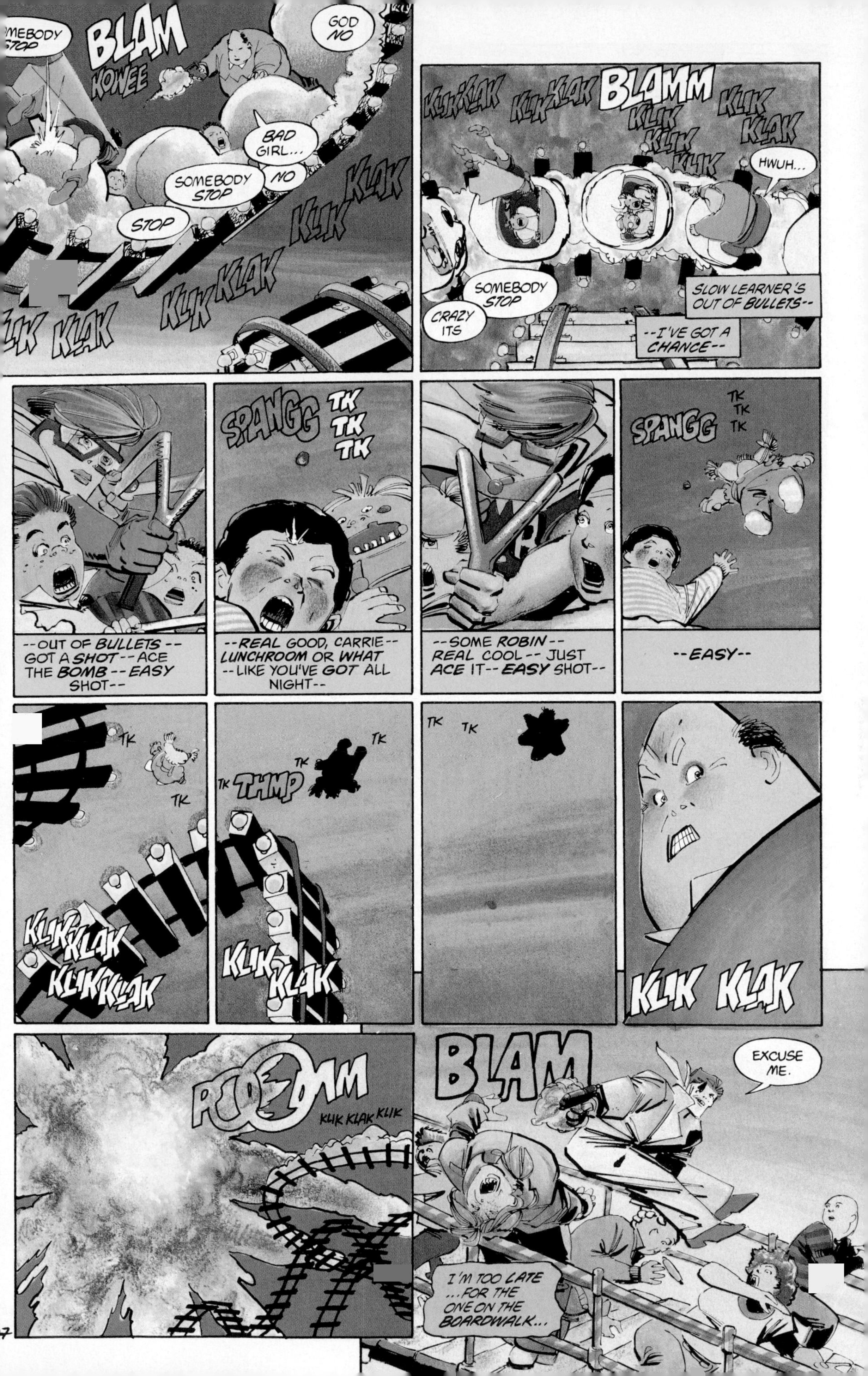

OMEBODY STOP
BLAM
KOWEE
GOD NO
BAD GIRL...
NO
SOMEBODY STOP
STOP
KLAK
KLIK
KLIK KLAK
LIK KLAK
KLIK KLAK
BLAMM
KLIK KLAK
KLIK
KLIK
KLIK
KLIK KLAK
HWUH...
SOMEBODY STOP
CRAZY ITS
SLOW LEARNER'S OUT OF BULLETS--
--I'VE GOT A CHANCE--
--OUT OF BULLETS-- GOT A SHOT--ACE THE BOMB--EASY SHOT--
SPANGG TK TK TK
--REAL GOOD, CARRIE-- LUNCHROOM OR WHAT --LIKE YOU'VE GOT ALL NIGHT--
--SOME ROBIN-- REAL COOL--JUST ACE IT--EASY SHOT--
SPANGG TK TK TK
--EASY--
TK
TK
KLIK KLAK
KLIK KLAK
TK THMP TK TK
KLIK KLAK
TK TK
KLIK KLAK
POOM
KLIK KLAK KLIK
BLAM
EXCUSE ME.
I'M TOO LATE ...FOR THE ONE ON THE BOARDWALK...

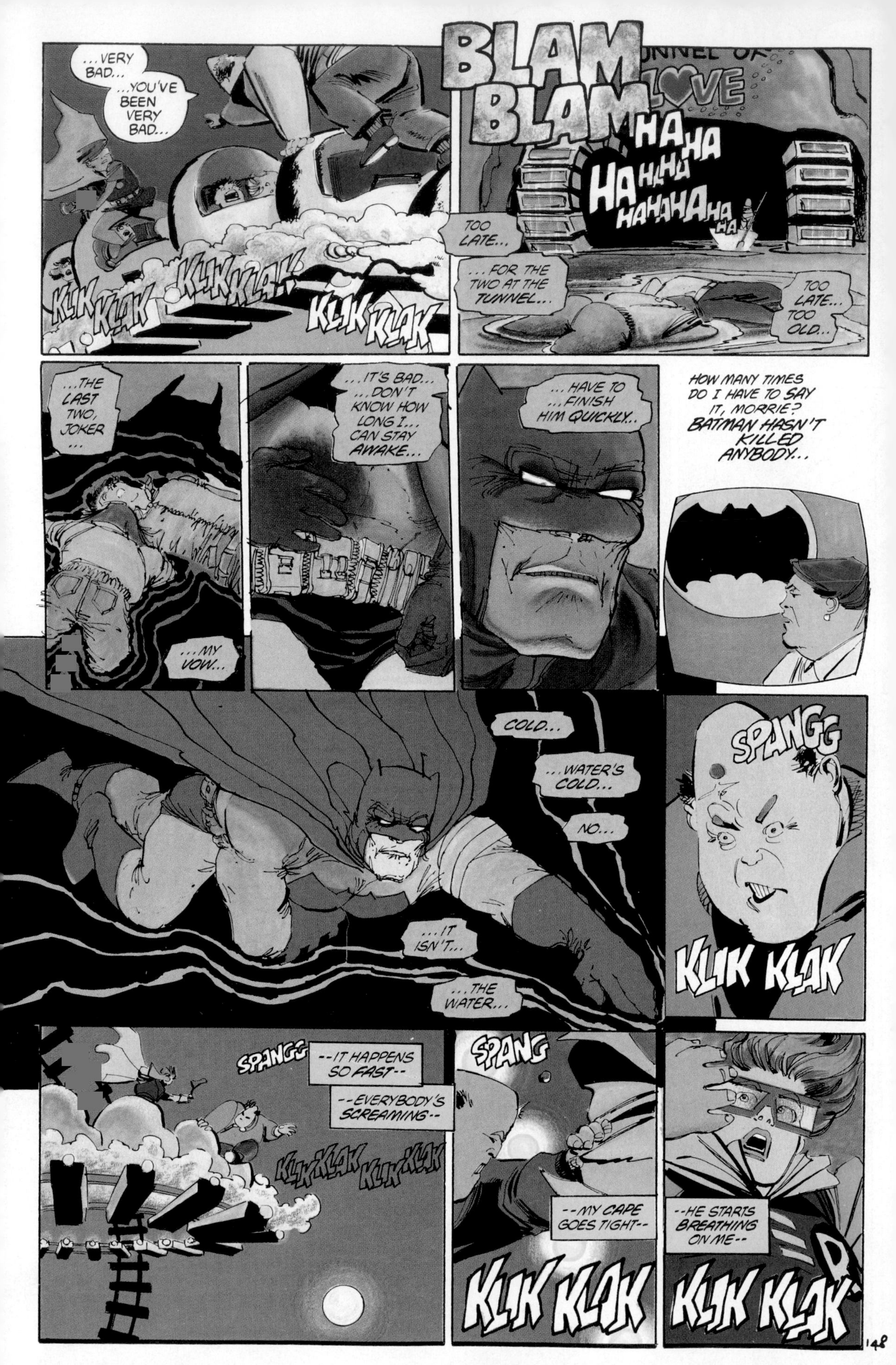
...VERY BAD... ...YOU'VE BEEN VERY BAD...
KLIK KLAK KLIK KLAK
KLIK KLAK
BLAM BLAM
TUNNEL OF LOVE
HA HA HA HA HAHA HAHAHAHA HA HA
TOO LATE...
...FOR THE TWO AT THE TUNNEL...
TOO LATE... TOO OLD...
...THE LAST TWO, JOKER...
...MY VOW...
...IT'S BAD... ...DON'T KNOW HOW LONG I... CAN STAY AWAKE...
...HAVE TO ...FINISH HIM QUICKLY...
HOW MANY TIMES DO I HAVE TO SAY IT, MORRIE? BATMAN HASN'T KILLED ANYBODY...
COLD...
...WATER'S COLD...
NO...
...IT ISN'T...
...THE WATER...
SPANGG
KLIK KLAK
SPANGG
--IT HAPPENS SO FAST--
--EVERYBODY'S SCREAMING--
KLIK KLAK KLIK KLAK
SPANG
--MY CAPE GOES TIGHT--
KLIK KLAK
--HE STARTS BREATHING ON ME--
KLIK KLAK

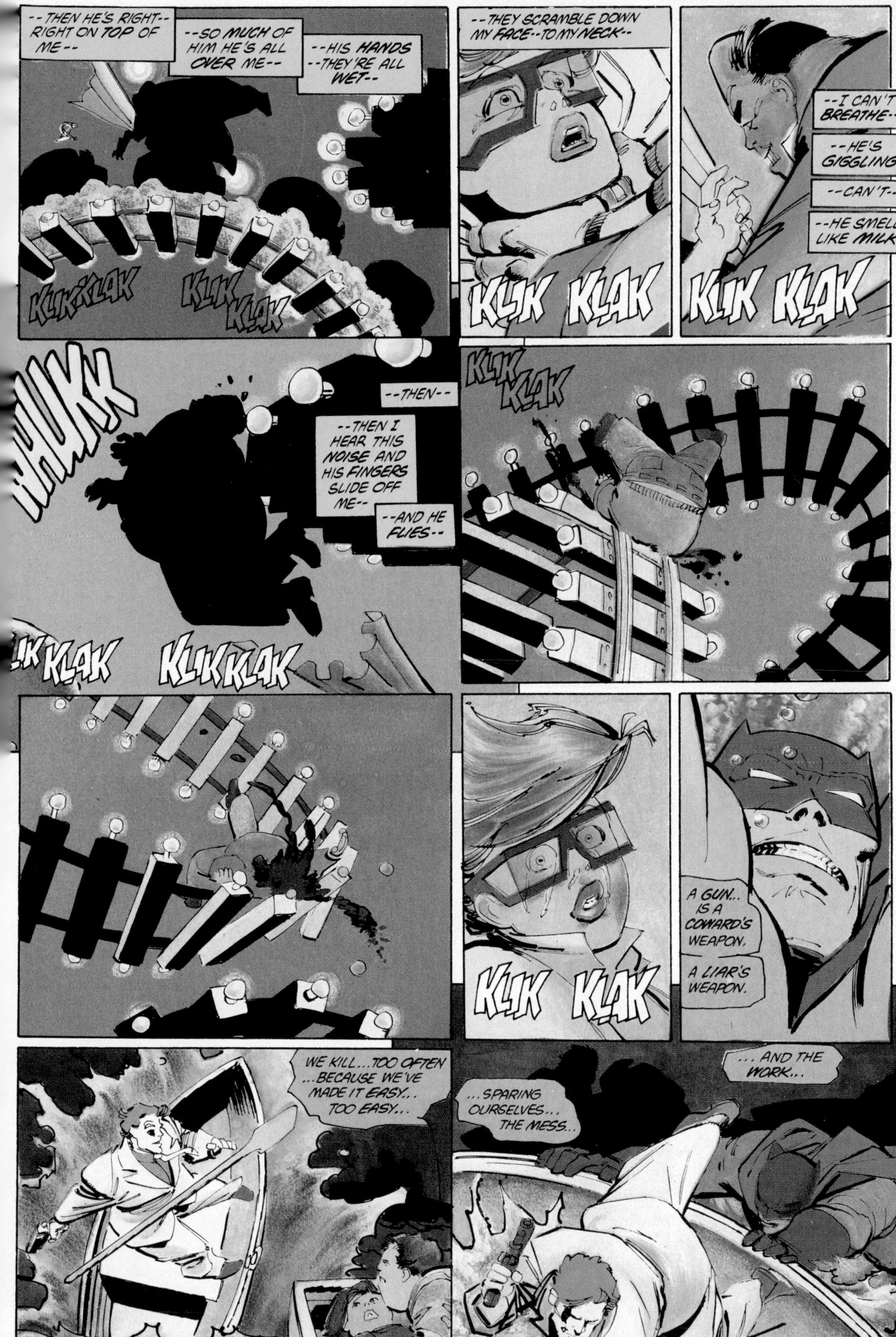
--THEN HE'S RIGHT--RIGHT ON TOP OF ME--
--SO MUCH OF HIM HE'S ALL OVER ME--
--HIS HANDS--THEY'RE ALL WET--
KLIK KLAK
KLIK KLAK
--THEY SCRAMBLE DOWN MY FACE--TO MY NECK--
KLIK KLAK
--I CAN'T BREATHE--
--HE'S GIGGLING--
--CAN'T--
--HE SMELLS LIKE MILK--
KLIK KLAK
THUKK
--THEN--
--THEN I HEAR THIS NOISE AND HIS FINGERS SLIDE OFF ME--
--AND HE FLIES--
KLIK KLAK
KLIK KLAK
KLIK KLAK
KLIK KLAK
A GUN... IS A COWARD'S WEAPON.
A LIAR'S WEAPON.
WE KILL...TOO OFTEN ...BECAUSE WE'VE MADE IT EASY... TOO EASY...
...SPARING OURSELVES... THE MESS...
...AND THE WORK...

IT HAPPENS... SO SLOWLY...

...IT HAPPENS ...IN FIVE SECONDS...

...THE BLADE IS SHARP...

...I BARELY FELT IT ENTER MY STOMACH...

...HE'S TALKING... I CAN'T HEAR HIM...

...SOMETHING IS ROARING... I CAN'T...HEAR ANYTHING...

...HIS NECK... ...WILL HAVE TO DO...

...HE'S MOVING ...MORE QUICKLY THAN I AM...

...STABBING...

SHKK

THNK

THNK

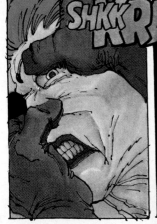

SHKK RAKKK

...THE ROAR... IS FADING...I HEAR... VOICES...

--SHEER PANDEMONIUM HERE AT THE COUNTY FAIR, LOLA! THE JOKER HAS BEEN SIGHTED--SIXTEEN CUB SCOUTS HAVE BEEN FOUND DEAD--DOZENS HAVE BEEN WOUNDED BY EXPLOSIONS--

--AND BATMAN HAS BEEN SEEN--HE AND THE JOKER EXCHANGED GUNFIRE IN A CROWD-- HEY-- WHAT--LOLA-- THEY'RE EVACUATING THE COUNTY FAIR--

...VOICES CALLING ME... A KILLER...

...I WISH I WERE...

THEY'RE GONE..?

...THE WITNESSES, I MEAN...

I'M REALLY...VERY DISAPPOINTED WITH YOU, MY SWEET... THE MOMENT WAS... PERFECT... ...AND YOU... DIDN'T HAVE THE NERVE...

PARALYSIS... REALLY...

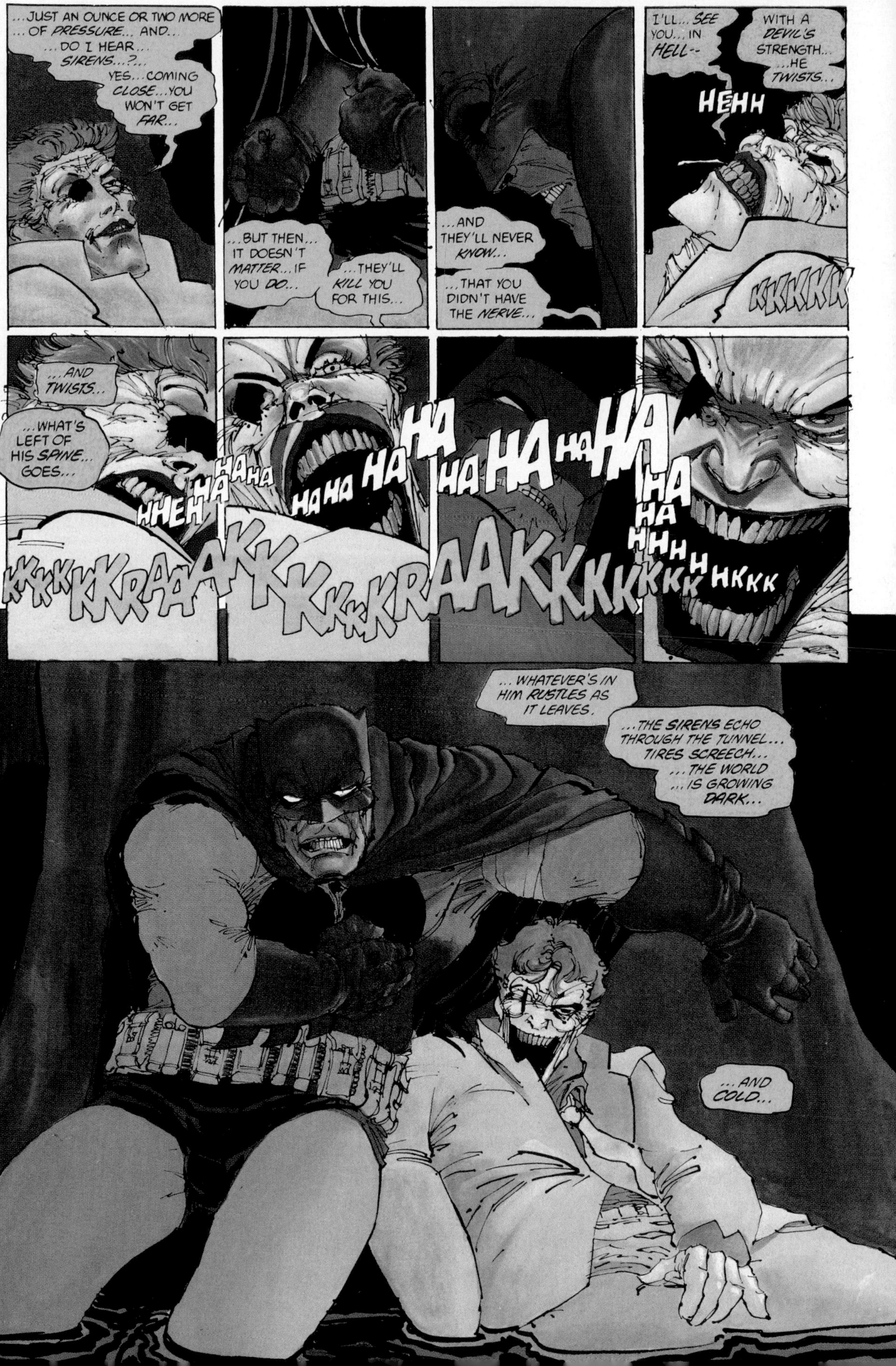
...JUST AN OUNCE OR TWO MORE ...OF PRESSURE... AND... ...DO I HEAR... SIRENS...?...
YES...COMING CLOSE...YOU WON'T GET FAR...
...BUT THEN... IT DOESN'T MATTER...IF YOU DO...
...THEY'LL KILL YOU FOR THIS...
...AND THEY'LL NEVER KNOW...
...THAT YOU DIDN'T HAVE THE NERVE...
I'LL... SEE YOU... IN HELL--
WITH A DEVIL'S STRENGTH... ...HE TWISTS...
HEHH
KKKKKK
...AND TWISTS...
...WHAT'S LEFT OF HIS SPINE... GOES...
HHEH HA HA HAHA HAHA HA HA HA HA HA HA HA HA HA HHH H HKKK
KKKKKRAAAKKKKKKRAAKKKKKKK
...WHATEVER'S IN HIM RUSTLES AS IT LEAVES.
...THE SIRENS ECHO THROUGH THE TUNNEL... TIRES SCREECH... ...THE WORLD ...IS GROWING DARK...
...AND COLD...

BOOK FOUR

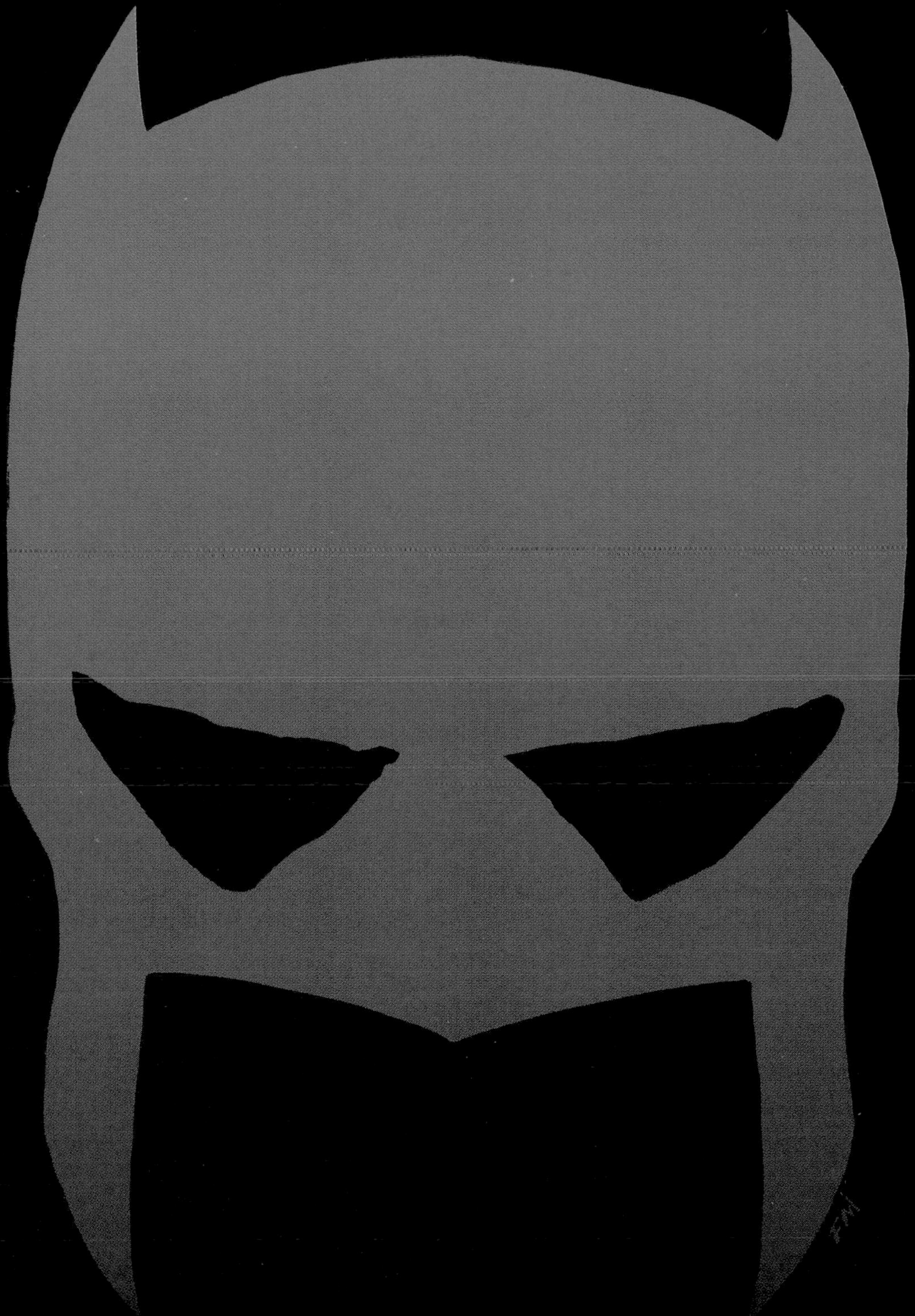

THE DARK KNIGHT FALLS

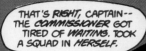

THAT'S RIGHT, CAPTAIN-- THE *COMMISSIONER* GOT TIRED OF *WAITING.* TOOK A SQUAD IN *HERSELF.*

--GOT THE *OTHER* END *SEALED* -- NO *WAY* THEY'LL GET PAST US--

YOU *LIKE* THAT BITCH, DON'T YOU, MERKEL?

--WITNESSES SAY THEY *BOTH* GOT *GUNS*--

--KEEP AN *EYE* OUT--

--GET SOME *BODY BAGS*-- GOT TWO *COLD* ONES--

...SHOWDOWN AT THE COUNTY FAIR, WHERE THE *JOKER* IS SAID TO HAVE *MURDERED* AT LEAST *TWENTY.* SIGHTED WAS THE *BATMAN,* IN HOT *PURSUIT* OF THE *JOKER...*

...LED BY COMMISSIONER *YINDEL,* POLICE WERE LAST SEEN *CONVERGING* ON THE *TUNNEL OF LOVE,* WITH *ARREST ORDERS* FOR BOTH THE *JOKER*-- AND FOR GOTHAM'S *VIGILANTE...*

SO *DARK,* MAN...

CAREFUL, NOW... QUIET...

--CAN'T SEE A DAMN *THING*--

-- SO *DARK*--

TAKE IT SLOW...

THE *INCENDIARIES...* ARE IN *PLACE...*

THE *ENEMY...* IS *SECONDS* AWAY...

I WASTE *ONE* SECOND... WITH A *GOOD-BYE...*

PTUI

SPLTT

COMMISSIONER-- OVER *HERE*--

IT'S THE *JOKER*--

--IT'S NO *SUICIDE*--

SERGEANT --DON'T *TOUCH* IT--

I SAID *DON'T TOUCH*--

JESUS--

RIGGED THE *BODY*--

--LIEUTENANT-- GET HIM *COVERED*--

AAAAA

--SON OF A BITCH *RIGGED* THE *BODY*--

NOW... WHILE THEY'RE *SCARED...*

WHILE MY *GUTS* ARE STILL... WHERE THEY *BELONG...*

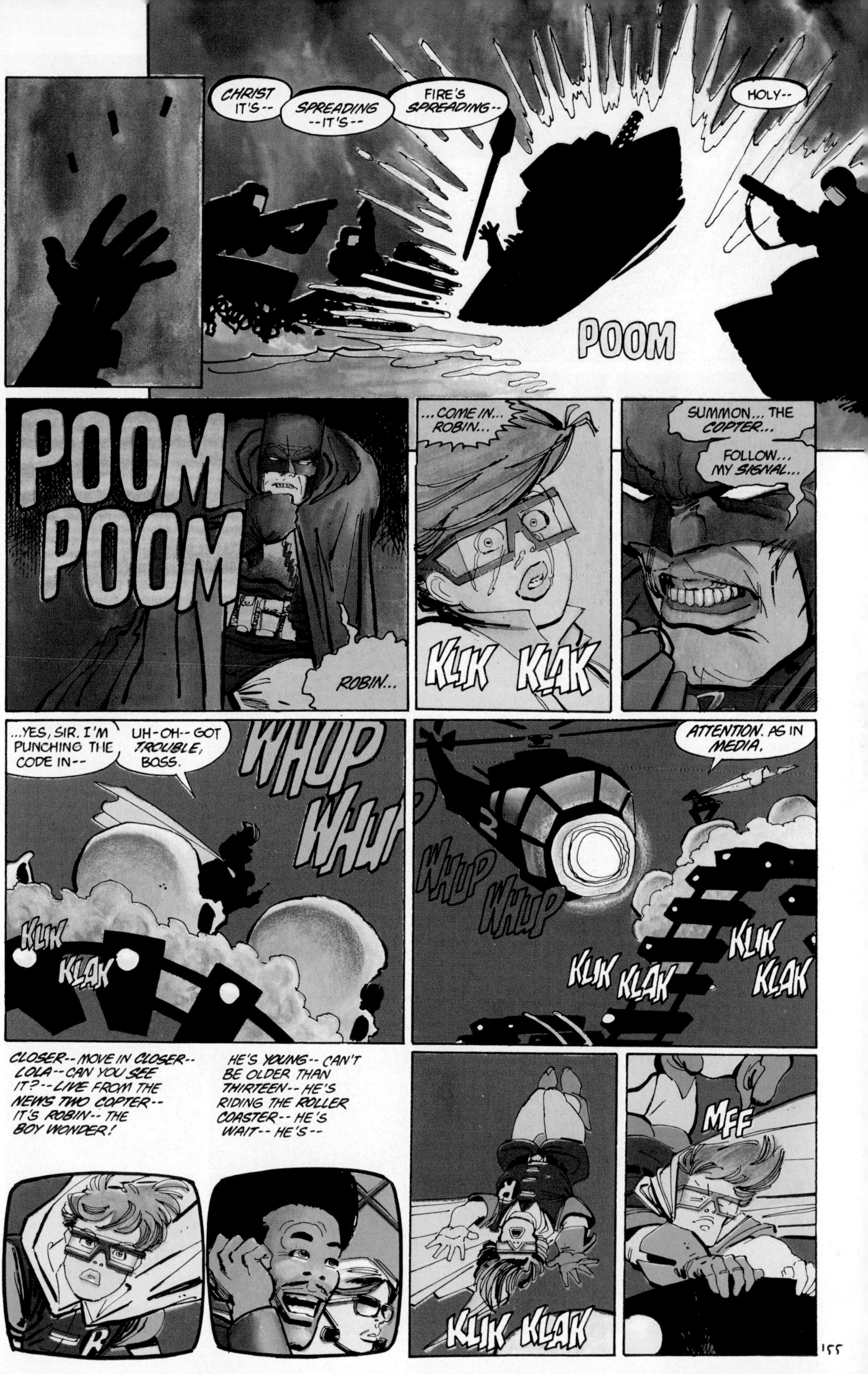
CHRIST IT'S--
SPREADING --IT'S--
FIRE'S SPREADING--
HOLY--
POOM
POOM POOM
ROBIN...
...COME IN... ROBIN...
KLIK KLAK
SUMMON... THE COPTER...
FOLLOW... MY SIGNAL...
...YES, SIR. I'M PUNCHING THE CODE IN--
UH-OH-- GOT TROUBLE, BOSS.
WHUP WHUP
KLIK KLAK
ATTENTION. AS IN MEDIA.
WHUP WHUP
KLIK KLAK KLIK KLAK
CLOSER-- MOVE IN CLOSER-- LOLA-- CAN YOU SEE IT?-- LIVE FROM THE NEWS TWO COPTER-- IT'S ROBIN-- THE BOY WONDER!
HE'S YOUNG-- CAN'T BE OLDER THAN THIRTEEN-- HE'S RIDING THE ROLLER COASTER-- HE'S WAIT-- HE'S--
KLIK KLAK
MFF

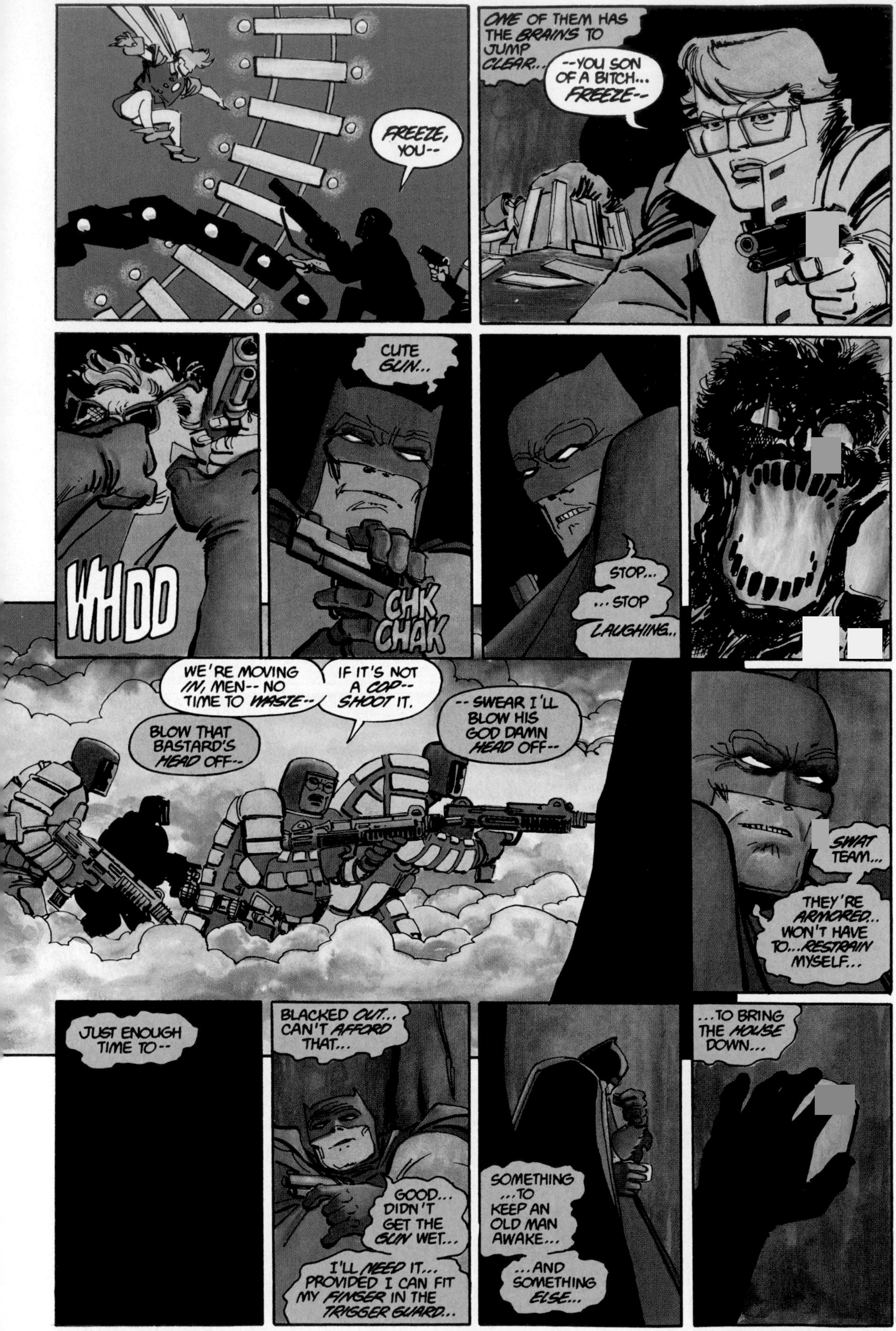
FREEZE, YOU--
ONE OF THEM HAS THE BRAINS TO JUMP CLEAR...
--YOU SON OF A BITCH... FREEZE--
WHDD
CUTE GUN...
CHK CHAK
STOP...
...STOP
LAUGHING...
WE'RE MOVING IN, MEN-- NO TIME TO WASTE--
IF IT'S NOT A COP-- SHOOT IT.
BLOW THAT BASTARD'S HEAD OFF--
--SWEAR I'LL BLOW HIS GOD DAMN HEAD OFF--
SWAT TEAM...
THEY'RE ARMORED... WON'T HAVE TO... RESTRAIN MYSELF...
JUST ENOUGH TIME TO--
BLACKED OUT... CAN'T AFFORD THAT...
GOOD... DIDN'T GET THE GUN WET...
I'LL NEED IT... PROVIDED I CAN FIT MY FINGER IN THE TRIGGER GUARD...
SOMETHING ...TO KEEP AN OLD MAN AWAKE...
...AND SOMETHING ELSE...
...TO BRING THE HOUSE DOWN...

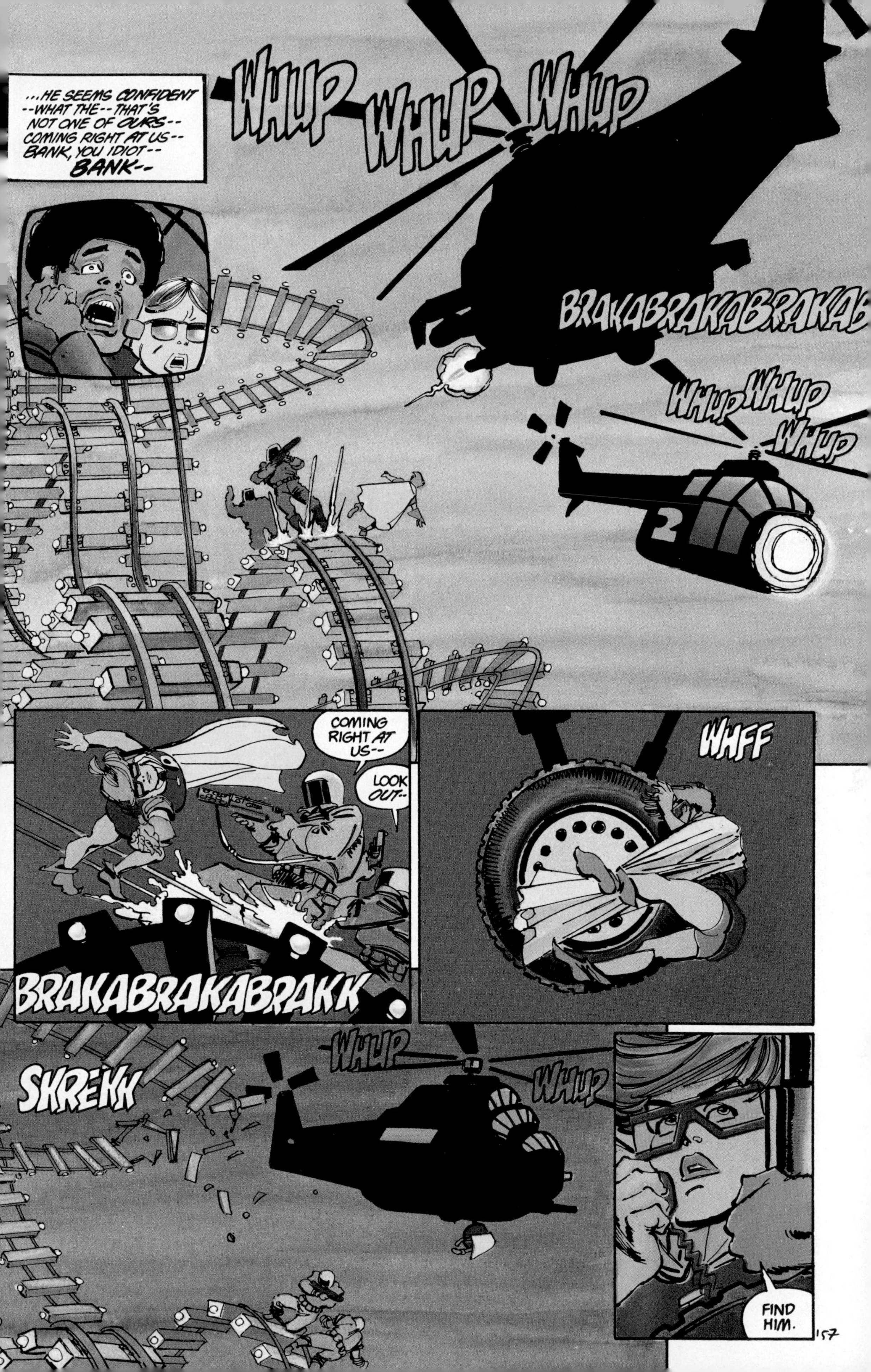
...HE SEEMS CONFIDENT --WHAT THE--THAT'S NOT ONE OF OURS-- COMING RIGHT AT US-- BANK, YOU IDIOT-- BANK--
WHUP WHUP WHUP
BRAKABRAKABRAKAB
WHUP WHUP WHUP
COMING RIGHT AT US--
LOOK OUT--
BRAKABRAKABRAKK
WHFF
SKREKK
WHUP
WHUP
FIND HIM.

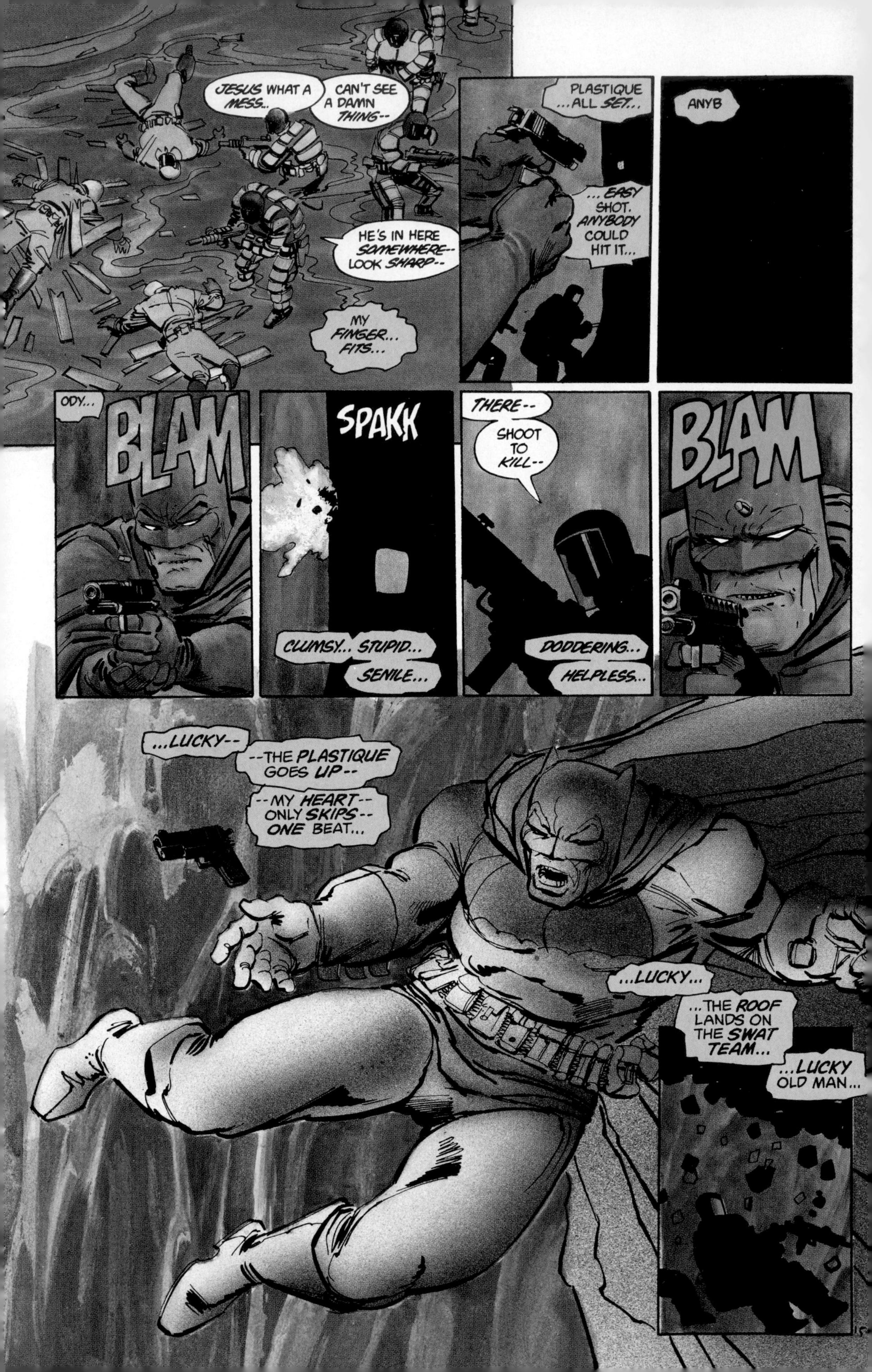
JESUS WHAT A MESS..
CAN'T SEE A DAMN THING--
HE'S IN HERE SOMEWHERE-- LOOK SHARP--
MY FINGER... FITS...
PLASTIQUE ...ALL SET...
...EASY SHOT. ANYBODY COULD HIT IT...
ANYB
ODY...
BLAM
SPAKK
CLUMSY... STUPID...
SENILE...
THERE--
SHOOT TO KILL--
DODDERING...
HELPLESS...
BLAM
...LUCKY--
--THE PLASTIQUE GOES UP--
--MY HEART-- ONLY SKIPS-- ONE BEAT...
...LUCKY...
...THE ROOF LANDS ON THE SWAT TEAM...
...LUCKY OLD MAN...
15

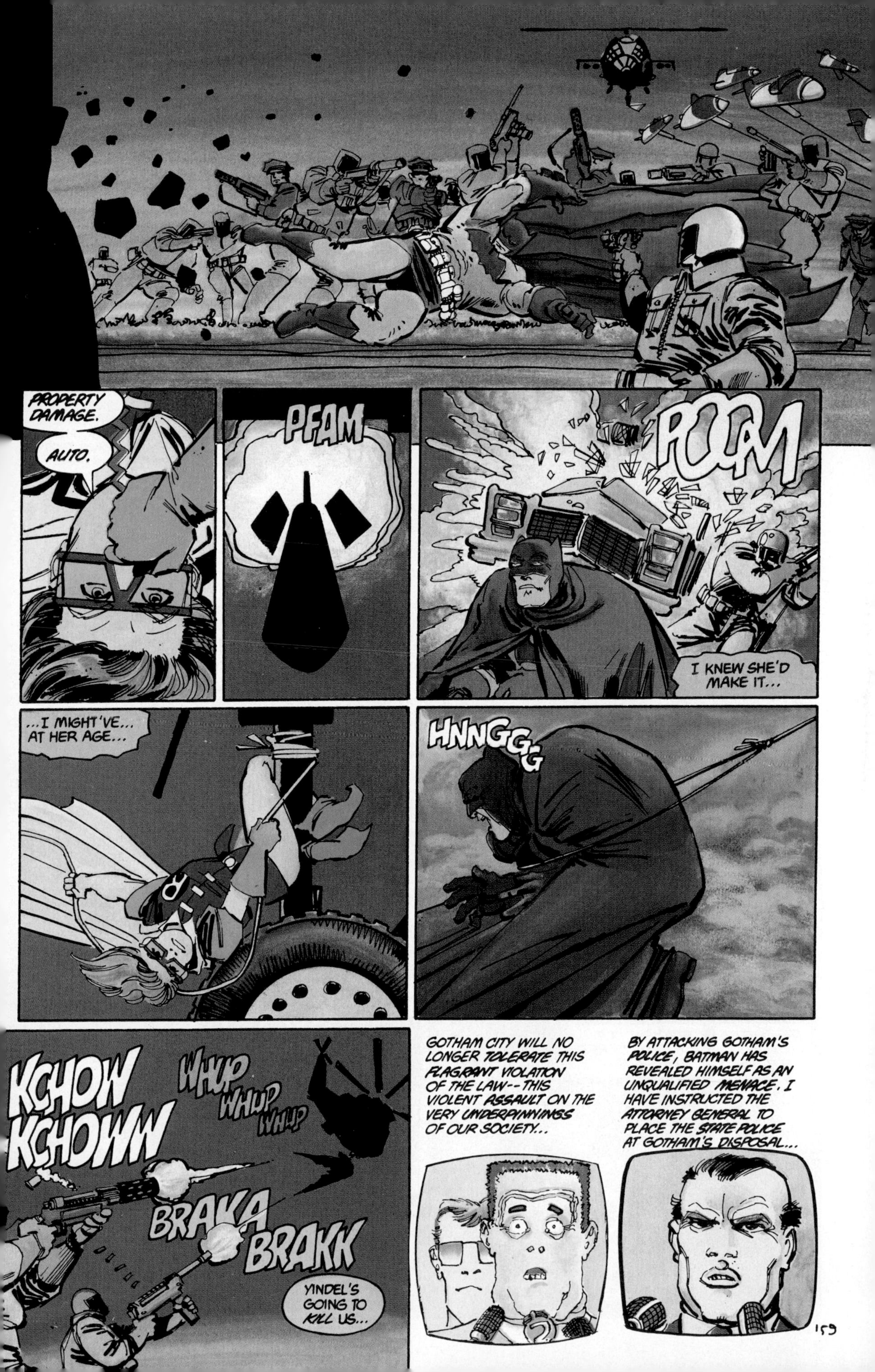

PROPERTY DAMAGE.
AUTO.
PFAM
POOM
I KNEW SHE'D MAKE IT...
...I MIGHT'VE... AT HER AGE...
HNNGGG
KCHOW KCHOWW
WHUP WHUP WHUP
BRAKA BRAKK
YINDEL'S GOING TO KILL US...
GOTHAM CITY WILL NO LONGER TOLERATE THIS FLAGRANT VIOLATION OF THE LAW--THIS VIOLENT ASSAULT ON THE VERY UNDERPINNINGS OF OUR SOCIETY...
BY ATTACKING GOTHAM'S POLICE, BATMAN HAS REVEALED HIMSELF AS AN UNQUALIFIED MENACE. I HAVE INSTRUCTED THE ATTORNEY GENERAL TO PLACE THE STATE POLICE AT GOTHAM'S DISPOSAL...

...THE JOKER'S BODY FOUND MUTILATED AND BURNED... MURDER IS ADDED TO THE CHARGES AGAINST THE BATMAN...

BRUCE. IT'S OVER.

YOU LOOK *TIRED*, KENT.

WELL, YOU'VE EARNED A GOOD NIGHT'S *SLEEP*.

HECK OF A POLICE ACTION, IF YOU ASK ME...

I DIDN'T...

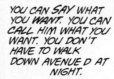

YOU CAN SAY WHAT YOU *WANT*. YOU CAN CALL HIM WHAT YOU WANT. YOU DON'T HAVE TO WALK DOWN AVENUE D AT NIGHT.

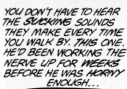

YOU DON'T HAVE TO HEAR THE *SUCKING* SOUNDS THEY MAKE EVERY TIME YOU WALK BY. THIS ONE. HE'D BEEN WORKING THE NERVE UP FOR *WEEKS* BEFORE HE WAS *HORNY* ENOUGH...

...NO, HORNY HE *WASN'T*. HE WAS JUST LOOKING TO *HURT* SOMEBODY AND HE'S THE KIND WHO HURTS *WOMEN*. I WISH THEY WERE *RARE*. HE GAVE HIMSELF AN *EXCUSE*...

SO NOW HE'S *GIGGLING* LIKE HE'S *TURNED ON*! I FIGURE HE'S *SERIOUS* ENOUGH TO RUN *AFTER* ME. I GO FOR THE *MACE*.

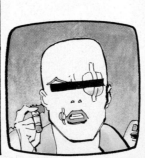

THE CREEP'S PULLING OUT HIS *WEAPON* WHEN THERE'S THIS *SHRIEK*.

STRAIGHT OUT OF HELL THERE'S THIS SHRIEK...

...IT TURNS INTO A *GROWL*-- FLAPPING OF *WINGS*--BIG *WINGS*--

-- SOMETHING *WET* HAPPENS TO THE *CREEP*--

160

--A SIDE OF *BEEF* SLAMS INTO THE *LAMPPOST*--

--A *SWITCHBLADE* SNAPS OPEN--

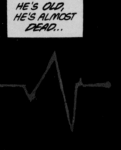

BONES START POPPING INSIDE THE *CREEP*-- HE'S SCREAMING AND *BEGGING*--

--WHAT *GRABBED* HIM IS *LAUGHING* AND SO AM I...

AND THE MAN WHO *ASSAULTED* YOU?

STILL IN THE *HOSPITAL*.

HE'S *OLD*, HE'S ALMOST *DEAD*...

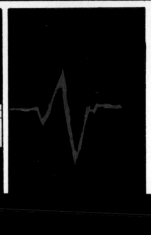

SUTURE.

HE'S GOING TO BE *OKAY*, RIGHT?

HE'LL *LIVE*...

DO NOT EXPECT ANY FURTHER *STATEMENTS*. THE *SONS* OF THE *BATMAN* DO NOT *TALK*. WE *ACT*. LET GOTHAM'S CRIMINALS *BEWARE*. THEY ARE ABOUT TO ENTER *HELL*.

THE MUTANTS ARE *DEAD*. THE MUTANTS ARE *HISTORY*. THIS IS THE *MARK* OF THE *FUTURE*. *GOTHAM CITY* BELONGS TO THE *BATMAN*.

...THE *SONS OF THE BATMAN* HAVE STRUCK AGAIN. JEFF STROCKEN WAS CLOSING UP THE SOUTH STREET 7-11 WHEN HE BECAME BOTH WITNESS-- AND VICTIM...

THEY'RE *YOUNGER* THAN YOU'D THINK--*THIS ONE* WAS, ANYWAY. COULDN'T HAVE BEEN OLDER THAN *SIXTEEN*... THAT'S *RIGHT*, THERE WAS JUST *ONE* OF THEM...

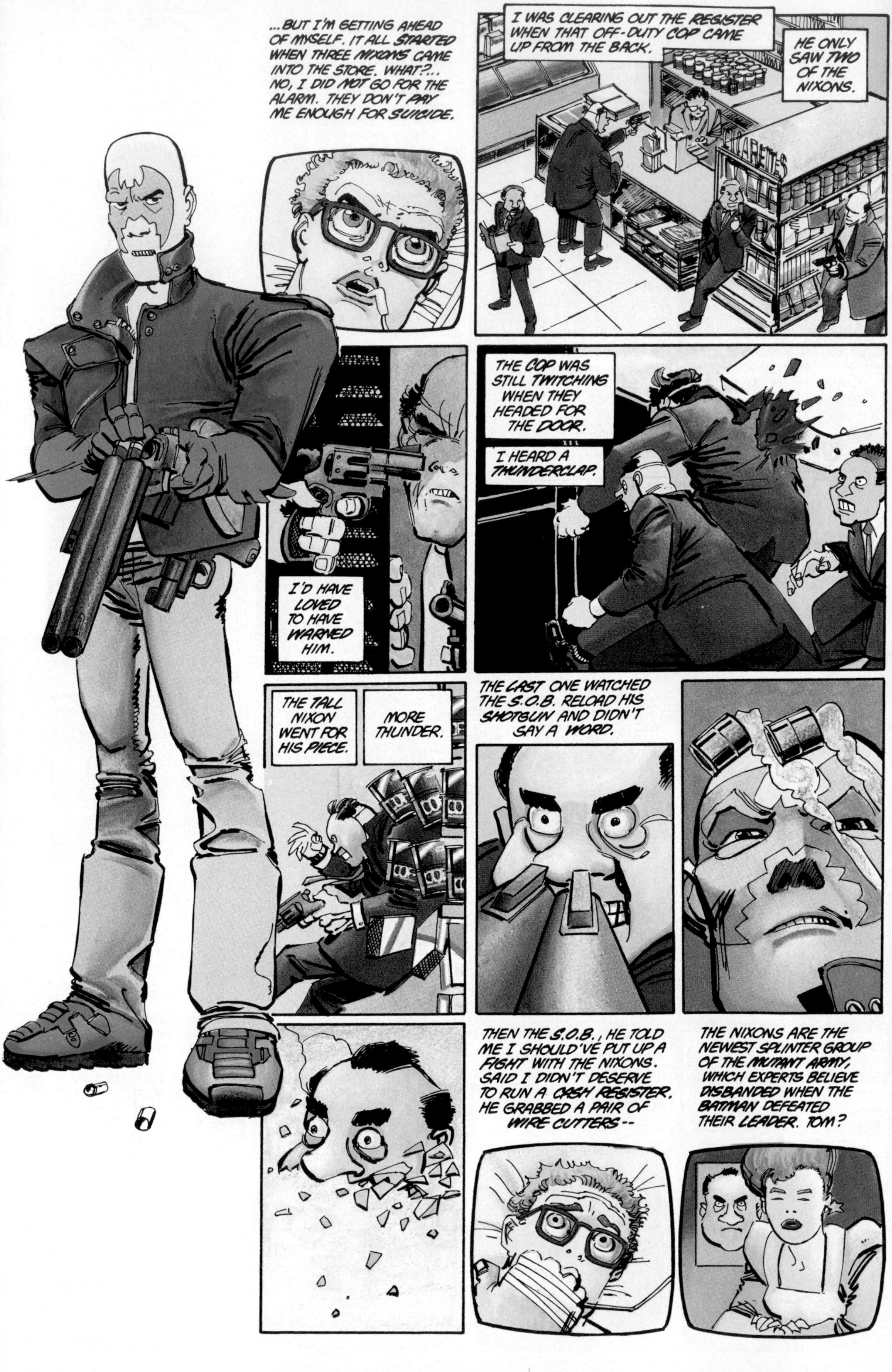
...BUT I'M GETTING AHEAD OF MYSELF. IT ALL STARTED WHEN THREE NIXONS CAME INTO THE STORE. WHAT?... NO, I DID NOT GO FOR THE ALARM. THEY DON'T PAY ME ENOUGH FOR SUICIDE.
I WAS CLEARING OUT THE REGISTER WHEN THAT OFF-DUTY COP CAME UP FROM THE BACK.
HE ONLY SAW TWO OF THE NIXONS.
CIGARETTES
I'D HAVE LOVED TO HAVE WARNED HIM.
THE COP WAS STILL TWITCHING WHEN THEY HEADED FOR THE DOOR.
I HEARD A THUNDERCLAP.
THE TALL NIXON WENT FOR HIS PIECE.
MORE THUNDER.
THE LAST ONE WATCHED THE S.O.B. RELOAD HIS SHOTGUN AND DIDN'T SAY A WORD.
THEN THE S.O.B., HE TOLD ME I SHOULD'VE PUT UP A FIGHT WITH THE NIXONS. SAID I DIDN'T DESERVE TO RUN A CASH REGISTER. HE GRABBED A PAIR OF WIRE CUTTERS--
THE NIXONS ARE THE NEWEST SPLINTER GROUP OF THE MUTANT ARMY, WHICH EXPERTS BELIEVE DISBANDED WHEN THE BATMAN DEFEATED THEIR LEADER. TOM?

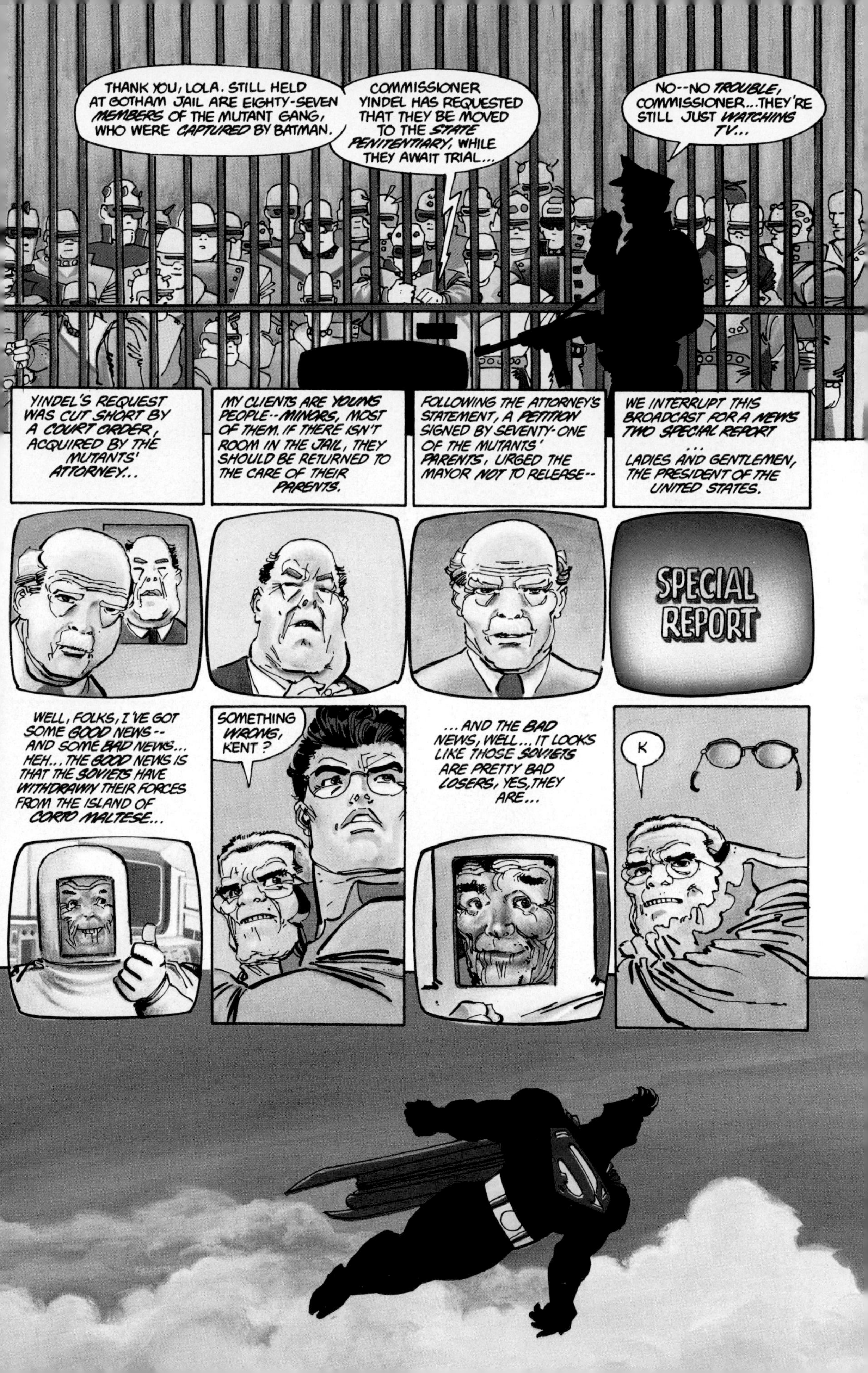
THANK YOU, LOLA. STILL HELD AT GOTHAM JAIL ARE EIGHTY-SEVEN MEMBERS OF THE MUTANT GANG, WHO WERE CAPTURED BY BATMAN.
COMMISSIONER YINDEL HAS REQUESTED THAT THEY BE MOVED TO THE STATE PENITENTIARY, WHILE THEY AWAIT TRIAL...
NO--NO TROUBLE, COMMISSIONER... THEY'RE STILL JUST WATCHING TV...
YINDEL'S REQUEST WAS CUT SHORT BY A COURT ORDER, ACQUIRED BY THE MUTANTS' ATTORNEY...
MY CLIENTS ARE YOUNG PEOPLE--MINORS, MOST OF THEM. IF THERE ISN'T ROOM IN THE JAIL, THEY SHOULD BE RETURNED TO THE CARE OF THEIR PARENTS.
FOLLOWING THE ATTORNEY'S STATEMENT, A PETITION SIGNED BY SEVENTY-ONE OF THE MUTANTS' PARENTS, URGED THE MAYOR NOT TO RELEASE--
WE INTERRUPT THIS BROADCAST FOR A NEWS TWO SPECIAL REPORT ... LADIES AND GENTLEMEN, THE PRESIDENT OF THE UNITED STATES.
SPECIAL REPORT
WELL, FOLKS, I'VE GOT SOME GOOD NEWS -- AND SOME BAD NEWS... HEH... THE GOOD NEWS IS THAT THE SOVIETS HAVE WITHDRAWN THEIR FORCES FROM THE ISLAND OF CORTO MALTESE...
SOMETHING WRONG, KENT ?
... AND THE BAD NEWS, WELL... IT LOOKS LIKE THOSE SOVIETS ARE PRETTY BAD LOSERS, YES, THEY ARE...
K

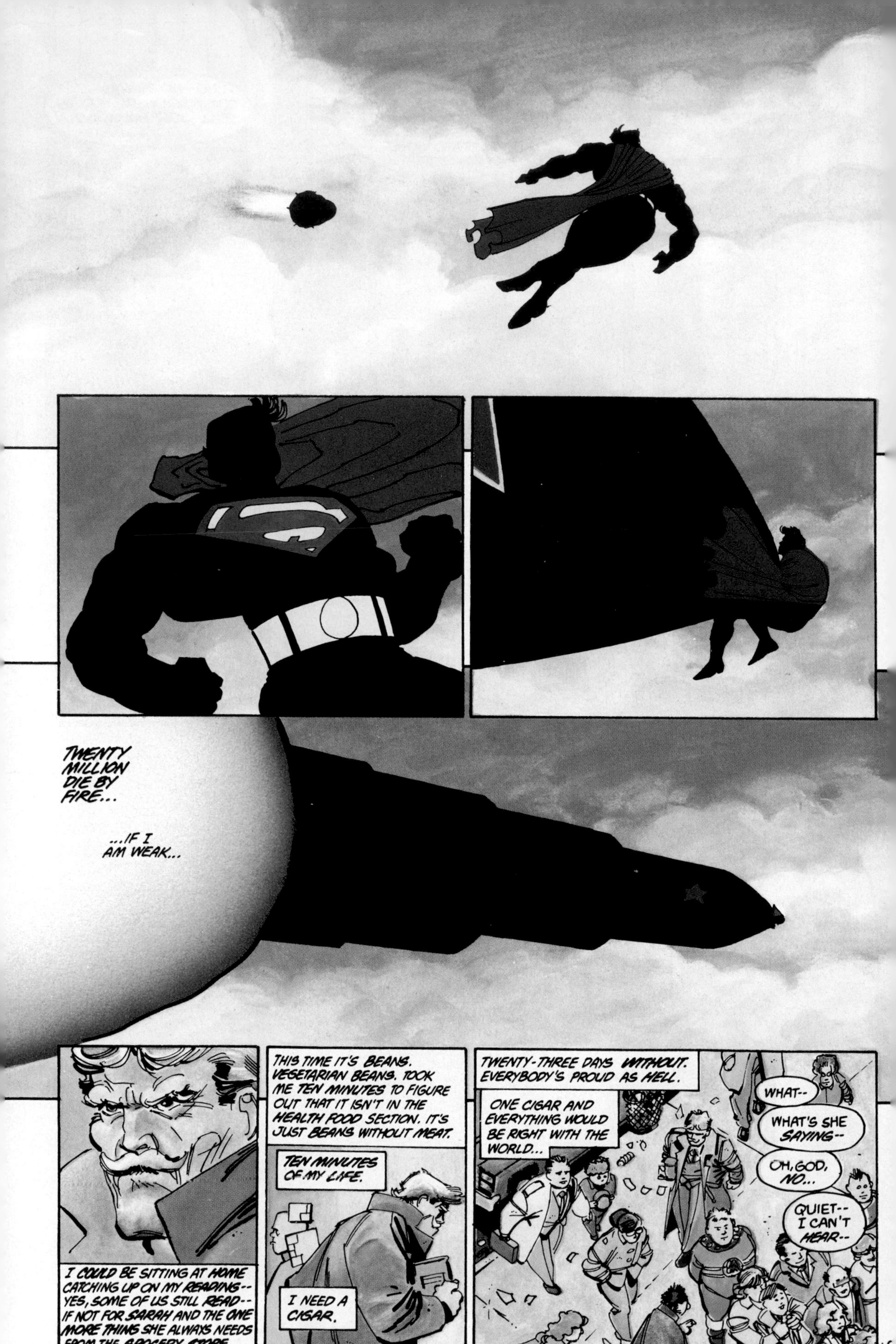
TWENTY MILLION DIE BY FIRE...
...IF I AM WEAK...
I COULD BE SITTING AT HOME CATCHING UP ON MY READINGS-- YES, SOME OF US STILL READ-- IF NOT FOR SARAH AND THE ONE MORE THING SHE ALWAYS NEEDS FROM THE GROCERY STORE.
THIS TIME IT'S BEANS. VEGETARIAN BEANS. TOOK ME TEN MINUTES TO FIGURE OUT THAT IT ISN'T IN THE HEALTH FOOD SECTION. IT'S JUST BEANS WITHOUT MEAT.
TEN MINUTES OF MY LIFE.
I NEED A CIGAR.
TWENTY-THREE DAYS WITHOUT. EVERYBODY'S PROUD AS HELL.
ONE CIGAR AND EVERYTHING WOULD BE RIGHT WITH THE WORLD...
WHAT--
WHAT'S SHE SAYING--
OH, GOD, NO...
QUIET-- I CAN'T HEAR--

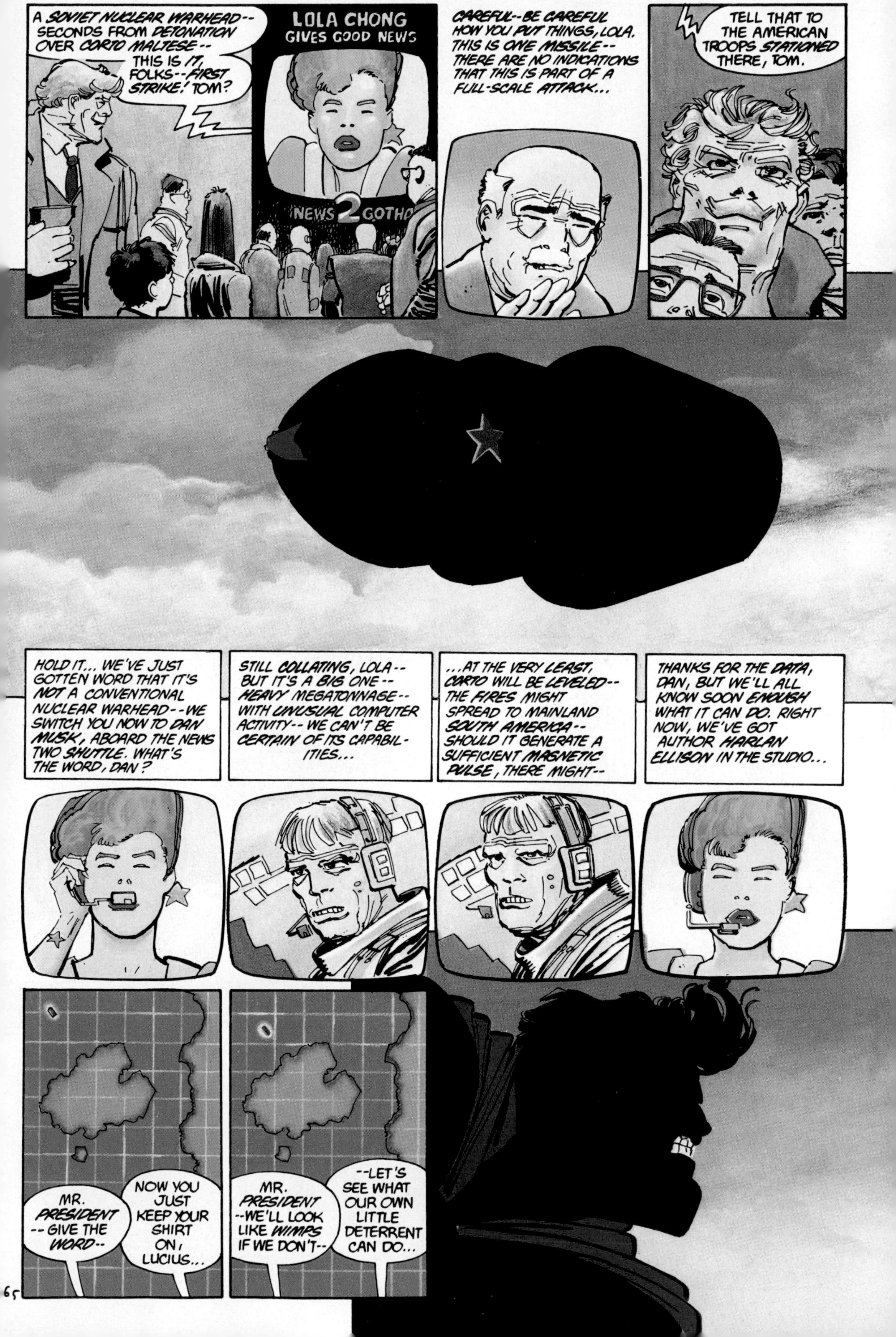
A SOVIET NUCLEAR WARHEAD-- SECONDS FROM DETONATION OVER CORTO MALTESE--
THIS IS IT, FOLKS--FIRST STRIKE! TOM?
LOLA CHONG GIVES GOOD NEWS
NEWS 2 GOTHA
CAREFUL--BE CAREFUL HOW YOU PUT THINGS, LOLA. THIS IS ONE MISSILE-- THERE ARE NO INDICATIONS THAT THIS IS PART OF A FULL-SCALE ATTACK...
TELL THAT TO THE AMERICAN TROOPS STATIONED THERE, TOM.
HOLD IT... WE'VE JUST GOTTEN WORD THAT IT'S NOT A CONVENTIONAL NUCLEAR WARHEAD--WE SWITCH YOU NOW TO DAN MUSK, ABOARD THE NEWS TWO SHUTTLE. WHAT'S THE WORD, DAN?
STILL COLLATING, LOLA-- BUT IT'S A BIG ONE-- HEAVY MEGATONNAGE-- WITH UNUSUAL COMPUTER ACTIVITY-- WE CAN'T BE CERTAIN OF ITS CAPABILITIES...
...AT THE VERY LEAST, CORTO WILL BE LEVELED-- THE FIRES MIGHT SPREAD TO MAINLAND SOUTH AMERICA-- SHOULD IT GENERATE A SUFFICIENT MAGNETIC PULSE, THERE MIGHT--
THANKS FOR THE DATA, DAN, BUT WE'LL ALL KNOW SOON ENOUGH WHAT IT CAN DO. RIGHT NOW, WE'VE GOT AUTHOR HARLAN ELLISON IN THE STUDIO...
MR. PRESIDENT --GIVE THE WORD--
NOW YOU JUST KEEP YOUR SHIRT ON, LUCIUS...
MR. PRESIDENT --WE'LL LOOK LIKE WIMPS IF WE DON'T--
--LET'S SEE WHAT OUR OWN LITTLE DETERRENT CAN DO...

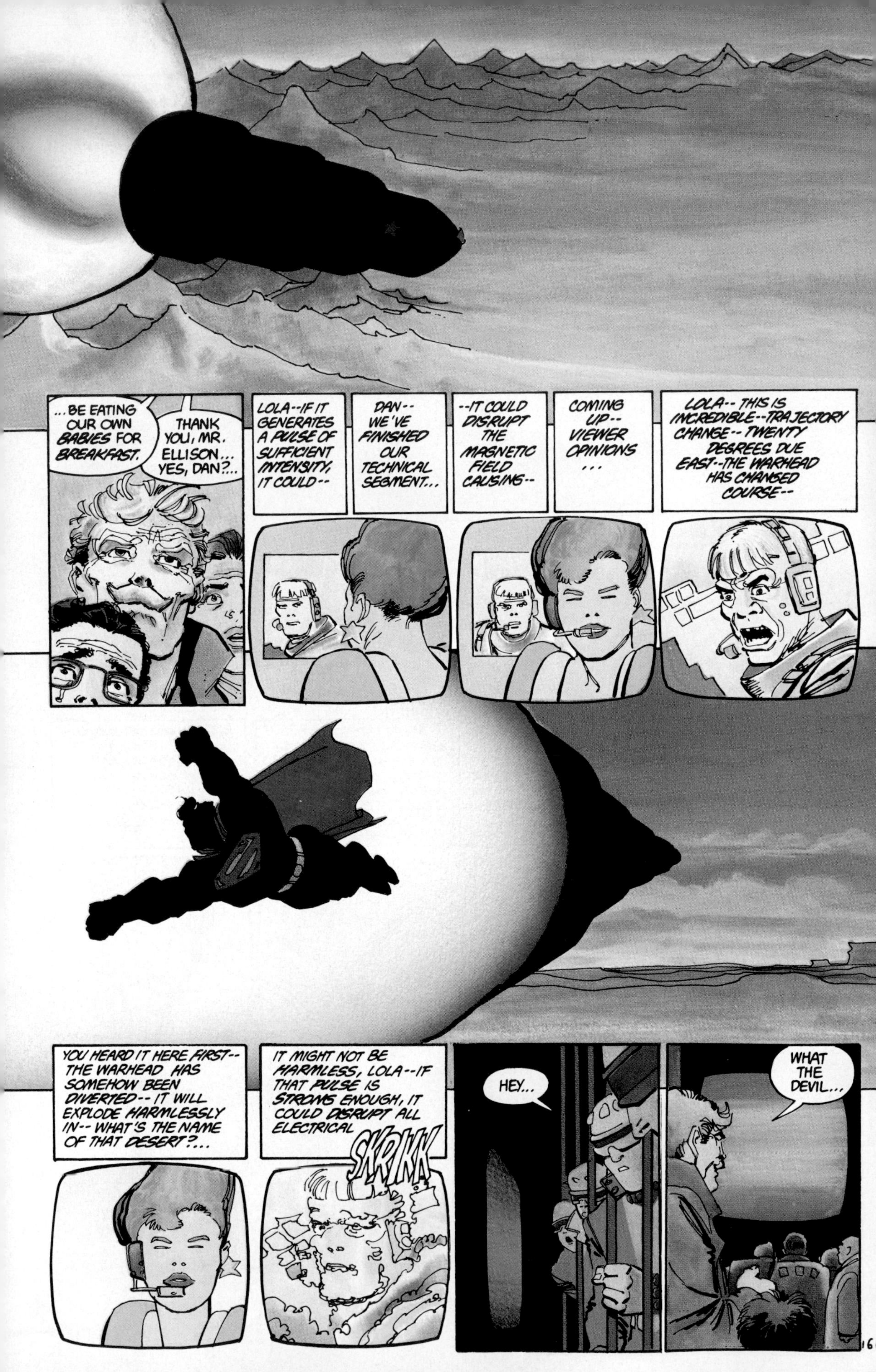

...BE EATING OUR OWN BABIES FOR BREAKFAST.
THANK YOU, MR. ELLISON... YES, DAN?...
LOLA--IF IT GENERATES A PULSE OF SUFFICIENT INTENSITY, IT COULD--
DAN-- WE'VE FINISHED OUR TECHNICAL SEGMENT...
--IT COULD DISRUPT THE MAGNETIC FIELD CAUSING--
COMING UP-- VIEWER OPINIONS ...
LOLA-- THIS IS INCREDIBLE--TRAJECTORY CHANGE-- TWENTY DEGREES DUE EAST--THE WARHEAD HAS CHANGED COURSE--
YOU HEARD IT HERE FIRST-- THE WARHEAD HAS SOMEHOW BEEN DIVERTED-- IT WILL EXPLODE HARMLESSLY IN-- WHAT'S THE NAME OF THAT DESERT?...
IT MIGHT NOT BE HARMLESS, LOLA--IF THAT PULSE IS STRONG ENOUGH, IT COULD DISRUPT ALL ELECTRICAL
SKRIKK
HEY...
WHAT THE DEVIL...

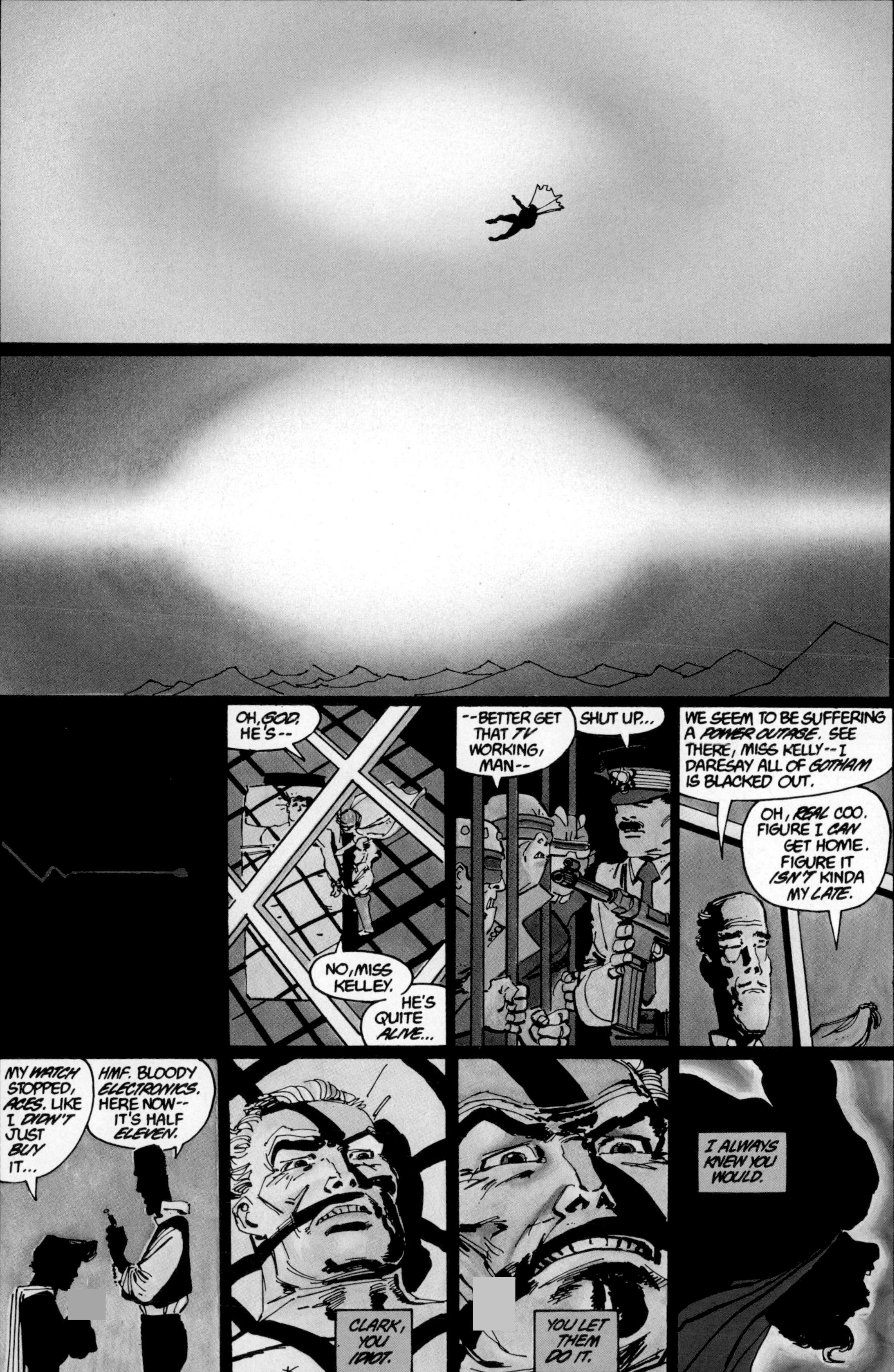
OH, GOD, HE'S--
NO, MISS KELLEY. HE'S QUITE ALIVE...
--BETTER GET THAT TV WORKING, MAN--
SHUT UP...
WE SEEM TO BE SUFFERING A POWER OUTAGE. SEE THERE, MISS KELLY--I DARESAY ALL OF GOTHAM IS BLACKED OUT.
OH, REAL COO. FIGURE I CAN GET HOME. FIGURE IT ISN'T KINDA MY LATE.
MY WATCH STOPPED, ACES. LIKE I DIDN'T JUST BUY IT...
HMF. BLOODY ELECTRONICS. HERE NOW--IT'S HALF ELEVEN.
CLARK, YOU IDIOT.
YOU LET THEM DO IT.
I ALWAYS KNEW YOU WOULD.

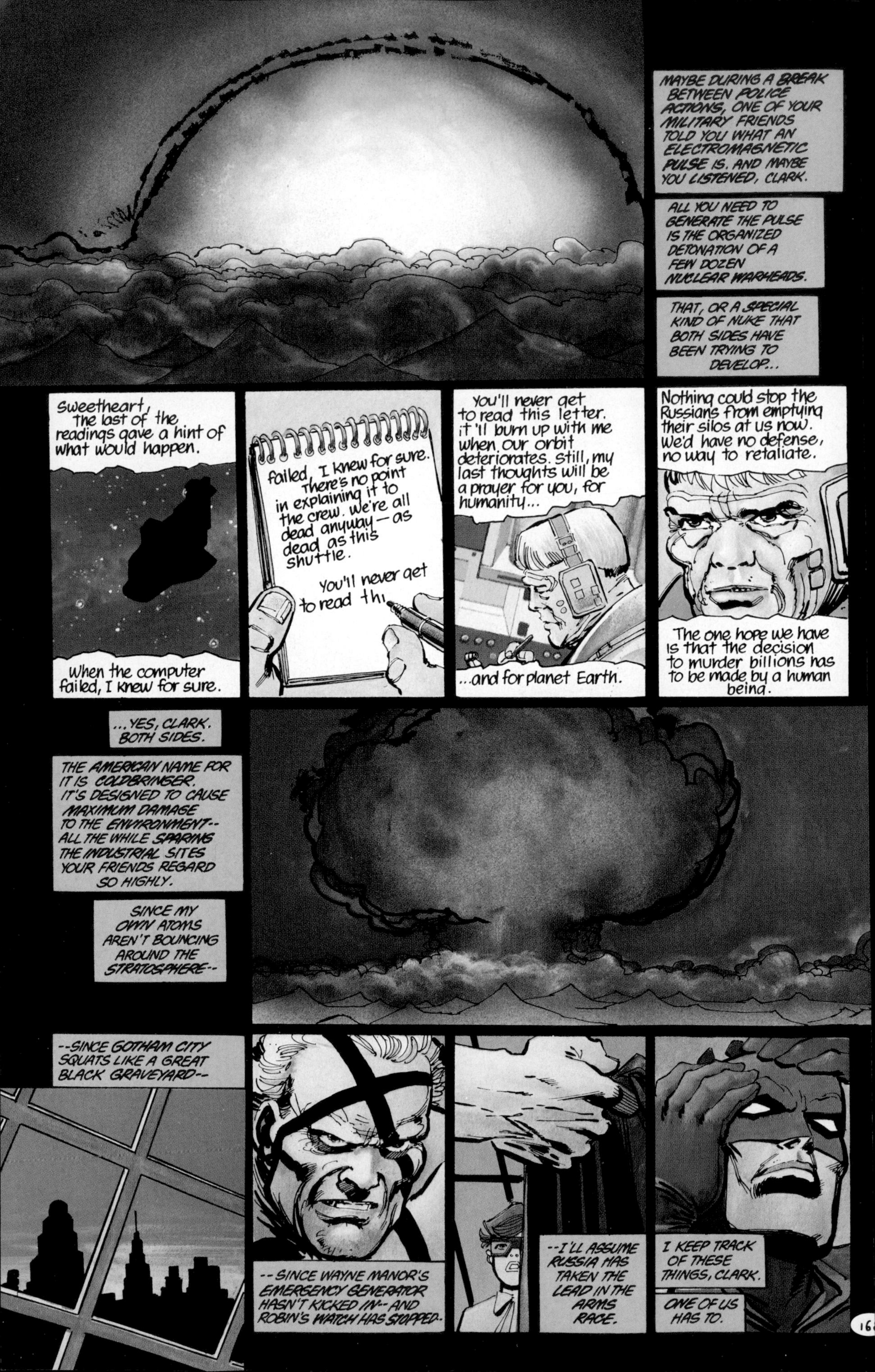
MAYBE DURING A BREAK BETWEEN POLICE ACTIONS, ONE OF YOUR MILITARY FRIENDS TOLD YOU WHAT AN ELECTROMAGNETIC PULSE IS. AND MAYBE YOU LISTENED, CLARK.
ALL YOU NEED TO GENERATE THE PULSE IS THE ORGANIZED DETONATION OF A FEW DOZEN NUCLEAR WARHEADS.
THAT, OR A SPECIAL KIND OF NUKE THAT BOTH SIDES HAVE BEEN TRYING TO DEVELOP...
Sweetheart, the last of the readings gave a hint of what would happen.
When the computer failed, I knew for sure.
failed, I knew for sure. There's no point in explaining it to the crew. We're all dead anyway—as dead as this shuttle.
You'll never get to read thi
You'll never get to read this letter. it'll burn up with me when our orbit deteriorates. Still, my last thoughts will be a prayer for you, for humanity...
...and for planet Earth.
Nothing could stop the Russians from emptying their silos at us now. We'd have no defense, no way to retaliate.
The one hope we have is that the decision to murder billions has to be made by a human being.
...YES, CLARK. BOTH SIDES.
THE AMERICAN NAME FOR IT IS COLDBRINGER. IT'S DESIGNED TO CAUSE MAXIMUM DAMAGE TO THE ENVIRONMENT-- ALL THE WHILE SPARING THE INDUSTRIAL SITES YOUR FRIENDS REGARD SO HIGHLY.
SINCE MY OWN ATOMS AREN'T BOUNCING AROUND THE STRATOSPHERE--
--SINCE GOTHAM CITY SQUATS LIKE A GREAT BLACK GRAVEYARD--
--SINCE WAYNE MANOR'S EMERGENCY GENERATOR HASN'T KICKED IN--AND ROBIN'S WATCH HAS STOPPED--
--I'LL ASSUME RUSSIA HAS TAKEN THE LEAD IN THE ARMS RACE.
I KEEP TRACK OF THESE THINGS, CLARK.
ONE OF US HAS TO.

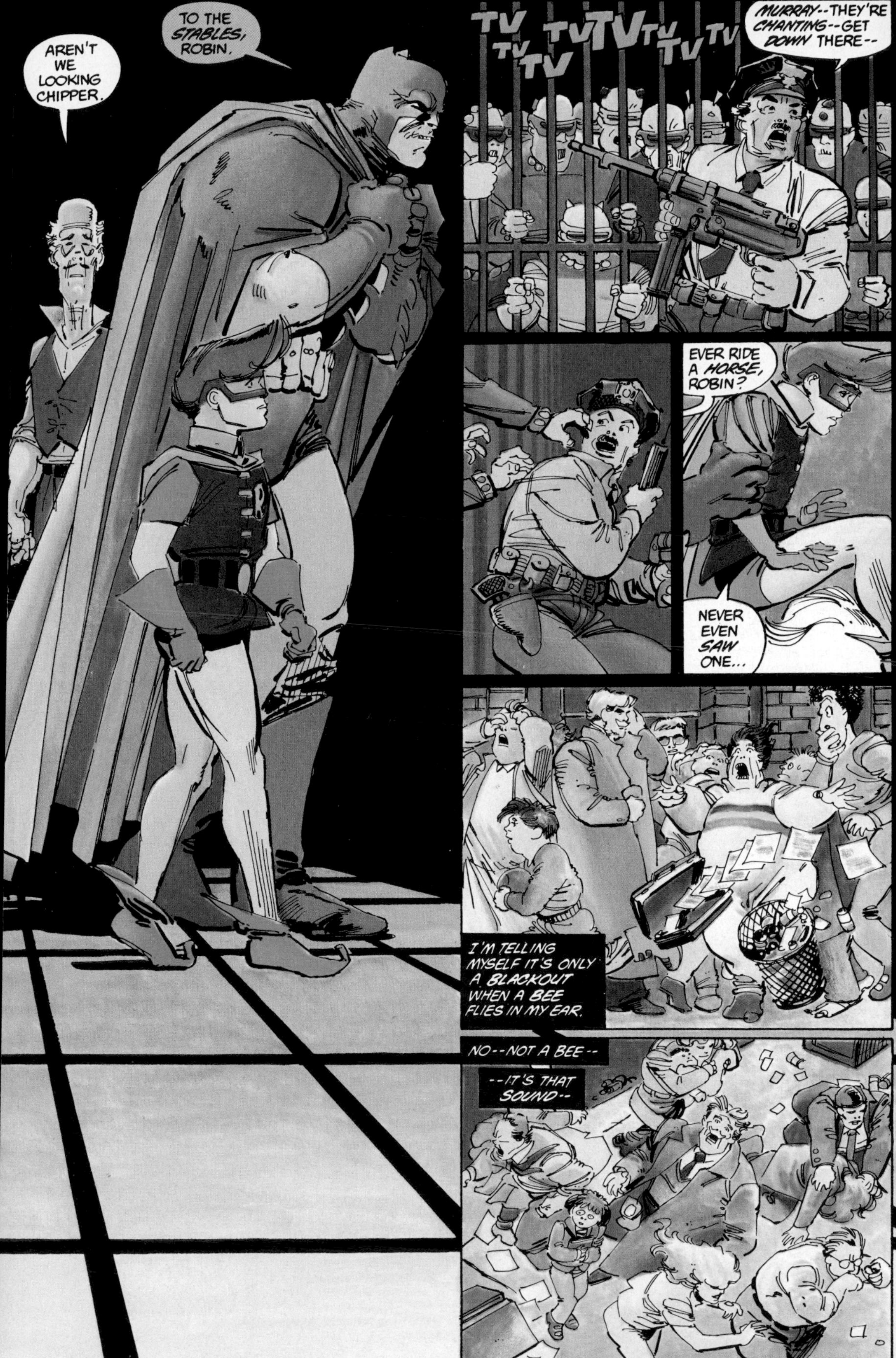

AREN'T WE LOOKING CHIPPER.
TO THE STABLES, ROBIN.
TV TV TV TV TV TV TV TV TV TV
MURRAY--THEY'RE CHANTING--GET DOWN THERE--
EVER RIDE A HORSE, ROBIN?
NEVER EVEN SAW ONE...
I'M TELLING MYSELF IT'S ONLY A BLACKOUT WHEN A BEE FLIES IN MY EAR.
NO--NOT A BEE--
--IT'S THAT SOUND--

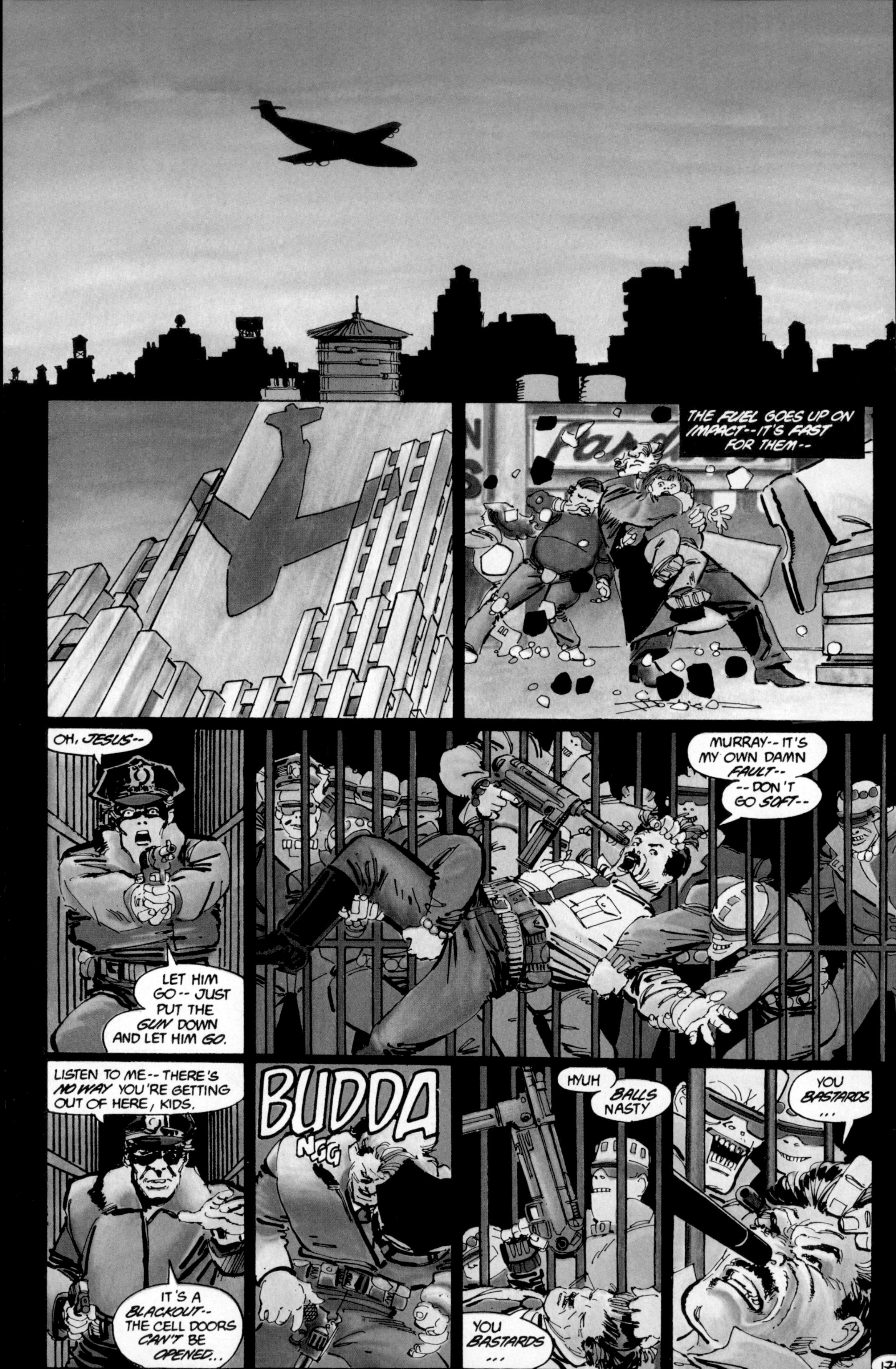

THE FUEL GOES UP ON IMPACT-- IT'S FAST FOR THEM--
OH, JESUS--
LET HIM GO-- JUST PUT THE GUN DOWN AND LET HIM GO.
MURRAY-- IT'S MY OWN DAMN FAULT--
--DON'T GO SOFT--
LISTEN TO ME-- THERE'S NO WAY YOU'RE GETTING OUT OF HERE, KIDS.
IT'S A BLACKOUT-- THE CELL DOORS CAN'T BE OPENED...
BUDDA
NGG
HYUH
BALLS NASTY
YOU BASTARDS ...
YOU BASTARDS ...

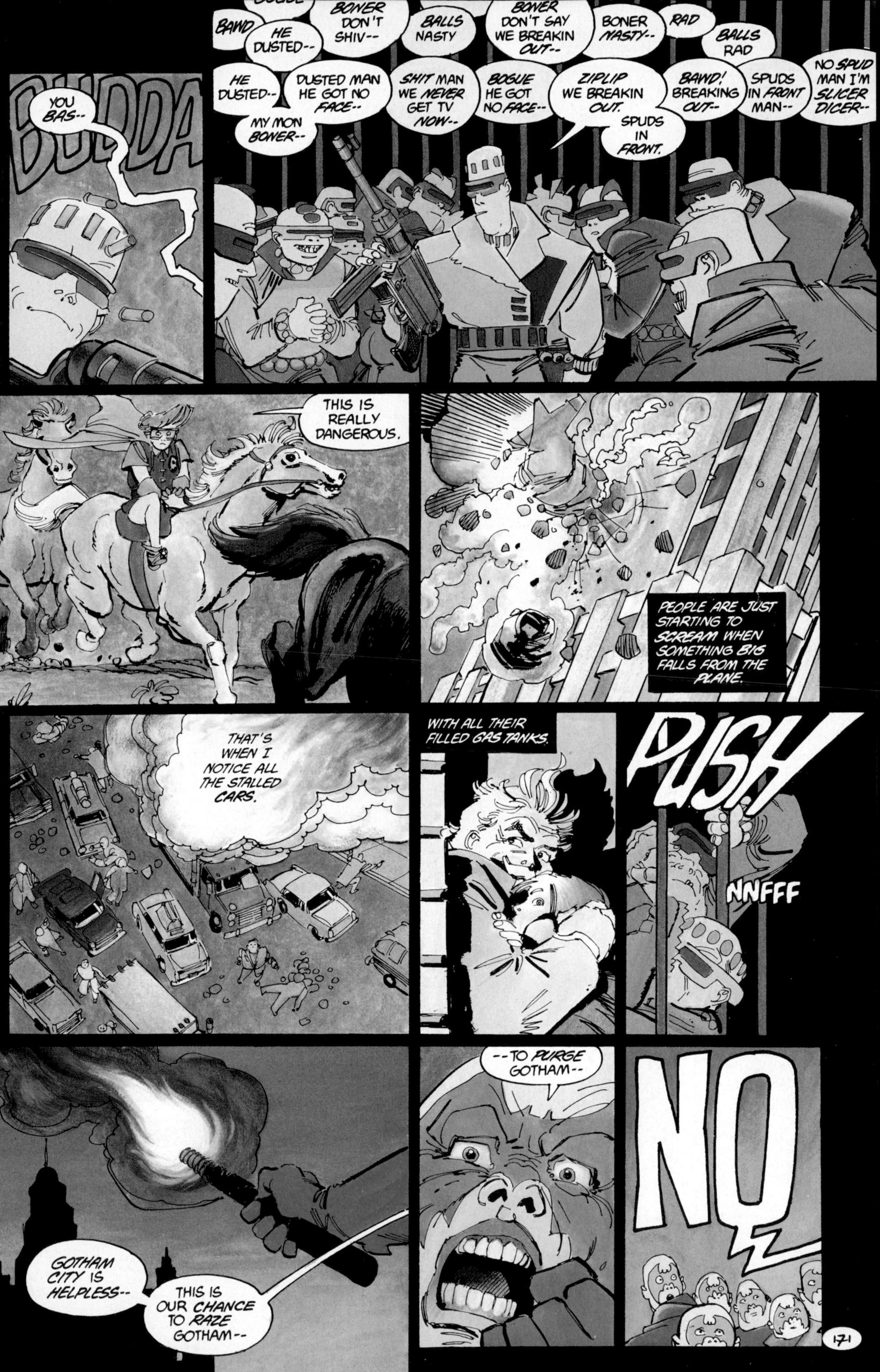
BUDDA
YOU BAS--
BAWD
HE DUSTED--
BONER DON'T SHIV--
BALLS NASTY
BONER DON'T SAY WE BREAKIN OUT--
BONER NASTY--
RAD
BALLS RAD
HE DUSTED--
MY MON BONER--
DUSTED MAN HE GOT NO FACE--
SHIT MAN WE NEVER GET TV NOW--
BOGUE HE GOT NO FACE--
ZIPLIP WE BREAKIN OUT.
SPUDS IN FRONT.
BAWD! BREAKING OUT--
SPUDS IN FRONT MAN--
NO SPUD MAN I'M SLICER DICER--
THIS IS REALLY DANGEROUS.
PEOPLE ARE JUST STARTING TO SCREAM WHEN SOMETHING BIG FALLS FROM THE PLANE.
THAT'S WHEN I NOTICE ALL THE STALLED CARS.
WITH ALL THEIR FILLED GAS TANKS.
PUSH
NNFFF
GOTHAM CITY IS HELPLESS--
THIS IS OUR CHANCE TO RAZE GOTHAM--
--TO PURGE GOTHAM--
NO

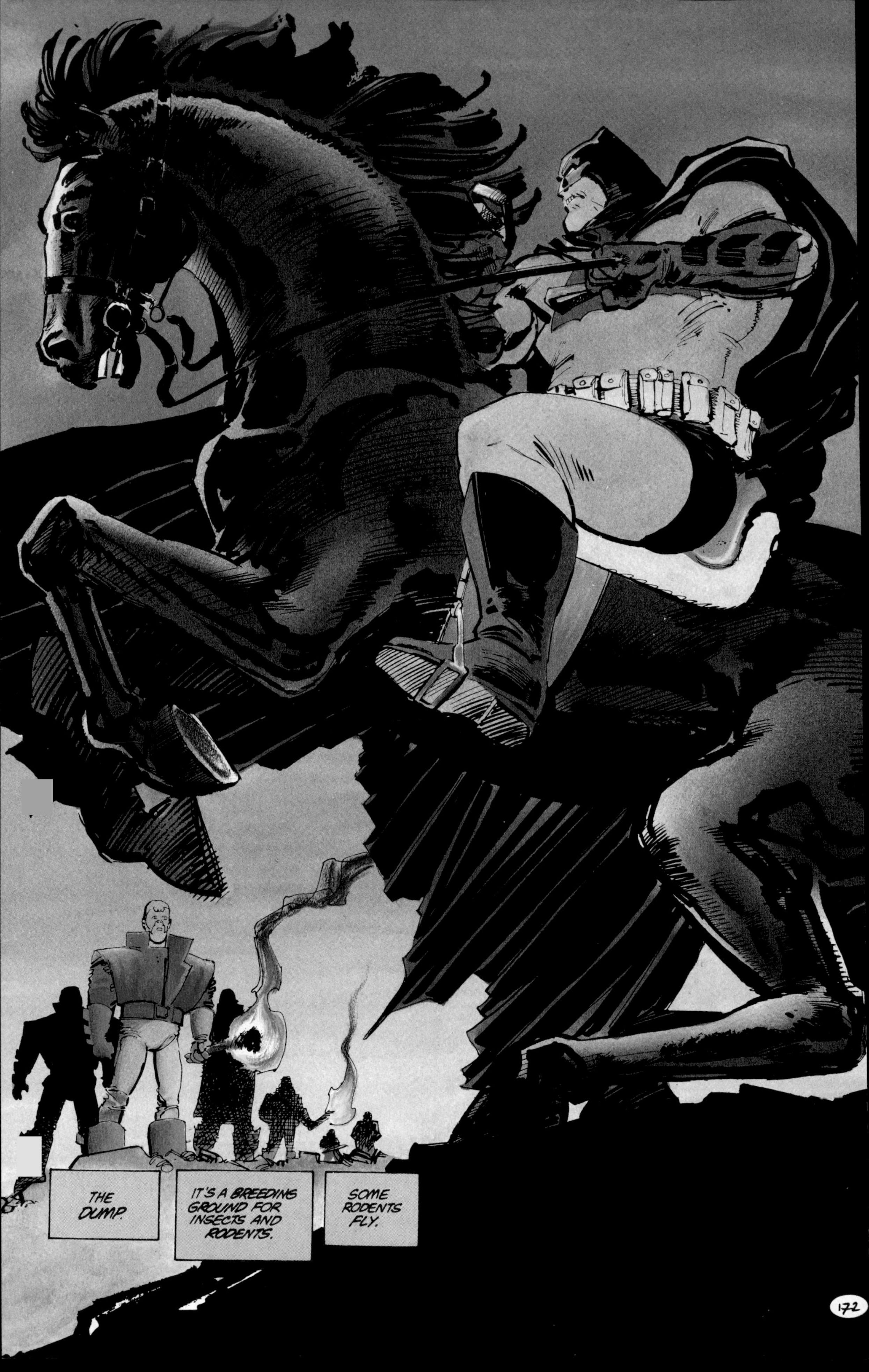
THE DUMP.
IT'S A BREEDING GROUND FOR INSECTS AND RODENTS.
SOME RODENTS FLY.

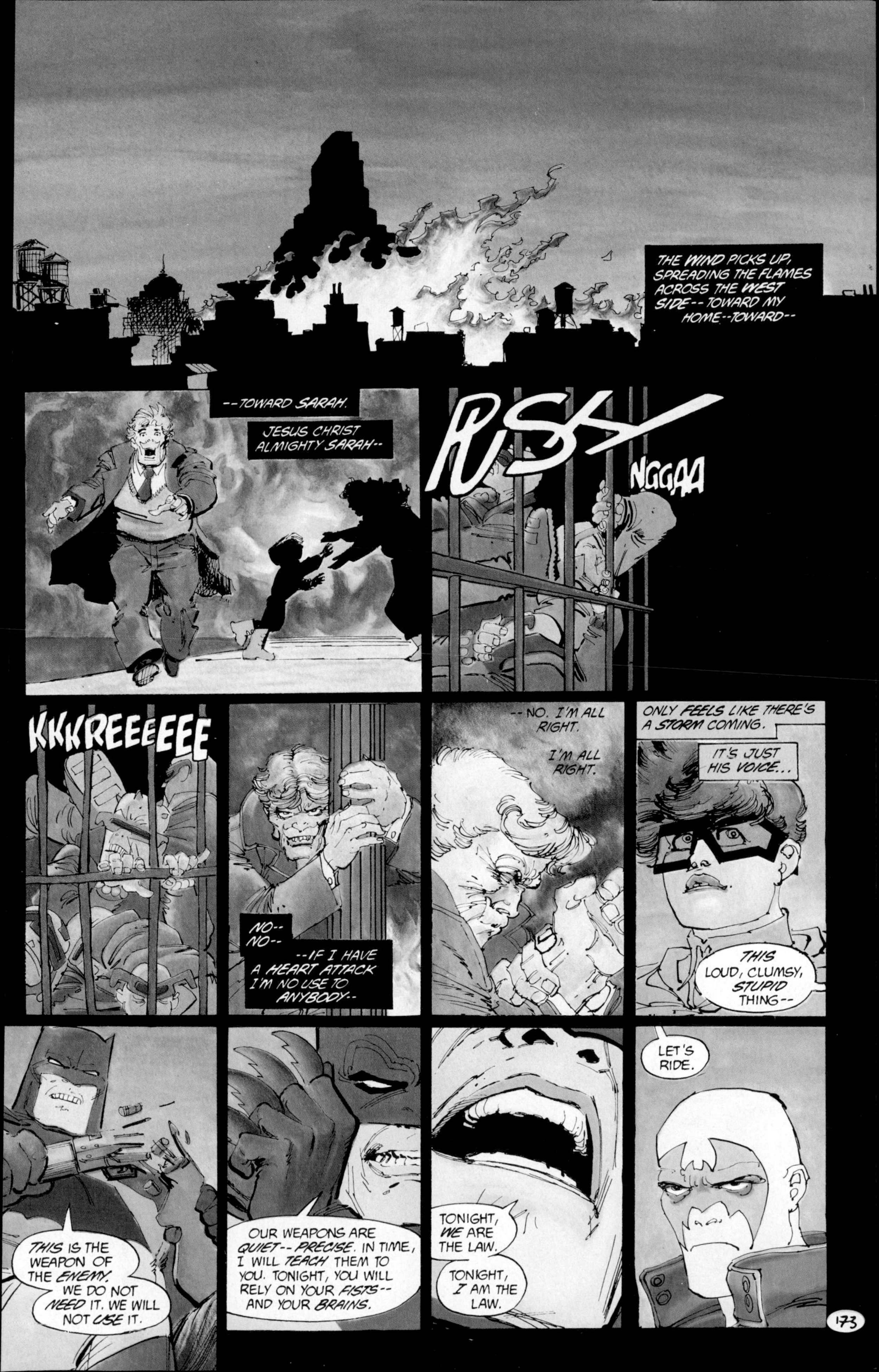
THE WIND PICKS UP, SPREADING THE FLAMES ACROSS THE WEST SIDE-- TOWARD MY HOME--TOWARD--
--TOWARD SARAH.
JESUS CHRIST ALMIGHTY SARAH--
NGGAA
KKKREEEEEEE
NO--
NO--
--IF I HAVE A HEART ATTACK I'M NO USE TO ANYBODY--
--NO. I'M ALL RIGHT.
I'M ALL RIGHT.
ONLY FEELS LIKE THERE'S A STORM COMING.
IT'S JUST HIS VOICE...
THIS LOUD, CLUMSY, STUPID THING--
THIS IS THE WEAPON OF THE ENEMY. WE DO NOT NEED IT. WE WILL NOT USE IT.
OUR WEAPONS ARE QUIET-- PRECISE. IN TIME, I WILL TEACH THEM TO YOU. TONIGHT, YOU WILL RELY ON YOUR FISTS-- AND YOUR BRAINS.
TONIGHT, WE ARE THE LAW.
TONIGHT, I AM THE LAW.
LET'S RIDE.

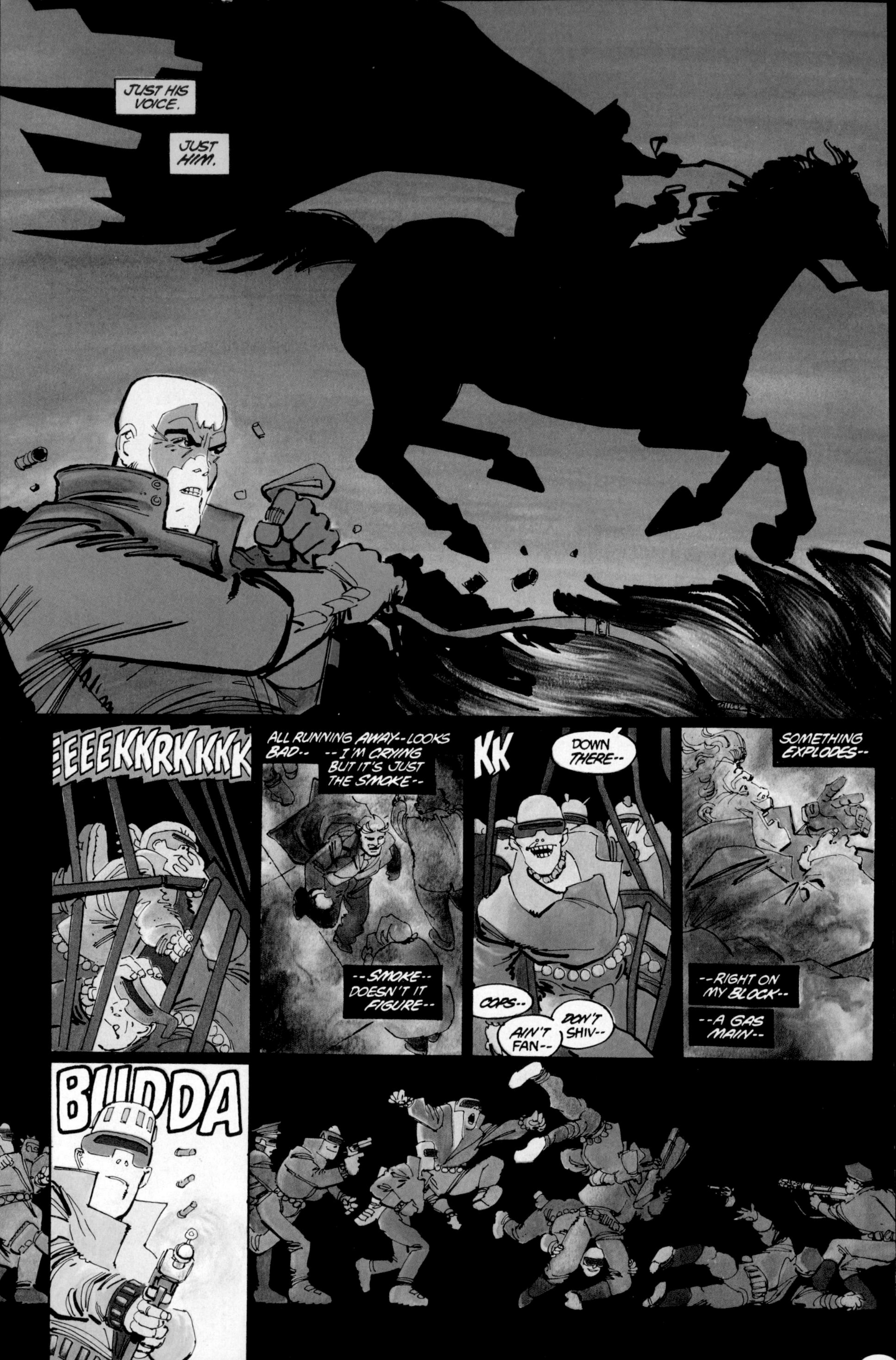
JUST HIS VOICE.
JUST HIM.
EEEEKKRKKKK
ALL RUNNING AWAY-- LOOKS BAD-- --I'M CRYING BUT IT'S JUST THE SMOKE--
--SMOKE-- DOESN'T IT FIGURE--
KK
DOWN THERE--
COPS--
AIN'T FAN--
DON'T SHIV--
SOMETHING EXPLODES--
--RIGHT ON MY BLOCK--
--A GAS MAIN--
BUDDA

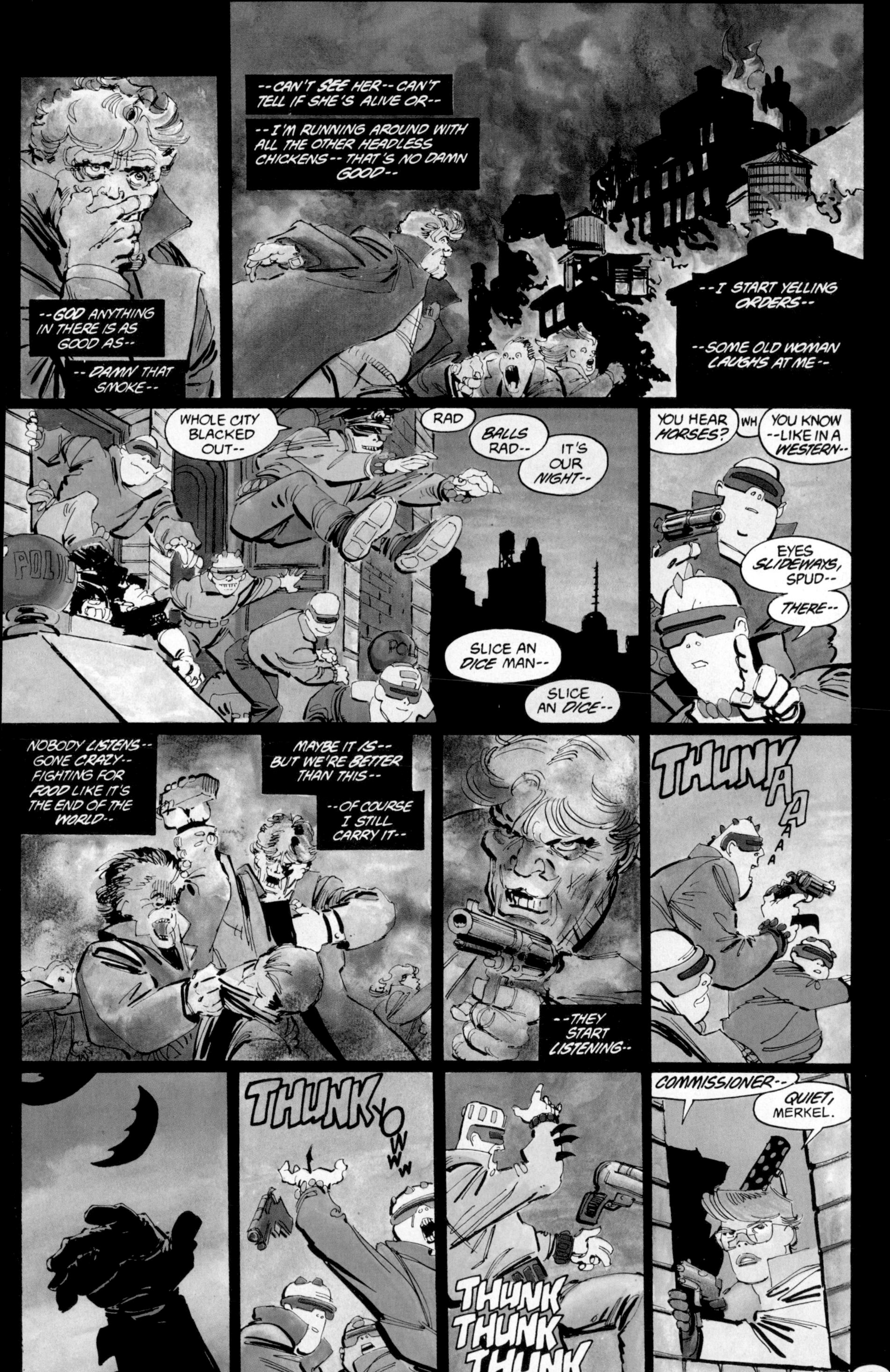
--CAN'T SEE HER--CAN'T TELL IF SHE'S ALIVE OR--
--I'M RUNNING AROUND WITH ALL THE OTHER HEADLESS CHICKENS--THAT'S NO DAMN GOOD--
--GOD ANYTHING IN THERE IS AS GOOD AS--
--DAMN THAT SMOKE--
--I START YELLING ORDERS--
--SOME OLD WOMAN LAUGHS AT ME--
WHOLE CITY BLACKED OUT--
RAD
BALLS RAD--
IT'S OUR NIGHT--
SLICE AN DICE MAN--
SLICE AN DICE--
YOU HEAR HORSES?
WH
YOU KNOW --LIKE IN A WESTERN--
EYES SLIDEWAYS, SPUD--
THERE--
NOBODY LISTENS--GONE CRAZY--FIGHTING FOR FOOD LIKE IT'S THE END OF THE WORLD--
MAYBE IT IS--BUT WE'RE BETTER THAN THIS--
--OF COURSE I STILL CARRY IT--
--THEY START LISTENING--
THUNK
AAAAAA
THUNK
OWWW
THUNK THUNK THUNK
COMMISSIONER--
QUIET, MERKEL.

BOYS, GIRLS... ...I'M HERE TO APPEAL TO YOUR COMMUNITY SPIRIT.

I'M SURE YOU'RE ALL *EAGER* TO HELP.

COMMISSIONER, WE--

NO. NO.

HE'S... TOO *BIG*...

THE SPIRIT SPREADS AS FAST AS THE FIRE.

TWO *NURSES* SHOW UP OUT OF *NOWHERE*-- THEY DON'T HAVE A *DAMN* THING TO WORK WITH...

THE ONES THEY CAN'T *COMFORT* THEY GET *DRUNK*.

A *HARDHAT* GRABS A *LUGWRENCH* FROM THE BACK OF HIS *DEAD TRUCK* AND SMASHES OPEN A *FIRE HYDRANT*.

THE MAN AT THE *HARDWARE STORE* PUTS HIS *SHOTGUN* AWAY AND EMPTIES *PAINT BUCKETS* ALL OVER HIS *NEW TILE FLOOR*.

A *LINE* FORMS.

PULSE IS *STEADY*, NO PROBLEM.

NO SIGN OF *SARAH*.

"HARMLESSLY..."

THE WOMAN... ON TELEVISION... SHE SAID THE BOMB WOULD DETONATE.... HARMLESSLY...

YOU CANNOT *TOUCH* MY PLANET WITHOUT DESTROYING SOMETHING *PRECIOUS*.

EVEN HER *DESERTS* ARE ABUNDANT.

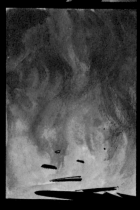

THERE WERE *BIRDS*, HERE, WHO SHE BLESSED WITH *CHEST FEATHERS* ABSORBENT ENOUGH TO CARRY WATER FOR MILES TO THEIR *CHILDREN*...

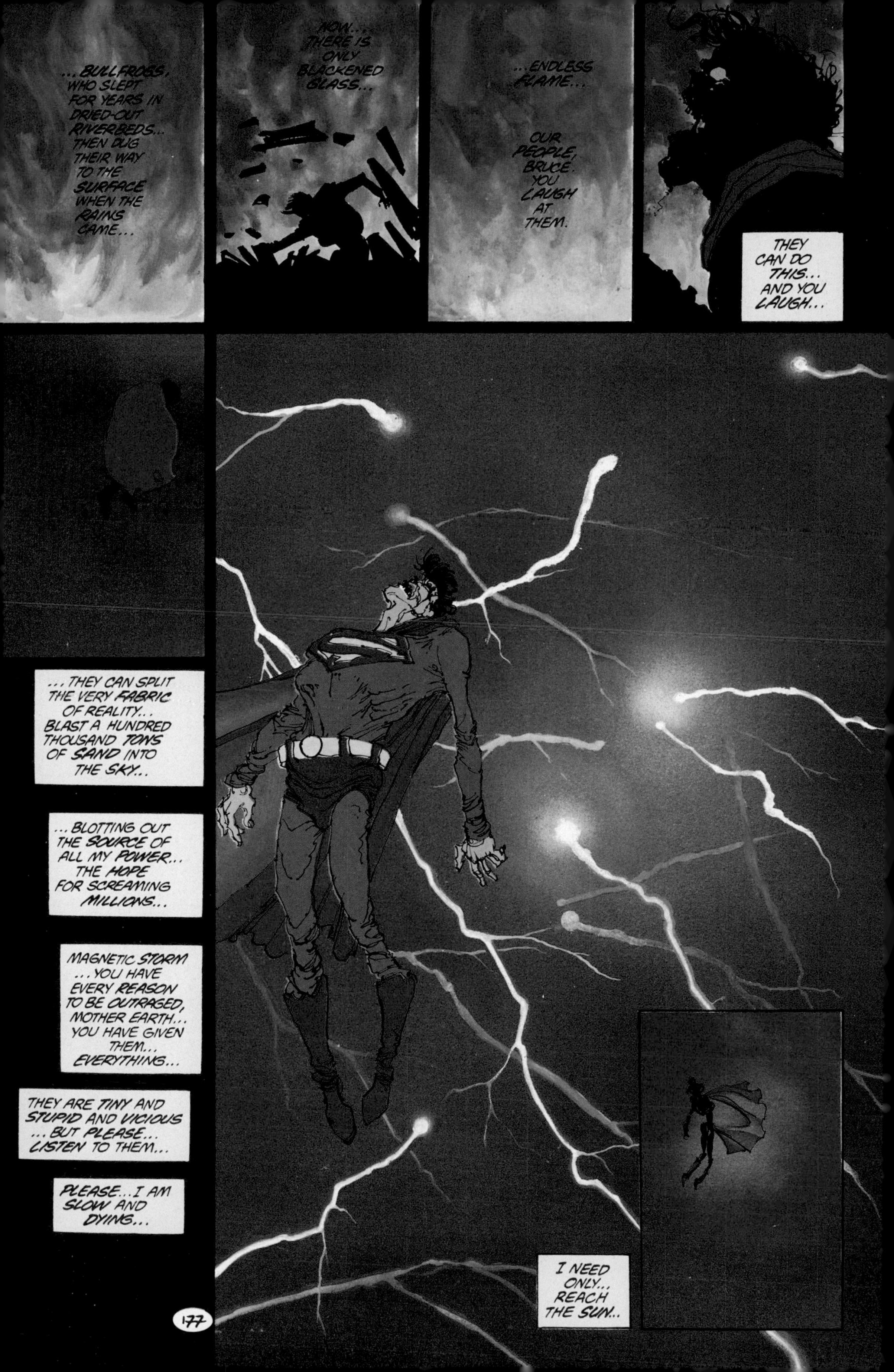

...BULLFROGS, WHO SLEPT FOR YEARS IN DRIED-OUT RIVERBEDS... THEN DUG THEIR WAY TO THE SURFACE WHEN THE RAINS CAME...
NOW... THERE IS ONLY BLACKENED GLASS...
...ENDLESS FLAME...
OUR PEOPLE, BRUCE. YOU LAUGH AT THEM.
THEY CAN DO THIS... AND YOU LAUGH...
...THEY CAN SPLIT THE VERY FABRIC OF REALITY... BLAST A HUNDRED THOUSAND TONS OF SAND INTO THE SKY...
...BLOTTING OUT THE SOURCE OF ALL MY POWER... THE HOPE FOR SCREAMING MILLIONS...
MAGNETIC STORM ...YOU HAVE EVERY REASON TO BE OUTRAGED, MOTHER EARTH... YOU HAVE GIVEN THEM... EVERYTHING...
THEY ARE TINY AND STUPID AND VICIOUS ...BUT PLEASE... LISTEN TO THEM...
PLEASE...I AM SLOW AND DYING...
I NEED ONLY... REACH THE SUN...

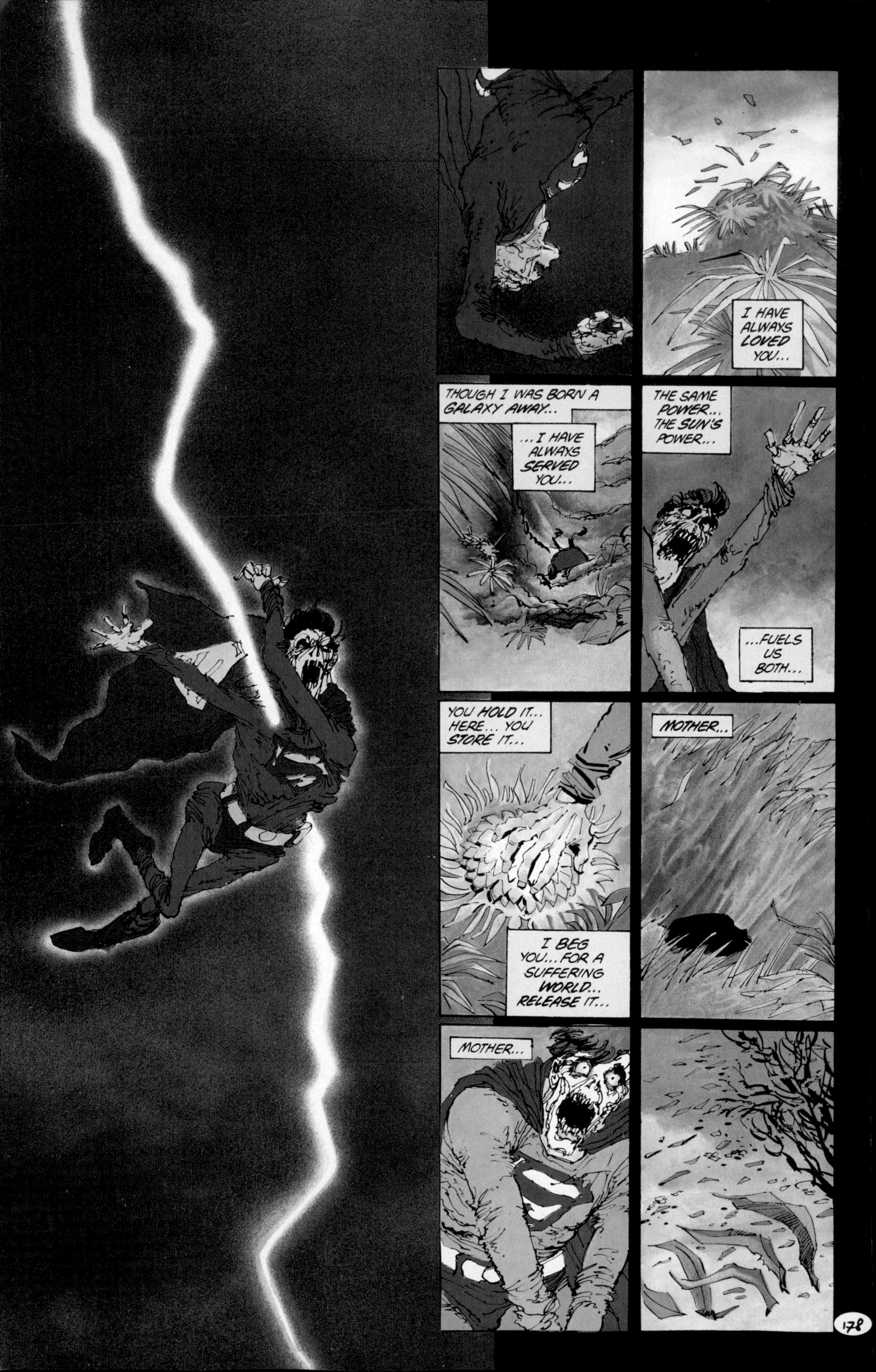
I HAVE ALWAYS LOVED YOU...
THOUGH I WAS BORN A GALAXY AWAY...
...I HAVE ALWAYS SERVED YOU...
THE SAME POWER... THE SUN'S POWER...
...FUELS US BOTH...
YOU HOLD IT... HERE... YOU STORE IT...
I BEG YOU... FOR A SUFFERING WORLD... RELEASE IT...
MOTHER...
MOTHER...

YOU ARE...SO GENEROUS...

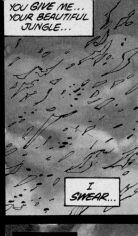

YOU GIVE ME... YOUR BEAUTIFUL JUNGLE...

I SWEAR...

...YOUR ADOPTED SON WILL HONOR YOU.

FROM MY BUILDING--

--SHE SCREAMS--

SARAH'S HEIGHT--

--SARAH'S HAIR--

A SKIRT--

--THAT COULD BE SARAH'S--

TRY NOT TO JUDGE THEM TOO HARSHLY. IT WAS A CRUEL TEST, FOR ALL OF US...

...AND, WE CAN HOPE, A LESSON...

NONE OF US CAN LOOK BACK ON THAT NIGHT WITHOUT SHAME. EVEN BEFORE IT ALL....I WAS WRAPPED IN MYSELF. YOU SEE, I HAVE ALWAYS BEEN RATHER SENSITIVE TO NOISE...

...AND THAT BOY-- HE SEEMED TO KEEP PACE WITH ME DELIBERATELY, TAKING THE JOY FROM MY EVENING WALK...

...WITH HIS HORRIBLY LOUD RADIO...

WHEN IT SHRIEKED, I BLAMED THE BOY. TRUTH TO TELL, I TURNED TO CONFRONT HIM...

...THEN I NOTICED HIS OWN CONFUSION -- AND THE DARKNESS THAT SEEMED TO FALL ACROSS THE ENTIRE CITY. I HEARD SHOUTS...

YES, I WAS SHOUTING. WHAT DO YOU EXPECT? I HAPPENED TO BE UP AGAINST A BITCH OF A DEADLINE. WHAT?... ...YES, OF COURSE I'D HEARD ABOUT THE BOMB. BUT I'VE GOT PROBLEMS OF MY OWN.

I'M NOT CRAZY ABOUT GETTING OUT OF MY CAR-- NOT IN THAT NEIGHBORHOOD--

--BUT I KNOW I BETTER CALL THE AGENCY AND MAKE SURE MY ASS IS COVERED.

SO I'M BARELY STANDING UP WHEN THERE'S THIS EXPLOSION KNOCKS ME FLAT--

MY ANKLE FEELS LIKE IT'S BROKEN-- SOMEBODY IS GOING TO GET SUED--

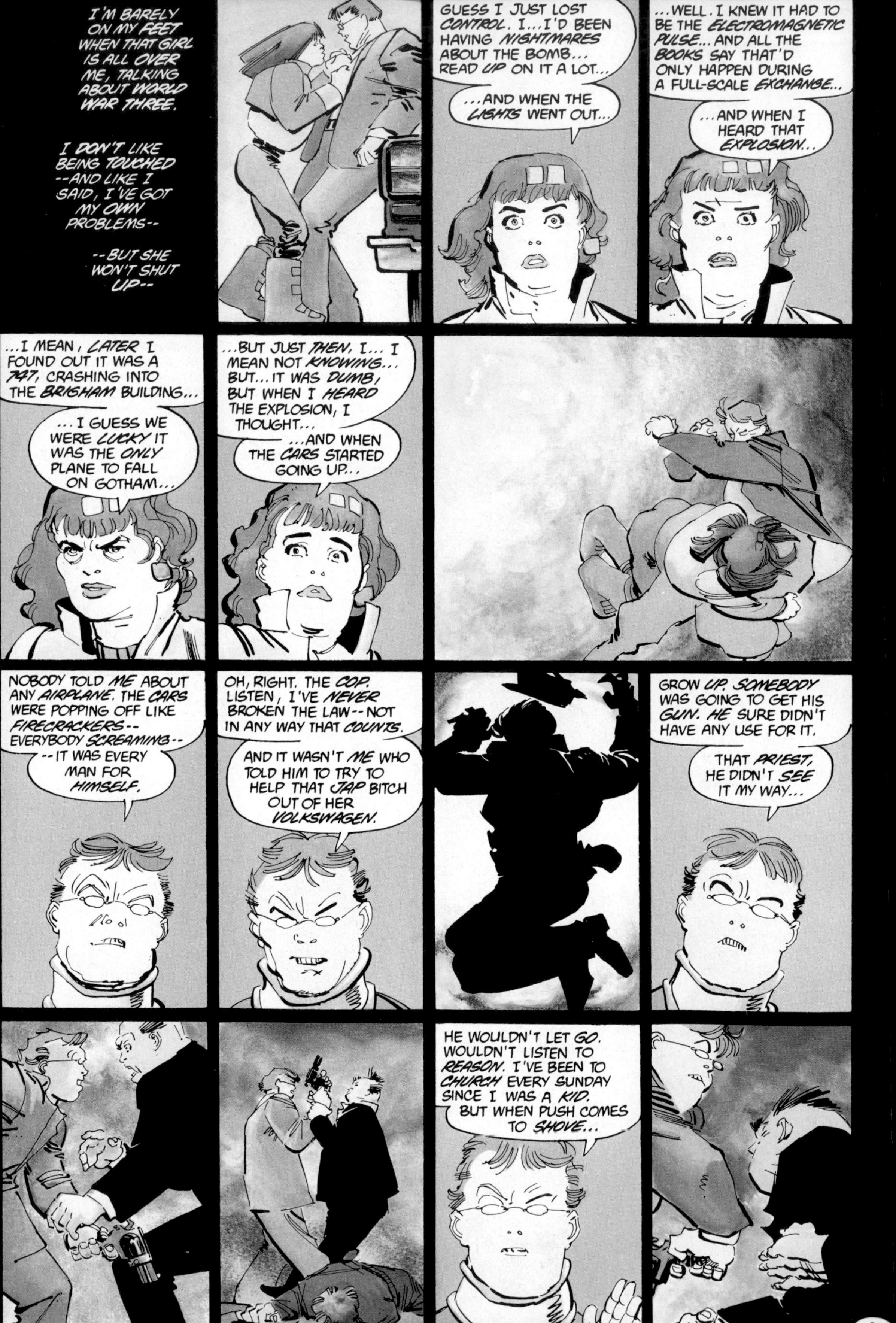
I'M BARELY ON MY FEET WHEN THAT GIRL IS ALL OVER ME, TALKING ABOUT WORLD WAR THREE.
I DON'T LIKE BEING TOUCHED --AND LIKE I SAID, I'VE GOT MY OWN PROBLEMS--
--BUT SHE WON'T SHUT UP--
GUESS I JUST LOST CONTROL. I...I'D BEEN HAVING NIGHTMARES ABOUT THE BOMB... READ UP ON IT A LOT...
...AND WHEN THE LIGHTS WENT OUT...
...WELL. I KNEW IT HAD TO BE THE ELECTROMAGNETIC PULSE... AND ALL THE BOOKS SAY THAT'D ONLY HAPPEN DURING A FULL-SCALE EXCHANGE...
...AND WHEN I HEARD THAT EXPLOSION...
...I MEAN, LATER I FOUND OUT IT WAS A 747, CRASHING INTO THE BRIGHAM BUILDING...
...I GUESS WE WERE LUCKY IT WAS THE ONLY PLANE TO FALL ON GOTHAM...
...BUT JUST THEN, I... I MEAN NOT KNOWING... BUT... IT WAS DUMB, BUT WHEN I HEARD THE EXPLOSION, I THOUGHT...
...AND WHEN THE CARS STARTED GOING UP...
NOBODY TOLD ME ABOUT ANY AIRPLANE. THE CARS WERE POPPING OFF LIKE FIRECRACKERS-- EVERYBODY SCREAMING-- --IT WAS EVERY MAN FOR HIMSELF.
OH, RIGHT. THE COP. LISTEN, I'VE NEVER BROKEN THE LAW--NOT IN ANY WAY THAT COUNTS.
AND IT WASN'T ME WHO TOLD HIM TO TRY TO HELP THAT JAP BITCH OUT OF HER VOLKSWAGEN.
GROW UP. SOMEBODY WAS GOING TO GET HIS GUN. HE SURE DIDN'T HAVE ANY USE FOR IT.
THAT PRIEST, HE DIDN'T SEE IT MY WAY...
HE WOULDN'T LET GO. WOULDN'T LISTEN TO REASON. I'VE BEEN TO CHURCH EVERY SUNDAY SINCE I WAS A KID.
BUT WHEN PUSH COMES TO SHOVE...

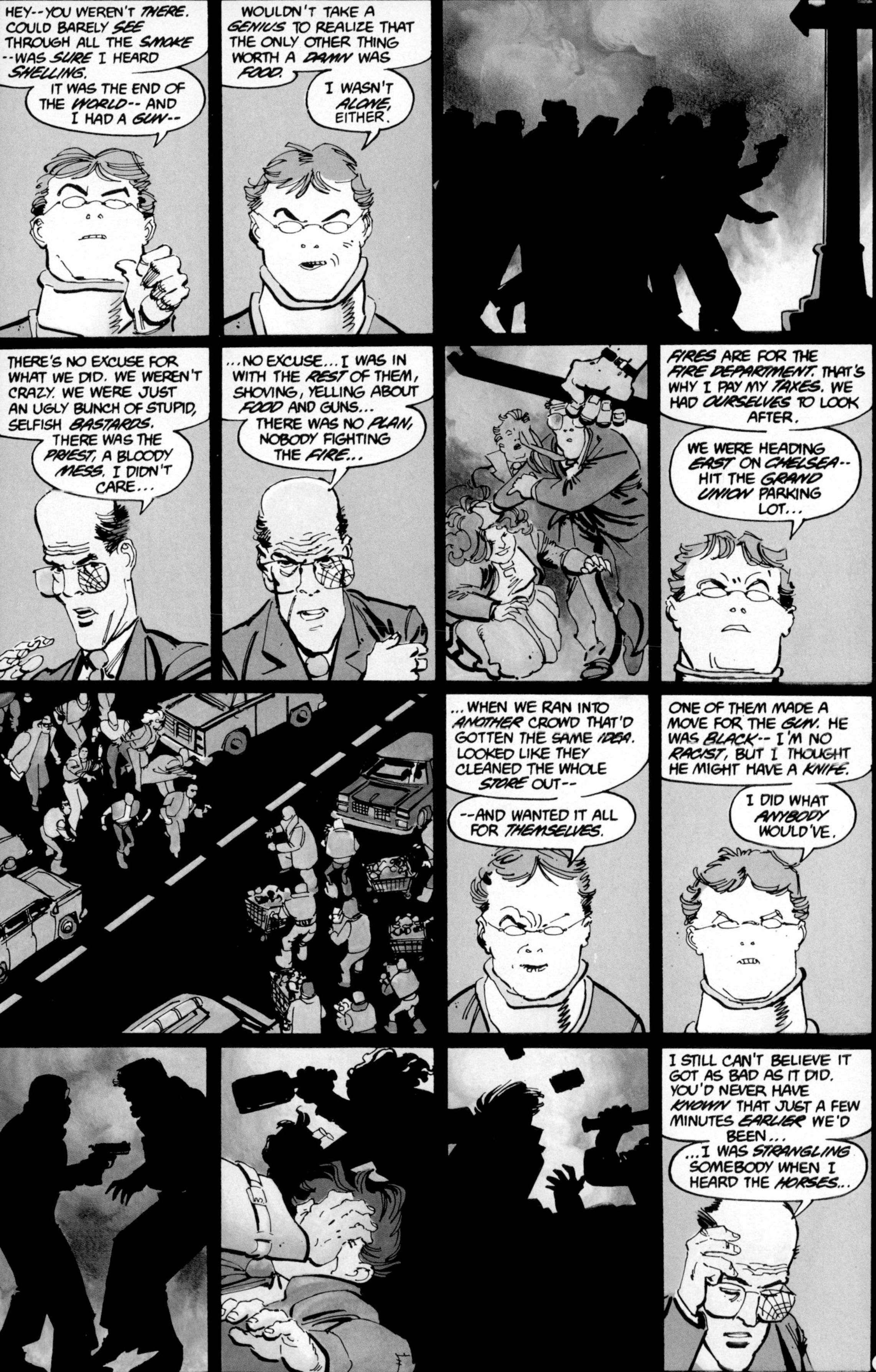

HEY--YOU WEREN'T THERE. COULD BARELY SEE THROUGH ALL THE SMOKE --WAS SURE I HEARD SHELLING.
IT WAS THE END OF THE WORLD-- AND I HAD A GUN--
WOULDN'T TAKE A GENIUS TO REALIZE THAT THE ONLY OTHER THING WORTH A DAMN WAS FOOD.
I WASN'T ALONE, EITHER.
THERE'S NO EXCUSE FOR WHAT WE DID. WE WEREN'T CRAZY. WE WERE JUST AN UGLY BUNCH OF STUPID, SELFISH BASTARDS.
THERE WAS THE PRIEST, A BLOODY MESS. I DIDN'T CARE...
...NO EXCUSE... I WAS IN WITH THE REST OF THEM, SHOVING, YELLING ABOUT FOOD AND GUNS...
THERE WAS NO PLAN, NOBODY FIGHTING THE FIRE...
FIRES ARE FOR THE FIRE DEPARTMENT. THAT'S WHY I PAY MY TAXES. WE HAD OURSELVES TO LOOK AFTER.
WE WERE HEADING EAST ON CHELSEA-- HIT THE GRAND UNION PARKING LOT...
...WHEN WE RAN INTO ANOTHER CROWD THAT'D GOTTEN THE SAME IDEA. LOOKED LIKE THEY CLEANED THE WHOLE STORE OUT--
--AND WANTED IT ALL FOR THEMSELVES.
ONE OF THEM MADE A MOVE FOR THE GUN. HE WAS BLACK-- I'M NO RACIST, BUT I THOUGHT HE MIGHT HAVE A KNIFE.
I DID WHAT ANYBODY WOULD'VE.
I STILL CAN'T BELIEVE IT GOT AS BAD AS IT DID. YOU'D NEVER HAVE KNOWN THAT JUST A FEW MINUTES EARLIER WE'D BEEN...
...I WAS STRANGLING SOMEBODY WHEN I HEARD THE HORSES...

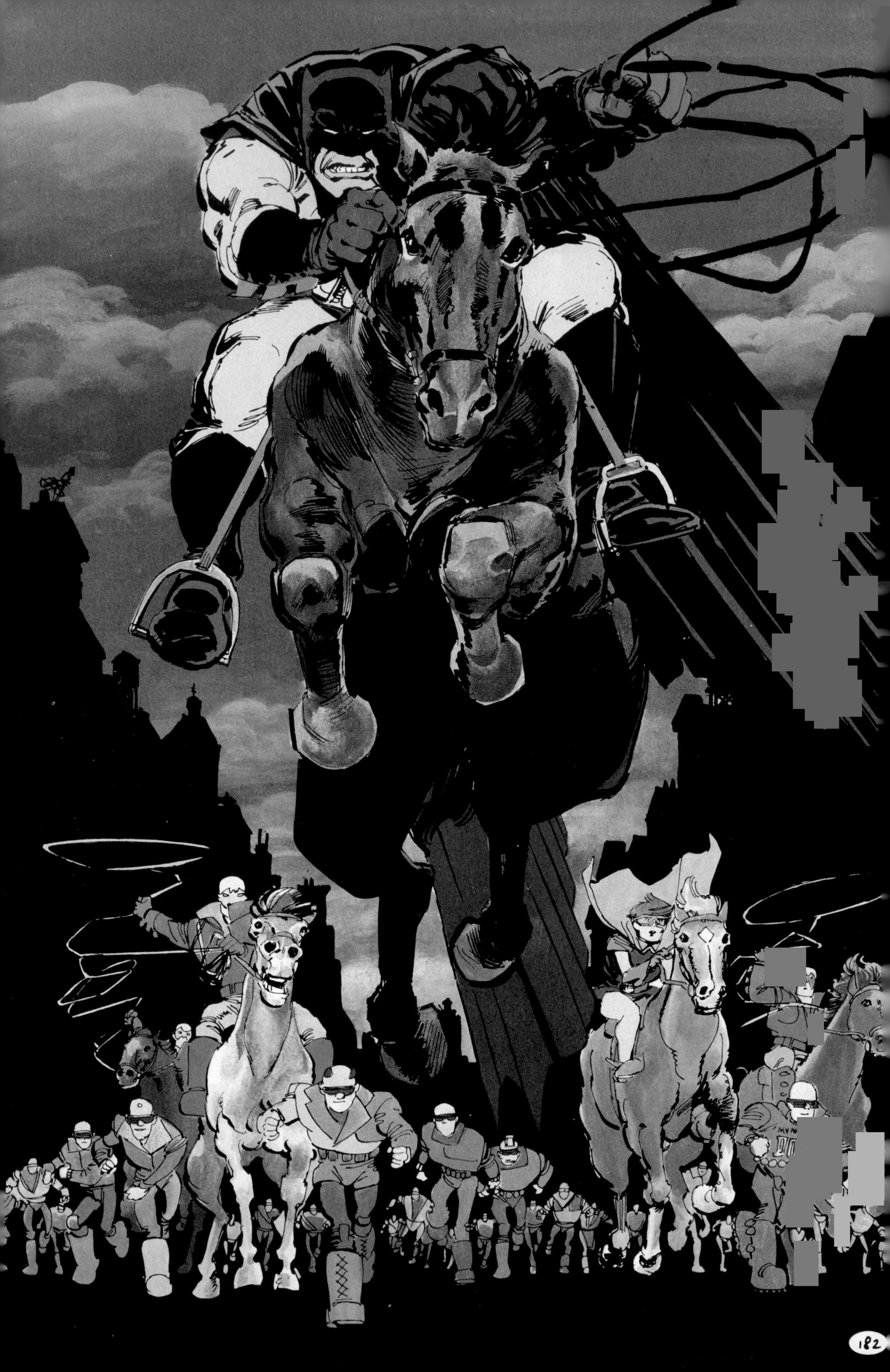

 LIKE THE *GESTAPO*, THEY MOVED IN ON US--*BATMAN* AND THAT *BRAT ARMY* OF HIS-- YOU'D HAVE THOUGHT WE WERE *CRIMINALS*.

I TRIED TO *DEFEND* MYSELF-- HE SINGLED ME *OUT*--

BROKE *THREE RIBS*-- AND THIS *BRACE* ISN'T FOR *LAUGHS*. WHENEVER THEY *CATCH* THAT LUNATIC, HE'LL HEAR FROM MY *ATTORNEY*.

WHO GAVE *HIM* THE RIGHT?

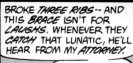

WHEN HE *TALKED*-- *BATMAN*, I MEAN-- IT WAS... IT'S HARD TO *DESCRIBE*... THERE WAS SOMETHING IN HIS *VOICE*...

... ANYWAY, HE TOLD US WE COULD SPEND THE NIGHT TIED *UP*-- OR HELP FIGHT THE FIRE...

SHE ONLY GOT TO SCREAM ONCE. IT WAS TOO LATE TO HELP HER.

SHE ISN'T *SARAH*. I DON'T *KNOW* HER.

IT'S ONLY ONCE... IN THE WHOLE NIGHT... THAT IT *SHOWS*...

HE'S GIVEN *ORDERS* AND ALL THE *MUTANTS* AND *S.O.B.S* AND *EVERYBODY* ARE *GONE* FOR A MINUTE...

... HE JUST *SAGS* IN HIS *SADDLE* LIKE AN OLD *MAN*...

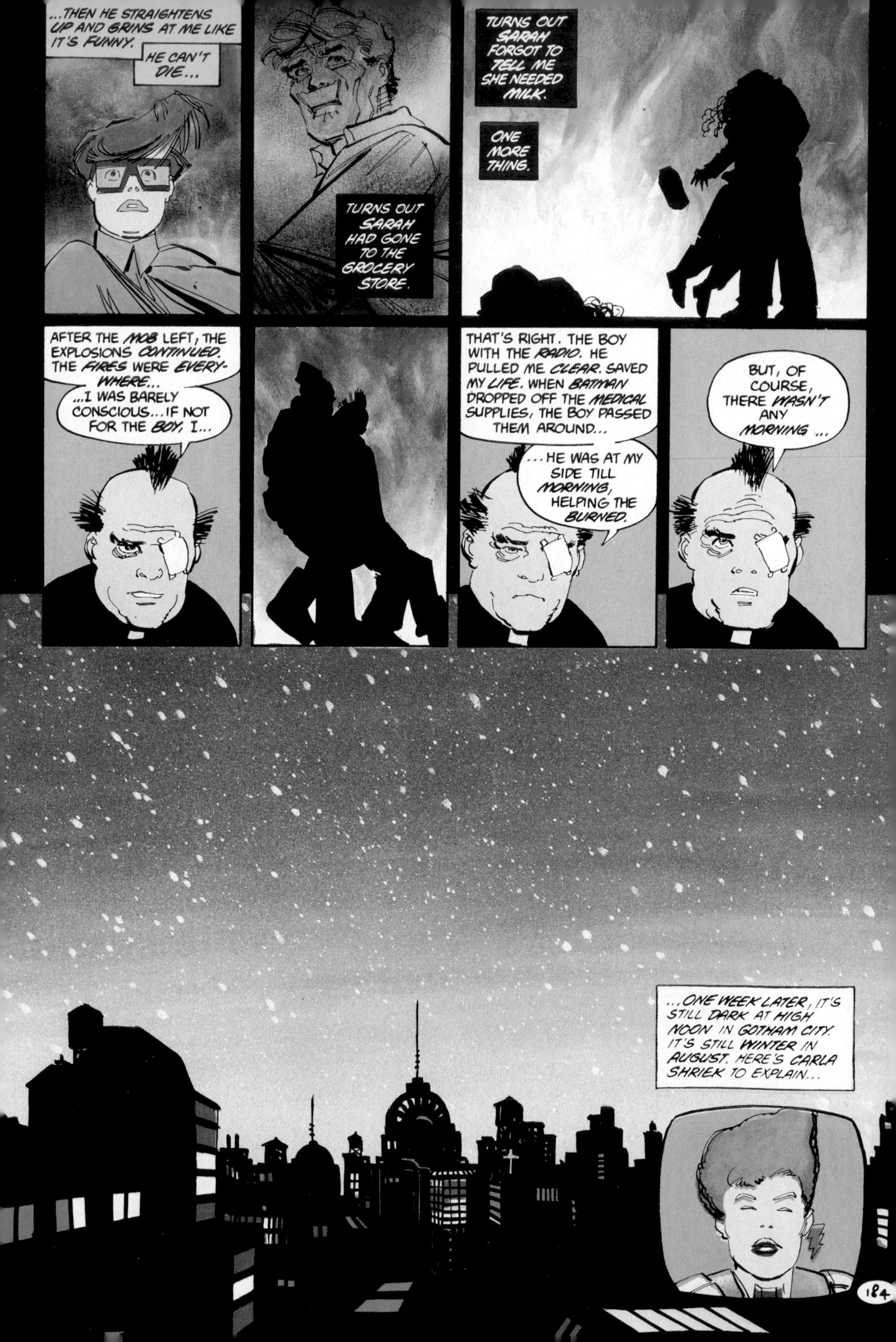

...THEN HE STRAIGHTENS UP AND GRINS AT ME LIKE IT'S FUNNY.
HE CAN'T DIE...
TURNS OUT SARAH HAD GONE TO THE GROCERY STORE.
TURNS OUT SARAH FORGOT TO TELL ME SHE NEEDED MILK.
ONE MORE THING.
AFTER THE MOB LEFT, THE EXPLOSIONS CONTINUED. THE FIRES WERE EVERYWHERE...
...I WAS BARELY CONSCIOUS... IF NOT FOR THE BOY, I...
THAT'S RIGHT. THE BOY WITH THE RADIO. HE PULLED ME CLEAR. SAVED MY LIFE. WHEN BATMAN DROPPED OFF THE MEDICAL SUPPLIES, THE BOY PASSED THEM AROUND...
...HE WAS AT MY SIDE TILL MORNING, HELPING THE BURNED.
BUT, OF COURSE, THERE WASN'T ANY MORNING...
...ONE WEEK LATER, IT'S STILL DARK AT HIGH NOON IN GOTHAM CITY. IT'S STILL WINTER IN AUGUST. HERE'S CARLA SHRIEK TO EXPLAIN...

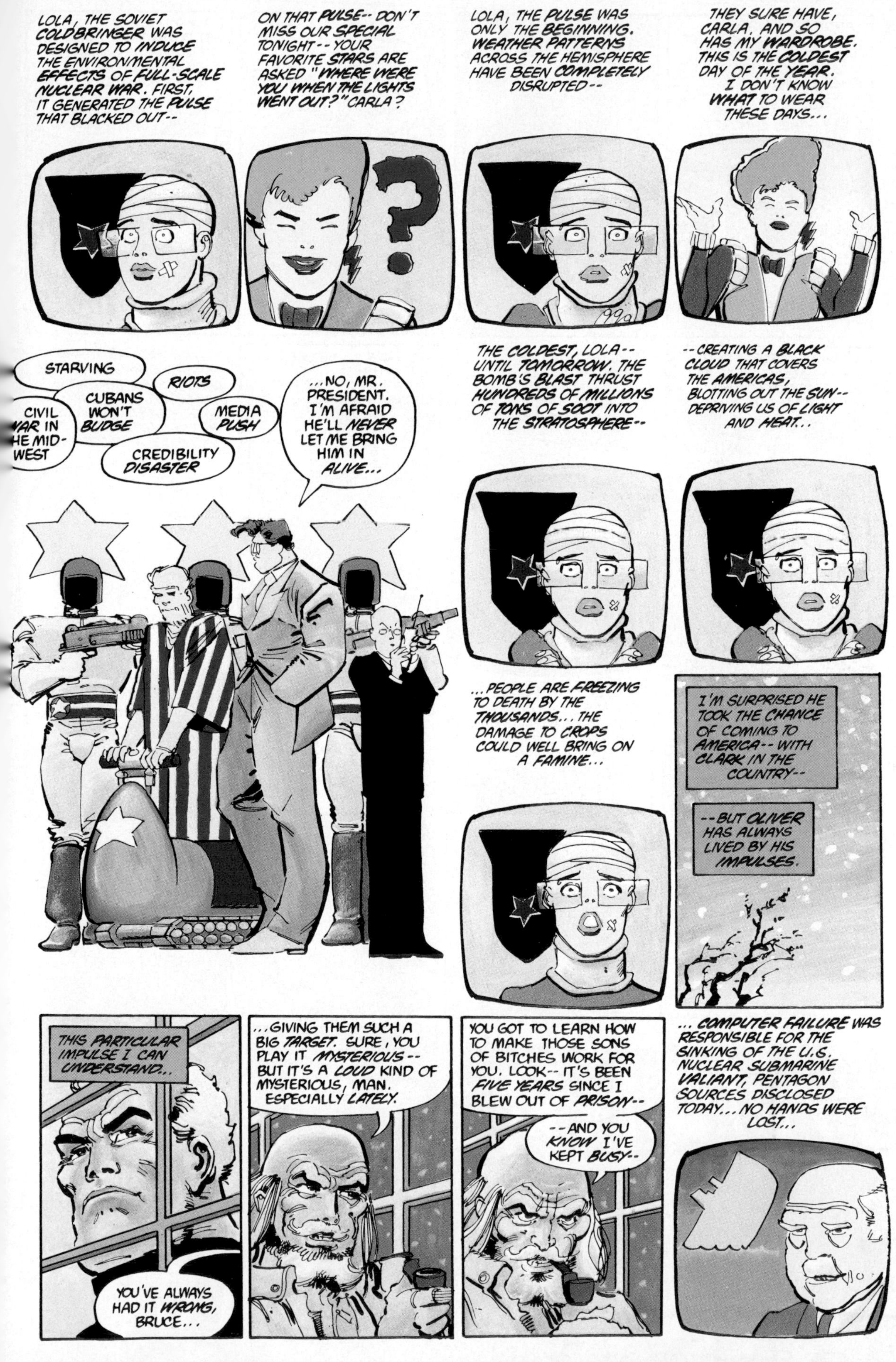
LOLA, THE SOVIET COLDBRINGER WAS DESIGNED TO INDUCE THE ENVIRONMENTAL EFFECTS OF FULL-SCALE NUCLEAR WAR. FIRST, IT GENERATED THE PULSE THAT BLACKED OUT--
ON THAT PULSE-- DON'T MISS OUR SPECIAL TONIGHT-- YOUR FAVORITE STARS ARE ASKED "WHERE WERE YOU WHEN THE LIGHTS WENT OUT?" CARLA?
LOLA, THE PULSE WAS ONLY THE BEGINNING. WEATHER PATTERNS ACROSS THE HEMISPHERE HAVE BEEN COMPLETELY DISRUPTED--
THEY SURE HAVE, CARLA. AND SO HAS MY WARDROBE. THIS IS THE COLDEST DAY OF THE YEAR. I DON'T KNOW WHAT TO WEAR THESE DAYS...
STARVING
RIOTS
CUBANS WON'T BUDGE
MEDIA PUSH
CIVIL WAR IN THE MID-WEST
CREDIBILITY DISASTER
...NO, MR. PRESIDENT. I'M AFRAID HE'LL NEVER LET ME BRING HIM IN ALIVE...
THE COLDEST, LOLA-- UNTIL TOMORROW. THE BOMB'S BLAST THRUST HUNDREDS OF MILLIONS OF TONS OF SOOT INTO THE STRATOSPHERE--
--CREATING A BLACK CLOUD THAT COVERS THE AMERICAS, BLOTTING OUT THE SUN-- DEPRIVING US OF LIGHT AND HEAT...
...PEOPLE ARE FREEZING TO DEATH BY THE THOUSANDS... THE DAMAGE TO CROPS COULD WELL BRING ON A FAMINE...
I'M SURPRISED HE TOOK THE CHANCE OF COMING TO AMERICA-- WITH CLARK IN THE COUNTRY--
--BUT OLIVER HAS ALWAYS LIVED BY HIS IMPULSES.
THIS PARTICULAR IMPULSE I CAN UNDERSTAND...
YOU'VE ALWAYS HAD IT WRONG, BRUCE...
...GIVING THEM SUCH A BIG TARGET. SURE, YOU PLAY IT MYSTERIOUS-- BUT IT'S A LOUD KIND OF MYSTERIOUS, MAN. ESPECIALLY LATELY.
YOU GOT TO LEARN HOW TO MAKE THOSE SONS OF BITCHES WORK FOR YOU. LOOK-- IT'S BEEN FIVE YEARS SINCE I BLEW OUT OF PRISON--
--AND YOU KNOW I'VE KEPT BUSY--
...COMPUTER FAILURE WAS RESPONSIBLE FOR THE SINKING OF THE U.S. NUCLEAR SUBMARINE VALIANT, PENTAGON SOURCES DISCLOSED TODAY... NO HANDS WERE LOST...

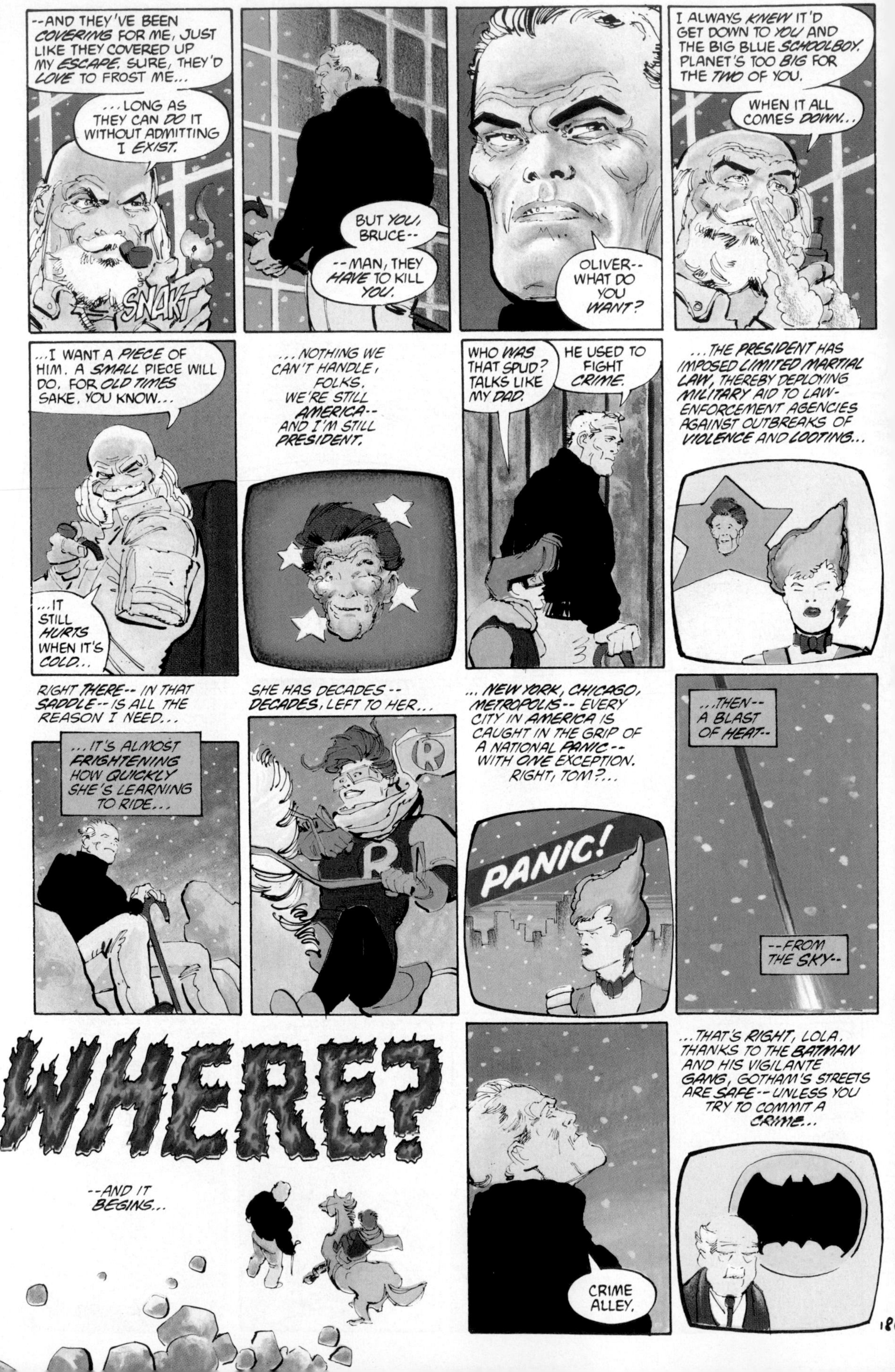
--AND THEY'VE BEEN COVERING FOR ME, JUST LIKE THEY COVERED UP MY ESCAPE. SURE, THEY'D LOVE TO FROST ME...
...LONG AS THEY CAN DO IT WITHOUT ADMITTING I EXIST.
SNAKT
BUT YOU, BRUCE--
--MAN, THEY HAVE TO KILL YOU.
OLIVER--WHAT DO YOU WANT?
I ALWAYS KNEW IT'D GET DOWN TO YOU AND THE BIG BLUE SCHOOLBOY. PLANET'S TOO BIG FOR THE TWO OF YOU.
WHEN IT ALL COMES DOWN...
...I WANT A PIECE OF HIM. A SMALL PIECE WILL DO. FOR OLD TIMES SAKE, YOU KNOW...
...IT STILL HURTS WHEN IT'S COLD...
...NOTHING WE CAN'T HANDLE, FOLKS. WE'RE STILL AMERICA-- AND I'M STILL PRESIDENT.
WHO WAS THAT SPUD? TALKS LIKE MY DAD.
HE USED TO FIGHT CRIME.
...THE PRESIDENT HAS IMPOSED LIMITED MARTIAL LAW, THEREBY DEPLOYING MILITARY AID TO LAW-ENFORCEMENT AGENCIES AGAINST OUTBREAKS OF VIOLENCE AND LOOTING...
RIGHT THERE-- IN THAT SADDLE--IS ALL THE REASON I NEED...
...IT'S ALMOST FRIGHTENING HOW QUICKLY SHE'S LEARNING TO RIDE...
SHE HAS DECADES-- DECADES, LEFT TO HER...
R
...NEW YORK, CHICAGO, METROPOLIS-- EVERY CITY IN AMERICA IS CAUGHT IN THE GRIP OF A NATIONAL PANIC-- WITH ONE EXCEPTION. RIGHT, TOM?...
PANIC!
...THEN-- A BLAST OF HEAT--
--FROM THE SKY--
WHERE?
--AND IT BEGINS...
CRIME ALLEY.
...THAT'S RIGHT, LOLA. THANKS TO THE BATMAN AND HIS VIGILANTE GANG, GOTHAM'S STREETS ARE SAFE-- UNLESS YOU TRY TO COMMIT A CRIME...

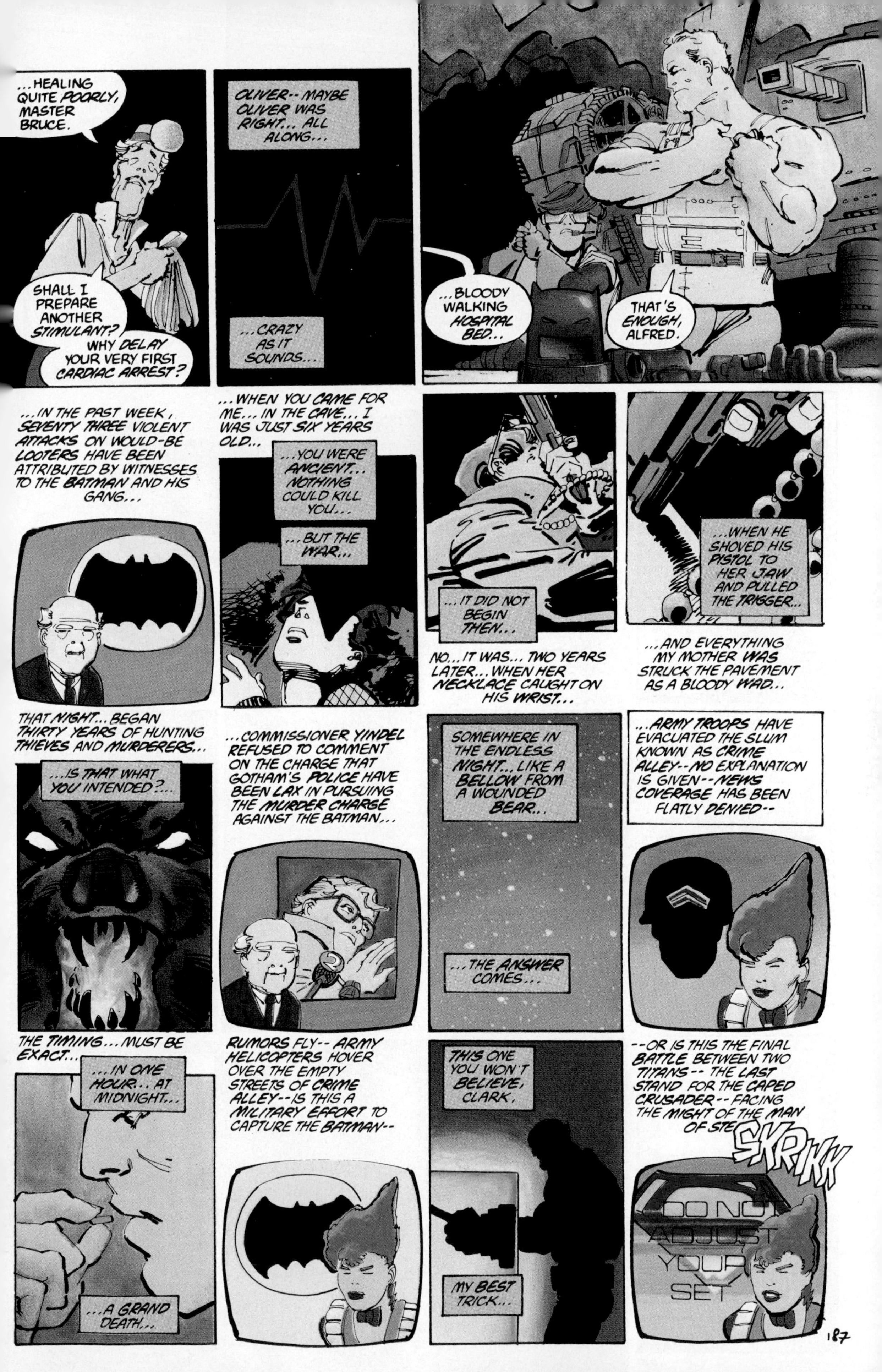
...HEALING QUITE POORLY, MASTER BRUCE.
SHALL I PREPARE ANOTHER STIMULANT? WHY DELAY YOUR VERY FIRST CARDIAC ARREST?
OLIVER-- MAYBE OLIVER WAS RIGHT... ALL ALONG...
...CRAZY AS IT SOUNDS...
...BLOODY WALKING HOSPITAL BED...
THAT'S ENOUGH, ALFRED.
...IN THE PAST WEEK, SEVENTY THREE VIOLENT ATTACKS ON WOULD-BE LOOTERS HAVE BEEN ATTRIBUTED BY WITNESSES TO THE BATMAN AND HIS GANG...
...WHEN YOU CAME FOR ME... IN THE CAVE... I WAS JUST SIX YEARS OLD...
...YOU WERE ANCIENT... NOTHING COULD KILL YOU...
...BUT THE WAR...
...IT DID NOT BEGIN THEN...
NO... IT WAS... TWO YEARS LATER... WHEN HER NECKLACE CAUGHT ON HIS WRIST...
...WHEN HE SHOVED HIS PISTOL TO HER JAW AND PULLED THE TRIGGER...
...AND EVERYTHING MY MOTHER WAS STRUCK THE PAVEMENT AS A BLOODY WAD...
THAT NIGHT... BEGAN THIRTY YEARS OF HUNTING THIEVES AND MURDERERS...
...IS THAT WHAT YOU INTENDED?...
...COMMISSIONER YINDEL REFUSED TO COMMENT ON THE CHARGE THAT GOTHAM'S POLICE HAVE BEEN LAX IN PURSUING THE MURDER CHARGE AGAINST THE BATMAN...
SOMEWHERE IN THE ENDLESS NIGHT... LIKE A BELLOW FROM A WOUNDED BEAR...
...THE ANSWER COMES...
...ARMY TROOPS HAVE EVACUATED THE SLUM KNOWN AS CRIME ALLEY-- NO EXPLANATION IS GIVEN-- NEWS COVERAGE HAS BEEN FLATLY DENIED--
THE TIMING... MUST BE EXACT...
...IN ONE HOUR... AT MIDNIGHT...
...A GRAND DEATH...
RUMORS FLY-- ARMY HELICOPTERS HOVER OVER THE EMPTY STREETS OF CRIME ALLEY-- IS THIS A MILITARY EFFORT TO CAPTURE THE BATMAN--
THIS ONE YOU WON'T BELIEVE, CLARK.
MY BEST TRICK...
--OR IS THIS THE FINAL BATTLE BETWEEN TWO TITANS-- THE LAST STAND FOR THE CAPED CRUSADER-- FACING THE MIGHT OF THE MAN OF STE
SKRIKK
DO NOT ADJUST YOUR SET

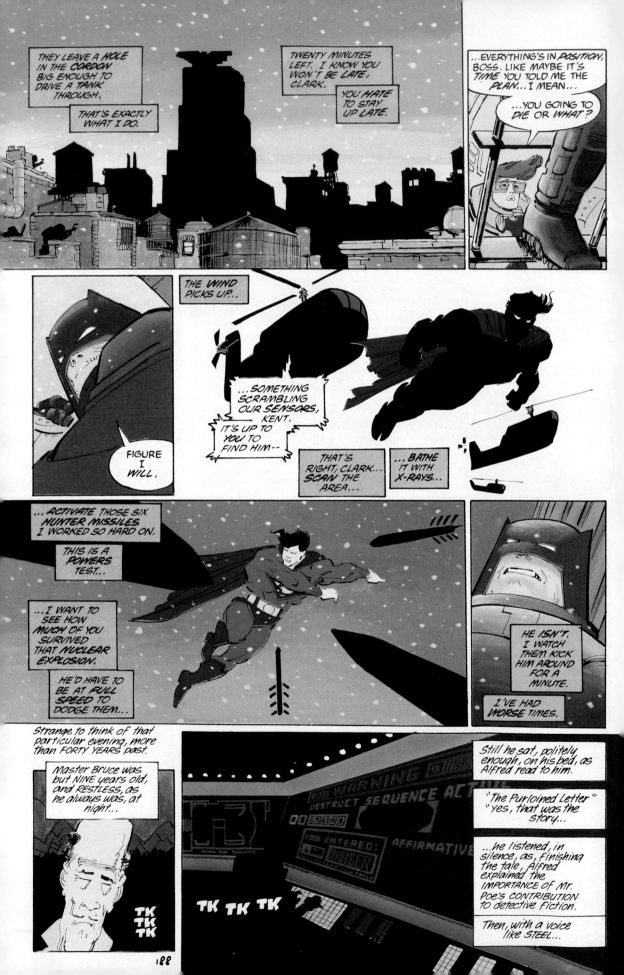

THEY LEAVE A HOLE IN THE *CORDON* BIG ENOUGH TO DRIVE A TANK THROUGH.

THAT'S EXACTLY WHAT I DO.

TWENTY MINUTES LEFT. I KNOW YOU WON'T BE LATE, CLARK.

YOU *HATE* TO STAY UP LATE.

...EVERYTHING'S IN *POSITION*, BOSS. LIKE MAYBE IT'S *TIME* YOU TOLD ME THE *PLAN*... I MEAN...

...YOU GOING TO *DIE* OR *WHAT*?

THE WIND PICKS UP...

...SOMETHING SCRAMBLING OUR *SENSORS*, KENT. IT'S UP TO YOU TO FIND HIM--

FIGURE I WILL.

THAT'S *RIGHT*, CLARK... *SCAN* THE AREA...

...*BATHE* IT WITH X-RAYS...

...ACTIVATE THOSE SIX *HUNTER* MISSILES I WORKED SO HARD ON.

THIS IS A *POWERS* TEST...

...I WANT TO SEE HOW *MUCH* OF YOU SURVIVED THAT *NUCLEAR* EXPLOSION.

HE'D HAVE TO BE AT *FULL* SPEED TO DODGE THEM...

HE *ISN'T*. I WATCH THEM KICK HIM AROUND FOR A MINUTE.

I'VE HAD *WORSE* TIMES.

Strange to think of that particular evening, more than FORTY YEARS past.

Master Bruce was but NINE years old, and RESTLESS, as he always was, at night...

WARNING SELF DESTRUCT SEQUENCE ACTIVE
02500
CODE ENTERED: AFFIRMATIVE
DANGER

TK TK TK

TK TK TK

Still he sat, politely enough, on his bed, as Alfred read to him.

"The Purloined Letter" "Yes, that was the story...

...he listened, in silence, as, finishing the tale, Alfred explained the IMPORTANCE of Mr. Poe's CONTRIBUTION to detective fiction.

Then, with a voice like STEEL...

...so *frightfully* FORMAL, his dark eyes *FLASHING*...

...*Master Bruce* asked--no, *DEMANDED*... *"the killer was CAUGHT. AND PUNISHED."*

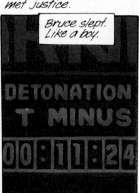

DETONATION T MINUS

00:11:24

Alfred *assured* him that the *villain* had met *justice.*

Bruce *slept.* Like a *boy.*

00:11:23

HE HITS THE *GROUND* ON *SCHEDULE.*

ONE *BLOCK* FROM ME.

BREATHING A LITTLE *FAST*--

IT'S *ROBIN'S TURN*--

THE *CHARGE* COULD SINK A *BATTLESHIP.* I think he *feels* it.

POOM

W H M P

SKREKK

ISN'T *TONIGHT* A *SCHOOL* NIGHT?

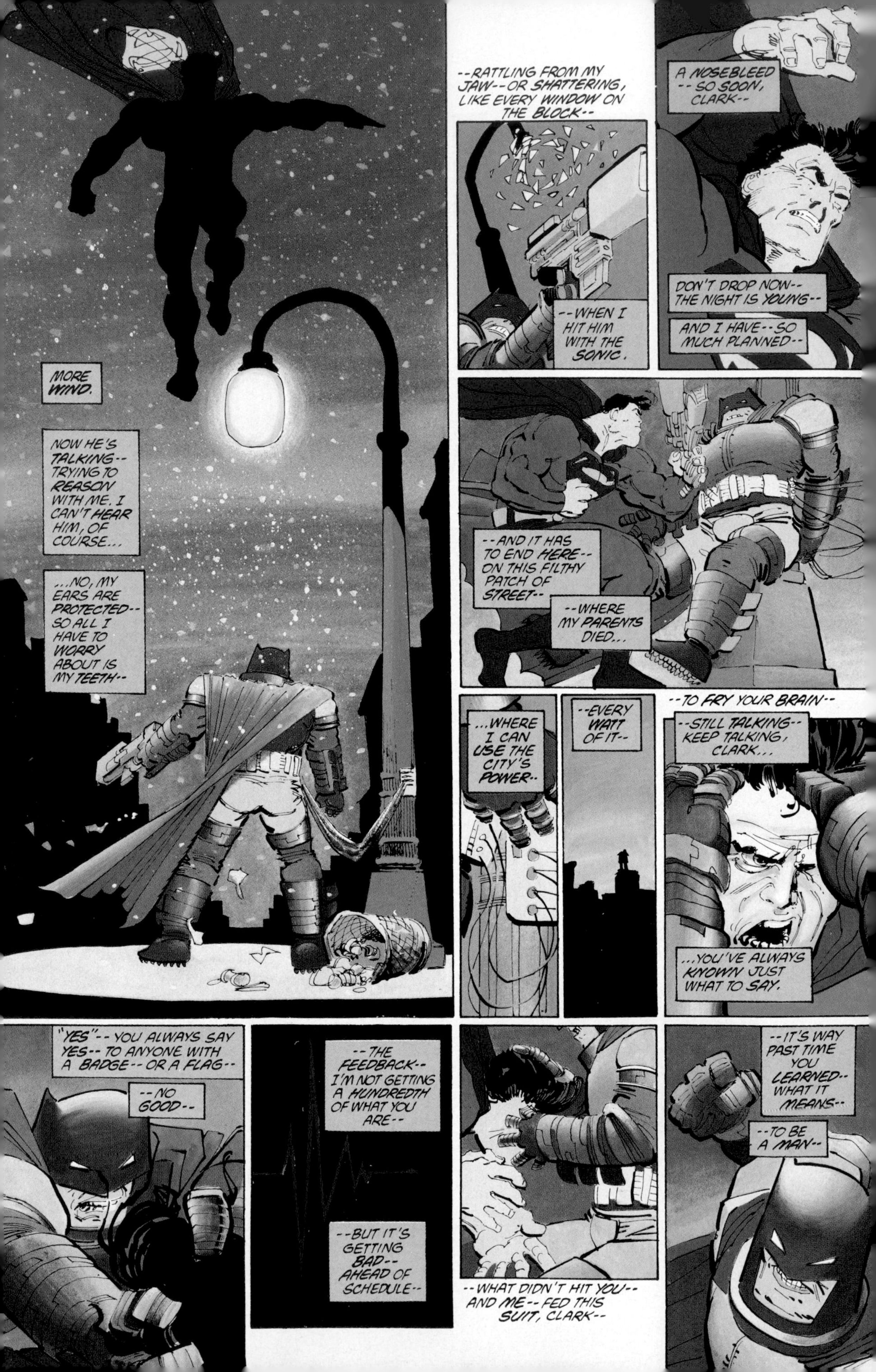
MORE WIND.
NOW HE'S TALKING-- TRYING TO REASON WITH ME. I CAN'T HEAR HIM, OF COURSE...
...NO, MY EARS ARE PROTECTED-- SO ALL I HAVE TO WORRY ABOUT IS MY TEETH--
--RATTLING FROM MY JAW--OR SHATTERING, LIKE EVERY WINDOW ON THE BLOCK--
--WHEN I HIT HIM WITH THE SONIC.
A NOSEBLEED -- SO SOON, CLARK--
DON'T DROP NOW-- THE NIGHT IS YOUNG--
AND I HAVE--SO MUCH PLANNED--
--AND IT HAS TO END HERE-- ON THIS FILTHY PATCH OF STREET--
--WHERE MY PARENTS DIED...
...WHERE I CAN USE THE CITY'S POWER..
--EVERY WATT OF IT--
--TO FRY YOUR BRAIN--
--STILL TALKING-- KEEP TALKING, CLARK...
...YOU'VE ALWAYS KNOWN JUST WHAT TO SAY.
"YES"-- YOU ALWAYS SAY YES-- TO ANYONE WITH A BADGE--OR A FLAG--
--NO GOOD--
--THE FEEDBACK-- I'M NOT GETTING A HUNDREDTH OF WHAT YOU ARE--
--BUT IT'S GETTING BAD-- AHEAD OF SCHEDULE--
--WHAT DIDN'T HIT YOU-- AND ME--FED THIS SUIT, CLARK--
--IT'S WAY PAST TIME YOU LEARNED-- WHAT IT MEANS--
--TO BE A MAN--

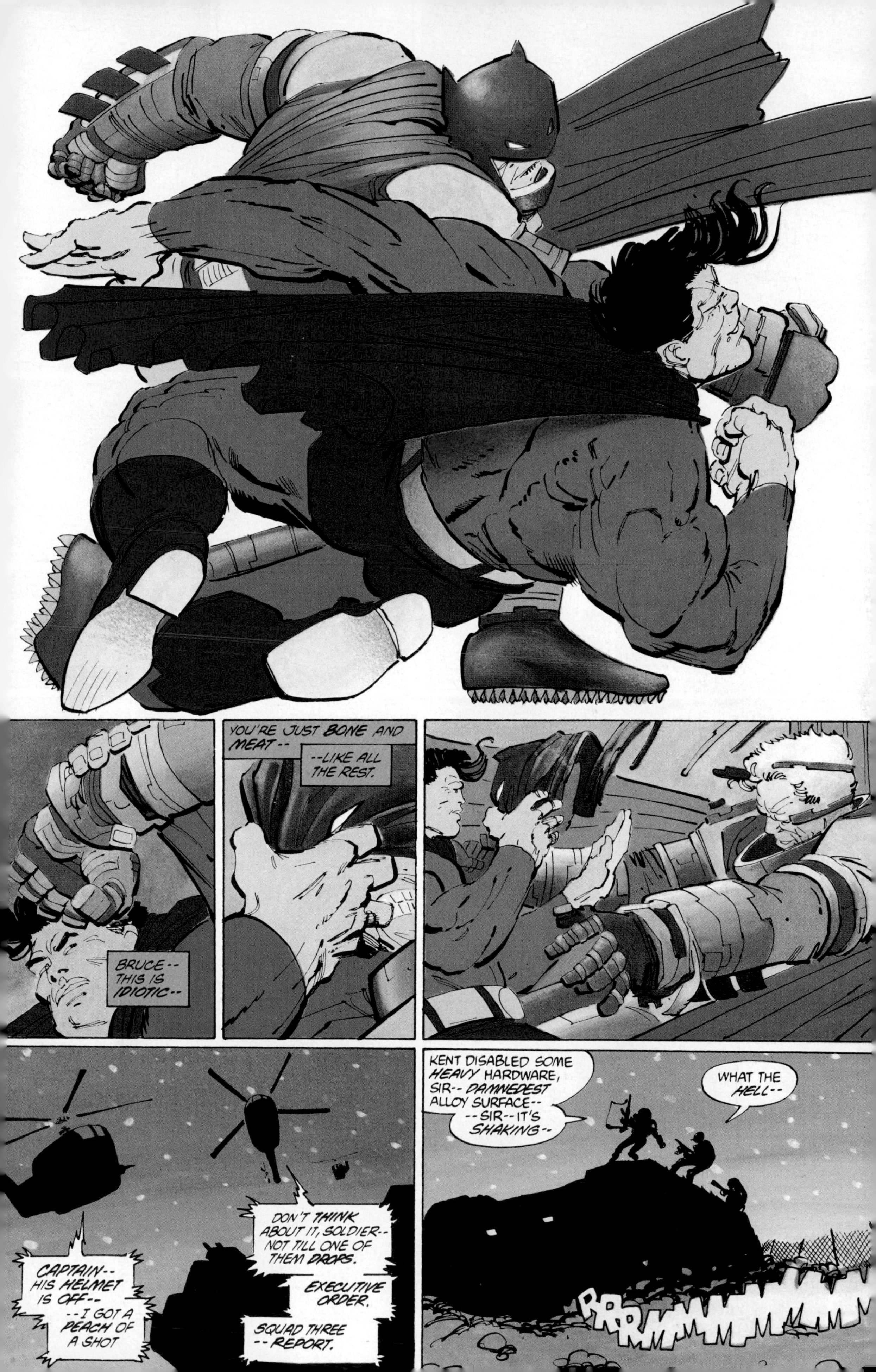
YOU'RE JUST BONE AND MEAT--
--LIKE ALL THE REST.
BRUCE--THIS IS IDIOTIC--
CAPTAIN--HIS HELMET IS OFF--
--I GOT A PEACH OF A SHOT
DON'T THINK ABOUT IT, SOLDIER--NOT TILL ONE OF THEM DROPS.
EXECUTIVE ORDER.
SQUAD THREE--REPORT.
KENT DISABLED SOME HEAVY HARDWARE, SIR--DAMNEDEST ALLOY SURFACE--
--SIR--IT'S SHAKING--
WHAT THE HELL--
RRRMMMMMMMM

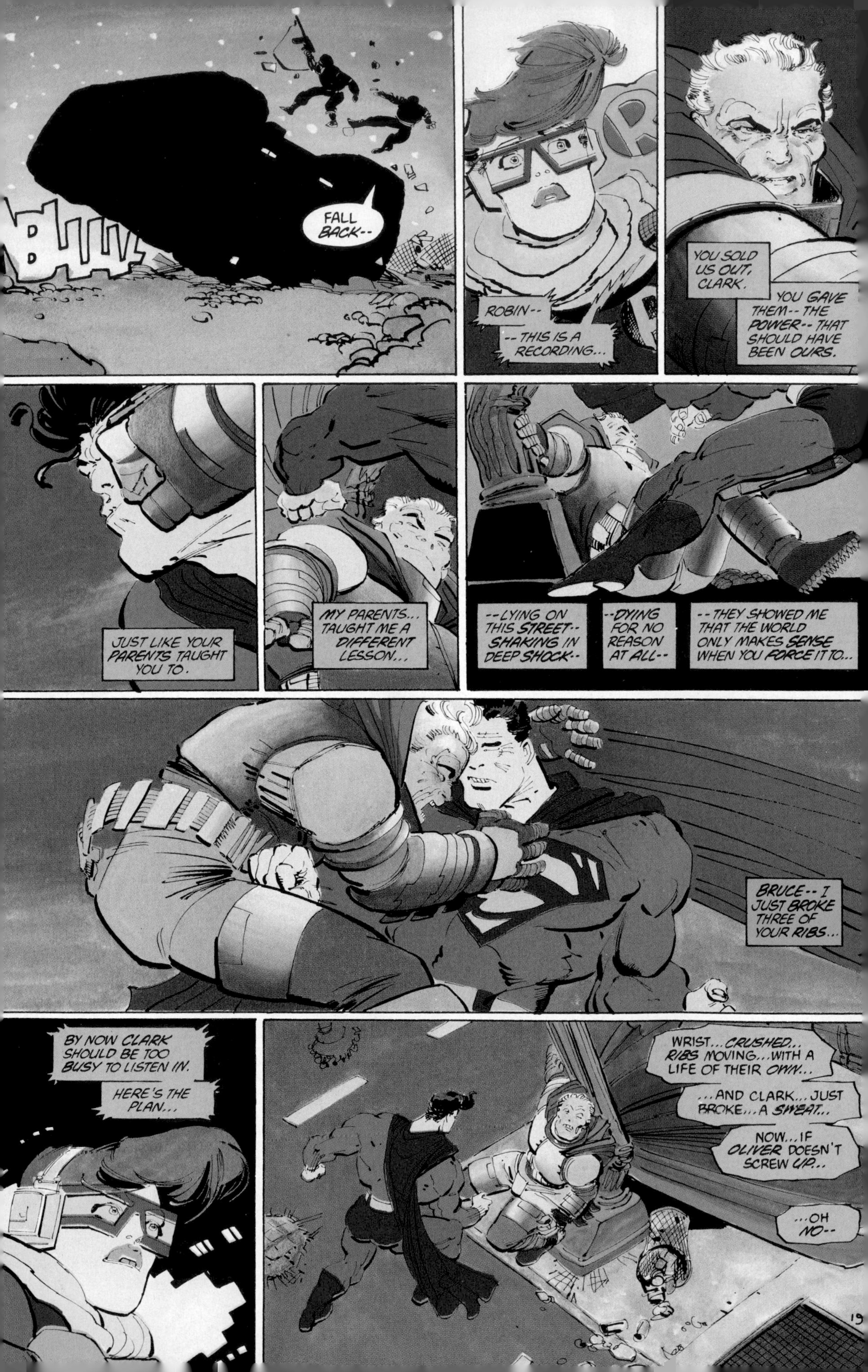
FALL BACK--
ROBIN--
--THIS IS A RECORDING...
YOU SOLD US OUT, CLARK.
YOU GAVE THEM-- THE POWER-- THAT SHOULD HAVE BEEN OURS.
JUST LIKE YOUR PARENTS TAUGHT YOU TO.
MY PARENTS... TAUGHT ME A DIFFERENT LESSON...
--LYING ON THIS STREET-- SHAKING IN DEEP SHOCK--
--DYING FOR NO REASON AT ALL--
--THEY SHOWED ME THAT THE WORLD ONLY MAKES SENSE WHEN YOU FORCE IT TO...
BRUCE-- I JUST BROKE THREE OF YOUR RIBS...
BY NOW CLARK SHOULD BE TOO BUSY TO LISTEN IN.
HERE'S THE PLAN...
WRIST... CRUSHED... RIBS MOVING... WITH A LIFE OF THEIR OWN...
...AND CLARK... JUST BROKE... A SWEAT...
NOW... IF OLIVER DOESN'T SCREW UP...
...OH NO--
19

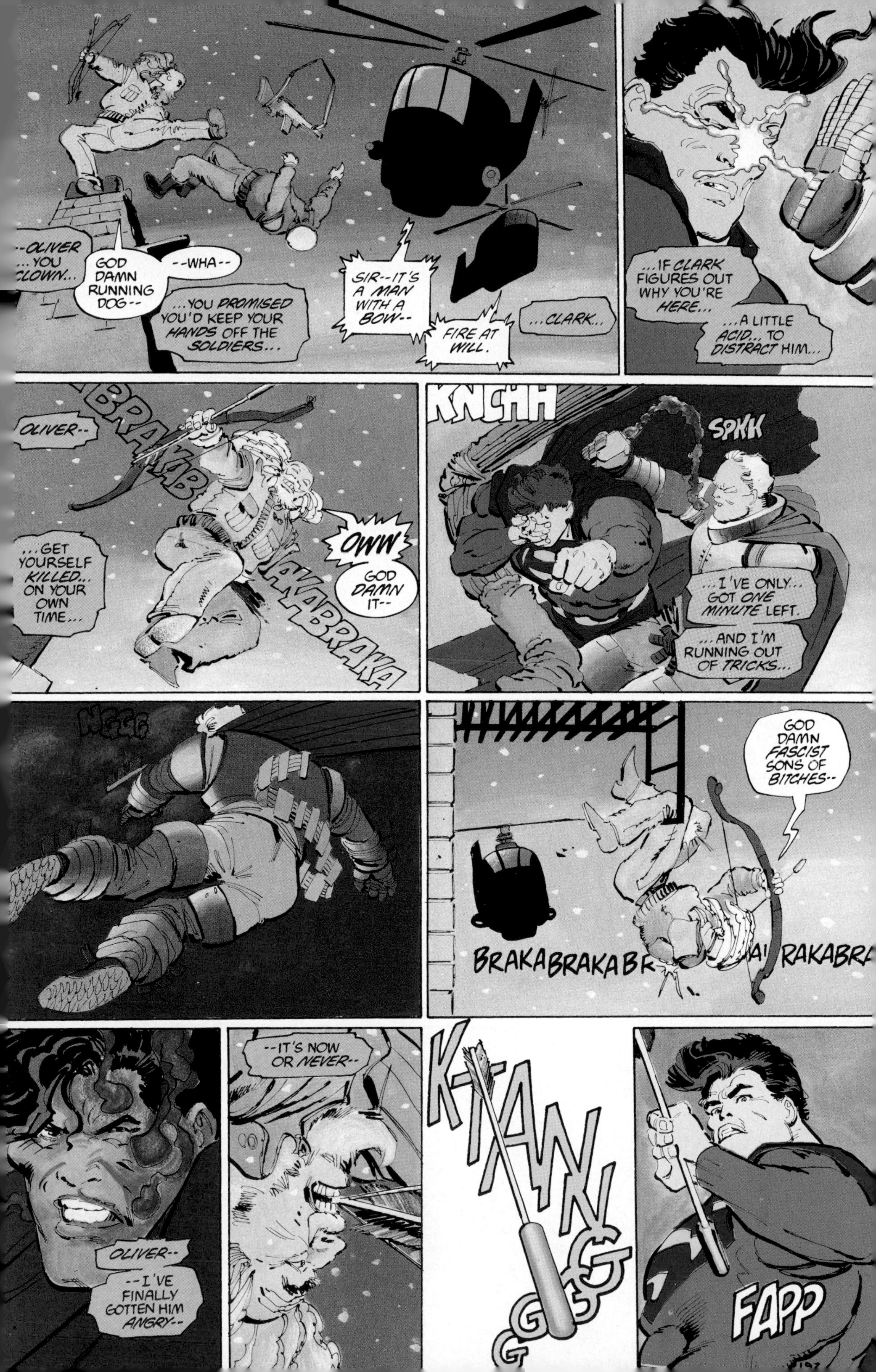
--OLIVER ...YOU CLOWN...
GOD DAMN RUNNING DOG--
--WHA--
...YOU PROMISED YOU'D KEEP YOUR HANDS OFF THE SOLDIERS...
SIR--IT'S A MAN WITH A BOW--
FIRE AT WILL.
...CLARK...
...IF CLARK FIGURES OUT WHY YOU'RE HERE...
...A LITTLE ACID... TO DISTRACT HIM...
BRAKAB
OLIVER--
...GET YOURSELF KILLED... ON YOUR OWN TIME...
OWW
GOD DAMN IT--
AKABRAKA
KNCHH
SPKK
...I'VE ONLY... GOT ONE MINUTE LEFT.
...AND I'M RUNNING OUT OF TRICKS...
GOD DAMN FASCIST SONS OF BITCHES--
BRAKABRAKABR
RAKABRA
OLIVER--
--I'VE FINALLY GOTTEN HIM ANGRY--
--IT'S NOW OR NEVER--
K-TANNNG
FAPP

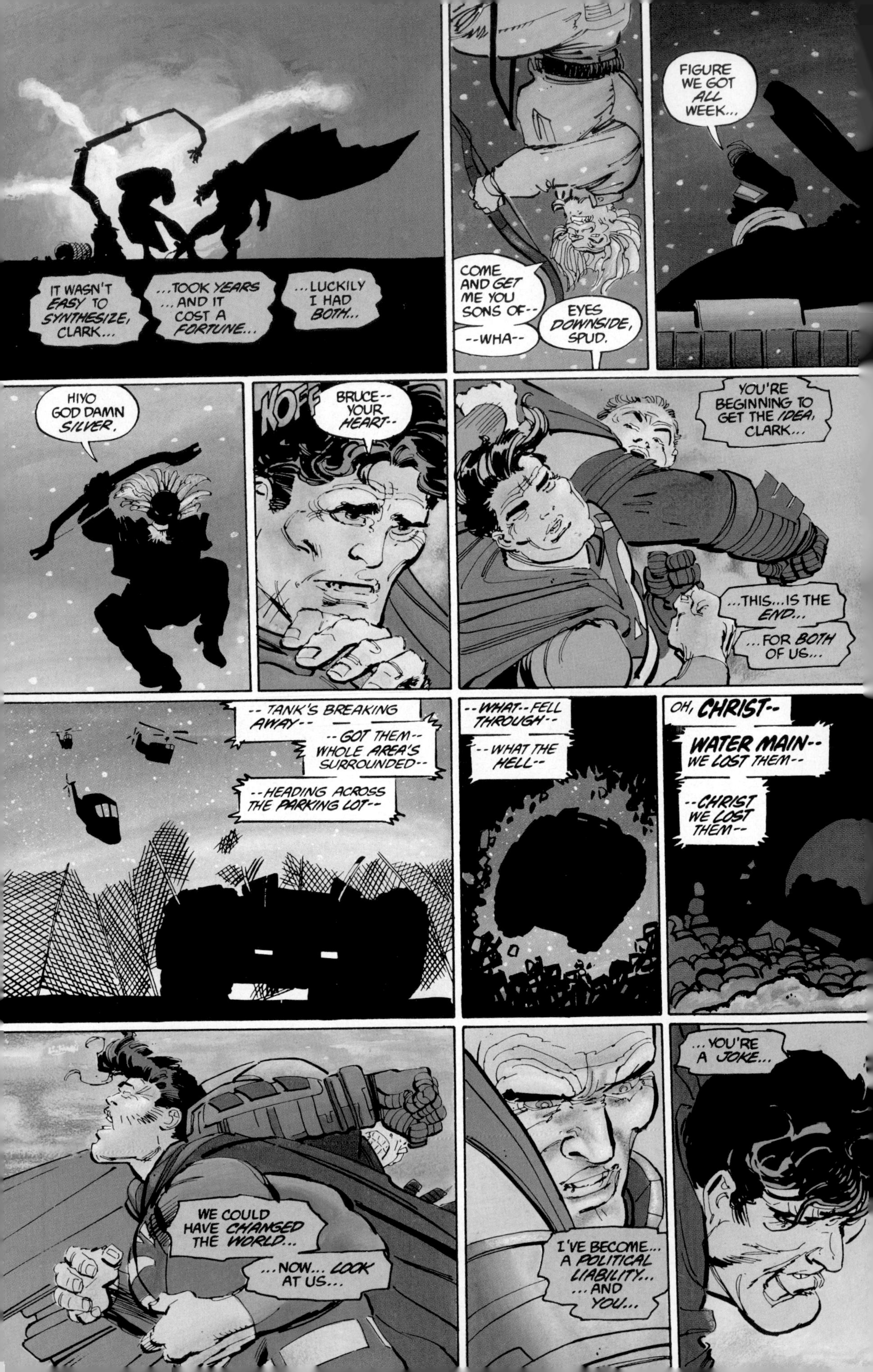
IT WASN'T EASY TO SYNTHESIZE, CLARK...
...TOOK YEARS ...AND IT COST A FORTUNE...
...LUCKILY I HAD BOTH...
COME AND GET ME YOU SONS OF--
--WHA--
EYES DOWNSIDE, SPUD.
FIGURE WE GOT ALL WEEK...
HIYO GOD DAMN SILVER.
KOFF
BRUCE-- YOUR HEART--
YOU'RE BEGINNING TO GET THE IDEA, CLARK...
...THIS...IS THE END...
...FOR BOTH OF US...
-- TANK'S BREAKING AWAY--
-- GOT THEM-- WHOLE AREA'S SURROUNDED--
--HEADING ACROSS THE PARKING LOT--
--WHAT--FELL THROUGH--
--WHAT THE HELL--
OH, CHRIST--
WATER MAIN-- WE LOST THEM--
--CHRIST WE LOST THEM--
WE COULD HAVE CHANGED THE WORLD...
...NOW... LOOK AT US...
I'VE BECOME... A POLITICAL LIABILITY... ...AND YOU...
...YOU'RE A JOKE...

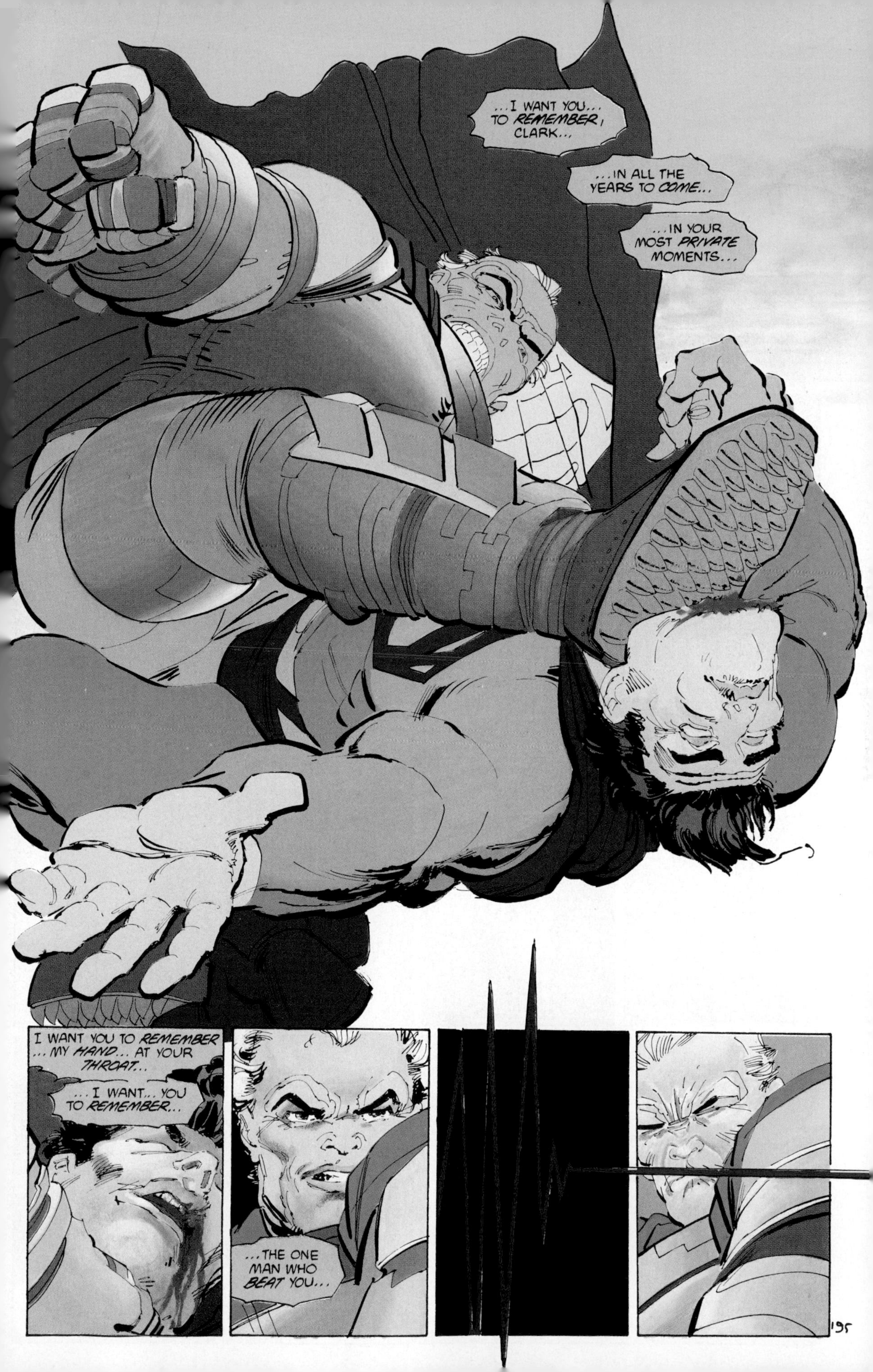
...I WANT YOU... TO REMEMBER, CLARK...
...IN ALL THE YEARS TO COME...
...IN YOUR MOST PRIVATE MOMENTS...
I WANT YOU TO REMEMBER ...MY HAND... AT YOUR THROAT...
...I WANT... YOU TO REMEMBER...
...THE ONE MAN WHO BEAT YOU...

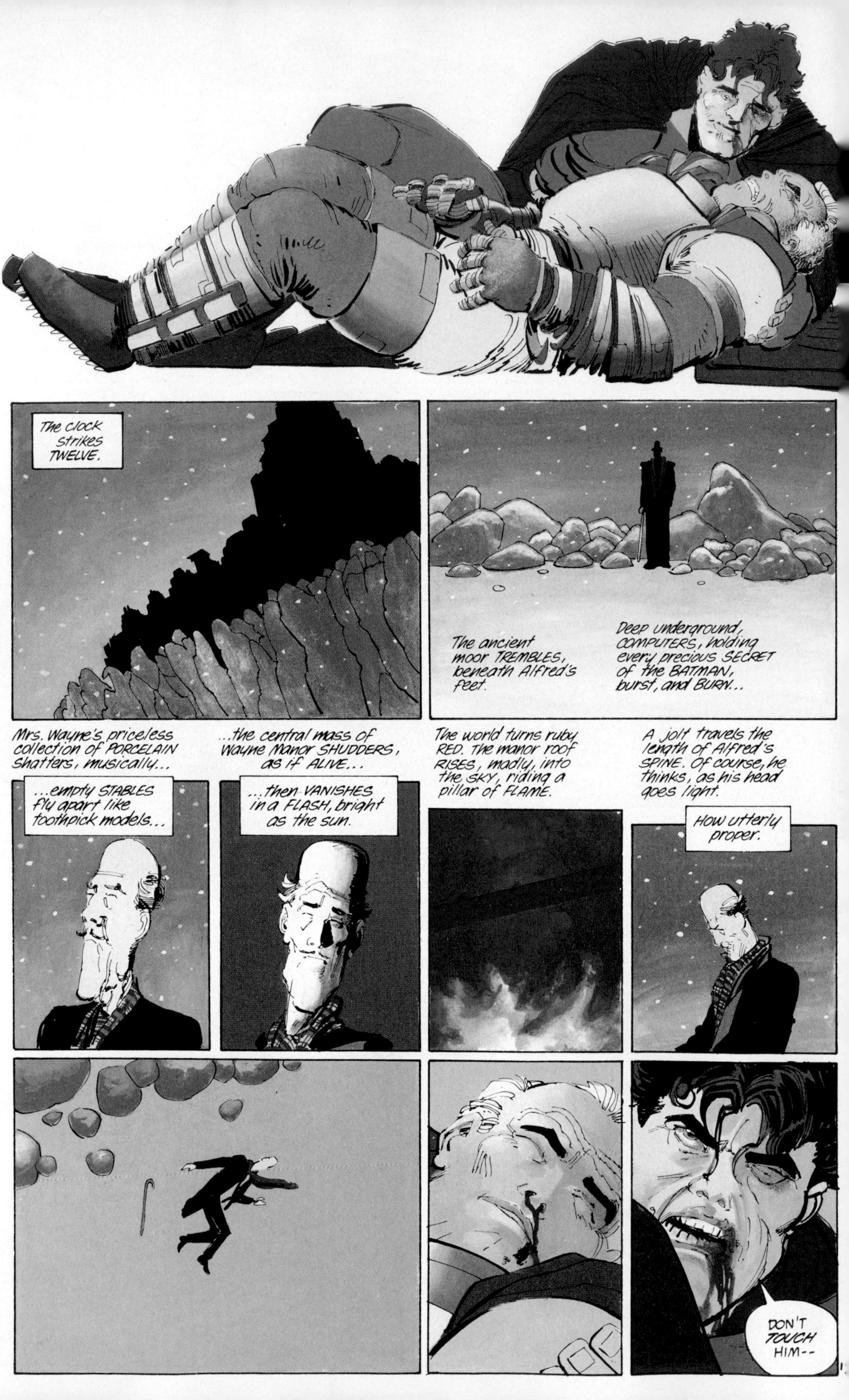
The clock strikes TWELVE.
The ancient moor TREMBLES, beneath Alfred's feet.
Deep underground, COMPUTERS, holding every precious SECRET of the BATMAN, burst, and BURN...
Mrs. Wayne's priceless collection of PORCELAIN shatters, musically...
...empty STABLES fly apart like toothpick models...
...the central mass of Wayne Manor SHUDDERS, as if ALIVE...
...then VANISHES in a FLASH, bright as the sun.
The world turns ruby RED. The manor roof RISES, madly, into the SKY, riding a pillar of FLAME.
A jolt travels the length of Alfred's SPINE. Of course, he thinks, as his head goes light.
How utterly proper.
DON'T TOUCH HIM--

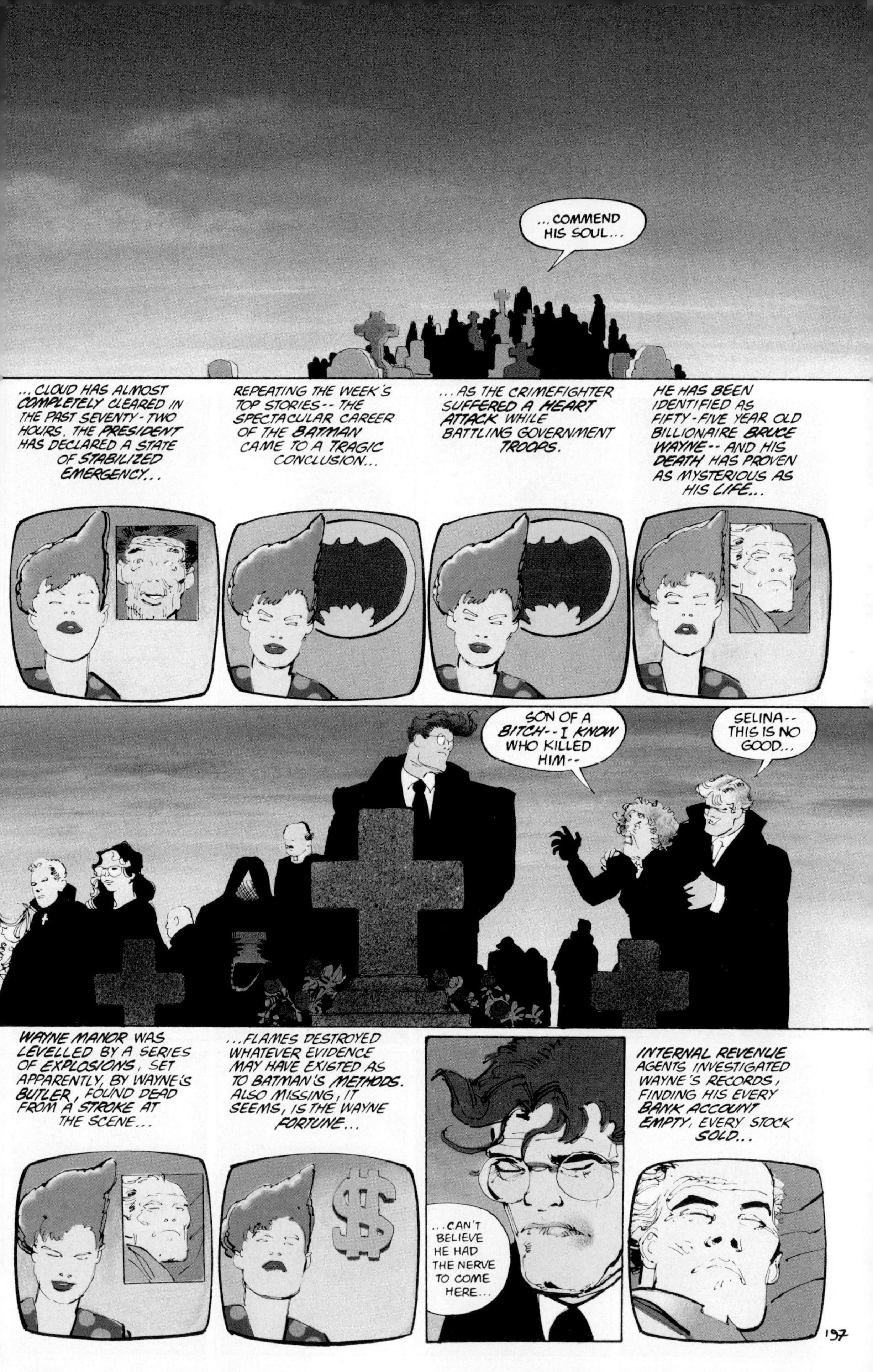

...COMMEND HIS SOUL...
...CLOUD HAS ALMOST COMPLETELY CLEARED IN THE PAST SEVENTY-TWO HOURS. THE PRESIDENT HAS DECLARED A STATE OF STABILIZED EMERGENCY...
REPEATING THE WEEK'S TOP STORIES-- THE SPECTACULAR CAREER OF THE BATMAN CAME TO A TRAGIC CONCLUSION...
...AS THE CRIMEFIGHTER SUFFERED A HEART ATTACK WHILE BATTLING GOVERNMENT TROOPS.
HE HAS BEEN IDENTIFIED AS FIFTY-FIVE YEAR OLD BILLIONAIRE BRUCE WAYNE-- AND HIS DEATH HAS PROVEN AS MYSTERIOUS AS HIS LIFE...
SON OF A BITCH--I KNOW WHO KILLED HIM--
SELINA-- THIS IS NO GOOD...
WAYNE MANOR WAS LEVELLED BY A SERIES OF EXPLOSIONS, SET APPARENTLY, BY WAYNE'S BUTLER, FOUND DEAD FROM A STROKE AT THE SCENE...
...FLAMES DESTROYED WHATEVER EVIDENCE MAY HAVE EXISTED AS TO BATMAN'S METHODS. ALSO MISSING, IT SEEMS, IS THE WAYNE FORTUNE...
$
...CAN'T BELIEVE HE HAD THE NERVE TO COME HERE...
INTERNAL REVENUE AGENTS INVESTIGATED WAYNE'S RECORDS, FINDING HIS EVERY BANK ACCOUNT EMPTY, EVERY STOCK SOLD...

...WHERE THE MONEY *WENT* IS ONE MORE SECRET WAYNE HAS TAKEN TO HIS GRAVE... HIS BODY WAS CLAIMED BY HIS ONLY LIVING RELATIVE, A DISTANT COUSIN...

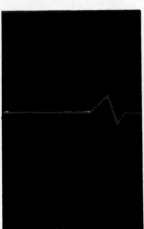

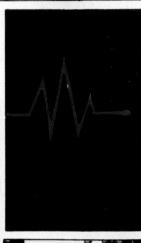

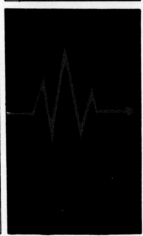

MY *TIMING* WASN'T QUITE *PRECISE* ENOUGH.

CLARK *HEARD.*

THAT WAS THE FIRST THING ROBIN *TOLD* ME--

--WHEN SHE DUG ME *UP.*

NOT THAT IT *MATTERED.* HE'D HAVE GUESSED SOONER OR LATER.

HE KNOWS HOW GOOD I AM WITH *CHEMICALS.*

I WAS *COUNTING* ON WHAT *OLIVER* SAID. AND WITH A *WINK*--

--*CLARK* PROVED *OLIVER* RIGHT.

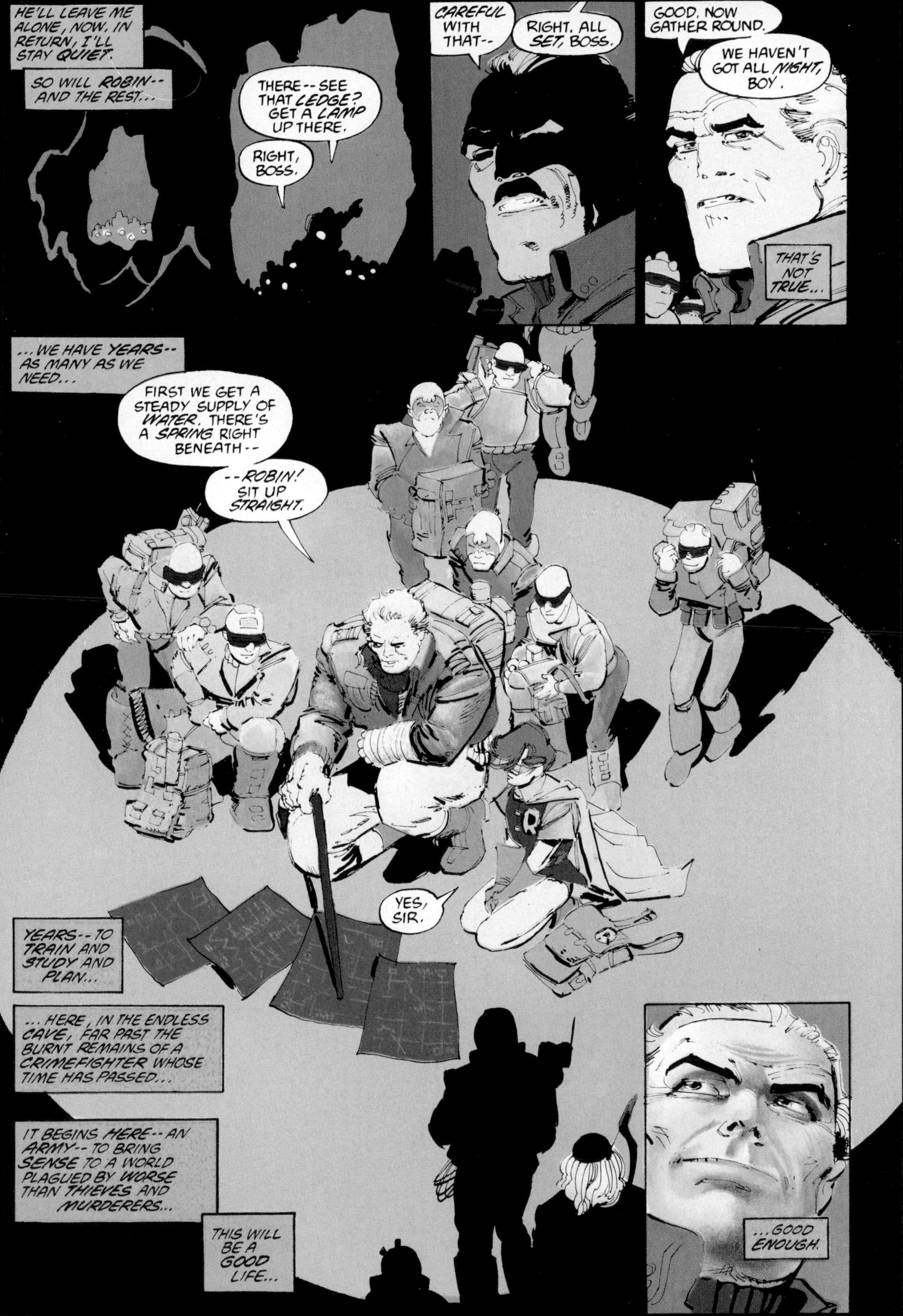
HE'LL LEAVE ME ALONE, NOW. IN RETURN, I'LL STAY QUIET.
SO WILL ROBIN-- AND THE REST...
THERE--SEE THAT LEDGE? GET A LAMP UP THERE.
RIGHT, BOSS.
CAREFUL WITH THAT--
RIGHT, ALL SET, BOSS.
GOOD. NOW GATHER ROUND.
WE HAVEN'T GOT ALL NIGHT, BOY.
THAT'S NOT TRUE...
...WE HAVE YEARS-- AS MANY AS WE NEED...
FIRST WE GET A STEADY SUPPLY OF WATER. THERE'S A SPRING RIGHT BENEATH--
--ROBIN! SIT UP STRAIGHT.
YES, SIR.
YEARS--TO TRAIN AND STUDY AND PLAN...
...HERE, IN THE ENDLESS CAVE, FAR PAST THE BURNT REMAINS OF A CRIMEFIGHTER WHOSE TIME HAS PASSED...
IT BEGINS HERE--AN ARMY--TO BRING SENSE TO A WORLD PLAGUED BY WORSE THAN THIEVES AND MURDERERS...
THIS WILL BE A GOOD LIFE...
...GOOD ENOUGH.

WITH ACKNOWLEDGMENTS
TO THE WORKS OF

BILL FINGER

DAVE FLEISCHER

MAX FLEISCHER

JERRY ROBINSON

JOE SHUSTER

JERRY SIEGEL

DICK SPRANG

BATMAN CREATED BY
BOB KANE

GALLERY

THE ORIGINAL COVERS

BOOK ONE

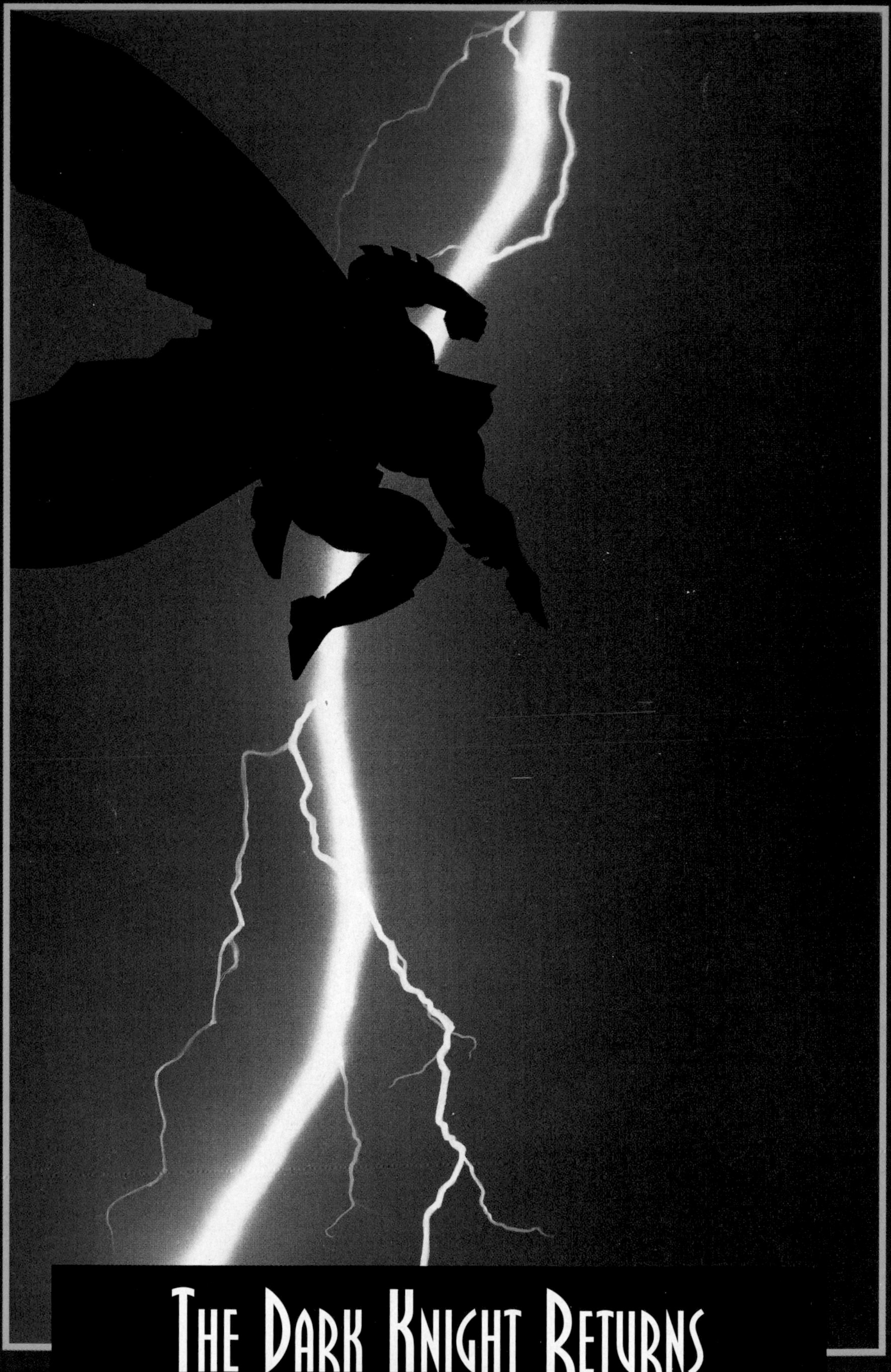

THE DARK KNIGHT RETURNS

BOOK TWO

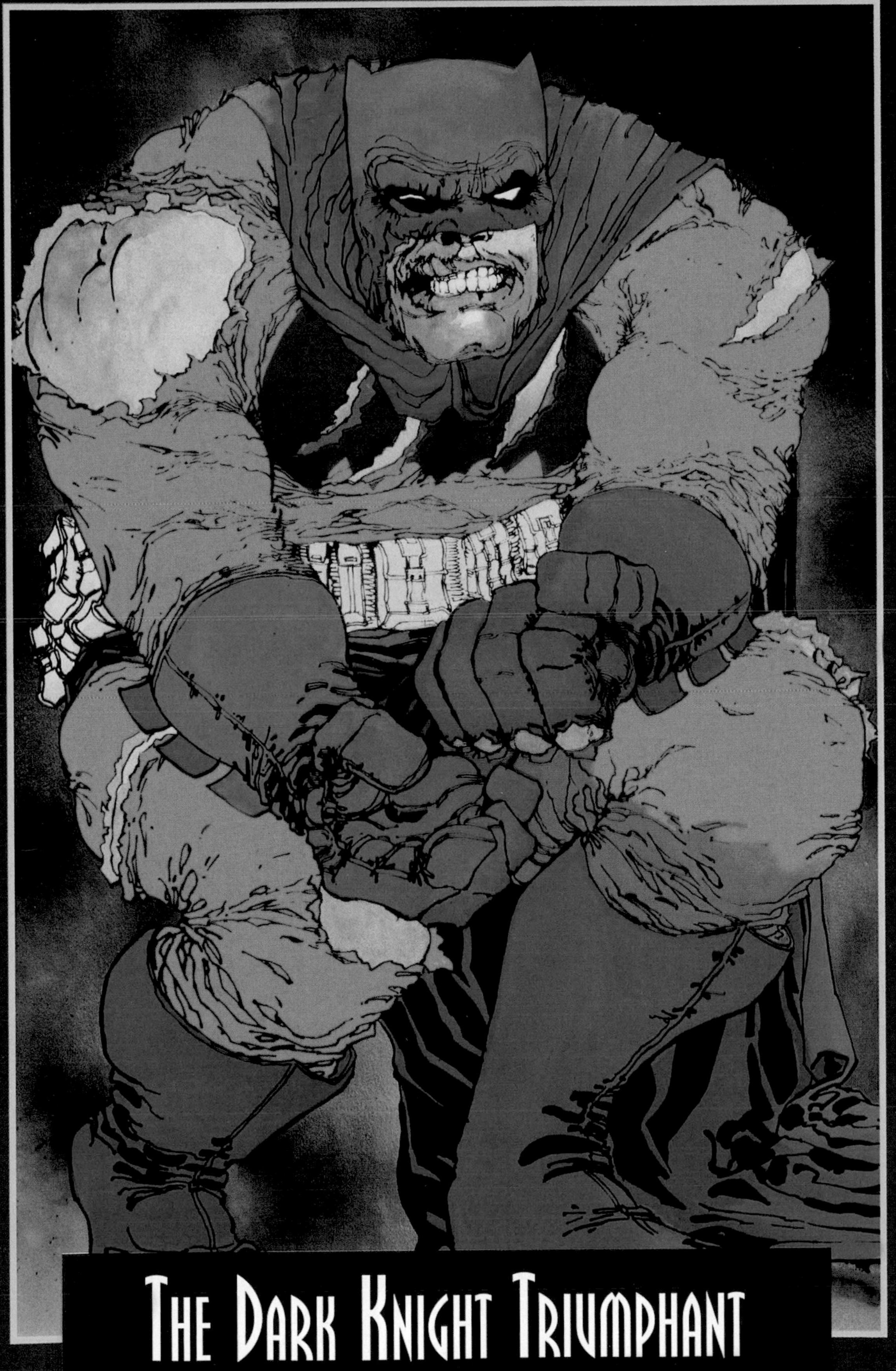

THE DARK KNIGHT TRIUMPHANT

BOOK THREE

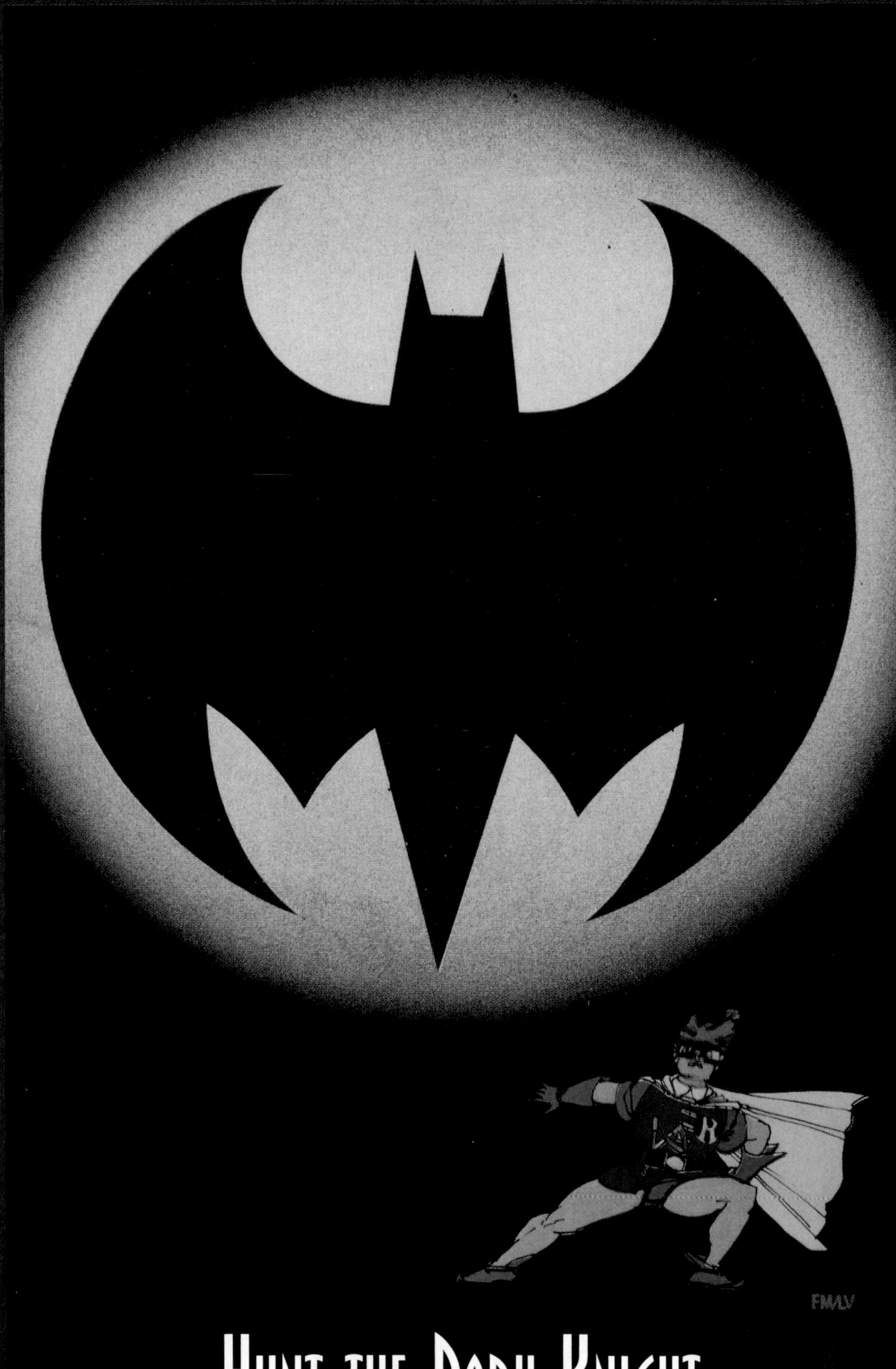
FM/LV

HUNT THE DARK KNIGHT

BOOK FOUR

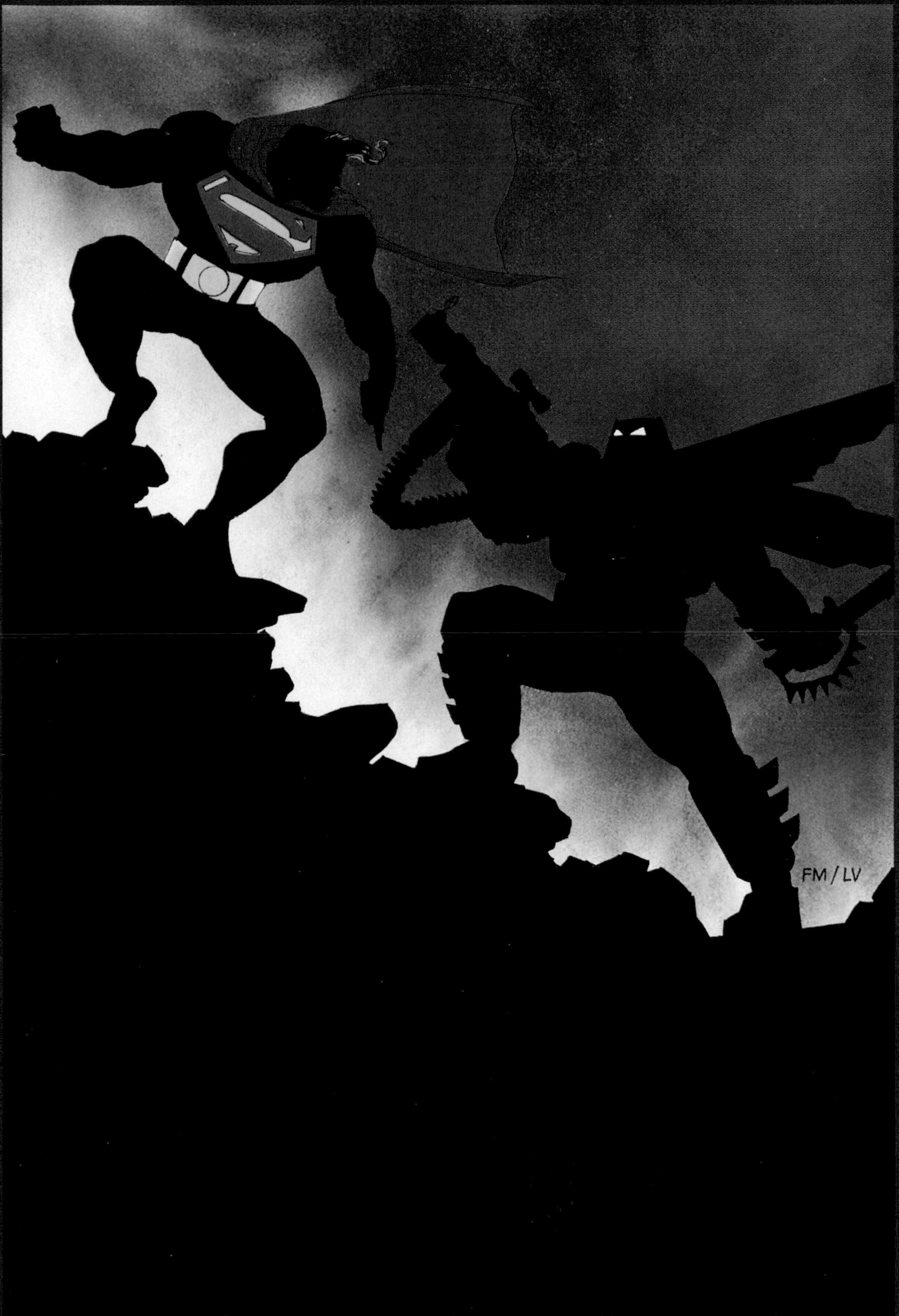
FM / LV

THE DARK KNIGHT FALLS

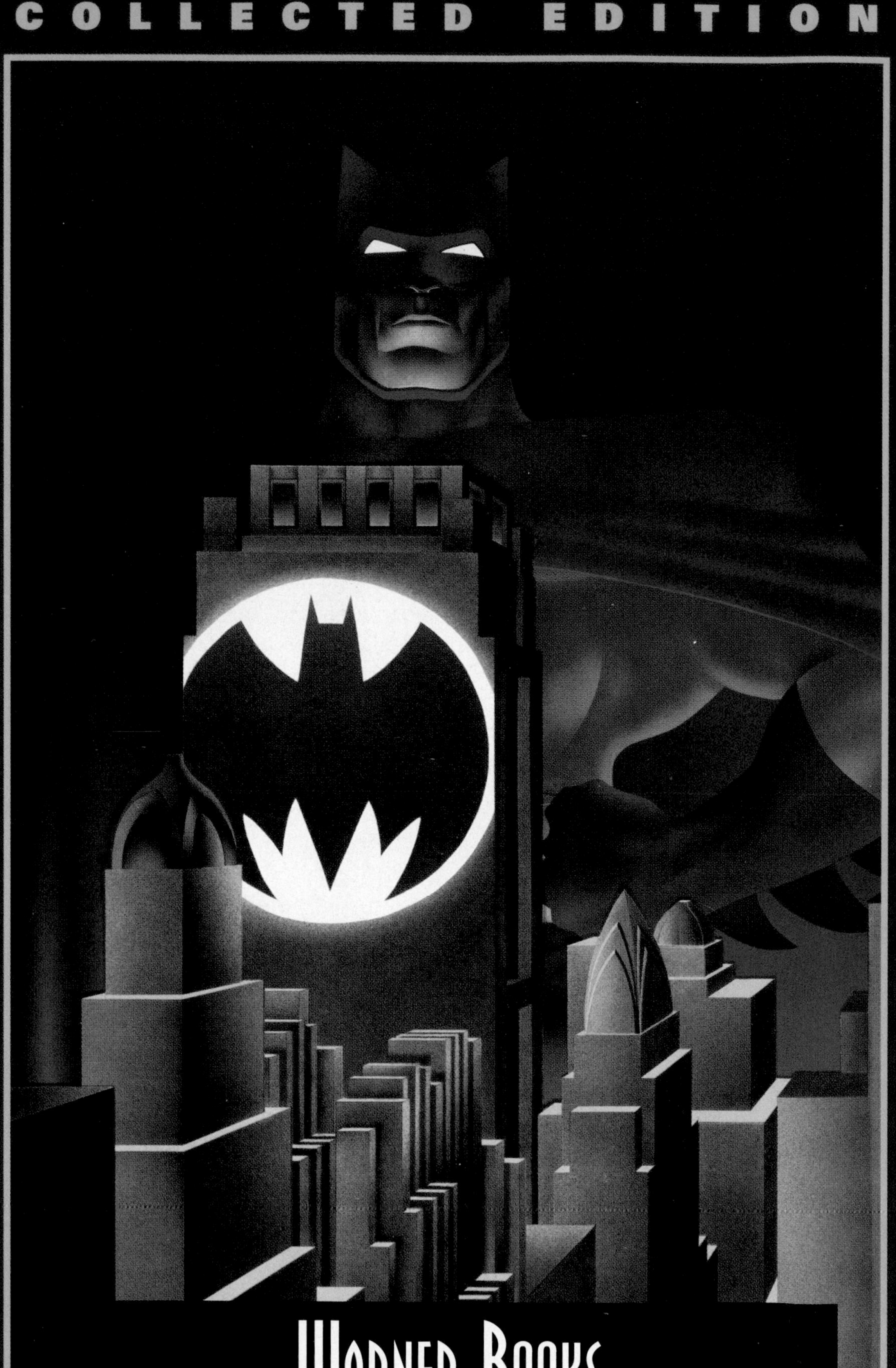
COLLECTED EDITION
WARNER BOOKS

Book One cover used for DC edition

THE FIRST 48-PAGE CHAPTER OF
THE DARK KNIGHT RETURNS WAS DONE IN A
FULL SCRIPT VERSION (ART DESCRIPTIONS, PANEL-BY-PANEL
PAGE BREAKDOWNS, FINISHED CAPTIONS AND DIALOGUE).
SUBSEQUENT CHAPTERS, AS DEADLINE PRESSURES INCREASED
AND THE CREATIVE PROCESS BECAME MORE CONFIDENT, WERE
DONE FROM DETAILED PLOTS SUCH AS THE ONE THAT
FOLLOWS, WITH DIALOGUE AND CAPTIONS WORKED OUT AT
THE ROUGH PENCIL STAGE AND WITH CHANGES UP UNTIL THE
FINAL LETTERING WAS DONE (AND OCCASIONALLY AFTER
THAT). ALL OF THESE GIVE INSIGHT INTO THE DEVELOPMENTS
AND DECISIONS IN BRINGING A MAJOR WORK TO FRUITION.

THE PLOT FOR THE LAST CHAPTER,
THE DARK KNIGHT FALLS, IS PARTICULARLY
INTERESTING FOR THE WAY IT BUILDS TO A SUBTLY
DIFFERENT AND DARKER ENDING. THE CHANGES THAT BECAME
THE PUBLISHED VERSION GAVE US TRUER AND MORE
EMOTIONALLY SATISFYING VERSIONS OF BOTH BATMAN AND
SUPERMAN AND THE CLIMAX IN GENERAL. STILL, THERE IS
GREAT FASCINATION IN SEEING BATMAN FALL BY HIS OWN
HAND RATHER THAN BATTLING SUPERMAN, IN OBSERVING
THAT THERE IS NO ROLE PROVIDED FOR GREEN ARROW
(A CREEPY GOVERNMENT AGENT FULFILLS A SIMILAR
FUNCTION IN A MUCH MORE CYNICAL WAY), AND IN
ADMIRING THE SWITCH FROM THE FINAL IMAGE SUGGESTED
HERE TO THE ONE ULTIMATELY USED.

THE DARK KNIGHT FALLS

A DC GRAPHIC NOVEL
A STORY FOR 46 PAGES

BY FRANK MILLER
12/26/85

PUT TOGETHER POLITICAL FACTS
—KNOWLEDGE OF BOMB IS LEAD-IN
TO BATS' POLITICAL AWARENESS...

ACT 1
[PP 1–12]

Commissioner Yindel and a squad of armed cops pilot boats into the tunnel of love, looking for Batman and the Joker. Both ends of the tunnel are blocked, surrounded by cop cars and dozens of cops. In the middle of the tunnel, a cop calls out to Yindel. He's found the Joker's corpse. In the darkness, Yindel and her men converge on the corpse—but the cop who called out has vanished.

On the roller coaster, Robin sits, still in shock. She is struck by a brilliant arc light. A huge voice booms, ordering her not to move. It's from a police helicopter, hovering by the moving roller coaster, trying to track it with the arc light. Robin does not respond or react. She's crying, shivering, and stunned. A voice crackles over her wrist communicator. Robin, it says, I need you. Robin shakes herself, for the first time aware of her situation. As the helicopter banks and turns, trying to keep her in sight, Robin tumbles from the coaster to a lower track, swings herself under it, invisible to the copter. She pulls a small device from her glove, the same device she used to summon the Wing, earlier. She expertly presses buttons on the device. I need firepower, she thinks. It'll take ten minutes to get here. She looks down. Armed cops are climbing the coasters toward her. She doesn't have ten minutes.

In the tunnel, Yindel and her men shine searchlights across the water, looking for Batman, with orders to shoot. Yindel's light catches the shape of a man, coming up from the water. The cop in the boat with Yindel aims his rifle. Yindel shoves his gun down as he fires. The cop who found the Joker is the man who surfaced. He's unconscious.

Two of the cops bring their boat up next to the Joker's corpse. They move to pull him onto the boat. As soon as they move the corpse, something explodes from behind the Joker. Tear gas fills the tunnel. He rigged the body, says Yindel, donning a small gas mask. Keep those lights shining. He can't breathe underwater.

Underwater, wearing a small device in this mouth, Batman places a device on the underside of Yindel's boat. Blood drifts from him.

Outside the tunnel, cops see tear gas drift out of the tunnel. The sound of explosions erupts from the tunnel. The cops charge in.

Inside the tunnel, the cops find Yindel and her men in the water, surrounded by fragments of their boats. The water is only waist deep, though, and the cops wade, guns out, in military formation. The gas clears. One cop, nervous, jumps in terror as something wet splatters on the top of his helmet. He looks up. A second drop of blood strikes his visor. He gestures upward to a cop near him, who shines a spotlight upward, at Batman, who clings to the tunnel roof. Batman dives, into the water, as the cops open fire. He begins fighting the cops, hand to hand. Have to get to the mouth of the tunnel, he thinks. Then I'm counting on Robin.

On the roller coaster, the cops close in on Robin, who climbs up the tracks. One cop gets her in his sights. Another cop stops him from firing. No guns, he says. Not with the kid. Yindel's orders. The cops are about to reach Robin as she leaps from one track to another, then bounds into space, flipping, landing on the coaster as it begins its descent. The coaster roars on, along a curve, then rockets down the track, right at the cops. The cops jump to either side, dodging the coaster. The police copter tracks Robin, staying close. Suddenly the Batcopter appears in the night sky. As Robin shouts an order, the Batcopter flies in, between tracks, to hover directly over the coaster. Robin grabs a lowered wheel, is lifted away, as the police copter, knocked sideways by the wind created by the larger Batcopter, banks, trying to stay aloft.

Cops pile on Batman as he reaches the mouth of the tunnel. Suddenly, machine gun fire rips across the water. The cops fall away as Batman staggers out of the tunnel and collapses. Robin dives from the Batcopter. As bullets strike the water around her, she grabs Batman's arm, struggles to lift him.

Throughout all of this, TV coverage continues, with Hernando Hernandez and Lola Chong. Batman and Robin escape the police. Murder is added to the charges against the Batman.

In a 7–Eleven, somewhere in Gotham City, an off-duty police detective opens a refrigerator cabinet and reaches in for a six-pack of beer. He hears a commotion from the front of the store, and peers down an aisle to see four hoods harassing the store's clerk, waving pistols, knocking over cans and bottles, and demanding the clerk empty the cash register. The detective moves down the aisle, slowly, drawing his gun. He comes up behind the hoods, tells them not to move. A fifth hood, out of sight until now, raises his pistol to the detective's temple and giggles.

Outside the store, a sixth hood, waiting in the would-be getaway car, recoils at the sound of a gunshot, curses, and shifts the car to drive, as three men on motorcycles pull into the parking lot. The hood in the car looks in terror at the motorcycles, whose riders are as yet silhouetted by streetlight, their features indistinguishable. The hood floors the accelerator, and the car roars across the lot. One of the bikers gestures. Another lights a Molotov cocktail, and throws it into the passing car. The car catches fire. The hood, aflame, tumbles out, onto the parking lot. He looks up. A sawed-off shotgun barrel presses to his face. The shotgun blast is lost in the roar of the car exploding.

Inside the store, the hoods wheel, lit by the flame of the explosion. They freeze, not knowing what to do. Suddenly, the glass front of the shop explodes inward, from shotgun blasts.

Silhouetted by the flame, three Sons of the Batman step forward, to stand framed by broken glass, their shotguns held casually by their sides. They wait until the hoods in the store raise their pistols to fire. They blow the hoods apart with shotgun blasts.

The clerk is left, in the mess of blood, produce, and bodies, screaming in horror. Add SOB tape—"Let Gotham criminals beware."

Taped commentary by the late Dr. Bartholomew Wolper leads into commentary by Wolper's widow, who claims that Batman's murder of the Joker should be enough to link Batman to the actions of the Sons of the Batman.

Commentary continues, as the governor and mayor are briefly interviewed. They are no longer sidestepping the issue. It has become a political necessity to attack the Batman. People on the street are interviewed, as well. Batman has apparently few supporters. The only supporter quoted is a survivalist lunatic.

At Gotham's jail, Yindel is harassed by an attorney as she passes cells filled with captured Mutants. The attorney is protesting the overcrowded conditions. Yindel is wondering what she's going to do with them. The Mutants are angry, confused. Their gang is dead. Members of it are now the Sons of the Batman. They don't know what to do with themselves.

In the Batcave, Robin sits nervously outside a closed door. The door opens, and Alfred steps out, exhausted, wearing a surgical gown, his arms bloody to the elbow. He'll make it, asks Robin. He'll live, says Alfred.

TV news coverage resumes, with the president announcing that Soviet forces have withdrawn from Corto Maltese.

Clark Kent rides in a jeep across the burned-out remains of Corto Maltese. He's weary, tired, but can't help listening to news broadcasts. He hears about the Joker's apparent murder. Bruce, he thinks. You're finished. Sitting beside Clark is an Air Force general, who talks triumphantly about the victory. Clark looks up, then, skyward, alarmed. He silences the general, and listens.

A Soviet nuclear warhead roars through the sky.

The general, startled, looks at the seat next to him. Clark's clothes collapse, empty.

An advisor wakes the President, in the middle of the night, to inform him that the Soviets have launched a nuclear missile. The missile will explode over Corto Maltese in fifteen minutes. Get me my Pepto, says the President. And call the usual gang together.

A computer screen lights, showing the missile as a blip approaching Corto. General Lockheed screams at the President. This is an act of war, he says. Give the word. Not just yet, says the President. Let's see what our own little deterrent can do.

Superman tackles the rocket, two minutes from detonation. Slowly, he pushes, veering its course. You laughed at them, Bruce, he thinks. They can make this and you laugh at them. Superman counts the number of lives who will be lost at Corto if he fails, and keeps pushing.

Superman and the missile fly over a mountain range. He counts the victims again, including every animal and plant. He strains, shifts the course of the missile again. He and the missile fly over open desert. The count of victims now is twelve snakes and three dozen scorpions. Superman describes desert life, too, in detail—frogs that hybernate underground, hyenas, etc. He settles for that. He lets go of the rocket, and flies away from it, as fast as he can.

The President addresses the nation.

Don't worry, he says. It's not World War III. We're still America, he says, smiling. And I'm still President. Suddenly, the TV screen goes blank.

Superman is caught in the flash as the warhead detonates.

Robin and Alfred sit, in Wayne Manor. Bruce is in a hospital-style bed, unconscious, surrounded by monitors that show his vital signs. Robin watches the cardiogram, fixed on it, as Alfred tries to convince her to eat. Robin recoils, horrified, as the cardiogram goes flat, then stops. Then she realizes the room is dark, as well. A blackout, she says. Alfred, at the window, tells her that it must be a huge blackout. Gotham City is dark. How am I getting home, asks Robin. It must be late. Alfred pulls his watch from his pocket. The watch has stopped.

Bruce's eyes open. Clark, he thinks. You idiot. You let them do it. I always knew you would.

Superman is tossed like a burning ragdoll in the nuclear fireball. The desert vanishes in an enormous mushroom cloud.

Using SOBs is Robin's idea—+ she makes it work.

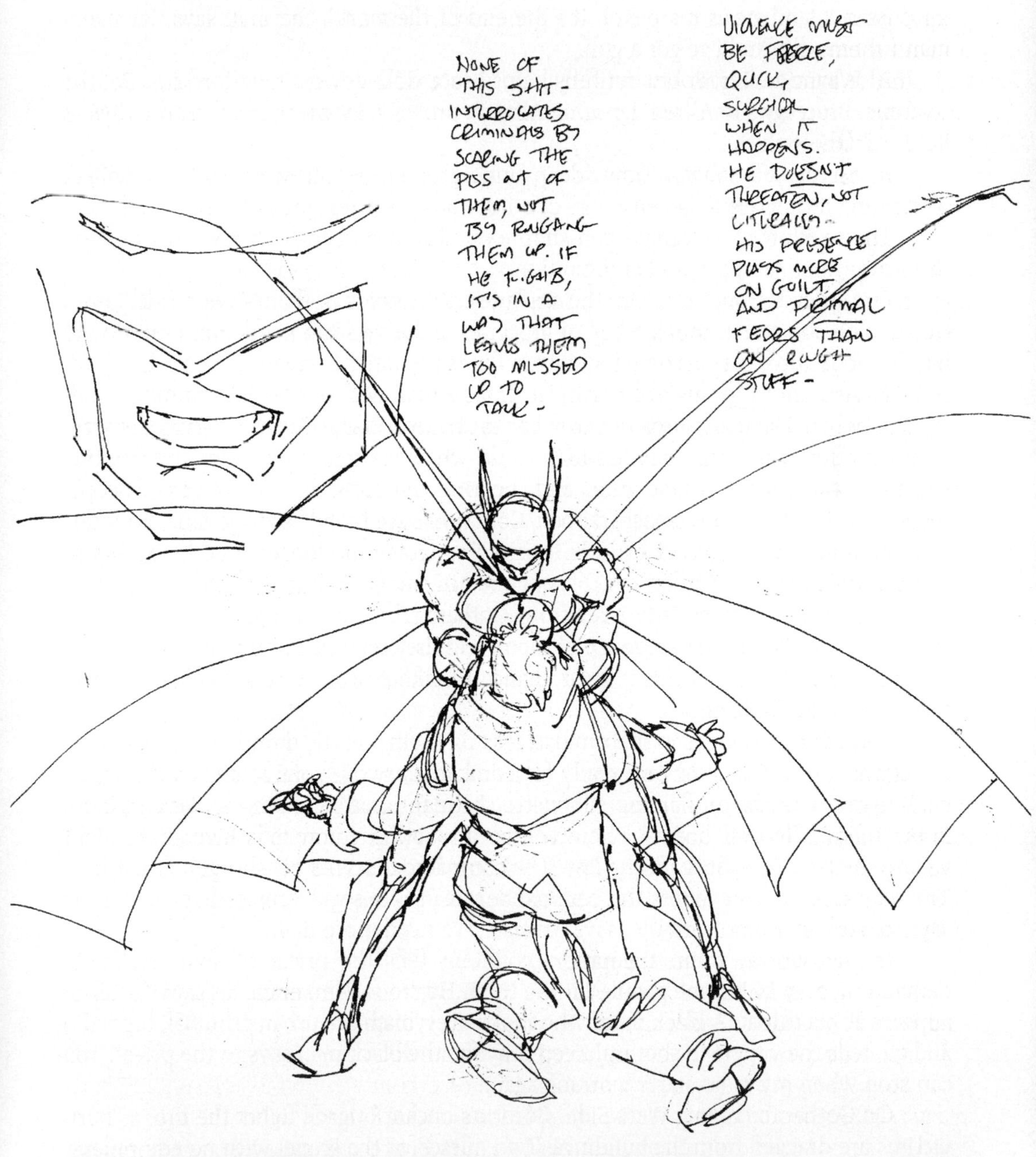
NONE OF THIS SHIT - INTERROGATES CRIMINALS BY SCARING THE PISS OUT OF THEM, NOT BY ROUGHING THEM UP. IF HE FIGHTS, IT'S IN A WAY THAT LEAVES THEM TOO MESSED UP TO TALK -
VIOLENCE MUST BE FIERCE, QUICK, SURGICAL WHEN IT HAPPENS. HE DOESN'T THREATEN, NOT LITERALLY - HIS PRESENCE PLAYS MORE ON GUILT AND PRIMAL FEARS THAN ON ROUGH STUFF -

ACT II
[PP 13-24]

A commercial jet flies over the black silhouette of Gotham City. The pilot screams into a dead microphone. A stewardess screams to the pilot that the passengers are panicking. The jet falls through the night sky, collides with a skyscraper. Flames burst from the skyscraper. Glass, stone, then the plane itself, now aflame, fall toward the street, into a crowded intersection of stalled cars. The cars explode, one by one, as their gas tanks ignite. A lone traffic cop tries to maintain order amid the explosions and screaming crowd. He fires a shot into the air. A man tackles him, strikes him unconscious, and steals his pistol. It's the end of the world, the man says. It's every man for himself. And I've got a gun.

At Wayne Manor, Robin dutifully helps Bruce walk down a long corridor. Get the costume, Bruce says to Alfred, ignoring Alfred's protests. Down this way, Bruce says to Robin. To the stables.

In a crowded subway train, deep underground, people wait, silent, terrified, wondering if they are to be survivors of a holocaust. A priest prays aloud.

The window to a Gotham gun shop explodes inward. A frightened mob enters the store, grabs weapons and ammunition.

Fire spreads from the site of the airplane crash, across Gotham's West Side. James Gordon, on the street, drops a bag of groceries as he sees the pandemonium around him. He looks up to see his own building in flames. Sarah, he screams, then calms himself. He can't afford to think of Sarah. He grabs a man near him, who's running, holding a crowbar. The man raises the crowbar to strike Gordon. Gordon shoves his magnum into the man's face, tells the man to do what he's told. Gordon starts shouting orders to the people around him, and, hearing the authority in his voice, people respond. A fire hydrant is smashed open. Containers are found, garbage cans, milk cartons, all kinds, and a bucket brigade forms. The crowd, no longer panicking, gets to work against the fire. Gordon coughs, engulfed in smoke, and continues his orders.

At the dump, across the river from Gotham, the Sons of the Batman, holding torches, argue. There are two dozen of them, and they can't agree on what to do. Their commander screams that this is their chance to take power, to rape Gotham, spread fires—to purge Gotham.

Something explodes in their midst, tossing them and the dump's wreckage in all directions. They rise, guns out, ready for combat, as two figures approach on horseback. Against Gotham's flaming silhouette, Batman appears, riding a black stallion. Robin follows, leading horses. There will be no looting, commands Batman. Tonight we are the law. Tonight, I am the law. The commander points his shotgun at Batman. The man next to him shoots the commander dead. We await your orders, leader, he says to Batman. Come with me, says Batman. We need more men.

In the subway train, a yuppie accountant tells the priest to shut up, starts demanding they kick some people off the train. He stops demanding, as a switchblade appears at his throat. A black man, who looks every inch the urban criminal, big radio and all, tells the yuppie to shut up. Keep praying, the black man says to the priest. You can stop when my radio starts working again.

On Gotham's flaming West Side, Gordon's bucket brigade fights the fire, as burn victims are dragged from the buildings. Two nurses, at the scene, with no equipment,

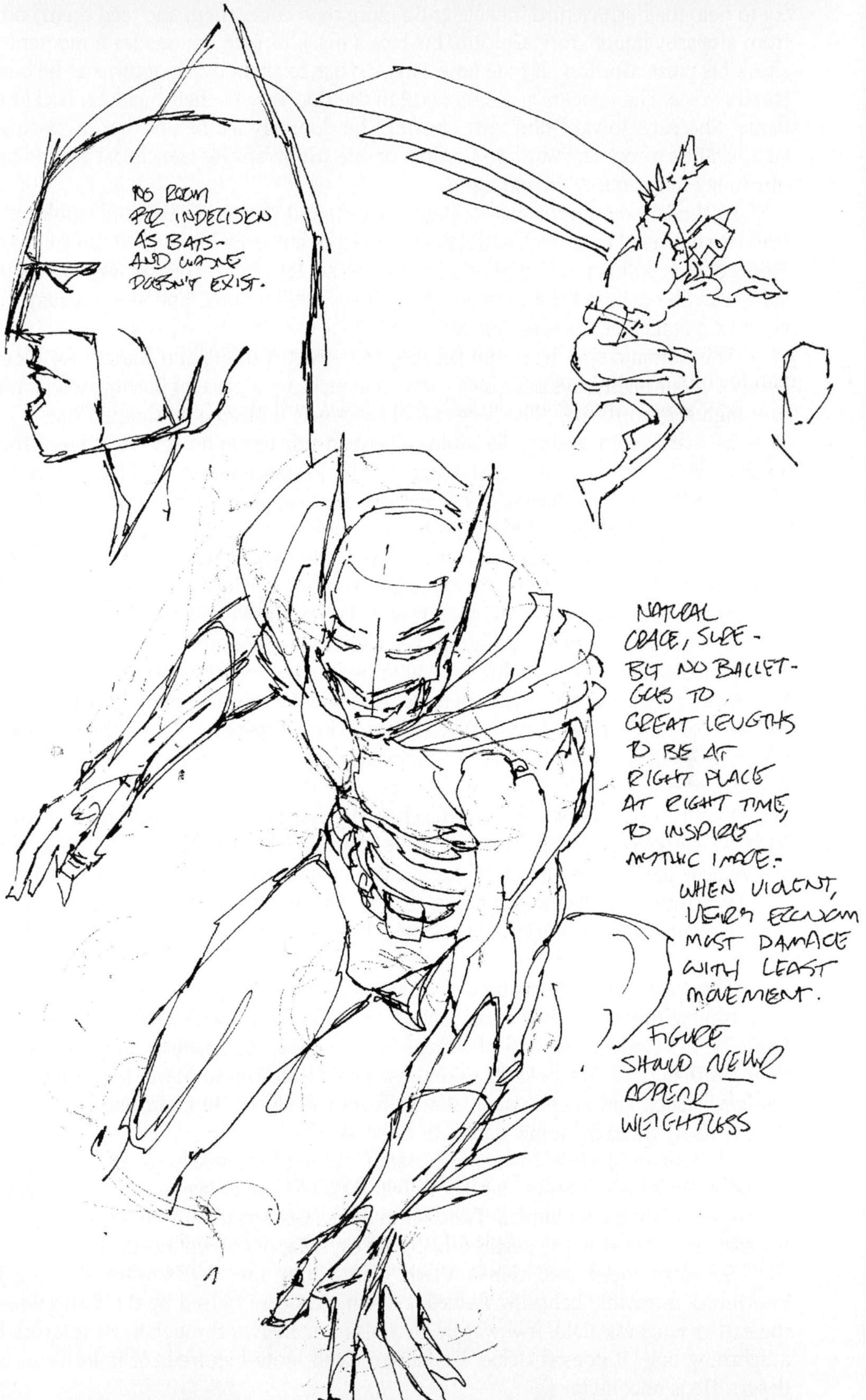
NO ROOM FOR INDECISION AS BATS— AND WAYNE DOESN'T EXIST.
NATURAL GRACE, SURE— BUT NO BALLET— GOES TO GREAT LENGTHS TO BE AT RIGHT PLACE AT RIGHT TIME, TO INSPIRE MYTHIC IMAGE—
WHEN VIOLENT, VERY ECONOM MOST DAMAGE WITH LEAST MOVEMENT.
FIGURE SHOULD NEVER APPEAR WEIGHTLESS

try to help the burn victims, unable to do more than cover them and feed them booze from a nearby liquor store. Gordon, his face a mask of pain, pauses for a moment to check his pulse, Gordon: If I die now, I'm—no use to anybody. then turns as he hears Sarah's voice. She appears as a silhouette in the doorway to their building, backlit by flame. She runs toward him, just clearing the doorway as, behind her, a gas main ignites. She's thrown forward, to Gordon, on fire. He wraps his trenchcoat around her, screaming her name again and again.

In the jail, the imprisoned Mutants scream and thrash. They smell smoke. The fire has continued to spread, and flames leap from a nearby building to the jailhouse. Yindel shouts orders to her frightened men. Merkel tells her there's no way to save the jailhouse. She pauses for a moment, looks over the Mutants. She sees a young one burst into tears. Let them go, she says.

The Mutants spill from the jail into the street, yelping and hungry for blood. Tonight is our night, says one. Let's party. One picks up a piece of burning wood, raises it high above his head. The fiery end of the wood is blasted by shotgun fire.

Batman, Robin, and the Sons of the Batman ride up on horses. Two dozen shotguns are aimed at the cornered Mutants. Swear allegiance to me, says Batman, or die. The Mutants pause, confused. Then, behind them, appears Yindel and several cops, guns drawn. Batman eyes them. It won't end tonight, he declares. The nightmare has only begun. The power will return by morning. But there will be no morning. The bomb, he says, furious, the bomb exploded over a desert. That desert is now in the sky, spreading across the hemisphere. It will blacken the sky over Gotham. It will blot out the sun—and the moon. As he speaks, the moon is obscured by black clouds. The shadow crawls across the frightened Mutants. One by one, they remove their visors. Yindel steps back, ordering her men to do the same. Merkel asks her why. He's too big, she says, distantly. Kneel, says Batman. Swear. The Mutants fall to their knees. One of the Sons of the Batman fires his shotgun into the air. Gotham City belongs to the Batman, he says.

In the desert, now a sheet of blackened glass, a tank-like vehicle, powered by hydraulics, moves through sheets of flame. The sky above is black. Hoses pop from the vehicle, spraying foam, quenching the fire on a small patch of glass. Men emerge, heavily armored, with large devices that resemble stethoscopes. They attach the devices to the floor. Through hand gestures they indicate that there is no sign of Agent Kent.

They're about to board their vehicle when they are knocked to their feet by a deep rumble that shakes the earth. The glass cracks, and a blackened, almost skeletal figure breaks through the crust. He looks like a zombie, his costume hanging from little more than bone. He looks up to the sky. There is no sun to power him. He rises to his feet, shaky, and keeps rising, slowly, from the earth. He must find the sun, he thinks, rising through atomic flames into the sky.

In Gotham, Gordon hovers over Sarah, talking hysterically to her, feeding her whiskey. She's badly burned, but she'll live. He looks up, to see black faces, awaiting orders, as building after building bursts into flame. Gordon lifts Sarah, still wrapped in his coat. We can't save the neighborhood, he says. Carry the wounded.

So many need me, thinks Clark, rising into the sky, toward the clouds. Enormous, unearthly lightning flashes, a magnetic storm caused by the disruption of the earth's magnetic field. Awkwardly, he tries to maneuver through it. He is struck by a lightning bolt. It doesn't tickle. He falls to earth, now hundreds of miles from the desert. He is unconscious.

In Gotham, the mob who robbed the gun shop breaks into a grocery store. An armed guard points his pistol and tells them to stop. Someone in the mob fires a rifle, and the guard falls dead, crashing into a shelf of canned food. The canned stuff, screams somebody in the mob, and they begin filling grocery carts with cans. They're exiting the store when they hear the sound of horses approaching.

Two Sons of the Batman, on horseback, lead a dozen armed Mutants to the grocery stores. Drop your weapons, says an SOB. And drop the food. One of the mob raises a pistol. The SOB blows him apart with a shotgun blast. To the west side, says the SOB to the mob. Get to work on the fires. We speak for the Batman.

What seems to be a meteor strikes a South American jungle, making the ground shudder and smashing through foliage. Clark lies in a crater, dying. He crawls, slowly, to the edge of the crater. He can't reach the sun. But the sun's power is held on earth. Photosynthesis, he thinks. So many need me. He reaches the edge of the crater, touches a patch of earth, then a beautiful jungle flower. The flower wilts, and dies. Then, spreading outward from Clark, the jungle dies, for miles around. Clark rises, looking like a man again, severely depowered, but Superman again. He rises into the air. The world is screaming to him.

Batman gives orders to SOBs, like a general commanding troops, giving each group of Mutants and SOBS different neighborhoods to protect. He sags, momentarily, in his saddle, then continues. Robin looks at him.

An airplane falls from the sky toward Rio. Superman flies beneath it, struggles with its weight. He can't keep it aloft, but uses his body to cushion its landing. He rises from beneath its crumpled front end, shakes himself, and leaps skyward.

In the subway train, the priest prays, then stops as he hears the crackle of a radio.

ACT III
[PP 25-36]

Gotham City squats beneath a black layer of clouds. The city's lights are on. Snow falls.

On TV, the Vice President addresses the nation. The President is dead, he says grimly. As a precaution, the President was flown high above the earth in Air Force One. Air Force One fell from the sky like a rock when all electrical activity ceased on the hemisphere. The bomb, he continues, was of a kind that the U.S. had not suspected existed—a Soviet creation called the Coldbringer, designed to cause maximum ecological damage. So, while its immediate effects were what experts expected, the magnetic pulse it produced, and the dirt and soot it spread, were comparable to that of a much larger nuclear strike. The Soviets wished to teach us a lesson, says the Vice President. But, to everyone's surprise, they did not take advantage of the blackout, which paralyzed U.S. nuclear capability, by following through with a total attack. We taught them a lesson, though, once the lights came on. We blew Cuba from the face of the earth.

Days pass. Superman and Batman work nonstop to maintain order. The Vice President declares a state of stabilized emergency.

Commissioner Yindel orders the Sons of the Batman arrested, but none are to be found, thanks to Batman's continued leadership. The warrant for murder against the Batman sparks cautious discussion about costumed individuals who set themselves apart from the rest of humanity.

A huge locomotive pulls into Gotham Central Station. From it steps Clark Kent. He buys a newspaper, reads an editorial complaining, in folksy terms, about so-called heroes who think they're better than everybody else. Something ought to be done, it says. Something is going to be done, thinks Clark, folding the newspaper. You crossed over the line, Bruce. I'm bringing you in. But first, I'm taking care of your fan club.

A truck, carrying desperately needed medical supplies, stops on a Gotham avenue at the scene of an apparent accident. A sedan rests upside down on the icy street. Next to it, a woman lies on her back. Her belly is swelled, as if she's pregnant. A man leans over her, desperate. As the truck stops, the man turns, declaring that this is his wife, that despite the ban on cars, he was rushing her to the hospital to have a baby when the car overturned. In the truck, the driver tells the guard next to him to check it out. The guard balks, says that they aren't allowed to stop for anything, since several medical shipments have been robbed. The driver insists. We're still human, for Christ's sake, he says. Cautiously, the guard steps from the truck, his hand on his holstered pistol. From a snowbank pops a man, wearing a ski mask, pointing a submachine gun at the guard. The guard curses, and raises his hands. The woman rises, leering, and pulls a pistol from her false stomach. Out of the truck, she says, and the driver complies. What the hell, she says, cocking her pistol. Let's kill them. Wait a minute, says the man. You hear horses?

Three Sons of the Batman ride up, carrying shotguns. They aim them. The thieves pivot, about to open fire. Suddenly, a huge wind rips down the avenue, an icy blizzard that tosses the SOBs from their horses and sends the thieves skittering along the icy street. Fiercer it blows. The snow is blinding white. After a few moments it dies down, leaving the guard and driver with their truck, alone on the avenue.

TV news reveals that SOBs are appearing at Gotham Jail in alarming numbers, trussed up, helpless, but refusing to explain who or what brought them in. An SOB lieutenant makes a brief statement: Our leader will come for us.

Establish Robin as reason Bats stays alive.

Batman and Robin ride horses down another icy street, somewhere in Gotham. Robin wears earmuffs, and tights, in addition to her costume. Batman wears a chest-plate, one he designed, that electronically monitors his vital signs and keeps them stable. He's not healing as quickly as he expected. He watches Robin, amazed at how quickly she is learning to ride. He smiles as she goads the horse into leaping a high snowbank. She's a miracle, he thinks.

His own horse rears, abruptly, as a blast of heat strikes the street in front of him. He topples from the horse. Ice explodes on the street. There is a blast of steam. When it clears, a message is left, burned into the street, a single word: WHERE? Very softly, Batman says, Crime Alley. Robin helps him rise. What does this mean, she asks. He touches her cheek. It means you're fired, he says gently. He rides off. She follows.

TV news reports that the city's jail is overflowing with SOBs, far worse than it was with the Mutants earlier. It's obvious that the SOBs have grown, from a couple of dozen to an army. Yindel requests help from nearby prisons, just to find a place for all of them. Her request is refused. Alone in her office, Yindel wonders what she can do with them—and how long she can hold them.

At Wayne Manor, Batman, Robin, and Alfred stand in the Batcave. Batman is partially covered in black body armor. He snaps orders to Robin, telling her what her part is in the coming fight. He turns to Alfred, holds him by the shoulders. It's time, he says, old friend. You know what to do. Alfred nods solemnly. Batman and Robin work on arming a series of bombs as Alfred walks off.

TV reports that Crime Alley is evacuated by the National Guard, and cordoned off, with no explanation.

In her TV office, Lola Chong explodes at her superiors. She tells them that they and everyone in the media knows who brought the SOBs in, and that this evacuation may be the prelude to the story of the decade. She wants to investigate it, and broadcast it, FCC regulations be damned. Her superiors get nervous. She threatens to quit.

At Wayne Manor, alone, Alfred carefully polishes the Wayne family crest.

A cold wind blows down Crime Alley. A very cold wind.

A blip appears on a radar screen. Lit by the screen, Robin whispers into a microphone. I think he's here, she says. She listens to an earphone, presses a series of buttons.

A red boot touches the pavement.

The street erupts in a massive explosion. As it settles, a searchlight flashes down, probing the wrecked street. It strikes a figure, rising to his knees in the rubble. Superman looks up, to see a helicopter above him. He's in pain, and furious. His eyes turn red. Then, he turns away, violently. Superman: Innocents. They told me there weren't going to be any. The facade of a nearby building catches fire.

In the helicopter, Lola Chong excitedly orders the pilot to come in lower. We've found him, she says. Screw the FCC.

Superman dashes through an alleyway, not flying. He probes the neighborhood, his eyes glowing blue now, with X-ray vision. The X-rays ignite several hunter missiles, which fly toward him from all directions. He blasts three from the air, with heat. The fourth strikes him, smashing him through the front of a tenement as it explodes. The tenement collapses on him.

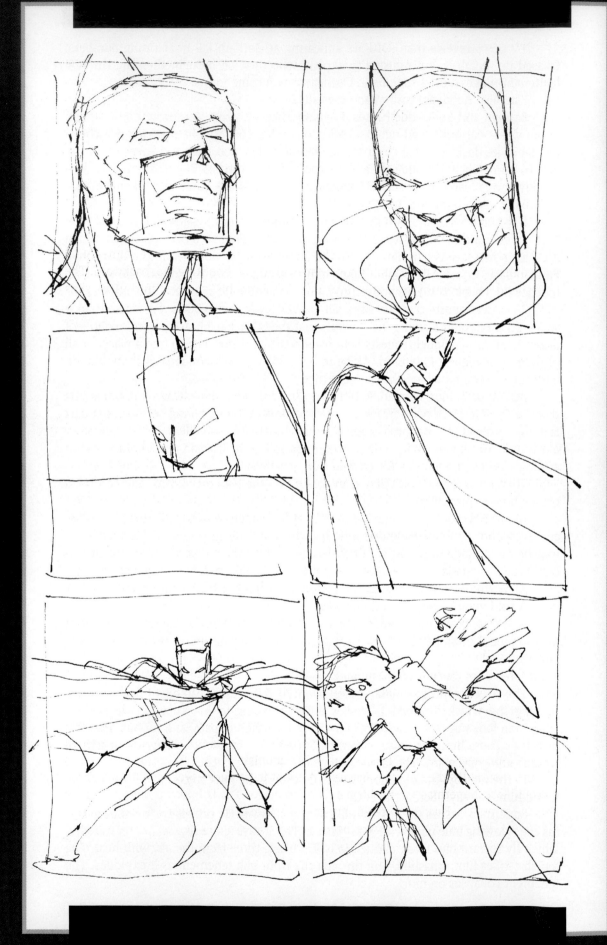

Lola Chong describes a battle of the gods in Crime Alley. She's interrupted as a fighter copter bearing Army insignia roars up beside hers, orders them to clear the area or be shot from the sky. Do as they say, says Lola. But fly low. As the News copter dips, turning from the area, Lola, carrying a portable camera and audio device, leaps from the copter to the street. Machine gun fire strikes the pavement behind her as she scrambles out of sight. She makes her way toward the collapsed tenement, taping, no longer broadcasting.

At Wayne Manor, Alfred stands before an enormous fireplace, with a roaring fire. He holds a large, leatherbound scrapbook, open, in his hands. It's open to an early page, featuring twenty-five-year-old clippings that announce the Batman's earliest assaults on crime in Gotham City. He runs his fingers gently over the clippings. He smiles and tosses the scrapbook into the fire.

Superman once again rises, his nose bloody now, his manner more calm—more irritated than angry. Machine gun fire rips across his chest, knocking him backward. The earth shudders. A nearby wall falls outward. The Batmobile rumbles into view, guns blazing.

Superman dodges the machine gun fire, as best he can. He smiles, says, isn't tonight a school night?

Inside the Batmobile, Robin talks into the microphone. Thought he couldn't see through lead, she says. He can hear through it, a voice tells her.

Superman cocks his head at the sound of Batman's voice, instantly pinpointing Batman's location two blocks away. As he turns to move in the direction of the voice, a load of napalm sprays across him. He bursts into flame. The Batmobile continues to rumble toward him. Setting his jaw, Superman, still aflame, faces off with it. He concentrates, but cannot summon his heat vision. A cannon pivots, aimed at him at point-blank range. He leaps to it, twists it upward, his teeth gritted with the effort. He lets go, falls under the Batmobile's track. The Batmobile rolls over him, then rises, and topples on its side. Superman grabs the hatch, rips it off. Inside squats Robin, terrified, her slingshot aimed. She watches as he rises into the sky.

From his vantage point, we see the street where Bruce's parents were murdered. Standing solemnly under the lamppost is Batman, dressed head to toe in gleaming black body armor. He watches Superman land, facing him ten feet away. Not good, thinks Batman. He can still fly.

Superman walks up to Batman. It's over, he says. Come along. Don't make me hurt you. Don't touch me, says Batman, holding a hand up. His other hand holds the lamp. Superman grabs the hand. His back arches, his hair stands on end, as a huge electrical charge rips through him. Batman sags against the lamp, holding fast to it and to Superman's hand. The lights dim in Gotham. Superman sags to his knees.

Lola steps into the street, filming and narrating.

In agony, Superman grabs Batman by the chestplate, pulls him from the post, slams him back into it. Batman punches Superman, his strength enormously amplified by the armor, and Superman falls on his back, astonished and enraged, now bleeding from the mouth. It's the sun, says Batman. Without it, you grow weaker by the minute. You could lose. Superman swings his fist. Batman ducks. The lamppost is bent in half by Superman's punch. Batman steps in, punches Superman in the solar plexus. You're a slob, Clark, he says. You've always been a slob. He kicks Superman in the throat. Superman falls, curled, coughing, on the street. Batman slaps a device on Superman's head, backs away as it explodes.

Lola is seized by government agents. They smash her camera and put her in handcuffs.

Superman is flat on the ground, still alive. Say uncle, says Batman. Superman struggles to rise. Batman kicks him in the face. Superman lies on his back. Batman turns, and walks away. Half a block from Superman, Batman stops, noticing that it is no longer snowing. No, he thinks. Oh, no. He looks skyward.

Sunlight creeps through the dark sky.

Sunlight strikes Superman. His wounds begin to heal. Batman turns to face him as he rises to one knee. Batman draws a huge pistol from a leg sheath and fires. An explosive bullet strikes Superman between the eyes. Superman punches the pavement. Batman topples to the street. Superman rises, walks toward him. The sky is red now, as if on fire. Batman fires again, the bullet exploding against Superman's chest— for tradition, thinks Batman. Superman seizes the gun, crushes it easily. Sadly, he says, Bruce, it's really over. Just listen to your heart. That portable hospital bed you're wearing doesn't make you invulnerable.

Nobody's invulnerable, says Batman, as green gas pours from his suit, enveloping both of them in a cloud. Superman falls back, coughing, horrified. It was tough to synthesize, says Batman. Took years. You see, I always knew I'd have to do something about you someday. Superman reels, takes a step backward. Batman chuckles, daunting Superman. He grabs him by the hair. Talk to Lois lately, says Batman.

Superman roars, in rage. Windows shatter. Batman is smashed into the air, into a brick wall, which gives way. Batman staggers to his feet. Superman leaps, tackling him, smashing through empty rooms. Wild with rage, he punches Batman, knocking his helmet off. Then he stops, and steps backward, seeing Bruce's face. Blood streams from Bruce's mouth and nose. Truce, says Clark. Your heart. Bruce collapses. His face is pale. His eyes are squinted in agony. He smiles crookedly, and passes out. His heart stops.

No, mutters Superman. You planned it this way. I won't let you get away with it. He grabs Bruce and lifts him as soldiers converge. Medic, he screams.

At Wayne Manor, Alfred carefully dusts a matched set of photographs of Thomas, Martha, and Bruce Wayne. He sets them neatly on a shelf. He opens a grandfather clock, and rearranges the weights. He walks from Wayne Manor, out to the moors, turns and faces the huge mansion. He stands, unsteadily, as the ground trembles. Wayne Manor shakes with the sound of underground explosions. It collapses in on itself, then falls in pieces into the earth, into the Batcave.

Alfred brushes a tear away, smiles, and falls dead in the grass.

ACT IV
[PP 37-47]

Soldiers converge on the damaged Batmobile, guns out. It lies on its side. The soldiers fall back as it rights itself, and roars forward, down the street. An army helicopter fires a rocket at it, to no effect. Another helicopter joins the scene. An intense Federal Agent, named Haggard, rides in the new copter. Track it, he orders. It'll take us to the son of a bitch's headquarters.

The Batmobile rumbles into a run-down, abandoned tenement. It smashes through a wall at full speed, and crashes down, through the rotted floor. Soldiers swarm the tenement, shining lights down into the tenement's basement. The Batmobile is gone. A wall of the basement is smashed through, revealing a huge unused water main.

Robin, inside the speeding Batmobile, punches a program and leans back in the seat, tense but unafraid. He won't die, she thinks. I won't even think about that. There's too much to do...

A fiery sky paints Gotham red. Looking stunned, Lola Chong appears on TV, announcing that Batman has been arrested by federal agents.

At an Army hospital, Haggard shows his identification to an armed guard, then enters a room, in which lies Bruce Wayne, plugged into all sorts of life support machinery. He lies still, eyes open, staring forward. Clark Kent leans by a window, intense. Haggard smiles at Clark, holds his hand out. Clark ignores the hand. He's stabilized, says Clark. You'll have to watch out for suicide attempts. When you question him, you are not to harm him in any way. Haggard's smile is awkward. Kent, he says, you're needed in the Midwest. The crop failure's causing serious trouble. It's practically civil war. Clark grimaces. It's much worse than you told me, he says. And I let you do it. Hey, says Haggard, it was the Russians, remember? Clark leaves.

Alone with Bruce, Haggard grows more confident. You're not going to trial, he says. Or to jail. As a matter of fact, you'll probably get your very own Agency. Once we're done with the questioning, of course. We've got a lot to learn from you. Bruce looks at Haggard and grins, amused. We're going to be great friends, says Haggard.

On TV, Lola Chong announces that Federal sources have divulged that Batman is Bruce Wayne—and is in critical condition. Doctors are not hopeful. In a related story, Wayne Manor has been destroyed. An enormous cave has been discovered beneath the site of Wayne Manor, apparently the Batman's base of operations. However, whatever secrets it might have revealed have been lost, burned to ashes. The cave's only entrance has been sealed by authorities.

The Batmobile rumbles out of an abandoned subway station. Robin presses a button on its controls. An inner lid seals the cab, making it airtight. She drives it into the river. It rumbles along the river bed. A flashing signal appears on the screen. Robin frowns. I'm running late, she thinks.

A nurse checks Bruce's vital signs, then lifts his head, fluffs up his pillow, and sets his head back down. Bruce smiles at her, warmly. She kisses his forehead. A lot of us love you, she says, and leaves the room.

Alone, Bruce becomes alert. His face is eager. He sits up in bed, and pulls a tube from his arm. His arm begins to bleed. Ignoring it, he gouges his forearm with the needle from the tube, cutting through his flesh. It's very painful, and bloody, but he looks like he's enjoying it. He digs into his arm with his fingers, extracts a small capsule. He puts it in his mouth and bites. He shudders, from head to foot. He arches his back. His vital signs go wild, then stop. His cardiogram becomes a straight red line.

On TV, it is reported that Bruce Wayne died in surgery. A surgeon is interviewed, briefly.

Carrying a freight car loaded with grain, Superman turns, in horror.

Bruce Wayne lies on a slab in the hospital morgue. Haggard screams at agents, points at the corpse. Bruce is naked; there are no marks of surgery on him. An agent, looking harassed, points at a cut on Bruce's forearm. Jesus, he says to Haggard. We checked him from head to toe. We checked his teeth, and every orifice in his body. He had the cyanide hidden under his goddamn skin. You want an autopsy, asks a bored attendant. Forget it, says Haggard. Son of a bitch is no use to us now.

At Gotham Jail, Commissioner Yindel walks past cells filled with SOBs, who sit, calmly, silently. Yindel is suspicious, and nervous.

On TV, it is announced that the IRS, investigating the Wayne Estate, has found every part of Wayne Enterprises has self-destructed, every stock has been sold, every penny of the Wayne fortune has ceased to exist. Bruce Wayne died broke, says the anchorman.

The Batmobile rises from the river, drives to the mudhole where Batman fought the Mutant leader in DARK KNIGHT TRIUMPHANT. Robin climbs from the mudhole as the Batmobile sinks, slowly, into the mud. She climbs to the pipe, and crawls inside.

At Gotham Jail, one SOB whispers to another. Bitch is late, he says. The cell door opens. You coming or what, a voice says.

On TV, it is reported that the SOBs vanished from their cells. Despite an intensive search, no sign of them has been found.

Bruce Wayne is buried, with a surprising crowd in attendance. The funeral is broadcast on TV. Featured are James Gordon, overcome with grief, Clark Kent, tight-lipped, looking somewhat older, Ellen Yindel, strangely respectful, and Selina Kyle, inarticulate with rage. The crowd hangs on long after the service, finally thinning, to Selina, Clark, Gordon, and Carrie Kelley, who does her best to look sad. The sun is rising as Selina collapses across Bruce's grave. Gordon pulls her away, takes her to his car. Clark and Carrie stand together by the grave. Clark pats Carrie on the shoulder, and turns to walk away, then stops, and turns back, staring at the fresh earth, startled. Clark breaks into a painful grin. Carrie stares at him, frightened. Clark gives Carrie a classic Superman wink, and walks off.

Carrie stands alone at the grave for a few seconds. Then she grabs a shovel.

Night falls on Gotham City. TV news reviews the international situation. Limited Nuclear War is now a reality, and tensions continue to mount. Every nation on earth is equipped with nuclear weapons, and a fearsome Terrorist Alliance is likewise equipped.

The remains of Wayne Manor seem tiny on the floor of the Batcave. The ashes that were once Batman's arsenal coat a patch of the cave floor. But the cave itself is enormous beyond belief. It stretches back, and down into the earth, for miles. Far down, far from what was once Batman's headquarters, a hundred torches burn.

Lit by the torches, on a throne made of living oak, sits the Batman. Robin stands at his side. Behind them, in military formation, holding the torches, stand the Sons of the Batman.

Bruce Wayne is dead. The Dark Knight lives.
And he has learned that there is more wrong with the world than crime.

-30-

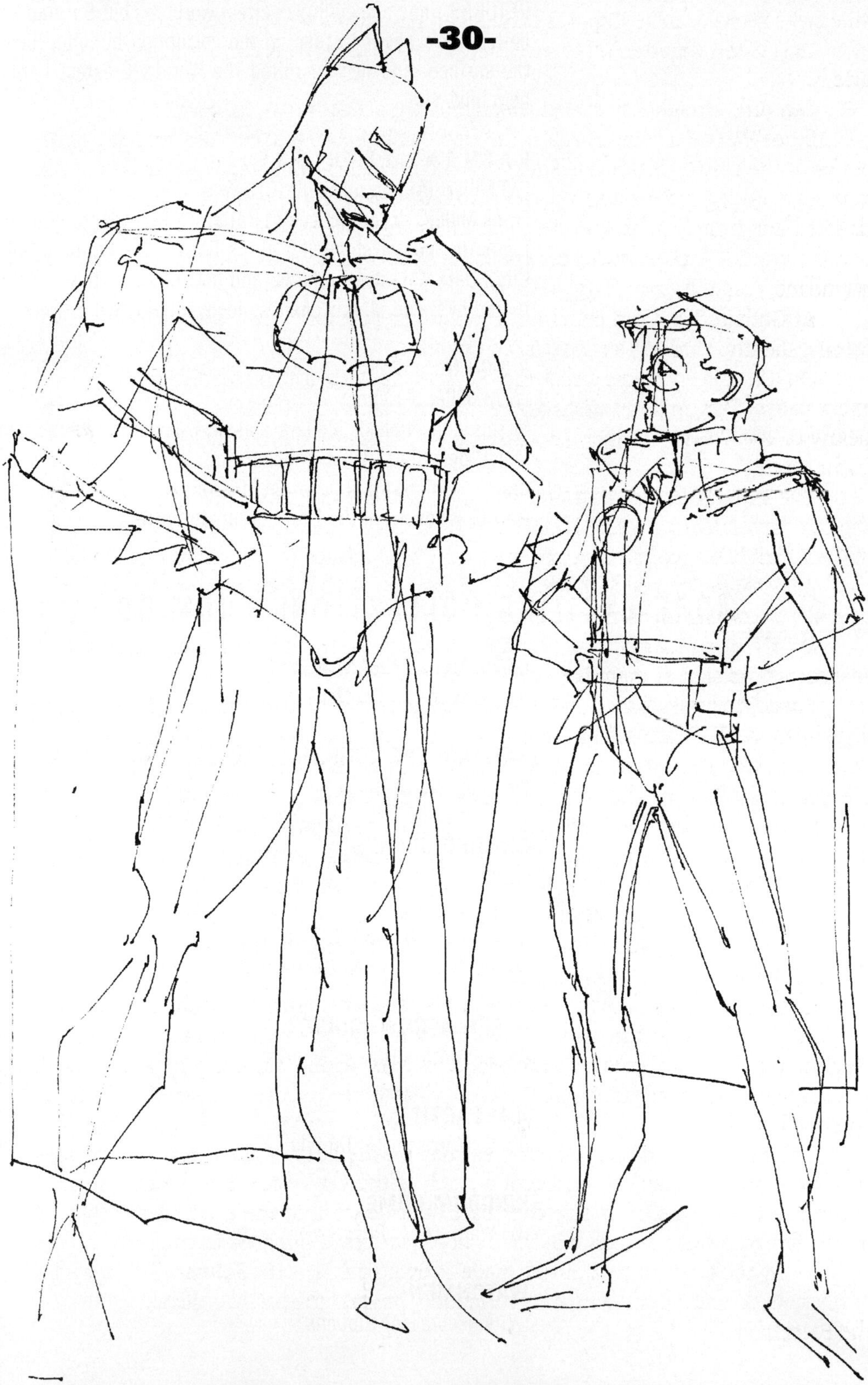

ALSO BY FRANK MILLER:

BATMAN: THE DARK KNIGHT STRIKES AGAIN
(W) Miller (A) Miller/Varley
The sequel to Frank Miller's classic BATMAN: THE DARK KNIGHT RETURNS finds a seemingly perfect world — but Batman knows better. He's about to take on the corruption bubbling beneath the surface, and he's recruited the World's Greatest Heroes to help him!

BATMAN: YEAR ONE
(W) Miller (A) Mazzucchelli (C) Lewis
Frank Miller's dramatic look at Batman's first year of crimefighting is the master storyteller at his finest. The origin of Gotham City's Dark Knight, who he is, and how he came to be is accentuated by David Mazzucchelli's moody, distinctive artwork.

RONIN
(W/A) Miller (C) Varley
In this collection of Miller's classic 6-issue miniseries (which Miller describes as a "super-hero, science fiction, samurai drama, urban nightmare, gothic romance"), a 13th-century warrior is reborn in the 21st century to battle a demonic foe.

MORE EXCITING COLLECTIONS FROM DC COMICS!

BATMAN: ARKHAM ASYLUM
(W) G. Morrison (A) McKean

BATMAN: THE LONG HALLOWEEN
(W) Loeb (A) Sale

BIZARRO COMICS
(W/A) Various

CRISIS ON INFINITE EARTHS
(W) Wolfman (A) Pérez/Ordway/Giordano

GREEN ARROW: QUIVER
(W) K. Smith (A) Hester/Parks

JLA: EARTH 2
(W) G. Morrison (A) Quitely

KINGDOM COME
(W) Waid (A) A. Ross

WATCHMEN
(W) A. Moore (A) Gibbons

FOR THE NEAREST COMICS SHOP CARRYING COLLECTED EDITIONS AND MONTHLY TITLES FROM DC COMICS, CALL 1-888-COMIC BOOK.